Frank W. Pierce Memorial Lectureship and Conference Series
Number 8

DO COMPENSATION POLICIES MATTER?

Ronald G. Ehrenberg, editor

ILR PRESS
CORNELL UNIVERSITY ITHACA, NEW YORK

The papers in this collection were originally published as a special
issue of volume 43 of the *Industrial and Labor Relations Review*.

Library of Congress Cataloging in Publication Data

Do compensation policies matter? / Ronald G. Ehrenberg, editor.
      p.   cm. — (Frank W. Pierce Memorial lectureship and
conference series : no. 8)
    "Originally published as a special issue of volume 43 of the
Industrial and labor relations review"—Verso t.p.
    Includes bibliographical references.
    ISBN 0-87546-166-2 (alk. paper)
    1. Compensation management—United States—Congresses.
2. Executives—Salaries, etc.—United States—Congresses.
I. Ehrenberg, Ronald G.   II. Series.
HF5549.5.C67D6   1990
658.3'22—dc20   89-71733
                                       CIP

Copies of this book may be ordered through
bookstores or directly from

ILR Press
School of Industrial and Labor Relations
Cornell University
Ithaca, NY 14851–0952

Printed on acid-free paper in the United States of America
5 4 3 2 1

CONTENTS

DO COMPENSATION POLICIES MATTER?

Support for this volume was provided in part by the Frank W. Pierce Memorial Lectureship Fund. This fund was established in 1965 to honor Frank W. Pierce, a pioneer in industrial relations, who graduated from Cornell University in 1916. Pierce served as head of industrial relations for Standard Oil of New Jersey and was a member of the Advisory Council of the New York State School of Industrial and Labor Relations and the Cornell University Council. The Pierce Fund supports lectures at the ILR School by distinguished scholars and professionals in the field of industrial relations.

INTRODUCTION:
DO COMPENSATION POLICIES MATTER?

RONALD G. EHRENBERG*

IT has been clear for some time that although various theories exist about why firms choose the compensation policies they do and what the effects of these policies are likely to be, there is very little empirical evidence on whether compensation policies have their intended incentive effects at either the individual or corporate level.[1] The time was therefore ripe in 1987 for a major interdisciplinary research effort on this subject. Such an effort was made possible by the generous support of the Alfred P. Sloan Foundation, including the support necessary to produce this volume.

A group of leading academic economists, industrial relations researchers, and personnel and human resource scholars from around the country was assembled in 1987 to conduct, individually and in teams, empirical research on compensation issues. A working conference of these researchers was held in Cambridge, Massachusetts, in November 1988 at the offices of the National Bureau of Economic Research, which also provided supplementary financial support for the project. At this meeting, the researchers and a few invited guests debated the technical merits of preliminary versions of the researchers' papers.

The project's final conference was held at Cornell University on May 23 through May 25, 1989. Attendance at this conference was limited to about 85 people, split roughly in thirds among project researchers, other (primarily young) academics doing research on the subject, and corporate executives who are at the forefront of compensation practices.[2] The major goals of the conference were to give the corporate practitioners a sense of current academic research on this subject, to get from the practitioners a sense of the relevance of the research to them and their views on aspects of the subject in which new research is needed, and, most important, through the interaction of the researchers and the corporate professionals, to stimulate further research on compensation issues. It is fair to say that all these goals were achieved.

This volume is an attempt to convey to a broad audience the exciting empirical research that has recently taken place on compensation topics and to try to stimulate still further research on these topics. Included in the volume are revised versions of 13 of the 15 papers presented at the conference that referees felt warranted publication in the *Industrial and*

* Ronald Ehrenberg is Irving M. Ives Professor of Industrial and Labor Relations and Economics at Cornell University and Research Associate at the National Bureau of Economic Research. He thanks John Abowd, Richard Freeman, and George Milkovich for serving as the Advisory Committee for the project that led to this volume, the Alfred P. Sloan Foundation for providing financial support for the project and the publication of this volume, and Donald Cullen for comments on an early draft of this paper.

[1] This point is developed in Ehrenberg and Milkovich (1987).

[2] A list of conference participants appears in the appendix. I am grateful to both the academic discussants (Edward Lazear, Henry Farber, Katharine Abraham, Charles Brown, Daniel Hamermesh, and Barry Gerhart) and corporate discussants (Michael Guthman, Robert Ochsner, Robert Burg, Jean Baderschneider, Stephen O'Byrne, Sharon Smith, and Ray Olsen) at the conference for their comments, many of which led to substantial improvements in the papers that appear here.

Labor Relations Review. A paper on managerial pay and performance that was not presented at the conference, but that had been submitted to the *Review* and accepted for publication, is also included because it fits into the volume so well.[3] Finally, a commissioned paper on data sets available to people interested in doing research on compensation issues is included to facilitate future research.

Executive and Managerial Compensation and Performance

The first three papers—one by Jonathan Leonard, one by Robert Gibbons and Kevin J. Murphy, and one by John Abowd—deal with the level and structure of executive and managerial compensation. Of key concern to the authors is whether executive and managerial compensation changes are related to measures of corporate performance; two of the papers also address whether firms in which compensation changes have been closely related to performance have outperformed other firms.

The Leonard and Abowd papers analyze compensation practices affecting over 25,000 executives at a large number of major companies, using data that are collected annually by a major compensation consulting company. Leonard focuses on accounting measures of performance, whereas Abowd examines not only accounting measures (for example, net income/assets) but also economic return on asset measures (such as return on equity) and financial or stock market–based measures (such as shareholder total return). Using different methodologies, both studies find weak evidence that firms that tie their executives' compensation changes to accounting measures of performance tend to have better financial performance. Abowd finds stronger results for economic return on asset measures and market-based performance. That is, he finds that firms that tie their executives' compensation to either of these two measures tend to have better performance on that measure in the future.

Gibbons and Murphy study the relationship between the compensation of chief executive officers (CEOs) and stock market measures of corporate performance, using a longitudinal sample of over 1,600 CEOs in large publicly held corporations. The authors' theoretical analysis suggests that CEOs' compensation changes should be related to measures of corporate performance relative to some comparison group rather than to measures of absolute corporate performance. Empirically, they find that CEO compensation increases are in fact positively related to their corporations' relative financial performance and that the probability that a CEO leaves his corporation is negatively related to his corporation's relative financial performance. In both cases, their evidence suggests that CEO performance is more likely to be evaluated relative to aggregate market measures than relative to industry measures of performance.

In the discussion of this set of papers at the Cornell conference, it was pointed out that the definition of compensation used by all the authors excludes benefits and long-term incentives. Because these forms of compensation have become increasingly important under current tax laws, their omission from these studies is unfortunate. Indeed, this omission may help explain why all the authors find relatively low elasticities of compensation changes with respect to performance. The authors were all well aware of this limitation in their data sets, and at least one author is currently working to value long-term incentives and include them in his compensation measures.

Do Pay Structures Have Incentive Effects at the Individual Level?

Economists and compensation specialists often assume that pay policies can influence employee behavior and have desirable incentive effects. Yet, little empirical testing by economists has been directed at whether incentive effects actually exist at the individual employee level.

---

[3] Lawrence Kahn and Peter Sherer (this volume).

The next four papers in the volume address this issue from very different perspectives. The paper by Michael Bognanno and myself and that by Beth Asch deal with occupations that, at first glance, appear far removed from the corporate world, namely, professional golfers and military recruiters. In both situations, however, one can measure with precision both the incentive structure the individuals face and the output they produce. Thus, data from these occupations permit strong tests of whether pay structures have incentive effects at the individual level.

Much attention has been devoted to studying models of tournaments or situations in which an individual's payment depends only on his or her output relative to that of other competitors.[4] Under certain assumptions tournaments are postulated to be a desirable way to structure compensation because of the incentive structure they provide.

The Ehrenberg-Bognanno paper uses data from professional golf to investigate whether tournaments actually elicit desired effort responses. The study focuses on golf because information on the incentive structure (prize distribution) and measures of individual output (players' scores) are both available for golf. Under suitable assumptions, players' scores can be related to players' effort and inferences drawn as to how both players' overall tournament scores and their scores on the last round of a tournament should depend upon the level and structure of prizes. In addition, data are available to control for factors other than the incentive structure that should affect scores, such as player quality, the quality of the rest of the field, and the difficulty of the course. Using data from the 1987 European Men's Professional Golf Association Tour, the authors find strong support for the proposition that both the level and structure of prizes in PGA tournaments influenced players' performance.

Asch examines how U.S. Navy recruiters, who are assigned to recruiting duty

for three-year tours and whose output (the number and quality of recruits generated) is perfectly observed, respond to the compensation structure they face. Key components of this structure include the presence of recruitment station quotas, piece rates, and prizes that individual recruiters are eligible to win every 12 months. Although her study focuses on military employees, Asch stresses its relevance to private sector employees, such as production workers or sales persons who compete each year for prizes, nontenured college professors competing for tenure, and workers nearing retirement (that is, approaching the end of their "tours").

Analyzing data on recruiters in the Chicago area during a five-month period in 1986, Asch finds that recruiters increase their output in the months immediately prior to qualifying for a prize and decrease it in later months. Since prizes are based at least partially on the number of recruits generated, those who have performed poorly (produced few recruits) in the early part of the year produce more recruits, but generally of lower "quality" as measured by educational achievement and AFQT scores, in later months in an attempt to increase their chances of winning a prize. Finally, recruiters near the end of their tour who have little chance of winning a prize appear to reduce their work effort. This last finding suggests the need for employers to consider ways to motivate employees who are nearing retirement.

The third paper in this group, by Lawrence Kahn and Peter Sherer, analyzes data for a single company that employs workers in a number of different locations. Bonus pay policies for this company vary across locations, positions in the managerial hierarchy, and worker seniority levels. The authors first estimate the extent to which the relationship between bonuses and supervisors' subjective productivity ratings varies across these three dimensions and then test whether the improvement in an individual's rating over time is positively related to the steepness of the bonus-productivity schedule he or she implicitly faces (that is, the

---

[4] See, for example, Lazear and Rosen (1981).

extent of bonus pay). They find that the steeper the bonus-productivity relationship, the more an employee's rating improves over time.

Finally, Daniel Hamermesh's paper focuses on a different type of incentive, namely, how the provision of "break time" (defined to include lunch breaks, coffee breaks, and other breaks) to workers affects their productivity per hour of work for which they are *paid*. He analyzes data collected by the University of Michigan Institute for Social Research in several household time use studies. Since information on productivity is not available, he assumes that the earnings workers are paid is a reasonable proxy for their productivity. On average, he finds that providing workers with additional break time has no effect on their earnings, suggesting that further growth of on-the-job leisure will not increase the productivity of most workers. On the other hand, additional break time does increase the productivity of the minority of workers with very short break times.

Do High-Wage Policies Pay?

Recently there has been extensive discussion in the academic literature concerning why firms might choose to be high-wage employers. Among the reasons suggested are increased ability to attract high-quality employees, increased ability to retain workers (lower turnover), increased work effort by workers and reduced shirking on the job by them (to reduce their chances of being fired from the high-paying jobs), and, because of the last reason, a reduced need for firms to closely supervise workers. This discussion often goes under the rubric of "efficiency wage" theories.[5] Surprisingly, there is very little empirical evidence that firms pursuing high-wage strategies actually outperform other firms. Indeed, in contrast to his findings on the relationship between executive and managerial compensation changes and corporate performance, Leonard also finds in

his paper in this volume that there is no correlation across firms between executive and managerial pay *levels* and accounting measures of performance.

The next two papers in the volume use different data bases to investigate the question of whether "paying high wages pays." Erica Groshen and Alan Krueger use data drawn from the Bureau of Labor Statistics' 1985 *Hospital Industry Wage Survey* to study the trade-off between the wages paid to various occupational groups and the intensity with which staff workers are supervised. They find that hospitals that pay higher wages to staff nurses tend to employ fewer nurse supervisors; no similar trade-off between supervision and pay is found, however, for other hospital occupations.

The authors' data do not permit them to determine whether the higher wages for staff nurses reduce the need for supervisory nurses because higher-quality staff nurses are attracted or because staff nurses of average quality work harder. The authors also do not provide any analysis of whether the high-wage hospitals have reduced costs of nursing services, because they cannot measure all of the benefits that the high-wage policies may bring (such as reduced turnover costs and higher-quality nurses). The direct cost saving (in terms of decreased supervisory costs) does, however, appear to be less than the increased costs of the higher wages for staff nurses.

Harry Holzer uses data from the 1982 wave of the national *Employment Opportunity Pilot Project* survey of firms—specifically, data on starting salaries, worker characteristics, and job characteristics for a market that is predominantly comprised of workers with a high school education in clerical, sales, and service jobs. He finds that firms that pay higher wages spend fewer hours on informal training; their workers have longer current job tenure, more years of previous job experience, and higher subjective performance ratings; and the firms have lower job vacancy rates and a higher perceived ease of hiring new employees. The magnitudes of these relationships, however, are quite sensitive

---

[5] See, for example, Akerlof and Yellen (1986).

to the specific statistical models used. Using admittedly crude measures of the overall benefits and costs to the firm of paying higher wages, he finds that some, but not all, of the costs of higher wages are offset by reduced costs in other areas.

Determinants of Firms' Compensation Policies

Each of the papers discussed so far focuses on the effects of firms' compensation policies rather than on the reasons compensation policies vary across firms. For example, neither the Groshen-Krueger paper nor the Holzer paper explains why some firms in their samples chose to pursue a high-wage policy while others chose to pursue a low-wage one. The next two papers are directed at exploring why compensation policies vary across firms and across establishments within a single firm.

Charles Brown distinguishes among three types of pay-setting methods: piece rates, in which pay is "mechanically" linked to output; merit pay, in which subjective ratings by supervisors determine salary levels; and standard rates, in which pay depends upon a worker's seniority but not his or her performance. His theoretical discussion suggests that a firm's choice among these methods depends on balancing the gains from more precise links between performance and pay against the costs of having to make precise or judgmental estimates of workers' performance.

Based upon this discussion, Brown hypothesizes that piece rates will be more common and merit pay less common in larger establishments; that the fewer the occupations in an establishment of a given size, the more likely it will adopt piece rates; and that work in which quality is easily verifiable is amenable to piece rates. Institutional considerations also suggest that standard rates should be more common in unionized establishments. Brown tests these and other hypotheses using both individual- and establishment-level data obtained from various governmental

sources. His results are generally in line with his theoretical predictions.

The importance of this paper for compensation research cannot be stressed enough. If pay policies are systematically chosen by firms, then analyses of the effects of pay policies cannot treat these policies as exogenous. Put another way, Brown's findings suggest that researchers must simultaneously analyze the causes and effects of pay policies.

Casey Ichniowski and John Delaney's paper analyzes union contract data from a single large company in the retail food industry that operates in a national market but that bargains at the local or regional level with its unionized employees. Their interest is in the factors that are correlated with whether the company won a *reduction* in the average rate of total compensation in a contract negotiation.

The authors find that unions were more likely to agree to concessions in situations in which accounting measures of store profits were low or negative. The largest concessions came from reductions in straight-time hourly earnings; the authors show, however, that a wide variety of provisions in the union contracts, not only wages, were changed to reduce costs. Finally, they show that wage concessions did serve to increase store profits on nearly a dollar-for-dollar basis. The last result implies that, at least in the short run, worker productivity was not seriously affected by the wage concessions.

Do Compensation Policies Matter?

The next two papers adopt novel (to many readers of the *Industrial and Labor Relations Review*) approaches to analyze "whether compensation policies matter." The first addresses the question of whether financial markets act as if compensation policies matter by analyzing how stock market prices react to announced changes in compensation and other human resource policies. The second paper uses micro-simulation models to gain an understanding of the extent to which various "pay for performance" systems (such as bonuses and merit increases) are translated into observed relationships between pay levels and productivity.

John Abowd, George Milkovich, and John Hannon investigate whether public announcements of selected human resource management decisions, including those involving compensation and benefit increases and decreases, staffing changes, and relocations or shutdowns, have any effects on the stock market performance of major corporations. They use an event study methodology, borrowed from finance theory, that enables them to estimate the effect of these announcements on the level and variability of abnormal total shareholder return (the movements in a corporation's stock market prices and dividends that cannot be predicted from what is happening to the stock market as a whole) around the announcement date.

The authors find no consistent pattern of increased or decreased valuation of a company's stock in response to such announcements. They do find, however, an increased variation in abnormal total shareholder return in response to announcements of permanent staff reductions and shutdowns or relocations. Thus, announcements of such policy changes do provide information that influences stock market prices.

Donald Schwab and Craig Olson's contribution is the only one in the volume that does not analyze "real-world" data. Rather, using simulation techniques, they investigate relationships between employee pay and performance produced under varying organizational practices among managerial and professional employees just below the levels of those studied by Leonard, Gibbons and Murphy, and Abowd. They study these relationships both cross-sectionally and longitudinally over ten time periods.

Among the more interesting outcomes, Schwab and Olson find that, contrary to a common supposition, bonus systems are generally not superior to conventional merit systems in linking pay to performance. They also find that error in the measurement of performance is not as serious a problem in pay-performance relationships as is typically believed. Their

study is unusual for the methodology used and permits the authors to address several issues that have not been amenable to previous empirical research.

Profit Sharing

Group incentive plans, such as profit sharing or gain sharing, are of interest for at least two reasons. On the one hand, it is often postulated that they create incentive effects for workers that will lead to improved firm performance. On the other hand, some economists have argued that firms with profit-sharing plans will have compensation levels that are more flexible than other firms' compensation levels over a business cycle, and thus firms with profit-sharing plans should exhibit fewer layoffs and greater employment stability than firms without such plans.[6]

The final research paper in the volume, that by James Chelius and Robert S. Smith, addresses the latter issue. The authors analyze the effects of profit-sharing on the employment of nonsupervisory workers in firms facing reduced demand using data from a special survey they conducted of small businesses and other data from a national sample of employees obtained from the 1977 Michigan *Quality of Employment Survey*. The authors first use the employer data base to test whether profit sharing increases employment stability in the face of negative demand shocks and then use the employee data base to test whether it reduces layoff probabilities. In both cases, they find weak support for their hypotheses.

Data Bases for Research on Compensation Issues

A major goal of this volume is to stimulate further research on compensation issues. To facilitate such research, the volume concludes with an annotated bibliography prepared by Julie Hotchkiss of machine-readable data bases that are available to people interested in doing

---

[6] See, for example, Weitzman (1984).

research on compensation issues. Each entry in this bibliography contains detailed information on a data base, including where it can be obtained and whom to contact for further information. Hotchkiss also includes information on several data bases that are not machine readable, usually collected either by the Bureau of Labor Statistics or by private compensation consulting firms.

Concluding Remarks

The papers in this volume should give the reader a sense of the exciting empirical research that has recently taken place on compensation-related issues. As a set, these papers considerably expand our empirical evidence on the effects of compensation policies. Several papers show that executive compensation is structured in a way that at least implicitly ties executive compensation changes to measures of corporate performance, and—crucially—that doing so leads to improved corporate performance (Leonard, Murphy/Gibbons, Abowd). Others show that compensation systems that pay workers for performance, in the sense of providing explicit or implicit incentives for high levels of performance, can motivate individuals to increase their effort levels (Ehrenberg/Bognanno, Hamermesh, Asch, Kahn/Sherer). Still others show that high-wage policies do have some of the effects that proponents of efficiency wage theories claim for them (Krueger/Groshen, Holzer). Finally, one shows that profit-sharing plans appear, at least weakly, to increase employment stability (Chelius/Smith).

The papers also make important methodological contributions. One shows that compensation policies are systematically chosen by firms and thus that analyses of the effects of pay policies cannot treat these policies as exogenous (Brown). Others introduce to the readers of this volume two somewhat novel methodological approaches that can be used to study compensation-related issues, namely, event study methods borrowed from finance

theory (Abowd/Milkovich/Hannon) and microsimulation methods (Schwab/Olson).

Even a set of 14 research papers, however, can only begin to touch on the range of interesting issues in the field of compensation. Notably missing from this volume are discussions of how employee ownership, employee participation, profit-sharing, and other group incentive plans (such as gain-sharing) can affect the performance of firms. Fortunately, the Brookings Institution recently commissioned survey papers that deal with these topics, and these papers will shortly appear in published form.[7]

Also missing from this volume is any mention of employee benefits, such as pensions, and the roles that the level and mix of benefits play in helping firms to attract, motivate, and retain workers and in helping firms to encourage older employees to either retire or stay on the job. Although much research has been done on these topics, this subject is likely to be of increasing importance as the proportions of older workers and women in the work force continue to expand. Increasingly, through voluntary corporate action, through collective bargaining, and through state and proposed federal legislation, the growth of the proportion of women in the work force will lead to increased interest in family leave and child care policies. Research is clearly needed on the incentive effects of such policies and on what types and mixes of such policies are cost-effective.

Similarly, none of the papers in this volume discusses the implications for compensation policies of the changing corporate environment in the United States, where fewer managers or employees can count on spending their entire careers with one firm than in the past. Some research has been conducted on how mergers and corporate acquisitions, including leveraged buy-outs, affect union and nonunion compensation and employment levels, but there have been no studies of how these restructurings will affect the set of compensation policies

---

[7] Blinder (forthcoming).

firms should offer.[8] For example, in a world in which the long-term attachment of workers to firms can no longer be presumed, does it still make sense for firms to offer their employees defined-benefit pension plans based on final salaries?

The papers in this volume should also give the reader a sense of the wide variety of data bases that can be used to conduct research on compensation. Several of the papers make use of corporate stock market data or accounting performance data and merge these data with either data on executive or managerial compensation collected by *Fortune Magazine* and a compensation consulting company or data on "human resource events" obtained from the *Wall Street Journal* (Abowd, Leonard, Murphy/Gibbons, and Abowd/Milkovich/Hannon). Two other papers use data for specialized occupational groups (Ehrenberg/Bognanno and Asch), and two use data from a single large corporation based on union contracts or corporate personnel records (Ichniowski/Delaney and Kahn/Sherer). Two use Bureau of Labor Statis-

tics data at the establishment level (Brown and Krueger/Groshen), three use survey data on firms or individuals collected by nongovernmental agencies for other purposes (Hamermesh, Holzer, Chelius/Smith), and one paper employs data from the authors' own survey (Chelius/Smith). Finally, the authors of one paper generate their data via microsimulation models (Schwab/Olson). Taken together, these papers suggest that a researcher's ability to study compensation issues is limited only by his or her ingenuity.

Corporate participants at the Cornell conference encouraged researchers to become more involved with the corporate world so that the researchers can learn the rapidly changing issues that corporate practitioners are confronting. Once these issues are known, the corporate participants stressed, there will be a need for more cooperation between economists and behavioral scientists in framing hypotheses and research designs, and subsequently between these researchers and corporations to produce data bases that will both be of use to the researchers and aid in corporate decision-making. I hope that some readers of this volume will act on these considerations.

---

[8] See Brown and Medoff (1988), Lichtenberg and Siegel (1989), and Rosett (1989).

Appendix

Participants in the ILR-Cornell Research Conference, "Do Compensation Policies Matter?"

John Abowd* ILR-Cornell	Charles Brown* University of Michigan	Ann Davis Marist College
Katharine Abraham* University of Maryland	Walton Burdick IBM Corporation	John Delaney Columbia University
Beth Asch Rand Corporation	Robert Burg Colgate-Palmolive	Anita Denning Mobil Corporation
Ronald Ash University of Kansas	Richard Chaykowski Queen's University	Joseph Duggan Data General Corp.
Jean Baderschneider Mobil Oil Corporation	James Chelius Rutgers University	E. G. Egea AT & T
Chris Berger Purdue University	Yuri B. Chernyak Auburndale, Mass.	Ronald Ehrenberg* ILR-Cornell
Michael Bognanno ILR-Cornell	Michael Conte University of New Orleans	Henry Farber* Mass. Inst. of Technology
Rene Broderick ILR-Cornell	James H. Curnow 3M Company	Charles Fay Rutgers University

Beth Florin-Thuma
Data General Corp.

Richard Freeman*
Harvard University

William N. Geary
UNISYS Corporation

Barry Gerhart
ILR-Cornell

Bob Gibbons*
Mass. Inst. of Tech.

I. Dwight Greenspan
GTE Corporation

Erica Groshen
Federal Reserve Bank of
Cleveland

Michael Guthman
Hewitt Associates

Daniel Hamermesh*
Michigan State University

John Hannon
ILR-Cornell

Harry Holzer
Michigan State University

Julie Hotchkiss
Georgia State University

Casey Ichniowski*
Columbia University

Derek Jones
Hamilton College

Larry Kahn
University of Illinois

Robin Kaiser
Sony Corp. of America

Jeffrey Keefe
Rutgers University

Richard Killeen
NYNEX Corporation

Morris Kleiner
University of Minnesota

Alan Krueger*
Princeton University

Douglas Kruse
Rutgers University

Edward Lazear*
University of Chicago

Dan G. Leach
U S WEST, Inc.

Michael Lee
San Jose State University

Jonathan Leonard*
University of California

Kathleen Malmgren
Welch Allen, Inc.

Carl Marinacci
AMOCO Corporation

William J. Meaken
Morgan Guaranty Trust Co.

John M. Mercier
Digital Equipment Corp.

George Milkovich
ILR-Cornell

Olivia Mitchell*
ILR-Cornell

Robert D. Mulkey
Digital Equipment Corp.

Janice D. Murphy
Bureau of Labor Statistics

Kevin J. Murphy
University of Rochester

Haig Nalbantian
National Economic Research
Assoc., Inc.

Stephen P. Neun
Utica College

Jerry Newman
SUNY-Buffalo

David Nurenberg
Exxon Corporation

Roberta F. Obler
Johnson & Johnson

Stephen F. O'Byrne
TPF & C

Robert Ochsner
Hay Group

Ray Olsen
TRW, Inc.

Craig Olson
University of Wisconsin

C. Thomas Parker
Air Products and Chemicals,
Inc.

Bonnie Rabin
University of Illinois

Walter Read
IBM Corporation

Albert Rees
Sloan Foundation

Daniel Rees
ILR-Cornell

Michael G. Reiff
Citibank, N.A.

Charles W. Rogers
Pepsico, Inc.

Vida Scarpello
University of Florida

Donald Schwab
University of Wisconsin

Peter Sherer
University of Illinois

Robert Smith
ILR-Cornell

Sharon Smith
Princeton University

Jan Svejnar
University of Pittsburgh

Michael A. Thompson
Hay Management Consultants

Lexie L. Walton
Morgan Guaranty Trust Co.

Yoram Weiss
NORC

* Denotes participant also affiliated with the National Bureau of Economic Research.

REFERENCES

Akerlof, George A., and Janet L. Yellen, eds. 1986. *Efficiency Wage Models of the Labor Market.* New York: Cambridge University Press.

Blinder, Alan, ed. Forthcoming. *Paying for Productivity: A Look at the Evidence.* Washington, D.C.: Brookings Institution.

Brown, Charles, and James Medoff. 1988. "The Impact of Firm Acquisitions on Labor." In Alan Auerbach, ed., *Corporate Takeovers: Causes and Consequences.* Chicago: University of Chicago Press.

Ehrenberg, Ronald G., and George T. Milkovich. 1987. "Compensation and Firm Performance." In Morris Kleiner et al., eds., *Human Resources and the Performance of the Firm.* Madison, Wis.: Industrial Relations Research Association, pp. 87–122.

Lazear, Edward, and Sherwin Rosen. 1981. "Rank Order Tournaments and Optimum Labor Contracts." *Journal of Political Economy,* Vol. 89 (October), pp. 841–64.

Lichtenberg, Frank, and Donald Siegel. 1989. "The Effect of Take-Overs on the Employment and Wages of Central-Office and Other Personnel." Cambridge, Mass.: National Bureau of Economic Research Working Paper No. 2895.

Rosett, Joshua. 1989. "An Empirical Investigation of Corporate Takeovers, Management Changes, Union Wages, and Employee and Target Firm Shareholder Wealth." Ph.D. diss., Princeton University, June.

Martin Weitzman. 1984. *The Share Economy.* Cambridge, Mass.: Harvard University Press.

EXECUTIVE PAY AND FIRM PERFORMANCE

JONATHAN S. LEONARD*

This study examines the effects of executive compensation policy and organizational structure on the performance of 439 large U.S. corporations between 1981 and 1985. Companies with long-term incentive plans enjoyed significantly greater increases in ROE (return on equity) than did companies without such plans, and by 1985 long-term incentive plans had been nearly universally adopted by large corporations. Corporate success was not significantly related to the level of, or degree of equity in, executive pay, or to the steepness of pay differentials across executive ranks; it was, however, positively related to the extent of hierarchical structure, which appears to have been the primary mechanism for sorting individuals by human capital endowments and performance.

An executive who earns tens of millions of dollars in pay per year provokes a certain critical regard no matter how efficient his operations. Extremely high compensation tends to raise questions concerning the competitive nature of the labor market determining executive compensation, and the effective degree of shareholder oversight and control. It has been justified, however, as part of incentive systems designed to align executives' interests more closely with those of shareholders.

This paper examines evidence on the competitive nature of executive and managerial labor markets. Most previous studies of executive compensation have been limited to the CEO and a few other officers whose compensation must be divulged in accord with SEC regulations. This paper instead makes use of a large sample of executives without regard to whether their pay is in the public domain. Specifically, I examine executive pay patterns for more than 20,000 executives at 439 corporations between 1981 and 1985, with particular attention to the role of human capital, hierarchical structure, and employer in determining executive pay, and to evidence of persistent pay differentials across firms. I also present evidence on the extent of sorting across hierarchies, and on the responsiveness of executive base and bonus pay to unit and corporate performance.

Evidence on those matters cannot, in its nature, conclusively establish whether the net effect of high executive salaries is to transfer wealth from shareholders or, through their incentive effects, to elicit effort from executives that results in improved firm performance and a gain

* The author is Harold Furst Professor of Management Philosophy and Values at the Haas School of Business, University of California–Berkeley, and Research Associate at the National Bureau of Economic Research. For helpful comments, he thanks seminar participants at U.C.–Santa Barbara, U.C.–Berkeley, Stanford University, the National Bureau of Economic Research, and the Cornell Conference on Compensation and Firm Performance. He also thanks Edward Lazear, Graef Crystal, and Michael Guthman for their comments, Susan Sassalos for research assistance, and the Institute of Industrial Relations for its support.

The proprietary data used in this analysis were provided on a confidential basis.

for shareholders. To explore that question, I discuss some problems in the design of incentive mechanisms and issues in estimating their effects, and I examine the impact on corporate performance of long-term incentive systems, bonus schemes, hierarchical structure, promotion rates, and pay equity.

Theories of Firm Effects

In the simplest model of a spot market for labor, firms have no pay policies and do not differ in their pay for a given skill employed under the same conditions. Pay is set by the market clearing conditions. A precondition for any discussion of pay policy is the absence of perfect information or of costless mobility.

Consider the puzzle raised by firm pay effects—differences in pay across firms that are widely shared among different occupations. Several theories may be employed to attempt an explanation of such effects. First, the classical theory of compensating differentials can account for firm pay effects among executives if those effects stem from omitted factors that differ across firms but are common to all executives within a firm. Among the omitted factors may be unmeasured components of compensation, such as long-term incentives and various perquisites, as well as unmeasured corporate characteristics, such as expected profitability, specificity of human capital, promotion probabilities, and the threat of unfair discharge. Second, equity theory may be consistent with firm effects, provided it is assumed that executives care more about internal equity than external equity and that some mechanism exists that causes key wages to differ across employers. Third, if the cost of shirking or monitoring differs across firms but is similar across positions within a firm, efficiency wage theories may predict such firm effects. In all three cases, the underlying causal factors plausibly change only slowly, so these models may explain persistent firm effects.

Also possibly useful in explaining firm pay effects for executives are rent sharing models, in which imperfect monitoring by shareholders (executive theft) or large fixed costs of turnover are responsible for interfirm differences in pay. Under such conditions, executives may succeed in appropriating part of the rents that a firm with market power achieves. Only if the underlying rents persist, however, are such models consistent with persistent firm effects.

Data

Much can be learned about the nature and operation of the labor market by matching information for firms and employees over time. All of the information analyzed in this study is derived from a private survey of executive and managerial compensation conducted between 1981 and 1985. The survey was not designed to cover a representative sample, and there was considerable turnover of survey firms from year to year. Nonetheless, the firms span a broad spectrum of the largest corporations in the United States, and their Betas (Valuelines) averaged 1.03 in 1983, so along this dimension they closely represent the stock market. In 1985, survey companies had employment-weighted average sales of $3.9 billion, assets of $3.3 billion, and profits of $182 million. Employment ranged from 132 to 252,000 employees, with an average of 33,000.

Participating firms were asked to report on the pay and personal characteristics of a representative sample of 75 to 100 incumbents in a variety of job families, managerial levels, and organizational units. *Pay* in this paper shall refer to the sum of base plus bonus paid in a given year. It does not include fringe benefits, pension benefits, or long-term incentive pay such as stock options, which can be substantial components of total compensation for some top executives. The combination of information on the personal characteristics of managers, with data on their employers in a longitudinal sample of firms, facilitates the testing of a number of fundamental models of the labor market. It also allows an examination of how pay, power, and prestige are allocated in major American corporations.

Analysis of Variance of Executive Pay

Although the firm wage effects estimated here cover a wide range, they are not of great significance in accounting for individual variation in executive pay. The standard deviation of estimated firm wage effects is .21 for the logarithm of pay including bonus. This value is roughly similar to the magnitude of dispersion of firm effects for production workers estimated by Groshen (1987) in some industry and area wage surveys, although it is considerably greater than Leonard's (1988) estimates for the electronics industry.

Table 1 presents an analysis of the variance of the logarithm of pay in a pooled non-rectangular sample of executives from 1981 to 1985. This table reports the proportion of variance that can be unambiguously attributed to each of six

Table 1. Components of Variation of Logarithm of Executive Pay (Base + Bonus), 1981–1985.

Factor	Percent of Total Sum of Squares (Degrees of Freedom)
1. Company	7.9 (439)
2. Occupation	2.2 (144)
3. Hierarchical Position	10.4 (36)
4. Human Capital	1.1 (4)
5. Unit Sales	0.1 (1)
6. Year	2.0 (4)
7. Joint Effects	63.6
8. Total	87.3 (626)
9. Interactions	12.7

Notes: Each of the main effects in lines 1 through 6 is conditional on the other 5. Line 8 is the R-squared of the full model presented in Table 2. Line 7 is the difference between line 8 and the sum of lines 1 through 6. Line 9 is one minus line 8. Hierarchical position includes sets of dichotomous variables indicating levels beneath board of directors (11), subordinate levels (16), chief responsibilities at corporate, division, or plant levels (3), international responsibility (1), and board membership (1), as well as continuous variables for number of subordinate exempt and non-exempt employees. Human capital includes variables for age, tenure with the firm, job tenure, and education. N = 98,587. TSS (Total Sum of Squares) = 34566.

main factors. Conditional on the other controls listed in Table 2, the marginal contribution to R^2 of each factor is presented. Individual company effects can unambiguously account for 8% of pay variance, with controls for occupation, hierarchy, human capital, unit sales, and year. This percentage is a measure of the importance of firm effects that persist over the period (up to five years) that firms remain in the sample. The variance decomposition for each of the five years closely resembles that for the pooled sample. Despite sample turnover, the relative importance of each of the main factors remains stable over time. Firm effects thus appear to be of minor direct consequence in all years studied.[1]

Pay differences across these firms appear to have been slowly fading. The correlation between firm wages in 1981 and 1985 (with all the controls in Table 2) is .77. After a decade at this rate of decay, half of the distinctive firm effects would remain. There is evidence of both error correction and mean reversion in the time series behavior of firm pay effects. Above-average wage growth in a firm in one year tended to be followed by below-average growth the next year. Firms with above-average wage *levels* also tended to have below-average wage growth in the subsequent year.

There are considerable lags in the adjustment process. Firm pay in 1985 was significantly and strongly related to pay in 1982, even with controls for pay in 1983 and 1984. Above-average pay raises in 1983 depressed subsequent raises in 1984 and 1985. Thus, pay does adjust, but slowly.

In the organizations studied here, pay is strongly hierarchically structured. Position in the corporate hierarchy unambiguously accounts for 10% of pay variance. The occupations considered here, on the other hand, appear surprisingly homogeneous

---

[1] Although it is possible that firms choose not to participate in surveys in which they will be outliers, firms that compete for talent in the same managerial labor markets are more likely to self-select into the same surveys.

Table 2. The Logarithm of Executive Pay (Base + Bonus) as a Function of Personal and Firm Characteristics, 1981–1985.

Variable	Coefficient	(Standard Error)
Age	.0082	(.0001)
Tenure with Firm	.0001	(.0001)
Job Tenure	.0008	(.0002)
Years of Schooling	.0174	(.0005)
Unit Sales	.0051	(.0002)
International Responsibility	.0657	(.0020)
Corporate Responsibility	.0534	(.0026)
Division Responsibility	−.0117	(.0019)
Plant Responsibility	−.0169	(.0043)
Board Member	.174	(.0027)
Eligibility for Long-Term Incentive	.159	(.0021)
Exempt Subordinates	.0055	(.0006)
Non-exempt Subordinates	.0021	(.0003)
Number of Subordinate Levels:		
0	−1.08	(.151)
1	−.99	(.151)
2	−.91	(.151)
3	−.84	(.151)
4	−.75	(.151)
5	−.67	(.151)
6	−.59	(.151)
7	−.51	(.151)
8	−.46	(.151)
9	−.41	(.151)
10	−.36	(.151)
11	−.38	(.151)
12	−.43	(.152)
13	−.45	(.155)
14	−.46	(.178)
15	−.38	(.172)
16	.53	(.211)
Number of Superior Levels:		
1	.64	(.109)
2	.64	(.095)
3	.48	(.095)
4	.38	(.095)
5	.30	(.095)
6	.23	(.095)
7	.17	(.095)
8	.12	(.095)
9	.09	(.095)
10	.07	(.096)
11	.06	(.103)
Year:		
1981	−.292	(.0025)
1982	−.198	(.0024)
1983	−.155	(.0024)
1984	−.076	(.0023)
R^2	.873	
N	98587	
SEE	.211	

Note: Controls indicating employment in one of 439 companies and one of 144 occupations are also included. "Subordinate Levels" refers to the number of layers of management an incumbent supervises. "Superior Levels" are the number of levels between the position and the Board of Directors; the CEO is Level 1.

in terms of pay. Differences in occupation (which range from CEO to foreman) can unambiguously account for only about 2% of pay variance.

The other main effects are of minor importance in terms of their unambiguous effects. Human capital variables can unambiguously account for 1.1% of pay variance, unit sales for 0.1%, and calendar year for 2.0%.

Sorting models predict a high correlation between measures of human capital and hierarchy or occupation, as firms sort the most able managers into the most important positions.[2] Given that prediction, the highly correlated main effects shown in Table 1 are not surprising. In combination, the variables included here can account for 87% of the variance in pay. Seventy-four percent of this "explained" variance—64% of total pay variance—occurs through joint effects that cannot be unambiguously credited to a single factor. This result is consistent with the prevalence of sorting, as are the highly correlated measures of corporate position and human capital.

The maximum proportion of pay variance that each factor could account for includes part of these joint effects and is simply the R^2 obtained with only that factor on the right-hand side of the equation. By themselves, the human capital variables can account for 28% of pay variance, not unlike standard log-wage equations with education and experience controls. Pay is very much a function of position, and measures of hierarchical position and of occupation can account for 69% and 52% of pay variance, respectively. By themselves, company effects account for 33% of pay variance.

The proportion of pay variance accounted for here (.87) is far higher than that usually estimated (~.30) for individual workers. It might be supposed that this high level of explanation simply reflects

---

[2] The latter two factors are themselves likely to be highly correlated in this study, given the type of occupational definitions used here: vice-presidents for marketing tend to be at the top of executive hierarchies, branch managers near the bottom.

the homogeneity of the sample; but a human capital wage equation similar to those typically estimated yields a similar R^2 (.28). At least along this dimension, the residual variation in this sample is similar in magnitude to that commonly observed. Instead, the high level of explanation is likely due to the additional controls used here. Position in the corporate hierarchy, employer, and detailed occupation all are significant correlates of pay.

In the executive suite, where individual performance is supposed to matter greatly and is often closely observed by colleagues and superiors, pay is often presumed to depend more on individual performance than on a job title. Although bargaining costs might be reduced (or merely redirected) by making pay a function of position, individual tailoring of pay is almost certainly less costly when used for a few executives than it would be if used for the mass of non-exempt workers. Executives are also more likely to voice allegiance to pay for performance systems than to group solidarity. Yet, we observe a strong systematic component in pay even near the tops of these hierarchies. The nonstandard and complex output of executives may be more difficult to measure than that of other employees. To the extent that individual performance and human capital endowments affect pay, they do so primarily by affecting the allocation of people to occupations and positions in the corporate hierarchy.

The tightness with which executive pay is administered can be judged from the fact that, with salary range mid-point controlled for, the standard error of base salary is 13%, allowing some individualistic pay adjustment. If individuals are sorted into companies, hierarchical levels, or occupations partly on the basis of productivity, then these variables will pick up part of the effect of unmeasured absolute productivity. Thus, Table 1 indicates that within position an executive has only modest scope to increase his or her salary, relative to that of the average incumbent in the same company, hierarchical position, and occupation, by means of exceptional performance.

Internal Labor Markets

Models of internal labor markets are commonly assumed to apply to corporate hierarchies with firm-specific skills, a strong policy of promoting employees within the firm, and external hiring limited to a few lower-level entry positions. In such models, market forces most directly affect wages in the entry-level positions. Competitive forces could be expected to equalize the expected present value of career earnings across employers. If this condition is fulfilled (and post-entry interfirm mobility is barred, and all executives have the same discount rate and expected working life), then the distribution of earnings over a career is indeterminate. Post-entry-level positions may then differ in pay across firms, and the relative pay of occupations within a job ladder may differ across firms. If such internal labor markets were prevalent in the firms studied here, we would expect to see strong occupation-employer interactions. On the contrary, no more than 13% of pay variance is accounted for by all possible interactions and omitted variables. These firms apparently tend not to differ greatly in terms of pay structure or average pay.[3]

Internal labor market models predict that the lowest cross-firm variance in pay will be found in entry-level positions directly exposed to market pressure.[4] Among the executives studied here, however, the cross-firm pay variance is similar across levels of the job ladder.[5] For example, the standard error of pay for executives to whom no managers report is .15, the same as for executives to whom between 1 and 10 levels of management report. (This correspondence is less per-

---

[3] This uniformity may, in part, reflect an endogenous response to previous surveys.

[4] More homogeneous pay is also expected in jobs that are more exposed to outsiders, so that competition is not limited by firm-specific information. Note also that some hierarchy levels may contain numerous salary grades.

[5] From the perspective of tournament models, in which absolute rather than percentage differences are relevant, equal proportionate variation indicates greater absolute heterogeneity across firms at higher levels.

fect at the top of more extensive hierarchies.) Within functional groups (finance, marketing, manufacturing, purchasing, and so on), there is no case in which the standard error of the lowest observed position is less than that of the top position in the job ladder. The only exception is the position of CEO, which shows the least homogeneity of any position. CEO pay is the least mechanically determined and the most subject to individual negotiation. To the extent that market forces impose wage uniformity, this effect appears to be similar across levels of the job ladder below CEO.

In fact, the premise of this internal labor market model appears not to hold for most sample firms. Rates of entry into high-level positions from outside the firm are substantial (Leonard 1989). The average employer in this sample does not pursue a pure promote-from-within policy. On the one hand, at all levels of the corporate hierarchies sampled here, at least 80% of the 1985 incumbents were hired before 1981; company tenure averages 15.6 years; and no pure entry-level positions are observed. But on the other hand, these companies do frequently hire top executives from outside. Two levels beneath the CEO, one in five of the 1985 incumbents have been with the company less than 5 years.

Most individuals in the sample for this study did some shopping among firms before being appointed as executives; the average age at which a 1985 executive was hired by his current employer was 34. An additional sign of the value of job shopping (or of those who job-shop) is that although managers at the lowest observed levels of the hierarchy are no older than managers at higher levels, they have, on average, accumulated 2 to 3 years more company tenure. By Baye's rule, those who settle with a company earlier in life are less likely to ascend or be hired into the top. Managers who settle with their current employer at an earlier age are more likely

to remain at the lower levels. They are unlikely to ascend or to leave.[6]

Hierarchical Pay

Position in the corporate hierarchy is one of the strongest determinants of pay. In a number of economic models, this link is attributed to the greater sensitivity of corporate success to the acts of higher-level executives than to those of lower-level executives. Executives with a wider span of control are expected to have greater marginal revenue products. In contrast to such efficiency explanations, however, equity theories may predict that hierarchical structure generates pressure for pay differentials across steps even in the absence of productivity differentials.[7] Why shareholders should agree to such transfers and what determines reference groups are questions left unanswered in such models.

One approach for testing these competing models is to consider two executives in the same occupation with the same numbers of exempt and non-exempt employees reporting to them directly or indirectly, a condition that, in principle, holds the span of control—the organizational multiplier on individual decisions—fixed. Now consider the effect on pay of differences in the number of hierarchical levels that these subordinate employees are organized into. In the sample for this study, executives in flat organizations (with only one subordinate level of management) received 32% lower pay than executives in hierarchical organizations

---

[6] Asymmetric information models allow for complex equilibria. For example, it is possible that moves early in a career do not carry negative signals, but that a lower-level manager seeking to move late in a career is suspect. The results reported here may also be an artifact of the sample design: managers who move with less success are more likely to be employed in smaller companies or in lower positions, and so drop out of the sample. Furthermore, a firm's reports may have varied from year to year in the extent of their coverage of the corporate hierarchy and in the kinds of positions included.

[7] This argument is in contrast to the argument that title differentiation serves as a *substitute* for pay differentiation.

(with five subordinate levels, an increase of about two standard deviations). (See Table 2.) This finding is obtained with controls on the number of subordinate exempt and non-exempt employees, unit sales, occupation, and location in corporate headquarters or plant.

An efficiency explanation for this result is that some differences among employers that remain uncontrolled are accompanied by both greater hierarchy and higher productivity.[8] In pure tournament models, executive pay serves as an incentive only for those in lower positions, not as a return to productivity in the current position.[9] The pay differentials observed in more hierarchical structures, however, cannot be rationalized purely in tournament terms. Conditional on the number of exempt subordinates (contestants), adding runner-up prizes (intermediate levels in the hierarchy) should reduce the first-prize payoff. Here, we observe higher pay with more levels of subordinate hierarchy, suggesting at the least that part of managerial pay is a return to current productivity. Alternatively, hierarchical pay differentials may satisfy equity norms without clear efficiency support. In the absence of a model of the determinants of hierarchical structure, the possibility that some other factor produces both greater hierarchy and greater productivity cannot be ruled out.[10] (At the end of this paper I return to an analysis of the effect of hierarchical structure on corporate performance and test for the efficiency of hierarchy.)

Pay differentials across levels do increase with level in the hierarchy, consistent with tournament theory. The proportional pay differences between adjacent levels, starting from those reporting directly to the CEO, are 16, 10, 8, 7, 6, 5, 3, 2, and 1 percent. In other words, 1% of pay separates level 10 from level 11 below the CEO, whereas 16% separates level 2 from level 3. This increasing spread between higher levels is consistent with models in which greater pay differentials are necessary to motivate managers at higher levels, for whom there are fewer superior positions to be promoted into and (often) less remaining time to reap rewards.

Other measures of position in the corporate hierarchy are also strongly associated with pay. Executives with corporate-wide responsibilities are paid 7% more than those at the plant level. International responsibilities bring 7% higher earnings than for those with only domestic responsibilities; board membership, 17% higher earnings than for those without board membership.[11] Although the value of long-term incentives is unmeasured here, eligibility for such incentives is known and is associated with 16% higher pay (not including the value of long-term incentives). Heterogeneity across jobs swamps any reduction in base pay by the risk-adjusted expected value of long-term incentives.

Sorting and the Returns to Education and Experience

Executives are rewarded for both experience and education. In regressions that control only for tenure in the firm and tenure in a particular job, each additional year of education is associated with an 11% increase in pay and each additional year of experience with a 3% increase. (See Table 3.) The return to firm-specific tenure is 0.6%, much less than the return to general experience.[12] This finding, which is consistent with the

---

[8] Hierarchical structure that itself increases managerial productivity may create firm-specific rents that should not be captured by employees under competitive conditions.

[9] The market equilibrium conditions for such tournament models are not well established.

[10] Relative rather than absolute position in a hierarchy may be relevant in some contexts. Table 2 identifies some of these effects as combinations of the coefficients on superior and subordinate levels.

---

[11] O'Reilly (1989) argues that such a pattern is due in part to social norms affecting standards for pay comparison in small groups.

[12] General experience is measured here as age, with years of schooling controlled for, and may include industry-specific components of human capital.

Table 3. The Logarithm of Executive Pay (Base and Bonus) as a Function of Tenure, Age, and Education, 1981–85.

Variable	Coefficient	(Standard Error)
Age	.0280	(.0002)
Tenure with Firm	.0057	(.0002)
Job Tenure	−.0208	(.0005)
Years of Schooling	.1064	(.0009)
Intercept	8.2077	(.0172)
R^2	.276	
N	98587	
SEE	.504	

earlier finding that pay diversity is no higher in upper-level positions than in lower-level positions, implies that managers make little investment in firm-specific human capital.[13]

Sorting does occur in lower-level executive positions. Some managers remain stuck in position rather than advancing through the ranks, and so they have job tenure that increases along with company tenure. Each additional year in the same position is associated with 2% less pay than would be received if the manager were promoted. This pattern is exactly what we would expect if the most productive managers were quickly promoted into higher positions, with the less productive managers accumulating longer job tenure and earning smaller raises.[14]

Almost all of these effects occur through the process of allocation to positions within the corporation. In regressions with the full set of controls, firm tenure and job tenure have no effect on pay, and an additional year of experience and of education increase pay by only 1% and 2%, respectively. These last two effects cannot be ascribed to the receipt of new information about managers' productivity by those setting pay. Observable measures of potential productivity, such as age, experience, and education, are important

determinants of starting pay. Their importance fades over time with the company, however, as information about the employee's true productivity in the company is revealed (Leonard 1989).

Fixed-Effects Estimates of the Change in Pay

Wage rigidity is nearly everywhere held to be a sin, and unions the chief sinners. Executives commonly preach the virtues of wage flexibility, a sermon delivered with greatest fervor when profits and sales are falling. Of course, of all workers, executives presumably have the greatest investment in firm-specific human capital, and so should have more inelastic labor supply and more variable pay. At the same time, executive pay increases that might otherwise seem exorbitant are justified as efficient incentives in view of increased profits supposedly resulting from gain-sharing mechanisms.

In this section I report the results of a longitudinal analysis of changes in pay over time for a sample of 2,511 executives who maintained employment in the same occupations in the same firms from 1981 to 1985. There are 10,043 observations of pay change (about four per manager). Fixed effects estimates allow us to difference out the stable effects of unchanging omitted factors such as individual productivity or working conditions. Table 4 presents results of a regression of the annual change in the logarithm of pay on changes in corporate profits and sales,[15]

---

[13] An alternative interpretation of the observed return to tenure is that good matches result in both higher pay and longer eventual tenure. However, pay is only 6% higher when uncompleted spells of tenure are a decade longer.

[14] For models of this sort, see Weiss and Landau (1985). This type of behavior may help explain an anomaly noted by Medoff and Abraham (1980).

[15] It is possible that the sales and profit measures used here measure with error some index of corporate performance, such as share price, that is more relevant to the reward of executives, and so underestimates the true elasticity of response. The estimated relationship between corporate earnings and stock returns is typically weak (Lev 1989). Also, part of corporate performance, however measured, is beyond executive control, and so should not affect executive pay. The independent variables are the change in the logarithm of billions of current dollars of corporate and unit sales, equity and assets, measured at the end of the most recent fiscal year. Because profits are often negative, the measure used here is the change in billions of dollars of profits, and the coefficient is not an elasticity.

Table 4. Change in the Logarithm of Executive Pay (Base + Bonus) as a Function of Firm Characteristics, 1982–1985.

Variable	Coefficient	(Standard Error)
Change in Logarithm of:		
Unit Sales	.028	(.003)
Corporate Sales	.122	(.011)
Equity	−.011	(.009)
Assets	−.011	(.010)
Employment	.003	(.009)
Change in Profits	.135	(.010)
1982–1981	.043	(.003)
1983–1982	−.023	(.003)
1984–1983	.024	(.002)
Intercept	.075	(.057)
R²	.196	
N	10,043	
SEE	.105	

Notes: Controls indicating employment in one of 119 companies and one of 137 occupations are also included. Estimated in a sample of executives who did not change occupation or employer.

and on sets of dichotomous variables controlling for company, occupation, and year. Pay includes bonuses, but does not include long-term incentives such as stock options, stock appreciation rights, or other long-term capital accumulation plans. For the 53% of sample executives eligible for such long-term incentives, compensation variability over time may well be understated.[16]

For most managers, pay (base plus bonus) is inflexible with respect to sales. The elasticities of executive pay (base plus bonus) with respect to unit sales and corporate sales are, respectively, .028 and .122. These are both significant but inelastic responses.[17] A corporation that saw its sales fall by half could expect to see executive pay reduced by about 9%. Of course, if the value of stock rights were included in these calculations, the elasticities might be higher.

Executive pay appears to be more significantly linked to profits, although the effect is still modest. The elasticity is not directly estimated because profits are often negative. A corporation in which profits fall by $157 million (1 standard deviation below the mean change) could expect to see executive pay reduced by about 2%. This yields a standardized Beta of .18, which is a modest response. The level of executive pay cannot be justified in terms of contingent pay schemes when such a small proportion of executive pay is so weakly contingent. The threat of opportunistic behavior by executives, who cannot be bound to the firm when a bad state (poor firm performance) occurs, may limit the use of contingent pay.

Executive pay shows other patterns that are puzzling if it is viewed as an incentive device. Absent other complications, pay that is supposed to elicit optimum performance should be linked most closely to the success of the corporate unit for which an executive is responsible. On the contrary, pay appears to be more significantly and strongly related to corporate sales than to unit sales. The stronger link with corporate sales may reflect equity norms that call for uniform corporate gain sharing. It may also be that unit performance measures are more subject than corporate measures to strategic manipulation or to measurement error, or that units have large potential negative spillovers.[18] That sales are linked to pay even independently of profits may simply reflect the divergence of accounting profits from economic profits.

There are several theoretical reasons why contingent pay should be used more in high- than in low-level positions. Top executives have a more direct impact on corporate profits than do their subordinates. Given this connection, the CEO's

---

[16] Murphy (1986) and Jensen and Murphy (1988) suggest this understatement is minor, and that inside stock holdings are of greater importance than stock options.

[17] Over longer periods of time pay is more responsive to corporate performance, indicating longer and more complex lags in adjustment (Leonard 1989).

[18] Alternatively, if pay contingent upon unit performance would provide outsiders with information about unit performance that management would prefer to keep confidential, the costs of such finely contingent contracts might exceed their benefits. However, neither the pay formulas necessary to infer unit performance nor the pay of lower-level executives need typically be disclosed.

performance is also more directly observable by outsiders. Since other firms may be willing to hire him based on his current firm's performance, his current firm will have to compensate him on the same basis to keep him. At lower levels, the potential for promotions within the company offers an alternative incentive mechanism not applicable to the CEO. Profit-sharing and share ownership embody the common problem of group piece-rate incentive schemes: the larger the group, the less manageable the free-rider problem. A tenth-level manager who shirks will have only a small effect on the company's profits, but will derive the full personal benefit of shirking. This free-rider problem generally extends to the co-supervision that group incentives are sometimes asserted to induce. For all these reasons, less contingent pay should be expected at lower levels in the corporate hierarchy than at higher levels.

That pattern is exactly what we observe. The estimated change in pay as a function of change in profits, with controls for employer, year, and changes in equity, assets, and employment, is .22, .18, .10, and .02, respectively, when estimated separately for the following levels of the hierarchy: (1) the CEO; (2) level 2 reporting to the CEO; (3) levels 3 and 4; and (4) all other levels. Replacing profits with sales growth in the above regressions yields estimated responses of .007, .003, .002, and .001. In regressions including both profits and sales, the same pattern obtains, although the effects are small: contingent pay is most important at the top, but even at the top it is a small effect.

The estimated response of pay to profits is conditional on changes in assets, equity, and total employment. None of these three variables has a strong or significant effect on pay. Neither changes in capital-labor ratios nor in scale significantly affect pay.

Over the five years studied, there was no significant realignment of occupational pay structure. Occupation dummies are insignificant jointly and singly. This finding is consistent, of course, with a policy by firms of maintaining fixed pay relationships between occupations. Alternatively, it could be that the occupations are close substitutes or that they experience parallel shifts in supply and demand.[19]

Executives enjoyed real wage gains in each year. Deflated by the GNP implicit price deflator, real executive wages increased by 5.3, 1.4, 5.8, and 4.2 percent, respectively, in each year from 1982 to 1985. The last three changes very roughly parallel the growth of real GNP, but in 1982 real wages rose by 5.3 percent while real GNP fell by 2.5 percent. These executives have little reason to fear that either recession or inflation will dramatically cut their base plus bonus pay. Perhaps the supply of skilled executives has fallen relative to demand, leading to an increase in their pay relative to that of other workers.

The results described above pertain to a sample of managers who did not change employer or occupation between 1981 and 1985, but expanding the sample does not make much practical difference. When occupation indicators are dropped from the equation and the sample is extended to include managers who changed occupations, resulting in 49,627 observations of pay change (up to four observations per manager), even smaller responses to sales and profits are obtained. The elasticities of pay with respect to unit and company sales are then .004 and −.005, respectively. Both are significant. If firms enjoying great success were more likely to promote managers, then restricting the sample to those in the same occupation would underestimate responsiveness. These results do not support such a selection bias. Rather, promotion rates appear higher in firms suffering sales declines.

One might also suspect that growing firms hire more people into entry positions at lower pay, and that these low-

---

[19] Of the 118 company effects estimated, 23 are significantly different from zero at the .05 level. Since only six effects could be expected to be significant at random, this result is evidence of significantly different trends in corporate pay, even after controlling for changes in profits, sales, and assets.

tenure, low-pay employees are the first to be let go in a downturn. The sample evidence does not suggest this type of selection bias either.[20] The mean pay of newly hired managers and that of departing managers are both equal to the mean pay of all managers in the same firm. This result holds true both in firms with sales gains and in those with sales declines.

A fundamental characteristic of incentive pay schemes is compensation that is an increasing function of desired performance. Although nonlinear compensation structures may well be optimal under certain conditions, compensation that falls with better performance cannot serve as an incentive for such performance. The data analyzed here show significant, although small, asymmetries in the response of pay to sales gains and losses. The elasticity of pay is .005 with respect to sales increases and − .015 with respect to sales losses. In other words, among firms with declining sales, pay gains are greater the greater the loss of sales. Both of these responses are quite small, although both are precisely measured and the difference is significant. Thus, in general, executive pay is not very responsive to sales changes; but to the extent that the two are linked, the relationship appears U-shaped, with bigger pay raises in firms with bigger sales losses. The response to profits shows a similar U-shaped pattern that is inconsistent with simple incentive models.

One possible explanation for the finding of higher executive pay in firms with high losses than in those with more moderate losses is that failing firms may need to pay a compensating differential to attract and retain skilled managers. Executives may discount future compensation more heavily when they consider employment with a failing firm, demanding a greater share of compensation in the form of current cash. Excessive executive pay raises may also reduce profits, which are measured net of compensation.

---

[20] Selection on the change rather than the level of pay might still lead to underestimation of the elasticity of pay offers with respect to sales, if managers who were offered the greatest pay cuts quit.

Managers' raises do depend somewhat on their employer's fortunes, but the response is not immediate. The relationship is smoothed over a number of years. F-tests fail to reject the joint significance of firm effects on pay changes in Table 4. Even after controlling for the past year's change in accounting measures of firm performance, 23 of the 118 firm effects are significantly different from zero at the .05 level. In part, these trends in the rate of change of pay at individual firms appear to be a response to long-run changes in firm performance.

First difference estimates such as the one in Table 4 emphasize transient elements, including noise. Here, over 80% of the variance in the change in wages remains unaccounted for, and only about half of the remaining variance is related to changes in corporate profits, sales, or assets. Although the portion of wage variance explained by those factors is high compared to the corresponding value in most wage change estimates, most executive pay changes are not driven by contemporaneous changes in observed corporate performance.

Bonus Pay Compared to Base Pay

Bonus pay that never changes is really just base pay under a different guise. Differences among the bonuses observed in this sample, however, persist far less than do differences in base pay. The correlation between firm effects on bonus pay in 1981 and in 1985 is .23. Thus, bonus pay in a given year provides only a negligible indication of what bonus pay will be a decade hence.

Still, autoregressions indicate that one-third of a given year's firm bonus effect carries forward into the next year. The stock market returns for 1981–85 give little reason to suppose that this carry-over reflects similarly persistent good corporate performance; a more plausible explanation is that smoothing is built into the bonus plans of executives (as, indeed, we know it is in at least some cases). Lags in adjustment are evident because an above-average increase in bonus in 1982 is followed by below-average increases in bonus in each of the three succeeding years.

There are persistent differences across firms in their use and level of bonuses. In pooled regressions from 1981 to 1985, 302 of 438 company dummies are significant at the .01 level, even though changes in unit sales are controlled for. The elasticity of bonus pay with respect to unit sales is .022—a low value, but more than four times as high as the elasticity of base pay with respect to unit sales. Bonus pay is also far more variable over time than is base pay. For example, from 1984 to 1985 average base pay increased 5.6%, whereas bonus pay increased 64%. Although it is not strongly tied to unit performance, bonus pay is far more flexible over time than is base pay.

The Effect of Compensation Systems and Organizational Structure on Profits

The owners of a firm face a moral-hazard problem in attempting to elicit optimum performance from executives. In theory, one solution to this principal-agent problem is for the shareholders to sell the company to the risk-neutral managers. The moral-hazard problem may then be replicated at lower levels of the corporate hierarchy, but at the top it will have been collapsed. The closer the executive payout function is to that of shareholders, the more closely aligned executives' actions should be to those desired by shareholders. Both short-term bonus schemes and long-term incentive systems have been offered as approximations to such a solution. But such systems are not without problems. Not only do they increase the uncertainty of executives' earnings, but lower-level executives who are offered such plans in lieu of cash may suspect the offerers have inside information indicating a decline in the firm's success.

The apparently simple proposition that an incentive system that ameliorates the principal-agent problem creates greater incentives for executives to maximize profits, and so increases profits, is not easily tested. First, consider tests that are at heart correlations of total executive compensation with earnings. By themselves, such correlations cannot reveal anything about the desirability or effectiveness of various compensation policies. In particular, from a correlation between high compensation and high profits, no causation can be inferred. If compensation is a function of profits, as incentive design suggests it should be, any accident that increases profits will increase compensation, producing a positive correlation between the two even if compensation systems have no direct effect on profits. Conversely, the absence of a correlation need not indicate the absence of desirable incentive effects. For example, suppose the executives capture all rents, and that corporate profits are measured net of compensation. In that case, even if an incentive system does produce greater gross profits, there will be no correlation between net profits and compensation.[21]

These difficulties suggest that a more fruitful approach is to test whether the presence or absence of certain incentive structures (rather than the level of pay) is associated with higher profits. Of course, such a test cannot be made using a sample with homogeneous firms and executives; a profit-enhancing mechanism is, in that case, adopted by all, leaving no testable variation. Under such conditions we must suspect the assumption that all relevant unobservable conditions are identical when we observe a non-adopter. In the present case, it is necessary to model the underlying heterogeneity of the firms sampled. Any heterogeneity that makes adoption of long-term incentives profitable for only some firms may also independently cause differences in profits. The omitted vari-

---

[21] Replacing profits with return on equity in the above argument leaves other problems. The expected impact of any policy on future earnings streams should be capitalized in current share prices. Risk-adjusted returns on equity (at market rather than book value) should be arbitraged to equality. Differences in returns on equity (at market value) are then due to noise or to news that has not yet been capitalized.

able may cause both profits and the adoption of an incentive structure, yielding correlation without causation between the two.

Consider next the innovation model, in which long-term incentive plans are desirable, but diffuse slowly across employers. Slow adopters might be slow in other ways (low ability), leading to overstatement of the effects of the incentive plan itself.

Yet another kind of test with difficulties is a study of changers—a before and after test of those who switch compensation systems. Such an approach is prone to all the criticisms above and one more. Executives with inside information that corporate profits are about to jump should be eager to adopt bonus or incentive plans. Observing ex-post that adoption of such plans is correlated with increases in profits may then tell us no more than that executives timed adoption to take advantage of inside information.

There are also non-trivial problems of incentive mechanism design, as well as a number of puzzles raised by the nature of actual incentive systems currently in use. Commonly observed bonus and incentive plans make pay a function of (a) sales, (b) earnings, (c) market share, or (d) share value. The last criterion is rare (nonexistent?) in bonus plans, but common in long-term incentive plans. Systems based on such indicators of corporate performance have a number of undesirable properties. Two of them (those based on "a" or "c") are subject to profit-decreasing manipulation by lowering output price. Three (those based on a, b, or d) reward executives for nominal changes such as inflation, particularly if the reward schedule is concave; they reflect industry- or economy-wide shifts outside the executives' control. Systems based on "a" or "b" (or, indirectly, "d") are also subject to accounting manipulation. Concavities in reward structure create incentives for bunching in time sales or earnings.[22]

Finally, share price is a very noisy measure of corporate performance.

An alternative mechanism free from some of these defects ties executive compensation to excess returns measured in a Capital Asset Pricing Model. This mechanism has several virtues: it rewards real rather than nominal improvements; it filters out general increases in the market index and, presumably, economy- and industry-wide changes outside the executive's control; it rewards relative rather than absolute performance; and it is not as subject to strategic manipulation as are the other mechanisms.

If such an incentive mechanism has so many advantages, the interesting question is why no firms have adopted it.[23] Clearly, the excess returns are noisy measures of success, and depend on the appropriateness of the underlying CAPM model. These excess returns are not as easy for an executive to verify as are sales or earnings results. Paying bonuses to the executives of a company that is dying, but dying more slowly than expected or more slowly than its competitors, may be desirable *ex ante* for an incentive structure, but may be difficult to explain to shareholders *ex post*. Furthermore, executives could limit their company-specific risk by selling options in their own company, or buying their competitors' options, thereby undoing the incentive system.[24]

The use of both sort-term bonuses and long-term capital incentives increased over time in the cross-sections studied here, reaching near universal coverage by 1985. Between 1981 and 1985 the proportion of sampled corporations using bonus systems increased from 95.6% to 98.3%, and the proportion of those using long-term incentive systems increased from 91.8% to

---

[22] If the return to market share is concave, an incentive is also created for collusion. Executives of two competing firms would then stand to gain by

taking turns serving the entire market, rather than splitting it evenly each year.

[23] Some function of the variables commonly observed in incentive pay schemes might approximate excess returns in the CAPM.

[24] Furthermore, it is not clear that excess returns are the proper measure of corporate success. Corporate restructuring allows strategic manipulation of the correlation between firm and market performance.

97.2%. The increasing and near-universal use of such plans makes a prima facie case for their desirability.[25] It also leaves only a small number of non-adopters for tests of the plans' impact on firm performance.

Firms implementing a bonus system have significantly higher average return on equity than do firms without bonus systems (Table 5). Firms with long-term incentive plans have a lower average return on equity (ROE). The degree of hierarchical structure is not significantly correlated with average ROE. These findings are based on regressions for 80 companies of ROE on dummy variables indicating the presence of a long-term incentive plan or a bonus plan, an index of the number of levels of hierarchy per 100 employees, indicators for other personnel practices, and vectors of dichotomous variables for companies' 2-digit industry codes.

An additional test is provided by examining changes in ROE over time within firms. On average, ROE fell in sample firms between 1981 and 1985. The presence of a bonus system did not significantly affect this result; but ROE declined significantly less in firms with long-term incentive plans and more hierarchical structure.

These results are subject to many of the criticisms noted above. Overall, they present a mixed picture of the impact of long-term incentives, bonuses, and hierarchy on corporate success. Bonuses are associated with higher average ROE, but have no significant effect on changes in ROE. Firms with long-term incentive plans and more hierarchy average lower ROE, but their ROE falls significantly less from 1981 to 1985. The early 1980s appear to have been poor years for such firms. The results on change in ROE may be more persuasive, because unchanging differences across firms are differenced out. Long-term incentives and hierarchy may both serve useful purposes.

---

[25] I have ignored possible tax and misinformation advantages of long-term incentives. The costs of long-term incentives are much less obvious to shareholders than are immediate cash payments, both because accounting rules do not in general value such options correctly and because payment is often ultimately made in the form of share dilution.

Table 5. Corporate Performance, 1981–1985, in Relation to Compensation Policies and Internal Organization.

Variable	Mean ROE	Change in ROE
Long-Term Incentives	−.34	2.38
	(.06)	(.29)
Bonus Pay Policy	.18	−.38
	(.06)	(.28)
Hierarchy	−.10	1.38
	(.10)	(.50)
Promotion Rate	.06	−.53
	(.09)	(.44)
Exit Rate	−.10	.20
	(.08)	(.38)
Steepness of Pay Profile	.10	.36
	(.32)	(1.53)
Mean Pay	.01	.16
	(.03)	(.16)
Standard Deviation of Pay	.29	−.98
	(.16)	(.78)
R^2	.70	.73
SEE	.064	.316
Mean of the Dependent Variable	.138	−.113

Notes: N = 80. Standard errors in parentheses. Both equations also control for 20 approximate 2-digit industry groups. Only corporations reporting data for all 5 years are included. Long-Term Incentives and Bonus Pay are dummies indicating use of these policies in 1981. The hierarchy index is measured as the number of levels of management in the firm's longest chain, divided by the number of employees in hundreds, with mean .10 and standard deviation .14. Promotion Rate (mean = .13) is the proportion of 1981 managers with the firm in a higher position by 1985. Exit rate (mean = .56) is the proportion of 1981 incumbents departing the sample by 1985. Steepness (mean = 1.11) is the ratio of mean pay in levels 1 and 2 to mean pay in levels 5 and 6 in 1981. The mean and standard deviation of pay are for all managers in 1981.

Corporate Performance, Pay Equity, and Tournaments

What impact does internal pay structure have on firm performance? In the absence of much systematic evidence, a number of conflicting theories have been advanced. Some assert that reducing pay differentials improves employee morale and cooperation and leads to greater productivity. The opposite effect is claimed by those who assert that the positive incentive effects of pay differentials—including the inducement of both effort and self-selection—dominate.

The regressions in Table 5 show how the level of and change in ROE vary as a function of the variance of managerial pay, the steepness of the managerial pay hierarchy, and the promotion rate. Again, such tests rely heavily on the *ceteris paribus* assumption. The data reveal no strong association between managerial pay equity and corporate performance. There is no significant correlation between the variance of managerial pay within a firm and the firm's subsequent change in ROE.

There is some evidence consistent with a tournament or lottery view of executive compensation. In such models, high pay in top executive positions is used to motivate lower-level executives to compete for promotions. The expected value to executives of such a scheme can be maintained if the pay differential across levels narrows while promotion probabilities increase.

Steeper pay differentials are indeed associated with lower promotion rates. (See Table 6.) The promotion rate is measured as the proportion of level 5 and 6 managers in 1981 staying with the company through 1985 who reached a higher level by 1985. The steepness of the pay hierarchy in 1981 is given by the ratio of mean pay in levels 1 and 2 to mean pay in levels 5 and 6. The correlation between

Table 6. Steepness of Pay Profile in Relation to Promotion and Exit Rates and Within-Level Pay Variance.

Variable	Coefficient	(Standard Error)
Promotion Rate	−.073	(.025)
Exit Rate, levels 1 + 2	−.010	(.017)
Exit Rate, levels 5 + 6	−.029	(.023)
Standard Deviation of Pay, levels 5 + 6	−.0003	(.048)
Intercept	1.16	(.025)
R^2	.11	
N	80	
SES	.034	
Mean of the Dependent Variable	1.11	

Note: Dependent Variable is ratio of mean pay in levels 1 and 2 to mean pay in levels 5 and 6 in 1981. The Promotion Rate (Mean = .20) is the proportion of 1981 level 5 and 6 managers with the firm in a higher level by 1985. Exit Rates are the proportion of 1981 incumbents departing the sample by 1985.

these two variables across firms is significantly negative.

Desire for pay equity within a managerial level is apparently not a great enough constraint to force the use of promotions across levels as a substitute for pay increases within each level. The variance of pay in levels 5 and 6 in 1981 is uncorrelated with the subsequent promotion rate out of these levels. Mean pay is also uncorrelated with the promotion rate. If both promotion rates and relative mean pay are stable over time, this suggests few managers are willing to accept better promotion possibilities as a substitute for current pay.

Conclusion

The impact of incentive mechanisms on executives' performance is likely to be important, particularly at the highest executive levels, where individual output is crucial to the success of the firm but nonstandard. This paper has analyzed new data on pay for executives ranging from CEO to foreman at a few hundred major U.S. corporations from 1981 to 1985. The major findings include the following:

Executive pay (base plus bonus) is widely dispersed across firms, but not much more so than for many production workers. Although firm effects persist, they account unambiguously for only 8% of individual pay variance.

Pay is strongly hierarchically determined. Level in the corporate hierarchy is the single most important correlate of executive pay. Consistent with tournament theory, pay differentials between ranks are greater higher up the ladder, and are also greater the lower the promotion rate. Managers in more hierarchically structured organizations are paid more than those in flat organizations: executives whose subordinates are more hierarchically ranked earn up to a 60% pay premium over those in flat organizations. Hierarchical structure is also associated with greater growth in ROE.

Human capital and individual performance affect pay primarily by affecting the allocation of individuals to jobs, rather than by affecting pay within each position. This finding is evidence of extensive sorting of people into positions. There is considerable turnover at every executive level, and pure promote-from-within systems are rare. One-fifth of the top executives in the sample for this study had been with their current company less than five years.

The odds of eventual employment in the highest ranks are higher for executives who do not lock themselves into one corporation early in their careers. Bonus pay should be particularly useful as an incentive for those left behind who remain stuck in the same position in the same company. The best managers are promoted out; those who remain for long periods in the same position suffer slower wage growth.

Accounting measures of corporate success are not significantly related to the level of, or degree of equity in, executive pay, or to the steepness of pay differentials across executive ranks. Corporations appear able to succeed with a variety of internal pay and promotion practices.

Most executive pay (base plus bonus) changes are unrelated to contemporaneous changes in company performance. The base and bonus pay of managers responds hardly at all to changes in corporate sales or profits, or to unit sales. The elasticity of pay with respect to corporate sales is only .122. Bonuses are smoothed over time, but they are far more variable over time than is base pay.

Higher-level executives are more likely to be motivated by contingent pay than by promotion. Because higher-level executives are also more directly responsible for corporate success, and less affected by free-rider problems, their pay is more heavily contingent upon corporate performance. The relationship of pay to corporate performance is U-shaped: executive pay is higher in successful than in failing companies, but among failing companies it is higher in those with heavy losses than in those with small losses. This pattern, which may reflect the difficulty of retaining skilled managers in a firm with poor prospects, is not compatible with the usual description of pay as an incentive device that rewards superior corporate performance.

As for whether long-term incentive plans are in the shareholders' best interests, the evidence of this study suggests that firms with such plans enjoyed significantly greater increases in ROE during the 1980s than did other firms. By 1985, such plans had been nearly universally adopted by large corporations, along with bonus pay plans.

REFERENCES

Abowd, John. 1989. "Does Performance-Based Compensation Affect Subsequent Corporate Performance?" Unpublished paper, Cornell University.

Benston, George. 1985. "The Self-Serving Management Hypothesis: Some Evidence." *Journal of Accounting and Economics*, Vol. 7 (April), pp. 67–84.

Brickley, James, Sanjai Bhagat, and Ronald Lease. 1985. "The Impact of Long-Range Managerial Compensation Plans on Shareholder Wealth." *Journal of Accounting and Economics*, Vol. 7 (April), pp. 115–29.

Coughlin, Anne, and Ronald Schmidt. 1985. "Executive Compensation, Management Turnover, and Firm Performance: An Empirical Investigation." *Journal of Accounting and Economics*, Vol. 7 (April), pp. 43–66.

Groshen, Erica. 1987. "Sources of Wage Dispersion: The Contribution of Interemployer Wage Differentials Within Industry." Federal Reserve Bank of Cleveland Working Paper, December.

Healy, Paul. 1985. "The Effect of Bonus Schemes on Accounting Decisions." *Journal of Accounting and Economics*, Vol. 7 (April), pp. 85–107.

Jensen, Michael, and Kevin Murphy. 1988. "Performance Pay and Top Management Incentives." Unpublished paper, University of Rochester.

Kalleberg, Arne, and James Lincoln. 1988. "The Structure of Earnings Inequality in the United States and Japan." *American Journal of Sociology*, Vol. 94, pp. s121–153.

Larcker, David. 1983. "The Association Between Performance Plan Adoption and Corporate Capital Investment." *Journal of Accounting and Economics*, Vol. 5, pp. 1–30.

Lazear, Edward. 1986. "Raids and Offer Matching." *Research in Labor Economics*, Vol. 8, Part A, pp. 141–65.

Lazear, Edward, and Sherwin Rosen. 1981. "Rank-order Tournaments as Optimum Labor Contracts." *Journal of Political Economy*, Vol. 89, pp. 841–64.

Leonard, Jonathan. 1989a. "Wage Structure and Dynamics in the Electronics Industry." *Industrial Relations*, Vol. 28, pp. 251–75.

———. 1989b. "Career Paths of Managers and Executives." Unpublished paper, U.C.–Berkeley.

Lev, Baruch. 1989. "On the Usefulness of Earnings: Lessons and Directions from Two Decades of Research." Unpublished paper, U.C.–Berkeley.

Lewellen, Wilbur, and Blaine Huntsman. 1970. "Managerial Pay and Corporate Performance." *American Economic Review*, Vol. 60, pp. 710–20.

Masson, Robert. 1971. "Executive Motivation, Earnings, and Consequent Equity Performance." *Journal of Political Economy*, Vol. 79, p. 1278–92.

Medoff, James, and Katharine Abraham. 1980. "Experience, Performance and Earnings." *Quarterly Journal of Economics*, Vol. 95, pp. 703–36.

Murphy, Kevin. 1985. "Corporate Performance and Managerial Remuneration: An Empirical Analysis." *Journal of Accounting and Economics*, Vol. 7 (April), pp. 11–42.

———. 1986. "Incentives, Learning, and Compensation: A Theoretical and Empirical Investigation of Managerial Labor Contracts." *Rand Journal of Economics*, Vol. 17, pp. 59–76.

O'Reilly, Charles. 1989. "Board Composition and Executive Pay." Unpublished paper, U.C.–Berkeley.

Rosen, Sherwin. 1982. "Authority, Control and the Distribution of Earnings." *Bell Journal of Economics*, Vol. 13, pp. 311–23.

———. 1986. "Prizes and Incentives in Elimination Tournaments." *American Economic Review*, Vol. 76, pp. 701–15.

Simon, Herbert. 1957. "The Compensation of Executives." *Sociometry*, Vol. 20, pp. 32–35.

Tehranian, Hassan, and James Waegelein. 1985. "Market Reaction to Short Term Executive Compensation Plan Adoption." *Journal of Accounting and Economics*, Vol. 7 (April), pp. 131–44.

Weiss, Andrew, and Henry Landau. 1985. "On the Negative Correlation Between Performance and Experience and Education." NBER Working Paper No. 1613.

RELATIVE PERFORMANCE EVALUATION
FOR CHIEF EXECUTIVE OFFICERS

ROBERT GIBBONS AND KEVIN J. MURPHY*

Relative performance evaluation (RPE) provides employees with an incentive to perform well while insulating their compensation from shocks that also affect the performances of other workers in the same firm, industry, or market. This paper reviews the benefits and costs of RPE and tests for the presence of RPE in the compensation contracts of chief executive officers (CEOs) using data on 1,668 CEOs from 1,049 corporations from 1974 to 1986. The results, in contrast to the findings of previous research, strongly support the hypothesis that RPE is used in compensation and retention decisions affecting CEOs: the revision in a CEO's pay and the probability that a CEO remains in his position for the following year are positively and significantly related to firm performance, but are negatively and significantly related to industry and market performance.

It is common for workers to be rewarded not simply for their own performance but rather for their performance measured relative to the performances of co-workers. Examples are explicit contests and tournaments, the allocation of a fixed bonus pool at the corporate or divisional level, forced-distribution performance appraisals, and promotions awarded to one worker from a group of subordinates.

Economic theory provides a rationale for relative performance evaluation (RPE) based on risk-sharing. Compensation based solely on observed individual performance provides incentives for a worker to be productive, but measured performance (and therefore compensation) is almost always affected by random factors beyond the worker's control. The random factors that affect one worker's performance often affect the observed performances of other workers in the same division, firm, industry, or market. In these cases, RPE can provide incentives while partially insulating the worker from the common uncertainty.

Although RPE offers benefits when there exists an important source of common risk or uncertainty, it also entails costs. Basing pay on relative performance generates incentives to sabotage the measured performance of co-workers (or any other reference group), to collude with

* Robert Gibbons is Assistant Professor of Economics at the Massachusetts Institute of Technology and Kevin J. Murphy is Associate Professor of Economics at the William E. Simon Graduate School of Business Administration, University of Rochester. The authors are grateful for many helpful comments from John Abowd, Joshua Angrist, James Brickley, David Card, Jeffrey Coles, Ronald Ehrenberg, Henry Farber, Lawrence Katz, Alan Krueger, Edward Lazear, Meg Meyer, Sherwin Rosen, Sharon Smith, Ross Watts, and Michael Weisbach as well as from participants in seminars at NBER, NYU, and the Princeton Labor Lunch. This research is supported by the Sloan Foundation (both authors); the NSF (grant SES 88-09200) and the Industrial Relations Section at Princeton University (Gibbons); and the John M. Olin Foundation and the Managerial Economics Research Center, University of Rochester (Murphy).

co-workers and shirk, and to apply for jobs with inept co-workers. Relative-performance contracts also are less desirable when the output of co-workers is expensive to measure or when there are production externalities, as in the case of team production.

One occupation for which the risk-sharing advantages of RPE likely exceed its counterproductive side-effects is top-level corporate management. Executive compensation contracts based only on firm performance subject executives to vagaries of the stock and product markets that are clearly beyond management control. Measuring managerial performance relative to the performance of other firms in the same industry or market partially insulates executives from such industry and market shocks. Relative-performance contracts for chief executive officers (CEOs) are inexpensive to administer, since the stock performance of rival firms is available on a daily basis at trivial cost. In addition, because CEOs tend to have limited interaction with CEOs in rival firms, sabotage and collusive shirking seem unlikely.

The purpose of this paper is to investigate empirically the extent to which CEOs are rewarded on the basis of relative performance. We begin with a review of the benefits and costs of RPE in the workplace, and then apply the analysis to the case of top-level management. We test for the presence of RPE in executive compensation by analyzing a longitudinal sample of over 1,600 CEOs from more than one thousand publicly held corporations.

This paper builds on previous research in agency theory, especially that by Holmström (1982), who developed the economic theory of relative performance evaluation, and Antle and Smith (1986), who tested for the existence of RPE in executive compensation contracts. We extend Holmström's analysis by discussing the costs as well as the benefits of relative-performance contracts. Our debt to other related research is discussed below.

The Theory of Relative Performance Evaluation

A Simple Model of the Benefits of RPE

This section presents an informal review of the economic theory of relative performance evaluation. Two early papers on this subject are Baiman and Demski (1980) and Lazear and Rosen (1981); Wolfson (1985) applies the theory to shared-equity real estate contracts. The analysis in this section applies to all employees in a workplace; we defer our application of the theory to top-level management until the next section.

Suppose that output, y, depends on the worker's effort, a, but is stochastic. For example,

$$(1) \qquad y = a + \epsilon,$$

where ϵ is a noise term with zero mean. Because the worker's effort is unobservable, the employer and worker cannot sign a contract specifying that the employee supply a particular level of effort. Instead, the employer offers the worker a compensation contract, $w(y)$, that determines the worker's wage as a function of the realized output of the production process. The worker then chooses whether to sign the contract or to take up alternative employment yielding utility U^0. After signing the contract, the worker chooses a level of effort, and production occurs.

Suppose that the employer is risk-neutral: he cares only about output net of compensation, $y - w$. The worker, on the other hand, dislikes effort and is averse to compensation risk. Under these assumptions, full efficiency (the "first-best") is defined by two conditions: (a) the worker must supply the productively efficient level of effort (that is, the level of effort at which the expected value of the output resulting from an additional unit of effort equals the disutility to the worker from this additional unit of effort); and (b) the worker must be perfectly insured against compensation risk.

If the worker were risk-neutral, insurance would be unnecessary and the first-best could be achieved via a contract $w(y)$ = $y - F$ that, in effect, sells the worker the firm: the worker receives the entire output, y, as compensation, but pays the employer an up-front fee, F, so that the worker's expected utility just equals his reservation utility. When workers are risk-averse, however, the optimal contract is necessarily "second-best," both because the worker bears income risk and because the worker's effort choice is smaller than is productively efficient. The optimal contract for a risk-averse worker reflects a trade-off between the goals of insuring the worker and providing incentives for efficient effort choice.

The fact that the best possible contract of the form $w(y)$ induces a risk-averse worker to supply less than the productively efficient amount of effort suggests that employers may be able to improve the contract by making pay contingent on a second variable, z, in addition to output, y. Holmström (1979) showed that the optimal contract has the form $w(y,z)$ whenever z contains incremental information valuable in assessing the worker's unobservable effort.[1] Intuitively, the role of z in the contract $w(y,z)$ is either to provide more insurance without reducing incentives for effort or to provide greater incentives without increasing risk exposure.

As a concrete example, suppose that the worker's output depends not only on effort and idiosyncratic noise, ϵ, but also on an additional noise term, θ, where θ is a common shock experienced by some set of workers in the same division, firm, industry, or market:

(2) $y = a + \epsilon + \theta.$

The shock θ could reflect, for example, seasonal or random variations in industry demand, market-wide stock movements, or the fixed-effect of a single supervisor evaluating each member of a group of workers. If θ is perfectly observable, contracts of the form $w(y - \theta)$ clearly improve on contracts of the form $w(y)$.

The presence of θ makes y a noisier signal about effort than it would be in the absence of θ. Therefore, the employer can reduce the noise in his evaluation of the worker's effort by basing contracts on $y - \theta$ rather than on y alone. Even if the common shock θ is not perfectly observable, the employer still can improve on contracts of the form $w(y)$ by incorporating an estimate of θ, denoted by $\hat{\theta}$, into the contract. Since $\hat{\theta}$ measures the common shock θ with error, optimal contracts incorporating the estimate $\hat{\theta}$ will generally be of the form $w(y,\hat{\theta})$ rather than of the simpler form $w(y - \hat{\theta})$, and the common risk will be only *partially* filtered out of the worker's compensation.

To see how $\hat{\theta}$ might be computed, consider the following elaboration of the example above.[2] Suppose that there are n identical workers whose outputs are given by $y_i = a_i + \epsilon_i + \theta$, for $i = 1, \ldots, n$, where a_i and ϵ_i are the ith worker's effort and idiosyncratic noise, respectively. Then, assuming that the ϵ_i's are independently and identically distributed with zero mean, an estimate of the common shock is $\hat{\theta} = \bar{y} - \bar{a}$, where $\bar{y}$ is the average output of all other workers subject to the common shock θ, and $\bar{a}$ is the average anticipated effort level of these $n - 1$ other workers conditional on their compensation packages.[3] Under the assumption that the ϵ_i's are normally distributed, Holmström (1982) showed that the optimal contract for the ith worker is $w_i(y_i, \bar{y})$.[4] Typically, the wage paid to the ith worker will be

---

[1] More precisely, the optimal contract will depend on z if y is not a sufficient statistic for the pair $\{y,z\}$ with respect to the worker's effort.

[2] Alternative methods of calculating $\hat{\theta}$ applicable to special situations include seasonal adjustments and prorating output to adjust for unanticipated plant closings.

[3] The estimate in the text, $\hat{\theta} = \bar{y} - \bar{a}$, is the OLS estimate of θ given the available information about the $n-1$ other workers. A more efficient OLS estimate of θ would also include the information available about the ith worker. If the joint distribution of the idiosyncratic noise terms is known, one can also compute the maximum likelihood estimate of θ. One can relax the assumption that the idiosyncratic noise terms are independently and identically distributed.

[4] Note that y_i plays two roles in this contract. First, it provides incentives in the usual way. Second, it improves the estimate of θ as described in footnote 3.

positively related to his own output but negatively related to the average output of all other workers subject to the same common shock. Holmström also showed that as the number of workers becomes very large (so that θ is a very precise estimate of θ), the optimal contract approaches the form $w_i(y_i - \bar{y})$, where $y_i - \bar{y}$ is the performance of the ith worker measured relative to the performance of others in the reference group.

Relative performance evaluation may be beneficial even in the absence of risk-aversion and incentive problems. Alternative models based on learning about ability, for example, also predict RPE when workers in a group are exposed to a common shock. Formally, let individual output, y_i, depend on ability and not effort:

(3) $$y_i = \eta_i + \epsilon_i + \theta,$$

where η_i is the ith worker's ability, ϵ_i is idiosyncratic noise, and θ is the unobservable common shock. Suppose that ability is not known precisely; rather, η_i is believed to be normally distributed with mean zero and variance σ_η^2. (Allowing for a non-zero mean is straightforward but uninformative.) Suppose further that θ and ϵ_i are normally distributed with mean zero and variances σ_θ^2 and σ_ϵ^2, respectively, and that the common shock and the n workers' individual abilities and noise terms are independent. Given these assumptions, it is straightforward to show (see, for example, Theorem 9.11 of Mood and Graybill 1963) that the expected ability of the ith worker, given his output and the outputs of the $n-1$ co-workers subject to the shock θ, is as described by equation (4). Suppose that individual outputs are observable and that wages are a function of expected ability. Then the wage offered to the ith worker will typically be positively related to his own output but negatively related to the average output of all other workers subject to the same common shock.

In both the incentive model and the learning model, RPE provides a way to filter common risk from workers' compensation contracts. The qualitative predictions of (and underlying economic rationales behind) both models are similar enough that we make no attempt to distinguish between these complementary theories of RPE.

Disadvantages of Rewarding Workers Based on Relative Performance

The benefits of RPE are straightforward—the risk exposure of risk-averse workers can be reduced by filtering out some or all of the common risk. This rationale for basing rewards on relative performance rather than on absolute performance accords with the general rule-of-thumb that workers should not be rewarded or punished for "things beyond their control." Before embracing the theory completely, however, we must also consider the costs of compensation systems based on relative performance.

An obvious cost of RPE is the cost of observing the average output of the workers subject to the same common shock. If the cost of measuring $\bar{y}$ is a fixed cost, C, it affects whether or not a firm uses RPE at all but does not affect the importance of relative performance in compensation contracts that use RPE: firms will use relative performance if C is less than the increased value of the best contract $w_i(y_i, \bar{y})$ relative to the best contract $w_i(y_i)$. Alternatively, the size of the reference group may be a choice variable for employers—employers will sample additional workers from the pool of workers subject to the common shock as long as the incremental gain from improved contracts (associated with more precise estimates of θ) exceeds the cost of measuring an additional worker's output.

There is another set of costs associated with RPE that may be much more impor-

$$E[\eta_i | y_1, \ldots, y_n] = \frac{\sigma_\eta^2}{\sigma_\eta^2 + \sigma_\epsilon^2} \left(y_i - \frac{\sigma_\theta^2}{\sigma_\eta^2 + \sigma_\epsilon^2 + n\sigma_\theta^2} \sum_{j=1}^{n} y_j \right).$$

Equation (4).

tant than the simple measurement costs described above. *Paying workers based on relative performance,* $y_i - \bar{y}$, *instead of on absolute performance,* y_i, *distorts the worker's incentives whenever the worker can take actions that affect the average output of the reference group,* $\bar{y}$. There are at least four ways in which a worker's action can have this kind of effect: *sabotage* (in which the worker takes unproductive actions to diminish the measured performance of another worker in the reference group); *collusion* (in which workers in the same reference group collude and shirk); *choice of reference group* (in which a worker chooses which of several groups of other workers to which to be compared); and *production externalities* (in which the productive actions of one worker affect the outputs of other workers).

Sabotage ranges from relatively subtle forms—such as concealing relevant information from, or spreading false gossip about, a fellow employee—to outright theft or destruction of co-worker output. Sabotage can be effective even if it diminishes one's own output provided that it has a larger negative effect on the average output of other workers. Lazear (1987) argues that the sabotage-related problems of RPE may be a driving force in the pay equality observed in many organizations. According to Lazear, reducing pay differences based on relative performance reduces uncooperative behavior that is detrimental to the firm. Withholding valuable comments on a colleague's paper or deleting data from a colleague's hard disk are examples of potential sabotage in academia.

Rewards based on relative performance also generate incentives for workers to collude and supply less effort than would be supplied in the absence of collusion (see Mookherjee 1984 and Dye 1984). In academia, for example, colleagues could agree not to work at night, on weekends, or during summers. The general conditions for cartel stability in the product market (Stigler 1964) apply to a workplace cartel as well—collusion is more likely when the number of potential colluders is small, for example, and collusion is more

effective when workers can observe the output and compensation of co-workers. It seems plausible that collusion in the workplace is more likely to be stable than collusion in the product market, both because workplace collusion is not an antitrust violation and because it may be easier to monitor co-workers who are close at hand than to monitor the costs and outputs of geographically dispersed rival establishments.

Relative performance evaluation also distorts incentives when agents can influence the determination of which of several possible reference groups is used in the evaluation process. Workers are often involved in interviewing, selecting, and recruiting potential colleagues. Workers paid on the basis of relative performance clearly have an incentive *not* to hire rookies of superior ability, and will instead desire incompetent co-workers. For example, Carmichael (1988) argued that non-tenured faculty have incentives to recruit less-able colleagues. The same rationale also applies to job search—RPE generates incentives for workers to self-select into firms with inferior co-workers. Dye (1988) argued that paying top executives based on industry-relative performance yields incentives to locate in industries with inept rivals, so that the manager appears to be both talented and hard-working relative to other managers in the (carefully selected) reference group. Similarly, RPE may adversely affect an executive's decision to leave a declining industry, and may cause a mediocre performer to leave a rapidly growing industry even if staying in the industry maximizes the value of the organization.

Finally, RPE will be less desirable when the effort levels of individual workers are complementary factors in the firm's production process, as in team production, for example. Workers paid on the basis of relative performance will not have incentives to develop innovations that uniformly increase the productivity of all other workers in the reference group. Optimal contracts in the presence of such production externalities typically involve rewarding individuals for group output,

$\partial w_i(y_i,\bar{y})/\partial\bar{y} > 0$, instead of rewarding individual performance measured relative to the performance of others, $\partial w_i(y_i,\bar{y})/\partial\bar{y} < 0$.

The costs and benefits of RPE suggest that filtering out common risk will be more effective in some situations than in others. Incentives to sabotage or collude with other agents subject to the same common shock are more important when the number of co-workers is small, and RPE will therefore be less effective for small groups than for large groups, *ceteris paribus*. Also, RPE will be more effective when the worker is unable to influence the choice of reference group, and will be less effective when there are externalities in the production process (such as team production), or when the output of co-workers is expensive to measure.

Rewarding Executives on Relative Performance

The relationship between the shareholders of a publicly owned corporation and the corporation's top manager is an archetypal example of a principal-agent relationship. Widely diffuse shareholders, assumed to be well diversified and therefore risk-neutral, want the manager to take actions that increase shareholder wealth. The imperfectly monitorable manager, however, takes actions that increase his expected utility. Managerial contracts tying pay and dismissal decisions to changes in shareholder wealth help align the interests of shareholders and the manager by giving the manager incentives to take actions that increase shareholder wealth.

Although the change in shareholder wealth is an appropriate measure of managerial output or firm performance, it is an imperfect measure of managerial effort, since many factors affect the value of a firm besides the actions taken by managers. (Managerial effort in this context refers not to how *hard* an executive works but rather to whether or not he takes actions or makes decisions that increase shareholder wealth.) Executives facing contracts based only on changes in shareholder wealth are subject to vagaries of the stock and product markets that are clearly beyond management control. The theory of relative performance evaluation suggests that optimal managerial contracts may base compensation and dismissal decisions on performance relative to other firms in the industry or market in order to filter common risk from the compensation of risk-averse managers.

Top-executive compensation and dismissal policy seems a likely place to observe RPE. First, it seems plausible that industry or market shocks (such as the October 1987 stock-market crash) are important and that filtering out these shocks can benefit risk-averse executives. Second, although there are of course important problems related to defining an industry, measuring the stock-market performance of other firms in a defined industry is easily accomplished on a daily basis at trivial cost. Third, because CEOs tend to have limited interaction with CEOs in rival firms, the potential for sabotage, collusive shirking, and production externalities is probably small. Another source of distorted incentives, the choice of a reference group, may be important, however (to the extent that the CEO plays a key role in choosing the industry in which his firm competes): under RPE, a manager who is among the best CEOs in a declining industry will not have the correct incentives to leave the industry. Finally, there may be production externalities across firms: for example, RPE makes oligopolistic collusion more difficult to sustain.

Another way to filter risks associated with industry and market shocks is to pay (or dismiss) executives in a given firm on the basis of their performance measured relative to the performance of other executives *in the same firm*. Lazear and Rosen (1981), for example, argue that top-management promotions are a form of RPE in which the vice president with the highest measured output is promoted to CEO. It is precisely this type of situation, however, in which the costs of RPE may be large. First, there are typically only a small number of vice presidents with a non-trivial chance of winning the promotion tournament, and therefore the opportunities for sabotaging or colluding with rival vice presidents seem large. Also, CEOs typically play an important role in selecting the team of vice presidents as well as their ultimate successor (Vancil 1987), so a CEO paid on the basis of his performance measured relative to the performance of subordinates may believe he can hold his position longer if he chooses incompetent vice presidents. Finally, because firm output (in this case, changes in shareholder wealth) is presumably jointly produced by the top management team, RPE may interfere with the shareholder's objective of maximizing team production.

Relative Performance and CEO Compensation

We test the importance of RPE in executive compensation and dismissal decisions by following all chief executive officers listed in the Executive Compensation Surveys published in *Forbes* from 1974 to 1986. These surveys include 2,214 executives serving in 1,295 corporations, or a total of 10,400 CEO-years of data. We focus on the CEO's *compensation* and *dismissal* rather than on his total incentives (which are created not only by compensation and threat of dismissal but also by changes in the value of his outstanding stock options and of his inside stockholdings) because changes in the value of previous holdings of stock and stock options are determined entirely by firm performance, independent of relative performance. Thus, if relative performance is important, its importance must arise in compensation and dismissal policy. We examine RPE in executive compensation contracts in this section; dismissals based on relative performance are examined in the next section.

We measure firm performance as the change in the logarithm of shareholder wealth, which equals the continuously accrued rate of return received by the firm's shareholders, including price appreciation and dividends. Reference-group stock-market performance is measured

using the population of 11,000 firms listed on the Compustat expanded industrial, full coverage, and historical research files. Several potential reference groups are analyzed: the entire Compustat population ("the market") and firms in the same one-, two-, three-, and four-digit SIC industries as the sample firm. Industry return is defined as the continuously accrued rate of return realized on a value-weighted portfolio of all Compustat firms (excluding the sample firm) in the same SIC industry; market return is the continuously accrued return on the value-weighted portfolio of all Compustat firms (excluding the sample firm).

Stock returns for New York Stock Exchange (NYSE) firms are calculated using fiscal-year stock-market data available from the Center for Research in Security Prices (CRSP). Fiscal-year industry classifications for NYSE and American Stock Exchange firms are also obtained from CRSP. Compustat industry classifications and stock data are used for firms included in Compustat files but not on CRSP files.[5] After matching these performance variables with the *Forbes* compensation sample and eliminating observations with missing data, our final sample contains 9,425 observations and includes 1,668 executives from 1,049 corporations. All rates of return and monetary variables are adjusted for inflation (using the consumer price index for the closing month of the fiscal year) to represent 1986-constant dollars.

Agency theory predicts that compensation will depend on relative performance but gives little guidance as to the form of the contract. We estimate the following relation between pay and firm, industry, and market performance:

---

[5] Compustat industry designations are appropriate only for the current or final year (generally 1987), whereas CRSP data allow the firm's industry to change from year to year. Compustat stock returns are based on calendar-year and not fiscal-year data, but when we replicated our analysis (including the construction of industry returns) for the subset of firms with December fiscal closings, our results were qualitatively unchanged.

Table 1. Coefficients of Ordinary Least Squares Regressions of Δln (CEO Salary + Bonus) on Firm, Industry, and Market Rates of Return on Common Stock.
(t-Statistics in Parentheses)

Independent Variable	Dependent Variable: Δln(CEO Salary + Bonus)			
	(1)	*(2)*	*(3)*	*(4)*
Intercept	.046	.055	.068	.068
Firm's Rate of Return on Common Stock	.1562 (19.5)	.1781 (19.4)	.1805 (21.0)	.1824 (19.9)
2-Digit SIC Industry Value-Weighted Return	—	−.0750 (−4.9)	—	−.0112 (−0.6)
Market Value-Weighted Return on Common Stock	—	—	−.1490 (−7.6)	−.1407 (−5.8)
R^2	.0467	.0496	.0537	.0538

Note: Sample size is 7,757 for all observations. The sample is constructed from longitudinal data reported in *Forbes* on 1,668 CEOs serving in 1,049 firms from 1974 to 1986.

(5) $\Delta \ln$(CEO Pay) = α + β(Shareholder Return) + γ(Industry and/or Market Return).

Rewarding CEOs for taking actions that increase shareholder wealth implies that $\beta > 0$. RPE implies that, holding the firm's rate of return constant, CEO pay revisions should be negatively related to the industry and market return, $\gamma < 0$.

Table 1 reports estimated coefficients from regressions relating the growth rate of CEO salary and bonus to the rates of return realized by shareholders in the firm, two-digit SIC industry, and market. Column (1) shows that CEO salaries and bonuses are positively and significantly related to firm performance as measured by the rate of return on common stock. The return coefficient of .1562 ($t = 19.5$) implies, for example, that CEO pay changes by about 1.6% for each 10% return on the common stock.[6]

Note that we interpret our estimate as having identified a compensation formula, rather than a causal relation from the compensation formula to observed performance. The latter interpretation would be incorrect, because it ignores the role of the capital market in bidding up the stock price to reflect a firm's expected profit. That is, although it is true that a higher piece rate (for example) will induce more effort and so may improve expected future profits, the stock price will adjust for this effect on the day the piece rate is announced, well before future profits are observed. Subsequent movements in our independent variable, the firm's rate of return, are thus independent of the compensation formula in place.

The estimated coefficient for industry rate of return in column (2) of Table 1 is negative and statistically significant, suggesting that boards of directors make some adjustment for industry trends when determining executive compensation. The coefficients in column (2) suggest, for example, that a CEO receives an average pay increase of 5.5% in years when shareholder return is zero in both the firm and the industry. The same CEO receives an average pay increase of 9.1% in years when shareholder return is 20% and industry return is zero, but receives an increase of only 7.6% in years when *all* firms in the industry realize 20% rates of return. This result is consistent with the hypothesis that uncertainties shared with

---

[6] The estimated return coefficient in column (1) is highly significant, but its economic magnitude is small. The sample medians for CEO pay and firm size (measured by market value) are $465,000 and $812,000,000, respectively. Thus, a 10% return in a median-size firm is $81,200,000 and corresponds to a pay raise for the median-pay CEO of $7,300, or less than nine cents for each $1,000 of increased shareholder wealth. See Jensen and Murphy (1990) for further discussion of the magnitude of the empirical relation between pay and performance.

Table 2. Coefficients of Ordinary Least Squares Regressions of Δln(CEO Salary + Bonus) on
Shareholder Return, Industry Return, and Market Return for
Three Alternative Industry Definitions.
(t-Statistics in Parentheses)

Independent Variable	Regression Coefficients Dependent Variable is Δln(CEO Salary + Bonus)					
	(1)	(2)	(3)	(4)	(5)	(6)
Intercept	.064	.051	.050	.069	.068	.068
Firm's Rate of Return	.1850 (20.6)	.1722 (18.7)	.1637 (18.4)	.1855 (20.7)	.1810 (19.5)	.1771 (19.5)
1-Digit SIC Industry Rate of Return	−.1266 (−7.1)	—	—	−.0554 (−2.0)	—	—
3-Digit SIC Industry Rate of Return	—	−.0452 (−3.5)	—	—	−.0018 (−0.1)	—
4-Digit SIC Industry Rate of Return	—	—	−.0303 (−2.8)	—	—	−.0019 (−0.2)
Value-Weighted Market Rate of Return	—	—	—	−.1027 (−3.4)	−.1462 (−6.6)	−.1444 (−6.9)
Sample Size	7,757	7,687	7,429	7,757	7,687	7,429
R^2	.0528	.0483	.0479	.0542	.0536	.0539

Note: The sample is constructed from longitudinal data reported in *Forbes* on 1,668 CEOs serving in 1,049 firms from 1974 to 1986.

other firms are partially filtered out of the CEO's compensation contract.[7]

Column (3) of Table 1 reports coefficients from regressions of CEO pay growth on shareholder return and the rate of return in the market. The negative and significant market-return coefficient suggests that market risks are also partially filtered out of executive compensation. The explanatory power of column (3) exceeds that of column (2), suggesting that CEO compensation contracts are more closely linked to market-relative returns than to two-digit industry-relative returns. The regression in column (4) includes both industry and market returns. The market-return coefficient is negative and statistically significant, indicating that CEOs are rewarded on the basis of market-relative performance and not only on

absolute performance. The industry-return coefficient is no longer significant after controlling for market-wide stock-price movements, although the point estimate is still negative.

The theory of RPE suggests that common uncertainties will be filtered out of executive compensation, but is of course silent on whether industry or market uncertainties are the most important source of common risk. The results in column (4) of Table 1 suggest that CEO performance is more likely to be evaluated relative to aggregate market movements than relative to industry movements, where the industry is defined as all other firms in the same two-digit SIC industry. We explored the robustness of this conclusion by re-estimating columns (2) and (4) of Table 1 for three alternative industry definitions: one-digit, three-digit, and four-digit SIC industries. Results from these regressions are presented in Table 2.

Columns (1), (2) and (3) of Table 2 show that CEO pay growth is positively related to shareholder return and negatively related to the value-weighted returns for other firms in the same one-digit, three-digit, and four-digit SIC industry. These

_____

[7] In keeping with the discussion in footnote 6, the economic magnitude of the industry adjustment implied by column (2) is not large. In particular, a median-paid CEO in a median-size firm receives ten cents for each $1,000 of increased shareholder wealth when his firm's return is 20% and the industry return is zero, but receives only six cents per $1,000 when both his firm and the industry realize returns of 20%.

results suggest that CEO pay is more closely linked to broad industry definitions than to narrow industry definitions. In fact, interpreting the market return as our broadest industry definition, the regressions in Tables 1 and 2 suggest that the magnitude and significance of the industry coefficient, and the explanatory power of the regression, decline monotonically as the industry becomes more narrowly defined.

The regressions in columns (4), (5), and (6) of Table 2 include market return as an additional explanatory variable and replicate the regression in column (4) of Table 1 for the three alternative industry definitions. The market-return coefficient is negative and significant in all three regressions, indicating that market risks are partially filtered out of executive compensation after controlling for industry returns. Holding market returns constant, however, CEO pay growth is negatively and marginally significantly related to one-digit industry returns, but is not significantly related to three-digit or four-digit industry returns. These results support the finding that CEO performance is more likely to be evaluated relative to aggregate market movements than relative to industry movements. An alternative interpretation of these results, however, is that firms are rarely engaged in a single industry, in which case our inability to detect an industry effect after controlling for market movements could simply reflect the fact that industry definitions based on a single SIC code for each firm are inappropriate for purposes of relative performance evaluation. Other alternative interpretations based on a connection between the performance of the stock market and conditions in the labor market for CEOs may also be possible.

The RPE hypothesis predicts that CEO pay will be more strongly related to market movements the higher the correlation between the firm's return and the return on the market portfolio. Using CRSP monthly stock returns for NYSE firms, we computed the correlation between firm and market return over each preceding two-year period. We then re-

estimated the regression in column (3) of Table 1 (CEO pay changes on firm and market return) for the subsamples of observations above and below the median value of this correlation statistic and found coefficients on the market return of $-.1775$ and $-.0916$, respectively. The difference between the coefficients is significant ($t = -1.8$). We interpret this result as strong additional support for the RPE hypothesis.

The regressions in Table 1 and Table 2 indicate that CEO salaries and bonuses are partially adjusted for industry- and market-wide stock price movements. This evidence is consistent with the RPE hypothesis.[8] These results are based only on salaries and bonuses, however, whereas CEOs in fact receive compensation in many additional forms—including stock options, profit-sharing arrangements, stock

---

[8] The evidence also is consistent with a subtly different hypothesis: CEOs are rewarded for shareholder return in excess of the market return *because this is the true objective of the shareholders*. This latter hypothesis is incorrect, because it confuses the shareholders' *ex ante* and *ex post* objectives. To understand the distinction between the shareholders' *ex ante* and *ex post* objectives, consider the following two-stage model of investment and production. During the investment stage of the model there are two kinds of agents, entrepreneurs and investors. Entrepreneurs have ideas but no capital; investors have capital but no ideas. If an entrepreneur receives capital from (at least) one investor, then the entrepreneur becomes a CEO, the investor becomes a shareholder, and the production stage of the model begins. The production stage is identical to the model in which $y_i = a_i + \epsilon_i + \theta$, where y_i is now the change in shareholder wealth (gross of wage payments) at the ith firm, ϵ_i is idiosyncratic (that is, completely firm-specific) noise, and θ is a market-wide shock. (Note that this model does not allow the CEO's action to affect either the variance of the firm's returns or its covariance with the market.)

According to the capital-asset pricing model, at the investment stage investors care about the covariance between the firm's return and the market (among other things). But at the production stage, shareholders at the ith firm face precisely the contracting problem described above (in the section entitled "Rewarding Executives on Relative Performance"): they have invested their capital and now want to make the most of it. Thus, in this model, the covariance between the firm's return and the market has *ex ante* relevance (because it helps determine which entrepreneurs will receive capital) but not *ex post* relevance.

grants, savings plans, long-term performance plans, and other fringe benefits.
These other forms of compensation may
also be adjusted for industry and market
movements, and it is therefore useful to
analyze the CEO's *total* compensation and
not only the cash component of compensation.

The annual *Forbes* surveys include data
on total compensation as well as on salary
and bonus. Unfortunately, although the
salary and bonus data are easily verifiable
and their definitions have remained constant throughout the sample period, the
Forbes data for other components of
compensation are neither easily verifiable
nor reliable. The most severe problems
relate to the largest non-cash component
of compensation—stock options. *Forbes*
surveys do not include any stock-option
data prior to 1978, and after 1978 the
surveys report *gains from exercising* stock
options but do not report stock options
granted during the year. The gains from
exercising options are typically associated
with options granted five to ten years

previously, and therefore using these data
imposes serious timing problems.

Columns (1) and (2) of Table 3 report
regressions based on the *Forbes* total-
compensation data, excluding both stock-
option grants and the gains from exercising stock options. The definition of total
compensation varies somewhat from year
to year, but typically includes salary,
bonus, value of restricted stock, savings
and thrift plans, and other benefits. The
one-digit industry coefficient in column
(1) is negative and significant, indicating
that the CEO's total compensation (exclusive of stock options) is based on industry-
relative as well as absolute firm performance. The regression in column (2)
suggests that market returns are a more
important determinant of total compensation than are industry returns, although
the industry coefficient is negative and
statistically significant. The results in columns (1) and (2) of Table 3 are qualitatively similar to the results in columns (1)
and (4) of Table 2, suggesting that our
earlier conclusions are not changed by

Table 3. Coefficients of Ordinary Least Squares Regressions of Δln(Salary + Bonus) and
Δln(Total Pay) on Firm and Industry Return for *Forbes* Sample and for Murphy (1985)
Sample of Manufacturing Firms.
(t-Statistics in Parentheses)

Independent Variable	Regression Coefficients					
	1,049-Firm Forbes Sample Dependent Variable: Δln[Total Pay]		73-Firm Murphy Sample Dependent Variable:			
			Δln[Salary + Bonus]		Δln[Total Pay]	
	(1)	(2)	(3)	(4)	(5)	(6)
Intercept	.074	.082	.024	.025	.031	.025
Firm's Rate of Return on Common Stock	.2048 (17.9)	.2055 (18.0)	.1441 (7.1)	.1455 (7.2)	.1991 (5.1)	.1918 (4.9)
1-Digit SIC Industry Value-Weighted Return	−.1859 (−8.2)	−.0827 (−2.4)	−.1533 (−4.7)	−.1089 (−1.2)	−.3282 (−5.2)	−.5670 (−3.3)
Market Value-Weighted Return on Common Stock	—	−.1487 (−3.8)	—	−.0522 (−0.5)	—	.2807 (1.5)
Sample Size	7,757	7,757	997	997	997	997
R^2	.0397	.0415	.0495	.0498	.0328	.0351

Note: Forbes sample constructed from longitudinal data on 1,668 CEOs serving in 1,049 firms from
1974–1986. The *Forbes* definition of total compensation typically includes salary, bonus, value of restricted
stock, savings and thrift plans, and other benefits but does *not* include the value of stock options granted or the
gains from exercising stock options. The Murphy (1985) data are based on 173 CEOs serving in 73 large
manufacturing firms from 1966 to 1983. Murphy's definition of total compensation includes salary, bonus,
value of restricted stock, savings and thrift plans, other benefits, and the estimated value of stock options
granted.

analyzing broader measures of compensation.

The total-pay variable used in columns (1) and (2) excludes stock options, but a better measure would include the value of stock options granted during the year. Although these data are not available for the *Forbes* sample, they are available for a longitudinal sample of 73 manufacturing firms first analyzed by Murphy (1985). This sample, constructed from proxy statements, includes data on salaries, bonuses, deferred compensation, stock options, and fringe benefits, and covers 173 CEOs from 1966 through 1983. Total compensation is defined as the sum of salaries, bonuses, fringe benefits, stock options, the face value of deferred compensation, and restricted stock awarded during the year (valued at the year-end stock price). Stock options are valued on the date of grant using a Black-Scholes (1973) valuation formula that allows for continuously paid dividends as described in Murphy (1985).

Columns (3) through (6) in Table 3 report coefficients from relative-performance regressions based on the 73-firm sample of manufacturing firms. As a robustness check on our earlier results, we re-estimated the one-digit industry salary-and-bonus regressions reported in Table 2 for the manufacturing firm sample. Column (3) in Table 3 shows that the growth rate of CEO cash compensation is positively related to firm performance and negatively related to industry performance, *ceteris paribus*. Neither the industry-nor market-return variables are individually statistically significant in the regression in column (4), although they are *jointly* significant at the .01% level. These results are qualitatively similar to those in columns (1) and (4) of Table 2, indicating that our earlier results are not specific to the particular sample analyzed there.

The industry-return coefficient in column (5) of Table 3 is negative and significant, indicating that the CEO's total compensation (including stock option grants) is based on industry-relative as well as absolute firm performance. Column (6) includes market returns as an additional explanatory variable, and shows that CEO pay growth is negatively and significantly related to one-digit industry returns, but positively (and insignificantly) related to market returns. Thus, our earlier finding that CEO performance is more likely to be evaluated relative to aggregate market movements than relative to industry movements is not robust across samples for broader definitions of compensation and industry performance. On the other hand, this finding may simply reflect a high correlation between market performance and one-digit industry performance for manufacturing firms. Indeed, when we re-estimate the regressions in columns (3) through (6) of Table 3 using two-digit industry definitions, we find that market movements are a more important determinant of CEO pay changes than are two-digit industry movements.

As an additional robustness check, we use the *Forbes* sample of 1,668 CEOs to estimate the levels equation analogous to the first-difference specification reported in Table 2, namely:

$$(6) \quad \ln(\text{CEO Pay})_{it} = \lambda_i + \alpha(\text{Age})_{it}$$

$$+ \beta \sum_{\tau=1}^{t} (\text{Shareholder Return})_{i\tau}$$

$$+ \gamma \sum_{\tau=1}^{t} (\text{1-Digit Industry Return})_{i\tau}.$$

where λ_i is a separate intercept or "fixed-effect" for the ith CEO, and the first difference of (6) is (5). Our results are reported in Table 4.

To ease comparison, column (1) of Table 4 repeats the regression reported in column (1) of Table 2. Column (2) of Table 4 reports estimated coefficients from the fixed-effects levels equation, (6). If the levels regression is correctly specified, the time-trend coefficient in column (2) should equal the intercept in column (1), and the coefficients for the cumulative firm and industry stock returns in column (2) should equal the coefficients for shareholder return and industry return in column (1), respectively. In fact, the

Table 4. Coefficients of Ordinary Least Squares Regressions of ln(CEO Salary + Bonus) on Firm and One-Digit Industry Shareholder Return for Level and First-Difference Specifications. (t-Statistics in Parentheses)

Independent Variable	Dependent Variable, in 1000s of 1986-Dollars			
	Change in ln(CEO Pay) (1)	ln (CEO Pay) (2)	Change in ln(CEO Pay) (3)	ln (CEO Pay) (4)
Intercept	.064	(CEO-specific)	.005	(CEO-specific)
Current Stock Return (R_{it})	.1850 (20.6)	—	.1801 (20.1)	—
Current 1-Digit Industry Return (I_{it})	−.1266 (−7.1)	—	−.0740 (−2.7)	—
Time Trend (Age_{it})	—	.0343 (15.5)	—	—
Cumulative Stock Return $\left(\sum_{\tau=1}^{t} R_{i\tau}\right)$	—	.1829 (25.0)	—	.1762 (24.3)
Cumulative 1-Digit Industry Return $\left(\sum_{\tau=1}^{t} I_{i\tau}\right)$	—	−.0011 (−0.1)	—	−.0449 (−2.2)
Year Dummies	(no)	(no)	(yes)	(yes)
Sample Size	7,757	9,361	7,757	9,361
R^2	.0528	.8926	.0758	.8964

Note: The sample is constructed from longitudinal data reported in *Forbes* on 1,668 CEOs serving in 1,049 firms from 1974 to 1986. Columns (2) and (4) include 1,668 individual intercepts.
Regression Specification:

Level:

$$\ln(w_{it}) = \lambda_i + \alpha\, Age_{it} + \beta\sum_{\tau=1}^{t} R_{i\tau} + \gamma\sum_{\tau=1}^{t} I_{i\tau} + \epsilon_{it}$$

First Difference:

$$\Delta\ln(w_{it}) = \alpha + \beta R_{it} + \gamma I_{it} + \nu_{it}$$

cumulative-stock-return coefficient in column (2) of Table 4 is very close to the stock-return coefficient in column (1), but the cumulative-industry-return coefficient in column (2) is insignificant whereas the corresponding coefficient in column (1) is significantly negative. This difference in the industry-return coefficient in columns (1) and (2) suggests the possibility that the model is misspecified.

The first-difference and fixed-effects specifications in columns (1) and (2) of Table 4 control for observable and unobservable individual characteristics that are fixed for a CEO over time, but do not allow for economy-wide shocks that vary from year to year. We allow for these time-effects in columns (3) and (4) by including year dummy variables. A comparison of the first-difference specifica-

tions in columns (1) and (3) shows that the rate-of-return coefficients are again similar, and the industry-return coefficient in column (3), though smaller in magnitude than the coefficient reported in column (1), remains negative and significant. Comparing the fixed-effects specifications in columns (2) and (4), the cumulative-stock-return coefficient is again essentially unchanged, but the cumulative-industry-return coefficient is negative and significant in column (4), in contrast to its insignificance in column (2). Thus, including year dummies appears to resolve the discrepancy between the first-difference and fixed-effects specifications.

Comparison with Previous Research

Antle and Smith (1986) conducted a careful examination of the relation between CEO salary and bonus and industry rates of return but found no evidence that two-digit industry risk is filtered out of executive cash compensation contracts.[9] In contrast, we find that industry risk is partially filtered out of contracts (although the effect diminishes when we include market movements as well). In an attempt to reconcile these conflicting findings, we investigated several differences between the Antle-Smith methodology and our own. First, whereas our regression specification relates changes in compensation to absolute and industry stock returns, the Antle-Smith specification relates pay changes to *changes* in absolute and industry stock and accounting returns. Also, whereas our sample pools data from over 1,000 firms in 58 two-digit SIC industries, the Antle-Smith results are based on separate regressions for 39 firms in three industries.

Column (1) of Table 5 reports results from relative-performance regressions using our data and the Antle-Smith specification,

$$(7) \quad \Delta \ln(\text{CEO Pay}) = \alpha + \beta \Delta \text{ (Shareholder Return)} + \gamma \Delta \text{(2-Digit Industry Return)}.$$

The coefficient on the change in shareholder return is positive and significant, indicating that CEOs are rewarded for taking actions that increase the value of their firm, *ceteris paribus*. Moreover, the coefficient on the change in industry return is negative and significant, indicating that boards of directors adjust for industry shocks when revising the CEO's compensation. This evidence is consistent with the RPE hypothesis, and indicates that specification differences do not explain the difference between our results and Antle and Smith's. Our specification does, however, have more explanatory power than the Antle-Smith specification, with $R^2 = .0496$ in column (2) of Table 1, compared to $R^2 = .0196$ in column (1) of Table 5.[10]

Our results in Tables 1 through 4 are based on pooled cross-sectional time-series data, whereas Antle and Smith report separate regressions for each firm. In a further attempt to replicate their results, we re-estimated the regression in column (1) of Table 5 separately for the 690 firms in our sample that had six or more usable observations. The average and median t-statistics associated with the coefficients on the change in industry return in these firm-specific regressions are -0.39 and -0.37, respectively. Two-thirds (450) of the 690 estimated coefficients are less than zero, and 89 (13%) of the associated t-statistics are less than -1.8. The estimated coefficients are based on varying degrees of freedom and it is therefore difficult to test the joint significance of the individual coefficients. As a whole, however, these firm-specific regressions provide fairly strong support for the RPE hypothesis.

---

[9] Antle and Smith (1986), Table 6B. Although Antle and Smith find no relation between salary and bonus and industry returns, they do document a weak relation between industry returns and a broader definition of compensation that includes the *net* returns on inside stockholdings. They measure these net returns on inside stockholdings as the change in the value of stockholdings minus the change in the value of the *S&P 500* portfolio. Thus, their results may be driven by correlations between industry returns and the *S&P* portfolio.

---

[10] Our specification in (5) restricts the coefficients on lagged shareholder and industry returns to be zero, whereas the Antle-Smith specification (7) implicitly restricts these coefficients to be equal in magnitude and opposite in sign to the analogous coefficients on the contemporaneous performance variables. The Appendix presents results of both first-difference and fixed-effects (level) regressions of compensation on performance and lagged performance. The results in columns (1) and (3) suggest that changes in CEO pay are positively related to shareholder return and (to a much smaller degree) lagged shareholder return. In addition, the results—in column (3), for example—show that pay changes are negatively related to contemporaneous industry return, but are *positively* related to lagged industry return. The estimated coefficients in the associated pay-levels regression in column (4) suggest that misspecification is not the cause of this perplexing result. Column (4) does, however, provide an alternative statement of the result: although current and lagged returns are important determinants of the level of pay, we find support for the RPE hypothesis with respect to current but *not* lagged industry returns.

Table 5. Coefficients of Ordinary Least Squares Regressions of Δln(CEO Salary + Bonus) on Δ(Shareholder Return), Δ(Industry Return), Δ(Return on Assets), and Δ(2-Digit Industry Return on Assets) for Full 1,668-CEO Sample, CEOs in Three Industries, and CEOs in 26 Firms. (t-Statistics in Parentheses)

	Dependent Variable is *Δln(CEO Salary + Bonus)*					
	Full Forbes Sample		*Three Antle-Smith Industries*		*26 Antle-Smith Firms*	
Independent Variable	*(1)*	*(2)*	*(3)*	*(4)*	*(5)*	*(6)*
Intercept	.065	.066	.061	.060	.051	.048
Change in Firm's Shareholder Return	.0731 (11.2)	.0583 (8.9)	.0646 (3.6)	.0436 (2.5)	.0431 (1.2)	−.0114 (−0.3)
Change in 2-Digit Industry Return	−.1071 (−11.0)	−.0828 (−8.4)	−.1494 (−5.5)	−.0738 (−2.6)	−.1370 (−2.5)	−.0026 (−0.0)
Change in Firm's Return on Assets	—	1.220 (15.2)	—	1.590 (8.0)	—	3.426 (7.1)
Change in 2-Digit Industry Return on Assets	—	.3730 (2.0)	—	1.804 (3.3)	—	1.682 (2.2)
Sample Size	7,693	7,468	1,079	1,059	247	247
R^2	.0196	.0539	.0273	.1036	.0264	.2162

Note: Full sample and subsamples constructed from longitudinal data reported in *Forbes* on 1,668 CEOs serving in 1,049 firms from 1974 to 1986. The three-industry subsample includes 218 CEOs serving in 135 chemical (SIC = 28), electronics (SIC = 36) and transportation (SIC = 37) firms. The 26-firm subsample includes 44 CEOs.

It seems likely that the use of RPE varies across industries, and it is possible that the particular firms in the three industries analyzed by Antle and Smith (electronics, aerospace, and chemical companies) are for some reason characterized by a lack of relative-performance evaluation. Column (3) of Table 5 reports coefficients from a regression of pay growth on changes in firm and industry rates of return for CEOs in the three industries examined by Antle and Smith: chemicals and pharmaceuticals (SIC code 28), electric machinery and equipment (SIC code 36), and transportation (SIC code 37).[11] The industry-return coefficient in column (3) is negative and significant (t = −5.5), suggesting that the specific industries analyzed by Antle and Smith do not account for the difference in our results. Twenty-six of the 39 Antle-Smith sample firms are included in

our data, and column (5) of Table 5 reports RPE regressions for this 26-firm subsample. (Most of the 13 remaining firms were delisted or merged prior to the beginning of our sample.) The industry-return coefficient is again negative and significant; thus, the difference between our results and Antle and Smith's does not appear to be due to differences between the two samples of firms.

In addition to stock performance, the Antle-Smith specification also includes changes in firm and industry return on assets. Columns (2), (4), and (6) of Table 5 replicate the Antle-Smith specification (including return on assets) for the *Forbes* sample, the three-industry sample, and 26-firm sample, respectively.[12] After controlling for accounting returns, the change in the industry-stock-return coefficient is negative and significant for the full sam-

---

[11] The Antle-Smith sample is from the aircraft-manufacturing subset of the two-digit transportation industry (which also includes automotive firms) and the chemical subset of the two-digit chemical and pharmaceuticals industry, but their industry-relative returns are based on the more broadly defined two-digit industries.

[12] Return on assets is constructed from Compustat data and is defined as the sum of after-tax income (before extraordinary items), interest, and interest tax shields, divided by total assets. Industry return on assets is defined as the asset-weighted-average return on assets for all other firms in the same two-digit industry.

ple in column (2) and the three-industry sample in column (4), but is insignificant for the 26-firm sample in column (6).[13] Therefore, a combination of differences in sample size and composition and in regression specification seems to reconcile our results with Antle and Smith's.[14]

Although Jensen and Murphy (1990) do not directly test the RPE hypothesis, they analyze *Forbes* compensation data and conclude that changes in CEO pay are much more closely related to changes in shareholder wealth than to changes in shareholder wealth measured relative to the market or two-digit industry. In the spirit of their specification, we estimate a regression of the change in CEO pay on the change in shareholder wealth and the change in wealth the shareholders would have received had they invested in an industry portfolio rather than in the sample firm. Shareholder-wealth changes are measured as $R_t V_{t-1}$, where R_t is shareholder return and V_{t-1} is the firm value at the end of the previous year. Industry-wealth changes are measured as $I_t V_{t-1}$, where V_{t-1} is as before and I_t is the rate of return on a value-weighted portfolio of all other firms in the two-digit industry. The estimated coefficients from this regression are

(8) Δ(Salary and Bonus) = 32.1
$+ .0133(R_t V_{t-1}) + .0021(I_t V_{t-1})$.
    $(t=6.3)$ $(t=1.0)$

The coefficient on the change in indus-

try wealth in (8) is positive and insignificant. This specification therefore yields no support for the RPE hypothesis. The regression in (8) differs from column (2) of Table 1 for two reasons. First, the dependent variable in (8) is the *change* in salary and bonus, as opposed to the *change in the logarithm* of salary and bonus (that is, the growth-rate of pay) in Table 1. Second, the independent variables (excluding the intercept) in (8) differ from those in (5) because the former are multiplied by V_{t-1}, the beginning-of-period market value. Both of these differences appear to have some bearing on the difference between our results in (8) and Table 1, although the latter seems to be the more important of the two.[15] In related work (Gibbons and Murphy 1989) we show that the rate-of-return specification of the independent variables reduces the impact of heterogeneity by firm size in pooled regressions.

Relative Performance and CEO Turnover

An important part of the contractual arrangement between a CEO and his board of directors (an arrangement that may be either explicit or implicit) is a specification of the conditions under which the CEO will be encouraged or forced to leave office. The CEO succession process serves a variety of purposes, including

---

[13] The return on assets and industry return on assets variables are positive and significant in columns (2), (4), and (6) of Table 5. Therefore, although our results support the RPE hypothesis with respect to the principal's objective (shareholder return), we do not find evidence for RPE with respect to accounting returns.

[14] There are other differences between the Antle-Smith methodology and ours that may have some bearing on the difference in results. Antle and Smith average the after-tax salary and bonus of the three highest-paid executives, for example, and their data cover an earlier time period (1946–77). Also, whereas our measure of industry returns is the value-weighted average return in the industry, Antle and Smith calculate weighted-average industry returns in which the weight for each firm in the two-digit industry is the correlation coefficient between the returns of that firm and the sample firm.

[15] Re-estimating (8) with the rate of growth of CEO pay as the dependent variable yields

$\Delta \ln$(Salary and Bonus) = .061
$+ .0000169(R_t V_{t-1}) - .0000025(I_t V_{t-1})$,
    $(t=6.4)$ $(t=-1.0)$

and re-estimating (8) with rates of return instead of wealth changes as independent variables yields

Δ(Salary and Bonus) = 28.4
$+ 110.7(R_t) - 38.89(I_t)$.
    $(t=15.0)$ $(t=-3.2)$

Both of these regressions yield negative point estimates for the industry variable, but the industry coefficient is significant only in the second case, where wealth changes are replaced by rates of return.

Table 6. Estimated Logistic Models Predicting CEO Turnover Using Shareholder, Industry, and Market Rates of Return.
(Asymptotic t-Statistics in Parentheses)

Independent Variable	Coefficient Estimates			
	(1)	(2)	(3)	(4)
Intercept	−2.10	−2.19	−2.22	−2.22
Firm's Rate of Return on Common Stock	−.4152 (−4.1)	−.7130 (−5.7)	−.7542 (−6.2)	−.7341 (−5.8)
1-Digit Industry Value-Weighted Return on Common Stock	—	.8330 (3.9)	—	−.2613 (−0.6)
Market Value-Weighted Return on Common Stock	—	—	1.114 (4.9)	1.350 (3.1)

Note: Sample size is 9,372 for all regressions. The dependent variable is equal to 1 if the CEO is serving in his last full fiscal year (1,000 observations) and 0 otherwise (8,372 observations); rates of return are calculated for fiscal year. The sample is constructed from longitudinal data reported in *Forbes* on 1,915 CEOs serving in 1,104 firms from 1974 to 1986. All regressions are significant at the .01% level.

bringing "new blood" into the helm, replacing tired or unhealthy CEOs, and providing promotion opportunities for other executives in the organization.

We focus on one important aspect of the succession process that provides direct incentives for the current CEO: the threat of dismissal for poor performance. Implicit contracts linking dismissal to changes in shareholder wealth may generate incentives for CEOs to take actions that increase shareholder wealth. As in the case of compensation, however, basing dismissals on absolute performance subjects CEOs to uncertainties associated with industry and market stock-price movements. Therefore, as long as CEOs cannot take actions to affect the measured performance of the other firms in the industry or market, basing dismissals on relative performance yields incentives to increase shareholder wealth while filtering out exogenous risks.

CEOs are rarely openly fired from their positions; Weisbach (1988), for example, analyzed 286 CEO changes over ten years and found only nine cases in which boards mentioned performance as a reason why the CEO was replaced. CEO turnover, however, occurs frequently: over half (1,000) of the 1,914 CEOs in our sample for whom performance data are available left office during the 1974–86 sample period. We estimate the importance of RPE in CEO dismissal decisions by estimating the effect of firm, industry, and market performance on the probability that a CEO will soon leave office. In particular, we estimate the following logistic regression:

$$(9) \quad \ln\left(\frac{\text{Prob[Turnover]}}{1 - \text{Prob[Turnover]}}\right)$$
$$= \alpha + \beta \text{ (Shareholder Return)} + \gamma(\text{1-Digit Industry and/or Market Return}).$$

The dependent variable equals one if the CEO is serving in his last full fiscal year, and zero otherwise.[16] The theory of relative performance evaluation predicts that CEOs are *more likely* to be dismissed following bad years in the firm, but are *less likely* to leave following bad years in the industry and market, *ceteris paribus*. We interpret $\beta < 0$ and $\gamma > 0$ as evidence that, although explicit dismissals are rare, many instances of turnover are in fact dismissals and are based on relative performance.

Table 6 reports coefficients from logistic

[16] The 1988 *Forbes* survey was examined to identify CEOs whose last fiscal year was 1986. The final CEO-year for firms leaving the *Forbes* survey was excluded, since we cannot determine whether or not this was the last year for that CEO. A total of 582 firms were deleted from the *Forbes* surveys during the 1974–86 sample period. Of these, 293 were still "going concerns" as of 1987, 214 were acquired by or merged with another firm, and 35 liquidated, went bankrupt, or went private. Current status data were unavailable for 40 of the 582 firms.

regressions predicting the probability of CEO turnover as a function of shareholder, industry, and market rates of return. Column (1) shows that, unconditional on industry and market performance, the probability that a CEO is serving in his last full fiscal year is negatively and significantly related to the rate of return realized by shareholders during that year. Converting the regression coefficients into estimated turnover probabilities, the regression in column (1) implies that a CEO has a .109 turnover probability in years when the firm earns a zero return, but a .131 dismissal probability in years when the firm realizes a −50% return.[17]

Columns (2) and (3) of Table 6 show that turnover probabilities are negatively and significantly related to shareholder return, but positively and significantly related to returns in the one-digit industry and market, *ceteris paribus*. The regression in column (3) implies, for example, that a CEO has a .098 turnover probability in years when both the firm and the market earn a zero return. The same CEO has a .137 turnover probability when the firm earns a −50% return while the market return is zero, but only a .083 turnover probability in years when both the firm and market earn a −50% return.

Column (4) in Table 6 includes both industry and market returns. As in column (3), the market-return coefficient in column (4) is positive and statistically significant, although it is much reduced in size. The industry-return coefficient in column (4) remains positive but is no longer significant after controlling for market-wide stock-price movements. We also re-estimated columns (2) and (4) using the two-, three-, and four-digit alternative industry definitions. Consistent with our earlier results on compensation, we find that the magnitude of the industry coefficient declines monotonically as the industry becomes more narrowly defined (although the results for one-digit and

two-digit industries are virtually identical). Thus, our results suggest that CEO turnover policy is more likely to control for aggregate market movements than to control for industry movements.

CEOs leave office for a variety of reasons and usually leave their position only after reaching normal retirement age; a third of the CEOs in our sample left when they were 64 or 65, and more than half left between the ages of 62 and 66. We attempt to exclude normal retirements by re-estimating the logit regressions in Table 6 for the subset of CEOs younger than 64. Our results for the younger subsample are qualitatively similar to the results for the full sample, although the asymptotic t-statistics and significance levels tend to be higher for the subsample.

Many factors can affect stock prices in addition to industry and market movements, and boards of directors may plausibly require more than a single bad year before forcing or encouraging a CEO to leave office. Table 7 reports coefficients from logit regressions predicting the probability of CEO turnover as a function of current *and lagged* shareholder, industry, and market rates of return. The results in Table 7 are very similar to the results in Table 6, and the effects of contemporaneous performance on turnover probability are uniformly greater than are the effects of lagged performance. We also re-estimated the regressions in Table 7 after incorporating an additional lagged performance variable (namely, performance measured two years before the CEO's final fiscal year) and obtained similar results. These results are consistent with the findings of Warner, Watts, and Wruck (1988) and Weisbach (1988), who concluded that decisions to replace CEOs are based on relatively recent performance data.

Comparison with Previous Research

Warner, Watts, and Wruck estimated logit regressions for 87 CEO changes and found that the probability of CEO turnover is negatively related to contemporaneous shareholder return and positively related to contemporaneous market return, whereas the relation between turn-

---

[17] Dismissal probabilities are computed as

$$p = \frac{e^x}{1 + e^x} \text{ where } x = -2.10 - .4152 \text{ (Return).}$$

Table 7. Estimated Logistic Models Predicting CEO Turnover Using Current and Lagged
Shareholder, 1-Digit SIC Industry, and Market Rates of Return.
(Asymptotic t-Statistics in Parentheses)

Independent Variable	Coefficient Estimates			
	(1)	*(2)*	*(3)*	*(4)*
Intercept	−2.10	−2.21	−2.25	−2.25
Current Stock Return	−.3499 (−3.4)	−.6531 (−5.2)	−.6922 (−5.7)	−.6747 (−5.3)
Lagged Stock Return	−.2660 (−2.7)	−.4114 (−3.3)	−.4114 (−3.4)	−.4295 (−3.4)
Current 1-Digit Industry Return	—	.8253 (3.9)	—	−.2905 (−0.7)
Lagged 1-Digit Industry Return	—	.3263 (1.6)	—	.2377 (0.6)
Current Market Return	—	—	1.120 (4.9)	1.379 (3.1)
Lagged Market Return	—	—	.4027 (1.8)	.1924 (0.4)

Note: Sample size is 9,291 for all regressions. The dependent variable is equal to 1 if the CEO is serving in his last full fiscal year (992 observations) and 0 otherwise (8,299 observations); rates of return are calculated for fiscal year. The sample is constructed from longitudinal data reported in *Forbes* on 1,896 CEOs serving in 1,092 firms from 1974 to 1986. All regressions are significant at the .01% level.

over probability and past performance is generally insignificant. Consistent with our results, Warner, Watts, and Wruck found that turnover is unrelated to industry performance after controlling for market performance. Although their sample is much smaller than ours (which is based on 1,000 CEO changes), the Warner-Watts-Wruck data may be less noisy than ours since they measure performance from the date when the CEO change was announced rather than over the preceding fiscal year.[18] The similarity of our results and theirs suggests that our evidence supporting RPE in CEO turnover policy is robust to these potentially important timing problems.

Several studies that did not directly test the RPE hypothesis nevertheless provide results that are consistent with our findings. Coughlan and Schmidt (1985) found an inverse relation between CEO turnover

and abnormal stock-price performance (estimated as the cumulative annual residual from the market model), and Weisbach (1988) obtained similar results by measuring performance as shareholder return minus the return on a value-weighted market portfolio. In addition, Morck, Schleifer, and Vishny (1988) found that the probability that the entire top-management team leaves is negatively related to abnormal performance minus abnormal performance in the industry.

Conclusion

Rewarding top-level executives based on performance measured relative to aggregate performance in the industry or market creates incentives to take actions increasing shareholder wealth while insuring executives against the vagaries of the stock and product markets that are beyond their control. We expect RPE to be a common feature of implicit CEO compensation and dismissal contracts because the potential benefit of filtering out common uncertainty is high, the cost of measuring the performance of other firms is small,

[18] In addition, Warner-Watts-Wruck also excluded cases in which the CEO title changed hands but the top-management team remained intact (for example, the chairman-CEO remained chairman but passed the CEO title to the president). We have no way of identifying these cases in our data.

and opportunities for sabotage and collusive shirking are limited.

The empirical evidence presented above supports the RPE hypothesis: the revision in a CEO's pay and the probability that a CEO remains in his position for the following year are positively and significantly related to firm performance, but are negatively and significantly related to industry and market performance, *ceteris paribus*. Our results also suggest that CEO performance is more likely to be evaluated relative to aggregate market movements than relative to industry movements, although our inability to detect an industry effect after controlling for market movements may reflect the inappropriateness of industry definitions based on SIC codes for purposes of relative performance evaluation.

The theoretical justification for rewarding top-level executives on the basis of relative performance is strong, and therefore the fact that previous research has failed to detect a significant relative-performance effect has been troublesome. The results in this paper begin to resolve the puzzle by documenting a significant negative relation between CEO compensation and industry and market performance, but more work remains to be done before the data can be said to provide completely convincing support for the RPE hypothesis. Although our results support the RPE hypothesis with respect to current shareholder return, we do not find evidence for RPE with respect to changes in shareholder wealth (equation 8), lagged shareholder return (Appendix), or accounting returns (Table 5). Finally,

we have made no attempt to distinguish between the incentive and learning versions of the RPE hypothesis.

Although the theory of relative performance evaluation predicts that optimal contracts will protect CEOs from industry and market shocks, there are many aspects of a CEO's wealth that are not protected from industry and market movements in stock prices. The gains and losses associated with stock options and inside stockholdings, for example, depend solely on the firm's absolute stock-market performance and not on performance measured relative to the industry or market. Therefore, although the CEO's compensation and probability of dismissal are partially insured against industry and market risk, other potentially more important components of his wealth are not.

It would be straightforward, however, to design a compensation plan that duplicates the rewards and losses from stock ownership or stock options *after* adjusting for industry- or market-wide stock movements, and it is puzzling that few firms have adopted such explicit RPE compensation systems. It may be that current stock-option and restricted-stock plans are easy to administer and offer tax advantages, and that the costs of switching to new systems outweigh the potential benefits. Alternatively, the distorted incentives induced by RPE—in terms of sabotage, collusion, choice of reference group, or production externalities—may in fact be important for top-level managers. Determining why RPE is not more comprehensive is an important goal for future research.

Appendix
Coefficients of Ordinary Least Squares Regressions of ln(CEO Salary + Bonus) on Firm and Industry Shareholder Return for Level and First-Difference Specifications
(t-Statistics in Parentheses)

Independent Variable	Dependent Variable, in 1000s of 1986-Dollars			
	Change in ln(CEO Pay) (1)	ln (CEO Pay) (2)	Change in ln(CEO Pay) (3)	ln (CEO Pay) (4)
Intercept	.046	(CEO-specific)	.043	(CEO-specific)
Current Stock Return (R_{it})	.1793 (20.2)	.0166 (1.9)	.1746 (19.5)	.0223 (2.5)
Lagged Stock Return (R_{it-1})	.0284 (3.3)	—	.0275 (3.2)	—
Current 1-Digit Industry Return (I_{it})	−.0893 (−5.0)	−.1443 (−9.5)	−.0856 (−3.1)	−.0636 (−2.3)
Lagged 1-Digit Industry Return (I_{it-1})	.0849 (6.1)	—	.0584 (2.1)	—
Time Trend (Age_{it})	—	.0256 (10.8)	—	—
Cumulative Stock Return $\left(\sum_{\tau=1}^{t} R_{i\tau}\right)$	—	.1779 (22.0)	—	.1676 (20.8)
Cumulative 1-Digit Industry Return $\left(\sum_{\tau=1}^{t} I_{i\tau}\right)$	—	.0830 (4.7)	—	−.0244 (−1.1)
Year Dummies	(no)	(no)	(yes)	(yes)
Sample Size	7,696	9,361	7,696	9,361
R^2	.0652	.8941	.0769	.8965

Note: The sample is constructed from longitudinal data reported in *Forbes* on 1,668 CEOs serving in 1,049 firms from 1974 to 1986. Columns (2) and (4) include 1,668 individual intercepts.
Regression Specification:

Level:
$$\ln(w_{it}) = a_i + \alpha\, Age_{it} + (\beta_0 - \beta_1)R_{it} + \beta_1 \sum_{\tau=1}^{t} R_{i\tau} + (\gamma_0 - \gamma_1)I_{it} + \gamma_1 \sum_{\tau=1}^{t} I_{i\tau} + \epsilon_{it}$$

First Difference:
$$\Delta\ln(w_{it}) = \alpha + \beta_0 R_{it} - (\beta_0 - \beta_1)R_{it-1} + \gamma_0 I_{it} - (\gamma_0 - \gamma_1)I_{it-1} + \nu_{it}$$

REFERENCES

Antle, Rick, and Abbie Smith. 1986. "An Empirical Investigation of the Relative Performance Evaluation of Corporate Executives." *Journal of Accounting Research,* Vol. 24, No. 1 (Spring), pp. 1–39.

Baiman, Stanley, and Joel Demski. 1980. "Economically Optimal Performance Evaluation and Control Systems." *Journal of Accounting Research,* Vol. 18 (Supplement), pp. 184–220.

Black, Fischer, and Myron Scholes. 1973. "The Pricing of Options and Corporate Liabilities." *Journal of Political Economy,* Vol. 81, No. 3 (May/June), pp. 637–54.

Carmichael, H. Lorne. 1988. "Incentives in Academia:

Why Is There Tenure?" *Journal of Political Economy,* Vol. 96, No. 3 (June), p. 453–72.

Coughlan, Anne T., and Ronald M. Schmidt. 1985. "Executive Compensation, Management Turnover, and Firm Performance: An Empirical Investigation." *Journal of Accounting and Economics,* Vol. 7, Nos. 1–3 (April), pp. 43–66.

Dye, Ronald A. 1984. "The Trouble with Tournaments." *Economic Inquiry,* Vol. 22, No. 1 (January), pp. 147–49.

———. 1988. "Relative Performance Evaluation and Project Selection." Unpublished paper, Northwestern University.

Gibbons, Robert, and Kevin J. Murphy. 1989.

"Optimal Incentive Contracts in the Presence of Career Concerns: Theory and Evidence." Unpublished paper, M.I.T.

Holmström, Bengt. 1979. "Moral Hazard and Observability." *Bell Journal of Economics,* Vol. 10, No. 1 (Spring), pp. 74–91.

———. 1982. "Moral Hazard in Teams." *Bell Journal of Economics,* Vol. 13, No. 2 (Autumn), pp. 324–40.

Jensen, Michael C., and Kevin J. Murphy. 1990. "Performance Pay and Top-Management Incentives." *Journal of Political Economy* (forthcoming).

Lazear, Edward P. 1987. "Pay Equality and Industrial Politics." Unpublished paper, Hoover Institution.

Lazear, Edward P., and Sherwin Rosen. 1981. "Rank-Order Tournaments as Optimum Labor Contracts." *Journal of Political Economy,* Vol. 89, No. 5 (October), pp. 841–64.

Mood, Alexander, and Franklin Graybill. 1963. *Introduction to the Theory of Statistics,* 2nd Edition. New York: McGraw-Hill.

Mookherjee, Dilip. 1984. "Optimal Incentive Schemes with Many Agents." *Review of Economic Studies,* Vol. 51, No. 3 (July), pp. 433–46.

Morck, Randall, Andrei Schleifer, and Robert W.

Vishny. 1988. "Alternative Mechanisms for Corporate Control." Unpublished paper, NBER.

Murphy, Kevin J. 1985. "Corporate Performance and Managerial Remuneration: An Empirical Analysis." *Journal of Accounting and Economics,* Vol. 7, Nos. 1–3 (April), pp. 11–42.

Stigler, George J. 1964. " A Theory of Oligopoly." *Journal of Political Economy,* Vol. 72, No. 1 (February).

Vancil, Richard F. 1987. *Passing the Baton: Managing the Process of CEO Succession.* Boston: Harvard Business School Press.

Warner, Jerold B., Ross L. Watts, and Karen H. Wruck. 1988. "Stock Prices, Event Prediction, and Event Studies: An Examination of Top Management Changes." *Journal of Financial Economics,* Vol. 20, No. 1/2 (January/March), pp. 461–92.

Weisbach, Michael S. 1988. "Outside Directors and CEO Turnover." *Journal of Financial Economics,* Vol. 20, No.1/2 (January/March), pp. 431–60.

Wolfson, Mark. 1985. "Tax, Incentive, and Risk-sharing Issues in the Allocation of Property Rights: The Generalized Lease-or-Buy Problem." *Journal of Business,* Vol. 58, No. 2 (April), pp. 159–72.

DOES PERFORMANCE-BASED MANAGERIAL COMPENSATION AFFECT CORPORATE PERFORMANCE?

JOHN M. ABOWD*

The author, using 1981–86 data on more than 16,000 managers at 250 large corporations, investigates whether the sensitivity of managerial compensation to corporate performance in one year is positively related to corporate performance in the next year. Accounting-based measures of performance yield only weak evidence of such an association, but economic and market measures yield stronger evidence. Payment of an incremental 10% bonus for good economic performance is associated with a 30 to 90 basis point increase in the expected after-tax gross economic return in the following fiscal year; and payment of an incremental raise of 10% following a good stock market performance is associated with a 400 to 1200 basis point increase in expected total shareholder return.

In order to quantify the potential gains from performance-based managerial compensation, in this study I specify and estimate two related models of the connection between increased performance-sensitivity in compensation and increased subsequent corporate performance. These models control for the historical levels of both compensation and performance so that it is possible to focus on the extent to which changes in the correlation between current compensation and current performance affect future performance.

The first model, a discrete formulation, focuses on the conditional probability of good future corporate performance given current corporate performance and the current association between pay and performance. In this model increased performance-sensitivity is accomplished by increasing the probability of high pay when there is high performance and low pay when there is low performance.

The second model, a continuous formulation, focuses on the conditional expectation of future corporate performance given an elaborate, nonlinear function of current performance and compensation.

* John M. Abowd is Professor of Labor Economics and Management at Cornell University and Research Associate at the National Bureau of Economic Research. The author is grateful to George Milkovich and a major compensation consulting company for providing the data for this study. The author also thanks Ronald Ehrenberg, Robert Gibbons, Edward P. Lazear, and Kevin J. Murphy for extensive comments on earlier drafts. The Alfred P. Sloan Foundation and the National Science Foundation (grant number SES-8813847) provided financial support. The data were converted to research files with the support of the Center for Advanced Human Resource Studies at Cornell University.

A data appendix describes the procedures used to assemble the managerial compensation data base used in this study. The compensation data are confidential but the author's access is not exclusive. The executive compensation data used by Jonathan Leonard (this issue) are substantially the same as those used in this study. The financial data used in this study may be licensed from Standard and Poor's COMPUSTAT service.

In this model performance-sensitivity in the compensation system can be varied continuously. The effects of this performance-sensitivity are captured by two interaction terms that measure the association between future performance and current compensation when current performance is below average and when current performance is above average.

The models are specified and interpreted using a general principal-agent framework in which the stockholders' compensation contract with the managers varies across companies and years in the extent of performance-sensitivity. The data used to test the models, obtained from a survey conducted by a major compensation consulting firm, cover some 25,000 managers at 600 corporations for the period from 1981 to 1986.

The Essential Features of Principal-Agent Models

Performance-based managerial compensation has recently attracted considerable attention in the professional literatures of economics, accounting, and human resource management. (See Ehrenberg and Milkovich 1987 for a comprehensive review.) This interest is justified by the belief that contingent, performance-based compensation provides a viable solution to the problem of aligning the interests of managers with those of the owners of the corporations that they manage. In the conventional agency cost formulation, the shareholders of the corporation are the principals and the managers are their agents. Manipulating the degree of performance-sensitivity in the manager's compensation contract is the principal's method of controlling the tradeoff between better management and increased compensation costs.

Ross (1973) first posed the basic principal-agent problem as it pertains to corporate managers. In his formulation the compensation contract is chosen so as to elicit actions by the agent that maximize the principal's utility subject to the constraints of a reservation utility level for the agent (feasibility) and private optimality of

the agent's action (incentive compatibility). Becker and Stigler (1974) and Lazear (1979) recast the problem in terms of implementing a long-term implicit contract in which the manager's compensation over time provides the correct incentives. Holmström (1979) and Grossman and Hart (1983) analyzed in considerable detail the theoretical structure of performance-based compensation systems designed to mitigate single-period principal-agent problems. (See Hart and Holmström 1987 for a comprehensive review.)

The Grossman-Hart model solves the agency problem by showing that there are two conceptual steps to an optimal program. First, the principal chooses a different contingent compensation plan relating pay to performance outcomes for each action the agent might take. Second, by choosing a particular plan, the principal chooses an optimal action for the agent that maximizes the principal's utility net of the expected cost of the chosen pay plan.

It is the Grossman-Hart formulation of the problem that makes clear the fundamental tradeoffs involved in performance-based compensation. Actions that the agent dislikes (relative to their alternatives) are more costly to implement and require a greater degree of performance-sensitivity in the compensation plan. The expected cost of a compensation system must increase as it becomes more performance-based—expected payroll costs and the degree of performance-sensitivity in the compensation plan are positively correlated. By the same token, the expected performance of the corporation also increases as the degree of performance-sensitivity in the compensation plan increases—expected corporate performance and the slope of the pay-for-performance relation are positively correlated. Because expected payroll costs and expected managerial performance are both increasing as the degree of performance-sensitivity in the compensation contract increases, the solution to the principal-agent problem generally occurs when the incremental payroll costs just equal the value of the incremental performance gains associated with the chosen level of performance-sensitivity.

In the financial economics literature, Jensen and Meckling (1976) and Fama and Jensen (1983a, 1983b) demonstrated that the agency costs associated with running a large corporation are intrinsic to organizations in which ownership and control are separated. Furthermore, it is efficient to encourage the separation of ownership and control because the limited wealth of all individual investors prevents undertaking large positive net present value investments unless investors pool resources, thus creating organizational control problems. Agency costs reduce the gains from the separation of ownership and control but do not eliminate them.

The principal-agent literature, in spite of its apparent applicability to the design of compensation systems, has not been easy to translate into empirically tractable models. There are two basic problems. Lazear (1986) showed that the appropriateness (optimality) of contingent performance-based managerial compensation contracts depends critically on the assumption that direct monitoring of the agent's actions is prohibitively costly. When a relatively inexpensive monitoring system is available, both managers and principals will prefer noncontingent (salary-based) compensation systems with performance appraisals based on the information generated by the monitoring system. To the extent that monitoring costs vary across firms the predicted positive relation between strong incentive pay and corporate performance may not hold. The present study cannot control for differential monitoring costs in any meaningful way.

A second problem in testing principal-agent models of managerial compensation, identified by Miller and Scholes (1982) and also studied in Lewellen et al. (1987), is that many apparently performance-based compensation systems are actually designed to minimize the total tax burden of the principal and the agent. Hence, the measured performance-sensitivity in the compensation system is a veil for tax avoidance. Contingent, performance-based compensation that is specifi-

cally designed to increase the joint tax liability of the corporation and the managers may be explained on incentive grounds alone. Most contingent compensation systems, however, reduce the joint tax liability of the corporation and its managers, so that the tax consequences of the compensation system must be controlled before the incentive effects can be determined. The present study considers only annual corporate performance and annual cash compensation (including amounts that the manager elects to defer). This focus reduces the potential for tax-related considerations to confound the results.

Most studies of managerial compensation have investigated the empirical relation between the level or rate of change of managerial compensation and corporate financial, economic, and market performance indicators. (See, for example, Lewellen 1968; Lewellen and Huntsman 1970; Masson 1971; Murphy 1985, 1986; Antle and Smith 1986; Jensen and Murphy 1987, 1988; Baker et al. 1988; Leonard, this issue; and Gibbons and Murphy, this issue.) When current compensation is shown to be sensitive to these performance indicators, the system is declared performance-based, whether or not an explicit formula exists that links current compensation to the indicators. Disputes arise as to whether or not the observed degree of sensitivity of compensation to performance is adequate to solve the principal-agent problem between the owners and the managers. (See Baker, Jensen, and Murphy 1988.)

In contrast to the fairly large number of studies investigating the sensitivity of managerial compensation to corporate performance measures, comparatively little research exists on the efficacy of performance-based compensation systems. The notable exception is Larker's (1983) study of the returns on investment decisions made by managers paid with different types of executive compensation systems. Masson (1971) also attempted to address this question as a part of his analysis of executive compensation and common stock performance. In financial economics the event study methodology has been used to assess the performance effects of some kinds of contingent compensation. (See Bhagat et al. 1985; Brickley et al. 1985; Coughlan and Schmidt 1985; Lambert and Larker 1985; and Tehranian and Waegelein 1985.) Recent work in compensation (Gomez-Mejia et al. 1987; Rabin 1986, 1987), accounting (Lambert and Larker 1987), and financial economics (Lewellen et al. 1987) also begins to address these issues. Healy (1985) considered the agency cost–related problem of manipulation of accounting quantities when contingent compensation is based on accounting performance measures rather than on economic or market measures.

Tests of Compensation System Design and Effectiveness

When the sensitivity of compensation to performance measures is increased, under what conditions does the subsequent performance of the corporation improve, worsen, or remain the same? Since an optimal compensation system balances the gain from additional performance-sensitivity, which takes the form of incremental corporate performance, against the cost of additional performance-sensitivity, which takes the form of higher average compensation, the answer to this question is at the heart of the study of the design and effectiveness of compensation systems. The gains are achieved because the manager's extra effort induced by the greater return to performance in the compensation system increases the probability of favorable corporate outcomes. The costs are incurred because a feasible performance-based compensation system must deliver greater expected total compensation the greater the effort level the system tries to induce from the managers. Neither the expected total cost of the compensation system nor the expected corporate performance improvement can be calculated without quantitative measures of the relation between the performance-sensitivity of compensation and future corporate outcomes.

It may be that the apparent complexity of determining the optimal compensation design and then validating that design by quantifying the improvements in performance that it caused has obscured the important and practical implications of quantifying the relationship between characteristics of the current managerial pay system and subsequent corporate performance. If the existence of this relationship and some estimate of its magnitude could be inferred from the sensitivity of corporate performance to the pattern of performance-based contingencies in a sample of corporate compensation plans, then compensation designers could use the estimated change in corporate performance from such a sample to justify a modification of the structure of a particular plan. The ability to evaluate existing compensation plans using formulas that reflect the consequences of incentives would greatly facilitate the comparison of such plans.

Statistical Models for Contingent Compensation Effects on Performance

Any statistical model of the relation between compensation and current performance must begin with the equation describing pay for the individual manager. To specify that function, define:

y_{ijt} = the compensation measure for manager i in company j for year t;

x_{ijt} = the personal characteristics of manager i (including job level at company j) for year t.

Since corporate performance does not vary for managers within a particular company, a general form for the compensation equation is:

$$(1) \qquad y_{ijt} = \alpha_{jt} + (x_{ijt} - \bar{x})\beta + u_{ijt}$$

where α_{jt} = the effects on compensation of being at company j for year t, called the company · year effects on compensation; β = the effect of x_{ijt} on compensation; u_{ijt} = the statistical error term associated with (1); and $\bar{x}$ = the grand mean of x_{ijt}. The individual characteristics are expressed as deviations from the grand mean in order to force the estimated α_{jt} through the grand mean of y_{ijt}.

Because all the information about the link between corporate pay and performance is contained in the company · year effects α_{jt}, I specify a statistical model relating these effects to annual performance. Let q_{jt} = the estimated α_{jt} from equation (1) and p_{jt} = the performance of company j for year t. Then the implications of principal-agent models for compensation design and annual performance reviews are:

(2a) $\qquad q_{jt} = a_{jt} + b_{jt}p_{jt} + v_{jt}$

(2b) $\qquad p_{jt+1} = \theta_0 + \theta_1 a_{jt} + \theta_2 b_{jt}$
$\qquad\qquad + \theta_3 p_{jt} + e_{jt+1}$

where a_{jt} = the intercept of the compensation-performance relation (2a); b_{jt} = the slope of the compensation-performance relation (2a); v_{jt} = the statistical error in equation (2a); θ_k = the parameters of the future performance relation (2b); and e_{jt+1} = the statistical error in equation (2b). A pay system is performance-based if the slope b_{jt} is positive. A performance-based system is consistent with a solution to the principal-agent problem if, as b_{jt} increases, the intercept a_{jt} falls. The payoff to low performance outcomes must be lower and the payoff to high performance outcomes must be higher the greater the work effort the compensation contract induces. The performance-based pay system is valid if $\theta_1 < 0$ or $\theta_2 > 0$, indicating that increasing the performance-sensitivity in compensation does increase subsequent performance.

It is not possible to test equation (2b) directly, because we do not have repeated observations on the p_{jt} and q_{jt} variables for each company year; hence, equation (2a) cannot be estimated. The predictions regarding the system in equations (2) can be explored under the maintained hypothesis that comparison of the pair (p_{jt}, q_{jt}) with the median outcomes for performance and pay for all companies in year t provides information about the values of a_{jt} and b_{jt}.

Figure 1 illustrates this maintained hypothesis. In the figure, performance is

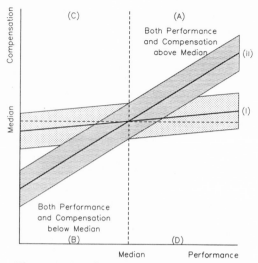

Figure 1. An Illustration of the Maintained Hypothesis About the Location of More vs. Less Performance-Sensitive Outcomes.

plotted along the horizontal axis and compensation along the vertical axis. The graph is divided into four regions by the dashed lines at the medians of performance and compensation. Region (A) contains points that are above both medians. Region (B) contains points that are below both medians. Regions (C) and (D) contain points that are above one median but below the other. The maintained hypothesis is that systems in which compensation is more performance-based are more likely to produce outcomes in regions (A) and (B).

The argument, which can be made rigorous for certain conditional probability distributions of the error term v_{jt}, is illustrated by the lines (I) and (II) and the shaded areas surrounding them. Line (I) represents a pay-for-performance relation that is not very sensitive (high intercept a_{jt} and low slope b_{jt}); line (II), a pay-for-performance relation that is very sensitive (low intercept, high slope). In both cases the shaded area around the lines contains the likely scatter of outcomes around the basic relation. The proportion of the outcomes for line (II) that lie in regions (A) and (B) is greater than the similar proportion of outcomes for line (I). Hence, an outcome in region (A) or (B) is more likely to have come from a highly performance-sensitive compensation system than is an outcome in region (C) or (D).

The Discrete Model

The following model incorporates the maintained hypothesis in a test of the efficacy of certain pay-for-performance systems. The test has the advantage of being simple and direct. It has the disadvantage of being difficult to translate into an estimate of the magnitude of the effect of increasing performance-sensitivity on future performance. This problem is handled in the continuous model.

Let:

$$p^*_{jt} = \begin{cases} 1 \text{ when } p_{jt} > \text{median over } j \text{ for year} \\ t \text{ of all } p_{jt}; 0 \text{ otherwise.} \end{cases}$$

$$q^*_{jt} = \begin{cases} 1 \text{ when } q_{jt} > \text{median over } j \text{ for year} \\ t \text{ of all } q_{jt}; 0 \text{ otherwise.} \end{cases}$$

$$x^*_{jt} = \begin{cases} 1 \text{ when the total assets of company} \\ j \text{ for year } t \text{ exceed the median total} \\ \text{assets for year } t \text{ on the New York} \\ \text{Stock Exchange; 0 otherwise.} \end{cases}$$

The test of the average sensitivity of compensation to performance is based on the following log linear model for the probabilities:

$$(3) \quad \log \Pr\{q^*_{jt} = 1 \mid p^*_{jt}, x^*_{jt}\} \\ = \phi_0 + \phi_1 p^*_{jt} \\ + \phi_2 x^*_{jt}.$$

Equation (3) is called the compensation equation in the discrete model. The parameter ϕ_1 measures the average sensitivity of compensation to the particular performance measure specified. Since I cannot verify that every performance measure I consider is appropriate, the compensation equation is used as a test that the average effect of a particular performance measure on compensation is actually positive. Such a test is germane because the average b_{jt} from equation (2a) over all companies and years must be positive, which implies that the parameter ϕ_1 will be positive. The variable x^*_{jt} is

included to control for sample design problems in the statistical analysis.[1]

The test of whether greater sensitivity of compensation to performance is associated with increased future performance is based on the following log linear model for the conditional probability of next year's performance given this year's compensation, performance, and size control.

$$(4) \quad \log \Pr\{p^*_{jt+1} = 1 \mid p^*_{jt}, q^*_{jt}, x^*_{jt}\} \\ = \delta_0 + \delta_1 p^*_{jt} + \delta_2 p^*_{jt} q^*_{jt} \\ + \delta_3 (1 - p^*_{jt}) \cdot (1 - q^*_{jt}) + \delta_4 x^*_{jt}.$$

Equation (4) is called the performance equation in the discrete model. The parameter δ_2 should be positive because it captures the effect of being above the median for both performance and compensation in the current year (region (A) in Figure 1). The parameter δ_3 should also be positive, since it captures the effect of being below the median for both performance and compensation in the current year. The parameter δ_1 will generally be positive for most accounting, economic, and market performance measures. It is included in the model because performance measures, especially those based on accounting data, are known to possess positive serial correlation for a variety of reasons unrelated to the compensation system design (Foster 1986). The sign of δ_4 is unknown a priori, since the variable x^*_{jt} is included as a control for sampling design problems in the analysis sample.[2]

The Continuous Model

In order to calculate an estimate of the

---

[1] This variable is introduced because the analysis sample is not a random sample of companies from the comparison group. Larger companies are more apt to be in the sample. In a discrete model, inclusion of this size variable adequately controls for the selectivity bias created by this sampling plan.

[2] It is important to note that equation (4) is saturated in the p^*_{jt} and q^*_{jt} effects as specified because there are only four possible combinations of outcomes for these variables and three independent effects (δ_1, δ_2, and δ_3) are included. The remaining outcome ($p^*_{jt} = 0$, $q^*_{jt} = 1$) is the reference point for the contrasts.

magnitude of the effect of increasing the sensitivity of managerial compensation to performance, I specify the following system, which also incorporates the maintained hypothesis. The model is specified in terms of the conditional expectations of the estimated company · year effects in compensation and performance next year, given the appropriate controls.

The compensation equation for the continuous model is:

$$(5) \quad E[q_{jt} \mid p_{jt}, x_{jt}] = \phi_0 + \phi_1 p_{jt} + \phi_2 x_{jt}$$

where x_{jt} is total assets for company j in year t, and the other variables are defined above. The parameters ϕ_k have the same interpretation as in equation (3), so I have not used new symbols. In particular, $\phi_1 > 0$ is required for compensation to be performance-based, on average.

The performance equation for the continuous model is:

$$(6) \quad E[p_{jt+1} \mid p_{jt}, q_{jt}, x_{jt}] = \delta_0 + \delta_1 p_{jt} \\ + \delta_2 T^+ (p_{jt} - m_t) q_{jt} + \delta_3 T^- (p_{jt} - m_t) q_{jt} \\ + \delta_4 x_{jt} + \delta_5 q_{jt}$$

where m_t is the median of p_{jt} over j for year t; the function $T^+(z) = z$ if $z > 0$ and 0 otherwise; and the function $T^-(z) = z$ if $z < 0$ and 0 otherwise. The interpretation of the parameters is similar to the interpretation in equation (4), so I have not changed the symbols. In particular, if performance is above the median, then increasing compensation is associated with increasing the sensitivity of pay to performance (region (A) in Figure 1); therefore, δ_2 should be positive. If performance is below the median, then decreasing compensation is associated with increasing the sensitivity of pay to performance (region (B) in Figure 2); therefore, δ_3 should also be positive (because $T^- (p_{jt} - m_t) < 0$ in this case).[3]

---

[3] Notice that since equation (6) is not saturated by the inclusion of δ_1, δ_2, and δ_3, it is possible for current compensation to have an independent effect, δ_5, that is not modeled.

The Managerial Compensation and Financial Data

The managerial compensation data used in this study were derived from the annual cash compensation survey of a major compensation consulting firm. The data cover approximately 75 top management employees for the period from 1981 to 1986 for each of about 600 corporations. The company, executive, and position are all identified in the survey data. Therefore, it is possible to follow both individuals and positions across years within a single company. All financial data used in this study were derived from Standard and Poor's COMPUSTAT data base (1988). The data appendix contains a detailed description of the methods used to create the analysis file.

Two important selection rules were applied to the companies in the original survey to derive the analysis file. First, a company must appear in the compensation survey at least three years (not necessarily consecutive) to have sufficient data for my analysis. Second, I used only publicly held U.S. companies for which the COMPUSTAT financial data and the respondent's self-reported financial data matched exactly. The strenuous requirement of an exact match on total assets was imposed to guarantee that the financial data used were always from the most recently completed fiscal year prior to the March 1 survey reference date and to guarantee that the position of the managers within the corporate hierarchy was comparable across companies (see the data appendix). Only about 225 companies and 99,200 executive years were used in each of the basic statistical analyses, with slight variations depending on the particular analysis. Fewer executive years but the same number of companies were available for the analyses involving changes.

Since the data were originally collected by a compensation consulting firm, it is appropriate to discuss the implicit sampling frame used to generate the survey responses. The original data were collected from client submissions to the consulting firm. A human resource management professional employed by the respondent company completed the survey form for each executive the company wished to have appraised. Unlike normal social science surveys, but consistent with industry practice in compensation surveys, the respondent company paid a fee to be included in the survey. The company controlled how often it participated and which executive positions were submitted in a given year. The consulting company had an active client relationship with many of the participating companies; the primary product of the survey, however, was an analysis of the competitive position of the respondent company's managers with respect to the managers of a comparison group of companies. The consulting company did not design most of the compensation systems in the survey.

Because the managers and companies in the sample are self-selected, it is important to know how representative they are of various populations. The companies in the sample I analyzed, all of which had public financial data, are primarily large U.S. corporations. On average, they have total assets 2.7 times greater than the average New York Stock Exchange company followed in the COMPUSTAT files (in 1986). For this reason, I included a company size control based on total assets in all analyses.

The compensation survey includes salary and annual bonus. The annual bonus was defined as any cash payment earned during the previous twelve months that was based exclusively on performance during a single year. Cash bonuses for meeting multiyear performance goals were not included in the annual bonus. (The information is actually collected in a different survey.) Cash that was received during the last twelve months but that was earned during an earlier period (with payment deferred) was not included in the bonus. Hence, the bonus data really are for annual performance. Long-term incentive pay was not available. For this reason, I tried to design the empirical analysis so that it focuses on annual performance criteria. To the extent that annual performance influences long-term incentive pay,

I am not able to capture the effect of performance on compensation. To the extent that there is a substantial difference between the performance-sensitivity of annual pay and long-term incentive pay, the annual pay for performance analysis is inappropriate.

Consider next the dating of the financial and compensation variables. In the theoretical framework, current compensation is based on current performance, that is, current compensation is paid at the end of the current period when current performance can be observed. In the empirical analysis, current performance is defined as the financial data for the most recently completed fiscal year prior to March 1 of the survey year, the reference date for the base salary. Future performance is defined as the performance during the fiscal year that includes March 1 of the survey year. Current compensation is defined as the base salary as of March 1 of the survey year and the most recently awarded bonus prior to March 1. I have made every effort to ensure that the bonus used in the statistical analysis was determined when the results of the most recently concluded fiscal year prior to March 1 were known. The data appendix describes the method for checking the dating of the financial information vis-à-vis the compensation data.

I used four distinct financial performance variables. Two of the performance measures, after-tax return on assets and after-tax return on equity, are conventional accounting measures of asset profitability, generically called return on investment. Actual definitions of these ratios differ greatly from one application to the next. Since there is no commonly agreed-upon method for calculating the ratios, I used the formulas in Bernstein (1983, Chapter 19).

The numerator of after-tax return on assets is net income plus the interest expense, adjusted to an after-tax basis at the marginal corporate tax rate. The denominator is average total assets over the fiscal year.

After-tax return on equity was defined for common stock equity, adjusted for unconsolidated minority interests. The numerator of after-tax return on equity is net income less income to minority interests less preferred stock dividends paid. The denominator is average common stock equity over the fiscal year.

The third performance measure I used is a measure of gross cash flow, net of taxes, divided by an estimate of the replacement cost of total assets. This ratio is called after-tax gross economic return. The numerator, operating income less income taxes, corresponds approximately to the after-tax cash flow into the business. The denominator, an estimate of the current replacement cost of total assets at the beginning of the fiscal year, corresponds approximately to the wealth tied up in the business at the beginning of the fiscal year. The data appendix contains a detailed description of the calculation of this variable.

The final performance measure is a market measure—total shareholder return, which is the calendar year holding period return per share of common stock. The numerator of total shareholder return is dividends per share earned over the calendar year plus the capital gain per share between the end of last year and the end of the current year. The denominator is the price per share of common stock at the end of the previous calendar year. Stock prices and dividends per share were adjusted to reflect the effects of stock splits and stock dividends during the calendar year.

Table 1 contains a summary of all variables used in my statistical analyses. The table shows that the average executive in the sample earned $106,689 per year in total cash compensation over the period from 1981 to 1986. The executives were employed by companies that had an average of $3,334 million in total assets and earned an average of 6.7% per year in after-tax return on assets. The shareholders of these companies earned an average of 17.3% per year total return. The notes to the table contain the short definitions of all variables; the data appendix contains long definitions.

Statistical Results

The first requirement of the empirical analysis is to estimate the company · year effects in equation (1) for each of the compensation variables used in the analysis. Table 2 contains a summary of the results for the four compensation measures—log of total salary, percent increase in total salary, log of base salary, and bonus as a percent of base salary.[4] The table contains no surprises and is presented to show that the adjustment to the various compensation measures is consistent with analysis of individual compensation data from many sources.[5]

Table 3 presents the results of the discrete model using the annual percentage increase in total salary as the compensation measure and using after-tax return on assets (ROA), after-tax return on equity (ROE), after-tax gross economic return (ERET), and total shareholder return (TSR) as the performance measures. The compensation equation clearly shows that compensation is performance-based with respect to each of the performance measures, on average.

The performance equation gives mixed results for the two accounting measures (ROA and ROE), indicating that increased performance sensitivity is not always associated with increased performance. The coefficients on the "Current Performance and Current Compensation Both Above Median" variable for the two accounting measures are both positive, although the coefficient in the ROE equation is impre-

---

[4] Throughout the paper, the exact form of the percent increase in total salary is $100 · (\log(\text{total salary current year}) - \log(\text{total salary previous year}))$; only consecutive years are used. The exact form of the bonus-to-base ratio is $100 · \log(1 + \text{bonus/base})$. This form was chosen because it makes the decomposition of the logarithm of total salary into the logarithm of base salary plus the bonus/base ratio exact, except for the multiplication by 100, which facilitates comparison of statistical models using the bonus-to-base ratio with models using the percentage change in total salary.

[5] The company · year effects from the "Log of Total Salary" and "Log of Base Salary" columns are never used as dependent variables in a compensation equation. They are used as control variables in the continuous model.

Table 1. Summary of the Managerial Compensation and Corporate Performance Data for All Firms Used in the Analysis (1981 to 1986).

Definition of Variable	Mean	Std. Dev.	Sample Size	Definition of Variable	Mean	Std. Dev.	Sample Size
Individual Data							
Base Salary[a]	85,599	61,513	99,219	Total Shareholder Return[t]	17.3%	35.1%	1,114
Logarithm of Base Salary	11.2	.5	99,219	Total Assets at Beginning of Year[u]	3,334	6,814	1,117
Bonus Payment[b]	21,090	39,321	99,219				
Total Salary[c]	106,689	94,826	99,219	Log of Total Assets (Beg. of Year)	7.2	1.3	1,117
Logarithm of Total Salary	11.4	.6	99,219	Proportion of Companies with Adj. Average Increase Above Median	.497	na	857
Percentage Increase in Total Salary[d]	9.2%	1.4%	60,227				
Bonus as a Percent of Base[e]	16.0%	15.1%	99,219	Proportion of Companies with Bonus as a Percent of Base Above Median	.498	na	1,107
Years of Education[f]	16.4	1.8	99,219				
Years of Labor Force Experience[g]	26.2	9.0	99,219				
Years at Employer[h]	14.7	10.4	99,219	Proportion of Companies with After-Tax Return on Assets Above Median	.554	na	1,107
Percentage Job Level 1[i]	1.2%	na	99,219				
Percentage Job Level 2[j]	6.6%	na	99,219				
Percentage Job Level 3[k]	19.9%	na	99,219	Proportion of Companies with After-Tax Return on Equity Above Median	.505	na	1,104
Percentage Job Level 4[l]	30.6%	na	99,219				
Company Data							
Average Adjusted Log Total Salary[m]	11.4	.3	863	Proportion of Companies with After-Tax Gross Economic Return Above Median	.560	na	1,052
Average Adjusted Increase in Total Salary[n]	8.8%	10.5%	863				
Average Adjusted Log Base Salary[o]	11.2	.3	1,114	Proportion of Companies with Total Shareholder Return Above Median	.493	na	1,114
Average Adjusted Bonus/Base (percent)[p]	15.5%	10.7%	1,114				
After-Tax Return on Assets[q]	6.7%	5.7%	1,107	Proportion of Companies with Total Assets (Beginning of Year) Above Median	.873	na	1,107
After-Tax Return on Equity[r]	10.8%	13.7%	1,104				
After-Tax Gross Economic Return[s]	11.4%	5.6%	1,052				

[a] Base Salary is the annual salary (exclusive of bonus and long-term incentive compensation) in effect on March 1 of the survey year.

[b] Bonus is the most recent payment (prior to March 1 of the survey year) determined by an annual review cycle. Bonus payments determined on review cycles longer than one year are considered long-term incentive compensation and are not included.

[c] Total salary is the sum of base salary and bonus.

[d] Percentage increase in total salary is $100 \cdot (\log(\text{total salary as of March 1 of the survey year}) - \log(\text{total salary as of March 1 of the previous year}))$, for consecutive surveys only. The variable is only available when the same executive is surveyed in two consecutive years.

[2] Bonus as a percent of base is $100 \cdot \log(1 + \text{Bonus/Base})$.

[f] Years of education is imputed for survey year 1986 using the history of the executive, when available, or the value 16.4 if there is no history.

[g] Years of labor force experience is Current age − Years of Education − 5.

[h] Years at employer is the executive's actual tenure with the surveyed company.

(table notes continue)

[i] Job level 1 is the highest position in the corporate hierarchy (usually Chairman and Chief Executive Officer) as reported on the survey.

[j] Job level 2 reports to the CEO (usually President and Chief Operating Officer).

[k] Job level 3 reports to the level 2 position.

[l] Job level 4 reports to the level 3 position. All other positions are level 5 or below.

[m] Average adjusted log total salary is the estimated company · year effect from the regression of log total salary on years of education, labor force experience, labor force experience squared, years at employer, indicators for job levels 1, 2, 3, and 4 (level 5 and above is the reference group), and unrestricted year within company fixed effects. The estimated company · year effects were forced through the grand mean of log total salary. See Table 2.

[n] Average adjusted increase in total salary is the estimated company · year effect from the regression of the percentage increase in total salary on the variables listed in note m (except labor force experience squared). See Table 2.

[o] Average adjusted log base salary is the estimated company · year effect from the regression of log base salary on the variables listed in note m. See Table 2.

[p] Average adjusted bonus/base (percent) is the estimated company · year effect from the regression of $100 \cdot \log(1 + \text{bonus/base})$ on the variables listed in note m. See Table 2.

[q] After-tax return on assets: $100 \cdot$ (Net Income + Interest $(1 - \text{Tax Rate})$) divided by (Beginning Total Assets + Ending Total Assets)/2.

[r] After-tax return on equity: $100 \cdot$ (Net Income) divided by (Beginning Shareholder's Equity + Ending Shareholder's Equity)/2.

[s] After-tax economic return is operating income less taxes as a percentage of beginning of period total assets, valued at replacement cost: $100 \cdot$ (Operating Income − Taxes) divided by (Beginning Total Assets, valued at replacement cost).

[t] Total shareholder return: $100 \cdot$ (Dividends per beginning share + Capital gain per beginning share) divided by (Beginning price per share).

[u] Total assets at the beginning of the year is the book value of all assets at the end of the previous fiscal year (in millions of dollars). In all cases, this value is for a fiscal year that ended prior to March 1 of the compensation survey year.

Sources: (1.) All financial data are from Standard and Poor's COMPUSTAT service for fiscal years 1980 to 1986 based on the September 1988 annual industrial tape. Only the 2,423 New York Stock Exchange companies available during this period were used for comparisons. (2.) All compensation data are from the annual surveys of a major compensation consulting firm (1981 to 1986 surveys). Surveys were conducted in March and April of the survey year.

cise. The coefficients on the "Current Performance and Current Compensation Both Below Median" variable for the two accounting measures are both negative, although both coefficients are imprecise. The results are also mixed for total shareholder return (TSR), although, given the rapidity with which the stock market moves, it is always possible that the effect of the incentive compensation was capitalized during the current year and not during the next year. The performance equation indicates a very substantial effect of increased performance-sensitivity, in the predicted positive direction, when the performance measure is after-tax gross economic return (ERET).

Table 4 presents a parallel analysis of a discrete model using as the compensation measure the bonus as a percent of base. The results are not substantially different from the results in Table 3. Compensation is performance-related for all perfor-

mance measures. Only the after-tax gross economic return shows evidence of a performance improvement when performance-sensitivity in the compensation equation increases.

Table 5 shows the results for a continuous model in which the compensation measure is the percentage increase in total salary. All compensation equations indicate that pay is performance-related, on average. The performance equations for after-tax return on assets and after-tax gross economic return give mixed evidence for an effect of increased performance-sensitivity on future performance. There is no evidence that sensitivity to after-tax return on equity affects future performance, but substantial evidence that total shareholder return has such an effect.

In the total shareholder return performance equation in Table 5, the estimated δ_2 is .0109 ($\pm$.0034) and the estimated δ_3 is

Table 2. Summary of the Regression Models Used to Adjust the Various Compensation Measures Defined at the Company Level Estimated by Least Squares with Fixed Company · Year Effects.[a]

Independent Variable[b]	Log of Total Salary	Percent Increase in Total Salary	Log of Base Salary	Bonus as a Percent of Base
Years of Education	.0429	−.2260	.0377	.5136
	(.0006)	(.0278)	(.0006)	(.0209)
Years at Employer	.0033	−.0356	.0016	.1620
	(.0001)	(.0059)	(.0001)	(.0044)
Years of Experience	.0379	−.1774	.0325	.5323
	(.0006)	(.0069)	(.0005)	(.0195)
Years of Experience Squared	$-.479 \cdot 10^{-3}$	na	$-.397 \cdot 10^{-3}$	−.0082
	$(.116 \cdot 10^{-4})$	na	$(.965 \cdot 10^{-5})$	(.0004)
Job Level 1	1.9145	3.60	1.7126	20.18
	(.0010)	(.3765)	(.0083)	(.3109)
Job Level 2	1.0478	3.98	.9014	14.65
	(.0048)	(.1930)	(.0040)	(.1511)
Job Level 3	.5505	2.34	.4647	8.58
	(.0033)	(.1352)	(.0027)	(.1020)
Job Level 4	.2737	1.28	.2284	4.54
	(.0027)	(.1166)	(.0023)	(.0857)
Standard Error of Equation	.333	10.86%	.277	10.40%
R^2	.697	.395	.713	.528
Degrees of Freedom for Company · Year Effects	1,151	896	1,151	1,151
Sample Size	99,219	60,227	99,219	99,219

[a] Coefficients are shown with standard errors in parentheses.
[b] Table 1 contains variable definitions and summary statistics.
Source: All data are from the annual surveys of a major compensation consulting firm (1981 to 1986 surveys).

.0095 (±.0058). These coefficients translate into rather substantial performance effects. A one standard deviation increase in the raise (an extra 10.5% of last year's salary) delivered when current total shareholder return is one standard deviation above the median (3,510 basis points above the median) yields a 400 basis point expected increase in next year's total shareholder return. The estimated effect is only 11% of the standard deviation of total shareholder return, which would be difficult, but not impossible, to detect in a sample of total shareholder returns for which there was only compensation announcement information. The expected effect of delivering the same incremental raise when total shareholder return is three standard deviations above average is 1,200 basis points of additional total shareholder return, which is about one-

third of the standard deviation. These results suggest that general managerial compensation policy may affect the stock market value of a company on a year-to-year basis. This conclusion is surprising in view of the timing difficulties associated with measuring the effects of managerial and other compensation policy changes on stock returns (see Abowd, Milkovich, and Hannon, this issue); it is not inconsistent, however, with efficient capital markets. If the compensation policies are announced after the current fiscal year results, the reported effects could legitimately be associated with the performance-sensitivity of compensation.

Table 6 reports the results for a continuous model in which the compensation measure is the bonus as a percent of base. The compensation equations indicate that pay is performance-related, on

Table 3. Summary of the Statistical Analysis of the Discrete Model Using the Annual Percentage Increase in Total Salary as the Compensation Measure and a Variety of Performance Measures. (Standard Errors in Parentheses)[a]

Performance Measure	ROA[b]	ROE[c]	ERET[d]	TSR[e]
Compensation Equation[f]				
Performance Measure	.614	.701	.777	.908
	(.140)	(.139)	(.145)	(.140)
Total Assets at	.598	.579	.655	.488
Beginning of Year	(.219)	(.220)	(.234)	(.222)
Intercept	−.876	−.866	−1.027	−.866
	(.226)	(.222)	(.243)	(.218)
Performance Equation[g]				
Current Performance	1.704	1.857	2.931	.534
Measure	(.233)	(.238)	(.287)	(.221)
Current Performance &				
Current Compensation	.437	.218	.624	−.098
Both Above Median	(.208)	(.217)	(.266)	(.203)
Current Performance &				
Current Compensation	−.404	−.479	.365	.277
Both Below Median	(.245)	(.241)	(.273)	(.196)
Total Assets at	−.375	−.360	−.593	.247
Beginning of Year	(.248)	(.251)	(.304)	(.214)
Intercept	−.665	−.723	−.994	−.512
	(.292)	(.291)	(.355)	(.248)
Number of Observations	857	853	814	863
Number of Firms	227	228	214	228

[a] The reported results are maximum likelihood estimates of the logistic regression coefficients for an equation that estimates the conditional probability of a one for the dependent variable, given the variables shown in the rows of the table. Summary statistics are reported in Table 1.
[b] ROA is after-tax return on assets, defined in Table 1.
[c] ROE is after-tax return on equity, defined in Table 1.
[d] ERET is after-tax gross economic return (cash flow) as a percentage of beginning of period total assets, valued at replacement cost, defined in Table 1.
[e] TSR is total shareholder return, defined in Table 1.
[f] The dependent variable in the compensation equation is based on the average adjusted value of $100 \cdot (\log(\text{total salary year } t) - \log(\text{total salary year } t\text{-}1))$, called the average adjusted increase in total salary. These are the company · year effects implied by the "percent increase in total salary" column of Table 2. If the average adjusted increase in total salary for a particular company exceeds the median average adjusted increase in total salary for all the firms in the sample, then the compensation measure is one for that company; otherwise, zero. The performance measure on the right-hand side of the equation is described in note g. The variable total assets at beginning of year equal one if total assets for the company exceed the median of total assets for the New York Stock Exchange companies listed on COMPUSTAT; otherwise, zero.
[g] The dependent variable is a performance measure based on the next fiscal year's value of the performance variable indicated by the column heading relative to the median of the New York Stock Exchange companies listed on COMPUSTAT for that year. If the performance variable for a particular company exceeds the annual median performance on the NYSE, then the performance measure equals one for that company; otherwise, zero. Current performance and current compensation both above median equals one when the performance measure is above the median for NYSE companies in the current fiscal year and the compensation measure is above the median for the compensation sample companies for the current year; otherwise, zero. Current performance and current compensation both below median is defined similarly when both measures are below the appropriate medians.
Sources: (1.) Annual median ROA, ROE, ERET, and TSR, Total Assets at Beginning of Year, and all other financial data are from the 2,423 New York Stock Exchange companies in Standard and Poor's COMPUSTAT for the fiscal years 1980 to 1986 (September 1988 annual industrial tape). (2.) All compensation data are from the annual surveys of a major compensation consulting firm (1981 to 1986 surveys).

Table 4. Summary of the Statistical Analysis of the Discrete Model Using the Bonus as a Percentage of Base Salary as the Compensation Measure and a Variety of Performance Measures.
(Standard Errors in Parentheses)[a]

Performance Measure	ROA[b]	ROE[c]	ERET[d]	TSR[e]
Compensation Equation[f]				
Performance Measure	.817	.938	.882	.489
	(.126)	(.126)	(.130)	(.126)
Total Assets	1.191	1.185	1.250	1.090
	(.203)	(.204)	(.216)	(.200)
Intercept	−1.518	−1.510	−1.611	−1.186
	(.212)	(.208)	(.226)	(.198)
Performance Equation[g]				
Current Performance	1.796	1.993	2.753	.065
Measure	(.214)	(.221)	(.252)	(.182)
Current Performance & Current Compensation Above Average	.045	.164	.533	.029
	(.191)	(.199)	(.228)	(.173)
Current Performance & Current Compensation Below Average	−.470	−.389	.012	−.071
	(.210)	(.212)	(.245)	(.172)
Current Total Assets	−.487	−.351	−.654	.255
	(.221)	(.220)	(.262)	(.185)
Intercept	−.236	−.652	−.805	−.272
	(.265)	(.264)	(.321)	(.215)
Number of Observations	1107	1104	1052	1114
Number of Firms	228	227	216	229

[a] The reported results are maximum likelihood estimates of the logistic regression coefficients for an equation that estimates the conditional probability of a one for the dependent variable, given the variables shown in the rows of the table. Summary statistics are reported in Table 1.

[b] ROA is after-tax return on assets, defined in Table 1.

[c] ROE is after-tax return on equity, defined in Table 1.

[d] ERET is after-tax gross economic return (cash flow) as a percentage of beginning of period total assets, valued at replacement cost, defined in Table 1.

[e] TSR is total shareholder return, defined in Table 1.

[f] The dependent variable in the compensation equation is based on the average adjusted value of $100 \cdot \log(1 + \text{Bonus/Base})$, called bonus as a percent of base. These are the company·year effects from the "Bonus as a Percent of Base" column of Table 2. If the adjusted average bonus as a percent of base for a particular company exceeds the median adjusted average bonus as a percent of base for all the companies in the sample, then the compensation measure is one for that company; otherwise, zero. The performance measure on the right-hand side of the equation is described in note f. The variable total assets at beginning of year equal one if total assets for the company exceed the median of total assets for the New York Stock Exchange companies listed on COMPUSTAT; otherwise, zero.

[g] The dependent variable is a performance measure based on the next fiscal year's value of the performance variable indicated by the column heading relative to the median of the New York Stock Exchange companies listed on COMPUSTAT for that year. If the performance variable for a particular company exceeds the annual median performance on the NYSE, then the performance measure equals one for that company; otherwise, zero. Current performance and current compensation both above median equals one when the performance measure is above the median for NYSE companies in the current fiscal year and the compensation measure is above the median for the compensation sample companies for the current year; otherwise, zero. Current performance and current compensation both below median is defined similarly when both measures are below the relevant medians.

Sources: (1.) Annual median ROA, ROE, ERET, and TSR, Total Assets at Beginning of Year, and all other financial data are from the 2,423 New York Stock Exchange companies in Standard and Poor's COMPUSTAT for the fiscal years 1980 to 1986 (September 1988 annual industrial tape). (2.) All compensation data are from the annual surveys of a major compensation consulting firm (1981 to 1986 surveys).

Table 5. Summary of the Statistical Analysis of the Continuous Model Using the Annual Percentage Increase in Total Salary as the Compensation Measure and a Variety of Performance Measures.
(Standard Errors in Parentheses)[a]

Performance Measure	ROA[b]	ROE[c]	ERET[d]	TSR[e]
Compensation Equation[f]				
Performance Measure	.353	.182	.306	.048
	(.061)	(.028)	(.066)	(.010)
Total Assets Beginning of Year	.654	.518	.601	.561
	(.267)	(.265)	(.290)	(.267)
Intercept	1.547	2.909	.891	3.898
	(2.061)	(1.985)	(2.335)	(1.992)
Standard Error of Eqn.	10.367	10.261	10.513	10.388
R^2	.042	.051	.029	.032
Performance Equation[g]				
Current Performance Measure	.463	.551	.685	−.203
	(.036)	(.042)	(.033)	(.044)
Current Adjusted Log of Total Salary	1.046	3.854	1.562	−7.109
	(.866)	(2.008)	(.648)	(5.363)
(Current Performance Above Median, if > 0) · Current Increase[h]	.0066	−.0020	.0043	.0109
	(.0031)	(.0024)	(.0022)	(.0034)
(Current Performance below Median, if < 0) · Current Increase[i]	−.0140	.0012	−.0065	.0095
	(.0043)	(.0037)	(.0042)	(.0058)
Total Assets Beginning of Year	−.373	−.772	−.404	−2.219
	(.209)	(.478)	(.160)	(1.289)
Intercept	−6.406	−34.761	−11.727	87.484
	(8.799)	(20.388)	(6.509)	(54.682)
Standard Error of Eqn.	5.354	12.597	3.947	34.694
R^2	.228	.235	.516	.028
Number of Observations	857	853	814	863
Number of Firms	227	228	214	228

[a] The reported results are least squares estimates of the regression coefficients for an equation that estimates the conditional expectation of the dependent variable, given the variables in the rows of the table. Summary statistics are reported in Table 1.

[b] ROA is after-tax return on assets, defined in Table 1.

[c] ROE is after-tax return on equity, defined in Table 1.

[d] ERET is after-tax gross economic return (cash flow) as a percentage of beginning of period total assets, valued at replacement cost, defined in Table 1.

[e] TSR is total shareholder return, defined in Table 1.

[f] The compensation measure is the average adjusted increase in total salary based on the company · year effects implied by the "percent increase in total salary" column of Table 2.

[g] The performance measure is the value of the variable indicated by the column heading for the next fiscal year.

[h] The current performance above median · compensation interaction is (the value of the performance variable minus the annual median of New York Stock Exchange companies for this performance variable, if this is positive; zero, otherwise) times the adjusted average increase in total salary.

[i] The current performance below median · compensation interaction is (the value of the performance variable minus the annual median of New York Stock Exchange companies for this performance variable, if this is negative; zero, otherwise) times the adjusted average increase in total salary.

Sources: (1.) Annual median ROA, ROE, ERET, and TSR, Total Assets at Beginning of Year, and all other financial data are from the 2,423 New York Stock Exchange companies in Standard and Poor's COMPUSTAT for the fiscal years 1980 to 1986 (September 1988 annual industrial tape). (2.) All compensation data are from the annual surveys of a major compensation consulting firm (1981 to 1986 surveys).

Table 6. Summary of the Statistical Analysis of the Continuous Model Using the Bonus as a Percentage of Base Salary as the Compensation Measure and a Variety of Performance Measures.
(Standard Errors in Parentheses)[a]

Performance Measure	ROA[b]	ROE[c]	ERET[d]	TSR[e]
Compensation Equation[f]				
Performance Measure	.540	.304	.577	.029
	(.051)	(.024)	(.053)	(.008)
Total Assets	2.303	2.138	2.433	2.179
Beginning of Year	(.221)	(.217)	(.240)	(.233)
Intercept	−5.354	−3.762	−8.848	−.901
	(1.698)	(1.620)	(1.937)	(1.730)
Standard Error of Eqn.	9.660	9.533	9.871	10.238
R^2	.154	.195	.158	.081
Performance Equation[g]				
Current Performance	.563	.518	.635	−.201
Measure	(.039)	(.046)	(.035)	(.040)
Current Adjusted Log	−1.321	−1.364	.732	−.298
of Base Salary	(.805)	(1.950)	(.638)	(5.523)
(Current Performance Above Median, if > 0)	.0075	−.0020	.0050	.0005
· Current Bonus/Base[h]	(.0025)	(.0025)	(.0017)	(.0028)
(Current Performance Below Median, if < 0)	−.0217	.0048	.0031	.0187
· Current Bonus/Base[i]	(.0030)	(.0051)	(.0036)	(.0047)
Total Assets	−.095	−.181	−.301	.160
Beginning of Year	(.165)	(.402)	(.136)	(1.143)
Intercept	17.489	20.934	−2.265	25.907
	(8.197)	(19.842)	(6.482)	(56.158)
Standard Error of Eqn.	4.918	11.961	3.834	34.526
R^2	.301	.241	.538	.036
Number of Observations	1,107	1,104	1,052	1,114
Number of Firms	228	229	216	228

[a] The reported results are least squares estimates of the regression coefficients for an equation that estimates the conditional expectation of the dependent variable, given the variables in the rows of the table. Summary statistics are reported in Table 1.

[b] ROA is after-tax return on assets, defined in Table 1.

[c] ROE is after-tax return on equity, defined in Table 1.

[d] ERET is after-tax gross economic return (cash flow) as a percentage of beginning of period total assets, valued at replacement cost, defined in Table 1.

[e] TSR is total shareholder return, defined in Table 1.

[f] The compensation measure is the average adjusted bonus as a percent of base implied by the "Bonus as a Percent of Base" column in Table 2.

[g] The performance measure is the value of the variable indicated by the column heading.

[h] The current performance above median · compensation interaction is (the value of the performance variable minus the annual median of New York Stock Exchange companies for this performance variable, if this is positive; zero, otherwise) times the adjusted average bonus as a percent of base.

[i] The current performance below median · compensation interaction is (the value of the performance variable minus the annual median of New York Stock Exchange companies for this performance variable, if this is negative; zero, otherwise) times the adjusted average bonus as a percent of base.

Sources: (1.) Annual median ROA, ROE, ERET, and TSR, Total Assets at Beginning of Year, and all other financial data are from the 2,423 New York Stock Exchange companies in Standard and Poor's COMPUSTAT for the fiscal years 1980 to 1986 (September 1988 annual industrial tape). (2.) All compensation data are from the annual surveys of a major compensation consulting firm (1981 to 1986 surveys).

average. The performance equation for after-tax return on assets gives mixed evidence for an effect of increased performance-sensitivity on future performance. There is no statistical evidence that increasing performance-sensitivity for after-tax return on equity affects future performance. The evidence that after-tax gross economic return and total shareholder return have an effect, however, is substantial.

I will illustrate the magnitude for the gross economic return. The estimated δ_2 is .0050 ($\pm$.0017) and the estimated δ_3 is .0031 ($\pm$.0036). Only δ_2 is statistically precise. The effect of increasing the bonus-to-base ratio by one standard deviation (10.7% of the base salary) when after-tax gross economic return is one standard deviation above the median (560 basis points) is an expected 30 basis points of economic return. The expected effect is 5% of the standard deviation of economic return. The expected effect from the same change in the bonus-to-base ratio when economic return is three standard deviations above the median (1680 basis points) is 90 basis points, which is 16% of the standard deviation of after-tax gross economic return. The estimated magnitudes of the effects of increasing the performance-sensitivity based upon the economic return measure are slightly smaller than the estimated effects for total shareholder return after standardizing. Given the variability of the estimates, however, the results are basically comparable.

Conclusions

I have specified an internally consistent framework for measuring the degree of performance-sensitivity in a compensation system and assessing the validity of the performance-base. The method shows clearly that measuring the effects of a change in the extent to which compensation is related to performance requires an analysis of the effects of interactions between current performance and current compensation on subsequent performance.

The estimated models produce some weak results and some fairly strong results. It is perhaps surprising that the accounting performance measures did not fare as well as the economic measure or the market measure. Accounting-based performance measures are widely used in businesses as a basis for compensation. There are two reasonable explanations for the weak results I obtained. First, most corporate performance plans explicitly using accounting data are multiyear plans, which have been excluded from my data. Second, since after-tax return on assets, after-tax return on equity, and after-tax gross economic return are all correlated (in all cases > .6), using any one of these measures as the basis for pay could produce the desired results on after-tax gross economic return, which is a better measure of the profitability of the assets than either of the usual accounting ratios.

This study suggests that pay-for-performance systems based on after-tax gross economic return and total shareholder return may be effective, since I find evidence that increasing the sensitivity of compensation to either of these measures may be associated with better performance on that measure in the future. None of the estimated equations approached the degree of precision that would warrant uncritical adoption of the plans under study. The results do lend credence, however, to claims that benefits can be gained by increasing the pay-for-performance component of managerial compensation.

Data Appendix

This appendix describes the sources and methods used to assemble the managerial compensation and corporate performance data used in this study. The appendix discusses the variables derived from the compensation surveys, Standard and Poor's COMPUSTAT database service, the U.S. Department of

Commerce Bureau of Economic Analysis time series, and miscellaneous additional sources. To improve the readability of this appendix I have not used acronyms for the variables. Instead, variable names are set in italics when first defined and capitalized throughout.

Compensation Variables

The managerial compensation data were developed using the cash compensation survey of a major compensation consulting company. The survey collects data for both the corporation and the individual manager. Data for individual managers are identified by company, person, and year. Thus, any particular executive who appears in the survey more than once can be followed over time. The respondent company decides how many executives to include and how often to participate. For this reason, sample mobility of the managers does not reflect career mobility. Exits from the sample do not imply either separations or promotions. Data on individual managers are available for survey years 1981 to 1986, inclusive. Corporate data are identified by company and year, making it possible to follow companies over time.

Variables from the Compensation
Survey Individual Data

Annual Base Salary: Salary (exclusive of long- and short-term bonuses) as of March 1 of the survey year.

Bonus: The dollar amount of any short-term incentive granted for the latest bonus period (prior to March 1 of the survey year). The figure includes any incentive awards based on one period's performance regardless of whether the cash was paid in full or deferred (completely or partially). Excluded from the figure are cash bonuses that are dependent on fulfillment of some future or longer-term organizational performance objectives; cash payments paid during the previous year for performance during an earlier period; and sales commissions. (This definition is a paraphrase of the survey instructions.)

Job Level: The position reporting level. The Chief Executive Officer is reporting level 1. Reporting level 2 reports directly to the CEO. For managers in divisions or subsidiaries, the divisional president or general manager cannot have a reporting level higher than 2. This definition is supposed to guarantee that only the corporate-level CEO has reporting level 1.

Years of Education, Birthday, and *Date of Hire* are defined in the conventional manner.

Variables from the Corporate-Level
Compensation Data

Company Name: The name of the business participating in the survey. This variable was used to build the link to COMPUSTAT data.

Assets: Corporate total assets as reported by the respondent to the survey (usually a member of the corporate-level human resource management staff). This variable was used to verify that the company was participating in the survey at the corporate level. Respondent companies from subsidiaries, divisions, and separate business units of a corporation could

elect to participate as if they were stand-alone companies. In this case, the variable Assets would contain total assets for the relevant business unit, an amount less than corporate total assets. Such companies were excluded from the present study. The Assets variable was also used to verify that the relevant fiscal year closed prior to March 1 of the survey year. Only companies with an exact match between the Assets variable in the compensation file and the Total Assets variable from COMPUSTAT were included in the study. This procedure ensured that the COMPUSTAT fiscal year information dated 1980 was available to make the compensation decisions reported in the 1981 compensation data, and so forth for the succeeding years.

Shareholders' Equity: Corporate common equity as reported by the survey respondent. This variable was used to check the match to COMPUSTAT based on the company name and assets. (Definitions of shareholders' equity are complicated by the treatment of preferred stock, so an exact match was not required.)

COMPUSTAT Variables

The descriptions below are based on COMPUSTAT (Standard and Poor's 1988) documentation of standard financial accounting concepts. The item numbers refer to the variable locations on the annual industrial files.

Net Sales: Sales revenue net of discounts and returns (COMPUSTAT Item 012).

COGS: Cost of goods sold (COMPUSTAT Item 041).

Selling and Administrative Expenses: Selling, overhead, and general administrative expenses (COMPUSTAT Item 012 less Item 041 less Item 013).

Operating Income: Net Sales − COGS − Selling and Administrative Expenses.

Interest Expense: Gross interest expense (COMPUSTAT Item 015).

Income Taxes: Total income taxes (COMPUSTAT Item 016).

Net Income: Income before extraordinary items (COMPUSTAT Item 018) plus gain (or loss) on extraordinary items (COMPUSTAT Item 048).

Minority Interest Income: The part of net income due to unconsolidated minority interests in the company (COMPUSTAT Item 049).

Preferred Stock Dividends: Dividends paid to holders of preferred stock (COMPUSTAT Item 019).

Total Assets: End of fiscal year book value of all assets on the balance sheet. This value must equal the sum of all liabilities and shareholders' equity (COMPUSTAT Item 006).

Inventory: Asset consisting of the value of raw, intermediate, and finished goods inventory (COMPUSTAT Item 003). The method of book valuation is discussed below.

Inventory Valuation Method: Last-in-first-out (LIFO) is distinguished from all other methods; other methods are treated as first-in-first-out (FIFO). The inventory adjustment method is based on COMPUSTAT Item 059.

Current Assets: Cash and short-term investments,

accounts receivable, inventory, and other short-term assets (COMPUSTAT Item 004).

Gross Property, Plant, and Equipment: Asset consisting of undepreciated historical cost of property, plant, and equipment (COMPUSTAT 007).

Net Property, Plant, and Equipment: Asset consisting of depreciated historical cost of property, plant, and equipment (COMPUSTAT 008).

Other Long-Term Assets: Total Assets less current assets less net property, plant, and equipment (COMPUSTAT Item 006 less Item 004 less Item 008).

Current Liabilities: Short-term debt, accounts payable, and other short-term liabilities (COMPUSTAT Item 005).

Current Debt: Short-term debt component of current liabilities (COMPUSTAT Item 034).

Common Equity: End of fiscal year book value of common stock equity (COMPUSTAT Item 060).

Gross Investment: Gross spending on new property, plant, and equipment (COMPUSTAT Item 030).

Dispositions: Proceeds from the sale of property, plant, and equipment (COMPUSTAT Item 107).

Cumulative Adjustment Factor: Restates common stock data so that all previous fiscal years are on the same basis as the most recent fiscal year in the file, usually 1987 (COMPUSTAT Item 027).

Bureau of Economic Analysis Variables

The variables described below are based on the National Income and Product Accounts (NIPA, *Survey of Current Business,* monthly). NIPA variables are referenced by their standard table numbers. NIPA variables extracted from CITIBASE (Citicorp Database Services 1978) are referenced by the CITIBASE name as well. The Bureau of Economic Analysis (BEA) in the Department of Commerce maintains estimates of fixed reproducible tangible wealth. Variables from this BEA data base are referenced by their table numbers in *Fixed Reproducible Tangible Wealth in the United States, 1925–85* (called *FRTW* below). (See also Musgrave 1986.)

Equipment Proportion of Industry Fixed Nonresidential Investment: Derived from the ratio of Fixed Nonresidential Private Capital, Equipment Investment, in millions of current dollars, to Fixed Nonresidential Private Capital, Total Investment, in millions of current dollars; *FRTW* Table B1, by two-digit Standard Industrial Classification. This variable was supplied by Shapiro (See Brainard et al. 1988) as extracted from the BEA *Wealth* tape, which contains the *FRTW* data.

Structure Proportion of Industry Fixed Nonresidential Investment: Derived from the ratio of Fixed Nonresidential Private Capital, Structure Investment, in millions of current dollars, to Fixed Nonresidential Private Capital, Total Investment, in millions of current dollars; *FRTW* Table B1, by two-digit Standard Industrial Classification. This variable was also supplied by Shapiro. Equipment and structure proportions of industry fixed nonresidential investment sum to one.

Industry Implicit Price Deflator for Plant Investment: Derived as the ratio of Fixed Nonresidential Private Capital, Plant Investment (millions of current dollars) to Fixed Nonresidential Private Capital, Plant Investment (millions of 1982 dollars); *FRTW* Table B1, by two-digit Standard Industrial Classification. This variable was also supplied by Shapiro.

Industry Implicit Price Deflator for Equipment Investment: Derived as the ratio of Fixed Nonresidential Private Capital, Equipment Investment (millions of current dollars) to Fixed Nonresidential Private Capital, Equipment Investment (millions of 1982 dollars); *FRTW* Table B1, by two-digit Standard Industrial Classification. This variable was also supplied by Shapiro.

Industry Implicit Price Deflator: Derived as the ratio of GNP by Industry, billions of current dollars (NIPA Table 6.1) to GNP by Industry, billions of 1982 dollars (NIPA Table 6.2), by two-digit SIC. This variable was supplied by Shapiro as extracted from the BEA NIPA tape.

Implicit Price Deflator for Fixed Nonresidential Investments in Structure: Derived as the ratio of Fixed Investment by Type, Structures, billions of current dollars (NIPA Table 5.12) to Fixed Investment by Type, Structures, billions of 1982 dollars (NIPA Table 5.13); extracted from CITIBASE as GDIS and converted to annual average.

Miscellaneous Variables

Tax Rate: U.S. Federal marginal corporate tax rate (.46 for 1980 to 1986, .40 for 1987, and .34 thereafter).

Derived Variables Used in the Compensation and Performance Analysis

The estimate of the replacement cost of total assets was developed using the methods of Brainard et al. (1988) and Hall et al. (1988). The flow of the calculation is described here. Programming is available from the author. Abowd and Tracy (1989) contains a detailed discussion of the methodology. The result of the calculation is an estimate of the cost of reproducing a company's current total assets (primarily property, plant, equipment, and inventory) without purchasing the company outright (by purchasing all of its outstanding stocks and bonds).

For each company, a complete history was assembled from annual industrial data, research data, back data, and research back data files supplied by COMPUSTAT. Some company histories begin in 1950, others in 1960, and still others in 1968 (the start date of the September 1988 annual industrial file for most companies). The company histories were used to impute a series of structure, equipment, inventory, and other investments that were converted from historical cost to current replacement cost, depreciated according to economic life, and summed over the economic life of each asset to produce an estimate of the replacement cost of the asset.

Plant investments were assumed to have an economic life of 26 years; equipment investments were assumed to have an economic life of 14 years. The first five years of data for each company were used to estimate the growth rate of the asset Gross

Property, Plant and Equipment (subject to a minimum of zero and a maximum of 10% per annum). This growth rate was used to impute a history of gross structure and equipment investments prior to the initial data year the sum of which was exactly equal to the earliest value of Gross Property, Plant and Equipment. For each subsequent year, gross investment in property, plant, and equipment was set equal to Gross Investment less Dispositions. Current and (imputed) historical cost gross investments were then adjusted (by imputing a writeoff or addition, as appropriate) so that the historical cost investment series always summed to the current Gross Property, Plant and Equipment asset.

The vintage history of gross investments was divided into structure and equipment using the Structure as a Proportion of Industry Investment and Equipment as a Proportion of Industry Investment series for the appropriate years. The historical cost plant investments were then converted to current replacement cost by multiplying by the ratio of the current value of the Industry Implicit Price Deflator for Structure Investments to the appropriate historical value of the same series. Historical cost equipment investments were similarly converted to current replacement cost using the Industry Implicit Price Deflator for Equipment Investment. Current replacement cost investments were depreciated using straight line depreciation over the economic lives assumed for plant and equipment, respectively. The sum of the current replacement cost structure investments for the current and 25 preceding years plus the sum of current replacement cost equipment investments for the current and 13 preceding years is *Gross Property, Plant, and Equipment, Replacement Cost.*

Net Property, Plant, and Equipment, Replacement Cost was calculated according to the same formula as Gross Property, Plant, and Equipment, Replacement Cost using the depreciated replacement cost estimates for structure and equipment investments.

Inventory was only adjusted to the extent that LIFO accounting was used. Up to three different inventory valuation methods were allowed. The proportion of Inventory valued using LIFO was estimated from the COMPUSTAT Inventory Method variable. For Non-LIFO Inventory the replacement cost and historical cost are equal. LIFO Inventory was converted to replacement cost by multiplying the LIFO proportion of last year's Inventory, valued at replacement cost, by the ratio of the current value of the Industry Implicit Price Deflator to last year's

Industry Implicit Price Deflator and adding the change in historical cost LIFO Inventory between the current and previous fiscal years. The sum of LIFO and non-LIFO Inventory, valued at replacement cost, is the series *Inventory, Replacement Cost.* The value of replacement cost and historical cost Inventory are equal for the first year a company appears in the COMPUSTAT data regardless of Inventory Method.

Other Assets were converted to replacement cost by multiplying last year's Other Assets, valued at replacement cost, by the ratio of the current value of the Implicit Price Deflator for Fixed Nonresidential Investments in Structure to last year's Implicit Price Deflator for Fixed Nonresidential Investments in Structure and adding the change in historical cost Other Assets between the current and previous fiscal years. The resulting series is *Other Assets, Replacement Cost.* The value of replacement cost and historical cost Other Assets are equal for the first year a company appears in the COMPUSTAT data.

Replacement Cost of Total Assets: Net Property, Plant, and Equipment, Replacement Cost + Inventory, Replacement Cost + Other Assets, Replacement Cost + (Current Assets − Inventory) − (Current Liabilities − Current Debt).

After-Tax Return on Assets: Ratio defined as $100 \cdot$ (Net Income + Interest Expense $\cdot$ (1 − Tax Rate))/((Total Assets + Total Assets previous fiscal year end)/2).

After-Tax Return on Equity: Ratio defined as $100 \cdot$ (Net Income − Minority Interest Income − Preferred Dividends Paid)/((Common Equity + Common Equity previous fiscal year end)/2).

After-Tax Gross Economic Return: Ratio defined as $100 \cdot$ (Operating Income − Income Taxes)/Replacement Cost of Total Assets previous fiscal year end.

Total Shareholder Return: Ratio defined as $100 \cdot$ ((Dividends per Common Share/Cumulative Adjustment Factor) + (Common Stock Price/Cumulative Adjustment Factor) − (Common Stock Price previous calendar year end/Cumulative Adjustment Factor previous calendar year end))/((Common Stock Price previous calendar year end/Cumulative Adjustment Factor previous calendar year end)).

A thorough discussion of accounting measures of profitability can be found in Bernstein (1983, Chapter 19). Some of the pitfalls are discussed in Foster (1986, Chapter 3). The definitions of after-tax return on assets and after-tax return on equity are from Bernstein and appear to conform to current accounting practice.

REFERENCES

Abowd, John M., George T. Milkovich, and John M. Hannon. 1990. "The Effects of Human Resource Management Decisions on Shareholder Value." *Industrial and Labor Relations Review,* this issue.

Abowd, John M., and Joseph S. Tracy. 1989. "Unions and Market Power." Unpublished working paper, Cornell University.

Antle, Rick, and Abbie Smith. 1986. "An Empirical

Investigation of the Relative Performance Evaluation of Corporate Executives." *Journal of Accounting Research,* Vol. 24, No. 1 (Spring), pp. 1–39.

Baker, George P., Michael C. Jensen, and Kevin J. Murphy. 1988. "Compensation and Incentives: Practice vs. Theory." *Journal of Finance,* Vol. 43, No. 3 (July), pp. 593–616.

Becker, Gary S., and George J. Stigler. 1974. "Law

Enforcement, Malfeasance, and Compensation of Enforcers." *Journal of Legal Studies,* Vol. 3 (January), pp. 1–18.

Bernstein, Leopold A. 1983. *Financial Statement Analysis: Theory, Application, and Interpretation.* Homewood, Ill.: Richard D. Irwin.

Bhagat, Sanjai, James Brickley, and Ronald C. Lease. 1985. "Incentive Effects of Stock Purchase Plans." *Journal of Financial Economics,* Vol. 14, No. 2 (June), pp. 195–215.

Brainard, William C., Matthew D. Shapiro, and John B. Shoven. 1988. "Fundamental Value and Market Value." Yale University working paper, May.

Brickley, James, Sanjai Bhagat, and Ronald C. Lease. 1985. "The Impact of Long-Range Managerial Compensation Plans on Shareholder Wealth." *Journal of Accounting and Economics,* Vol. 7, No. 1–3 (April), pp. 115–29.

Citicorp Database Services. 1987. *CITIBASE: Citibank Economic Database (Machine-Readable Magnetic Data File, 1946–Present).* New York: Citibank.

Coughlan, Anne T., and Ronald M. Schmidt. 1985. "Executive Compensation, Management Turnover, and Firm Performance: An Empirical Analysis." *Journal of Accounting and Economics,* Vol. 7, No. 1–3 (April), pp. 43–66.

Ehrenberg, Ronald G., and George T. Milkovich. 1987. "Compensation and Firm Performance." In Morris Kleiner et al., eds., *Human Resources and the Performance of the Firm.* Madison, Wis.: Industrial Relations Research Association, pp. 87–122.

Fama, Eugene F., and Michael C. Jensen. 1983a. "Separation of Ownership and Control." *Journal of Law and Economics,* Vol. 26 (June), pp. 301–25.

Fama, Eugene F., and Michael C. Jensen. 1983b. "Agency Problems and Residual Claims." *Journal of Law and Economics,* Vol. 26 (June), pp. 327–49.

Foster, George. 1986. *Financial Statement Analysis,* 2d Edition. Englewood Cliffs, N.J.: Prentice-Hall.

Gibbons, Robert, and Kevin J. Murphy. 1990. "Relative Performance Evaluation for Chief Executive Officers." *Industrial and Labor Relations Review,* this issue.

Gomez-Mejia, Luis R., Henry Tosi, and Timothy Hinkin. 1987. "Managerial Control, Performance, and Executive Compensation." *Academy of Management Journal,* Vol. 30, No. 1, pp. 51–70.

Grossman, Sanford J., and Oliver D. Hart. 1983. "An Analysis of the Principal-Agent Problem." *Econometrica,* Vol. 51, No. 1 (January), pp. 7–46.

Hall, Bronwyn H., Clint Cummins, Elizabeth S. Laderman, and Joy Mundy. 1988. "The R&D Master File Documentation." NBER Technical Working Paper No. 72, December.

Hart, Oliver, and Bengt Holström. 1987. "The Theory of Contracts." In Truman F. Bewley, ed., *Advances in Economic Theory, Fifth World Congress.* Cambridge, England: Cambridge University Press.

Healy, Paul M. 1985. "The Effect of Bonus Schemes on Accounting Decisions." *Journal of Accounting and Economics,* Vol. 7, No. 1–3 (April), pp. 85–107.

Holmström, Bengt, "Moral Hazard and Observability." *Bell Journal of Economics,* Vol. 10, No. 1 (Spring), pp. 74–91.

Jensen, Michael C., and William H. Meckling. 1976. "Theory of the Firm: Managerial Behavior, Agency Costs, and Ownership Structure." *Journal of Financial Economics,* Vol. 3 (October), pp. 305–60.

Jensen, Michael C., and Kevin J. Murphy. 1987. "Are Executive Compensation Contracts Structured Properly?" University of Rochester unpublished working paper.

Jensen, Michael C., and Kevin J. Murphy. 1988. "Performance Pay and Top Management Incentives." University of Rochester unpublished working paper.

Lambert, Richard A., and David F. Larker. 1985. "Golden Parachutes, Executive Decision-Making, and Shareholder Wealth." *Journal of Accounting and Economics,* Vol. 7, No. 1–3 (April), pp. 179–203.

Lambert, Richard A., and David F. Larker. 1987. "An Analysis of the Use of Accounting and Market Measures of Performance in Executive Compensation Contracts." *Journal of Accounting Research,* Vol. 25 (Supplement), pp. 85–125.

Larker, David F. 1983. "The Association Between Performance Plan Adoption and Corporate Capital Investment." *Journal of Accounting and Economics,* Vol. 5 (April), pp. 3–30.

Larker, David F. 1986. "Choosing a Performance Measure: An Analysis of the Alternatives." *Topics in Total Compensation,* Vol. 1, No. 1 (Fall), pp. 57–71.

Lazear, Edward P. 1979. "Why Is There Mandatory Retirement?" *Journal of Political Economy,* Vol. 87, No. 6 (December), pp. 1261–84.

Lazear, Edward P. 1986. "Salaries and Piece Rates." *Journal of Business,* Vol. 59, No. 3 (July), pp. 405–31.

Leonard, Jonathan S. 1990. "Executive Pay and Corporate Performance." *Industrial and Labor Relations Review,* this issue.

Lewellen, Wilbur G. 1968. *Executive Compensation in Large Industrial Corporations.* New York: National Bureau of Economic Research.

Lewellen, Wilbur G., and Blaine Huntsman. 1970. "Managerial Pay and Corporate Performance." *American Economic Review,* Vol. 60, No. 4 (September), pp. 710–20.

Lewellen, Wilbur G., Claudio Loderer, and Kenneth Martin. 1987. "Executive Compensation and Executive Incentive Problems: An Empirical Analysis." *Journal of Accounting and Economics,* Vol. 9, No. 3 (December), pp. 287–310.

Masson, Robert T. 1971. "Executive Motivations, Earnings, and Consequent Equity Performance." *Journal of Political Economy,* Vol. 79, No. 6 (November), pp. 1278–92.

Miller, Merton H., and Myron S. Scholes. 1982. "Executive Compensation, Taxes and Incentives." In William F. Sharpe and Cathryn M. Cootner, eds., *Financial Economics: Essays in Honor of Paul Cootner.* Englewood Cliffs, N.J.: Prentice-Hall, pp. 179–201.

Murphy, Kevin J. 1985. "Corporate Performance and Managerial Remuneration: An Empirical Analysis." *Journal of Accounting and Economics,* Vol. 7 (April), pp. 11–42.

Murphy, Kevin J. 1985. "Top Executives Are Worth Every Nickel They Get." *Harvard Business Review,* Vol. 64 (March–April), pp. 125–32.

Musgrave, John C. 1986. "Fixed Reproducible Tangible Wealth in the United States, 1982–85." *Survey of Current Business,* Vol. 66, No. 8 (August), pp. 36–39.

Rabin, Bonnie R. 1986. "Executive Compensation and Firm Performance: The Case of Employment Agreements." M.S. thesis, School of Industrial and Labor Relations, Cornell University.

Rabin, Bonnie R. 1987. "Executive Compensation and Firm Performance: An Empirical Analysis." Ph.D. thesis, School of Industrial and Labor Relations, Cornell University.

Ross, Stephen A. 1973. "The Economic Theory of Agency: The Principal's Problem." *American Economic Review* (Papers and Proceedings), Vol. 63, No. 2 (May), pp. 135–39.

Standard and Poor. 1988. *COMPUSTAT.* New York: Standard and Poor Corporation.

Tehranian, Hassan, and James F. Waegelein. 1985. "Market Reaction to Short Term Executive Compensation Plan Adoption." *Journal of Accounting and Economics,* Vol. 7, No. 1–3 (April), pp. 131–44.

U.S. Department of Commerce. Bureau of Economic Analysis. *Survey of Current Business,* monthly.

U.S. Department of Commerce. Bureau of Economic Analysis. 1987. *Fixed Reproducible Tangible Wealth in the United States, 1925–85.* Washington, D.C.: GPO.

THE INCENTIVE EFFECTS OF TOURNAMENTS REVISITED: EVIDENCE FROM THE EUROPEAN PGA TOUR

RONALD G. EHRENBERG and MICHAEL L. BOGNANNO*

This analysis of data from the 1987 European Men's Professional Golf Association (PGA) Tour strongly supports the hypothesis that the level and structure of prizes in PGA tournaments influence players' performance. Specifically, players' performance appears to vary positively with both the total money prizes awarded in a tournament and the marginal return to effort in the final round of play (a value that varies among players largely depending on how the prize money is allocated among finishers of different ranks). The authors suggest that these results, together with the similar results of their earlier study of the 1984 U.S. Men's PGA Tour, may have implications for the design of compensation systems for certain groups of workers, such as corporate executives, college professors, and salespeople.

ECONOMISTS have recently devoted considerable attention to models of tournaments, or situations in which an individual's payment depends only on his output or rank relative to other competitors.[1] Such models are of more than academic interest, as they may well describe the compensation structures applicable not only to professional sports tournaments but to many corporate executives (who can be thought of as competing with colleagues for promotions), young college professors (who may be thought of as competing with colleagues for tenure), and sales people (whose bonuses often depend on their relative outputs).

Academic interest in tournament models derives from the incentive effects that such compensation structures are thought to have. In particular, under certain sets of assumptions tournaments are thought to give participants an incentive to provide optimal levels of effort.[2]

Very few attempts have been made, however, to test either if tournaments actually elicit desired effort responses or if executive compensation is generated by a tournament-type reward structure.[3] The

* Ronald Ehrenberg is Irving M. Ives Professor of Industrial and Labor Relations and Economics at Cornell University and Research Associate at the National Bureau of Economic Research, and Michael Bognanno is a Ph.D. candidate in Labor Economics at Cornell University. This paper is based on work supported by the National Science Foundation under Grant No. SES-8719592, and the authors thank the Foundation for its support. The data set used in the paper will be archived at the Inter-University Consortium for Political and Social Research (P.O. Box 1248, Ann Arbor, Michigan 48106) as of January 1, 1991.

[1] See Lazear and Rosen (1981), Carmichael (1983), Green and Stokey (1983), Malcomson (1984), Nalebuff and Stiglitz (1984), O'Keefe, Viscusi, and Zeckhauser (1984), Rosen (1986), and McLaughlin (1988) for discussions of tournament theory.

[2] These assumptions relate to the costs of monitoring effort, asymmetric information, and the nature of random shocks to output/productivity.

[3] Bull, Schotter, and Weigett (1987) is an experimental study that used paid undergraduate student volunteers as subjects to test whether tournaments elicit desired effort responses. O'Reilly et al. (1988) is

lack of studies that use corporate data is undoubtedly due to the difficulty of measuring both individual executives' effort levels and the incentive structures they face.

In previous research we have examined data from professional golf tournaments in the United States to test whether tournaments do have the postulated incentive effects (Ehrenberg and Bognanno 1988). Our focus was on golf tournaments because data were available for them on the incentives players face (the prize distribution in each tournament) and measures of each individual's output (the player's score). In addition, data were available to control for factors other than the prize structure that should affect a player's score in a tournament, such as the player's "quality," the "quality" of his opponents, the difficulty of the tournament's course, and the weather conditions during the tournament. Thus, our analysis could isolate the effect of the prize structure on player performance. In the main, the results presented in that paper indicated that tournaments' prize structures *do* affect players' performance.

In the present paper we seek to test the robustness of our previous findings by performing a similar analysis using data from the 1987 European Men's Professional Golf Association (PGA) Tour.

Analytical Framework

Our econometric work is based on implications derived from simple two-contestant models that capture the essence of the incentive problem.[4] If one wishes, one can view the two-person tournament as a situation in which a contestant competes against "the rest of the field."

Each individual's score in a tournament is assumed to depend on his effort/concentration level, a pure random or luck component, and tournament-specific factors such as the difficulty of the course and the adversity of weather conditions. For simplicity, the last two factors are assumed to affect all players in a tournament equally. A key assumption in the model is that players choose their effort/concentration levels.

Of course, one may argue that treating the effort/concentration levels of professional golfers as choice variables does not make sense because professionals *always* play as hard as they can.[5] What this criticism ignores, however, is how difficult it is even for professionals to maintain their concentration levels over tournaments that typically last four days per week and that involve four to five hours of physical effort per day. Furthermore, playing on the PGA European Tour involves weekly international travel and living out of hotel rooms. At the very least, one might expect fatigue to set in during the latter days of each tournament and players' ability to maintain their concentration to diminish at these times. To capture this effect, we assume that each individual faces a "cost of effort/concentration" function and that the marginal cost of effort is positive and increases as effort increases.

Given a prize differential for winning, each player is assumed to choose his effort level to maximize his expected utility. If, furthermore, we posit that each player assumes his opponent is similarly choosing *his* optimal strategy, a solution can be found for each player's optimal effort/concentration level and thus his score. In particular,

$$(1) \quad q_{ji} = u_{ji}((w_{1i} - w_{2i}), A_{jo}, A_{jc}) + \epsilon_{ji} + \delta_i.$$

Here q_{ji} is individual j's score in tournament i, $w_{1i} - w_{2i}$ is the prize differential for winning, A_{jo}, A_{jc} are measures of the player's own ability and his competitor's ability respectively, δ_i reflects the tourna-

---

a recent attempt to test whether executive compensation corresponds to a tournament structure.

[4] Details of these models can be found in Lazear and Rosen (1981) and Ehrenberg and Bognanno (1988). Generalizations to the n-contestant case are found in Green and Stokey (1983) and elsewhere.

[5] In fact, the U.S. PGA Tour's *1984 Player's Handbook* (1984) states that "in making a commitment to play in a PGA Tour cosponsored or approved event, a player obligates himself to exercise his maximum golf skill and to play in a professional manner" (p. 58).

ment-specific factors, and ϵ_{ji} is a random error term. Equation (1) states that a player's score in a tournament depends on the prize differential for winning, how "good" the player is relative to his opponent, tournament-specific factors such as the weather and course difficulty, and a random error term. One crucial implication of this model is that higher prize differentials for winning should lead players to exert more effort/concentration and thus should result in better (that is, lower) scores.

The 1987 Men's European Professional Golf Tour

The typical golf tournament has four rounds. Half the field is "cut" at the end of the second round, two additional rounds are played, and then prizes are awarded on the basis of the players' ranks after the final round. Of the 29 tournaments on the 1987 European Men's Professional Golf Association Tour, 27 were of this type, and data from 23 of these are used in our analysis.[6]

Across these tournaments the *structure* of the allocation of prize money by rank was virtually identical, although the *level* of prize money varied across tournaments.[7] Figure 1 summarizes this structure. An important effect of the prize structure is that it gave a much higher marginal return for improving one's performance by one rank (or not seeing one's performance decline by one rank) to players who

were close to the leaders after three rounds than to players who were far from the leaders. For example, the marginal prize received for finishing second instead of third was approximately 5 percent of the total tournament prize money, whereas the marginal price received for finishing nineteenth instead of twentieth was less than 0.1 percent of the total tournament prize money.[8]

This structure of prizes, coupled with variations in the level of prizes across tournaments, suggests two types of tests of the theory sketched in the preceding section. First, since the structure of prizes is constant across tournaments, the prize differential for "winning" depends only on the level of total prize money. Thus, one can focus on a tournament as a whole and ask, other things equal, if higher total prize money leads to lower scores for the tournament as a whole. Second, one can focus only on the last round of a tournament and ask if a player's performance in the last round depends, other things equal, on the marginal return to effort. The marginal return to effort will depend, in turn, on the total prize money in the tournament, the player's rank after the third round, and how many players are tightly bunched around him after three rounds. The results of both of these types of analysis are reported in the next section.

Before turning to the empirical results, however, we must discuss one institutional complication. Not every pro golfer who wanted to enter any given European PGA tournament in 1987 could do so. Rather, a system of exemptions and priorities existed. At the risk of simplifying a very complex system, we would describe it as follows:[9]

---

[6] See *Pro-Golf '88: The Official PGA European Tour Guide* (1988). The six tournaments not included in the sample were two match-play tournaments that had different formats and much smaller fields (Epson Grand Prix of Europe Match-Play, Dunhill Cup Nations Tournament), two tournaments that were interrupted after three rounds because of the weather (Volvo Belgian Open, Portuguese Open), a tournament open only to golfers aged 50 and older (Senior British Open), and the Open Golf Championship, in which the eligibility criteria and the prize structure differed from those in the other tournaments. A listing of the 23 tournaments included in the sample and the total prize money awarded in each appears in Appendix Table A1.

[7] See *Pro-Golf '88: The Official PGA European Tour Guide* (1988).

[8] Appendix Table A2 presents data on the mean level and share of prize money won *expost* for players at various ranks in these tournaments. Because of ties in some tournaments for some ranks, the *expost* share of the prize money won at each rank is not identical across tournaments.

[9] See *Pro Golf '88: the Official PGA European Tour Guide* (1988), pp. 55–57. In addition to the distinctions noted in the text, members of the European Ryder Cup Team fell in group (ii), past winners of a

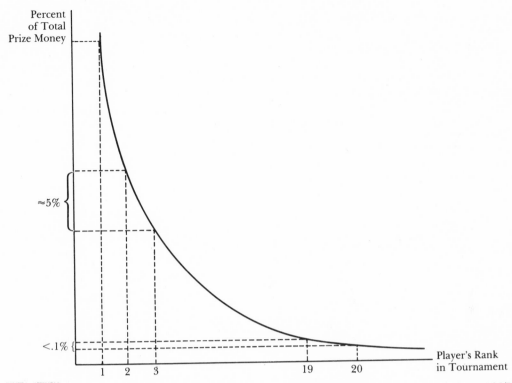

Figure 1. Share of Total Prize Money Going to Players of Different Ranks: Sample from 1987 Men's European PGA Tournament.

(i) Any golfer who had won any "major" tournament after 1977 or any European PGA Tour tournament in 1986 could enter any tournament he wanted in both 1987 *and* 1988.

(ii) Any golfer who failed to qualify under (i) and had won a specified major tournament in 1977 or any European PGA Tour tournament in 1985 could enter any tournament he wanted in 1987 but had no promise of entry for tournaments in 1988.

(iii) If all positions in a 1987 tournament were not filled by individuals from categories (i) and (ii), any golfer who was among the top 40 career money winners as of 1986 or was among the top 128 money winners on the 1986 European PGA Tour could enter the tournament.

(iv) Any remaining vacancies in a tour-

nament were filled with players who met other criteria (for example, lower-ranked players on the 1986 tour, and leaders from the European PGA Tour Qualifying School).

As we shall show, this system of exemptions and priorities helps to explain which players entered which 1987 PGA Tour tournaments. This consideration is important because analyses that use data on the scores of entrants to tournaments may be subject to potential selectivity biases. In addition, individuals in categories (ii), (iii), and (iv) had to be very concerned about their total tour earnings in 1987, for unless they won a PGA Tour tournament during the year, they had to finish in the top 128 money winners during the year in order to be assured of virtual automatic entry (if they desired) to European PGA Tour tournaments in 1988 (that is, to be in category (iii) in 1988). In contrast, no matter what individuals in category (i) accomplished during the 1987 tour, they

specific tournament received an exemption for that specific tournament, and each tournament sponsor was allowed to invite a specified number of players to participate in his or her tournament.

were assured the option of entry into any European PGA Tour tournament that they wanted to enter in 1988.

Suppose that the latter (category (i)) group, whom we refer to henceforth as the *exempt* players, exhibited effort levels that were sensitive to the level and structure of prizes in a tournament. Because the former (category (ii), (iii), and (iv)) group, whom we henceforth refer to as the *nonexempt* players, had to worry about qualifying for the next year's tour, the level and structure of prize money in a tournament may not be an accurate indicator of their marginal financial return to effort. Rather, one would need to know also how an increase in effort for one of them increased both the probability that he would be classified as an exempt player in 1988 and his expected future earnings if he was so classified. As such, even if the exempt and nonexempt players' marginal responses to financial returns were equal, one might intuitively expect nonexempt players' effort levels, and hence scores, to be less sensitive than those of exempt players to tournament-specific prize variables.[10]

Empirical Analysis

Our empirical analysis proceeds in two stages: first we estimate final score equations for players on the 1987 European Men's PGA Tour; then we estimate final round score equations.

Final Score Equations

Pro Golf '88: The Official PGA European Tour Guide (1988) provides data for each 1987 Men's PGA European Tournament on the score by round, final rank, and prize money won for all players who entered and made the cut.[11] Data on each player's scoring average on all rounds

during the year, a measure of his "ability," are available only for the top 130 money winners during the year; consequently, the analysis reported below is restricted to these individuals.[12]

Equations were estimated (pooling the data across individuals and tournaments) of the form

$$(2) \quad s_{ji} = a_0 + a_1 \text{TPRIZE}_i + a_2 \text{MAJ}_i \\ + a_3 x_i + a_4 y_j + a_5 z_i + v_{ji}$$

Here, s_{ji} is the final score of individual j in tournament i, TPRIZE_i is the total prize money awarded in the tournament, MAJ_i takes on the value of one if tournament i is a major tournament and zero otherwise, x_i is a vector of variables to control for the difficulty of the tournament course, y_j is a vector of proxies for player j's ability, z_i is a vector of variables to control for the quality of other players in the tournament, and v_{ji} is a random error term.[13] If the theory of tournaments is correct, higher prizes should lead to lower scores, and estimates of a_1 should therefore be negative. Similarly, since winning a major tournament typically provides a golfer with endorsement opportunities and also provides him with guaranteed entry to all tournaments for a number of years, estimates of a_2 should also be negative.[14]

The controls for the difficulty of the course are PAR, the par for the tourna-

---

[10] The appendix to Ehrenberg and Bognanno (1988) presents a simple omitted variable model that indicates the precise conditions under which this expectation is correct.

[11] The restriction to players who entered and made the cut leads to potential selectivity problems, and we discuss this issue below. (See note 16.)

[12] As a result, virtually no individuals from category (iv) are included in the sample.

[13] Our earlier study of U.S. golf tournaments included a measure of the weather conditions during each tournament as an explanatory variable. Unfortunately, such a measure could not be constructed for this paper, as detailed descriptions of the weather on each day of each tournament were not readily available to us. As long as weather conditions are uncorrelated with the other explanatory variables in the model, the omission of that factor will reduce the model's explanatory power but not lead to biased estimates of any of the other coefficients.

[14] The five "major" tournaments are the PGA Championship, the Open Championship, the TPC, the European Open, and the European Masters. The TPC was not played in 1987 and, as noted above, the Open Championship was not included in our sample. Hence, MAJ takes on the value of unity in our sample for the PGA, European Open, and European Masters tournaments.

ment course; and YARDS, the total course yardage. Player ability is proxied by SAVE, his scoring average on all rounds played during the 1987 European tour; and SPARR, his average number of strokes per round worse ($+$) or better ($-$) than par for all rounds he played during the 1987 European tour. Finally, the quality of the other players in the field is proxied by MSAVE and MSPARR, the mean values of SAVE and SPARR respectively, for all players who finished in the tournament, and by TOP20, the number of the top 20 money winners on the 1987 Men's PGA European Tour who finished in the tournament.

Estimates of equation (2) are reported in Table 1 and descriptive statistics for the variables used are found in Table 2. More difficult courses, as measured by higher pars or longer yardage, are associated with high scores. Similarly, the better the player, as measured by lower values of either SAVE or SPARR, the lower the player's score will be. Most striking, the coefficients of MAJ in columns (1) and (2) of Table 1 imply that players' scores, *ceteris paribus*, average more than one stroke lower in the major tournaments. Similarly, the coefficient of TPRIZE is negative as anticipated. TPRIZE is measured in thousands of pounds; hence, the results in columns (1) and (2) imply that increasing the total prize money by £60,000 would be associated with each player scoring, on average, about three strokes less during a tournament. During 1987, the exchange rate averaged about .6 pounds per dollar, so this change in prize money is roughly equivalent to $100,000.[15] In our earlier paper, we found that an increase in prize money of this magnitude would cause the score of the typical golfer on the 1984 U.S. PGA Men's Tour to fall (improve) by about 1.1 strokes during a tournament (Ehrenberg and Bognanno 1988, Table 1). Apparently, golfers' performances are more sensitive to prize levels on the European tour than on the U.S. tour.

Columns (3) and (4) of Table 1 present

estimates of specifications in which TPRIZE and MAJ are interacted with a variable that indicates whether, as of the start of the 1987 tour, the player has already automatically qualified to enter tournaments on the next year's (1988) Men's European PGA Tour (EXEM). The negative coefficient of the interaction term with TPRIZE suggests, as noted above, either that exempt players' effort levels are more responsive to financial variables, or that the nonexempt players' TPRIZE coefficient is biased toward zero because their marginal return to effort also depends both upon how doing well in a tournament increases their probability of being classified as exempt in the next year and upon their expected increase in the present value of future income if so classified.[16]

Although not central to our discussion here, it is also of interest to know which factors influence players' decisions to enter tournaments. Columns (1) and (2) of Table 3 present estimates of probit probability of entry equations. The probability is specified to be a function of a player's total career earnings prior to 1987 (PRCASH), his age (AGE), the order of the tournament in the year and its square (TCODE, TCODE2)

---

[15] *Economic Report of the President* (1988), Table B-108.

---

[16] The results in Table 1 may be subject to two types of selection bias because the sample is restricted to the subset of players who both entered *and* made the cut in each tournament. Consequently, we may confound the effect of the total prize variable on players' final scores with its effect on their probability of entering and making the cut in a tournament. Controlling for this possible problem requires the use of information on the players who entered each tournament and failed to make the cut; fortunately, such information is found in *Pro Golf '88: The Official PGA European Tour Guide* (1988).

To model separately the decision to enter a tournament and the probability of making the cut and then to estimate a bivariate selection model is a difficult task. Instead, we approximated this process and estimated a univariate probit probability of entering and making the cut equation. Following the approach initially suggested by James Heckman (1979), we then used estimates from this equation to compute an estimate of the inverse Mills ratio for each individual and entered the latter as an additional explanatory variable in equation (2) to control for selectivity bias. When these "augmented" equations were estimated, the selectivity bias adjustment procedure was seen to have virtually no effect on the TPRIZE coefficients.

Table 1. Final Score Equations for the 1987 PGA Men's European Tour: Data Pooled Across Tournaments and Players.
(Absolute Value t-Statistics in Parentheses)

Variable	(1)		(2)		(3)		(4)	
Intercept	−1,208.233	(6.2)	21.442	(1.0)	−1,201.470	(6.2)	21.764	(1.0)
TPRIZE	−.050	(10.6)	−.050	(11.1)	−.049	(10.4)	−.050	(11.0)
TPRIZE*EXEM					−.004	(1.7)	−.004	(1.5)
MAJ	−1.177	(2.0)	−1.307	(2.2)	−1.287	(2.0)	−1.400	(2.2)
MAJ*EXEM					.451	(0.3)	.377	(0.3)
PAR	2.411	(6.0)	3.216	(8.3)	2.412	(6.0)	3.214	(8.3)
YARDS	.004	(2.4)	.003	(1.8)	.003	(2.4)	.003	(1.8)
SAVE	3.026	(16.9)			2.903	(15.1)		
MSAVE	14.892	(5.4)			14.921	(5.4)		
SPARR			3.042	(17.2)			2.935	(15.3)
MSPARR			18.511	(6.9)			18.546	(6.9)
TOP20	1.309	(10.3)	1.495	(11.7)	1.315	(10.3)	1.500	(11.7)
$\overline{R}^2$	.434		.444		.438		.445	
n	1,386		1,386		1,386		1,386	

TPRIZE: total tournament prize money, in hundreds of British pounds.
EXEM: 1 = player has automatically qualified to enter tournaments on the *1988* Men's European PGA tour; 0 = not automatically qualified.
MAJ: 1 = PGA, European Masters, or European Open Tournament; 0 = other.
PAR: par for the tournament course.
YARDS: course yardage.
SAVE: player's scoring average on all rounds played during the 1987 European tour.
MSAVE: mean value of SAVE for all players who finished the tournament.
SPARR: player's average number of strokes worse ($+$) or better ($-$) than par for all rounds played during the 1987 European tour.
MSPAR: mean value of SPARR for all players who finished the tournament.
TOP20: number of the top 20 money winners on the 1987 PGA Men's European tour who finished the tournament.
Source: Authors' calculations from data in *Pro-Golf '88: Volvo Tour, The Official PGA European Tour Guide* (1988).

to allow for seasonal patterns, the total tournament prize money (TPRIZE), whether the tournament is a major tournament (MAJ), and the player's quality (SAVE in column (1), SPARR in column (2)). Coefficient estimates are permitted to vary between exempt and nonexempt players, and an "A" before a variable's name indicates that the coefficient is for exempt players, whereas a "B" indicates that it is for nonexempt players.

Both exempt and nonexempt players are seen to be more likely to enter major tournaments and tournaments in which the total prize money is higher.[17] An income effect on labor supply is evident for exempt players since, *ceteris paribus*, the greater an exempt player's lifetime earn-

Table 2. Descriptive Statistics for the Variables Used in the Final Score Equations.

Variable	Mean	Standard Deviation	Minimum Value	Maximum Value
TSCORE	286.57	8.66	259.00	319.00
TPRIZE	199.32	56.45	98.17	339.09
EXEM	0.19	0.39	0.00	1.00
MAJ	0.13	0.33	0.00	1.00
PAR	71.83	0.68	69.00	73.00
YARDS	6,837.58	210.58	6,198.00	7,362.00
SAVE	72.02	0.97	69.19	74.63
MSAVE	72.03	0.17	71.61	72.33
SPARR	0.31	0.98	−2.58	2.98
MSPARR	0.31	0.18	−0.11	0.60
TOP20	12.63	3.59	5.00	20.00

TSCORE: player's total number of strokes over the four rounds of the tournament.
All other variables are defined in Table 1.

[17] Recall that only the top 130 money winners on the tour are included in our sample. Thus, if a decrease in a variable reduces the likelihood of entry for both exempt and nonexempt players in a tournament, an implication is that the decrease also permits more players who are not among the top 130 money winners to enter the tournament.

Table 3. 1987 PGA Men's European Tour: Probit Probability of Entry. (Absolute Value t-Statistics in Parentheses)

Variable	Probability of Entry	
	(1)	(2)
Intercept	−12.889 (5.3)	−.125 (0.6)
EXEM	10.613 (2.0)	.338 (0.6)
APRCASH[a]	−.129 (4.7)	−.094 (3.3)
AAGE	−.112 (1.2)	−.012 (1.2)
ATCODE[b]	−.211 (0.1)	.237 (0.1)
ATCODE2[b]	−.002 (0.0)	−.003 (0.0)
ATPRIZE[b]	.268 (1.7)	.265 (1.7)
AMAJ	.645 (2.8)	.628 (2.8)
ASAVE	.041 (0.7)	
ASPARR		.010 (2.6)
BPRCASH[a]	.115 (4.0)	.116 (3.8)
BAGE	−.014 (2.5)	−.012 (2.1)
BTCODE	.070 (4.3)	.070 (4.4)
BTCODE2	−.003 (4.9)	−.003 (4.9)
BTPRIZE[b]	.106 (1.6)	.108 (1.6)
BMAJ	.421 (4.4)	.419 (4.3)
BSAVE	.185 (5.5)	
BSPARR		.009 (4.6)
χ^2 (DOF)	149.169 (15)	145.670 (15)
PE = 0	828	828
PE = 1	2,185	2,185

[a] Coefficient has been multiplied by 10^5.
[b] Coefficient has been multiplied by 10^2.
An "A" before a variable name indicates the variable's coefficient for exempt players, and a "B" before a variable's name indicates its coefficient for nonexempt players.
PRCASH: total career earnings prior to 1987.
AGE: age.
TCODE: tournament code, in chronological order (equals 1 for the first tournament).
TCODE2: tournament code squared.
PE: 1 = entered the tournament; 0 = did not enter the tournament.
See Table 1 for all other variable definitions.

ings, the lower his probability of entering a tournament. In contrast, the greater the lifetime earnings of nonexempt players, the more likely they will enter tournaments. Older nonexempt players enter fewer tournaments. Finally, better players, as measured by lower values of SPARR, enter fewer tournaments.

Final Round Score Equations

Consider a golfer playing in two tournaments with the same total prize money. Suppose he scores a 72 on each of the first three days of both tournaments but,

because of random factors that influence his opponents' performance, he finds himself in third place in the first tournament but in twentieth place in the second tournament. Given the structure of PGA tournament prizes (Figure 1), he faces a greater marginal return to effort/concentration in the first tournament, should exert more effort/concentration there, and, on average, should have a lower final round score in that tournament. Put another way, we should expect to observe, *ceteris paribus,* a positive correlation between a player's rank after the third round of tournaments and his final round scores.

The results of an initial test of this hypothesis are shown in Table 4. Here, we have estimated final round score equations, using data pooled across individuals and tournaments. A player's score on the final round of a tournament is specified to be a function of his scores on the first three days of the tournament (SCORE1, SCORE2, SCORE3), his rank after the third round (RANK3RD), and the total tournament prize money (TPRIZE). A player's scores on the first three days, which are probably the best predictor of how well he is currently playing, should be positively associated with his score on the final day. Given his scores on the first three days, higher rank (poorer relative position) after the third round should lead to higher final round scores, and higher total prize money should lead to lower final round scores. The total prize level should matter because a higher average prize level leads to larger prize differences between players of different ranks.

A player's scores on the first three days of a tournament are not exogenous, but rather depend (from equation (1)) on the prize differential for winning, measures of his ability and his opponents' ability, and tournament-specific factors such as course difficulty. Similarly, neither is a player's rank after the third round exogenous. It depends on his scores and his opponents' scores on the first three days—both of which depend, in turn, on the factors described above. As such, we treat SCORE1, SCORE2, SCORE3, and RANK3RD as endoge-

Table 4. Final Round Score Equations for the 1987 PGA Men's European Tour: Data Pooled
Across Tournaments and Players.[a]
(Absolute Value t-Statistics in Parentheses)

Variable	All Players (1)	Nonexempt Players (2)	Exempt Players (3)
Constant	23.889 (3.2)	24.894 (3.1)	28.508 (1.7)
SCORE1	.330 (1.5)	.271 (1.1)	.064 (0.2)
SCORE2	.726 (3.8)	.693 (3.2)	.790 (3.0)
SCORE3	−.384 (2.4)	−.307 (1.8)	−.242 (0.7)
RANK3RD	.095 (5.2)	.089 (3.9)	.075 (2.4)
TPRIZE	−.012 (4.8)	−.012 (4.2)	−.013 (2.3)
$\overline{R}^2$	.128	.111	.176
n	1,377	1,117	260

SCORE1: player's first round score in the tournament.
SCORE2: player's second round score in the tournament.
SCORE3: player's third round score in the tournament.
RANK3RD: player's rank after the third round of the tournament.
TPRIZE: total tournament prize money (in thousands).

[a]Instruments for SCORE1, SCORE2, SCORE3, RANK3RD were obtained using TPRIZE, PAR, YARDS, TOP20, MSPARR, MSAVE, SPARR, SAVE, and MAJ (which are all defined in Table 1) and:
AGE: player's age (in years).
MERIT: player's official prize money winnings rank in the year.
SCORE3A: player's scoring average on all third rounds he played on the 1987 tour.

nous, and the estimates in Table 4 are obtained using an instrumental variable method.[18]

Quite striking, as expected, is the evidence in Table 4 that the higher the rank of a player (the poorer his relative position) after the third day of a tournament, the higher his final round score will be. Moreover, again as expected, the higher the total prize money in a tournament, the lower his score will be.[19]

---

[18] The specific variables used to obtain the instruments are listed in the notes to Table 4. Formal specification tests permit us to reject the hypothesis that this set of variables should be treated as exogenous. See Hausman (1978) for these tests.

[19] These results are contingent upon SCORE1, SCORE2, SCORE3, and RANK3RD being treated as endogenous. When they are treated as exogenous, the coefficient of TPRIZE remains negative but the coefficient of RANK3RD switches sign and becomes negative (significantly so for the all player and nonexempt samples). As noted in footnote 18, formal specification tests allow us to *reject* the hypothesis that the above set of variables should be treated as exogenous.

The results in Table 4 also suggest that a player's score on the second round of a tournament is an important explanatory variable for his final round score, but that the scores on this first and third rounds are less important. It may be that players play "harder" on the second round, when they are aware what it will take to make the cut, and on the fourth round, when the "money is at stake." Of course, such

Of course, entering a player's rank after three rounds and total tournament prize money separately only approximates the marginal return to effort/concentration that he faces if he improves his rank by a given number of units. Such a specification also does *not* take into account how closely his competitors are "bunched" around him. To obtain more precise measures of the relevant marginal returns, we defined six different variables, all of which are illustrated in Figure 2.

Suppose that the curve PP in Figure 2 shows the relationship between a player's final rank in a tournament and the prize money he will be awarded. Consider an individual who after the third round is at rank R. If he remains at that rank, he will be awarded the amount OA at the end of the tournament.

The first three marginal return variables we compute ignore how tightly competitors are bunched around the player and are based on the return to improving performance, or of having it get worse, by

---

an explanation suggests that players' behavior is somewhat irrational, as it is their *total* score after two rounds that determines if they make the cut, and their *total* score after four that determines their prize winnings.

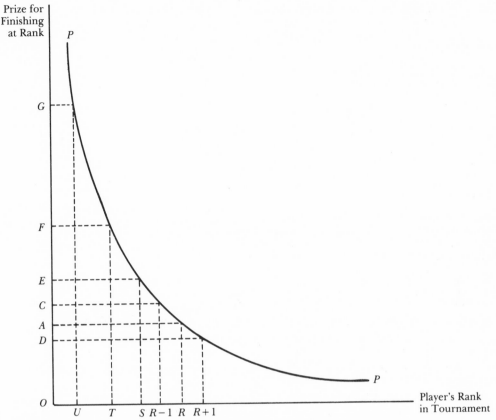

Figure 2. Alternative Measures of Marginal Return to Effort/Concentration in a Tournament.

one rank.[20] DPRIZE3 is the estimated decrease in prize money if the individual's rank at the end of the tournament was one higher (worse) than his current rank. It is given by our estimate of AD. UPRIZE3 is the estimated increase in prize money the individual would gain if he improved his rank by one; this is given by AC in the figure. MIDPRIZ3 assumes the individual takes into account the cost of losing one

rank and the benefit from improving one rank. It is defined as the estimated average absolute change in prize money if the rank at the end of the tournament is either one lower or one higher than R, and it is given in the figure by the average of the lengths of AC and AD.

Presumably, increased effort/concentration directly affects a player's score, not his rank. The effect of increased concentration on rank then depends on the number of competitors closely bunched around the player. The next three measures take this factor into account; they are the estimated increase in prize money the individual would receive if he improved his scores relative to his competitors by one stroke (LES1PRIZ), two strokes (LES2PRIZ), or three strokes (LES3PRIZ). Assuming that improvements of one, two, and three strokes would cause the individual's rank to improve respectively to S, T, and U in the

---

[20] The marginal return variables were computed from the following equation, which was estimated using data on all players who finished each of the tournaments in the sample:

$$\log(S_{ri}) = 5.384 - 1.031(\log(ri)) \qquad \overline{R}^2 = .920$$
$$\qquad (.025) \quad (.008)$$

Here, S_{ri} is the share of the total prize money in a tournament that went to the person who finished in the rth place in tournament i, ri is that individual's rank in the tournament, and standard errors of the estimates are found beneath the estimated coefficients.

Table 5. Coefficients of the Marginal Return to Effort Variables in the Final Round Score Equations for the 1987 PGA Men's European Tour: Data Pooled Across Tournaments and Players.
(Absolute Value t-Statistics in Parentheses)

Specification	All Players	Nonexempt Players	Exempt Players
(1) DPRIZE	−.570 (4.9)	−.936 (3.0)	−.148 (1.5)
(2) UPRIZE	−.794 (4.2)	−.895 (3.2)	−.159 (1.0)
(3) MIDPRIZE	−.692 (4.9)	−.961 (3.3)	−.208 (1.5)
(4) LES1PRIZ	−1.050 (3.7)	−1.103 (3.4)	−.384 (1.3)
(5) LES2PRIZ	−.435 (4.1)	−.500 (3.5)	−.145 (1.6)
(6) LES3PRIZ	−.244 (3.5)	−.271 (3.0)	−.091 (1.1)

DPRIZE: estimated marginal reduction in prize money (in 000's) if rank at the end of the tournament is one higher (worse) than the player's third round rank.

UPRIZE: estimated marginal increase in prize money (in 000's) if rank at the end of the tournament is one lower (better) than the player's third round rank.

MIDPRIZE: estimated average marginal absolute change in prize money (in 000's) if rank at the end of the tournament is one lower or one higher than the individual's third round rank.

LES1PRIZ: estimated marginal increase in prize money (in 000's) if the individual improved his rank after the third round by reducing his score by 1 stroke relative to the rest of the field (LES2PRIZ—2 strokes; LES3PRIZ—3 strokes).

[a] All specifications also include SCORE1, SCORE2, and SCORE3 and use instruments for these variables *and* the marginal return to effort variables.

figure, these variables' magnitudes in turn would be given by AE, AF, and AG.

Each of these six variables was estimated for each individual in each tournament. Each variable in turn was substituted for RANK3RD and TPRIZE, and equations similar to those reported in Table 4 were estimated. Because each of these marginal return to effort variables depends on a player's rank after the third round and the latter is endogenous, instruments were also used for each of these variables.

Estimates of the coefficients of the marginal return to effort variables from these equations are reported in Table 5. The pattern of results is remarkably consistent across specifications. The marginal prize variables do affect players' scores on the final round, with larger marginal rewards to effort resulting in lower final round scores.[21] In contrast to the findings in our total score equations (Table 1), the size and significance of these

responses appear to be larger for nonexempt players.

One may argue that, in theory, a player's effort on the last round of a tournament also depends on his ability relative to the players who are closely bunched around him. To see how inclusion of such measures would influence the importance of financial variables, we computed for each player in each tournament the average ability of players who were within one, two, and three strokes of him, in either direction, at the end of the third round of play in the tournament. These variables (one at a time), plus a measure of the player's ability, were added to the specifications that underlie Table 5, and these extended equations were estimated for the entire sample. Since the average quality of the players around a player after the third round is endogenous, instruments for these average quality variables were also used.

Table 6 summarizes the coefficients of the marginal prize variables that result when those changes are made. Column (1) simply repeats the coefficients found in column (1) of Table 5 that came from specifications that did not control for the quality of "nearby" opponents. Columns (2), (3), and (4), respectively, present the

[21] Again, formal specification tests allow us to reject the hypotheses that the set of earlier round score variables, and each of these variables, should be treated as exogenous. This finding is important, because if one erroneously treats those variables as exogenous, the coefficients of all the marginal prize variables switch signs and become positive (significantly so in most cases for the nonexempt and all player samples).

Table 6. Coefficients of the Marginal Return to Effort Variables in the Final Round Score Equations for the 1987 Men's European PGA Tour: Controlling for Quality of Players Nearby After Three Rounds.[a]
(Absolute Value t-Statistics in Parentheses)

Marginal Return Variable	Control for "Quality"			
	None (1)	AVESPAR1 (2)	AVESPAR2 (3)	AVESPAR3 (4)
(1) DPRIZE	−.570 (4.9)	−.296 (2.1)	−.231 (1.6)	−.231 (1.6)
(2) UPRIZE	−.794 (4.2)	−.428 (2.1)	−.330 (1.6)	−.338 (1.7)
(3) MIDPRIZE	−.692 (4.9)	−.371 (2.2)	−.290 (1.7)	−.292 (1.7)
(4) LIES1PRIZ	−1.050 (3.7)	−.693 (2.5)	−.622 (2.3)	−.611 (2.2)
(5) LES2PRIZ	−.435 (4.1)	−.280 (2.5)	−.248 (2.2)	−.247 (2.3)
(6) LES3PRIZ	−.244 (3.5)	−.152 (2.0)	−.126 (1.7)	−.130 (1.7)

[a] Specifications are the same as those found in Table 5, with the addition in all but the first column of measures of the player's ability (SPAR) and the ability of other players close to him after the third round (AVESPAR1, AVESPAR2, or AVESPAR3). Since the latter variable is endogenous, instruments for it are also used.

AVESPAR1: average number of strokes from par per round during the year of all players within one stroke of the player after third round of the tournament.
AVESPAR2: same as AVESPAR1 but within two strokes.
AVESPAR3: same as AVESPAR1 but within three strokes.

coefficients from specifications that control for the quality of other golfers within one, two, and three strokes of the player, respectively, after the third round.

Quite strikingly, although the magnitudes and the statistical significance of the marginal prize variables decline when the controls for average competitor quality are present, larger marginal prizes are still associated with lower final round scores. Furthermore, the coefficients on all of the marginal prize variables remain statistically significantly different from zero.

Table 7 presents descriptive statistics for each of the marginal prize variables. One can use these data and the estimates in Table 6 to obtain estimates of the influence of these variables on players' performance. For example, *ceteris paribus,* one can estimate for LES1PRIZ and LES2PRIZ how much better those players will perform whose marginal prize is one standard deviation above the mean marginal prize in the sample by multiplying the standard deviations in Table 7 by the corresponding regression coefficient in Table 6.[22] When the quality of players nearby after the third round is not included in the equation (Table 6, column (1)), such calculations suggest that these players would score 3.4 to 4.5 strokes lower on the final round of the tournament. When it is included (Table 6, columns (2)–(3)), these effects fall to roughly 1.9 to 3.0 strokes. Notably, even the latter effects are somewhat larger than the similar effects we found in our earlier paper that used U.S. data.

Concluding Remarks

This paper and our earlier paper have provided nonexperimental evidence that tournaments do have incentive effects. In our earlier paper, we analyzed data from the 1984 United States Men's PGA Tour and the 1984 United States Senior Men's PGA Tour and found that the level and structure of prize money did influence players' performance. Higher prize levels led, *ceteris paribus,* to lower scores, although this effect occurred primarily in the later rounds of a tournament, when fatigue had set in and it was

---

[22] We say LES1PRIZ and LES2PRIZ are probably the two "best" marginal prize variables because they take account of how closely bunched competitors are around the player and because improving one's performance by three strokes relative to one's

competitors is not an easy task. On average, players in our sample improved their performance by .3 strokes between the third and fourth rounds, and the standard deviation of their change in performance was 3.97 strokes.

Table 7. Descriptive Statistics—Marginal Prize Variables.[a]

Variable	Mean	Standard Deviation	Minimum Value	Maximum Value
DPRIZE	.789	3.746	b	76.980
UPRIZE	.909	4.541	b	76.980
MIDPRIZE	.849	3.433	b	50.395
LES1PRIZ	1.058	4.327	b	76.980
LES2PRIZ	2.415	7.846	b	112.160
LES3PRIZ	3.895	8.791	b	126.035

[a] See Table 5 for variable definitions. All variables are measured in thousands of pounds.
[b] Less than 0.5.

more difficult for players to maintain concentration. Given a player's performance on the first three rounds of a tournament, his performance on the last round also appeared, *ceteris paribus,* to depend on the marginal returns to effort he faced, with players who faced larger marginal returns achieving better scores. The level of prize money in tournaments also influenced who entered the tournaments, with higher prize money attracting better players.

The influence of tournament prizes on performance was observed in the data primarily for exempt players. As discussed in our earlier paper, this result may indicate either that exempt players are more responsive to the reward structure or that a tournament's prize level does not adequately reflect the reward structure that nonexempt players face, since these players must be concerned with how their finish in a tournament will influence their probability of qualifying for exempt status on the next year's tour. Evidence from the U.S. senior tour provided some support for the former hypothesis—that better players are, in fact, more responsive to financial incentives.

Our analysis here, using data from the 1987 Men's European PGA Tour, supports most of the above findings. Higher prize levels appear to lead to lower player scores in the European PGA tournaments, and higher marginal return to effort that players face on the last round of tournaments apparently leads to lower final round scores. The responsiveness of per-

formance to prize money also appears to be greater on the European than on the U.S. tour. In contrast to the U.S. data, however, the European data yield only mixed evidence to support the view that exempt players are more responsive to financial incentives.

Together, our two papers provide only an exploratory analysis of the incentive effects of tournaments, and there are a number of directions that future research might take. First, replication and extensions using data from other sports in which absolute measures of output are available, the level and structure of prize money differs, and the form of tournaments differs would obviously be desirable. Professional bowling is particularly attractive in this regard, because bowling tournaments have a match play element.[23]

Second, all of our analyses are derived from simple two-person models that yield implications for the output/scores of an individual player. Generalization to n-person tournaments would yield implications about the entire distribution of scores one might expect to observe, and empirical analyses of the distribution of final scores could then be undertaken.

Third, our analyses assume that the tournament prize structure influences output/scores through its effect on effort/concentration levels. Players can also choose conservative strategies (for example, hitting down the center of the fairway) or risky strategies (for example, trying to cut across a dogleg), and depending on a player's ability relative to the rest of the field, his rank after each round, or both, different strategies may be pursued. Models that also included the choice of strategies that differ in risk undoubtedly would yield additional empirical implications.

Fourth, there are normative issues relating to the level and structure of prizes that we actually observe in tournaments. Can

---

[23] Research using data from professional bowling is currently being undertaken by Bognanno (forthcoming).

we infer from this structure what the objective functions of the PGA Tour and tournament sponsors actually are? Can we estimate whether the marginal cost to sponsors of higher prize tournaments is less than, equal to, or greater than the marginal benefits they receive? To answer such questions will require going far beyond the scores of players in tournaments and analyzing more generally the operations of the PGA Tour and its sponsors.

Finally, although studies of sports tournaments are of interest in themselves, there is the broader question of the extent to which tournament theory can help to provide an explanation for the structure of compensa-

tion we observe among corporate executives. As is well known, situations in which opportunities exist for one executive to sabotage another's performance are not conducive to tournament-type pay structures. One might, therefore, expect to see tournament-type pay structures used more frequently when rivals can be effectively "separated" (for example, for managers of different branches of a firm) than when they work closely together.[24] Nevertheless, devising ways to empirically address the relevance of tournament theory should rank high on the research agenda of economists interested in compensation issues.

---

[24] For an extended discussion of this point, see Lazear (1989).

Appendix
Table A1: 1987 European PGA Tournaments Included in the Sample

Tournament	Total Prize Money (in Pounds)	Tournament	Total Prize Money (in Pounds)
1. Moroccan Open	165,398	13. Bell's Scottish Open	200,594
2. Jersey Open	98,170	14. KLM Dutch Open	181,170
3. Suze Open	153,105	15. Scandinavian Enterprise Open	193,436
4. Cepsa Madrid Open	165,000	16. PLM Open	145,998
5. Lancia Italian Open	141,637	17. Benson & Hedges International Open	201,544
6. Peugeot Spanish Open	175,200	18. Lawrence Batley International	141,544
7. Whyte & MacKay PGA	220,000	19. German Open	274,555
8. London Standards Four Stars	138,500	20. Ebel European Masters Swiss Open	339,093
9. Dunhill British Masters	200,000	21. Panasonic European Open	221,908
10. Peugeot French Open	253,200	22. Lancome Trophy	300,750
11. Johnnie Walker Monte Carlo Open	204,604	23. German Masters	267,684
12. Carrolls Irish Open	216,895		

Distribution of Tournaments by Prize Money:

< 100,000£	1
100,000–150,000£	4
151,000–200,000£	7
200,500–250,000£	6
251,000–300,000£	3
> 300,000£	2

Table A2: Mean Percentage and Level of Prize Money Awarded Expost by Rank in the Tournaments Included in the Sample: Selected Ranks[a]

Final Rank	Mean Percentage of Total Prize	Mean Level of Prize Money (in Pounds)
1	16.3	34,867
2	10.4	23,342
3	5.8	11,918
4	4.7	10,601
5	3.6	7,642
19	1.18	2,378
20	1.13	1,975
30	0.87	1,616
40	0.61	1,479
50	0.43	1,053

[a] Authors' calculations from observations included in the sample. As noted in the text, the sample is confined to observations on the top 130 money winners during the year. The means for each rank are computed across a different number of observations because two or more golfers may tie for a rank in a given tournament, because no one may finish in a given rank in a given tournament (e.g., if two golfers tie for tenth, there is no eleventh-place finisher), or because a golfer who finished in a given rank in a tournament is not in our sample.

REFERENCES

Bognanno, Michael. 1988. "Performance Incentives in Tournaments: An Empirical Test." M.S. Thesis, Cornell University, January.

Bognanno, Michael. In progress. "Performance Incentives, Relative Ability Effects, and Tournament Structure." Ph.D. Diss., Cornell University.

Bull, Clive, Andrew Schotter, and Keith Weigelt. 1987. "Tournaments and Piece Rates: An Experimental Study." Journal of Political Economy, Vol. 95 (February), pp. 1–33.

Carmichael, H. Lorne. 1983. "The Agent-Agents Problem: Payment by Relative Output." Journal of Labor Economics, Vol. 1 (January), pp. 50–65.

Economic Report of the President, 1988. Washington, D.C.: GPO.

Ehrenberg, Ronald G., and Michael L. Bognanno. 1988. "Do Tournaments Have Incentive Effects?" NBER Research Working Paper No. 2638, June.

Green, Jerry, and Nancy Stokey. 1983. "A Comparison of Tournaments and Contracts." Journal of Political Economy, Vol. 91 (June), pp. 349–65.

Hausman, J. A. 1978. "Specification Tests in Econometrics." Econometrica, Vol. 46 (November), pp. 1251–71.

Heckman, James. 1979. "Sample Bias as a Specification Error." Econometrica, Vol. 47 (January), pp. 153–62.

Lazear, Edward. 1989. "Pay Equality and Industrial Policies." Journal of Political Economy, Vol. 97 (June), pp. 561–81.

Lazear, Edward, and Sherwin Rosen. "Rank Order Tournaments as an Optimum Labor Contract." Journal of Political Economy, Vol. 89 (October), pp. 841–64.

Malcomson, James M. 1984. "Work Incentives, Hierarchy, and Internal Labor Markets." Journal of Political Economy, Vol. 92 (June), pp. 486–507.

McLaughlin, Kenneth J. 1988. "Aspects of Tournament Models: A Survey." In Ronald G. Ehrenberg, ed., Research in Labor Economics, Vol. 9. Greenwich, Conn.: JAI Press, pp. 225–56.

Nalebuff, Barry J., and Joseph E. Stiglitz. 1984. "Prizes and Incentives: Towards a General Theory of Compensation and Competition." Bell Journal of Economics, Vol. 2 (Spring), pp. 21–43.

O'Keefe, Mary, W. Kip Viscusi, and Richard Zeckhauser. 1984. "Economic Contests: Comparative Reward Schemes." Journal of Labor Economics, Vol. 2 (January), pp. 27–56.

O'Reilly, Charles, Brian S. Main, and Graef S. Crystal. 1988. "CEO Compensation as Tournaments and Social Comparisons: A Tale of Two Theories." Administrative Science Quarterly, Vol. 33 (June), pp. 257–74.

Pro Gold '88: The Official PGA European Tour Guide. 1988. Virginia Waters, Surrey, United Kingdom: PGA European Tour.

Rosen, Sherwin. "Prizes and Incentives in Elimination Tournaments." American Economic Review, Vol. 76 (September), pp. 701–16.

DO INCENTIVES MATTER?
THE CASE OF NAVY RECRUITERS

BETH J. ASCH*

This study examines how Navy recruiters in April–August 1986 responded to a multiperiod incentive plan that included piece rates, quotas, prizes, and standards. Recruiters generally produced more enlistments as they gained experience and as the date of their eligibility for a prize approached. Those with higher past output (who were thus more likely to win a prize), however, produced less as they approached the prize eligibility date. Recruiters also enlisted markedly fewer recruits immediately after winning a prize. This evidence that recruiters varied their effort over time in response to an incentive system, the author suggests, has implications for such private sector jobs as sales and tenure-track teaching.

In recent years a plethora of articles have addressed problems related to the principal-agent relationship. Although the main motivation behind this literature is to derive compensation structures that elicit desired levels of efforts, few empirical studies have examined the effect of a given compensation structure on worker effort and, therefore, output. Generally, empirical studies are sparse because data are unavailable on worker output and company incentive plans or because worker output is imperfectly measured.

To surmount these data problems, many previous studies have focused on earnings rather than productivity. A large body of empirical work has studied executive compensation and firm performance. (See, for example, Murphy 1986; Antle and Smith 1986; and Coughlin and Schmidt 1985.) Other studies have examined the effects of piece rates and wages on earnings (Seiler 1984; Pencavel 1977). Bull, Schotter, and Wiegert (1987) focused on productivity rather than earnings by using data collected during an experiment, with students as participants, rather than "natural" data on "real" workers. In their study, they examined the effects of piece rates versus tournaments on effort.

The purpose of this study is to examine empirically how workers vary their productivity in response to a given incentive structure. I use data on a group of "real" workers whose output (but not effort) is perfectly observed, and who participate in a multiperiod incentive plan that utilizes piece rates, quotas, fixed prizes, and standards. This group consists of Navy recruiters.

Navy recruiters are military personnel in various occupations who are assigned to recruiting duty, typically for a three-year period. Their purpose is to enlist 17-

* The author, an Associate Economist at the RAND Corporation, thanks James Dertouzos, Henry Farber, Glenn Gotz, James Hosek, Lynn Karoly, and Michael Murray for valuable comments on earlier drafts, and the Chicago Navy Recruiting District for data and assistance. This research was sponsored by the Office of the Assistant Secretary of Defense for Force Management and Personnel. The release of the data and computer programs used in this study must be authorized by the research sponsor and by the commander of the Navy recruiting command.

to-21-year-old youths in the Navy. Since recruiters' military pay is independent of their productivity as a recruiter, a moral hazard problem arises. To address this problem, the Navy requires recruiters to participate in an incentive program designed to reward good performance. Under this plan, recruiters earn points for every enlistment they make. At the end of a twelve-month period, they become eligible to win rewards that have monetary value, if their accumulated points exceed predetermined values. Recruiters also face quotas each month, but their compensation is independent of meeting them.

In this study, I examine how recruiters vary productivity over time in an attempt to win prizes. In particular, I examine whether recruiters make intertemporal effort decisions over the twelve-month reward period and over their three-year tour. Although the analysis focuses on workers in the military, it has applications to workers in the private sector. For example, workers who receive bonuses at the end of the year, salesmen who compete over time for fixed prizes, and junior professors striving to make tenure can make intertemporal effort decisions to win a reward.

Institutional Background

The Navy's recruiting system is organized into five operational levels. Below the national level, the country is divided into six recruiting areas, each of which, in turn, is divided into recruiting districts. The national market is divided into 42 recruiting districts. Below the district level are recruiting zones, which are the areas served by individual recruiting stations. Finally, the fifth level is that of the individual recruiter. The number of recruiters assigned to a station varies from one to seven.

Quotas

At the national level, the Navy determines the number and quality[1] level of

recruits to meet its military objectives. These requirements are translated into quantity and quality quotas for each month for each recruiting district using a regression model that takes into account the district's share of recruiters, the 17-to-21-year-old population, extent of urbanization, and minority population. Thus, quotas vary geographically. Currently, the national quota calls for 90% of all enlistees to be high school graduates and approximately 60% to be in the upper half of the Armed Forces Qualifying Test score (AFQT) distribution.

Below the district level, goals are set in a highly decentralized and diverse manner. Usually the managers at each level of the hierarchy assign quotas based on some analysis of the size and quality composition of the zone's, station's, and recruiter's market. Some managers use informal observation and others use census data or data on the quality of enlistments made in the past.[2] District, zone, station, and recruiter quotas vary from month to month due to seasonal variations in the supply of potential enlistees.

Recruiters do not receive rewards for meeting or exceeding their quotas. Moreover, recruiters who fail to meet their quota can blame poor performance on poor market conditions, since the supply of enlistees is subject to random fluctuations that allow recruiters to "hide" their true effort levels. As a result, recruiter activity is extensively monitored by station managers. Managers require recruiters to first meet their quotas of high-quality enlistments so that if they underproduce relative to the quantity quota, they underproduce mostly low-quality enlistments. Recruiters who meet or exceed their quotas of high-quality enlistment are free to overproduce low-quality enlistments.

---

[1] The "quality" of a recruit is determined by whether or not the individual is a high school graduate and by his or her score on the Armed Forces Qualification Test (AFQT). High school graduates scoring in the top 50th percentile on the AFQT are considered high-quality recruits and all others are considered low-quality.

[2] An individual recruiter's quota is generally based on his territory's market and seasonal factors rather than individual performance, thus reducing the likelihood of a ratchet effect.

Although recruiters are monitored, many of their activities, such as visits to local high schools, occur outside the station. Thus, monitoring is imperfect.

The Freeman Plan

The Freeman plan is a national incentive system that designates points and rewards for recruiting success. More points are assigned to higher-quality recruits than to low-quality recruits because the former are thought to be more productive in the military and because they are harder to enlist due to their better private sector opportunities. The point values, which presumably reflect the Navy's valuation of each quality category, are shown in Table 1.

These points are accumulated and averaged over a 12-month production period. After 12 months, if the recruiter's average points per month exceeds 300, a reward is granted and the production period begins again. If the average falls short of this standard, the production cycle becomes a 12-month moving window whereby points in the earliest month are dropped and those in the new month are added until an average of 300 points is achieved. Any distribution of enlistments across quality levels can be used to achieve a reward.

Table 2 presents the rewards and the average accumulated points required to win them. The availability of several levels of reward is intended to induce already successful recruiters to further increase effort. The highest reward is a promotion. The recruiter can win this prize only once during his or her tour. The second reward

Table 1. Freeman Plan Point Values.

(1) AFQT Category[a]	(2) High School Graduates	(3) Non-High School Graduates
I (93–100)	116	100
II (65–92)	107	90
IIIA (50–64)	100	85
IIIB (31–49)	90	65
IV (10–30)	70	N/A
V (1–9)	N/A	N/A

[a] AFQT category is based on the recruit's Armed Forces Qualification Test score. The range of scores that define a category is in parentheses.

Table 2. Recruiter Rewards and Required Average Accumulated Points over 12 Months.

(1) Reward[a]	(2) Required Average Accumulated Points
1. Promotion	525
2. Voluntary Extension	400
3. Navy Achievement Medal (2 promotion points)	350
4. Certificate of Commendation (1 promotion point)	300

[a] Numbers indicate ranking, 1 being the highest ranking.

provides recruiters with an opportunity to extend their tour for one year. An extension of recruiting duty—a shore job—is valuable to Naval personnel, for whom heavy sea duty can mean prolonged separation from their families.

The third and fourth rewards have no immediate value to recruiters other than the value of recognition. The promotion points associated with these rewards can, however, increase their chances of a promotion at a later date. When individuals are considered for promotion, they take several proficiency exams in their occupational specialty. If the exam point totals meet a minimum standard, and if other performance indicators are satisfactory, the individual receives a promotion. Promotion points earned as a recruiter are added to the exam point total. Since the variance of exam scores tends to be small, extra points can make a significant difference.

The Interaction Between Quotas and the Freeman Plan

The Navy's first recruiting priority is meeting its quotas, particularly its high-quality quotas. Although the Freeman Plan places a premium on high-quality enlistments, recruiters can win prizes under that plan by enlisting only low-quality recruits, counter to the Navy's high-quality enlistment objectives. The Navy attempts to counteract this potential conflict between its high-quality quotas and the Freeman Plan through monitoring. As noted above, however, monitoring is imperfect.

Economic Implications

Below, I first examine recruiters' enlistment choices at a specific time for a given level of effort and then examine how recruiters choose their level and allocation of effort over time. A formal model is not developed because many factors can affect effort in the same way and a given factor may increase or decrease effort depending on individual preferences. Thus, I simply provide a framework for interpreting the empirical findings.

Enlistments at any given time are affected by random changes in market potential. I analyze the case of perfect certainty by assuming that recruiters make their choices after they have become aware of the random change.

Recruiter Choices at a Point in Time

Given the scarcity of resources available to recruiters and the size and composition of the market they face, they must allocate their effort between high- and low-quality enlistments. The tradeoff they make can be illustrated by a production possibilities curve, shown in Figure 1, which indicates all feasible combinations of high- and low-quality enlistments at a particular time, given the limited amount of recruiting resources.[3] The slope of the curve is negative and concave because recruiters typically first obtain the most visible or most willing high-quality recruits, but thereafter must work harder, sacrificing more low-quality enlistments to obtain an additional high-quality one.

Enlistments increase when recruiters supply more effort, given market potential and resource availability. In Figure 1, the curve bb' can represent not only a larger market but also a greater level of effort than aa'. The outer curve, cc', represents the production possibilities when effort is maximized. The placement of this curve depends on recruiter ability—for more

able recruiters, the curve will be farther from the origin.

Point Q in the figure represents a possible quota. Because of monitoring, underproducers—those with the curve aa'—can only choose points to the left of L_q. Those who exceed the quota can overproduce solely low-quality enlistments (points along $\overline{QB}$), Solely high-quality enlistments (points along $\overline{QH}$), or some combination. Alternatively, they can underproduce low-quality enlistments and overproduce high-quality ones (points above $\overline{QH}_q$ but to the left of $\overline{QA}$).

The number of Freeman points earned in a given month is a linear combination of enlistments and the points per enlistment shown in Table 1. If the recruiters' utility equals their monthly Freeman points, their indifference curves are linear and each curve represents all the combinations of high- and low-quality enlistments yielding the same points. Lines mm' and nn' illustrate two indifference curves.

The recruiter's objective is to maximize the number and level of rewards he or she obtains subject to the production possibility curve. To do this, the recruiter must choose, in each month of the 12-month production cycle, the combination of high- and low-quality enlistments that maximizes points for a given level of effort as well as the optimal level of effort.[4] For a given level of effort, the recruiter maximizes points where the marginal benefit, equal to the relative points assigned to each quality type, equals the ratio of the marginal costs. Points C and D in the figure illustrate two such points.

Recruiter Choices Over Time

Given effort, recruiters' optimal enlistment choices will vary over time because of anticipated changes and different out-

---

[3] For ease of exposition, I assume that there are only two quality categories of enlistments.

[4] To simplify the problem conceptually, I assume recruiters maximize their reward attainment by maximizing the number of points they earn each month. In actuality, recruiters probably care more about maximizing average accumulated points, since rewards are based on these. The assumption, however, does not interfere with the identification of the essential elements affecting recruiters' decisions.

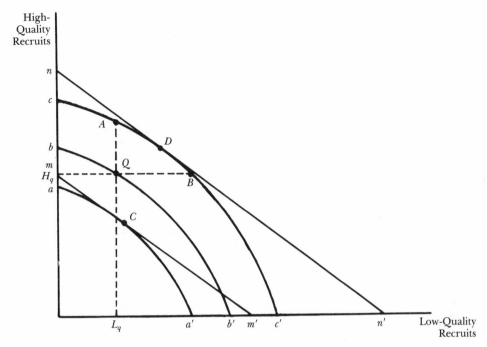

Figure 1. The Tradeoff Facing Recruiters Between High-Quality and Low-Quality Enlistments.

comes of random changes in market potential, recruiting resources, and quotas. These factors change the shape and position of the production possibilities curve as well as the number of over- and underproducers.

Over time, recruiters choose the allocation and type of effort that maximizes their chances of winning a prize.[5] I first examine these choices over the production cycle and then over a recruiter's tour.

Productivity over the 12-month production cycle. Whether recruiters supply more effort at a *particular* time depends on the difficulty of winning rewards, quota levels, and the recruiters' preferences for rewards versus leisure. In turn, the difficulty of winning depends on the Freeman

Plan's point structure and reward requirements, recruiter ability, market potential, and resource availability.

Rewards will be harder to win if the number of points that can be earned for any quality category is low, the points required to win are high, recruiter ability is low, and market opportunities are limited. In these cases, the potential for earning points is lower, given effort, and recruiters must supply more effort to earn more points. If the points required to win are too high, winning may be impossible for less able recruiters and those in smaller markets, even when effort is maximized. Such recruiters may supply only sufficient effort to meet their quotas.

If monitoring is effective, higher quotas will induce more effort. Recruiters who value rewards the most relative to leisure will supply more effort. But those who value rewards the least relative to leisure will supply less effort and possibly only enough to meet their monthly quotas.

The allocation of effort *over time* depends on how quotas, market size and

[5] Previous studies of moral hazard in a multiperiod setting have examined the optimal conditions for a one-period versus a multiperiod contract, as well as the optimal compensation structure (Lambert 1983; Rogerson 1985; Malcomson and Spinnewyn 1988; Rubinstein and Yaari 1983; Spear and Srivastava 1987). These studies do not, however, examine intertemporal substitutions in effort when payment is deferred beyond one period.

composition, and resource levels change over the cycle, whether or not these changes are anticipated; recruiters' point accumulation; and recruiters' preferences for allocating time. If market or quota changes are anticipated, recruiters can preplan an effective strategy at the beginning of the cycle for distributing effort over time that capitalizes on available opportunities. If unexpected changes occur, however, the preconceived strategy may no longer be optimal.

For example, recruiters may anticipate that market opportunities will be best at the end of the cycle, when seasonal variations result in a greater supply of potential recruits. Their strategy may be to supply less effort initially and then more effort when the recruiting environment improves. Thus, they plan to increase productivity over the cycle. If, on the contrary, it happens that market opportunities are unexpectedly poor at the end of the cycle, a better strategy, ex post, would have been to supply greater effort initially.

When unanticipated changes occur, recruiters at the end of their cycle may update their strategy when they have insufficient average accumulated points to win a reward. If they increase effort to increase their point accumulation, productivity will rise at the end of the cycle. If they reduce effort because they believe their chances of accumulating sufficient points to win is small, productivity will fall. Thus, it is not clear whether productivity will rise or fall given the past pattern of points collected.

More generally, recruiters may vary effort during the production cycle based on their success to date on the Freeman Plan. Recruiters with more average accumulated points as of the beginning of the month may increase effort during the month to further raise their average points. In this case, current productivity and past average points would be positively related. On the other hand, more successful recruiters may reduce effort, consume more leisure, and "rest" on past achievements. Such recruiters may value leisure more than winning better rewards.

In this case, current productivity and past average points would be negatively related.

Recruiters' preferences for the time-path of leisure will also affect the allocation of effort over time. Those who value large blocks of leisure may maximize effort at the beginning or end of the cycle and consume leisure for the remaining months. Alternatively, those who prefer the same amount of leisure each month may supply a constant level of effort each month. In part, these choices depend on their discount rate. Recruiters who discount future costs and benefits more will end-load effort. Because of "procrastination," productivity will rise over the cycle. Whether recruiters can "front-load" or "end-load" enlistments, however, will depend on their quotas.

In addition to varying their level of effort over time, recruiters may vary their type of effort. In the initial months, they may devote considerable time to activities that build their inventory of future recruits, such as visiting job fairs and giving lectures at high schools, rather than working to gain enlistments immediately. Later in the cycle, as they approach the eligibility month for winning a reward, they would deplete their inventory, enlist more recruits, and increase their Freeman point attainment. If their points are insufficient at the end of the cycle to win a reward, they may "steal" future enlistments—deplete their inventory even further—to ensure winning. Such a strategy would result in productivity rising over the first cycle and dropping at the beginning of the second.

Productivity over a recruiter's tour. Past studies have shown that recruiter productivity, in the absence of an incentive plan, rises at a decreasing rate with experience (Carroll, Rao, and Lee 1986; Kostiuk and Follmann 1989). These studies explain the relationship between productivity and experience in terms of learning on the job.

Freeman status may alter how recruiter productivity varies with experience. How recruiters vary their level and type of effort over and between production cycles will affect how productivity varies with tenure because as recruiters gain months of production, they also gain months of tenure.

Since recruiters' tours are generally 36 months, the opportunities for winning rewards are limited and some recruiters may reduce effort. With a 12-month production cycle, recruiters can win only three rewards at most. Recruiters aiming to win all three must supply sufficient effort to win every twelve months. Those who have the usual three-year tour and who fail to win immediately after the first year become ineligible to win all three rewards. Such recruiters may reduce effort because they have more than twelve months to win each of the two rewards for which they remain eligible.

The timing of rewards can also affect effort at the end of a recruiter's tour. If recruiters have insufficient time remaining to finish their production cycle, they may reduce effort. If enough time does remain, they may increase effort depending on how many months they need to complete their production cycle, their average accumulated points, and the value they place on leisure relative to rewards.

Data

The data for this study cover recruiters in the Chicago Navy Recruiting District for the five-month period from April through August 1986. During that time, the Chicago district was one of the top-performing districts in the country relative to its quotas. Thus, recruiter behavior and the Freeman Plan were examined in an environment in which overall performance was more than satisfactory. These data include information on enlistments, recruit attrition,[6] station and zone affiliation, station size and quotas, time devoted to recruiting, Free-

man Plan status including month of production, past rewards, accumulated points, average accumulated points, and points earned each month.

Unfortunately, there are no data on individual quotas, only station quotas. I proxy individual quotas by dividing each recruiter's station quota by the number of recruiters in the station.[7]

The database has a short time series because of the considerable effort required to hand-enter and clean the data. Thus, to examine productivity over time, comparisons across recruiters with different tenures and months of production are made. Below, I discuss the estimation procedure used to eliminate differences in recruiter attributes, such as ability, that may confound the analysis of how a single recruiter varies effort and productivity over time.

The Chicago Navy Recruiting District database has 540 observations representing five complete months of data on 90 recruiters and less than five months of data on an additional 35 recruiters who either joined the District or ended their tour during the sample period or who had incomplete data. Therefore, the sample consists of 125 recruiters.

Table 3 presents the sample means and standard deviations. On average, recruiters made 2.59 gross contracts per month. Net of recruit attrition, recruiters enlisted 2.41 recruits, exceeding the average net contract quota of 2.39 recruits.

Recruiters' average tour length is 36 months, and 80% of the recruiters in this sample had tours between 35 and 37 months. Tour lengths in the sample vary, however, from 11 months to 70 months, and recruiters with abnormal tour lengths have fewer or more opportunities to win rewards.

The majority of the recruiters in the sample (55%) were in their first year of

---

[6] Enlistments in the military are also referred to as contracts. Recruit attrition equals the number of recruits who enlist but do not enter the military, or the number of unfilled contracts. Net contracts, the Navy's definition of recruiter productivity, equals gross contracts minus the number of unfilled contracts each month.

[7] This proxy is reasonable to the extent that the average station has only two recruiters. If the station includes one junior and one senior recruiter, however, the proxy probably overstates the quota of the junior recruiter (who probably gets assigned a lower quota) and understates the senior recruiter's quota.

Table 3. Means and Standard Deviations of Recruiter Level Variables: Chicago Navy Recruiting District, April–August 1986.
(N = 540)

(1) Variable	(2) Mean	(3) Standard Deviation
Enlistments		
Gross Contracts	2.59	1.78
Net Contracts	2.41	1.79
Quotas		
Net Contract Quota	2.39	.47
Recruiters Exceeding Quota	.52	.50
Black I–IIIA AFQT Quota	.17	.26
Hispanic I–IIIA AFQT Quota	.12	.20
Recruiter Resources		
Percent of Month on Leave	.12	.20
Station Chief Status	.38	.49
Length of Stay		
Tour of Duty Length	36	5.67
Months of Tenure	13.94	11.17
Freeman Plan Status		
Months on Production Cycle	7.57	4.20
Percent of Sample in Cycle 1	.79	.41
Percent of Sample in Cycle 2	.18	.39
Percent of Sample in Cycle 3	.02	.15
Current Month Points	231	175
Accumulated Points	1840	1182
Ave. Accumulated Points	232	101
Lagged Ave. Accumulated Points	231	99
Tenure When Reward Won	15.1	3.08

recruiting duty, probably because the Navy nationally increased the number of recruiters in 1986. Twenty-six percent of the recruiters were in their second year, 14% were in their third year, and 4% were in their fourth year. Because of the large number of first-year recruiters, few recruiters in the sample had won Freeman rewards, since these recruiters had not reached the reward eligibility month of the production cycle. Twenty-five recruiters, out of a total of 125, had won a reward. Also, because of the small number of senior recruiters, few recruiters were at the end of their tour. As a result, we cannot adequately examine end-of-period patterns using this sample.

Table 3 also presents average Freeman Plan status and performance. One hundred recruiters remained in the first production cycle throughout the sample period, 16 remained in the second cycle, and 2 remained in the third cycle. During the sample period, 7 recruiters won a reward—5 recruiters entered the second cycle and 2 entered the third cycle. Thus, 105 recruiters were in the first cycle for at least part of the sample period, 23 were in the second cycle, and 4 were in the third cycle.[8] Out of the 125 recruiters, 56 were eligible to win a reward by the end of the sample period. Of these, 21 had won one reward and were in cycle two, and 4 had won two rewards and were in cycle three. Recruiters, on average, had 15 months of tenure when they won their reward.

[8] In terms of observations, 428 are attributed to the first cycle, 99 to the second cycle, and 15 to the third cycle.

Estimation

Reduced form regression equations are estimated using Ordinary Least Squares. The dependent variable in these models is enlistments (net contracts), and the independent variables include factors that vary with recruiter and time or simply with recruiter.

Recruiters may differ in ability, an unobserved attribute, and the regression results will be biased if the independent variables are correlated with ability. Moreover, it will not be possible to interpret the results in terms of recruiters' effort decisions. In an attempt to eliminate ability differences empirically, I estimate fixed-effect, or dummy variable, regression models that exclude recruiter attributes that are fixed over time, such as ability, and include attributes that change over time, such as effort.

For example, net contracts made by recruiter i in month t are specified as

$$(1) \qquad C_{it} = Z_i\gamma + Y_{it}\delta + \eta_{it}$$

where Z_i is a vector of observable time invariant recruiter attributes; Y_{it} is a vector of variables that vary with time, recruiter, effort, and ability; and η_{it} is equal to (ϵ_{it} + μ_i), where ϵ_{it} is a random error that varies with time and recruiter and has a zero mean and standard deviation equal to σ, and μ_i equals unobservable, time-invariant recruiter attributes, such as ability.

The variable Y_{it} is a function of both observed characteristics, Q_{it}, and unobserved characteristics, ability μ_i and effort v_{it}, or:

$$(2) \qquad Y_{it} = Q_{it}\alpha + \mu_i + v_{it}$$

Thus, the effect of Y_{it} on contracts may be due to ability. Moreover, Y_{it} is correlated with the error term η_{it} implying that estimates of δ will be biased. The objective is to estimate equation (1) net of ability, or:

$$(3) \qquad C_{it} = Z_i\gamma + W_{it}\delta + \eta_{it}$$

where W_{it} is defined as ($Q_{it}\alpha + v_{it}$). To do this, equation (1) is first estimated as a fixed-effect model to derive the parameter estimate for δ. Operationally, the change between t and $t-1$ is computed for each

variable in (1). If we assume that effort, v_{it}, is uncorrelated with η_{it}, the estimation results will be unbiased.[9]

To obtain the parameter estimate for γ in (1), we estimate:

$$(4) \qquad \overline{C}_i - \overline{Y}_i\hat{\delta} = Z_i\gamma + \mu_i$$

where $\hat{\delta}$ is obtained from estimating the fixed-effect model, and $\overline{C}_i$ and $\overline{Y}_i$ equal the means of each variable over time for each recruiter. The parameter estimate for δ will be biased by differences in ability. Below, I report the estimation results for the fixed-effect model, denoted Model 1, and for equation (4), denoted Model 2 (or the recruiter attribute model).

Number of Observations

Since few recruiters have won two rewards, the observations for cycle three recruiters are excluded, thereby decreasing the sample size from 540 to 527. To estimate the fixed-effect model, observations are lagged by one month, thereby further decreasing the number of observations to 404.[10] To estimate equation (4), the sample size is 123, which equals the number of recruiters in the sample.[11]

Variable Definitions

Month of production. For estimation purposes, I assume that the production cycle runs from 1 to 13 months. Recruiters whose cycle is a running 12-month average are in the 13th month of production. I distinguish the 13th production month from the other months because, at this month, recruiters do not progress further

---

[9] Autocorrelation of the error terms is built into the model. To correct for autocorrelation, the sample size is reduced. As a result, time series variations in a five-month period are reduced. The results after correcting for autocorrelation are qualitatively the same as when the sample size is simply reduced without correcting for this problem. Thus, I do not correct for autocorrelation in estimated regressions.

[10] Of the 404 observations, 323 are attributed to cycle one and 81 to cycle two.

[11] The two recruiters who remained in cycle three during the sample period are excluded. Thus, the number of recruiters drops from 125 to 123.

on the cycle and accumulated points become a moving average.

Two spline variables are used to represent months of production. The first variable, denoted PROD, runs from one to twelve. In the 13th production month, PROD equals twelve. The second variable, denoted MONTH13, equals one if the recruiter is in the 13th month and equals zero otherwise.

Other variables. Recruiters' market potential is proxied by dummy variables that indicate their zone affiliation. Also included is a dummy variable that indicates whether recruiters were reassigned to a new station (within their zone) during the sample period. Both this variable and calendar month capture changes in market potential during the sample period.

I define resource availability in terms of each recruiter's time availability. Time available is proxied by a dummy variable indicating whether a recruiter is in command of a station. In smaller stations (the majority of the Chicago Navy Recruitment District stations) a station chief not only has managerial responsibilities but is also a production recruiter. Thus, these recruiters have less time to devote to recruiting than non-managers. The number of weeks excused per month from recruiting duty is excluded, despite its importance, because this variable may be endogenously determined. Recruiters may decide when to take leave time based on their performance on the Freeman Plan and whether they are eligible to win a reward. The regression results are qualitatively the same whether this variable is excluded or not.

The Shape of the Productivity Curve

To ascertain how productivity varies over the production cycle for recruiters in each cycle, I estimate a model that relates net contracts to the recruiter's month of production, where dummy variables represent each of the 13 months. Tenure also increases as months of production increase, and continues to rise when the recruiter reaches the 13th month. To separate the effect of tenure from that of the production cycle for recruiters in their second cycle, variables that capture the change in tenure are also included. Tenure is also included for first-cycle recruiters, although the effects of tenure and month of production are indistinguishable for recruiters whose tenure is less than 12 months. The relationship between tenure and months of production is explored further below.

Results

The key finding of the analysis is that productivity rises over the production cycle. Table 4 shows the regression results. When only month of production is allowed to vary, productivity rises from zero to 4.69 for non-reward winners in the first cycle and from − .35 to 5.94 for those who have won one reward. For reward winners, however, only the last three months of the cycle have statistically significant coefficients.

The shape of the productivity curve when the effect of tenure is allowed to vary and when all other variables are set equal to their mean values is shown in Figure 2 for non-winners and in Figure 3 for reward winners. In Figure 3, it is assumed that recruiters begin their second cycle in their 16th month of tenure (see Table 3). The solid lines in the figures indicate the standard errors.

For recruiters in their first production cycle, Figure 2 shows that net contracts rise by 3 over the cycle. One interpretation of this rise is that recruiters obtain human capital in their first year. For more senior recruiters who have won a reward, however, Figure 3 shows that net contracts rise by 5.36 over the second cycle. Since productivity rises more over the second than the first cycle, especially in the last four months, the attainment of human capital cannot be the only explanation for rising productivity.

The rise in productivity is consistent with two interpretations. First, recruiters may stockpile future recruits initially and deplete their stock at the end of the cycle, when they become eligible to win a reward. Alternatively, recruiters may vary their level of effort over the cycle. They may simply procrastinate until they near

Table 4. Productivity over the Production Cycle.
(Dependent Variable = Net Contracts)

Variable (1)	Cycle 1[a]		Cycle 2[a]	
	Coeff. Estimate (2)	t-Stat. (3)	Coeff. Estimate (4)	t-Stat. (5)
Model 1[b]				
Tenure	−.116	−.22	.09	.34
Tenure Squared	−.00165	−.11	−.0031	−.25
Month 2	.01	.11	.17	.19
Month 3	.91	1.28	.13	.09
Month 4	.79	.93	.61	.36
Month 5	1.10	.99	1.46	.73
Month 6	2.11	1.66**	.96	.44
Month 7	2.42	1.68**	2.15	.92
Month 8	2.10	1.33	2.56	1.07
Month 9	2.53	1.42*	2.65	1.09
Month 10	3.26	1.63**	2.17	.94
Month 11	3.48	1.58*	3.58	1.66**
Month 12	4.14	1.69**	4.64	2.21***
Month 13	4.69	1.86**	5.94	2.49****
Net Contract Quota	.35	1.52*	−.12	−.27
Black I–IIIA AFQT Quota	−1.36	−2.21***	.37	.29
Hispanic I–IIIA AFQT Quota	−1.81	−2.65****	1.02	.52
Change Station	.65	1.49*	−.54	−.69
May	−.16	−.74	.39	.78
June	.15	.61	.42	.79
July	.43	2.08***	.13	.27
	R²=.10, N=323		R²=.21, N=81	
Model 2[b]				
Intercept	.12	.07	.45	.17
Station Chief	−.70	−2.12***	−.45	−.40
Tour Length	.05	1.04	.06	1.01
Zone 2	−1.30	−2.35***	−4.96	−2.46***
Zone 3	−.56	−1.02	−3.52	−2.17***
Zone 4	−.82	−1.60*	−2.41	−1.37
Zone 5	−1.03	−1.83**	−.73	−.41
Zone 6	−1.22	−2.22***	−1.80	−1.08
Zone 7	−1.34	−2.56****	−1.77	−.84
Zone 8	−1.04	−1.94***	−5.32	−2.10***
	R²=.16, N=105		R²=.48, N=23	

[a] Cycle 1 refers to non-reward winners; Cycle 2 refers to reward winners.
[b] Model 1 is fixed effect model; Model 2 is recruiter attribute model.
* Significant at the .15 level; ** significant at the .10 level; *** significant at the .05 level; **** significant at the .01 level.

the reward month in the cycle, thereby supplying less effort initially and more effort at the end of the cycle. Put differently, rewards far in the future may not adequately elicit current effort. Both interpretations imply that recruiters make intertemporal effort decisions in an attempt to win a reward.

Factors Affecting the Shape of the Productivity Curve

Variations in quotas, past Freeman Plan success, calendar month, and changing recruiting stations may alter the observed rise in productivity over the production cycle. If more experienced recruiters receive higher quotas, quotas will rise over the production cycle. Given that quotas induce greater productivity, the productivity curve will steepen as quotas increase. After controlling for tenure in the equation, however, quotas may have little additional effect on the curve's shape.

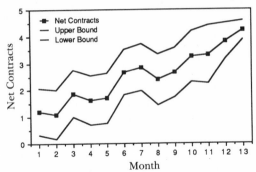

Figure 2. Productivity by Production Month:
Non-Winners.

Less productive recruiters may improve their performance when they are reassigned to new stations, implying that their productivity profile will be steeper. On the other hand, if more productive recruiters are reassigned to improve the performance of less productive stations, productivity will rise less over the production cycle.

As shown in Figures 2 and 3, the profiles of reward winners and non-winners are roughly similar in shape—both appear linear—but the profile for reward winners is steeper. Thus, reward status may affect how productivity varies over the production cycle.

Greater success on the Freeman Plan, defined in terms of lagged average accumulated points, may steepen or flatten the productivity profile. If more successful recruiters rest content with their past achievements and decrease effort to consume more leisure, productivity will rise less when (lagged) average points are greater. If, on the other hand, more

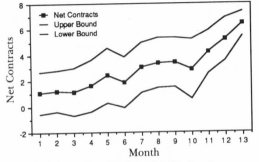

Figure 3. Productivity by Production
Month: Winners.

successful recruiters increase productivity to ensure winning a reward, the curve will steepen as the lagged average points rise.

Similarly, it is unclear whether the profile for less successful recruiters will be relatively steep or flat. Such recruiters may have attained fewer average points because they diverted their effort toward building their stock of future recruits rather than making more enlistments; if so, when they draw down their stock in future months their productivity will rise. On the other hand, less successful recruiters may become discouraged and reduce effort in future months, resulting in a flatter profile.

I assume that the productivity curve is linear. As seen in Figures 2 and 3, this assumption is roughly borne out by the observed patterns. Months of production is represented by PROD and MONTH13. To determine how quotas, calendar month, change of station, and performance on the Freeman Plan affect the shape of the curve, each of these variables is interacted with PROD and MONTH13. I also include the levels of each of these variables and control for the effect of tenure by including a linear and quadratic term in tenure.

Results

Table 5 shows the regression results. Tour length and station chief status do not have a statistically significant effect on the position of the curve. In terms of the shape of the curve, quotas and calendar month do not have a statistically significant impact. Ignoring the effects of tenure, which will be investigated below, the effect on net contracts of increasing month of production by one, when production month is less than 13, is [1.99 − (.29 × Change Station) − (.00365 × Lagged Points)]. The effect of a transfer to a different station is statistically significant only at the .10 level, whereas the effect of past average points is significant at the .01 level. The results indicate productivity rises by 1.99 net contracts in each month when lagged points equal zero and recruiters do not change station.

Table 5. Factors Affecting the Shape of the Productivity Curve.
(Dependent Variable = Net Contracts)

(1) Variable	(2) Coefficient Estimate	(3) t-Stat.	(1) Variable	(2) Coefficient Estimate	(3) t-Stat.
Model 1[a]			June × MONTH13	−.24	−.47
Tenure	−.99	−2.34****	July × PROD	.05	.73
Tenure Squared	.0124	1.41*	July × MONTH13	−.02	.04
PROD	1.99	4.39****	Change Station	2.01	2.15***
MONTH13	3.69	1.50	Lagged Average Points	.00016	.06
Change Station			Cycle 2	11.19	2.48****
× PROD	−.29	−2.26***	Net Contract Quota	−.48	−.67
Change Station			Black I–IIIA AFQT Quota	.28	.18
× MONTH13	2.55	2.37****	Hispanic I–IIIA		
Lagged Average			AFQT Quota	−1.44	−.66
Points × PROD	−.00365	−4.86****	June	−.45	−.91
Lagged Average			July	−.13	−.27
Points × MONTH13	−.014	−1.62**	R² = .30, N = 283		
Cycle 2 × PROD	.19	.49			
Cycle 2 × MONTH13	−1.11	−.88			
Net Contract Quota			**Model 2**[a]		
× PROD	.06	.70	Intercept	2.60	.93
Net Contract Quota			Station Chief Status	−.60	−.78
× MONTH13	.15	.24	Tour Length	−.02	−.24
Black I–IIIA AFQT			Zone 2	−3.27	−2.26***
Quota × PROD	−.07	−.37	Zone 3	−2.80	−2.13***
Black I–IIIA AFQT			Zone 4	.15	.12
Quota × MONTH13	−.47	−.37	Zone 5	.95	.65
Hispanic I–IIIA AFQT			Zone 6	.07	.05
Quota × PROD	.07	.27	Zone 7	.32	.24
Hispanic I–IIIA AFQT			Zone 8	−.91	−.67
Quota × MONTH13	−.09	−.10	R² = .13, N = 123		
June × PROD	.08	1.22			

[a] Model 1 is fixed effect model; Model 2 is recruiter attribute model.
* Significant at the .15 level; ** significant at the .10 level; *** significant at the .05 level; **** significant at the .01 level.

Although this result is somewhat tenuous, it suggests that relocated recruiters have a flatter productivity curve; net contracts rise by 1.7 per month. More successful recruiters also have a flatter profile. Lagged average points equal 231, on average. Using this average figure, productivity rises by only 1.15 contracts per month, assuming recruiters did not change stations. When lagged average points are greater than 231, productivity rises even less.

For recruiters at month 13 of the production cycle, lagged points and change of station also affect productivity. The effect of past points, however, is significant only at the .10 level. For recruiters in their last production month, the change in net contracts is [3.69 + (2.25 × Change Station) − (.014 × Lagged Points)]. When lagged points equal zero, net contracts rise by 3.69 at the end of the cycle, but this effect is only marginally statistically significant. Productivity rises more when recruiters are reassigned to a new station and rises less when recruiters have been more successful on the Plan. Given that lagged average points, on average, equal 204, net contracts rise by .83 when recruiters are eligible to win a reward.

The negative effect of relocation when recruiters have less than 13 months of production suggests that recruiters are reassigned to improve the performance of a poorly performing station. Since reassignment significantly improves the performance of recruiters in their 13th month, however, the results can be interpreted as suggesting, on the contrary, that these recruiters were reassigned because their performance in their former station was poor.

As suggested above, the rise in productivity over the production cycle could be explained by an inventory argument or by variations in recruiter effort. The negative relationship between current productivity and past Freeman Plan success (or past output) in Table 5 lends support to the latter interpretation. For the inventory argument to be consistent with the inverse relationship between current and past output, recruiters would have to deplete their inventory at the beginning of the production cycle (implying greater past output) and make fewer enlistments when they become eligible to win a reward. On the other hand, the effort argument suggests that recruiters modulate their effort over time. In other words, productivity regresses toward the mean. When past performance is good, recruiters reduce effort, implying a flatter productivity profile over time. Conversely, when past performance is poor, recruiters increase effort. When recruiters become eligible to win at the end of the cycle, productivity rises in response to poorer performance.

These results suggest that recruiters are sensitive to the reward structure but that the timing of rewards affects current effort levels. When successful recruiters must wait longer to win a reward, they may reduce effort. Shortening the length of the production cycle could induce greater effort. Linking rewards to short-term output, however, would increase recruiters' risk when random market fluctuations are large.

How Does Productivity Vary with Experience?

I assume that recruiters win one reward during their tour. The estimation includes tenure, tenure squared, and separate variables for the recruiter's month of production by reward status.

In the recruiter's first year, tenure and months of production move in unison.

Thus, from an estimation standpoint, the effect on net contracts of tenure and the production cycle in the first twelve months is indistinguishable. After the first year, however, a recruiter in the first cycle is in the 13th production month even though tenure continues to progress. Thus, to represent the relationship between tenure and production month for recruiters in their first cycle, I only include a variable indicating the interaction between MONTH13 and tenure.

For recruiters in their second cycle, the month of production equals one the month after winning a reward. Twelve months later, the production month equals 13. Recruiters remain at month 13 until the end of their tour. To represent the relationship between tenure and the production cycle for second-cycle recruiters, I include interaction variables between month of production and tenure.

Three spline variables, MONTH1–5, MONTH6–12, and MONTH13, are used to represent months of production.[12] By allowing productivity to rise between months one and five at a rate different from that between months six and twelve, two additional effects can be captured. First, for reward winners, we can examine whether there is a difference between how recruiters vary productivity immediately after winning and later in their production cycle. Second, for non-reward winners, we can capture the effect of learning on the job when recruiters begin their tour.[13]

The model to be estimated is:

---

[12] The conclusions do not depend on the specific month intervals selected. When the intervals are defined as month one to four and five to twelve, or as month one to nine and ten to twelve, for example, the estimated tenure profiles have the same key features as those discussed in the text.

[13] The three variables are defined as follows. When month of production is less than or equal to five, MONTH1–5 equals the month of production, and MONTH6–12 and MONTH13 equal zero. When production month is greater than five but less than or equal to twelve, MONTH1–5 equals five, MONTH6–12 equals the month of production minus five, and MONTH13 equals zero. Finally, when the production month equals thirteen, MONTH1–5 equals five, MONTH6–12 equals seven, and MONTH13 equals one.

(5) Net Contracts =
    f(tenure, tenure-squared,
    cycle1 × (MONTH1–5, MONTH6–12,
      MONTH13),
    cycle1 × tenure × (MONTH13),
    cycle2 × (MONTH1–5, MONTH6–12,
      MONTH13),
    cycle2 × tenure × (MONTH1–5,
      MONTH6–12, MONTH13),
    cycle2, Z)

The vector Z equals the other variables of the model, which include the quotas, calendar month, change of station, station chief status, tour length, and zone.

Results

Columns 2 and 3 of Table 6 show the estimation results. The lack of statistical significance for most of the variables, despite the relatively high R^2, suggests that the independent variables are highly correlated. Assuming that the model is correctly specified, the equation can still be used to predict the tenure profile. Alternatively, the model can be estimated using a specification that eliminates collinear variables. The solution is to estimate a second specification of the model and compare its prediction for the tenure profile to the predictions generated by the column 2 estimates.

Columns 4 and 5 of Table 6 present the results of an estimation that excludes the interaction variables between tenure and production month and the variables MONTH1–5 and MONTH6–12 for recruiters in their first cycle. The estimated coefficients on the tenure variables are statistically significant (although only marginally for tenure) and confirm the finding of other studies that recruiter productivity rises with tenure but the rise declines as recruiters gain experience. For recruiters in their second cycle, the production cycle variables are all positive and statistically significant. The relative size of the coefficients indicates that productivity rises faster in the first five months of the cycle than in the last seven. At the end of the cycle, recruiter productivity jumps by 1.43 net contracts.

Figure 4 shows the predicted tenure profile based on the estimates in column 4. For comparison, Figure 5 shows the predicted profile generated from the original model's estimates in column 2.[14] The dotted lines indicate the standard errors. Although the profiles differ in shape somewhat, particularly between months 13 and 15 and months 21 to 27, they both have the same key feature— productivity drops sharply after a recruiter wins a reward. The difference in productivity between month 15 and month 16 of tenure is statistically significant. Thus, productivity rises over tenure as the recruiter gains months on the production cycle. After the recruiter wins, productivity falls by 2.4 net contracts (Figure 4). Within five to six months, however, the recruiter's productivity in the second cycle is back to its level prior to winning the reward; and productivity rises dramatically thereafter, reaching 5.7 net contracts when the recruiter is at the 27th month of tenure. Although Figures 4–5 indicate that productivity falls at the end of the tour, no conclusions can be drawn from this result given the lack of observations for recruiters in their final months.

The drop in net contracts after a reward is won is consistent with the notion that recruiters deplete their inventory of potential recruits to win the reward. Put differently, recruiters may "steal" future enlistments to improve their chances of winning a reward in the current month. Once recruiters win their reward, they must divert their effort toward building their inventory rather than making enlistments. As a result, productivity is lower once the reward is won but rises again five months later after the stock is replenished.

An alternative interpretation is simply that recruiters "rest" after exerting effort to achieve the reward. Thus, productivity rises over the first production cycle as recruiters increase effort. When they become eligible to win, they exert the most effort. Once they have won, however, they rest and start the process again.

The estimated relationship between tour

---

[14] Recruiters are assumed to begin their second cycle at month 16. (See Table 3.)

Table 6. Productivity over Tenure.
(Dependent Variable = Net Contracts)

Variable (1)	Specification 1		Specification 2	
	Coefficient Estimate (2)	t-Stat. (3)	Coefficient Estimate (4)	t-Stat. (5)
Model 1[a]				
Tenure	−.41	−1.04	.25	1.46*
Tenure Squared	.0059	.75	−.0082	−1.79**
Cycle 2	5.54	1.33	−2.76	−2.61****
MONTH1–5 × Cycle1	.69	1.68**		
MONTH 6–12 × Cycle1	.69	2.10***		
MONTH13 × Cycle1	−1.05	−.81	.42	1.08
MONTH1–5 × Cycle2	2.02	1.87**	.65	1.69**
MONTH6–12 × Cycle2	−.30	−.36	.49	1.96***
MONTH13 × Cycle2	3.80	1.36	1.43	1.61**
Tenure × MONTH1–5 × Cycle2	−.05	−1.30		
Tenure × MONTH6–12 × Cycle2	.03	1.13		
Tenure × MONTH13 × Cycle2	−.07	−.90		
Tenure × MONTH13 × Cycle1	.09	1.28		
Net Contract Quota	.23	1.18	.24	1.24
Black I–IIIA AFQT Quota	−1.36	−2.65****	−1.46	−2.84****
Hispanic I–IIIA AFQT Quota	−1.60	−2.79****	−1.61	−2.80****
Change Station	.26	.75	.32	.93
May	−.12	−.60	−.11	−.59
June	.05	.22	.05	.26
July	.29	1.60*	.36	2.01***
	R^2 = .15, N = 412		R^2 = .12, N = 412	
Model 2[a]				
Intercept	−5.83	−2.92****	−4.04	−3.73****
Station Chief Status	.15	.33	−.67	−1.98***
Tour Length	.18	4.46****	.18	6.00****
Zone 2	−1.58	−1.92***	−1.79	−2.96****
Zone 3	−1.55	−2.03***	−1.08	−1.92***
Zone 4	−.58	−.77	−1.31	−2.35***
Zone 5	−.48	−.57	−1.43	−2.27***
Zone 6	−1.05	−1.35	−1.49	−2.59****
Zone 7	−1.26	−1.61**	−1.11	−1.94***
Zone 8	−1.40	−1.73**	−1.22	−2.05***
	R^2 = .21, N = 119		R^2 = .31, N = 119	

[a] Model 1 is fixed effect model; Model 2 is recruiter attribute model.
* Significant at the .15 level; ** significant at the .10 level; *** significant at the .05 level; **** significant at the .01 level.

length and net contracts suggests that recruiters with more opportunities to win Freeman rewards produce more.

Conclusions

Although the results of this study of how Navy recruiters respond to compensation structure are subject to several interpretations, they do strongly suggest that incentives matter. Recruiters appear to vary effort in an attempt to win rewards, and the timing of the rewards affects the allocation of effort over time. The study's main findings can be summarized as follows.

Recruiter output is greatest in the months immediately prior to becoming eligible to win a prize. In part, this effect could be due to human capital attainment, since recruiters gain experience as they gain months on the 12-month production cycle. Since the same effect is apparent for more senior recruiters, however, it seems likely that individuals vary either their level or type of effort over the 12-month

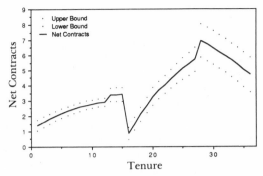

Figure 4. Tenure Profile: Model 2.

period. More specifically, recruiters may "procrastinate" until they approach the reward deadline. Alternatively, recruiters may vary their type of effort by first devoting their time to building an inventory of future recruits rather than making enlistments, and later depleting their inventory when they become eligible to win a reward.

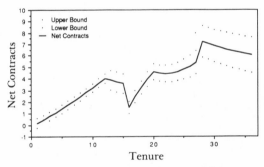

Figure 5. Tenure Profile: Model 1.

The evidence supporting the notion that recruiters vary their level rather than their type of effort is provided by the finding that current productivity is negatively related to past output, defined as success to date on the incentive plan. More successful recruiters have lower productivity, suggesting that recruiters reduce effort when they are already in a good position to win a reward. Thus, rewards that are some distance in the future may have a negative impact on current effort levels.

The analysis also shows that productivity rises with tenure but drops precipitously after an individual has won a prize. This finding is consistent with both the human capital model and the notion that recruiters vary effort between production cycles. Productivity may drop after a reward is won either because individuals "rest" after expending effort to win a reward or because in order to win a reward they pursued enlistments that they otherwise would have made in future months. In following the latter strategy, they increase their chances of winning a reward, but have lower productivity in future months.

Although the Navy recruiter compensation structure does not have a direct counterpart in the private sector, the results are suggestive of the type of behavior one might observe among workers whose compensation structure allows for intertemporal substitutions in effort.

REFERENCES

Antle, Rick, and Abbie Smith. 1986. "An Empirical Investigation of the Relative Performance Evaluation of Corporate Executives." *Journal of Accounting Research*, Vol. 24, No. 1 (Spring), pp. 1–39.

Asch, Beth J. 1989. "Recruiter Productivity and the Freeman Plan." The RAND Corporation, R-3713-FMP, forthcoming.

Bull, Clive, Andrew Schotter, and Keith Weigert. 1987. "Tournaments and Piece Rates: An Experimental Study." *Journal of Political Economy*, Vol. 95, No. 1 (February), pp. 1–33.

Carroll, Vincent P., Hau L. Lee, and Ambar F. Rao. 1986. "Implications of Salesforce Productivity Heterogeneity and Demotivation: A Navy Re-

cruiter Case Study." *Management Science*, Vol. 32, No. 11 (November), pp. 1371–88.

Coughlan, A., and R. Schmidt. 1985. "Executive Compensation, Management Turnover, and Firm Performance: An Empirical Investigation." *Journal of Accounting and Economics*, Vol. 7 (April), pp. 43–66.

Kostiuk, Peter F., and Dean A. Follmann. 1989. "Learning Curves, Personal Characteristics, and Job Performance." *Journal of Labor Economics*, Vol. 7, No. 2 (April), pp. 129–46.

Lambert, Richard A. 1983. "Long-Term Contracts and Moral Hazard." *Bell Journal of Economics*, Vol. 14, No. 2 (Autumn), pp. 441–52.

Lazear, Edward P. 1986. "Salaries and Piece Rates."

Journal of Business, Vol. 59, No. 3 (July), pp. 405–31.

Malcomson, James M., and Frans Spinnewyn. 1988. "The Multiperiod Principal-Agent Problem." *Review of Economic Studies,* Vol. 55, No. 3 (July), pp. 391–408.

Murphy, Kevin S. 1986. "Incentives, Learning, and Compensation: A Theoretical and Empirical Investigation of Managerial Labor Contracts." *RAND Journal of Economics,* Vol. 17, No. 1 (Spring), pp. 54–76.

Pencavel, John. 1977. "Work-Effort and on the Job Screening and Renumeration." In Ronald G. Ehrenberg, ed., *Research in Labor Economics, Vol. 1.* Greenwich, Conn.: JAI Press, pp. 225–58.

Rogerson, William P. 1985. "Repeated Moral Hazard." *Econometrica,* Vol. 53, No. 1 (January), pp. 69–76.

Rubinstein, Ariel, and Menahem E. Yaari. 1983. "Repeated Insurance Contracts and Moral Hazard." *Journal of Economic Theory,* Vol. 30, No. 1 (June), pp. 74–97.

Seiler, Eric. 1984. "Piece Rates vs. Time Rates: The Effects of Incentives on Earnings." *Review of Economics and Statistics,* Vol. 66 (August), pp. 363–76.

Spear, Stephen E., and Sanjay Srivastava. 1987. "On Repeated Moral Hazard with Discounting." *Review of Economic Studies,* Vol. 54, No. 4 (October), pp. 599–617.

CONTINGENT PAY AND MANAGERIAL PERFORMANCE

LAWRENCE M. KAHN and PETER D. SHERER*

This paper uses longitudinal data on managers from one company to examine the relationship between financial incentives and performance. One important finding is that bonuses for managers who are in high-level positions, work at corporate headquarters, and have low seniority are more sensitive to performance than are the bonuses given to managers without those three characteristics. A second important finding is that the managers for whom bonuses are most sensitive to performance have higher subsequent performance levels than other managers, even when past performance levels are controlled for. Merit pay, in contrast to bonuses, appears to be awarded on the same basis across managerial levels, plant locations, and seniority levels, and differences in the sensitivity of merit pay to performance appear to have no significant effect on subsequent performance.

THE issue of worker performance, which has long been of crucial importance to firms and to students of management, has received increasing attention by economists as well.[1] Labor productivity was at one time viewed by the latter as solely a function of investments in human and physical capital. Economists have increasingly recognized, however, that worker effort is also an important determinant of output, given such investments.[2]

The effect of company compensation policies on worker effort and performance is of both theoretical and practical interest. First, expectancy theory (Lawler 1973) and economic theory (Lazear 1986; Brown 1988) both argue that performance-contingent reward systems can lead to higher performance levels than systems that do not tie pay to performance. Under either of these theories, workers in contingent reward systems anticipate that current effort will lead to future rewards. Empirical evidence is needed to allow us to assess these theories. Second, the effect of compensation systems on performance is of obvious importance to organizations. A company, for example, must weight the costs and benefits of such alternative systems in order to maximize its effectiveness.

This paper uses longitudinal data on middle- and upper-level managers from one company to estimate the impact of company pay raise policy and pay levels on worker performance. Longitudinal data allow us to estimate the parameters of this pay raise policy and to use these results to estimate the determinants of subsequent performance. Further, longitudinal data

---

*Lawrence M. Kahn is Professor of Economics and Labor and Industrial Relations at the University of Illinois at Urbana-Champaign, and Peter D. Sherer is Associate Professor of Management at the Wharton School of the University of Pennsylvania.

To preserve confidentiality, the authors are unable to release the name of the company from which they obtained the data for this study or the data base itself.

[1] See, for example, Lawler (1968, 1973, or 1981) for an organizational behavior perspective on the performance question.

[2] See Lazear (1979, 1981, or 1986), Shapiro and Stiglitz (1984), and Bowles (1985) for examples of economic modeling of work incentives.

on individual performance enable us to deal with the problem of unobservable determinants of performance, a problem that has plagued many attempts to estimate the impact of company compensation systems on firm performance.[3]

We use a two-stage procedure to study the pay-performance issue. First, we estimate the determinants of 1985 bonus and merit pay awards. In this analysis, the effects of past performance on rewards are explicitly allowed to vary across workers within the company. This variability across workers provides a "natural" experiment for estimating the impact of the contingent pay system on subsequent performance. From this first stage estimation, for each worker we compute the derivative of bonus and merit pay with respect to performance. Second, we use these estimated derivatives along with pay levels and other variables (including past performance) to estimate the determinants of subsequent performance.

This paper adds in two important ways to the literature on pay and performance. First, many existing studies of the subject fail adequately to separate the effects of pay levels and pay increases on performance (Ehrenberg and Milkovich 1987; Milkovich and Newman 1987). We provide an integrated treatment of pay levels, bonuses, and merit pay. Further, our study uses as explanatory variables the estimated parameters of the bonus and merit pay systems, whereas other studies have often used the presence or absence of a merit pay system as the key explanatory variable (Locke et al. 1980). Thus, our approach comes closer to a structural model than does the previous literature.

Second, our use of panel data allows us to handle the difficult issues of causality that arise when researchers examine the correlation between pay and performance. We are able to control for unobserved fixed differences across managers in measured performance levels. In addition, panel data allow us to estimate the bonus and merit pay system parameters on data

taken prior to the period for which performance is measured, increasing our confidence that the causation in our tests runs from pay to performance.

Theories of Pay and Performance

Economic and organizational behavior literature both suggest that the manner in which pay increases are awarded, as well as pay levels themselves, can affect worker performance levels. First, regarding company raise policy, both types of literature have argued that systems that tie pay to performance can lead to higher effort levels by workers than would be the case under noncontingent reward systems. For example, according to expectancy theory (Lawler 1973), contingent pay systems can lead workers to anticipate that hard work today will be rewarded later.[4] The economic literature on contingent pay systems also models the worker as weighing the gains to harder work (effort-contingent pay increases) against the disutility incurred by working harder (Lazear 1986; Brown 1988). A rise in the reward to higher effort induces a utility-maximizing worker to increase his or her effort level: at the previous effort level the marginal returns to higher effort are now greater than their marginal costs (disutility).

Second, economists and organizational behavior theorists postulate that pay levels can also influence work effort, apart from any effect of the pay raise system. For example, the efficiency wage literature (Shapiro and Stiglitz 1984; Bulow and Summers 1986) suggests that paying workers higher wages than they could obtain with other companies can lead to higher worker effort than a policy of paying workers just what they could earn elsewhere. This outcome can occur if there is some probability that a worker will be discharged for poor performance and that the worker can reduce this probability by

---

[3] See Ehrenberg and Milkovich (1987) and our discussion below.

[4] According to Lawler (1973), for contingent pay systems to be effective, workers must be convinced that higher effort will lead to better performance and that better performance will be rewarded.

working harder. The pay premium a worker earns relative to his or her outside opportunity gives the worker a reason to want to keep the job (that is, to avoid being discharged).

Equity theory provides an additional framework predicting that high pay levels can lead to high performance (Adams 1965; Lawler 1968). According to this theory, individuals bring inputs (for example, performance) to an organization and receive outcomes (for example, pay) from it. A person compares the relationship of outcomes to inputs with that of a referent other, who could be either a different person or the same person at an earlier time. When individuals perceive that they are overrewarded for their inputs as compared to a referent other, they feel inequity and seek to redress it. One means of doing so is to increase performance as an input. Conversely, it is reasoned that those who feel underpaid will respond by lowering their performance.[5]

Although equity theory and efficiency wage theory both predict that high wages can increase work effort, the two theories emphasize different mechanisms by which this outcome occurs. Efficiency wage theories, as noted, assume that the worker compares current pay with outside opportunities; some threat of discharge and a perceived ability to reduce this threat are necessary in order for high wages to motivate workers. In contrast, equity theory does not require a discharge mechanism or comparisons with outside jobs in order to generate a high pay–high effort connection. Internal pay comparisons may be sufficient for this outcome. Of course, workers might compare their situation with the situations of workers outside the firm, and the possibility of discharge could still motivate workers (Lawler 1968).

Previous Research

A number of studies have estimated the impact of pay systems on objective performance.[6] A review of 44 studies on the adoption of incentive systems showed in almost all cases a substantial improvement in performance.[7] This evidence is consistent with a positive effect of tying pay to performance. In many instances, however, the implementation of such plans may coincide with other changes in the workplace, such as a change in overall pay levels; and few studies on pay and performance have given much attention to the need to disentangle the impact of pay level and pay increases (Ehrenberg and Milkovich 1987; Milkovich and Newman 1987). In this paper we explicitly break down the effects of pay levels and various types of pay increases on performance. Furthermore, our study examines an intact contingent pay system, whereas most of the studies alluded to above have focused on the implementation phase. Since contingent pay systems may take considerable time to become fully operative, an examination of an existing system differs from a study of the implementation of a new system.

Our study departs from much previous work on this subject by examining managerial performance. Managers are a particularly good sample on which to test theories about pay and performance, because they typically have more discretion about their work than other employees do. Of the relatively few studies of managerial performance that have been done, many examine the impact of the adoption of incentive bonuses or stock option plans on the market value of the company. These studies have tended to find that adoption of such incentive schemes is followed by increases in shareholder wealth.[8] It is not clear, however, whether there are actual incentive effects or, on the contrary, the adoption of

---

[5] The link between overpayment and subsequent performance has been tested in experimental research; the construct validity or correspondence between the experimental induction and the construct of inequity has been questioned, however. See Schwab (1980).

[6] See Milkovich and Newman (1987) and Ehrenberg and Milkovich (1987) for summaries of this literature. For recent evidence, see other papers in this issue of the *Industrial and Labor Relations Review*.

[7] See Locke et al. (1980).

[8] See Bhagat, Brickley, and Lease (1985), Brickley, Bhagat, and Lease (1985), or Tehranian and Waegelein (1985).

executive bonus plans is proposed by managers only when they expect to benefit from such schemes (Ehrenberg and Milkovich 1987). The use of panel data in this study to some degree helps us avoid such problems of interpretation.[9]

The only existing study of managerial merit pay examined federal employees and found no impact of merit pay on performance; many of these managers, however, thought that the merit pay system was political window dressing (Pearce, Stevenson, and Perry 1985).

Our study differs from most other research on pay for performance not only in its focus on managers and its use of panel data, but also in its focus on subjective, as opposed to objective, measures of performance.[10] Although objective measures of performance (for example, physical output or sales quotas) may have less measurement error than subjective measures, they cannot be used when there is no readily available way of quantifying performance. Perhaps not surprisingly, the Bureau of National Affairs (1981) reports that contingent pay systems involving subjective measures are more common than those involving objective measures and are almost always relied upon for white-collar and managerial employees.[11]

Finally, unlike earlier work, our study provides an integrated treatment of bonuses, merit pay, and pay levels. Our focus on the bonus system provides a test of some conjectures about the efficacy of this type of reward.

Bonuses have been recommended by Lawler (1981) as an especially useful mechanism for eliciting higher performance, and recent data indicate their growing popularity (Bureau of National Affairs 1984; Peck 1986). Bonuses may be effective in inducing high performance because they are not subject to the same constraints as the typical merit system. Whereas merit systems almost always involve a rate range that restricts the size of increases to those low and high in the range, bonuses typically do not entail such restrictions (Milkovich and Newman 1987).

In addition, bonuses may be attractive from the company's point of view because they do not become part of the base salary in the way that merit pay does. Of course, regularly paid bonuses of a constant percentage could take on the characteristics of an entitlement; but the literature on bonuses points to their flexibility in tying reward to performance as an advantage of this form of pay.[12] A simulation study by Schwab and Olson (1988) indeed found that bonus systems can maintain a performance-reward linkage better than merit systems, due to their greater flexibility.

Although contingent compensation systems may have benefits, companies must weigh the benefits of contingent compensation plans against their costs. These costs include administration as well as the disutility to workers of the risks associated with such plans.

Data

Personnel data were obtained from a moderate-sized firm involved in production. The firm's corporate office and main production facility are located in the

---

[9] One study attempted to avoid such problems by relating measures of the level, risk, and structure (namely, bonus component) of top executive compensation to subsequent firm performance. The estimated effects were, however, too sensitive to lag structures to allow firm conclusions about the impact of various dimensions of executive compensation. See Rabin (1988).

[10] For some discussion of this distinction, see Heneman, Schwab, Fossum, and Dyer (1986). We note below that raters are instructed to use specific criteria in giving their performance evaluations. Even so, a subjective component remains.

[11] The distinction between subjective and objective measures can be important in evaluating the impact of merit systems. For example, Pearce, Stevenson, and Perry (1985) attempted to evaluate a merit pay system in which a manager's evaluation was based 60 percent on subjective factors and 40 percent on objective measures of performance in the manager's department. Unfortunately, the authors examined only objective factors in assessing the effect of the merit pay plan on managerial performance.

[12] This flexibility has been cited as a particular advantage of the Japanese employment system, with its heavy emphasis on bonuses. See Hashimoto (1979).

upper Midwest, and the company has other units in several midwestern states.[13] We analyze a sample of 92 middle- to upper-level managers whose 1985 salaries ranged from about \$32,000 to about \$72,000. The firm's merit pay system and bonus system have been operative for over ten years.

The firm requires that performance be made quantifiable, and numerical ratings are made through a Management by Objectives (MBO) system of performance appraisal. Managerial employees set goals with their immediate supervisors. Line positions make use of such quantitative measures as departmental productivity and energy costs. For staff positions, which are more difficult to quantify in terms of output, goals for project development and completion are established in a goal-setting session, and approximately a year later the employees are evaluated as to how well they achieved their goals. The immediate manager then makes an overall judgment of the employee's performance. An employee's performance is summarized on a six-point rating scale, with one being the lowest performance level (substantially below the target performance level) and six being the highest (exceptionally high performance).

MBO and performance appraisal done in this way provide an absolute measure of performance, and it is therefore meaningful to make performance comparisons across jobs.[14] Furthermore, the use of the same set of procedures and the same measurement scale by all raters may reduce inter-rater bias.

For all jobs, behavioral data on 13 dimensions (for example, whether one works effectively with others) are used to supplement the quantitative data concerning goal attainment. These data are used in consultations with employees to suggest behavioral explanations for their performance levels.

The performance data may contain errors. The firm has, however, taken steps to minimize error in the data, guided by the literature on performance appraisal and MBO. The firm runs two-day training sessions for raters on MBO and the performance appraisal process. One part of the training covers goal setting and performance appraisal. Managers are encouraged to set goals with their subordinates that accurately represent the performance domain of the job and that are challenging and specific—a process that helps ensure that the performance data will be meaningful and fair. This training helps guard against changes in performance standards over time (leniency effects).

Managers are also made aware of the most important common sources of error in performance appraisal, such as halo, primacy, and recency effects. It is possible that training employees to avoid specific errors simply results in their committing other specific errors (for example, becoming excessively severe in their effort to avoid leniency), with no net gain in validity (Bernardin and Buckley 1981), but the firm does not make this element of training the cornerstone of its training program, nor does it tell employees what specifically to correct; it simply makes employees aware of the errors commonly found. Finally, supervisors keep extensive diaries, further reducing recency and primacy biases.

The second part of the training program focuses on the interpersonal components of performance appraisal, particularly as they relate to evaluative and developmental feedback. Behavioral modeling and role playing are used to make managers more comfortable with giving feedback. Bernardin and Buckley (1981) have suggested that such training is critical because raters often are afraid to tell employees the truth about their negative

---

[13] To preserve confidentiality, we are unable to provide more specific information about the company's activities. The following description of the company's personnel policies is based on its personnel policy manual and on discussions with a top personnel executive at the firm.

[14] We discuss below the impact of possible rating errors in the evaluations. Furthermore, our empirical work pays some attention to the issue of functional form: is a move, say, from 3 to 4 in performance equivalent to a move from 5 to 6?

performance, resulting in distorted ratings.

The performance appraisal system is computerized and monitored by the director of human resources. Periodically, statistical analyses of performance data are conducted by the organization to assess how well the system is operating. Also, raters whose ratings appear particularly questionable are identified and, in some cases, given feedback about their ratings. This monitoring may increase the accuracy of ratings. Ilgen and Feldman (1983) argue that raters are more motivated to make accurate ratings when the organization has policies and procedures signaling that the organization considers performance appraisal to be important and that raters will be evaluated on the quality of their ratings.

Bonus and merit awards are made on criteria that are similar in some ways but different in others. As noted, both are influenced importantly by measured performance. Further, both are, in effect, given as percentage increments; for example, a $2,000 bonus or merit raise for a $60,000 per year executive is viewed by the company (although not necessarily by employees) as being similar to a $1,000 increment for a $30,000 base salary. The company reserves the right to vary bonus and merit goals across different plant and office locations.

On the other hand, company policy explicitly targets bonuses to particular employees in a way that the merit system does not. According to a top personnel executive and the personnel policy manual, bonuses are targeted to higher-level, higher-paid managers who are high performers. These executives have first claim on bonus dollars. Lower-paid managers who are high performers receive remaining amounts from the bonus pool. Further, maximum percentage bonuses are, by policy, higher for upper-level managers than for lower-level managers (up to 20 percent and up to 10 percent, respectively). Different employees thus operate under different bonus incentive structures.

In contrast to bonus awards, the merit system considers each person's salary in relation to the industry average for that job (based on a wage survey). Top performers are expected to be paid above this average, and average performers are expected to be paid at the middle of the range. One can, of course, "top out" either by receiving large merit increases (through high performance) or by achieving high seniority (with perhaps average to below-average performance); but the high performers are most likely to get promoted, and any increase in their base upon promotion is treated as a merit raise. To summarize, in contrast to the bonus system, the merit pay system follows no explicit policy of applying different ceilings (in terms of salary percentages) to awards available to high-level employees and those available to low-level employees with similar performance ratings.

Whereas the company's bonus and merit policies may be conducive to testing incentive-based theories of employment, the firm apparently does not use discharges or their threat as a motivating device. Specifically, the annual discharge rate for managers is about 0.5 percent.[15] We do not have information on the response of the individual's discharge probability to performance, but discussions with personnel management suggested that there was considerable job security. Thus, the variant of efficiency wage theory that relies on the threat of dismissal does not appear to operate for these managers. Finally, this group of managers has a very low quit rate—less than 0.5 percent per year—which, in conjunction with the low discharge rate, suggests the presence of a functioning internal labor market.[16]

Estimation Strategy

Our objective is to estimate the effects of

---

[15] This discharge rate is about one-tenth of the manufacturing average for the 1959–71 period (Medoff 1979).

[16] The monthly quit rate of 1.9 percent for manufacturing (1958–71) is thus about four times the annual quit rate among these managers (Medoff 1979).

pay levels and incentive pay on subsequent performance levels. In an "ideal" experiment for that purpose, two similar workers would be given different base salaries, bonus-performance schedules, or merit pay–performance schedules, and their performance would be observed. For example, we would expect the worker who perceives a relatively steep bonus- or merit-pay performance relationship to work harder, all else equal, than one who perceives a relatively small financial return to greater effort.

Similarly, given controls for opportunity wages, the discharge probability, and the impact of effort on the discharge probability, higher base salary should positively affect effort and thus future performance. In this case, a higher base salary raises the return to keeping one's job, and effort would increase as long as higher effort reduces the discharge probability. As noted, the extremely low discharge rate at the company we studied reduces the relevance for our purposes of the discharge-based efficiency wage model of Shapiro and Stiglitz (1984). On the other hand, models based on equity theory (Lawler 1968) might still imply a positive impact of pay level on subsequent performance (see our earlier discussion).

The data demands of this ideal experiment are severe. In a largely cross-sectional sample of managers from one company, one can test incentive-based theories of performance only if different employees perceive different rewards to higher effort levels. Further, even if reward schedules do vary across individuals, measures that capture the *perceived* differences in these schedules are needed. We believe that there are several types of situations in which individuals in the same company could perceive different reward schedules, and we propose a method for inferring such differences in perception. Specifically, we hypothesize that the explicit targeting of the firm's bonus system will produce these differences.

First, reward schedules may vary by location. Different plants have varying functions or use varying technologies that carry varying returns (productivity) to effort levels. To the extent that workers or company administrators perceive some costs to a performance-based reward system, different technologies could lead to different performance-reward schedules. Second, a given level of measured performance by a key worker may be valued more highly than the same level of measured performance by other workers. For example, many workers' outputs may depend on the efforts of one other worker in a position such as sales executive. Poor performance in such a job could have more serious consequences than poor performance in a lower-tier position such as sales representative. The company's policy of targeting bonuses is consistent with this consideration (see below).

To estimate the impact of performance-reward schedules on subsequent performance, we use a two-step procedure that our longitudinal data base allows us to implement. The first step is to use data on 1984 performance level and on subsequent bonus and merit pay to estimate the parameters of the reward schedules. Second, we use these estimated parameters and other information as right-hand variables in analyses of the determinants of 1985 performance levels.

To capture perceived differences in reward schedules, we estimate the following equations:

$$(1) \quad \text{DBON85} = a_0 + a_1\text{LPER84} + a_2\text{LOC} \\ + a_3\text{LBA84} + a_4\text{TEN} \\ + a_5\text{LPER84} \cdot \text{LOC} \\ + a_6\text{LPER84} \cdot \text{LBA84} \\ + a_7\text{LPER84} \cdot \text{TEN} + e_1$$

$$(2) \quad \text{DMER85} = b_0 + b_1\text{LPER84} + b_2\text{LOC} \\ + b_3\text{LBA84} + b_4\text{TEN} \\ + b_5\text{LPER84} \cdot \text{LOC} \\ + b_6\text{LPER84} \cdot \text{LBA84} \\ + b_7\text{LPER84} \cdot \text{TEN} + e_2,$$

where, for each manager, DBON85 = (1985 bonus in dollars)/(1984 base salary, annualized); DMER85 = (1985 merit pay in dollars, annualized)/(1984 base salary, annualized); LPER84 = log of 1984 measured performance level, as discussed above; LOC = 1 if the manager is located at company headquarters, 0 otherwise; LBA84

= log of annualized 1984 base salary; TEN = number of years of company service as of early 1986; and e_1 and e_2 are error terms.

Equations (1) and (2) allow the return to performance to vary across settings. First, the managers at corporate headquarters (LOC = 1) make decisions on the fate of the entire company. One might therefore expect the reward to higher performance to be particularly large at headquarters (and thus a_5 and b_5 to be positive). Second, we view LBA84 (log of 1984 base salary) as a measure of one's position in the organization. Presumably those with higher salaries are making decisions that affect more people than are those lower in the organization.[17] This consideration could explain the company's explicit targeting of bonus payments to high-level managers.

Third, equations (1) and (2) allow the effect of performance on reward to vary by seniority level. Senior workers' rewards may depend more on their accumulated performance records than on 1984 performance levels, compared to junior workers. This effect may be due to the higher levels of information the company has on more senior workers. Alternatively, the company may implicitly shield senior workers from the impact of changes in their performance levels.[18] Further, it should be noted that in (1) and (2) tenure may be a negative indicator of worker quality, since we control for salary level.

Finally, factors beyond a manager's control, such as exogenous financial events, may affect the size of his or her bonus or merit raise. If these events are uncorrelated with individual worker characteristics, individual performance, or location, however, then the events will not cause any bias in the estimated coefficients of (1) and (2).

Equations (1) and (2) allow the determinants of bonuses to have effects different from those of the determinants of merit pay, as our earlier discussion of the company pay setting suggested. The parameter estimates for (1) and (2) can be used as follows to proxy the pay-performance schedules facing an individual. For any person in our sample, we have:

$$(3) \quad \text{DERB} \equiv \frac{\partial(\text{DBON85})}{\partial \text{LPER84}} = a_1$$
$$+ a_5\text{LOC} + a_6\text{LBA84} + a_7\text{TEN}$$

$$(4) \quad \text{DERM} \equiv \frac{\partial(\text{DMER85})}{\partial \text{LPER84}} = b_1$$
$$+ b_5\text{LOC} + b_6\text{LBA84} + b_7\text{TEN}$$

These partial derivatives are computed and then used in the following equation for log 1985 performance level, the second step in our procedure:

$$(5) \quad \text{LPER85} = c_0 + c_1\text{DERB} + c_2\text{DERM}$$
$$+ c_3\text{LBA84} + c_4\text{MAR}$$
$$+ c_5\text{MALE} + c_6\text{PROMO}$$
$$+ c_7\text{LPER84} + e_5,$$

where LPER85 = log of 1985 measured performance level; MAR = 1 if respondent is married, 0 otherwise; MALE = 1 if respondent is male, 0 otherwise; PROMO = 1 if respondent had changed jobs within the firm in the previous year, 0 otherwise; and e_5 is an error term.

In equation (5), MAR and MALE serve as control variables. Recent job change (PROMO) is included to control for the possibility that performance in the first year on a new job differs from later performance. These three variables may also be related to opportunity wages, which, according to efficiency wage theories, influence a worker's effort level by affecting the value of keeping his or her job. As noted, DERB and DERM are the slopes of the bonus- and merit-pay performance relationship and should positively affect future performance. Since performance is measured in December, these variables precede LPER85. The LBA84 coef-

---

[17] We were able to obtain information on each manager's 1986 "grade level," a measure of his or her position in the hierarchy. This measure is really an *outcome* of the performance-reward process, however, not an explanatory variable. Lacking data on 1984 grade level, we use (log) 1984 base salary as a reasonable proxy for one's position in the company.
[18] See Medoff and Abraham (1980) for a discussion of the issue of seniority, performance, and reward.

ficient in principle measures the impact of pay level, net of the effect of pay level on DERB and DERM.[19]

Finally, inclusion of previous performance level (LPER84) helps alleviate problems of omitted variables (for example, unmeasured ability) that might affect performance and pay. Suppose, for instance, that jobs with a relatively steep bonus-performance relationship (that is, a high DERB) are attractive to high performers but that DERB does not actually affect their effort levels once they are employed.[20] One might then observe over time a positive correlation between DERB and performance levels even if bonuses have no incentive effects. By controlling for the worker's past performance level, we can be more confident than otherwise that actual incentive effects are being observed. Further, inclusion of LPER84 also in effect alleviates possible inter-rater reliability problems, to the extent that each manager is rated twice by the same supervisor.

Before presenting the results for equations (1), (2), and (5), we discuss several qualifications to the analysis and alternative formulations. First, these equations assume a particular functional form for the bonus, merit, and performance variables. We discuss additional results based on alternative functional forms: in particular, we use unlogged performance level as well as absolute dollar measures for bonus and merit pay. Recall that the personnel policy manual and discussions with company management suggest that DBON85 and DMER85 are the appropriate functional forms.

Second, (5) is a kind of structural equation in which some of the variables that theoretically affect performance are estimated from first-stage regressions (equations 1 and 2). We also present reduced-form estimates in which LPER85 is estimated as a function of previous pay variables (DBON85, DMER85,

and LBA84) as well as all of the other variables in the system. In particular, such an analysis asks whether, for example, two workers with the same 1984 performance levels but different subsequent bonus payments performed differently in 1985, all else equal. Although it is not as precise as the structural equations, the reduced-form approach provides an additional check on the basic findings.[21]

Third, equation (5) uses the point estimates of the derivatives of bonus and merit pay with respect to performance. These coefficients capture systematic effects of performance on pay, and ordinary least squares (OLS) in the second stage regressions will produce consistent estimates of equation (5), if the first stage estimates are consistent.[22] The asymptotic standard errors for equation (5) must, however, include a correction for the fact that the equation contains estimated regressors (DERB and DERM). We use a technique devised by Murphy and Topel (1985) to compute asymptotic standard errors for the second stage regressions.

Finally, the merit raises and bonuses combine the effect of progression within a job and any promotion raises or bonuses for those promoted in 1985 (see our earlier discussion). Thus, in principle, the DERB($\frac{\partial DBON85}{\partial LPER84}$) and DERM ($\frac{\partial DMER85}{\partial LPER84}$) variables capture the sums of the effects of performance on promotion raises and bonuses and within-job raises in salary and bonus payments. It would be interesting to break down the incentive effects into within- and across-job components; but our sample size of 92 does not permit the

[19] We use 1984 base salary because 1985 base salary includes the 1985 merit raise.

[20] Lazear (1986) makes a similar argument regarding the impact of piece rates: high-quality workers are more attracted to workplaces that reward individual output than are workers of less ability, other things equal.

[21] Both the structural and reduced-form estimates may suffer from an omitted variable bias to the extent that unmeasured factors (such as an improvement in the relationship between the manager and the manager's supervisor between 1984 and 1985) affect performance and subsequent pay or pay and subsequent performance. On the other hand, since in the LPER85 regressions we control for LPER84, the existence of long-term favoritism (a kind of fixed effect) cannot explain our findings for the pay effects. Unfortunately, lack of suitable instruments prevents any further analysis of such omitted variable problems.

[22] See note 21.

Table 1. Means and Standard Deviations.

Variable	Mean	Standard Deviation
MAR	.9239	.2666
MALE	.9674	.1786
PROMO	.3044	.4627
TENURE	17.208	9.902
LOC	.1848	.3903
BASE84	$43,174	$8,011
MERIT85	$4,418	$2,737
BONUS85	$4,851	$2,852
PERF84	4.4565	0.9483
PERF85	4.5870	0.7472

use of the switching regression technique needed to perform such a breakdown.[23]

Results

Table 1 contains means and standard deviations for the variables in our model. The sample largely comprises married men. The average current tenure is about 17 years. Base salary in 1984 was about $43,000; bonus income was about 10.6 percent of base, merit pay about 10.4 percent. These latter figures are consistent with overall U.S. data. Specifically, in 1982, among U.S. manufacturing firms with merit plans, the median merit increase was 8.7 percent of salary (for all workers covered); and among lower and middle managers in manufacturing firms with bonus plans, awards in 1982 averaged 10–20 percent of salary.[24]

Table 2 contains results from the first stage estimates.[25] The table indicates con-

siderably more systematic variations in the effect of performance on bonus than in the effect of performance on merit raises. Turning first to the effect of performance on bonuses, the table shows significantly higher returns to performance (all else equal) for those located at headquarters and for junior employees; further, all else equal, the effect of performance on bonuses is higher for high-paid than for low-paid managers, and this impact is significantly different from zero at the 10.5 percent level in a two-tailed test. (The interaction variables as a group are significant at better than the 5 percent level.)

The results suggest that the company particularly values high performance levels of those at company headquarters and those high up in the organization. As discussed above, those managers have greater influence on the output of other workers than do lower-level managers or managers at locations other than headquarters. The positive LBA84-LPER84 interaction

Table 2. First Stage Regression Results for the Determinants of Bonus and Merit Raises. (Standard Errors in Parentheses)

Explanatory Variable	Dependent Variable	
	DBON85	DMER85
CONSTANT	3.7367 (3.4629)	4.7309 (8.3977)
LPER84	−1.4582 (.9123)	−1.0154 (2.2125)
LOC	−.1698* (.0946)	.1665 (.2294)
LBA84	−.3478 (.3260)	−.4618 (.7906)
TEN	.0101** (.0051)	.00028 (.0012)
LPER84·LOC	.0464* (.0251)	−.0500 (.0610)
LPER84·LBA84	.1388 (.0858)	.1032 (.2081)
LPER84·TEN	−.0027** (.0013)	−.0011 (.0033)
R²	.6100	.1306
SAMPLE SIZE	92	92

Note: Performance has been multiplied by 10 for convenience.

* Significantly different from zero at the 10 percent level; ** significantly different from zero at the 5 percent level (two-tailed tests).

---

[23] We should point out that despite the company's efforts (described earlier), there may still be unsystematic differences in performance ratings across workers caused by reliability and validity problems. Such differences in LPER85 are reflected in the error term of equation (5) and do not bias the coefficients in that regression. To the extent that LPER84 also contains measurement errors, however, the derivatives from equations (3) and (4) may be biased. As long as measurement errors for LPER85 are uncorrelated with DBON85 and DMER85, the reduced-form type estimates are not biased by such errors.

[24] See Peck (1984:15–17). Neither the bonus figures cited by Peck nor those we use include stock options.

[25] Results for other functional forms were similar and are available upon request. All performance variables were multiplied by 10 in the regressions, so they vary from 20 to 60.

effect directly reflects company policy on bonuses (see above). The negative tenure-performance interaction may reflect the company's reasoning that one year's performance rating adds less information to a senior manager's personnel file than it does to a junior manager's.[26]

To illustrate the impact of performance on bonuses in different settings, consider a $60,000 manager with 10 years' seniority who works at corporate headquarters. This manager is a high-paid executive on the "fast track" at the company (seniority is below the average of 17 years) who works in a key location. For such a manager, the derivative of DBON85 with respect to LPER84 is .0880. This point estimate implies that for this fast-track manager, a fall-off in performance from 5 to 3 on the 6-point scale (measured as 50 to 30 in our regressions) means a fall in bonus by about 4.5 percentage points of salary, or about $2,700. The predicted bonus for this executive with a performance level of 5 is 18.6 percent, so this fall by 2 points on the performance scale reduces the bonus by about 24 percent.

$$\overset{***}{\underset{(.0391)}{}}$$

In contrast to a high-paid executive at corporate headquarters, a high-paid manager at other locations faces a lower return to performance. For the $60,000 manager with 10 years' tenure who is located outside headquarters, $\partial DBON85/\partial LPER84 =$ .0416 (.0256), about half of the effect for one at headquarters.[27] Finally, the impact of performance on bonus for a manager with the average salary level and 10 years' seniority working outside corporate headquarters is $\partial DBON85/\partial LPER84 = -$ (.0104)— $\overset{.00004}{}$ virtually no effect at all. Thus, with regard to bonus payments, different managers face different incentive structures at the company. We exploit this cross-sectional variation in incentives in the second stage estimates.

Whereas different employees apparently are subject to significantly different bonus incentives, there is little evidence that they face significantly different merit incentives. The LPER84 interaction terms are insignificant individually and as a group.[28] Further, the point estimates of the interaction terms in the DMER85 equation are generally smaller than those for the DBON85 equation. The standard deviation of DERM ($\partial MER85/\partial LPER84$) is about 2.9 percentage points, whereas the figure for DERB ($\partial DBON85/\partial LPER84$) is 3.6 percentage points, again illustrating the smaller magnitude of variations in merit rewards to performance. Evidently the merit system at the company gives more similar rewards to performance across workers than does the bonus system. Our discussions with company management (above) are consistent with this finding.

Table 3 presents structural and reduced-form estimates of the impact of pay incentives on managerial performance. The major findings are for DERB and DBON85. The structural equation results show that an increase in DERB raises performance, all else equal; further, this effect is significant at the 5.6 percent level (LPER84 excluded) or 11.9 percent level (LPER84 included) in two-tailed tests. A one standard deviation increase in DERB raises log performance by .36 to .42 standard deviations, *ceteris paribus*. The reduced-form estimates show similar effects for bonuses: the coefficients for DBON85 in Table 3 are positive and highly significant. A one standard deviation increase in DBON85 raises performance by .40 to .42 standard deviations.

The results for DERB and DBON85 suggest that variations in the company's bonus policy do produce differences in subsequent performance levels. Inclusion of LPER84 (previous performance level)

---

[26] As noted, TEN may also be a negative indicator of quality, since salary is controlled for. This interpretation is questionable, however, at least at low performance levels. For example, at the minimum performance level (20 out of a possible 60), the effect of TEN on DBON is positive and insignificant.

[27] This effect is significant at the 10.4 percent level in a two-tailed test.

[28] When the DBON85 and DMER85 equations were run without interaction terms, the LPER84 coefficients were $-$ .0134 for DBON85 and .0461 for DMER85.
$\quad\quad\quad\quad$ (.0308) $\quad\quad\quad\quad\quad\quad$ (.0308)

Table 3. Second Stage and Reduced Form Results for the Determinants of Log 1985
Performance Level.
(Asymptotic Standard Errors in Parentheses)

Explanatory Variable	Coefficients			
CONSTANT	4.9836	4.5628	5.1849***	5.7527***
	(3.1114)	(3.2703)	(1.4939)	(1.4440)
DERB	2.0231*	1.7075	—	—
	(1.0583)	(1.0954)		
DERM	−.4371	−.7193	—	—
	(1.3376)	(1.3921)		
LBA84	−.1032	−.1419	−.1462	−.2807*
	(.2958)	(.3107)	(.1454)	(.1467)
MAR	−.0309	−.0365	−.0170	−.0226
	(.0671)	(.0647)	(.0648)	(.0621)
MALE	.0214	.0369	.0197	.0232
	(.1034)	(.0998)	(.1038)	(.0994)
PROMO	−.0093	−.0295	.0020	−.0155
	(.0387)	(.0380)	(.0382)	(.0371)
LPER84	—	.2225***	—	.2263***
		(.0802)		(.0777)
TEN	—	—	−.0041**	−.0030*
			(.0018)	(.0018)
LOC	—	—	.1164***	.1138***
			(.0440)	(.0421)
DBON85	—	—	1.7359***	1.8448***
			(.6561)	(.6252)
DMER85	—	—	.4268	.3230
			(.2824)	(.2728)
R^2	.1437	.2156	.2249	.2976

implies that these bonus results do *not* merely reflect the placement of high performers in locations with high values of DERB or DBON85. The bonus system appears to have a behavioral impact.[29]

---

[29] Since MBO may be part performance appraisal and part motivational technique, it is possible that our results for DERB do not reflect financial incentives. Instead, the variable may be related to the intrinsic satisfaction of achieving one's goals. That is, jobs with a high sensitivity of bonus pay to performance (DERB) may also happen to be jobs in which goal achievement (and therefore intrinsic satisfaction) is highly sensitive to effort. Although our results strongly suggest that financial incentives have an important impact, we cannot rule out this alternative explanation.

On the other hand, if our results reflect only the effects of intrinsic satisfaction and not the effects of financial incentives, one must question why the company went to the trouble of designing different bonus arrangements for different workers. Our earlier speculation that the company weighs the costs

In contrast to the bonus results, Table 3 does not provide evidence that merit pay influences performance. The coefficients for DERM are small, negative, and only .33 to .52 times as large as their asymptotic standard errors in absolute value. The reduced-form DMER85 coefficients, although positive, are small and are 1.18 to 1.51 times their standard errors. It is still possible that the merit system affects performance; but the merit rewards to performance at this company may vary too little to provide a good test of the impact of merit systems.

The remaining major set of findings concerns the impact of LBA84, which is small, negative, and equal to less than half

---

of designing such a system against its benefits (enhanced performance) provides one possible answer to this question.

its asymptotic standard error in the structural estimates in Table 3; in the reduced form, its coefficient is larger and in one case is significant.[30] Recall that the structural estimates for LBA84 indicate the direct impact of base, whereas the reduced-form estimates combine this effect and the indirect effects of LBA84 on DERB and DERM. In any case, equity theories that emphasize base salary are not supported here, although the results for bonus levels are consistent with equity theory. Note that even if high pay levels do not lead to high effort levels, they could still benefit the firm if they cause low turnover (Krueger and Summers 1988).

Conclusions

We have used data on managers from one company to examine the relationship between incentives and performance. Our study uses a performance measure that, like virtually any indicator of performance, may well be subject to problems of reliability and validity. As we noted, however, our use of longitudinal data on managers and the company's emphasis on monitoring its performance appraisal system and training of supervisors to some degree alleviate these problems.

The study's basic findings are two-fold. First, the *bonus* system in this company appears to be directed toward a select group of high-performance managers: a high bonus premium for high performance levels is given to those who work at corporate headquarters in high-level positions and have low seniority. In contrast, there is little evidence that the *merit* pay

premium for high performance varies across managerial levels, plant locations, or seniority levels.

Second, differences across workers in the impact they expect their performance to have on bonus payments lead to differences in subsequent performance levels. Specifically, managers for whom the impact of performance on bonus is high have higher future performance levels than other managers, even controlling for past performance levels. Again, there is no apparent corresponding effect in the case of merit pay: we find the relationship between the impact of performance on merit pay and future performance to be small and insignificant.

Our findings for managers whose performance has a large effect on their bonus payment are supportive of expectancy theory. We cannot say what these managers perceive; but the pattern of our results suggests that high-wage, low-seniority managers at corporate headquarters can anticipate that their performance will have a large impact on the bonus the company chooses to pay them. Further, this aspect of the reward system appears to motivate future performance levels, as suggested by expectancy theory (Lawler 1973).

It thus appears that this company is using its bonus system to provide particularly strong incentives for those managers whose good performance is most crucial to the performance of the company. For some workers, bonuses may be viewed as almost an entitlement, independent of a wide range of performance levels. Less than excellent performance levels among such workers may be tolerated by the company. The benefits of raising performance may not be worth the perceived costs of tying bonuses to performance for these workers. For other workers, however, bonuses are benefits that can be lost if performance is inadequate. In these cases the company may be unwilling to tolerate poor performance, and a steep relationship between bonus payments and performance can play a role similar to that of the threat of discharge in companies that do not protect their workers' jobs. Our findings for the determinants of 1985 performance suggest that this system of differential targeting has its desired effect on performance.

---

[30] From Table 3, a one standard deviation increase in LBA84 lowers performance by .107 to .147 standard deviation (structural model) or raises it by .151 to .290 standard deviation (reduced form). Several of the pay variables in Table 3 are correlated with each other. For example, DBON85 and DMER85 have a simple correlation of −.19, whereas the correlations of DBON85 and DMER85 and LBA84 are .74 and −.15, respectively. DERB, DERM, and LBA84 are, of course, correlated by construction. More efficient tests of incentive effects could be made using experimental data in which the explanatory variables (treatments) have been orthogonalized.

REFERENCES

Adams, J. S. 1965. "Injustice in Social Exchange." In Leonard Berkowitz, ed., *Advances in Experimental Social Psychology,* Vol. 2. New York: Academic Press, pp. 267–99.

Bernardin, H. John, and M. Ronald Buckley. 1981. "Strategies in Rater Training." *Academy of Management Review,* Vol. 6, No. 2 (April), pp. 205–12.

Bhagat, S., J. Brickley, and R. Lease. 1985. "Incentive Effects of Employee Stock Purchase Plans." *Journal of Financial Economics,* Vol. 14, No. 2 (January), pp. 195–216.

Bowles, S. 1985. "The Production Process in a Competitive Economy: Walrasian, Neo-Hobbesian, and Marxian Models." *American Economic Review,* Vol. 75, No. 1 (March), pp. 16–36.

Brickley, J., S. Bhagat, and R. Lease. 1985. "The Impact of Long-Run Managerial Compensation Plans on Shareholder Wealth." *Journal of Accounting and Economics,* Vol. 7, No. 1 (April), pp. 115–29.

Brown, C. 1988. "Firms' Choice of Method of Pay." Mimeo, University of Michigan.

Bulow, J., and L. Summers. 1986. "A Theory of Dual Labor Markets with Applications to Industrial Policy, Discrimination and Keynesian Unemployment." *Journal of Labor Economics,* Vol. 4, No. 3 (July), pp. 376–414.

Bureau of National Affairs. 1981. "Wage and Salary Administration." PPF Survey No. 131. Washington, D.C.: BNA.

————. 1984. "Productivity Improvement Programs." PPF Survey 138. Washington, D.C.: BNA.

Ehrenberg, R., and G. Milkovich. 1987. "Compensation and Firm Performance." In M. Kleiner, R. Block, M. Roomkin, and S. Salsburg, eds., *Human Resources and the Performance of the Firm.* Madison, Wis.: Industrial Relations Research Association, pp. 87–122.

Hashimoto, M. 1979. "Bonus Payments, On-the-Job Training, and Lifetime Employment in Japan." *Journal of Political Economy,* Vol. 87, No. 5 (October), pp. 1086–1104.

Heneman, H. G. III, D. P. Schwab, J. Fossum, and L. Dyer. 1986. *Personnel/Human Resource Management.* Homewood, Ill.: Irwin.

Ilgen, Daniel R., and Jack Feldman. 1983. "Performance Appraisal: A Process Focus." In Barry M. Staw and Larry L. Cummings, eds., *Research in Organizational Behavior,* Vol. 5. Greenwich, Conn.: JAI Press, pp. 141–97.

Krueger, A., and L. Summers. 1988. "Efficiency Wages and the Inter-Industry Wage Structure." *Econometrica,* Vol. 56, No. 2 (March), pp. 259–93.

Lawler, E. 1968. "Equity Theory as a Predictor of Productivity and Work Quality." *Psychological Bulletin,* Vol. 70., No. 6 (December), pp. 596–610.

————. 1973. *Motivation in Work Organizations.* Belmont, Calif.: Wadsworth.

————. 1981. *Pay and Organizational Development.* Reading, Mass.: Addison-Wesley.

Lazear, E. 1979. "Why Is There Mandatory Retirement?" *Journal of Political Economy,* Vol. 87, No. 6 (December), pp. 1261–84.

————. 1981. "Agency, Earnings Profiles, Productivity, and Hours Restrictions." *American Economic Review,* Vol. 71, No. 4 (September), pp. 606–20.

————. 1986. "Salaries and Piece Rates." *Journal of Business,* Vol. 59, No. 3 (July), pp. 405–31.

Locke, E. A., et al. 1980. "The Relative Effectiveness of Four Methods of Motivating Employee Performance." In K. D. Duncan, M. M. Gruneberg, and D. Wallis, eds., *Changes in Working Life.* New York: John Wiley & Sons, pp. 383–88.

Medoff, J. 1979. "Layoffs and Alternatives Under Trade Unions in U.S. Manufacturing." *American Economic Review,* Vol. 69, No. 3 (June), pp. 380–95.

Medoff, J., and K. Abraham. 1980. "Experience, Performance, and Earnings." *Quarterly Journal of Economics,* Vol. 95, No. 4 (December), pp. 703–36.

Milkovich, G., and J. Newman. 1987. *Compensation,* 2nd ed. Plano, Tex.: Business Publications.

Murphy, K. M., and R. H. Topel. 1985. "Estimation and Inference in Two-Step Econometric Models." *Journal of Business and Economic Statistics,* Vol. 3, No. 4 (October), pp. 370–79.

Pearce, J. L., W. B. Stevenson, and J. L. Perry. 1985. "Managerial Compensation Based on Organizational Performance: A Time-Series Analysis of the Effects of Merit Pay." *Academy of Management Journal,* Vol. 28, No. 2 (June), pp. 261–78.

Peck, C. 1984. *Pay and Performance: The Interaction of Compensation and Performance Appraisal,* Research Bulletin No. 155. New York: The Conference Board.

————. 1986. *Top Executive Compensation: 1987 Edition,* Conference Board Report No. 889. New York: The Conference Board.

Rabin, B. 1988. "Executive Compensation and Firm Performance: An Empirical Analysis." In *Proceedings of the Fortieth Annual Meeting.* Madison, Wis.: Industrial Relations Research Association, pp. 323–31.

Schwab, D. P. 1980. "Construct Validity in Organizational Research." In Larry L. Cummings and Barry M. Staw, eds., *Research in Organizational Behavior,* Vol. 2. Greenwich, Conn.: JAI Press, pp. 3–43.

Schwab, D. P., and C. A. Olson. 1988. "Pay-Performance Relationships as a Function of Pay for Performance Policies and Practices." *Academy of Management Best Paper Proceedings,* pp. 287–91.

Shapiro, C., and J. Stiglitz. 1984. "Equilibrium Unemployment as a Worker Discipline Device." *American Economic Review,* Vol. 74, No. 3 (June), pp. 433–44.

Tehranian, H., and J. Waegelein. 1985. "Market Reaction to Short-Term Executive Compensation Plan Adoption." *Journal of Accounting and Economics,* Vol. 7, No. 1 (April), pp. 131–44.

SHIRKING OR PRODUCTIVE SCHMOOZING: WAGES AND THE ALLOCATION OF TIME AT WORK

DANIEL S. HAMERMESH*

This study uses detailed time diaries from household surveys for 1975 and 1981 to examine how changes in the use of time on the job affect earnings. Among nonunion workers, the marginal minute of break time apparently increases earnings, but not as much as does the marginal minute of work time. Among union workers, additional time in unscheduled breaks appears to be associated with significantly higher earnings, though other break time is not. The author concludes that further growth in on-the-job leisure would reduce productivity, that monitoring workers would yield returns to the firm, but that entirely eliminating breaks would be counterproductive.

Since World War II there has been a rapid increase in two types of leisure that may affect workers' productivity. The first of these is the well-known increase in paid time off from work—vacations, holidays, and sick days. Surveys by the U.S. Chamber of Commerce suggest that in larger manufacturing firms this type of payment for not working increased from 5.4 percent of total payroll cost in 1953 to 10.2 percent in 1986. (Comparable figures for paid holidays and sick time alone are 2.1 and 4.4 percent.) The less well-known increase is the rise in time spent at work but not working. In the same surveys, this source of paid on-the-job leisure increased from 2.1 to 3.3 percent of payroll costs. (U.S. Chamber of Commerce 1953, 1987.)

In an earlier study (Hamermesh 1986) I analyzed workers' demand for mixing work with leisure on the job and paid leisure off the job. No one, however, has examined how on-the-job leisure affects production or the demand side of the labor market.[1] Time spent on the job relaxing (loafing?) can increase workers' productivity by enabling them to rest when they are physically or mentally fatigued. The magnitude of this productivity-enhancing effect has implications for issues of interest to labor economists and economists generally. The simplest of those issues is how the structure of pay differs along the dimension of the alloca-

* Daniel Hamermesh is Professor of Economics, Michigan State University, and Research Associate, National Bureau of Economic Research. The author thanks the Alfred P. Sloan Foundation for research support, Neil Bjorksten for excellent research assistance, and Seung Chang Ahn, Jeff Biddle, Harry Holzer, John Owen, and participants at a seminar at the National Bureau for helpful comments. The suggestions of Henry Farber were especially useful.

A diskette containing the files used in this study, written in ASCII and easily usable in MICRO TSP, is available on request from the author at the Department of Economics, Michigan State University, East Lansing, MI 48824-1038.

[1] Hersch (1985) did include data on the *number* of work breaks in an equation describing the hourly earnings of a small group of piece-rate workers in one plant.

tion of time at work. That is, do we observe pay differences that are related to the amount of time workers spend on scheduled and unscheduled breaks?

Less straightforward, but also important, is the question of how alternative uses of time on the job affect predictions about the impact of various labor market policies. Legislated reductions in the standard workweek will affect the relative demand for workers and hours differently depending on the productivity of slack time (see Hart 1987:53). The more productive slack time is, the smaller is the margin available to employers for increasing the efficiency of hours paid for in response to an imposed change in standard hours. Increases in wage rates, be they legislated or bargained, are more costly to employers, and will have a greater disemployment effect, the lower the productivity of time on the job. Understanding the effects of on-the-job leisure on productivity informs us about the structure of the demand for workers and thus about the possible impact of such policies as overtime pay requirements, payroll taxes, and minimum wages.

Of particular recent interest to macro-economists and labor economists has been the role of shirking on the job and the incentives it gives employers to institute monitoring schemes. This question also bears, though less directly, on the issue of efficiency wages. Yet, in the burgeoning literature concerned with the hypothesis that wage differentials affect worker productivity, the evidence supporting the hypothesis is the documentation of wage differentials unexplained by conventional human capital, demographic, and other variables (Krueger and Summers 1988). The hypothesis is based on how time is used in the workplace; but no evidence on time use is provided.

This is the first comprehensive study to relate time use to wages. As such, it tries to answer whether on-the-job leisure represents unproductive shirking or productive

schmoozing—socializing with workmates that adds to productivity (see Schrank 1978).[2]

Background and Theory

As far back as Florence (1924), industrial engineers have charted the paths of output, spoilage, and other indicators of physical productivity as functions of the length of time the employee has been producing during the day. The evidence suggests that accident rates and work spoilage are lowest after breaks and at the start of a shift, and that output is highest at those times. A huge literature in industrial psychology has examined the effects of rest periods on the job on fatigue, boredom, and other counterproductive reactions. (See McCormick and Ilgen 1985 for a summary.) Among workers engaged in physical tasks there is clear physiological evidence of reductions in work capacity occurring at lower levels of rest and break time. Among workers in sedentary jobs no such physiological evidence exists. Those workers do, however, report feelings of fatigue when deprived of rest periods, and the literature indicates that rest periods provide psychological benefits that may enhance the well-being of these workers and hence their productivity.

This evidence is clearly important; but its implications for labor-market outcomes are not entirely clear. What is required is some consideration of how time use on the job affects the rewards—higher wages— that are the returns to productive uses of time on the job. Unless worker productivity is independent of the way time is used on the job, the phenomena must be modeled as being jointly determined by workers and employers. Throughout the discussion I assume that the wage paid reflects the worker's productivity. This assumption underlies a large part of the huge body of empirical work in modern labor economics, and is based on neoclassical theory. It allows me to make the

---

[2] The Yiddish word *schmooze* has by now clearly entered the American vernacular. (See, for example, *Newsweek*, April 24, 1989, p. 60.)

transition from the relationship between wages and time use on the job to that between productivity and time use.

Consider a simple model of the choice of hours of productive work and wages in a world of homogeneous workers and a firm typical of those in which leisure on the job is possible. The question of interest is the effect of an increase in the productivity of on-the-job leisure on the equilibrium values of wages and hours of productive work. One can easily show in an implicit-contract framework that an increase in the productivity of leisure at work lowers both the wage rate and hours of productive work, given a fixed total time spent on the job. Essentially, the increase encourages the firm to substitute toward on-the-job leisure and against normal work time, and the firm can still attract employees at a lower wage rate because workers are willing to make this trade-off.

In reality, workers will sort themselves among employers depending on their tastes for leisure on the job and the employers' ability to provide it. In an economy with heterogeneous firms and workers, let the ith firm's production technology be:

$$(1) \qquad Y_i = Y_i(H_{wi}, b_i[H^* - H_{wi}]),$$

where H_{wi} is normal (non-break) hours per worker, $b_i \leq 1$ is a parameter indicating the productivity of on-the-job leisure, and H^* is the fixed number of hours paid for in the firm. I assume that $Y_{i1}(x, x) > Y_{i2}(x, x) \geq 0$, that is, that the marginal minute of work is uniformly more productive than the same marginal minute of on-the-job leisure. Each firm has a different production technology, Y_i, and thus a differing ability to provide leisure at work. The product price is normalized at one, and I assume that the firm has already determined employment.

Workers j maximize utility defined over the probability of keeping the job in firm i:

$$(2) \qquad U_j = U_j(W_iH^*, H^* - H_{wi}) \\ \geq U_j(I^*, 0),$$

where I^* is the earnings available to the

worker in a job where no on-the-job leisure is possible. I ignore the worker's choice of how many hours to supply to the market, H^*, though the empirical work does address that issue.

Each firm maximizes profits subject to the competitively determined market locus shown in Figure 1 in W–H_w/H^* space. The firm's isoprofit curves slope upward because it can offer a higher wage rate if it can induce its workers to spend more time in normal work. Workers' indifference curves slope upward because they must receive a higher wage rate if they forgo more on-the-job leisure. As a result of both sets of behavior, WW, the market locus of equilibrium combinations ($\widetilde{W}$, $\widetilde{H}_w/H^*$), also slopes upward. With a fixed H^* this means that the locus of equilibrium combinations of wages and on-the-job leisure, $\widetilde{W}$ and $\widetilde{H}_l/H^*$, slopes downward.

Consider what happens if b_i rises in each firm, while workers' preferences for spending time in on-the-job leisure rather than work remain unchanged. Because on-the-job leisure is now more productive, competition among firms for workers forces employers to raise the wage at each level of H_{wi} less than H^*. The competitive pressures are especially increased among firms that had already chosen a low $\widetilde{H}_{wi}$ (and a high $\widetilde{H}_{li}$), for the productivity gains are greatest in those firms. (In the extreme case, at a firm in which $\widetilde{H}_{wi} = H^*$, a small increase in b_i will not change the firm's choices of $\widetilde{W}_i$ and $\widetilde{H}_{wi}$.) The market locus in Figure 1 thus rises and rotates clockwise, becoming $W'W'$, when on-the-job leisure becomes more productive. Obversely, the negatively sloped locus of equilibrium combinations of $\widetilde{W}$ and $\widetilde{H}_l/H^*$ becomes flatter also.

This observation on the possible effects of productive on-the-job leisure in an implicit market with heterogeneous workers and firms leads to a specific prediction: the more productive on-the-job leisure is, the flatter will be the market locus relating the wage rate to hours actually worked, *holding total hours on the job constant.* It implies that the market locus relating wage rates and on-the-job leisure will also

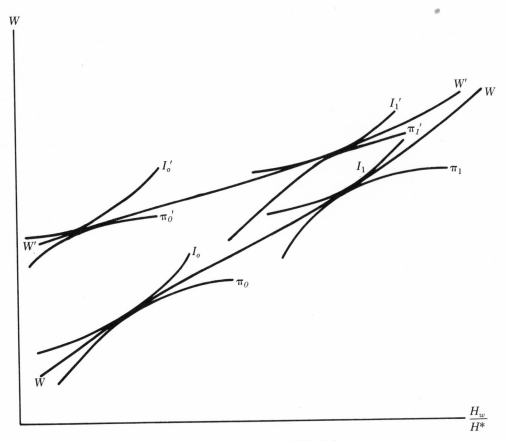

Figure 1. The Wage–Actual Work Locus.

be flatter, other things (*including total hours*) equal, the more productive is on-the-job leisure.

Estimating Equations

The model to be estimated is very similar to the reduced form implicit in the equilibrium locus in Figure 1:

$$(3) \quad W = \{\alpha_w + \Sigma[\gamma_j - 1]\alpha_j\}\exp(X\beta),$$

where $\alpha_w = \tilde{H}_w/H^*$, the α_j are the fractions of time on the job spent in each activity other than regular production. The γ_j are parameters, X is a vector of control variables, and β is a vector of parameters. Another version of (3) aggregates and replaces the $\Sigma[\gamma_j - 1]\alpha_j$ by $[\gamma - 1]\alpha_l$. Taking logarithms in (3) yields the approximation:

$$(4) \quad \log W = \Sigma[\gamma_j - 1]\alpha_j + X\beta.$$

The parameters γ_j measure the productivity of time in the particular activity relative to regular production time. Presumably $1 \geq \gamma_j$ for each activity: time devoted to on-the-job leisure is no more productive than regular work time.

If on-the-job leisure is assumed to be as productive as time spent working (is identical to it from the employer's standpoint), demand forces alone would equate the γ_j to one. If, as I assumed above, marginal workers find on-the-job leisure more attractive than normal working time, we will observe $\gamma_j < 1$ even if on-the-job leisure is as productive as regular work time. In that case, employers will be able to pay otherwise identical workers less if they offer an employment package that includes substantial leisure at work.

This discussion illustrates the difficulty of drawing inferences about the relative productivity of alternative uses of time on the job. We simply cannot be sure that any shortfalls of the γ_j from one that we observe are attributable to differences in productivity rather than to differences induced by workers sorting themselves into various jobs according to their relative tastes for time spent working and on-the-job leisure. Clearly, if we found $\gamma_j \ll 1$ we could interpret that result as reflecting the different relative productivity of the two activities, different relative tastes for the two activities, or some combination of both. Conversely, if we find $\gamma_j \gg 1$, we could be fairly sure that the activity is as productive as regular work, since supply forces tend to reduce the observed γ_j below one. In interpreting the results, I shall ignore the problems this difficulty may produce and interpret the effects as purely demand-induced. I leave it to the reader to decide how large are the potential biases that this assumption imparts to the conclusions about the relative productivity of the alternative uses of time.

Data

The following empirical examination of time use on the job uses data from the 1975–76 Time Use Study (Juster et al. 1979) and from the 1975–81 Time Use Panel Study (Juster et al. 1983). These data sets apparently have not been used much by economists outside the group that collected the data; and only one study, Stafford and Duncan (1980b), used them to examine time use on the job. The sample used in that study is quite similar to the one I create from the 1975–76 Time Use Study, but Stafford and Duncan did not analyze the relation between wages and alternative uses of time on the job.

The 1975–76 Time Use Study obtained data from four days of time diaries kept by members of 1,519 households. The days were at three-month intervals, with two being weekdays, one a Saturday, and the fourth a Sunday. The data on time use are combined into "synthetic weeks," and I

use these to estimate (4). The 1975–81 Time Use Panel Study data were collected similarly, with follow-up diaries kept for four days (again, at three-month intervals) in 1981 by 620 of the households that were included in the 1975–76 survey.

In the 1975–76 diaries workers could categorize time on the job as normal work; work at a second job; lunch at work; coffee breaks; and other breaks (before regular work, after regular work, and at other times during work). In the 1981 follow-up survey, information on work for pay done at home was also collected, and separate totals were reported for the three components of "other breaks." Reporting of break time does not merely include scheduled on-the-job leisure, but instead is designed to reflect all time on the job not spent working. Because of this survey feature, and because time use is reported by the worker, the data on time use should include much of what economists could regard as time spent "shirking" (that is, engaging in unproductive activities at work). The less structured category, "other breaks," is especially likely to yield such information. Any positive effects on wages of switching time from normal work to other breaks would be an especially strong indication that on-the-job leisure is productive.

The data on household heads in the surveys formed the basis for the analysis. Only those who responded that their weekly work hours on the main job were at least 20 during each of the four interview waves in 1975–76 and whose actual normal work time (in the time diaries) exceeded 15 hours on that job in the synthetic week were included in the extract. Also, in order to ensure that the data describe the same workplace, only workers who kept the same employer throughout the interview year were included. These disqualifiers account for most of the reductions in the number of data points, with the remaining reductions due to the exclusion of household heads for whom substantial amounts (at least one full day out of the four) of time-use information were missing, or for whom data on one of the X variables were not reported. When these exclusions were made, data on 343 persons surveyed in the 1975–76 Time Use Study remained.[3] Of these, 311 were employees, and 276 were employees whose only earnings were wages or salaries. The statistics and estimates are reported for those two groups as well as for the larger subsample of 343.

These same 343 people formed the basis of the subsample from the Panel Study. When the same exclusions were made—of individuals who changed employers during 1981 (though the employer in 1981 could differ from that in 1975–76); of those who stated that they worked less than 20 hours per week in 1980 when working, or for whom the time diaries showed less than 15 hours of normal work time; and of those for whom data on one of the X variables were not reported—the usable subsample contained 92 individuals, of whom 81 were employees. Because of the small size of the panel, it was not practical to break this subsample into still finer groups.

The vector X includes all the variables that have become standard controls in earnings equations and for which the Time Use Study and the Panel Study provide information. Thus, educational attainment, years of labor market experience (including a quadratic), self-reported health status, union membership, marital status (currently married or not), location in the South, residence in a large metropolitan area, and vectors of dummy variables for one-digit occupation and industry were all used as controls in estimating (4).[4] Also, the logarithm of total time at work was included in the vector X to allow for the possibility that supply behavior generates an earnings–total hours relationship that does not have an elasticity of one (Biddle and Zarkin 1989).

Normal work measures time (in minutes) reported for the synthetic workweek

(based on the four daily diaries). For the observations in 1981 this measure includes work time at home.[5] The α_j in (4) reflect reported break time in the three categories—lunch, coffee, and other. The earnings measure is monthly pay, and the dependent variable in all estimation is the logarithm of monthly pay. Monthly pay is calculated as the sum of reported earnings on the particular job during a recent month and the monthly bonus received during that month.[6]

Results from the Time Use Study, 1975–76

Table 1 presents descriptive characteristics of the three subsamples from the 1975–76 Time Use Study. In addition, I present separate data for the small group of self-employed workers, and for union and nonunion employees separately. The four categories defining time use on the job are listed in minutes per week. The mean from the time diaries is 42.5 hours per week, somewhat less than the 44.0 hours that sample members report when asked how much time they usually work per week.[7] This discrepancy suggests that CPS-type data overestimate the amount of time devoted to market production and lead to underestimation of the amount of time spent in household production and leisure. The allocations of time on the job do not differ much among the three subsamples. Unionized workers, however, took distinctly more "other" break time on the job than did nonunion workers, and

---

[3] The exclusions are quite similar to those in Stafford and Duncan (1980b). Their final subsample contained 375 workers, partly because their hours disqualifiers were less stringent than the ones I used.

[4] Experience was measured as age − education − 6.

[5] Of the 92 workers in the subsample of the Panel Study, only three, all of whom were self-employed, reported any working time at home.

[6] Hourly pay is not reported in the data for most workers. It could be measured by dividing monthly pay by 4.33 times the weekly hours workers report they normally work, but that procedure would be likely to produce a substantially noisier dependent variable than the earnings measure I use. In any case, when the equations were re-estimated using a wage measure, the qualitative conclusions did not differ from those reported in the text.

[7] Stafford and Duncan (1980b) note the same discrepancy between answers to questions about weekly hours and totals of time spent at work based on time diaries.

Table 1. Means (and Their Standard Deviations) of Variables in the 1975–76 Time Use Study.

Variable	All	Self-employed	Employees	Employees Union	Employees Nonunion	Employees, Wages Only
Weekly Minutes of:						
Normal Work	2,345	2,678	2,311	2,234	2,336	2,313
	(37)	(139)	(37)	(75)	(43)	(40)
Lunch Breaks	107	62	112	109	113	112
	(6)	(13)	(6)	(11)	(7)	(6)
Coffee Breaks	54	31	56	62	54	56
	(6)	(9)	(4)	(8)	(5)	(4)
Other Breaks (before, after, other)	43	15	46	56	43	48
	(4)	(3)	(6)	(9)	(8)	(7)
Usual Weekly Hours, Main Job	44.0	51.9	43.2	42.8	43.3	43.0
	(.6)	(2.7)	(.6)	(.93)	(.63)	(.5)
Pay Per Month	1,121	1,885	1,043	1,014	1,053	968
	(54)	(390)	(42)	(45)	(54)	(35)
N	343	32	311	78	233	276

coffee breaks were more widely available or longer (or both) among unionized workers.

Are the data on break times reasonable?[8] Consider first their means. Total weekly break time, 204 minutes for employees, seems at first glance to be disturbingly low (less than 45 minutes per working day for the average employee). It is quite comparable, though, with other available data. The Chamber of Commerce survey of larger firms (1987, Table 4) shows that only 3.4 percent of payroll costs are accounted for by lunch, coffee, and other paid breaks. Assuming a forty-hour week, this statistic implies that those paid breaks totaled only 82 minutes per week. Even if only half of the 161 minutes of coffee and lunch breaks reported by employees in our sample are paid for, we may conclude that the Time Use Study does not understate break time.

Now consider the variability of break time across the days on which the workers kept diaries. (Remember that the typical respondent kept time diaries for two work days.) The average correlation between time on coffee breaks within a pair of diary days was .32 for the sample of 343 workers. For lunch breaks it was .27, and for the less structured other breaks it was .16. These correlations are significant, suggesting the data are not just noise. That the correlation is lower for other breaks is consistent with their less formal nature.

The differences in diary times between self-employed workers and employees are striking. Self-employed workers reported 2,678 minutes of normal work, but *only 108 minutes of break time*. Self-employed workers, who presumably determine their own break time to maximize productivity, spend only half as much time on breaks on employees, and they do this during a longer workweek. Moreover, the biggest proportional difference is in the category of other breaks. This difference between self-employed workers and employees is the simplest but most striking evidence for the proposition that on-the-job leisure is not as productive as ordinary working time.

In Table 2 I show the parameter estimates of (4) for the various subsamples. Before examining the returns to

---

[8] Their demographic characteristics suggest the subsamples are quite typical along most dimensions. The workers' average age and educational attainment are roughly those observed for steady workers in subsamples from other large micro data sets. Twenty-five percent of employees in this subsample are unionized, roughly the same percentage as for all nonfarm employees in 1976 (see Hamermesh and Rees 1988:247). Along the dimensions of the other control variables, too, members of this subsample are representative of household heads in the mid-1970s.

Table 2. Estimates of Hedonic Wage Equations, 1975–76 Time Use Study.[a]
(Standard Errors in Parentheses)

Independent Variable	Employees and Self-Employed	Employees Only	Employees Union	Employees Nonunion	Employees, Wages Only
Log(Total Work)	.205 (.09)	.123 (.09)	.029 (.17)	.100 (.12)	.211 (.09)
$\hat{\gamma}_{Lunch}$	1.508 (.76)	2.076 (.72)	2.237 (1.83)	2.371 (.81)	1.97 (.72)
$\hat{\gamma}_{Coffee}$	.893 (1.03)	.503 (.99)	−.205 (2.13)	2.019 (1.16)	.907 (1.01)
$\hat{\gamma}_{Other}$	−.426 (.85)	−.505 (.80)	6.031 (2.02)	−1.232 (.88)	−.343 (.77)
$\overline{R}^2$	.407	.393	.208	.449	.399

[a] Dependent variable is the logarithm of pay per month. Also included in the regressions are measures of education, experience, health, union and marital status, gender, regional and metropolitan location, and vectors of dummy variables for 1-digit occupation and industry.

alternative time uses on the job, it is worth noting that the returns to other characteristics of the workers accord with those found in earnings regressions on other sets of data.[9] The elasticity of earnings with respect to total hours at work is small but usually significant. Thus, the marginal benefit from additional time spent working is positive, though it is well below the average wage in this subsample.

Only for time on lunch breaks is $\hat{\gamma}$ significantly different from zero (though it is not significantly different from one). Time spent on coffee breaks and on other, nonscheduled breaks yields less payoff than does time spent on lunch breaks. Although none of the other $\hat{\gamma}$ is significantly different from zero, some of them are significantly less than one. Indeed, the estimates for other breaks are negative. This finding suggests that, to the extent that such breaks are not contractual (explicit or implicit) benefits, it pays employers to spend resources on monitoring workers to induce them to shift time from unproductive breaks to productive work.

The results for lunch breaks are similar for union and nonunion workers. For coffee breaks, and even more so for "other" breaks, the effects on earnings are strikingly and significantly different. Among nonunion workers, an increased fraction of time at work on other breaks significantly reduces monthly pay; among union workers it significantly raises monthly pay. Given the rigid structuring of union jobs, these differences may not be surprising; unscheduled breaks are the workers' necessary and productive response to the rigidity. This view is consistent with the notion that higher union wages are in part a compensating differential for the structure of work (Stafford and Duncan 1980a). In the less rigidly structured nonunion sector, these unscheduled breaks detract from performance. These results clearly suggest that unstructured on-the-job leisure is shirking among nonunion workers, but may be productive leisure among unionized employees.[10]

Before accepting these conclusions, we should investigate their robustness in light of the evidence from industrial psychology that error rates, accidents, and other work problems are reduced following breaks in long spells of continual work. It may be

---

[9] For example, in the estimates of (4) over the entire subsample the rate of return to schooling was 6 percent, the union wage premium was 13 percent, and workers in the South earned 6 percent less than otherwise identical workers.

[10] If the sample is split by industry, we cannot reject the hypothesis that the structure of (4) is the same in manufacturing as in the rest of the economy. The same qualitative conclusions are provided by tests on the subsamples of all workers and workers who receive only wages or salaries.

Table 3. Estimates of γ_l, 1975–76 Time Use Study.[a]
(Standard Errors in Parentheses)

γ_l evaluated at:	Employees and Self-Employed	Employees Only	Employees		Employees, Wages Only
			Union	Nonunion	
Minimum Break	1.035	1.479	−.463	1.256	1.608
	(.82)	(.80)	(2.97)	(1.10)	(.93)
Mean Break	−.271	1.106	2.006	1.023	1.236
	(.35)	(4.90)	(.97)	(.58)	(.60)
Maximum Break	.500	.238	4.508	.425	.303
	(.76)	(16.28)	(2.42)	(1.00)	(.92)

[a] Based on equations containing the same controls as in Table 2, but with all break time as a fraction of total work, and with a complete second-order approximation to log(total work) and the fraction of work time on break.

that a few short breaks throughout the day raise productivity in nonunion jobs too, even though the average minute of time spent in breaks is not productive. To investigate this possibility, I reestimated (4) by combining the three categories of break time into one to form α_l and then adding quadratic terms in α_l and the logarithm of total work time, and an interaction term between it and α_l.[11]

The marginal effects of α_l and total work time on earnings at their minima, means, and maxima are shown in Table 3. Although the results are not very strong, they do expand somewhat on the story told by the estimates in Table 2. Except for unionized workers, the initial minute of break time, evaluated at the mean total time at work in the sample, generates a $\hat{\gamma}_l$ that is very close to one. Implicitly, the initial minutes devoted to breaks produce the same increases in earnings (and presumably in productivity) as the time that would otherwise be devoted to normal work (though the effect is not very significant). This pattern mirrors perfectly the results from industrial psychology on the declines in productivity that come with continual, uninterrupted work. At the mean fractions of break time in these samples, however, an additional minute switched from normal work to break time has a somewhat smaller positive effect on productivity. At the maximum break time in the sample, switching another minute to

break time reduces earnings, although the effect of that time is still positive. Among unionized workers the marginal effect on earnings of switching normal work time to breaks is increasing.

Admittedly, few of the partial effects in Table 3 are significantly different from one. The pattern of effects does, however, suggest that the initial few minutes of break time raise earnings as much as does the same amount of normal working time. On the other hand, the results also indicate that additional break time beyond the average adds less pay. These inferences are buttressed by the evidence that much less break time is taken by self-employed workers than by employees, but that the self-employed do take some breaks. Except among unionized employees, switching to more break time will reduce productivity. The average minute of time spent on the job but not in normal work is partly shirking, partly productive schmoozing.

Results from the Time Use Panel Study, 1975–81

There are several reasons for using panel data to explore further the relation between pay and time use on the job. Most important, the cross-section estimates reported above do not allow us to separate out the effects of worker–firm specific matches and unobserved worker characteristics that may be correlated with the uses of time. For example, we might expect that workers with positive unobserved

[11] This is essentially an expanded version of the market loci estimated by Biddle and Zarkin (1989).

characteristics that are correlated with earnings will obtain greater amenities, including on-the-job leisure. We will then observe a larger $\hat{\gamma}_j$ than would be estimated if we could control for the characteristics of the workers and the firms that affect this sorting. The results for γ_{lunch} in Table 2, all of which exceed one, indicate that this problem may be present. Also, the use of a panel of workers allows us to examine the stability of patterns of time use on the job. The cost of using the Panel Study is the reduction in the number of individuals included in the subsamples.[12]

Table 4 lists the means of the same variables shown in Table 1. A comparison of the two tables indicates that the workers included in the subsample from the Panel Study spent about the same time on the job as did the average worker in the 1975–76 cross-section. The mean amount of time spent actually working fell sharply in this subsample between 1975–76 and 1981, and the amount of break time reported fell proportionately. Whereas time on lunch and coffee breaks fell, however, time spent on other breaks rose.

What is most interesting about these data is the large deviation between the time spent on the job in 1981 as indicated by the diaries (a mean of 39.7 hours) and as reported by the workers in the background questionnaires (a mean of 43.3 hours). This discrepancy is twice as great as that in the 1975–76 data (see Table 1 and the data for 1975–76 in Table 4). Does this change reflect increasing overreporting of hours in CPS-like data? It is true that the questions on usual weekly hours differed in the two surveys: the 1975–76 question referred to the "main job at the current time," and the 1981 question referred to weekly hours when working in 1980.[13] Restricting the sample

to people with only one job in 1981 and adjusting for different economic conditions in 1980 and 1981 does not, however, alter the conclusion: the discrepancy between usual hours and diary reports of total work was 1.9 hours in 1975–76, but was 2.6 hours in 1981.[14] Not only may there be upward biases in reported hours of work from the major household surveys; these biases may be increasing.

There is remarkable stability in monthly earnings among the workers in the subsample across the two surveys, even though those surveys are separated by six years. Table 5 shows the autocorrelations to be around .80. That the six-year autocorrelations of time use by category are positive suggests that even those data do not solely represent serially independent noise.[15] It is interesting to note that the autocorrelation for total break time is not far below that for time spent actually working. Also, the lowest autocorrelation coefficients are in "other" break time, the least-structured category of time on the job that is not spent in normal work.

Equation (4) is estimated on the panel of two cross-sections from the Time Use Panel Study. I assume the error structure is characterized by:

$$(5) \qquad \epsilon_{it} = \mu_i + \upsilon_{it}, \; i=1, \\ \ldots, N, \; t=1975, 1981,$$

where ϵ is the error term in (4), μ is the individual–job-specific effect, and υ is an i.i.d. error term.[16] Equation (4) is esti-

---

[12] This problem is inherent in starting out with a very small basic sample. Thus, Stafford (1987) had only 77 observations from the Panel Study in his work on two-parent families with young children.

[13] The question in the 1975–76 survey was, "How many hours do you work in your main job in an average week?" In the 1981 follow-up the question was, "How many hours did you work in 1980 when you were working?"

[14] *Employment and Earnings,* January 1981 and January 1982.

[15] Whether they represent autocorrelated measurement errors or true observations cannot be inferred. Duncan and Hill (1985), however, suggest for a similar household survey that only part is measurement error.

[16] It is not completely clear whether the error component μ_i refers to the individual or the match between the individual and the job. Each interpretation is probably valid for one part of the subsample but not the other. One should note, however, that 15 percent of the workers in the subsample changed one-digit industry between 1975–76 and 1981, and undoubtedly many more changed two- or three-digit industries. For at least this group, the interpretation should be that μ_i represents an individual effect only.

Table 4. Means (and Their Standard Deviations) of Variables in the 1975–81 Time Use Panel Study.

Variable	Employees and Self-Employed		Employees	
	1975–76	1981	1975–76	1981
Weekly Minutes of:				
Normal Work	2,344	2,225	2,279	2,174
	(73)	(69)	(74)	(69)
Lunch Breaks	104	87	107	94
	(9)	(9)	(10)	(10)
Coffee Breaks	50	46	53	46
	(7)	(7)	(8)	(7)
Other Breaks	51	63	53	67
	(8)	(8)	(9)	(9)
Usual Weekly Hours (1975–76), Main Job; Weekly Hours (1980)	44.6	44.0	43.3	43.3
	(1.1)	(.9)	(.9)	(.8)
Pay per Month	1,283	1,933	1,149	1,853
	(120)	(145)	(86)	(108)
	92		81	

mated using a generalized least squares estimator based on this random-effects model. The particular estimator used is essentially a weighted average of the "within" estimator (in this case, based on the difference in the variables between the two observations for each worker) and the "between" estimator (in this case, based on the averages of the variables for each individual). (See Judge et al. 1980.) The parameters are calculated as OLS estimates of (4) computed over observations for all N workers for both years from which θ times the individual means have been subtracted for all variables, where θ is the ratio of the standard errors of the "within" to the "between" estimators.

The Lagrange Multiplier statistics that test for the presence of individual effects in the OLS estimators of (4) on the panel data suggest that it makes sense to

Table 5. Six-Year Autocorrelations, Pay and Time Use.

Variable	Employees and Self-Employed	Employees Only
log(Pay Per Month)	.813	.818
Normal Work	.435	.342
Breaks	.260	.279
Lunch Breaks	.334	.358
Coffee Breaks	.238	.261
Other Breaks	.151	.164
Weekly Hours	.537	.438

calculate the GLS estimates.[17] For the sample of 92 workers the statistic, distributed $\chi^2(1)$, equals 22.57; for the subsample of employees the statistic is 24.56. Both of these values are highly significant.

Table 6 shows the GLS estimates of (4) with the error structure embodied in (5).[18] The responses of earnings to increases in total time at work and to changes in the fraction of time spent on break are estimated with about the same lack of precision as in the cross-section data. The GLS estimates do, however, reinforce the conclusion that the marginal minute of time that the average worker spends on lunch break is as productive as normal work time, and that time spent on other breaks is relatively unproductive.

I also used GLS to estimate versions of (4) that contain a second-order approximation to a generalized earnings function in α_l and the logarithm of total time at work (analogous to the results in Table 3). The marginal effects on earnings of switching from normal work to break time are shown at their minima, means, and max-

[17] The test is discussed by Judge et al. (1980:338).
[18] It is worth noting that the OLS point estimates on the pooled cross-section time-series data differ little from the GLS estimates presented in the table. Similarly, the "within" and "between" estimators suggest the same qualitative conclusions.

Table 6. GLS Estimates of Hedonic Wage Equations, 1975–76 and 1981.[a]
(Standard Errors in Parentheses)

Independent Variable	Employees and Self-Employed		Employees Only	
log(Total Work)	.295	.288	.070	.062
	(.11)	(1.08)	(.099)	(.10)
$\hat{\gamma}_{\text{All Breaks}}$	1.006		.779	
	(.52)		(.99)	
$\hat{\gamma}_{\text{Lunch}}$		1.346		1.858
		(1.08)		(.93)
$\hat{\gamma}_{\text{Coffee}}$		1.274		−.396
		(1.39)		(1.22)
$\hat{\gamma}_{\text{Other}}$		.229		.213
		(1.07)		(.92)
θ	.099	.097	.134	.135
$\overline{R}^{2b}$	.520	.516	.564	.562

[a] Equations also include education, experience, union, marital and health status, and gender, and a dummy variable for 1981.
[b] Based on $[1 - \theta]$ differences.

ima in Table 7 for both subsamples. These results do not confirm the findings from the cross-section. The marginal effects are small and insignificant over the entire range of break time, although it is worth noting that at all values of α_l the $\hat{\gamma}_l$ are less than one, indicating that break time is less productive than normal work time.

Conclusion

Additional time spent on breaks at work apparently does raise earnings, but not to the same extent as does additional time spent working. The cross-section results do, however, suggest that the marginal effect of break time on earnings is as large

Table 7. Estimates of γ_l, 1975–81 Time Use Panel Study.[a]
(Standard Errors in Parentheses)

γ_l evaluated at:	Employees and Self-Employed	Employees Only
Minimum Break	−.340	−1.323
	(1.28)	(1.10)
Mean Break	.509	.308
	(.76)	(.57)
Maximum Break	.812	.994
	(.70)	(.51)

[a] Based on equations containing the same controls as in Table 6, but with all break time as a fraction of total work, and with a complete second-order approximation to log(total work) and the fraction of work time on break.

as that of normal work time among otherwise identical workers who spend little time on breaks. Moreover, the finding that self-employed workers give themselves unscheduled breaks (though of much shorter duration or frequency than employees) also suggests that some break time is productive. The empirical results support the notion that the marginal minute of break time, especially of breaks other than lunch breaks, is less productive for the average worker than the marginal minute of regular work time.

The results imply that additional time spent in on-the-job leisure at least partly represents unproductive shirking rather than productive schmoozing. Employers therefore have a substantial incentive to devote resources to monitoring workers' allocations of time on the job, since time switched from normal work to breaks reduces firms' revenues without reducing costs. To the extent that monitoring can, at the margin, shift the time allocations of workers who are paid on a time-rated basis away from breaks and toward normal work, it is reasonable to expect at least some monitoring expenditures to increase profits.

The relative unproductivity of some additional break time also implies that employers have ample latitude for responding to legislated cuts in standard hours or to higher overtime premia by tightening up their supervision of break time. The existence of this additional margin means that the employment effects of such legislation are even more complex than standard labor-demand models suggest. Finally, the results imply that workers who obtain additional on-the-job leisure at the expense of normal work time will see their relative pay fall (since they are substituting toward a less productive use of time on the job). To the extent that on-the-job leisure is a normal good, an increase in the variance of full incomes will, other things equal, lead to a smaller increase in the variance of observed earnings.

The evidence here is based on cross-section data and does not directly predict the effects of the trend toward steady increases in the fraction of time on the job that is spent in mixed leisure—the interspersing of leisure time with normal working time. Indirectly, however, the evidence suggests that the trend toward increased mixed leisure is costly in terms of lost output. People may well choose to spend more time at work in activities that are essentially leisure, but that choice comes at the cost of slower increases in productivity, and hence in living standards, than would otherwise occur. The U.S. economy is now far past the point where switching from normal work to additional break time raises productivity.

REFERENCES

Biddle, Jeff, and Gary Zarkin. 1989. "Choice Among Wage-Hours Packages: An Empirical Investigation of Labor Supply." *Journal of Labor Economics,* Vol. 7, No. 4 (October).

Duncan, Greg, and Daniel Hill. 1985. "An Investigation of the Extent and Consequences of Measurement Error in Labor-economic Survey Data." *Journal of Labor Economics,* Vol. 3, No. 4 (October), pp. 508–32.

Florence, P. Sargant. 1924. *Economics of Fatigue and Unrest.* New York: Henry Holt.

Hamermesh, Daniel. 1986. "Incentives for the Homogenization of Time Use." In Bela Balassa and Herbert Giersch, eds., *Economic Incentives.* London: Macmillan, pp. 124–39.

Hamermesh, Daniel, and Albert Rees. 1988. *The Economics of Work and Pay.* New York: Harper & Row.

Hart, Robert. 1987. *Working Time and Employment.* London: Allen & Unwin.

Hersch, Joni. 1985. "The Effect of Housework on Earnings of Husbands and Wives." *Social Science Quarterly,* Vol. 66, No. 1 (March), pp. 210–17.

Judge, George, William Griffiths, R. Carter Hill, and Tsoung-Chao Lee. 1980. *The Theory and Practice of Econometrics.* New York: John Wiley & Sons.

Juster, F. Thomas, Paul Courant, Greg J. Duncan, John Robinson, and Frank Stafford. 1979. *Time Use in Economic and Social Accounts, 1975–76.* Ann Arbor, Mich.: Institute for Social Research.

Juster, F. Thomas, Martha Hill, Frank Stafford, and Jacquelynne Eccles Parsons. 1983. *Time Use Longitudinal Panel Study, 1975–81.* Ann Arbor, Mich.: Institute for Social Research.

Krueger, Alan, and Lawrence Summers. 1988. "Efficiency Wages and the Wage Structure." *Econometrica,* Vol. 56, No. 2 (May), pp. 259–94.

McCormick, Ernest, and Daniel Ilgen. 1985. *Industrial and Organizational Psychology.* Englewood Cliffs, N.J.: Prentice-Hall.

Schrank, Robert. 1978. *Ten Thousand Working Days.* Cambridge, Mass.: MIT Press.

Stafford, Frank. 1987. "Women's Work, Sibling Competition, and Children's School Performance." *American Economic Review,* Vol. 77, No. 5 (December), pp. 972–80.

Stafford, Frank, and Greg J. Duncan. 1980a. "Do Union Members Receive Compensating Wage Differentials?" *American Economic Review,* Vol. 70, No. 3 (June), pp. 355–71.

———. 1980b. "The Use of Time and Technology by Households in the United States." *Research in Labor Economics,* Vol. 3, pp. 335–75.

U.S. Chamber of Commerce. 1953, 1987. *Employee Benefits.* Washington, D.C.: Chamber of Commerce.

THE STRUCTURE OF SUPERVISION AND PAY IN HOSPITALS

ERICA L. GROSHEN and ALAN B. KRUEGER*

Using BLS data on 300 hospitals in 1985, the authors examine pay in four occupations, with a particular focus on the effect of supervision on the pay of nonsupervisory employees. There was a strong hospital-specific effect on wages that cut across occupations; thus, if a hospital paid relatively high wages to one occupation, it was likely to pay high wages to workers in other occupations as well. The inter-occupational pattern of the ratio of supervisors to staff, on the other hand, was much less uniform among hospitals. The wages of staff nurses tended to fall with the extent of supervision, suggesting that workers do not receive a compensating wage premium in return for closer supervision.

MANY models of the labor market involve explicit or implicit assumptions about the role of supervision. For instance, the efficiency wage literature assumes that supervision serves a monitoring function and that, other things equal, increased supervision will be associated with lower wages. In contrast, if employees dislike being closely monitored, the theory of equalizing differences suggests that closely supervised workers will receive a wage premium.[1] Finally, agency and tournament models are predicated on the assumption that employees are imperfectly monitored and supervised.

Despite the importance of supervision in models of labor market behavior, very little is known about the relationship between supervision and pay, or about the organization and effectiveness of supervision within firms. A better understanding of the structure and impact of supervision is needed to understand its role in production. The goal of this paper is to document several facts regarding the extent of supervision at the workplace, and to measure its effect on the pay of nonsupervisory employees. We make use of a Bureau of Labor Statistics (BLS) industry wage survey of the hospital industry. The hospital industry is the focus of our analysis because it has well defined lines of supervision; because unusually rich employer-reported data are available for a sample of hospitals; and because independent local regulating authorities may impose particularly strong supervision requirements on hospitals, allowing us to avoid problems arising from the endogeneity of the supervisor-to-staff ratio that have hindered other studies of the subject.

Data

The data we examine are drawn from the Bureau of Labor Statistics' 1985 Hospital Industry Wage Survey. In 1985

* The authors thank Paula Laboda for research assistance; Lawrence Summers for making funds available allowing them to obtain the data set; and Joshua Angrist, Ronald Ehrenberg, and Barry Gerhart for helpful comments.

The computer programs and data used in this study are available on request to the authors.

[1] Of course, if workers prefer more supervision to less supervision, the opposite prediction follows.

the BLS sampled nearly 1,000 hospitals from 23 Standard Metropolitan Statistical Areas (SMSAs) to measure hospital pay and staffing.[2] To preserve confidentiality, the BLS subsequently provided us with a public-use sample containing information on employees of 300 hospitals from a random sample of 10 of the SMSAs and concealed the identity of the SMSAs. The data were coded in such a way, however, that it is still possible to identify the groups of hospitals that are located in the same SMSAs.[3] Consequently, in our analysis we can control for the SMSA in which the hospital is located without knowing *where* the hospital is located.

The survey contains wage and salary information, union status, and some demographic information for employees in selected occupations. In addition, several characteristics of the hospital are reported, such as the form of ownership. Most important, the Hospital Survey is the only BLS industry wage survey that contains salary and staffing information (employment and hours) for supervisory workers.

We focus on registered general duty nurses, radiographers, physical therapists, and food service workers because the data set allows us to derive the average supervisor-to-staff ratio for employees in these four occupations. Although only limited human capital controls are available in the data set, the occupations are narrowly defined (for example, radiographers must be accredited by the American Registry of Radiologic Technologists and must be educated in an approved program), which should reduce heterogeneity in worker quality. Furthermore, supervisory information for these workers is particularly meaningful because the lines of supervision are typically standard across hospitals and are narrowly drawn for these types of jobs.

The data appendix provides a more detailed description of the data set. Included are precise definitions of the four occupations in our sample, the derivation of the full-time equivalent supervisor-to-staff ratio for each occupation, and the means and standard deviations of the relevant variables for each occupation.

Basic Findings

The Inter-Occupational Structure of Wages

To examine the inter-occupational structure of wages across hospitals, we calculate the average wage paid to employees at the various hospitals for each occupation. Table 1 contains a correlation matrix of the average wage in the four occupations across hospitals. The table shows that the average hospital wage is highly correlated between pairs of occupations. For instance, the correlation between the average wage of registered nurses and that of radiographers across hospitals is .740.

Although it may not be surprising to find highly correlated hospital-level wage rates for two similar occupations, a high correlation is also found for dissimilar occupations. For instance, the correlation in wages between registered nurses and food service workers is .754. The average correlation in wages among the six different pairings of occupations is .673. These figures suggest that there is a substantial hospital-specific effect on wages that cuts

Table 1. Correlation of Average Hospital Wage by Occupation, 1985.
(Number of Hospitals in Parentheses)

	Food Service	Radi- ographer	Physical Therapist
Radiographer	.798 (254)		
Physical Therapist	.589 (214)	.639 (219)	
Registered Nurse	.754 (271)	.740 (270)	.517 (226)

Notes: Correlations are of average hourly wage rate. All correlations shown are statistically significant at the .0001 level.

---

[2] For further details on the original survey, see U.S. Department of Labor (1982, 1987).

[3] SMSA codes are scrambled, but unique identifiers are provided to allow the creation of SMSA dummy variables.

across occupations.[4] Therefore, if one occupation in a given hospital is paid a relatively high wage, the other occupations in the hospital are also likely to be paid a relatively high wage.

In Table 2, we report the correlation between the average wages of staff workers and their supervisors in the four occupations. These results, like those in Table 1, indicate a high degree of similarity in the wage structure across occupations. For instance, the correlation between the wage of registered nurses and that of their supervisors is .805.

What might explain the high similarity across occupations of the inter-firm wage structure? In particular, what role might supervision play?

Consider first the human resource management/personnel literature on compensation. This literature stresses three main factors that influence the firm's wage structure and location in the "wage hierarchy." First, internal equity is believed to be important in explaining wage structures.[5] According to this argument, if workers perceive their compensation as less than that of co-workers who are less skilled, they will become dissatisfied with their job and withhold effort. Moreover, one might expect a link between supervisor and staff wages across establishments because supervisors are likely to be more effective when they are paid more than the workers they supervise, since pay symbolizes a worker's

Table 2. Correlation of Average Staff Workers' Wage with Their Supervisor's Wage.

Occupation	Correlation	Sample Size
Registered Nurse	.805	296
Radiographer	.631	217
Physical Therapist	.541	169
Food Service	.652	214

prestige and authority.[6] If workers in one occupation in a firm are paid relatively well compared to workers in the same occupation in other firms for exogenous reasons, workers in the other occupations that the firm employs would also be relatively well paid because of vertical equity considerations. Thus, equity concerns would lead to a positive correlation in wages among workers in different occupations across firms.

Second, the traditional personnel literature also places much emphasis on the firm's ability to pay. Although a cost-minimizing firm would not consider its ability to pay in setting pay, workers may be able to extract rents from firms through collective bargaining—in which case the firm's ability to pay becomes a relevant factor. Alternatively, principal-agent problems may allow managers to share product market rents with workers even in the absence of collective bargaining.

Finally, and transcending the above concerns, the personnel literature has stressed the interrelationship between management strategy and personnel policy.[7] Among other factors, the type of supervision and the nature of the work that the firm provides would be aspects of managerial strategy taken into account in deciding wages.[8] Firms that closely moni-

---

[4] Other researchers have found a similar pattern at the industry level. For instance, Dickens and Katz (1986) estimate that the correlation in the inter-industry wage differential for managers and operatives (after controlling for education, age, region, and other variables) is .73. In addition, Groshen (1988) finds evidence that different occupations have highly correlated wages across firms in the chemicals, steel, plastics, wool textiles, cotton textiles, and men's and boys' shirts and nightwear industries. Leonard (1987), however, finds relatively low inter-firm correlations in wages among 6 occupations in the "high technology" industry, ranging from −.18 to .38.

[5] See Milkovich and Newman (1984), Kochan and Barocci (1985), and Heneman, Schwab, Fossum, and Dyer (1986) for statements concerning the importance of internal equity in pay setting. See Akerlof and Yellen (1987) for an economic model of vertical pay equity.

---

[6] As Taylor (1959) puts it, "For a man to believe he is in truth 'the boss,' he must know he is receiving more pay than the men and women he supervises and, with few exceptions, more than any employee in the operation who occupies a nonsupervisory job" (p. 126).

[7] Kochan and Barocci (1985) provide a discussion of the link between managerial strategy and personnel policy.

[8] See Lester (1952) for an early statement of the "range theory of wage differentials."

tor and control workers would be able to hire lower-quality workers and to pay lower wages than firms that allow workers more autonomy and responsibility.

Next, consider possible neoclassical economic explanations of the observed pattern of inter-firm earnings differentials for different occupations. First, there may be working conditions associated with employers that cut across all jobs and dictate compensating wage differentials. For example, a firm may be located at a great distance from residential areas, so that all employees (regardless of their occupation) must endure a long commute to work.[9]

Alternatively, the employer may closely supervise all employees to a similar extent. Such a uniform supervisory strategy would necessitate a positive wage premium if employees dislike being monitored. Employees may dislike supervision for two reasons: first, they may consider supervision a disagreeable intrusion on their privacy and independence; and second, supervisors may exact more work effort from workers than workers would provide in the absence of supervision. On the other hand, some employees may prefer more supervision because it helps them to achieve desired goals. If workers' preferences toward supervision are heterogeneous, we would expect workers to sort into firms that provide working conditions they deem desirable, and any compensating differential for supervision would in that case be determined by the preferences of the marginal worker.

Finally, workers may sort themselves into firms—or firms may recruit workers—on the basis of workers' ability. Although many components of the workers' abilities are unobserved by the econometrician, the firm may be able to discriminate among high- and low-ability workers and set their pay accordingly. This practice would lead researchers to spuriously conclude that

equally skilled workers are paid differently. To the extent that there is uniform, hospital-wide sorting on the basis of unobserved ability in all occupations, we would observe a wage pattern like the one described above. In addition, it seems likely that firms will more intensively supervise work units that on average have low-ability workers.

The Structure of Supervision

Table 3 reports the correlation in the supervisor-to-staff ratios across hospitals for the various occupations.[10] In comparison to the findings for wages, we find a much lower correlation in the supervisor-to-staff ratio across occupations. For example, the correlation in the supervisor-to-staff ratio between the radiographers and physical therapists among the hospitals is .281. The average correlation in the supervisor-to-staff ratios among the six different pairings of occupations is .239. These figures suggest that hospitals do not follow a general strategy of supervisory intensity that cuts across occupations. Instead, if a hospital supervises employees in one occupation closely (compared to the way other hospitals supervise that occupation), it is only slightly more likely to closely supervise employees in other occupations.

One possible explanation for this finding is that the number of supervisors or staff employees (or both) in hospitals is often highly regulated by state and local governments. If the mandated supervisor-to-staff ratio varies by occupation and city, one would not expect to find a hospital-wide influence on the supervisor-to-staff ratio. On the other hand, if the supervisor-to-staff ratios in all occupations are regulated to a similar extent in an area, the reported correlations may be biased upward. Thus, it is important to consider the impact of regulations in interpreting these correlations.

Nonetheless, the observed inter-occupational correlations of supervision among

---

[9] For example, Shultz and Rees (1970) find evidence of geographic wage differentials across different sections of the Chicago metropolitan area. The locations that require a longer commute to work tend to have higher wages. Eberts (1981) reaches a similar conclusion after examining the spatial pattern of wages of municipal employees in the Chicago area.

[10] See the appendix for a description of the calculation of supervisor-to-staff ratios for each occupation.

Table 3. Correlation of Supervisor-to-Staff Ratios, 1985.
(Number of Hospitals in Parentheses)

	Food Service	Radi-ographer	Physical Therapist
Radiographer	.116* (254)		
Physical Therapist	.174** (214)	.281** (219)	
Registered Nurse	.160** (271)	.549** (270)	.155** (226)

Note: One asterisk denotes a statistically significant difference between the correlation and 0 at the .10 level; two asterisks denotes a statistically significant difference between the correlation and 0 at the .01 level.

the hospitals suggests that the inter-occupational wage structure cannot be explained by arguments based on the premise that hospitals tend to have a similar level of relative supervisory intensity for all occupations.

Is There a Trade-Off Between Supervision and Pay?

There is considerable interest in estimating the relationship between supervision and pay. On the one hand, a positive relationship between supervision and pay would support a conclusion that employees dislike supervision, and that firms must pay a compensating wage differential to attract workers to jobs that are intensively supervised. Aoki (1984:29), for instance, writes:

Why do the team players [workers] accept the monitor's control, then? Since the possibility of shirking indicates that team members derive some utilities from a saving of effort expenditure, they are unlikely to accept the latter's control voluntarily for no compensation.

On the other hand, a negative relationship between supervision and pay would be consistent with two alternative hypotheses: the efficiency wage hypothesis and sorting by ability. First, according to the efficiency wage hypothesis, at the same level of effort one should observe a trade-off between self-supervision and external monitoring, in which increased

monitoring is assumed to increase the likelihood of detecting poor performance (see Shapiro and Stiglitz 1984 and Bulow and Summers 1986). Higher pay induces more self-supervision and therefore less shirking because workers value their jobs more as their pay increases, whereas more intensive supervision reduces shirking by raising the probability that workers who shirk will be disciplined. Thus, holding workers' effort level constant, the efficiency wage model predicts that increases in monitoring would be associated with lower wages.

The supervisor-to-staff ratio is an input in monitoring; a greater supervisor-to-staff ratio increases the likelihood that shirking workers will be detected and disciplined.[11] At a fixed level of worker effort, the firm will be indifferent between expending an additional dollar on monitoring (the marginal cost of a supervisor) and paying workers a dollar more in wages, since both supervision and pay are choice variables to the firm in this model. Therefore, a testable implication of the efficiency wage model is that the cost of an increase in supervision should be just offset by a decrease in the wage rate, all else equal.

Finally, if there is sorting on the basis of workers' abilities (within occupations), we should expect low-ability workers to be supervised more than high-ability workers. If low-ability workers are paid less than high-ability workers, and if the available data are not sufficiently detailed to allow us to completely control for workers' abilities, then we should also expect to find a negative relationship between wages and the extent of supervi-

---

[11] Odiorne (1963:30) defines a supervisor's tasks to include organizing work, planning performance targets, and "checking the actual performance and noting its level quality and direction against his previously set plan." Although supervisors have different functions at different firms, and firms may utilize other forms of technology to monitor employees (such as computers), the supervisor-to-staff ratio is likely to be highly correlated with the extent of employee monitoring. Moreover, mismeasurement of the extent of supervision is likely to lead to a downward-biased estimate of the effect of supervision on pay.

sion. Moreover, cost-minimizing firms will substitute low-quality labor for high-quality labor until the point is reached at which the increased supervisory costs associated with low-quality workers are exactly offset by reductions in the wage bill. This model yields the same prediction as does the monitoring efficiency wage model.

Previous Research

To test the monitoring efficiency wage model, Leonard (1987) regressed the wages of staff workers on the occupation-specific supervisor-to-staff ratio for each of six occupations in a sample of high-technology firms in California. His estimates generally indicated a positive, but statistically insignificant, relationship between pay and supervision. From this exercise he concluded that there is little evidence in favor of the shirking efficiency wage model.

It is unlikely, however, that a regression of the wage rate of staff workers on the supervisor-to-staff ratio will yield a convincing test of the effect of monitoring on wages, because supervision is a choice variable to the firm. For example, if we assume that the hospital has a Cobb-Douglas production function with $Q = L^\alpha S^\beta$, where L is the labor input, S is the input of supervisors, and Q is the hospital output, then the first-order conditions for cost-minimization will require that

$$(1) \qquad \frac{S}{L} = \frac{\beta w}{\alpha r},$$

where w is the wage of laborers and r is the wage of supervisors.[12]

From (1) it is apparent that holding the wage of supervisors constant, random variations in w will induce a positive relationship between staff workers' wages and the supervisor-to-staff ratio even if supervision has no direct effect on employee utility or monitoring. More generally, any production technology that has a

non-zero marginal rate of technical substitution between laborers and supervisors will induce a positive relationship between wages and the supervisor-to-staff ratio. As a result of the potential for substitution among factors of production, regressions of the wage rate of staff workers on the supervisor-to-staff ratio are likely to reflect "reverse causation," since an exogenously high staff wage would lead firms to substitute S workers for L workers.[13]

Only if r varies independently of w, or if the supervisor-to-staff ratio is exogenously determined, will it be possible to statistically identify the impact of supervision on wages by regressing the wage rate of staff workers on the supervisor-to-staff ratio. In Leonard's application, it is likely that any trade-off between supervision and pay would be biased and perhaps dominated by the substitution effect, since his data pertain to an industry without external restrictions on S/L.[14]

Estimation

The particular institutions of the hospital industry provide some hope of obtaining an estimate of the trade-off between supervision and pay that is not biased by the substitution of inputs. In particular, local regulatory authorities exercise a great deal of authority in directly and indirectly setting minimum standards for the supervisor-to-staff ratio in hospitals. For instance, the state of Georgia requires that all hospitals in the state provide at

---

[12] We ignore issues concerning monopsony power, which might be relevant in the labor market for nurses (see Sullivan 1987).

[13] Ehrenberg (1974) finds that hospitals substitute registered nurses (RNs) for licensed practical nurses (LPNs) when the wage of LPNs is high relative to RNs, especially in private-for-profit hospitals. It is likely that substitution also takes place between nurse supervisors and registered nurses. Estimating Ehrenberg's model with our data, we find a high elasticity of substitution between registered nurses and supervisors—nearly -4.

[14] Leonard notes that cost minimization implies that $w = \alpha Q/L$. Therefore, if Q could be held constant in his analysis, the regression of w on S/L would trace out the trade-off between supervision and pay along an isoquant. Given data limitations, however, he must use as a proxy for Q the total employment of the firm, which is likely to be a very imprecise measure of output.

least one supervisory nurse per 40 patients and at least 3.4 hours of general duty nursing time per patient each day. Other states in our sample that regulate staffing requirements for at least some hospital employees include California, Florida, New York, Illinois, and Wisconsin. In addition, some cities in our sample have local regulations that restrict a hospital's authority to autonomously determine its staffing arrangements.[15] In many hospitals these regulations are likely to require hospitals to use supervisor-to-staff ratios that they would not have voluntarily chosen in the absence of such regulation.

For our purposes, regional variations in the supervisor-to-staff ratio that are generated by state and local government regulations can be used to identify the hedonic relationship between wages and supervision. Ideally, the exact level of the government-mandated staffing requirements should be used to instrument for the supervisor-to-staff ratio. Unfortunately, this information cannot be matched to our data set, since SMSA locations are concealed in the BLS data. Instead, we use a set of SMSA dummy variables to instrument for the supervisor-to-staff ratio in the wage equations. Since we assume that government staffing requirements vary exogenously across SMSAs, this procedure provides a way to estimate the trade-off between wages and supervision without encountering the problems created by the endogeneity of the number of supervisors and staff workers.

A potential limitation of this approach is that if SMSA location is a direct determinant of wages, hospital location is not a valid instrument for supervision. Thus, we include a direct measure of the relative wage level in each SMSA to control for regional wage effects. An SMSA wage index was obtained as follows: using the full sample of occupations and hospitals,

log wages of workers were regressed on a set of SMSA dummy variables and occupation dummy variables. The estimated coefficients on the SMSA dummies are the components of the area wage index, which is included as an independent variable in the wage equations estimated below.

Table 4 reports two-stage least squares estimates of earnings equations for four occupations. The dependent variable is the log of the average *staff worker's* hourly wage in each hospital; the key independent variable is the supervisor-to-staff ratio. For reasons discussed above, the exclusion restriction of SMSA dummy variables—which are correlated with local staffing regulations—allows the identification of the supervisor-to-staff ratio. Comparable equations estimated by OLS are reported in Table 5.

When the equations are estimated by two-stage least squares to account for the endogeneity of supervisory intensity, the supervisor-to-staff ratio has a negative, statistically significant effect on the pay of nurses. The OLS regressions show a much smaller trade-off between pay and supervision for registered nurses than the two-stage least squares estimates, a finding that may result from reverse causality in the OLS regressions. Moreover, the three other occupations have small, statistically insignificant coefficients on the supervisor-to-staff ratio. In these occupations, either regulation does not provide exogenous variation in supervisory intensity or no trade-off exists between supervision and pay.

The chi-square statistics reported at the bottom of Table 4 indicate that the exclusion restrictions fail the Generalized Method of Moments (GMM) over-identification test for the three non-nursing occupations, but pass the test at the 5% level for nurses. In other words, the estimated trade-off between pay and supervision is sensitive to the choice of instruments for the non-nursing occupations, which suggests that the effect of the supervisor-to-staff ratio is not properly estimated in these occupations. On the other hand, the GMM test lends some support for using hospital location as an

---

[15] A histogram of the supervisor-to-staff ratio shows a substantial spike at low levels of supervision for nurses in nine of the ten cities. These spikes suggest that regulation is a binding constraint on the number of supervisors relative to staff in most cities. Spikes in the distribution of the supervisor-to-staff ratio are less apparent for other occupations.

Table 4. Estimates of the Trade-off Between Supervision and Pay.
(Dependent Variable: Log Average Wage; Two-Stage Least Squares Estimates)[a]

Explanatory Variable[b]	Registered Nurses	Food Service	Radiographers	Physical Therapists
Supervisor-to-Staff Ratio	− .866	− .115	.050	.114
	(.216)	(.159)	(.104)	(.068)
Covered by Union Contract	.044	.111	.022	− .038
	(.016)	(.016)	(.017)	(.029)
Proportion Full-Time	− .041	.105	.061	.013
	(.031)	(.029)	(.032)	(.041)
Proportion Male	1.059	− .047	.103	.043
	(.300)	(.040)	(.032)	(.045)
Proportion of Unknown Gender	.041	− .018	.049	.002
	(.021)	(.021)	(.019)	(.020)
Area Wage Index	.772	1.213	1.036	.791
	(.063)	(.079)	(.058)	(.077)
Hospital Size				
1–99	− .068	—	—	—
	(.111)			
100–249	.050	− .115	− .109	− .018
	(.046)	(.048)	(.056)	(.067)
250–499	.025	− .066	− .006	− .026
	(.034)	(.031)	(.030)	(.039)
500–999	.030	− .024	− .023	− .004
	(.025)	(.023)	(.021)	(.030)
1,000–2,499	− .005	− .008	− .011	.020
	(.020)	(.020)	(.019)	(.021)
Chi-Square Over-Identification Test (DF = 8)	14.7	25.3	91.5	76.2
Sample Size	297	273	271	226

[a] Nine SMSA dummy variables are excluded instruments for the supervisor-to-staff ratio.

[b] Equations also include dummy variables indicating whether the hospital is government-owned, proprietary, or nonprofit; a dummy variable indicating whether the hospital is a long-term care facility; two dummy variables indicating the type of hospital; and an intercept term.

instrument for supervisory intensity in the nursing occupation.[16] This finding is also consistent with our understanding of the hospital regulatory process, which appears to concentrate more on regulating supervisor-to-staff ratios for nurses than for other occupations.

The finding of a negative relationship between pay and supervision for nurses suggests that these workers do not receive a compensating differential when they are subject to close supervision. To the contrary, highly supervised workers tend to earn lower wages than those who are supervised less intensively. This result is consistent with either of the following interpretations: firms that hire low-quality workers tend to supervise them more intensively; or there is a trade-off between self-monitoring and external supervision for workers of a given quality level.

The point estimate of the coefficient on the supervisor-to-staff ratio indicates a substantial trade-off between pay and supervision for nurses. For example, consider the wage reduction associated with hiring an additional nurse supervisor. On average, there are 6.5 nurses assigned to a supervisor. Hiring an additional supervisor for the average work group will thus reduce the number of nurses monitored by a supervisor to 3.25 in two work groups. This change would enable the hospital to reduce these staff nurses'

---

[16] We note that if the equations are re-estimated excluding the area wage index, the over-identification test is overwhelmingly rejected for the sample of nurses.

Table 5. Estimates of the Trade-off Between Supervision and Pay.
(Dependent Variable: Log Average Wage; Ordinary Least Squares Estimates)

Explanatory Variable	Registered Nurses	Food Service	Radiographers	Physical Therapists
Supervisor-to-Staff Ratio	−.097	.028	.006	.077
	(.044)	(.041)	(.032)	(.022)
Covered by Union Contract	.039	.111	.023	−.030
	(.011)	(.016)	(.017)	(.024)
Proportion Full-Time	−.035	.096	.055	−.002
	(.022)	(.027)	(.029)	(.031)
Proportion Male	.126	−.043	.104	.043
	(.113)	(.039)	(.032)	(.045)
Proportion of Unknown Gender	−.001	−.017	.047	.003
	(.013)	(.021)	(.019)	(.020)
Area Wage Index	.756	1.255	1.041	.768
	(.043)	(.063)	(.056)	(.065)
Hospital Size				
1–99	−.067	—	—	—
	(.076)			
100–249	−.079	−.149	−.089	.011
	(.021)	(.030)	(.033)	(.044)
250–499	−.050	−.078	−.0002	−.016
	(.018)	(.028)	(.027)	(.034)
500–999	−.015	−.028	−.023	.005
	(.015)	(.022)	(.021)	(.026)
1,000–2,499	−.015	−.001	−.012	.023
	(.013)	(.019)	(.018)	(.021)
R^2	.714	.777	.691	.469
Sample Size	297	273	271	226

[a] Equations also include dummy variables indicating whether the hospital is government-owned, proprietary, or nonprofit; a dummy variable indicating whether the hospital is a long-term care facility; two dummy variables indicating the type of hospital; and an intercept term.

hourly pay by approximately 13.3%. Using the average nurse's pay of $12.18 per hour, the addition of a new supervisor would therefore lead to a payroll reduction of .133 × 12.18 × 6.5 = $10.53 per hour.[17]

Although nontrivial, this cost reduction falls short of the average hourly wage of nurse supervisors ($15.39). One would not, however, expect the optimality condition—which is identical for efficiency wage models and labor quality models—to hold exactly in this industry, since the government often regulates staff levels in hospitals. The estimated wage savings associated with hiring an additional nurse supervisor suggests that regulations re-

quire hospitals to employ more supervisors than they would voluntarily choose to employ.[18]

Another way to explore the trade-off between supervision and pay is to examine how it differs among hospitals depending on their ability and incentive to take advantage of the trade-off: in particular, unionized hospitals may be limited in their ability to adjust wages and staffing levels, and government-owned hospitals may not have the same cost-minimization incentives as privately owned institutions. These considerations suggest that the estimated trade-off may be stronger for nonunion privately owned hospitals than for govern-

---

[17] This calculation assumes that productivity is constant.

[18] Integer restrictions on the number of nurse supervisors is probably not a relevant constraint in this situation, since hospitals could hire part-time supervisors.

ment and union hospitals. In results not fully reported here, we find that both of these predictions are borne out for nurses. For example, the coefficient on the supervisor-to-staff ratio estimated for the subsample of privately owned hospitals is −2.068, which is much greater in absolute magnitude than the coefficient estimated for the sample as a whole.

Other variables in the wage equations. The estimates show that unions have a positive effect on wages in the hospital industry for most occupations. Interestingly, full-time nurses tend to earn lower wages than part-time nurses. Moreover, this pattern was found by the BLS in the majority of the cities that were surveyed. The coefficient on the area wage index variables are, as expected, highly statistically significant and are close to one in magnitude. Finally, the coefficients on the hospital size dummy variables (measured by total hospital employment) and wages vary among the occupations.

Summary and Conclusion

The first finding of this study of the structure of pay and supervision in the hospital industry is that there is a strong hospital-specific effect on wages that cuts across occupations—that is, in a given hospital, if wages for one occupation are well above the industry average, wages for the other occupations are likely to be relatively high as well. A second finding is that the inter-occupational pattern of supervisory intensity (as measured by the supervisor-to-staff ratio) is much less uniform among hospitals. Given the unusual number of state and local government regulations affecting staffing in the hospital industry, it is difficult to generalize from these results to other industries. Government regulation of supervision in hospitals, however, has allowed us to overcome problems of endogeneity of the supervisor-to-staff ratio that have affected previous studies.

We used regional variations in the supervisor-to-staff ratio to identify the effect of supervision on the wages of staff workers. This analysis finds that wages of staff nurses tend to fall with the extent of supervision. On the other hand, in wage equations for three other occupations (food service employees, radiographers, and physical therapists), the effect of supervision on pay is found to be statistically insignificant. The more limited government regulation of supervisory intensity and the rejection of the specification tests for these occupations suggest that the estimated trade-off between supervision and pay in the nursing occupation might be more reliable.

Since many theoretical models of the labor market (for example, agency and efficiency wage models) are predicated on assumptions about supervision, it is important to empirically examine the actual impact of supervision on pay and productivity. The analysis presented here suggests that workers do not require additional compensation to endure more intensive supervision. If anything, we find that hospitals that have a greater supervisor-to-staff ratio tend to pay lower wages to nurses. There are two plausible interpretations of this finding.

First, when staff workers are closely supervised, firms may substitute low-quality/low-pay workers for high-quality/high-pay workers. Although our analysis is intentionally confined to narrowly defined occupations (registered nurses, for example) in order to limit worker heterogeneity, there is still scope for heterogeneity in worker ability within occupations, which is observed by employers but not reflected in our explanatory variables. Second, an alternative interpretation of our results is that to elicit work effort from a homogeneous group of employees, firms can choose between paying the workers a relatively high wage or more closely supervising them. Unfortunately, from our analysis it is impossible to distinguish between these two alternative interpretations because they yield identical empirical predictions.

Data Appendix

Description of the data. The data analyzed are from the Bureau of Labor Statistics Industry Occupational Wage Surveys of the Hospital Industry in 1985. Hospitals in 23 SMSAs were surveyed for the wages paid to certain occupations. We use a subsample drawn from 10 of the 23 SMSAs surveyed. Actual SMSA of origin was masked by the BLS, but unique identifiers were provided to allow the creation of SMSA dummy variables.

The data set contains the wages, gender, occupation, and establishment identifier of individual employees. Wages reported are straight-time hourly wages (no overtime or shift premia are included). Although confidentiality restrictions prohibit the release of employers' names, the data include unique employer identifiers and the following hospital characteristics: SIC, approximate number of employees in

the hospital, union coverage, whether the hospital provides short-term or long-term care, and type of ownership (state, other government, proprietary, nonprofit-church, nonprofit-nonchurch, other).

We analyze the relationship between wages and supervision in the four occupations that have data on supervisors and staff: physical therapists, radiographers, nurses, and food service workers. Descriptive statistics for the relevant variables by occupation are provided in Table A1.

Construction of supervisor-to-staff ratios for hospital employees. The measure of supervisory intensity that we use is simply the number of supervisors divided by the number of staff workers in a given occupation for each hospital. The data only allow us to calculate the supervisor-to-staff ratio at the hospital (rather than work-group) level. The following conventions were

Table A1. Means and Standard Deviations.

Variable	Registered Nurse	Radiographers	Physical Therapists	Food Service
Hourly Wage of Staff	$12.18 (1.68)	$10.18 (1.90)	$12.21 (1.85)	$6.53 (1.45)
Hourly Wage of Supervisors	$15.39 (2.27)	$13.65 (2.47)	$15.46 (2.20)	$9.10 (1.79)
Supervisor-to-Staff Ratio	.152 (.143)	.239 (.312)	.389 (.426)	.162 (.184)
Covered by Union Contract	.374 (.485)	.251 (.434)	.146 (.354)	.447 (.498)
Proportion Full-Time	.641 (.251)	.716 (.253)	.765 (.292)	.615 (.256)
Proportion Male	.026 (.048)	.209 (.239)	.085 (.178)	.214 (.207)
Proportion of Unknown Gender	.191 (.392)	.191 (.392)	.196 (.397)	.198 (.397)
Government-Owned	.273 (.445)	.255 (.436)	.234 (.423)	.263 (.440)
General Hospital	.788 (.409)	.845 (.362)	.854 (.353)	.817 (.387)
Psychiatric Hospital	.118 (.323)	.070 (.256)	.040 (.196)	.088 (.284)
Specialty Hospital	.094 (.293)	.085 (.279)	.106 (.309)	.095 (.294)
Hospital Size				
1–99	.003 (.058)	—	—	—
100–249	.101 (.302)	.074 (.262)	.049 (.216)	.099 (.299)
250–499	.135 (.342)	.122 (.328)	.092 (.291)	.117 (.322)
500–999	.219 (.414)	.225 (.418)	.199 (.400)	.231 (.422)
1,000–2,499	.380 (.486)	.402 (.491)	.447 (.498)	.377 (.486)
>2,500	.162 (.369)	.177 (.382)	.213 (.409)	.176 (.381)

Table A2. Definitions and BLS Occupational Codes.

Occupation	BLS Code	Definition
Nurses		
Supervisors:	010	Director of nursing
	020	Supervisor of nurses
	021	Supervisor of nurses—day
	022	Supervisor of nurses—night
	030	Head nurse
Staff:[a]	040	Registered general duty nurse
	041	LPN—administers medications
	042	LPN—does not administer medications
	043	LPN—psychiatric
	044	LPN—nonpsychiatric
	049	LPN—no information about medications
Food Service Workers		
Supervisors:	410	Food service supervisor
Staff:	430	Food service worker
Physical Therapists		
Supervisors:	640	Physical therapist supervisor
Staff:	230	Physical therapist
Radiographers		
Supervisors:	270	Radiographer supervisor
Staff:	261	Registered radiographer
	262	Nonregistered radiographer
	269	Radiographer—unknown registration status

[a] It should be noted that although LPNs are included in the denominator of the supervisor-to-staff ratio for nurses, the analysis of wages only pertains to registered nurses.

used to obtain the number of workers and supervisors: (1) Each part-time supervisor was counted as half of a supervisor in the numerator of the ratio; each part-time staff member was counted as half of a staff member in the denominator of the ratio.[19] (2) If no su-

pervisors were reported in an occupation, we assumed the hospital had one supervisor for that occupation. This correction was made in less than 10% of the observations; moreover, the results are not sensitive to the alternative of treating the supervisor-to-staff ratio as zero in these cases.

Definition of supervisory and staff workers by occupation. Supervisor and worker definitions for the individual occupations, as well as BLS Occupational Codes for each job classification, are shown in Table A2.

---

[19] The estimated effect of the supervisor-to-staff ratio was not sensitive to counting part-time staff members as equivalent to full-time staff members, or to counting LPNs as less than RNs.

REFERENCES

Akerlof, George, and Janet Yellen. 1987. "The Fair Wage-Effort Hypothesis." Unpublished manuscript, University of California, Berkeley.

Aoki, Masahiko. 1984. *The Co-Operative Game Theory of the Firm.* Oxford: Oxford University Press.

Bulow, Jeremy, and Lawrence Summers. 1986. "A Theory of Dual Labor Markets with Application to Industrial Policy, Discrimination, and Keynesian Unemployment." *Journal of Labor Economics,* Vol. 4, pp. 376–414.

Dickens, William, and Lawrence Katz. 1986. "Industry and Occupation Wage Patterns and Theories of Wage Determination." Unpublished manuscript, University of California, Berkeley.

Eberts, Randall. 1981. "An Empirical Investigation of Intra-Urban Wage Gradients." *Journal of Urban Economics,* Vol. 10, pp. 50–60.

Ehrenberg, Ronald. 1974. "Organizational Control and the Economic Efficiency of Hospitals: The Production of Nursing Services." *Journal of Human Resources,* Vol. 9, pp. 21–32.

Groshen, Erica. 1988. "Sources of Wage Dispersion: The Contribution of Inter-Employer Differentials Within Industry." Federal Reserve Bank of Cleveland Working Paper 8802.

Heneman, Herbert, Donald Schwab, John Fossum, and Lee Dyer. 1986. *Personnel/Human Resource Management.* 3rd Edition. Homewood, Ill.: Irwin.

Kochan, Thomas, and Thomas Barocci. 1985. *Human Resource Management and Industrial Relations.* Boston: Little Brown.

Leonard, Jonathan. 1987. "Carrots and Sticks: Pay, Supervision, and Turnover." *Journal of Labor Economics,* Vol. 5, pp. s136–s152.

Lester, Richard. 1952. "A Range Theory of Wage Differentials." *Industrial and Labor Relations Review,* Vol. 5, pp. 483–499.

Milkovich, George, and J. Newman. 1984. *Compensation.* Plano, Tex.: Business Publications.

Odiorne, George. 1963. *Personnel Policy: Issues and Practices.* Columbus, Ohio: Charles Merrill Books.

Shapiro, Carl, and Joseph Stiglitz. 1984. "Involuntary Unemployment as a Worker Discipline Device." *American Economic Review,* Vol. 74, pp. 433–44.

Shultz, George P., and Albert Rees. 1970. *Workers and Wages in an Urban Labor Market.* Chicago: University of Chicago Press.

Sullivan, Daniel G. 1987. "Estimates of Monopsony Power in the Market for Hospital Workers." In "Three Empirical Studies of Firm Behavior in Imperfectly Competitive Markets." Ph.D. diss., Princeton University.

U.S. Department of Labor, Bureau of Labor Statistics. 1982. *Industry Wage Survey: Hospitals.* Bulletin 2142, December.

U.S. Department of Labor, Bureau of Labor Statistics. 1987. *Industry Wage Survey: Hospitals.* Bulletin 2273, February.

Taylor, James. 1959. *Personnel Administration.* New York: McGraw-Hill.

WAGES, EMPLOYER COSTS, AND EMPLOYEE PERFORMANCE IN THE FIRM

HARRY J. HOLZER*

Analyzing data from a 1982 survey of firms, the author finds evidence that firms' wage levels are positively associated with the previous experience of new hires, the tenure of employees with the firm, managers' perceptions of employee productivity, and managers' perceptions of the ease of hiring qualified workers; they are negatively associated with job vacancy rates and training time. Although the magnitudes of some of these relationships are not large, in combination they suggest that high-wage firms can sometimes offset more than half of their higher wage costs through improved productivity and lower hiring and turnover costs. The effects are generally stronger for firms that have chosen high wage levels than for firms in which unions have imposed high wage levels.

It has long been recognized that when firms are forced to pay above-market-clearing wages, they respond by altering their hiring behavior. If, for instance, unions raise the wages of unskilled workers for a firm or industry, the affected firm(s) will generally substitute capital for labor and more highly skilled workers for those less skilled, in order to prevent workers from fully extracting their monopoly rents.[1] Thus, workers at unionized firms should have higher skill levels and higher productivity than workers at nonunion firms. The amount of training provided to these workers once they are hired might be affected as well.[2]

Of course, these labor demand–side explanations often assume that the skills of workers are perfectly observable, that workers within skill categories are homogeneous, and that supplies of workers in

---

* Harry J. Holzer is Associate Professor of Economics, Michigan State University, and Faculty Research Fellow, National Bureau of Economic Research. He thanks seminar participants at Michigan State and the NBER for their helpful comments. Data and programs used are available from the author on request.

[1] Employer substitution in response to union wages was remarked as early as Lewis (1963), and was also stressed by Johnson (1975). Discussions of union effects on productivity and profits appear in Slichter et al. (1960), though they focus on institutional factors rather than direct wage effects. It should be noted that the effects of union wages predicted within a labor demand framework contrast with those predicted by the "efficient contracts" approach, which stresses union control over employ-

ment as well as wages (Farber 1986). Union effects may also be present for nonunion workers due to "insider" power (Lindbeck and Snower 1986) or the threat of unionization (Dickens 1985).

[2] The effects of unions on hours of training are theoretically ambiguous. If unions have a larger effect on starting wages than on subsequent wages, they might be expected to reduce on-the-job training in the same manner as does the minimum wage (Hashimoto 1981). But if unions raise wages independently of (or more than proportionately with) job tenure, it may pay for firms to invest more training in the new hires. On the other hand, employee incentives to invest in such training may be reduced (Mincer 1983). The specificity of the training involved and the expected tenure of the employee should also affect the firm's training choices.

each category are limitless (perfectly elastic).[3] If, however, these conditions are not met, profit-maximizing firms might choose to pay higher wages even in the absence of unions.[4] The recently burgeoning "efficiency wage" literature stresses the difficulties that firms may have in hiring, monitoring, and retaining high-productivity workers.[5] Because of these difficulties, firms might choose to pay higher wages in order to raise the quality or quantity (or both) of job applicants, reduce supervision costs, and reduce turnover. Employer search and matching models also suggest that firms might choose to pay high wages in order to lower the forgone profits associated with lengthy job vacancies and perhaps to lower hiring costs as well.[6] Finally, firms might change the structure and method of pay in addition to their average level of pay in order to give workers greater incentives for performing well.[7]

A great deal of empirical evidence has been produced on these general topics, but surprisingly few studies have investigated the direct effects of firm-level wages on employee characteristics and performance. For instance, the effects of unions on worker productivity, profits, training, and turnover have received widespread attention, but few studies focus on the direct effects of wages as opposed to the institution of unionism on these outcomes.[8] More generally, wage effects on turnover and absenteeism have been studied,[9] but a much broader range of employee costs and productive characteristics or outcomes among workers must be considered in order to correctly measure the firm's ability to offset the costs of higher wages. The magnitudes of the effects must be considered as well in any reasonable attempt to gauge the overall effects of wages on the firm.[10]

In this paper I use data from a survey of firms to estimate the effects of a firm's wages on its hiring costs and on the characteristics and performance of its workers. The focus on wages at the level of the firm (as opposed to the industry or individual worker) distinguishes this work from most previous studies on related issues. This focus is consistent with the evidence of wage differentials between firms for comparable workers of which economists have long been aware (for example, Dunlop 1957) but which remain poorly understood to date.

---

[3] Simple labor-demand models of wage-taking firms assume infinitely elastic supplies of labor in each category of workers. Instead, firms might face upward-sloping labor supply curves (especially in the short run), thereby causing equilibrium wages to respond to shifts in demand. But firms might still prefer to pay above-market wages to attract queues of highly skilled workers from which to choose.

[4] This possibility has, of course, long been recognized in the personnel and human resources literature. See, for example, Milkovich and Newman (1987).

[5] The different versions of efficiency wage theory are summarized in Yellen (1984) and Katz (1987).

[6] Employer search models include Barron et al. (1985), Jackman et al. (1985), and Albrecht and Axell (1985). These models frequently posit that employers choose wages and search intensities to maximize profits (which, in turn, depend on efficient matching of jobs and workers). Models in which wages depend on bargaining solutions once a match has occurred include Pissarides (1985) and Davidson et al. (1988). Evidence on employer search intensity also appears in Barron et al. (1985).

[7] See Brown (1990) and Ehrenberg and Milkovich (1987) for discussions of these issues.

[8] Union effects on productivity are reviewed in Addison and Hirsch (1986), and those on firm profits are discussed in Becker and Olson (1987). For union effects on turnover, see Mincer (1983) and Freeman and Medoff (1984). The turnover studies generally sort out wage and union effects. An alternative approach to this question is to use panel data in determining the extent to which the cross-sectional union wage effect is an actual wage premium as opposed to a return for higher-quality workers. Mincer (1983) and Freeman (1984) concluded that half or more of the observed effect is a union premium.

[9] See Pencavel (1970), Viscusi (1980), and Allen (1981) for evidence on turnover and absenteeism effects of wages.

[10] Two recent papers that consider the effects of wages on several employee outcomes and then compare potential benefits with the costs of higher wages are Raff and Summers (1987) and Leonard (1987). The former considers data on the Ford Motor Company before and after the introduction of the "Five-Dollar Day" in 1914. The latter analyzes effects of wages on supervisory personnel and turnover in six occupations for a sample of high-technology firms.

Data and Equations

In order to consider the effects of a firm's wage level on its cost and profits, we must distinguish between its effects on fixed hiring costs and on its variable operating costs and revenues. For a given period of time, a firm's profits can be written as follows:

$$(1) \quad \Pi = P \cdot Q(W, (1-V)J) - W \cdot (1-V) \cdot J - F_H C_H - C_O$$

where F_H and C_H reflect the frequency of hiring and direct cost per hire, respectively; V reflects the job vacancy rate at the firm; J is the number of jobs currently available in the firm; C_O reflects other costs (materials, energy, and so on); and P, Q, and W reflect prices, output, and wages at the firm. Both output and labor costs therefore depend on non-vacant jobs (that is, employment in the firm) as well as on wages in this formulation, although employment above the specified job level does not add to output or revenue here.

The frequency of hiring should reflect employee turnover as well as net employment growth at the firm. The cost per hire should reflect both the duration and intensity of hiring activity, which in turn should influence the number of hours spent by company personnel in recruiting, screening, and training new employees. The wages of company personnel and other direct hiring expenditures (such as for advertising) are included as well in this term. Finally, the vacancy rate also depends on both the frequency and duration of new hiring activity, as well as the fraction of each in which the positions being filled are actually vacant.

An above-market-clearing wage level might raise output levels by inducing the firm to hire more qualified workers. This effect is especially likely if the quantity or quality of job applicants attracted by the firm rises with the wage. The wage level might also effect direct hiring costs in a variety of ways. By reducing employee turnover (or, equivalently, raising employee tenure with the firm), higher wages will reduce the frequency with which new employees must be hired. Costs per hire might also be reduced

if a larger and better applicant pool leads to fewer hours spent recruiting and training by company personnel. Monetary costs of recruiting should be reduced as well. Finally, reductions in the frequency and duration of hiring will also reduce vacancy rates and thus the costs of forgone output associated with vacant jobs. Of course, large offsets of wage costs in terms of training or expected productivity should imply smaller ones in terms of vacancy rates and turnover, as the net attractiveness of high-wage jobs for workers becomes diminished.

Assuming that the price level and number of jobs are fixed, the effects of wages on firm profits can be seen by differentiating equation (1) as follows:

$$(2) \quad \frac{d\Pi}{dW} =$$

$$P \cdot \frac{\partial Q}{\partial W} - P \cdot \frac{\partial Q}{\partial (1-V)J} \frac{\partial V}{\partial W} \cdot J - (1-V)J$$

$$+ W \cdot J \cdot \frac{\partial V}{\partial W} - \frac{\partial F_H}{\partial W} \cdot C_H - \frac{\partial C_H}{\partial W} \cdot F_H$$

where the costs of higher wages must be balanced against the potential benefits of higher output, lower vacancies, and lower direct hiring costs. If the firm is free to choose its wage level, it will do so in the usual manner, by comparing these marginal costs and benefits. If, however, the wage is exogenously determined (by unions or otherwise), equation (2) simply enables us to measure the degree to which these higher costs can be offset by the firm.

The data I analyze to explore these issues are from the Employment Opportunity Pilot Project (EOPP) survey of firms in 1980 and 1982. This survey was administered in 28 local areas that were sites for the EOPP labor market experiments in the late 1970s. The sites are heavily concentrated in the South and Midwest, and about half are SMSAs. Large and low-wage firms were oversampled within each site.

The 1982 survey asked two general types of questions of employers, one regarding firm-wide characteristics (such

as number of employees, fraction unionized, number of vacancies, and perceived
hiring difficulties) and the other regarding the last worker hired during the
previous year. Information solicited by the
latter questions included (but was not
limited to) the occupation, gender, age,
and years of education of the worker, as
well as his or her wages, both starting and
current (or most recent if the employee
was no longer with the firm).

One measure of employee performance
that is available for these workers is a
subjective performance rating. Employers
were asked to score the productivity of the
last-hired worker in the previous year on a
scale from 0 to 100, with zero denoting no
productivity and 100 denoting the maximum feasible output on the job. The
question was asked for different points in
the employee's tenure at the firm: weeks
1–2, weeks 3–12, and currently or (if the
worker had left the firm) most recently.
The same questions were asked for "typical" employees on the same job so that
comparisons could be made.

As for more objective employee characteristics that might be performance-
related, a few different measures of
employee experience are available in these
data. One question asked how many
months of the employee's previous work
experience had some application to the
current job. Presumably, this question
gauges occupation- or industry-specific
experience. From the questions on the
employee's age and years of education, we
can also calculate a standard measure of
total labor market experience (age minus
years of education minus 6).

In the case of employees who were no
longer with the firm at the time of the
survey, employers were asked how long
the worker had remained with the firm.
For those still present, tenure can be
calculated from the date of hiring and the
survey date. In addition to the tenure
measures, several questions were asked
about the amount of time explicitly
invested in training the new employee.
Total hours of formal and informal
training provided by management, supervisors, or trained personnel, as well as time

spent with co-workers, are available. The
hours spent recruiting and screening
workers for the position are available as
well.

Using these data, we can estimate the
effects of firm-level wages on a variety of
labor outcomes. Note that an individual
employee's wages and quality (or productivity) can be decomposed into firm-wide
and individual-specific components:

$$(3) \qquad W_{ij} = W_j + w_{ij} \, (Q_{ij})$$

$$(4) \qquad Q_{ij} = Q_j \, (W_j) + q_{ij}$$

where W and Q reflect wages and quality,
respectively, and the subscripts i and j
denote the individual and firm, respectively. Thus, an individual's wage is
some function $w_{ij}(Q_{ij})$ of his or her
perceived quality in addition to a firm-
wide premium W_j, which in turn influences the quality of workers attracted and
retained by the firm. Other equations
comparable to (4) could be specified for
employee tenure or for time spent training the employee. In addition, some
firm-wide outcomes (such as vacancy rates
or ease of hiring) can be denoted as
follows:

$$(4') \qquad V_j = V(W_j) + v_j$$

with both wage-determined and random
components.

If direct observations on the firm wage
premium W_j were available, these equations could be estimated recursively. But
given that only individual employees'
wages are available in the data, I estimate
the following simultaneous equations:

$$(5) \qquad \begin{aligned} W_{ij} = a_w &+ b_w X_{ij} \\ &+ c_w Z_{ij} + d_w Y_j + \epsilon_{w,ij} \end{aligned}$$

$$(6) \qquad \begin{aligned} X_{ij} = a_x &+ b_x W_{ij} \\ &+ c_x Z_{ij} + \epsilon_{x,ij} \end{aligned}$$

$$(6') \qquad \begin{aligned} V_j = a_v &+ b_v W_{ij} \\ &+ c_v Z_{ij} + \epsilon_{v,ij} \end{aligned}$$

where the X_{ij} are the observed individual
characteristics or outcomes described above
(such as experience and productivity ratings), the Z_{ij} are exogenous worker and

job characteristics, and the Y_j are exogenous characteristics of the firm.[11]

The Z_{ij} variables used here include gender, occupation, and education (high school or college) dummies. The Y_j include 2-digit industry dummies as well as fraction unionized and a group of firm size variables. The latter include a continuous measure of firm size within the site as well as a set of dummies for total firm size (0–99 employees, 100–249, 250–499, 500–1,999, 2,000+).

The crucial assumption of this model is that the Y_j can be excluded from, and thereby used to identify, equations (6) and (6'). This assumption is tantamount to assuming that these variables affect the various labor outcomes strictly through the wage and not directly. This assumption is no doubt questionable, especially for industry (where technological differences independent of the wage may determine differences in hiring). Even firm size might directly affect the quality of job applicants independently of the wage.[12]

Furthermore, the exogeneity of industry and size with respect to the wage as well as the observed outcomes might also be in doubt, since wage differentials with regard to each might reflect maximizing behavior and therefore self-selection. Indeed, the "efficiency wage" theories noted above predict such self-selection, which may cause biases in estimated wage effects.[13]

For those reasons, I estimate different specifications of equations (6) and (6'). In some, the fraction unionized or plant and firm size (or both) will be used to identify the outcome equations; in others, industry dummies will be used as well. In all cases, I report the results of statistical tests for the validity of the exclusions used.

An additional concern in some cases below involves the *subjective* nature of certain outcome variables—namely, the productivity ratings and perceived ease of hiring. The former, in particular, are known to contain a good deal of measurement error (Bishop 1987). But since these subjective measures are used here only as dependent variables, random measurement error will result in upwardly biased standard errors but *not* in biased coefficients. Only if the subjective measures contain firm-specific components that are correlated with the instruments for firm-level wages will coefficient estimates be biased as well.[14]

Of course, the additional use of objective outcomes (experience/tenure instead of productivity scores and vacancy rates instead of ease of hiring) provides a check on any results obtained with the subjective outcomes. Furthermore, evidence will be provided below on the relationship between experience, productivity scores, and wages that will underscore the validity of both.

A few other aspects of the estimation should be noted. First, I estimate the various outcome equations independently of one another, thus abstracting from cross-equation effects and error correlations.[15] Thus, the outcome equations are of a reduced-form nature. Second, certain limited dependent variable functions are

---

[11] Individual wages, rather than firm-level wages, could be used in equation (4'). I continue to use firm-level wages, however, because the focus of this study is on wage differentials at that level. The firm-wide wages also lessen the problem of unobserved heterogeneity that would plague an analysis of wages at the individual level.

[12] Evidence presented in Holzer et al. (1988) shows that firm size affects the quantity of job applicants received per opening by firms independently of wages paid. Assuming that the quantity and quality of the best applicants are positively correlated, firm size might have independent effects on the quality of hires as well.

[13] If, for instance, all firms need workers of a certain performance level and all choose the wages needed to obtain such workers, there should be no observable relationship between wage levels and performance. Only to the extent that firms vary in

their need for high performance (because output and profits are more dependent on such performance for some than for others) will the wage effect be observed.

[14] This bias could be upward or downward, depending on the sign of the correlation between the firm-specific factor and the relevant independent variables.

[15] Seemingly Unrelated Regression estimates might have been appropriate here, but the identical specifications of right-hand side variables precluded their use.

estimated where appropriate, using predicted firm wages as the independent
variable.[16] Finally, continuous hazard models of the Weibull form are estimated in
order to gauge the effect of the firm's
wages on tenure outcomes.

Empirical Results

Table 1 contains the means and standard deviations of several key variables for
the sample used here. Two types of
variables are considered: those that describe the characteristics and performance
of the last worker hired in the previous
year, and those that describe the firm
itself.

Several characteristics of workers and
firms in the sample are noteworthy. The
starting wages are relatively low, reflecting
a sample that predominantly comprises
workers with high school educations in
clerical, sales, and service jobs. It is also a
fairly young sample, averaging 8–9 total
years of experience in the labor market.
Average tenure on the job thus far is just
under one year. These characteristics
reflect the fact that low-wage firms were
oversampled and also that last-hired workers generally over-represent high-turn-
over, low-wage jobs and low-tenure workers within firms. It is unclear to what
extent the results below hold for more
representative groups in the labor force or
for specific types of workers, such as
professional and managerial workers.

The vast majority of training hours
reported here are for informal training
by both co-workers and management.
Management spent less time hiring than
training. Current or most recent productivity scores average about 80, which
is significantly higher than the scores
attributed to workers at the time of hiring.

As for the firms themselves, they

Table 1. Means and Standard Deviations of
Key Variables.

Last Worker Hired:	
Starting Wage	$5.02
	(1.88)
Education:	
High School	.782
College	.087
Occupation:	
Professional/Technical	.042
Managerial	.040
Clerical	.154
Sales	.190
Crafts	.005
Operatives	.020
Laborer	.002
Service	.192
Missing	.355
Prior Experience (Years):	
General	8.581
	(8.925)
Related	2.446
	(4.420)
Tenure (Months)	11.380
	(7.152)
Hours of Training:	
Formal	8.991
	(38.779)
Informal (Management)	45.118
	(73.716)
Informal (Co-workers)	38.768
	(129.283)
Hours spent Hiring:	
Total	12.225
	(28.865)
Per Applicant	2.155
	(4.647)
Productivity Score	80.057
	(17.598)
Firm:	
Fraction Unionized	.113
	(.288)
Local Firm Size	68.185
	(227.933)
Vacancy Rate	.018
	(.059)
Perceived Ease of Hiring	
Qualified Workers:	
Very Easy	.315
Not Very Difficult	.267
Somewhat Difficult	.248
Very Difficult	.170

are apparently larger but less unionized than the average firm in random
national samples.[17] Vacancy rates are

---

[16] Tobit models will be used for vacancy rates,
since most firms (about 80%) report no vacancies.
They will also be used for applicable experience,
since about 40% of the sample reports no experience.
The use of predicted wage variables in these
equations is an approximation to a fuller treatment
of simultaneity in limited dependent variable models.

[17] Average private sector unionism in the United
States in 1982 was approximately 18%.

fairly low, and a majority of firms do not report difficulties in hiring qualified workers.

Fixed Costs: Hiring Time, Training Time

Tables 2 and 3 present estimates of the effects of the firm's wage levels on its hours spent hiring and training, respectively. These estimates are from versions of equation (6) in which hours spent hiring or training are the dependent variables. A similar set of equations are estimated for other outcomes and reported below.

The equations reported here and below are estimated using two-stage least squares. Several specifications are presented in which industry, fraction unionized, and firm size variables are used to identify the two stages and provide estimates of the firm wage. To test whether the effects of high wages caused by unions are different from the effects of high wages chosen by the firm, there are separate estimates of the union wage effect (column 3) and the size-wage premium effect (column 4). Coefficients on these variables when they appear as controls are presented as well. I use the individuals' starting wage to calculate this premium, and I control for a variety of personal characteristics (education, gender, occupation, site, and year hired) in the outcome equation.[18]

Table 2 contains the results for hours spent hiring. Because high-wage and large firms receive more job applicants than other firms, requiring more time for screening and interviewing applicants, I present estimates of equations for total hours spent as well as hours spent per applicant.[19]

The results show that high-wage firms generally must spend more total time on

their hiring activities than do other firms. Only when a strict union wage premium is considered (that is, when there are controls for industry and firm size) does this result not appear. Hours spent per applicant, however, show no such effect. If anything, high-wage firms tend to spend fewer hours per applicant for hiring (an effect that is not, however, statistically significant). Thus, the larger quantity (and perhaps quality) of job applicants received by high-wage firms requires them to spend more time on screening, though some small economies of scale may emerge.[20]

The effects of firm wages on hours spent training new employees appear in Table 3. Separate equations appear for the three types of training considered: formal training, informal training provided by management, and informal training provided by co-workers.

The results show generally negative effects of firm wages on all three types of training, although most effects are not significant. Only the effects on hours of informal training provided by management are marginally significant when we control for industry but not firm size.[21] Note that these results conflict somewhat with those presented by Barron et. al. (1985, 1989), who used the same data.[22]

A comparison of Tables 2 and 3 shows that the magnitudes of the combined negative training effects are generally larger than the positive effects on total time spent hiring. Although the lack of significant re-

---

[18] I use starting wages rather than current/most recent wages for calculation of the firm wage premia because the latter is strongly affected by job tenure, which is an outcome variable in this study. The correlation here between starting and current wages, however, is about .9, and estimated results using both variables are quite similar.

[19] See Footnote 12.

[20] These results are generally consistent with those of Barron, Bishop, and Dunkelberg (1985). An alternative interpretation of these findings might be that firms for which employee quality is crucial will both pay high wages and spend considerable time screening in order to obtain that quality.

[21] Industry controls appear to affect training independently of the wage, as F-statistics on these dummies are highly significant in all of the training equations.

[22] Barron et al. used log-odds specifications for the probabilities of workers receiving each type of training. Their use of discrete as opposed to continuous training variables, as well as individual rather than firm-level wages, probably accounts for the conflicting results.

Table 2. Firm Wage Effects on Hours Spent Hiring: The 1982 Wave of the
EOPP Survey of Firms.
(Two-Stage Least Squares)

	Equation			
Independent Variable	*1*	*2*	*3*	*4*
Total Hours Spent Hiring[a]				
Firm Wage	13.434**	21.970	−6.940	143.204*
	(5.361)	(14.911)	(13.906)	(75.099)
Fraction Unionized	—	—	—	−.344
				(.205)
Local Firm Size	—	—	3.444	—
			(.814)	
Firm Size Dummies	no	no	yes	no
Industry Dummies	no	yes	yes	yes
R^2	.055	.087	.103	.034
Hours Spent Hiring per Applicant[a]				
Firm Wage	.104	−1.095	−.965	−3.459
	(.859)	(1.919)	(2.242)	(7.424)
Fraction Unionized	—	—	—	.007
				(.020)
Local Firm Size	—	—	.041	—
			(.131)	
Total Firm Size Dummies	no	no	yes	no
Industry Dummies	no	yes	yes	yes
R^2	.069	.099	.101	.092

Notes: Education, gender, occupation, site, and year dummies are included. The sample size is 1,278. Industry dummies are 2-digit unless otherwise indicated. Standard errors are in parentheses. One asterisk indicates statistical significance at the .10 level; two asterisks indicate significance at the .05 level (two-tailed tests).
   For descriptions of the four specifications, see the text.
   [a] Hours spent hiring include hours spent recruiting, screening, and interviewing job applicants.

sults makes this pattern somewhat tenuous, the results at least suggest that total time spent and costs per new employee might be lower in high-wage firms.

Hiring Frequency: Tenure

A question not yet answered is how frequently these new employees must be hired, which depends on turnover. Previous research (cited above) has shown lower turnover among high-wage employees and industries as well as unionized firms. To investigate whether this pattern holds more generally for employees of high-wage firms, I estimated hazard functions in which the dependent variable is months of job tenure. Estimates are presented using the Weibull functional form. (See Table 4.)
   The results show that higher firm wages generally lead to higher tenure with the firm.[23] The effect of high wages in large firms is particularly strong; that in union firms, on the other hand, is negative but not significant.[24]

In summary, it appears that high wages in a firm generally enable it to reduce turnover and thus the number of new employees it must hire, as well as the total time associated with each new employee. Fixed hiring costs thus appear to be lower in high-wage firms.

_____

[23] Industry dummies are again significant in these outcome equations.
[24] It is important to remember when interpreting the coefficient on unions that this is a partial effect, controlling for the effects of firm wages, which in turn already capture industry, size, and union effects.

Table 3. Firm Wage Effects on Hours Spent Training.
(Two-Stage Least Squares)

Independent Variable	Specification			
	1	2	3	4
Formal Training by Management				
Firm Wage	−3.397	−10.878	−12.701	2.239
	(7.308)	(15.993)	(18.738)	(59.210)
Fraction Unionized	—	—	—	−.037
				(.162)
Local Firm Size	—	—	.458	—
			(1.096)	
Total Firm Size Dummies	no	no	yes	no
Industry Dummies	no	yes	yes	yes
R²	.035	.088	.089	.088
Informal Training by Management				
Firm Wage	−13.085	−50.603*	−28.982	−158.590
	(13.759)	(30.004)	(35.507)	(130.113)
Fraction Unionized	—	—	—	.306
				(.355)
Local Firm Size	—	—	−2.762	—
			(2.077)	
Total Firm Size Dummies	no	no	yes	no
Industry Dummies	no	yes	yes	yes
R²	.049	.084	.087	.066
Informal Training by Co-Workers				
Firm Wage	−45.258*	−26.412	−13.877	82.412
	(24.384)	(53.911)	(62.686)	(204.606)
Fraction Unionized	—	—	—	−.308
				(.558)
Local Firm Size	—	—	−2.558	—
			(3.667)	
Total Firm Size Dummies	no	no	yes	no
Industry Dummies	no	yes	yes	yes
R²	.035	.068	.074	.005

Notes: See *Notes* under Table 2.

Vacancies and Ease of Hiring

As noted above, a firm's output and labor costs reflect its vacancies as well as its direct wage costs, and vacancy rates can give us some indication of the frequency and duration of hiring activities. Estimates of vacancy rate equations are presented in Table 5. Given the large fraction of firms (about 85%) that report no vacancies, I estimate those equations using Tobit as well as OLS. In both cases, the firm-level wage is the predicted wage based on virtually the same instruments as were used in the previous tables.[25] Control variables are comparable as well.

The results show that higher wages are usually associated with lower vacancy rates, although, once again, the exact magnitudes are difficult to pin down. Coefficient magnitudes among the Tobit estimates are much more unstable than those among the estimates from OLS equations, varying in both sign and mag-

[25] For computational reasons, I use 1-digit rather than 2-digit industry dummies here. All other instruments and controls are comparable.

Table 4. Firm Wage Effects on Months of Job Tenure.
(Weibull Hazard Functions)

Independent Variable	Specification			
	1	*2*	*3*	*4*
Firm Wage	.048	.180**	−.048	.540**
	(.050)	(.085)	(.103)	(.192)
Fraction Unionized	—	—	—	−.0013
				(.0006)
Local Firm Size	—	—	.033	—
			(.008)	
Firm Size Dummies	no	no	yes	no
Industry Dummies	no	yes	yes	yes
Log L	−174.68	−146.78	−154.30	−164.21

Notes: See *Notes* under Table 2.

nitude. Also, the standard errors are consistently larger among the Tobit estimates. The largest and most significant negative effect is the one associated with union wages in the Tobit equations, whereas the Tobit effect of large firm size has the opposite sign.

An alternative method of testing for the effects of wages on hiring is to analyze the firm's perceived ease of hiring qualified workers. As noted above, this subjective variable may refer to any or all components of hiring costs and may also reflect firm-specific factors that could cause bi-

Table 5. Firm Wage Effects on Job Vacancy Rates.
(Two-Stage Least Squares and Tobit Analyses)

Independent Variable	Specification			
	1	*2*	*3*	*4*
Two-Stage Least Squares Analysis				
Firm Wage	−.020*	−.056**	−.014	−.069*
	(.011)	(.019)	(.023)	(.038)
Fraction Unionized	—	—	—	.0001
				(.0001)
Local Firm Size	—	—	−.006	—
			(.002)	
Total Firm Size Dummies	no	—	yes	no
Industry Dummies	no	yes	yes	yes
R²	.052	.059	.072	.059
Tobit Analysis				
Firm Wage	−.023	−.028	−.158	.388**
	(.048)	(.084)	(.104)	(.165)
Fraction Unionized	—	—	—	−.0017
				(.0006)
Local Firm Size	—	—	.014	—
			(.007)	
Total Firm Size Dummies	no	no	yes	no
Industry Dummies	no	yes	yes	yes
Log L	−547.7	−253.9	−250.3	−249.2

Notes: In these equations, firm wage is a predicted variable based on the regressors used in all of the previous tables. Industry dummies are 1-digit here.

Table 6. Firm Wage Effects on Ease of Hiring.[a]
(Two-Stage Least Squares)

	Specification			
Independent Variable	1	2	3	4
Firm Wage	.468**	.563**	.186	2.687*
	(.093)	(.209)	(.232)	(1.423)
Fraction Unionized	—	—	—	.006
				(.004)
Local Firm Size	—	—	.042	—
			(.014)	
Total Firm Size Dummies	no	no	yes	no
Industry Dummies	no	yes	yes	yes
R^2	.095	.116	.135	.040

[a] The dependent variable is equal to one if employer finds it very easy or not very difficult to hire qualified workers and zero otherwise.

Also, see *Notes* below Table 2.

ases if correlated with regressors. Still, it provides us with an additional measure of hiring costs with which to estimate the effects of a firm's wages.

Equations for the effects of wages on perceived ease of hiring appear in Table 6. In these equations, the dependent variable takes on a value of one if firms report that the hiring of qualified workers is "very easy" or "not very difficult" and zero if such hiring is "somewhat difficult" or "very difficult." Other specifications not reported here provided similar estimates.[26]

The results show that higher wages generally cause the perceived ease of hiring qualified workers to rise as well. Only the union wage effect is not significant here; the wage effect associated with firm size is quite large.

Overall, then, firm wage levels appear to be negatively associated with hiring costs and difficulties. Though hours spent recruiting and screening rise for high-wage firms, hours spent training per new hire usually fall by even larger amounts. The frequency of new hiring apparently is reduced, employee tenure rises, and the costs associated with vacant jobs are probably reduced as well.

Employee Characteristics and Performance

For employees of relatively long tenure, the variable costs of higher wages per hour or week of work will probably outweigh any reductions in fixed hiring costs that they might cause. These variable costs must therefore be evaluated in the light of improvements in the characteristics or performance of employees hired in these firms.

For want of direct evidence on worker output, I use two proxies for the performance of workers in the firm. One is the number of years of prior experience the employee has had (both a measure of general experience and a measure of experience related to the job at the firm). The other is the productivity score assigned to the worker either currently or at the end of his or her tenure with the firm. The experience measures have the advantage of being objective. There may be some doubt, however, as to whether prior experience is truly productivity-enhancing.[27]

To examine the viability of these proxies for worker productivity, OLS equations for wages and productivity scores of workers were estimated (see the appen-

---

[26] For instance, defining the dependent variable as one if hiring is very easy and zero otherwise produces quite comparable results.

[27] See, for instance, Medoff and Abraham (1981) for evidence that tenure with the firm may not enhance worker productivity.

dix). The wage equations correspond to equation (5) above. They appear with and without the productivity score included as an additional independent variable.

These equations show that both experience and productivity scores are positively associated with individuals' wages. The effects of related experience are several times larger than those of general experience. Furthermore, the effects of productivity scores on wages seem to be largely (though not totally) explained by prior experience. The productivity score equations also show particularly large effects of related experience.

Various wage-change and productivity-change equations in Holzer (1988) produce results that are fairly comparable to those presented in the appendix.[28] Since these change equations omit fixed effects of firms in the performance ratings (which should capture some of the subjective differences across managers of different firms in how they rate employees), we may conclude that both prior experience measures and subjective productivity scores are reasonable proxies for worker performance at the firm.

Tables 7 and 8 present results on the effects of firm-level wages on the proxies for worker performance. Table 7 contains equations for years of prior experience, and Table 8 contains the firm productivity scores.

Table 7 provides separate estimates for general and related experience. Because of the large fraction (about 40%) of workers with no related experience reported, Tobit estimates for this latter measure are provided as well.[29] The results show generally positive effects of

firm wages on years of prior experience. These estimates are generally not significant, however, once industry is controlled for. Furthermore, industry effects generally appear to exist independently of firm wages (according to F-tests on the industry dummies).

The results of productivity score equations (Table 8) provide strong support for the notion that worker productivity rises with the firm wage level. Effects of wages are positive and significant in all cases except for the firm-size-wage effect. In contrast, coefficients on the control variables for unionism and local firm size suggest that these factors have little direct effect.

All of these estimated effects of firm wages on hiring costs and employee characteristics and performance are summarized in Table 9. Specifically, the table shows the sign (plus or minus) of the wage effect of each outcome variable in Tables 2–8 under each of the four different exclusion restrictions. Results that are significant at the 10% level in a 2-tailed test are represented by 2 signs, and those that are significant at the 5% level or better are represented by three signs.

The table shows that the firm's wage level generally has positive and negative effects, respectively, on total hours spent hiring and training new workers. Effects on vacancy rates are also generally negative, whereas those on employee tenure, perceived ease of hiring, experience, and perceived productivity are positive. The vacancy, ease of hiring, and productivity score effects are significant in three of the four specifications presented, and the tenure effect is significant (at the 10% level) in two of the four. In general, the wage premia associated with firm size are more likely to be significant than are those associated with unionism.

A Summing Up of Wage Effects

To determine the extent to which wage costs can be offset for firms, it is necessary to sum the magnitudes of the estimated wage

---

[28] In those equations, I interpret employee tenure at the firm as the change in total experience for that worker. The effects of experience on productivity scores and on wages, as well as the effects of productivity scores on wages, continue to be positive and significant in those equations, with most magnitudes remaining quite comparable to those of cross-section estimates.

[29] As in the case of vacancy rate equations, the predicted wage variable is based on the same set of instruments as in all other equations except for the use of 1-digit dummies. Controls are comparable as well.

Table 7. Firm Wage Effects on Years of Prior Experience.

Independent Variable	Specification			
	1	2	3	4
General Experience: Two-Stage Least Squares				
Firm Wage	4.713**	2.627	4.468	7.572
	(1.630)	(3.621)	(4.199)	(14.912)
Fraction Unionized	—	—	—	.029
				(.041)
Plant Size	—	—	−.012	—
			(.245)	
Firm Size Dummies	no	yes	yes	no
Industry Dummies	no	yes	yes	yes
R^2	.048	.082	.087	.068
Related Experience: Two-Stage Least Squares				
Firm Wage	3.024**	1.837	1.912	4.172
	(.775)	(1.739)	(2.032)	(6.297)
Fraction Unionized	—	—	—	−.007
				(.107)
Plant Size	—	—	.017	—
			(.119)	
Firm Size Dummies	no	no	yes	no
Industry Dummies	no	yes	yes	yes
R^2	.079	.108	.110	.113
Related Experience: Tobit[a]				
Firm Wage	4.430**	1.795	1.139	2.521
	(1.153)	(2.007)	(2.392)	(4.094)
Fraction Unionized	—	—	—	−.003
				(.014)
Plant Size	—	—	.142	—
			(.171)	
Firm Size Dummies	no	no	yes	no
Industry Dummies	no	yes	yes	yes
Log L	−2,907.1	−2,902.1	−2,901.1	−2,902.1

[a] The tobit equations use 1-digit industry dummies rather than 2-digit for computational reasons. Also, see *Notes* beneath Table 2.

effects for hiring and training, vacancy rates, and worker quality/performance. Although this process requires some fairly heroic assumptions and therefore must be viewed as yielding only suggestive evidence, it does shed light on the relative magnitudes of the estimated effects and therefore on the net impact of these effects.

Equation (2) (page 149-S), which decomposes wage effects on profits into components based on output (directly and through vacancy rates), wage costs, and fixed hiring costs, can be adapted for this purpose:

$$(7) \quad \frac{d\ln\Pi}{d\ln W} = \left(\frac{d\ln PQ}{d\ln W} - \gamma_W \frac{d\ln WC}{d\ln W} - \gamma_H \frac{d\ln HC}{d\ln W} \right) \frac{1}{\gamma_\kappa}$$

where the revenue (PQ) and wage cost (WC) elasticities include the direct effects of wages (first and third terms of equation 2, respectively) as well as their indirect effects through the vacancy rate (second and fourth terms of equation 2, respectively). The hiring cost (HC) elasticity includes wage effects on both

Table 8. Firm Wage Effects on Current Productivity Scores.
(Two-Stage Least Squares)

Independent Variable	Specification			
	1	2	3	4
Firm Wage	7.053**	16.056**	15.487*	16.773
	(3.308)	(7.461)	(8.719)	(27.788)
Fraction Unionized	—	—	—	−.002
				(.076)
Local Firm Size	—	—	.270	—
			(.570)	
Total Firm Size Dummies	no	no	yes	no
Industry Dummies	no	yes	yes	yes
R^2	.044	.076	.077	.075

Notes: See *Notes* beneath Table 2.

frequency and cost per hire (fifth and sixth terms of equation 2), and γ_W, γ_H, and γ_K represent the shares of output accounted for by direct wage costs, hiring costs, and profits, respectively.

Equation (7) is obtained by dividing equation (2) by PQJ/W. The estimated effect of wages on profits can then be calculated from the estimated means and coefficients in previous tables.[30] To perform the calculation, .6, .1, and .3 are used as approximations for γ_W, γ_H, and γ_K, respectively. This approximation is based on the fact that employee compensation accounts for about 70% of private, nonagricultural national income. I assume that 10% of this amount goes directly to personnel-related activities, although the calculations below are not very sensitive to this particular assumption.[31]

In order to obtain estimates of the elasticity of revenue with respect to wages, two further assumptions are made: (1) proportional changes in performance ratings equal proportional changes in output per worker and therefore in revenue (since prices are being treated as constant); and (2) the effect of a percentage point change in the vacancy rate (and therefore of occupied jobs) on output is one percent—that is, there are constant returns to scale.

As for the elasticity of profit with respect to hiring costs, I assume that the hiring frequency is the inverse of expected job tenure and then use the estimated wage effects on duration (Table 4) to calculate the effects of wages on this frequency.[32] Hours spent recruiting and training each new employee are used as a measure of the cost per hire.[33] But since an hour spent by co-workers is presumably not as costly to the firm as an hour spent by management personnel, each of the latter is assigned twice the value of each of the former.[34] I also adjust time

---

[30] I divide by J for this term and all other terms of the equation, since the estimated effects apply only to the last worker hired. The estimated effect of ln$W$ on performance ratings is then divided by mean performance and added to the vacancy rate effect of ln$W$ to obtain the elasticity estimate. I use the OLS rather than tobit estimates of vacancy effects, since the former are more stable and plausible in magnitude.

[31] With the exception of the financial sector (in which compensation is only about one-third of income), compensation fractions in all 1-digit industries range from .7 to .8. Using .8 instead of .7 (and keeping .1 as the part attributable to hiring activities) raises the percent of profit lost by about one percentage point above the numbers presented in the bottom row of Table 10 (i.e., the new numbers range from −.0832 to −.1542). Using .65 and .05 as γ_W and γ_H, respectively (instead of .6 and .1), raises

this percent lost by under one percentage point (yielding numbers ranging from −.0831 to −.1512).

[32] If $F_H = 1/T$, then dlnF_H/dln$W$ = −dln$T$/dln$W$, which is simply the additive inverse of any of the Weibull hazard function coefficients presented in Table 4.

[33] I thus abstract from direct monetary costs of recruiting.

[34] Mean weakly wages in May 1978 for managers were $322, compared to $231, $175, and $152 for sales, clericals, and service workers, respectively, who are paid weekly. For those earning hourly rates the corresponding wages are $4.66, $2.93, $3.72, and

Table 9. Summary of Firm Wage Effects on Hiring Costs and Employee Performance.

Outcome	Industry, Union, Size Effects	Union, Size Effects	Union Effect	Size Effect
Hours Spent Hiring:				
Total	+ + +	+	−	+ +
Per Applicant	+	−	−	−
Hours Spent Training:				
Formal	−	−	−	+
Informal: Management	−	− −	−	−
Informal: Coworkers	− −	−	−	+
Month of Tenure	+	+ + +	−	+ + +
Job Vacancy Rates	− −	− − −	−	− −
Ease of Hiring	+ + +	+ + +	+	+ +
Prior Experience:				
General	+ + +	+	+	+
Related	+ + +	+	+	+
Productivity Scores	+ + +	+ + +	+ +	+

Note: Three plus or minus signs reflect statistical significance at the 5% level (2-tailed test); two reflect significance at the 10% level; and one reflects only the direction of a generally insignificant effect. The four columns here correspond to columns 1–4 in Tables 2 through 8. Job vacancy rate and experience level estimates reflect 2SLS with linear (rather than Tobit) second stage.

spent in formal training to account for the fact that managers usually train two or more employees at a time.[35] The elasticity of total hiring costs is then obtained by aggregating these effects and dividing by appropriately weighted means.

Table 10 presents calculations of how a 10% rise in the firm's wages will affect profits. Separate estimates are presented based on wage effects from each of the four specifications used in Tables 2 through 8. Table 10 also presents estimates of each of the three terms of equation (7), which are appropriately weighted and summed to produce estimates of total effects as well.

The results show that a 10% rise in wages will lower the share of output going to profits by 2.2% to 4.3%. Transformed into fractions of profits lost, these figures range from about 7.4% to 14.5%. More specifically, a wage increase of 10% caused by unions will reduce profits by 10.6%, and the same wage increase associated with firm size will reduce profits by about 8.3%. A comparison

of these results with the reduction in profits that would be caused without any offsetting effects suggests that about 46% of the higher wage costs associated with unions and about 58% of those associated with firm size is offset by firms.

These findings are, of course, heavily conditioned by the relatively large weight attached to the revenue effect and to the magnitude of the wage effect on revenue (output), which are similar in the union and firm size cases. The crucial assumption that observed wage effects on performance rating effects equal those on output is admittedly questionable; but note that the estimated magnitudes of the offset are consistent with various estimates of the fraction of the union wage differential that is accounted for by personal characteristics (see, for example, Mincer 1983; Freeman 1984). The evidence of lower profits in the union sector despite higher experience and productivity (Becker and Olson 1987) is also consistent with the finding here of a lower wage offset for unionized firms than for other firms.

$2.93, respectively. (BLS Bulletin 2096, September 1982). The two-to-one ratio of managerial to non-managerial wages is thus a reasonable approximation.

[35] See Bishop (1988), who assumes an average class size of two at formal training sessions.

Conclusion

I have provided estimates of how the wage level of a firm affects its hiring and training

Table 10. Effects of a 10% Wage Increase on Profits.

Components of Effects	Industry, Union, Size Effects	Union, Size Effect	Union Effect	Size Effect
1. Output Effect				
Direct Wage Effect	.0088	.0201	.0193	.0210
Vacancy Effect	.0020	.0056	.0014	.0069
Total	.0108	.0257	.0207	.0279
2. Labor Cost Effect				
Direct Effect	−.0982	−.0982	−.0982	−.0982
Vacancy Effect	.0020	.0056	.0014	.0069
Total	−.0962	−.0926	−.0968	−.0913
Weighted by Share	−.0577	−.0556	−.0581	−.0548
3. Hiring Cost Effect				
Cost per Hire Effect	.0295	.0582	.0606	−.0332
Weighted by Share	.0030	.0058	.0061	−.0033
Frequency Effect	.0048	.0180	−.0048	.0540
Weighted by Share	.0005	.0018	−.0005	.0054
4. TOTAL EFFECT				
Percent of Output Lost	−.0434	−.0223	−.0318	−.0248
Percent Profit Reduced	−.1446	−.0743	−.1060	−.0827

Note: The four columns correspond directly to columns 1–4 in Tables 2 through 8. Job vacancy rate estimates reflect 2SLS with linear (rather than Tobit) second stage.

costs as well as the observed characteristics and performance of its employees. The estimates were made using data from a nationwide survey of firms on the number of hours spent hiring and training a recently hired employee; the characteristics (experience and job tenure) and subjective ratings of the performance of that employee; and vacancy rates as well as other measures of hiring difficulties. Separate estimates are provided for union wage premia and for wage premia associated with firm size or industry.

The results generally show that high-wage firms have lower hiring and training costs as well as better employee performance. More specifically, I find fewer hours spent on informal training, longer tenure with the firm, more years of previous job experience, higher performance ratings, lower vacancy rates, and higher perceived ease in hiring for firms with higher wages. The magnitudes and significance levels (as well as the signs, in a few cases) of these effects are, however, quite sensitive to whether identification is achieved through fraction unionized or employee size.

I have also attempted to measure, although necessarily crudely, the overall costs and benefits to the firm of these higher wages. The calculations suggest that about 46% of the higher wage premia gained by unions and about 58% of those associated with large firms are offset by reduced costs and improved performance.

A number of important caveats must be kept in mind. First, the sample overrepresents young workers early in their tenure with these employers. Second, the statistical tests may be plagued by a number of biases, especially because of the nonrandom nature (due to self-selection) of firm wage levels. The overall direction of these biases, as well as their magnitudes, remain unclear. Finally, some very strong assumptions enter into the calculations of wage costs offset by firms. Consequently, the exact magnitudes of these effects are uncertain. All that can be said with confidence is that firms respond to higher wage costs in a variety of ways that offset substantial fractions of those costs.

Future research on these wage effects will require better measures of outcomes, especially those pertaining to worker output and performance. Financial data on the profits and capital values of firms might be preferable. More careful specifications of how various outcomes are related to each other and to wage measures would also be useful. Finally, there is a need for a better understanding of the extent to which results such as those presented in this paper depend on the particular characteristics of workers, jobs, and firms.

Appendix
Experience and Effects of Productivity Scores on Wages of Individuals: OLS Equations.

Independent Variable	Specification		
	1	*2*	*3*
	Wage Levels		
General Experience	.0113**	—	.0112**
	(.0027)		(.0026)
(General Experience)^2	−.0003**	—	−.0003**
	(.0001)		(.0001)
Related Experience	.0411**	—	.0393**
	(.0044)		(.0045)
(Related Experience)^2	−.0010**	—	−.0009**
	(.0002)		(.0002)
Productivity Score	—	.0019**	.0009**
		(.0004)	(.0003)
R^2	.511	.423	.514
	Productivity Score Levels		
General Experience		.1604	
		(.2181)	
(General Experience)^2		−.0007	
		(.0060)	
Related Experience		2.0327**	
		(.3655)	
(Related Experience)^2		−.0545**	
		(.0151)	
R^2		.150	

Note: In addition to the variables listed, the wage equations contain the following controls: gender, education, occupation, year, and site dummies, as well as hours of training. All but the year dummies also appear in the productivity score equations.

* Significant at the .10 level; ** significant at the .05 level (two-tailed tests).

REFERENCES

Addison, John, and Barry Hirsch. 1986. *The Economic Analysis of Unions.* London: Allen & Unwin.

Albrecht, James, and Bo Axell. 1984. "An Equilibrium Model of Search Unemployment." *Journal of Political Economy,* Vol. 92, No. 5 (October), pp. 824–40.

Allen, Steven. 1984. "Trade Unions, Absenteeism and Exit-Voice." *Industrial and Labor Relations Review,* Volume 37, No. 3 (April), pp. 331–45.

Barron, John, et al. 1985. "Employer Search: The Interviewing and Hiring of New Employees." *Review of Economics and Statistics,* Vol. 67, No. 1 (February).

Barron, John, et al. 1989. "Job Matching and On-the-Job Training." *Journal of Labor Economics,* Vol. 7, No. 1 (January), pp. 1–19.

Becker, Brian, and Craig Olson. 1987. "Labor Relations and Firm Performance." In R. Block et al., eds., *Human Resources and the Performance of the Firm.* Madison, Wis.: Industrial Relations Research Association.

Bishop, John. 1988. "Do Employers Share the Costs and Benefits of General Training?" Unpublished paper, Cornell University.

Brown, Charles. 1990. "Firm Choice of Method of Pay." *Industrial and Labor Relations Review,* this issue.

Davidson, Carl, et al. 1988. "The Structure of Simple

General Equilibrium Models with Frictional Unemployment." *Journal of Political Economy,* Vol. 96, No. 6 (December), pp. 1267–93.

Dickens, William. 1986. "Wages, Employment, and the Threat of Collective Action by Workers." National Bureau of Economic Research, Working Paper No. 1856.

Ehrenberg, Ronald, and George Milkovich. 1987. "Compensation and Firm Performance." In R. Block et al., eds., *Human Resources and the Performance of the Firm.* Madison, Wis.: Industrial Relations Research Association.

Farber, Henry. 1986. "The Analysis of Union Behavior." In O. Ashenfelter and R. Layard, eds., *Handbook of Labor Economics.* Amsterdam: North Holland.

Freeman, Richard. 1984. "A Longitudinal Analysis of Trade Unionism." *Journal of Labor Economics,* Vol. 2, No. 1 (January), pp. 1–20.

Freeman, Richard, and James Medoff. 1984. *What Do Unions Do?* New York: Basic Books.

Hashimoto, Masanori. 1982. "Minimum Wage Effects on Training on the Job." *American Economic Review,* Vol. 72, No. 5 (December), pp. 1070–87.

Holzer, Harry. 1988. "The Determinants of Employee Productivity and Earnings: Some New Evidence." National Bureau of Economic Research, Working Paper No. 2782.

Holzer, Harry, Lawrence Katz, and Alan Krueger. 1988. "Job Queues and Wages: New Evidence on Minimum Wages and the Inter-Industry Wage Structure." National Bureau of Economic Research, Working Paper No. 2561.

Jackman, Richard, et al. 1985. "On Vacancies." London School of Economics, Center for Labor Economics Working Paper.

Johnson, George. 1975. "Economic Analysis of Trade Unionism." *American Economic Review,* Vol. 65, No. 2 (May), pp. 23–28.

Katz, Lawrence. 1987. "Efficiency Wage Theories: A Partial Evaluation." in S. Fischer, ed., *NBER Macroeconomics Annual.* Cambridge: MIT Press.

Leonard, Jonathan. 1987. "Carrots and Sticks: Pay,

Supervisions and Turnover." *Journal of Labor Economics,* Vol. 5, No. 4, Part 2 (October), pp. S136–S152.

Lewis, H. Gregg. 1963. *Unionism and Relative Wages in the United States.* Chicago: University of Chicago Press.

Lindbeck, Assar, and Dennis Snower. 1986. "Wage Setting, Unemployment, and Insider-Outsider Relations." *American Economic Review,* Vol. 76, No. 2 (May), pp. 235–49.

Medoff, James, and Katharine Abraham. 1981. "Are Those Paid More Really More Productive? The Case of Experience." *Journal of Human Resources,* Vol. 16, No. 2 (Spring), pp. 186–216.

Milkovich, George, and Jerry Newman. 1987. *Compensation.* Texas: Business Publications.

Mincer, Jacob. 1981. "Union Effects: Wages, Turnover, and Job Training." National Bureau of Economic Research, Working Paper No. 808.

Pencavel, John. 1970. *An Analysis of the Quit Rate in American Manufacturing Industry.* Princeton, N.J.: Princeton University Press.

Pissarides, Christopher. 1985. "Short-Run Equilibrium Dynamics of Unemployment, Vacancies, and Real Wages." *American Economic Review,* Vol. 75, No. 4 (September), pp. 676–90.

Raff, Daniel, and Lawrence Summers. 1987. "Did Henry Ford Pay Efficiency Wages?" *Journal of Labor Economics,* Vol. 5, No. 4, Part 2 (October), pp. S57–S86.

Slichter, Sumner, et al., 1960. *The Impact of Collective Bargaining on Management.* Washington, D.C.: Brookings.

Viscusi, W. Kip. 1980. "Sex Differences in Worker Quitting." *Review of Economics and Statistics,* Vol. 64, No. 3 (August).

Weiss, Andrew. 1988. "High School Graduation, Performance, and Wages." *Journal of Political Economy,* Vol. 96, No. 4 (August).

Yellen, Janet. 1984. "Efficiency Wage Models of Unemployment." *American Economic Review,* Vol. 74, No. 2 (May), pp. 200–205.

FIRMS' CHOICE OF METHOD OF PAY

CHARLES BROWN*

Using data from the BLS Industry Wage Survey, the author tests the theory that firms choose their methods of pay by balancing the gains from more precise links between performance and pay against monitoring costs. The results confirm most of the predictions from the general theory. For example, large firms make significantly greater use of standard-rate pay than do small firms, and incentive pay (such as piece rates) is less likely in jobs with a variety of duties than in jobs with a narrow set of routines.

THE importance of differences in methods of pay is not a new topic,[1] but it is one that has received increasing attention from academic researchers and compensation specialists. Its claim to academic attention rests largely on the hypothesized relationship between methods of wage payment and the cost of monitoring workers in different contexts—a theme that, in turn, lies at the heart of recent theoretical insights about the structure of wages. Improvements in technology, particularly the growing use of computers in the office and the factory, and even in long-haul trucking, are reducing dramatically the cost of monitoring workers in some industries.[2] Compensation specialists have noted a decline in the link between pay and performance, and many predict the crisis of competitiveness facing U.S. firms will force a re-strengthening of this link for both managerial and nonmanagerial employees (McLaughlin 1986; Morse 1986).[3] Meanwhile, on the other side of the Pacific, "there is starting to be a shift away from pay by seniority and towards pay determined by merit" in Japan as well (Maidment 1987:S-18).

But problems in implementing contracts linking pay and performance run into monitoring problems that are stressed in the academic literature. One example of general interest is the contract of New York Jets quarterback Ken O'Brien,

* Charles Brown is Professor of Economics and Research Scientist at the Institute for Social Research at the University of Michigan, and a Research Associate of the National Bureau of Economic Research. This research was supported by the National Science Foundation (Grant 8708370). The author thanks Nancy Lemrow, Thomas Hungerford, and Marsha Silverberg for research assistance. For helpful suggestions, he also thanks seminar participants at the NBER and these universities: Chicago, Cornell, Georgetown, Illinois, Kentucky, Michigan, and Toronto.

Copies of the data and computer programs used to generate the results presented in this paper are available from the author at the Institute for Social Research, University of Michigan, Ann Arbor, MI 48109.

[1] Julius Caesar is said to have enhanced the effectiveness of the Roman army by implementing a performance-based salary system in lieu of booty (McLaughlin 1986:8).

[2] The *Washington Post* reported that a large hotel now requires each maid to punch her ID number on the room telephone when she enters and leaves each room. Similar opportunities are available for monitoring typists using word processing packages that can record the typist's work level while performing traditional word processing. For evidence of the potential of modern technology for more precise monitoring of workers, see National Research Council (1986) and Shaiken (1987).

[3] A survey of compensation committee members of 350 large U.S. corporations found this was "the most important objective in the next five years" (McLaughlin 1986:7).

under which part of O'Brien's pay is keyed to his NFL quarterbacks' rating, which penalizes incomplete passes but not sacks. Said former Jets quarterback Joe Namath, "I'm amazed at [O'Brien's] accuracy, but I see him hold the ball more than he should. I always thought it was better to have second and 10 than second and 18. I don't like incentive contracts that pertain to numbers" (Anderson 1988).

The existing theory of the determinants of method of pay is fairly straightforward: in essence, it asserts that different methods of pay offer different approximations to an idealized pay-for-performance incentive for workers, but carry different costs. In general, the link between pay and performance will be stronger where performance is more accurately observed (for example, where there are piece rates), but such accuracy is likely to be expensive. Hence, across firms or jobs within a firm, variations in costs and benefits of accurate monitoring are hypothesized to explain differences in method of pay.

This theory receives considerable support in the prescriptive treatments in personnel texts (though the topic appears to command less attention in such texts now than it once did) and in a quite limited set of empirical analyses. Perhaps little empirical work in the spirit of the new personnel economics has been devoted to these issues because data in household surveys and most establishment surveys are not very helpful. The purpose of this paper is to help fill this gap.

Existing Theoretical Models

A recent paper by Lazear (1986), which presents several models of the choice of method of pay,[4] provides a convenient

point of departure. Existing models generally assume the firm has two choices: paying piece rates (earnings tied to an objective measure of value of output) or paying time rates or salaries (earnings not linked to how much is produced). To simplify, I will assume the work-week is fixed, which means that earnings per period are fixed under the latter system.

In the simplest model of this sort, each worker's productivity is fixed (effort is not an issue), and the methods of pay sort workers among firms. Workers know their own productivity, but firms do not, unless they pay a monitoring cost θ. The firm can either pay θ to measure a worker's productivity q directly, in which case it pays the worker $q - \theta$, or not pay the cost of the piece-rate monitoring system and pay salary S. The piece rate structure obviously satisfies the zero-profit requirement. Firms using salaries must in equilibrium choose S so they, too, earn zero profits. Since workers know their own q's, they choose the type of firm in which their earnings are highest: workers with $q > S + \theta$ choose piece-rate firms and those with $q < S + \theta$ choose the firms paying salaries. (See Figure 1.) If q has density and c.d.f. $f(q)$ and $F(q)$ respectively, the zero-profit condition is

$$(1) \qquad S = \frac{1}{F(S + \theta)} \int_0^{S + \theta} q f(q) dq$$

Lazear shows that an $S > 0$ satisfying this condition exists so long as $\theta > 0$. Thus, the

---

[4] An alternative approach would be to emphasize the somewhat different principal-agent literature, as developed by Harris and Raviv (1979), Holmstrom (1979 and 1982), or Green and Stokey (1983). A fundamental difference between these papers and Lazear's is the assumed source of randomness. Lazear assumes that unless the cost of an accurate piece rate system is undertaken, the firm does not know how much the worker has produced. The principal-agent papers, on the other hand, assume

that firms *do* observe each worker's output (an exception is part of Holmstrom's 1982 paper) but this output depends on environmental factors the worker cannot control as well as on effort, so that paying piece rates introduces risk, which agents find undesirable. The extra information sought by the firm is some measure of effort, so that the worker can be partially insured in cases where output is low due to environmental randomness rather than worker shirking. This approach is very likely the right one for thinking about corporate CEOs or salespersons, for whom output is easily measured but environmental randomness is important. Lazear's approach seems better suited to the blue-collar workers in the IWS, for whom environmental randomness is relatively unimportant (the most important randomness, breakdown of machines or material unavailability, being easily measured) but measuring output (performance) is costly.

salary firms save on monitoring costs and pay lower wages, but these advantages are exactly counterbalanced by their having less productive workers.

The most obvious prediction of this simple model is that within an occupation, workers paid piece rates will have higher earnings than workers paid time rates. Available evidence supports this prediction (King 1975; Pencavel 1977; Seiler 1984).

A second prediction is that as the costs of directly monitoring output increase, fewer workers will work in piece-rate firms. This pattern is clear from Figure 1. An increase in θ shifts down the $w(q)$ function for piece rate firms. The initial effect of this change is to increase the number of workers receiving time rates, and to allow time-rate firms to earn positive profits (since the additional workers have $q_0'>q>q_0$ but they are paid S, the average of q from zero to q_0). This effect in turn raises the wages offered by time-rate firms, further increasing their share of the work force.

The above model emphasizes sorting of workers with different abilities. An alternative is to emphasize worker effort. The key distinction between ability and effort is that the latter is controlled by the worker, and can be manipulated by the firm by offering appropriate incentives. Because workers are assumed to find greater effort distasteful, however, we must assume that there is some minimum level of effort $\bar{E}$ that firms can observe cheaply;[5] workers who do not work at this level of effort are discharged by time-rate firms.

A worker who puts forth effort E produces E units of output, but at psychic cost $C(E)$. The piece rate firm pays a wage equal to $E-\theta$ and, if the worker works under a piece-rate system, his or her utility is $E-\theta-C(E)$. Utility is maximized at E^*, where $C'(E^*)=1$, and utility is U^*. Alternatively, if the individual works in a time-rate firm, an effort level $\bar{E}$ is required, and a salary $\bar{S}$ is paid. The worker achieves utility $\bar{U}=\bar{S}-C(\bar{E})=\bar{E}-C(\bar{E})$, since $\bar{S}$ must equal $\bar{E}$ to satisfy the zero-profit condition. The worker compares U^* to $\bar{U}$ and chooses the firm offering the greater utility.

To strengthen the comparison with the earlier model, assume that workers differ in their cost-of-effort functions. Let $C(E)=E^2/N$, where N represents the energy (or ability) of the worker: workers with higher N produce a given (increment to) E at lower (marginal) cost. Then $\bar{U}=\bar{E}-\bar{E}^2/N$ is the utility offered by time-rate firms. Under piece rates, the worker chooses $E^*=N/2$ and attains utility level $U^*=(N/4)-\theta$. Workers are sorted across firms by their value of N, as shown in Figure 2.[6]

---

[5] If there were no minimum level of effort the firm could easily verify, workers would presumably set E equal to zero and the firm could not survive. An alternative approach is to assume there is a minimal level of effort $\bar{E}>0$ below which less effort does not raise utility.

[6] Figure 2 is drawn on the assumption that $\bar{E}$ is low enough relative to the minimum value of N that all workers with low N work for the salary firm. As the above algebra makes clear, $U^*(N)$ and $\bar{U}(N)$ will cross twice. Call the two values N^0 and N_0. For $N>N_0$, the worker prefers the piece rate firm and exerts $E>\bar{E}$. For $N^0<N<N_0$, the worker prefers time rates. If there are any workers with $N<N^0$, however, they will prefer piece rates because piece rates permit a leisurely pace of work below $\bar{E}$. Given that $\bar{E}$ typically corresponds to a very low level of effort (just going through the motions) and that previous studies find piece rate workers earning more, this possibility seems unlikely to be important empirically.

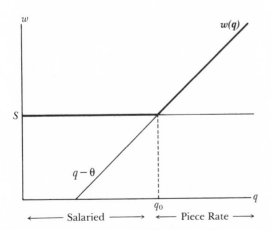

Figure 1. Salary and Piece Rate Firms.

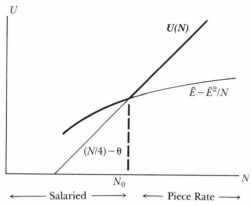

Figure 2. Salary and Piece Rate Firms.

The implications of this model, apparent in Figure 2, are similar to those of the previous model: piece-rate workers earn higher wages, and an increase in the cost of running a piece-rate system increases the fraction of workers (range of N values) who prefer time rates.

Three-Choice Models

The assumption that pay of time-rated workers is unrelated to productivity is overly restrictive—at least for *some* time-rated blue-collar workers and a clear majority of clerical and technical workers (Cox 1971; BNA 1981; Personnick 1987). Within the general category of time-rated workers, some receive wages that depend on job category and perhaps seniority but not performance, whereas others' wages are set individually based on supervisors' perceptions of their productivity. A generalization that allows the firm to choose among three wage-setting methods—one in which wages depend only marginally on performance ("standard rates"), one in which they depend on supervisors' evaluations ("merit pay"),[7] and a piece rate system—is developed in this section. (The empirical motivation for this way of defining the boundaries between methods

will be clearer when the data are described.)

Suppose there are three intensities of monitoring, and for any monitoring strategy j the expected wage offered a worker of quality q is a linear function of q:

$$(2) \qquad w_j = a_j + b_j q.$$

The statistical discrimination literature (Aigner and Cain 1977; Lundberg and Startz 1983; Garen 1985) shows that the relationship between expected wage and worker quality will be steeper (that is, b_j will be larger) the more accurate the available productivity indicator. If all three monitoring intensities are used, and $b_1 < b_2 < b_3$, it must be that $a_1 > a_2 > a_3$. Since the cost of monitoring workers is presumably lower if the monitoring strategy is less accurate, and the cost θ_j is subtracted from a worker's output in setting the wage, differences in θ contribute to this ranking of the a's.

As in Lazear's model, assume that piece rates correspond to a precise but expensive measuring of physical output. Merit pay offers a less expensive but less accurate alternative.[8] Part of the weaker link between pay and performance under

---

[7] Merit pay may take the form of "contests" in which each worker's rating depends on his measured performance relative to everyone else's, as described in Nalebuff and Stiglitz (1983).

[8] One might make two objections to this classification. First, it might be argued that, in some cases, piece rates are less accurate than supervisor ratings as an indicator of productivity (for example, where quality of output is very important). Such a situation, however, consistent with the framework developed here, can be described as one in which the cost of a precise piece-rate system is very high. Second, one might wonder whether merit ratings are very expensive, given that supervisors have a reasonably accurate estimate of workers' productivity that comes "free" from the act of supervising. A merit pay system in which considerable weight is placed on the evaluations, however (see next paragraph), imposes not only the cost of the supervisors writing down what they already know; morale considerations seem to demand that a serious merit-pay system be *formalized* so that workers will accept it as fair, and coordinated so that otherwise identical workers with different supervisors are not treated very differently. Finally, the personnel literature suggests it is difficult—perplexingly so to an economist—for top management to enforce sizable merit differentials for workers at lower levels. See Hamner (1983); Strauss and Sayles (1980).

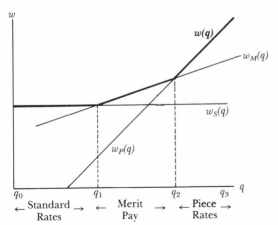

Figure 3. Standard Rate, Merit Pay, and Piece Rate Firms.

merit pay comes from errors in supervisors' ratings of performance; the peculiar feature of most merit-pay systems that increments feed into the base wage contributes as well (Schwab and Olson, this issue). Firms using standard rates presumably spend little on measuring performance, since they do not use it in wage-setting.[9]

Let S, M, and P denote standard rates, merit pay, and piece rates, respectively. Figure 3 shows a three-method generalization of Figure 1. Although b_S may be greater than zero and b_P may be less than one, the essential difference here is that merit pay is added as an intermediate method of pay.

If the costs of using a particular

monitoring intensity or the benefits of better performance indicators change, the use of the three monitoring intensities and their associated methods of pay will also change. An increase in θ_j leads $w_j(q)$ to shift downward, and the number of workers who opt for that method falls.

The benefits of better performance indicators are presumably larger where differences in worker productiveness are larger. In the limiting case in which all workers are equally productive, expenditures to assess their performance would not be profitable.

To be more precise, suppose wage offers are

$$(3) \qquad w_j = a_j + b_j v q$$

where v depends on the sensitivity of output to worker quality. Let v initially equal one, as in Figure 3. Now let v increase. The boundary between standard rate and merit pay workers, q_1, is defined by

$$(4) \qquad q_1 = \frac{a_S - a_M}{(b_M - b_S)v}$$

An increase in v thus reduces q_1 (and q_2), reducing the use of standard rates and increasing the use of piece rates.[10]

How does the three-alternative model work when workers vary their effort in response to wage incentives? A worker who exerts effort E produces E worth of output and earns an expected wage of $a_j + b_j E$ if he or she works under method of pay j. A worker with energy level N has utility $U_j = a_j + b_j E - E^2/N$. To maximize utility, the worker chooses effort level $E_j^* = b_j N/2$, earns $w_j^* = a_j + b_j^2 N/2$, and attains utility level $U_j^* = a_j + b_j^2 N/4$. If we now plot $U_j^*(N)$, we have a diagram like Figure 3, except that the axes are U^* and N rather than w_j and q. Recognizing that

---

[9] My focus is on the relationship between performance and pay in the short run. Even if it is granted that those who perform better under standard-rate regimes have a greater probability of promotion in the future, the relationship between pay and performance would still be "less than that associated with the other forms of compensation that are more closely tied to current output" (Barron and Loewenstein 1986:604). Future compensation is neglected in the text because it is not measured in the IWS.

It is worth noting that future promotions would probably depend on measured performance under any of the systems, so neglecting them may be a defensible simplification when the object is to compare systems. Also, to the extent that less accurate monitoring leaves standard-rate firms less able to identify the "right" workers to promote to higher positions, there is presumably a productivity loss that should be counted as part of the cost of using this system.

[10] I am assuming that these "first-round" effects are not completely undone by subsequent changes in response to positive profits.

the worker chooses the method of pay that offers the highest U_j^*, we again have the workers sorting according to N, and the merit-pay workers receiving wages between the low-wage standard-rate workers and the high-wage piece-rate workers.

Thus far, I have taken the supply of labor to the occupation or industry in question as given. Although it is clear that this is a strong assumption, it is not clear how best to relax it. One possibility is to assume that workers face an alternative wage $\bar{w}$, independent of q. This assumption is reasonable if workers do not know their abilities,[11] but when workers do know their abilities it is equivalent to assuming that ability in the occupation in question is uncorrelated with ability in alternative occupations.

A less restrictive option is to assume that there is an alternative wage function $w^a(q)$ that must be met if workers of quality q are to be attracted. Although the details depend on the shape and position of the $w^a(q)$ one chooses, the basic impact of including w^a is to eliminate part of the q distribution from Figure 3. For example, in Figure 4 workers with $q_0<q<q_1$ still work for standard rate firms, those with $q_1<q<q_4$ work for merit-pay firms, those with $q_4<q<q_5$ accept alternative employment, and only those with $q>q_5$ work for piece-rate firms. It remains true that a small increase in θ_P (shifting $w_P(q)$ downward) reduces the incidence of piece rates. The difference is that here a small increase in θ_P has no effect on the *number* of merit-pay or standard-rate workers, and their *share* of employment in this market rises when the workers with q slightly above q_5 leave for alternative employment.

Measurable Determinants of Method of Pay

The extension of the standard model leads to the prediction that the prevalence of each of the three methods of pay should be inversely related to the cost of using it, and that piece rates should be more com-

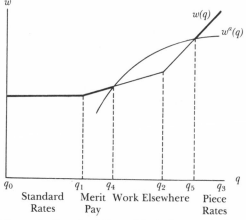

Figure 4. Standard Rate, Merit Pay, and Piece Rate Firms.

mon and standard rates less common where the differences in productivity among workers are greatest. Factors related to these determinants (and how they can be measured in the data described below) are summarized in Table 1. These factors include those mentioned in the method-of-pay literature and in personnel texts.

Perhaps the most commonly cited indicator of monitoring costs in the economics literature is the *size of establishment* or firm. The classic reference here is Stigler (1962), who argued that large employers have a significant disadvantage in monitoring workers. (More recent studies using this premise are Oi 1983 and Garen 1985.)

A closer look at the Stigler argument makes it clear that the greater monitoring costs correspond to an increase in θ_M — greater difficulty in monitoring through supervisors' ratings—rather than an increase in θ_P. Indeed, since piece-rate systems entail fixed costs that can be spread over more workers in larger establishments (Cleland 1955; ILO 1984), θ_P should be lower in such workplaces. This consideration demonstrates the practical importance of the three-way choice of method of pay. We expect larger establishments to make greater use of piece rates, less use of merit pay, and perhaps greater use of standard rates.

The argument that larger establishments have an advantage in implementing piece rate systems has a subtler implication

---

[11] Lazear (1986) introduces $\bar{w}$ when workers do not know their own abilities, but reverts to the fixed-supply model when the worker knows q.

Table 1. Variables, Hypothesized Impact on Method of Pay, and Data.

Variable	Hypothesized Impact[a]	Data[b]
Size of Establishment	↑ P, ↓ M	Estab. Size (IWS)
Occupational Concentration	↑ P	$\sum_k$ (share of occ k)^2 (IWS)
Diversified Duties	↓ P	DOT Variables
Skill (Variation in vmp)	↓ S, ↑ P	DOT Variables
Accuracy & Quality Important but Hard to Measure	↓ P	DOT Variables
Growth in Q/L	↓ P	Δ ln VA/L (COM)
Capital Intensity	↓ P?, ↓ M?	$\dfrac{VA - Payroll}{Shipments}$ (COM)
Importance of Teamwork	↓ P	$\dfrac{Holidays}{Total\ Time\ Off}$ (IWS)
Proportion Female	↓ S?, ↑ P	Female Empl. Share (IWS)
Union Coverage (U)	↑ S, ↓ M, ?P	Whether Unionized (IWS)
Threat of Unionization	↑ S, ↓ M, ?P	(1–U) U-hat (IWS)

[a] P = piece rates; M = merit pay; S = standard rates.
[b] IWS = Industry Wage Survey; DOT = *Dictionary of Occupational Titles*; COM = Department of Commerce, *County Business Patterns* for 1977. VA = value added; L = number of workers; U-hat = predicted value of U.

that has not been discussed in the literature. The more separate jobs within an establishment of given size, the greater the cost of setting up and maintaining piece rates. Greater *occupational dispersion* raises θ_P and should, other things equal, be associated with less use of piece rates. It may also increase the cost of a given level of accuracy for merit pay ratings in which each worker's performance is compared to the group average, because the group average would be based on fewer observations and contain more noise.

A related theme is that establishments with long, standardized production runs or those in which individual employees perform the same tasks *repetitively* are amenable to piece rates. Conversely, where (due to short production runs or the nature of the jobs involved) individual workers perform a wide range of duties and there is considerable day-to-day variation in the importance of various duties, it is difficult (that is, costly) to devise a piece-rate system that correctly prices each of the tasks (Cleland 1955; Cornell 1936; Carlson 1982).[12]

An interrelated set of job characteristics—*skill* level and the importance of *accuracy* and *quality* of output—have conflicting effects on method of pay. Almost by definition, high-skill jobs are jobs in which worker output is sensitive to differences in worker quality. Thus, high-skill jobs should have greater benefit from precise monitoring, and greater use of piece rates and less use of standard rates (Beach 1975:670). On the other hand, when accuracy and quality of work are important—characteristics that are often but not necessarily associated with skill level—θ_P is likely to be high and the use of piece rates less common (Cornell 1936: 537; Lansburgh and Spriegel 1940:416; Pencavel 1977:232). More precisely, since piece rate systems can penalize workers for defective pieces, situations in which accuracy and quality are important but not easily verified pose an obstacle to using piece rates.

A frequently mentioned disadvantage of a piece rate system is that *rapid growth of output per worker* due to technological change or increased capital intensity necessitates revisions in the piece rate structure, raising the cost of piece rates. If the piece rate is adjusted downward, morale is likely

---

[12] Cleland (1955) and Oi (1983) suggest that long standardized production runs are more characteristic of large than small establishments, reinforcing the predicted effect of establishment size.

to suffer, particularly if the workers believe that management used piece rates to get them to work hard and then adjusted the rate downward. In principle, adjustments to reflect the fact that new machinery has made the old piece rate too generous might be accepted, but in practice, determining whether the reduction is fair is difficult. Lansburgh and Spriegel (1940:419)[13] stated this problem quite clearly:

Really radical changes in production method, which so change the job as to make the past rate absurd, have been frequently looked upon by workers merely as *an excuse for cutting rates.* . . . This confusion between logical piece rate re-adjustments and rate-cutting results in numerous borderline cases which it is difficult to settle amicably, because there are no real data, convincing to both sides, which may be used as a basis.

Piece rates as understood in the theoretical literature link individual performance and pay. Consequently, where *team production* is important, measuring individual performance is more difficult and the cost of an accurate piece-rate system will be greater. Firms will avoid piece rates "if the cost of determining how much each individual employee has produced at each stage in a production process is excessive" (Beach 1975:681).

The relationship between *capital intensity* and method of pay is complicated by the fact that the literature has made use of capital intensity as an indicator of several forces. Lazear (1986) shows that an increase in the required value of capital per worker is like a simultaneous increase in all θ's—the cost of capital per worker is subtracted from the output of each worker under each payment system, and the use of particular payment schemes is not affected. Others have used capital intensity as a proxy for machine-paced production (for example, McKersie et al. 1964 and Carlson 1982; but see Pryor 1984:41 for evidence challenging this link), which reduces the attractiveness of piece rates

(Cornell 1936:537; Cox 1971:55) and increases the use of standard rates (Beach 1975:680). Alternatively, greater capital intensity may be interpreted as more machinery entrusted to the worker. Since maintenance of machinery is, like quality, something that may suffer unless special measures are undertaken in a piece rate system, I expect less use of piece rates where capital intensity is greater. Finally, capital intensity may have an indirect effect by changing the skill level of the work. To the extent that the occupation mix is affected, the skill measures of individual occupations would capture this effect. To the extent that the skill required within occupational titles changes, a capital intensity measure will pick up that effect as well. On balance, previous research suggests that capital intensity probably should reduce use of piece rates, but this prediction depends on hard-to-verify links between capital intensity and more basic determinants of method of pay, and in having controlled adequately for the skill level of the work involved.

Goldin (1986) has argued that the proportion of women in the firm's work force may have an important bearing on the method of pay. Her analysis compares a piece rate system to a time rate system, in which better performance is rewarded through future promotion, and less careful (less expensive) monitoring is employed. She argues that the latter system can be efficient for those planning stable attachment to the firm. Piece rates would be more common for female work forces, however, because the promise of future promotion is too bland a carrot for those planning short tenure with the firm. Goldin found that women were indeed more likely to be piece-rate workers, whereas men tended to be paid piece rates in integrated establishments but time rates in segregated male workplaces.[14]

A three-way method of pay categorization allows us to put Goldin's hypothesis to

---

[13] See also Cornell (1936:711); Pencavel (1977: 233); and Carlson (1982:20).

[14] Pencavel (1977) found only a very weak tendency for women to be piece-rate workers, in a relatively small sample of Chicago punch press operators.

a more precise test. Not only should women be more likely to be paid piece rates, they should be less likely to be paid standard rates, since presumably the relative importance of promotion as an incentive is greatest where few within-occupation distinctions are made. An alternative view is that women avoid systems where supervisors have great discretion (namely, merit pay systems) and concentrate in systems with the formal protection offered by either standard rates or piece rates. Both models predict women are more likely to work under piece rates (as Goldin demonstrated); they differ in their prediction about the distribution of women between merit pay and standard rate systems (which Goldin's data could not distinguish).

Thus far, the discussion has implicitly focused on nonunion establishments, or situations in which the presence of a union makes no difference for method of pay. Freeman (1982:4–5) has argued, however, that *unions* opt for standard-rate wage systems, both as protection against arbitrariness by low-level supervisors and because eliminating wage disparities strengthens a political sense of solidarity. Although Freeman's analysis focuses on the choice between standard-rate and merit-pay systems, a more explicit consideration of piece rates would be illuminating. Piece rates provide protection against supervisory discretion[15] but not solidarity-enhancing wage equality. Thus, the relationships between unionization and piece rates allows us to distinguish between these motivations. The distinction has potentially important policy implications. In an environment where heavily unionized industries need improvements in productivity to remain competitive, technological monitoring could provide incentives for better performance without sacrificing protection from arbitrary supervisory discretion.

Finally, the history of firms' response to the *threat of unionization* suggests another union-related hypothesis. Jacoby (1984) found that nonunion firms threatened with unionization often adopted more formal, standardized wage structures to fend off unionization. This finding suggests that merit-pay systems may be less common among nonunion firms threatened by unionization than among nonunion firms facing less serious threats.

Following the formal models on the topic, Table 1 emphasizes differences in "objective" conditions in the workplace. An alternative, more elusive factor is differences in management philosophy (Lewis 1960:462; Carlson 1982:20): some managers believe it is essential to reward productive employees, whereas others worry more about the harm done by distinctions that are perceived to be unjustified. Although there is no precise measure of managerial philosophy, it is possible to extend an idea recently introduced by Dickens and Katz (1986) in a related context. Given that office work has no obvious technological similarity to plant work across manufacturing establishments, it would be useful to know whether there is an important relationship between methods of pay of office and plant workers in an establishment.[16] A finding, for example, that establishments using standard rates for office workers have no particular tendency to use standard rates for their plant workers would tend to support the importance of factors like those in Table 1 rather than managerial style in determining methods of pay.[17]

Data

The Industry Wage Survey (IWS) program of the Bureau of Labor Statistics provides data on methods of wage determination and other establishment charac-

---

[15] Under an imperfect piece rate system, supervisors can still assign favored employees to jobs with "loose" rates—that is, jobs that are overpriced (Beach 1975:699). The union would need to restrict such flexibility in assignment.

[16] Of course, office workers are almost never paid piece rates. But there is variation in the importance given to individual differences in productivity, particularly in the importance of seniority versus merit in range-of-rate systems.

[17] Methods of pay of office workers are available for only a minority of the IWS industries.

teristics. The Survey itself collects, from a sample of establishments in approximately 60 industries (four-fifths of them in manufacturing), data on seven categories of establishment characteristics: proportion of production (and, in a few industries, office) workers paid by various "methods of pay"; fringe benefit policies (for example, number of holidays and vacation days at different seniority levels); number of workers employed; union coverage; region; metropolitan/non-metropolitan location; and details about the product and production technology, which vary from industry to industry.

Ten methods of pay are distinguished, five for time rates and five for incentive pay:[18]

Time rates. (1) In a single rate system, all those in a job category receive the same wage. When a range of rates is used for a job category, progression through the range is governed by (2) merit, (3) seniority, or (4) a combination of merit and seniority. Finally, (5) wages may be individually determined.

Incentive pay. Incentives may take the form of (1) individual piece rates, (2) individual bonus pay (pay for exceeding a production quota), (3) group piece rates, (4) group bonus pay, or (5) commissions.

The "single rate" and "range of rates–seniority" categories are standard-rate methods. The "range of rates–merit" and "individual determination" categories are merit-pay methods.[19] "Individual piece rates," "individual bonus pay," and (negligible in these data) "commissions" correspond closely to the piece rate system as characterized by the theory described above. "Range of rates–combination" straddles the boundary between merit pay and standard rates. "Group piece rates" and "group bonus pay" may act like individual piece rates if groups are small, but Weiss (1987) offers strong evidence that in large groups these incentive effects may be lost. Unfortunately, the data do not include the group size for those paid group incentives; but these categories are fairly rare in the 10 industries studied here.

In addition, for each production worker in "studied occupations," a subset of occupations that includes the major occupations in the industry, the Industry Wage Survey provides the hourly wage;[20] gender; whether paid by incentive or time rates; and occupation (roughly 30 occupations are distinguished for each industry).[21]

Table 2 shows the distribution of establishments by method of pay[22] for blue-collar workers in 10 industries.[23] Each

---

[18] A more precise definition of the IWS categories is provided in each report: Formal rate structures for time-rated workers provide single rates or a range of rates for individual job categories. In the absence of a formal rate structure, pay rates are determined primarily by the qualifications of the individual worker. A single rate structure is one in which the same rate is paid to all experienced workers in the same job classification. (Learners, apprentices, or probationary workers may be paid according to rate schedules that start below the single rate and permit the workers to achieve the full job rate over a period of time.) An experienced worker occasionally may be paid above or below the single rate for special reasons, but such payments are exceptions. Range-of-rate plans are those that specify minimum or maximum rates, or both, for experienced workers in the same job. Specific rates of individual workers within the range may be determined by merit, length of service, or a combination of the two. Incentive workers are classified under piecework or bonus plans. Piecework is work for which a predetermined rate is paid for each unit of output. Production bonuses are based on production over a quota or for completion of a task in less than standard time.

[19] This usage differs slightly from that in compensation textbooks, where merit pay means range of rate systems in which a worker's position in the range depends on merit reviews (and perhaps seniority), and thus usually would not include a less formal "individual determination" system. For a more detailed description of what is meant by merit pay in that context, see Schwab and Olson, this issue.

[20] The hourly wage includes piece rates and production bonuses but excludes annual non-production bonuses and premium pay for overtime, holidays, and shiftwork.

[21] A sense of the fineness of detail of the IWS's breakdown of occupations can be gained from a sampling of occupations it lists for the wood household furniture industry: router operators (distinguished by whether they do set up work or not), rip saw operators, furniture sanders (3 types), and furniture packers.

[22] Establishments that used more than one method are assigned to the three methods in Table 1 in proportion to the fraction of workers paid by each method.

[23] These are the same industries analyzed by Freeman (1982), with the addition of men's and boy's

Table 2. Method of Pay of Establishments, by Industry.

| Industry | Number of Establishments | % of Establishments Using:[a] | | | % Covered by Unions |
		Standard Rates	Merit Pay	Piece Rates	
Nonferrous Foundries	364	38	47	15	49
Paints	292	58	42	0	62
Textile Dyeing & Finishing	149	72	20	7	49
Industrial Chemicals	270	79	20	1	74
Cotton Textiles	342	66	9	26	16
Wool Textiles	57	61	17	22	33
Shirts	220	3	23	75	28
Plastics	876	43	52	5	45
Household Furniture	331	18	63	19	41
Steel	332	54	42	4	71

[a] Apart from rounding error, these three columns sum to 100%.
Source: Industry Wage Survey.

industry makes serious use of two or three methods, even though individual establishments typically use one or two. There is, therefore, considerable within-industry variation to explain. Although union status is related to method of pay—in particular, unionized establishments are more likely to use standard rates (Freeman 1982)—the variation in Table 2 is not just a reflection of differences in collective bargaining coverage. The distribution of piece-rate shares in Table 2 is similar to that in the broader set of IWS industries (Seiler 1984:365) except that industries in which 60% of more of the workers are paid piece rates are underrepresented.

The IWS data alone allow the measurement of several of the determinants of method of pay listed in Table 1. Size of establishment is coded in eight employment classes. These were converted to a continuous variable by assigning to each category the mean establishment size (for the establishment's 4-digit industry) using data from *County Business Patterns* for 1977 (U.S. Department of Commerce 1979, Table 1B). The measure of occupational concentration used here is the sum (over IWS occupations) of the squared share of the occupation in the establishment's employment (based on workers in the subset of "studied" occupations). If all workers work in a single occupation, the concentration index equals one; when workers are

uniformly distributed over N occupations, it is $1/N$ or close to zero.

A measure of the importance of teamwork that is admittedly crude and indirect can be constructed from the IWS data on holidays and vacations, if we assume that "teamwork" implies a need to coordinate the work schedules of team members (in other words, a cost to having some but not all members of the team present on any given work day). Thus, where teamwork is important, we should expect time off to take the form of coordinated leisure (holidays) rather than uncoordinated vacations. The share of holidays in total time off (holidays plus vacation days) is therefore an indirect measure of the importance of teamwork.[24] Unfortunately, this variable was strikingly unrelated to method of pay and, given the indirectness of its link to teamwork in the first place, it was deleted from the final regressions.

The female share of employment in the studied occupations can be computed directly from the IWS worker records. Moreover, when method of pay of individual workers is considered, a dummy variable for female workers is based directly on the worker's IWS record.

The IWS also determines whether a majority of the production workers in an establishment are covered by collective bargaining. The measure of threat of

shirts (which Freeman deleted because he was focusing on non-piece-rate pay).

[24] The IWS vacation data are presented separately at different levels of seniority. I convert these data to an overall average using distributions of workers by tenure by industry from Sekscenski (1980).

unionization used here is based on the predicted probability of unionization, U-hat, from a regression of a union-status dummy on the other exogenous variables. Clearly, the threat of unionization applies only to nonunion firms, so this variable equals U-hat for nonunion establishments and zero for establishments that are already unionized.

Because IWS gives the 4-digit SIC industry and employment size class of its establishments, the establishments can be matched to Census of Manufacturers' data by industry-by-size cell. Specifically, the growth in output per worker is measured by the change in the logarithm of value added per worker between 1967 and 1977,[25] and capital intensity by $1 - (\text{payroll} + \text{materials})/\text{shipments}$ in 1977.

The IWS also provides detailed occupation coding for workers in studied occupations—sufficiently detailed occupations to correspond closely (often with identical titles) to those in the *Dictionary of Occupational Titles*. From the DOT file, I matched three types of variables. First, the primary skill measures are the three indicators of General Educational Development (reasoning, mathematics, and language) and the required level of Specific Vocational Preparation. In addition, the DOT rates occupations on a 5-point scale for 11 aptitudes, ranging from math ability to foot-eye coordination; the *maximum* of these aptitude ratings is used as an additional skill indicator.[26] Second, the DOT indicates whether an occupation requires a tolerance for changing duties or a tolerance for repetitive work. The difference between these variables (which takes the values -1, 0, 1) is used as a measure of diversity of duties. Third, the DOT indicates whether the job requires "adaptability to situations

requiring the precise attainment of set limits, tolerances, or standards"—which seems to be a natural indicator of the importance of accuracy and quality. The precision described in this variable, however, may well be an easily checked sort, so penalties for substandard pieces (and hence piece rates) would be feasible after all. Alternative DOT variables indicate whether the job requires aptitude for making "generalizations, evaluations or decisions" based on "sensory or judgmental criteria" or based on "measurable or verifiable criteria." The sum of these two dummy variables is an index of the extent to which the job requires the sort of work in which care is important but haste is difficult to penalize. Therefore, less use of piece rates would be expected where such judgments are important.

Establishment-Level Regressions

Table 3 presents a set of equations showing the relationship between the proportions of workers paid incentive pay and standard rates (with merit pay the omitted category), using different combinations of the IWS methods of pay for these categories. Table 4 presents similar equations, but with the sample divided into union and nonunion establishments.

The results for (ln-) establishment size are as predicted by models in which difficulty in monitoring workers leads large employers to avoid merit pay and to use either standard rates or incentive pay instead. Larger establishments are more likely than smaller firms to use incentive pay in both union and nonunion settings; they are more likely to use standard rates in nonunion establishments and across nonunion and union establishments combined, but not in union workplaces. The related hypothesis that occupational concentration encourages piece rates and perhaps discourages standard rates is not supported by the data. The coefficients are wrong-signed, though not very precisely estimated.

As noted previously, "skill," which is measured here by a wage-weighted occupation index (based on workers in studied

---

[25] Although growth due to greater capital per worker cannot be distinguished from growth due to technological change, either cause of "overly" rapid growth should reduce the incidence of piece rates.

[26] Using the maximum rather than the mean reflects a belief that "skill" means that unusual levels of *something* are required; one would not down-rate the "skill" of mathematicians (or football players) because little hand-eye coordination (language aptitude) is required for the job.

Table 3. Effects of Various Factors on Method of Pay: 3,211 Establishments.

Independent Variable	Mean (Std. Dev.)	Dependent Variable = Proportion of Workers Paid by:			
		All Incentives	Individual Incentive or Bonus	Single Rates or Range:Seniority	Single Rates or Range:Seniority or Range:Combination
ln (Employment)	4.84	.022*	.019*	.034*	.051*
	(1.15)	(.004)	(.004)	(.008)	(.008)
Occupational Concentration	.29	−.029	−.034	.089	.017
	(.20)	(.023)	(.020)	(.047)	(.046)
Wage-Weighted Occupation Index	1.34	.092	.050	−.091	−.269*
	(.24)	(.068)	(.057)	(.136)	(.133)
Prop. Change in Value Added/Worker	.72	.080*	.064*	−.063	−.056
	(.13)	(.035)	(.030)	(.071)	(.069)
Capital's Share of Costs	.25	−.217	−.195	.392	.246
	(.05)	(.161)	(.136)	(.321)	(.314)
Prop. Female	.29	.038	.042*	.020	.099*
	(.32)	(.021)	(.018)	(.042)	(.041)
Union	.47	.004	.003	.303*	.296*
	(.50)	(.018)	(.015)	(.036)	(.035)
Union Threat	.19	−.001	−.019	−.146*	−.007
	(.24)	(.033)	(.028)	(.065)	(.064)
Mean of Dependent Variable		.14	.12	.47	.61

All equations have dummy variables for 4-digit industry, region, and metropolitan location, not shown separately.
*|t|≥1.96.

occupations), has theoretically indeterminate effects on methods of pay. In the data, there is little consistent relationship between the skill index and method of pay.

The hypothesis that rapid growth in value added per worker is a deterrent to use of piece rates does not fare well in this empirical analysis: the relevant coefficients are wrong-signed and sometimes significant. One technical explanation for this failure is that the variable is matched to IWS establishments based on industry and establishment size, and both industry dummies and establishment size are also entered in the equations. A considerable amount of variation in the industry by size cells, however, is not accounted for by the dummies and ln(establishment size): when the change in value added per worker is regressed on these variables, only 34% of the variation is explained. A more substantive explanation may be that large jumps in output per worker are characterized by dramatic changes in the type of machinery in use. Of so, worker opposition to changes in piece rates may be muted, since

the complaint that the change was unfair would be less credible.

The relationship between capital intensity and method of pay was theoretically ambiguous, depending on what one believes capital intensity is measuring, though it is most commonly conjectured that high capital intensity discourages the use of piece rates. The estimates suggest that more capital-intensive establishments are less likely to use piece rates and more likely to use standard rates, though the association is not even close to statistical significance. The "technical" problem cited above for growing output per worker may have more force here: industry dummies and ln(establishment size) account for 75% of the variation in our measure of capital intensity. Moreover, when industry dummies are excluded (so that the cross-industry relationship is not netted out), capital intensity *is* significantly (negatively) related to use of incentive pay.

As Goldin's model predicts, establishments with larger proportions of female workers are more likely to use piece rates. The effect on use of standard rates,

Table 4. Effects of Various Factors on Method of Pay: 1,523 Union and 1,688 Nonunion Establishments.

Independent Variable	*Union Establishments*			*Nonunion Establishments*		
		Dependent Variable			*Dependent Variable*	
	Mean (Std Dev)	All Incentive	Single Rates or Range:Seniority	Mean (Std Dev)	All Incentive	Single Rates or Range: Seniority
ln(Employment)	4.90 (1.13)	.023* (.006)	.007 (.012)	4.79 (1.17)	.020* (.006)	.043* (.010)
Occupational Concentration	.26 (.18)	−.070 (.036)	−.003 (.076)	.32 (.21)	−.007 (.031)	.176* (.057)
Wage-Weighted Occupation Index	1.41 (.25)	.073 (.103)	.276 (.217)	1.27 (.22)	.099 (.091)	−.387* (.166)
Prop. Change in Value Added/Worker	.73 (.13)	.080 (.050)	−.075 (.105)	.72 (.13)	.051 (.053)	.058 (.096)
Capital's Share of Costs	.26 (.05)	−.087 (.211)	.791 (.444)	.24 (.05)	−.199 (.259)	−.246 (.473)
Prop. Female	.21 (.29)	.031 (.032)	.028 (.067)	.37 (.33)	.045 (.027)	.045 (.055)
Mean of Dependent Variable		.11	.66		.17	.29

All equations have dummy variables for 4-digit industry, region, and metropolitan location, not shown separately.

* $|t| \geq 1.96$.

however, is either zero or positive. Goldin's model (which emphasizes the importance of providing immediate incentives to female employees) seems inconsistent with the latter finding.[27] It is tempting to argue simply that the labor force participation pattern assumed in Goldin's model is no longer strong enough to produce such differences. That argument, however, leaves unexplained the strong association between proportion female and piece rates.

As expected from others' research, unionized establishments make significantly greater use of standard-rate pay than do nonunion establishments. The effects on incentive pay are insignificant, both statistically and practically. Unions neither avoid incentive pay, as the egalitarian model of unions would suggest, nor use it more often, as the block-supervisory-discretion model would have it. Rather, both forces appear to be at work, more or less canceling each other out.

The final explanatory variable is the threat of unionization, defined so that high values represent establishments that are nonunion but have high "predicted" values of being union, and are therefore plausibly regarded as threatened by unionization. I hypothesized that such establishments would be more likely to use standard-rate pay systems in an attempt to head off unionization. Table 3 shows no evidence of such an effect. An admittedly after-the-fact explanation for this result may be that establishments that have remained nonunion despite being in industries that are unionized may be exactly the ones that have the most to lose from union practices like standard rates, and hence they devote more resources to remaining nonunion.

One further experiment is not reported in Table 3. The IWS file for paints contained methods of pay for office workers as well as production workers. Unfortunately, this is the one industry in which there are no incentive-pay workers (see Table 2). Moreover, 80% of the office workers had merit pay systems (and the rest had standard rates), so there was less variation than one would like in office

[27] When detailed methods of pay are used as dependent variables, the proportion female is associated with a significant *increase* in the proportion of workers paid by range of rates–seniority.

methods of pay. When the proportion of office workers paid standard rates was added to an equation similar to the equations for standard-rate pay in Table 3, but for paints alone, its coefficient was positive but very imprecisely estimated.

Worker-Level Regressions

The results in Table 5 are based on a sample of individual workers, one drawn at random from each establishment's set of workers in studied occupations.[28] Before turning to the establishment-level variables in Table 5, it is worth noting the ways in which these regressions differ from those in Table 3. First, the establishment-level methods of pay referred to all nonsupervisory production workers, whereas Table 5 is limited to individual workers in "studied" occupations. Second, about a tenth of the potential worker sample was lost due to a failure to match workers' IWS occupations to any DOT occupation. Finally, the coefficients reported in Table 5 control for the DOT characteristics (and include a variable for the gender of the *individual* worker), whereas those in Table 3 do not. Fortunately, the results for establishment-level variables in Table 5 are not very different from those in Table 3. The most obvious change is that the proportion female no longer increases use of incentive pay—but the individual worker's being female does. (There is still little evidence of employers' having a comparable aversion to women in standard-rate jobs.)

The most noteworthy results in Table 5 are those concerning the worker-level

Table 5. Effects of Various Factors on Method of Pay: Workers in Selected Occupations with DOT Matches.

Independent Variable	Mean (Std. Dev.)	Dependent Variable = Worker Paid by:	
		All Incentives	Single Rates or Range: Seniority
ln(Employ-ment)	4.79 (1.14)	.025* (.007)	.026* (.009)
Occupational Concentration	.29 (.20)	−.025 (.038)	.064 (.054
Wage-Weighted Occupation Index	1.35 (.24)	.137 (.114)	−.130 (.164)
Prop. Change in Value Added/ Worker	.72 (.12)	.094 (.058)	−.008 (.083)
Capital's Share of Costs	.25 (.04)	−.269 (.260)	.449 (.373)
Prop. Female	.29 (.33)	.001 (.037)	.072 (.053)
Union	.49 (.50)	−.012 (.029)	.364* (.041)
Union Threat	.19 (.24)	−.019 (.052)	−.055 (.075)
Gen Educ Dev: Reasoning	2.69 (.81)	.050* (.020)	−.032 (.029)
Gen Educ Dev: Mathematics	1.92 (1.07)	.010 (.014)	−.023 (.020)
Gen Educ Dev: Language	1.86 (.80)	−.051* (.014)	.037 (.021)
Specific Voc Preparation	3.90 (1.78)	.005 (.008)	.016 (.011)
Maximum Aptitude Score	3.04 (.52)	−.005 (.016)	−.030 (.023)
Diversified Duties	−.46 (.40)	−.046* (.017)	.026 (.024)
Precise Standards	.79 (.40)	.087* (.017)	−.093* (.024)
Generalize, Evaluate, Decide	.51 (.57)	−.073* (.016)	.061* (.024)
Female	.29 (.45)	.070* (.019)	−.030 (.027)
Mean of Dependent Variable		.16	.44

N = 2,888.
All equations have dummy variables for 4-digit industry, region, and metropolitan location, not shown separately.
* |t| ≥ 1.96.

[28] One drawback of the worker-level data is that the characterization of the method of pay is less detailed—only time-rated and incentive-paid workers are distinguished. Thus, for time-rated workers in establishments that use both standard rates and merit pay, it is not certain in which category the individual belongs. Since only about 10% of the establishments use both standard rates and merit pay for their production workers, however, this problem is not an overwhelming one. It was finessed in the obvious way: for time-rated workers, the "dummy" variable for standard-rate workers is in fact the proportion of the establishment's time-rated workers (standard rates plus merit pay) who received standard rates.

variables. The various skill measures show little overall relationship to method of pay. Incentive pay is positively related to a high requirement for general reasoning skills, and negatively related to a need for general language skills. The remaining coefficients are tiny and statistically fragile. Given the theoretically ambiguous relationship between skill and method of pay detailed above, these results should not be over-interpreted.

As predicted, there is less use of incentive pay (and greater use of standard rates) in jobs with diverse duties than in jobs with unchanging duties repetitively performed. Moreover, since the variable runs from -1 to $+1$, the estimated effect on use of incentive pay is practically quite significant.

The variables labeled "precision" and "generalize, evaluate, decide" were intended to capture, respectively, situations in which accuracy was important but relatively easily verified and situations in which judgments that would be hard to evaluate numerically were important. The former should encourage, and the latter discourage, use of piece rates (with perhaps opposite-signed impacts on use of standard rates). The data strongly confirm this prediction. Again, the practical significance of the coefficients is noteworthy.

Conclusions

The goal of this study was to determine whether the use of different methods of paying production workers is related in predictable ways to the costs of undertaking the monitoring that the methods require. For incentive pay, these are the costs of measuring output and setting up (and updating) the relationship between pieces and pay. For merit pay, they are the costs of obtaining sufficiently careful ratings from supervisors and of convincing the workers that these ratings should be taken seriously. The costs of standard rate pay systems are presumably negligible, although such systems forfeit the benefit of correct incentives that a well-conceived piece rate (or merit pay) system can provide. An attempt was also made, where possible, to account for institutional factors (specifically, unionization, or the threat of unionization).

In some cases, such as the effect of unionization on the use of incentive pay or the effect of skill level on methods of pay in general, there was no strong a priori basis for predicting the relationship between observable measures and methods of pay. In most of the other cases, bearing in mind the undeniable difficulty of measuring the factors that researchers have cited as likely to be important, the results of the empirical analysis seem to be generally in line with theoretical predictions. Specifically, the results confirm that larger establishment are less likely to use piece rates and predominantly female establishments more likely to do so; unionized establishments make significantly greater use of standard-rate pay than do nonunion establishments; incentive pay is less likely in jobs with a variety of duties than in jobs with a narrow set of routinized duties; and the ease of monitoring work quality is correlated with the use of incentive pay. Other hypotheses—that occupational dispersion, capital intensity, and rapid growth in value added per employee should all be negatively associated with the use of piece rates, and the threat of unionization should encourage greater use of standard rates—are much less well supported by the results. In my view, the failure to show the last three relationships may reflect problems in measuring variables the effects of which may not be terribly large in the first place. I hope this suggestion does not seem a mere excuse—the tired refrain of measurement problems, the first refuge of scoundrels—because the problems here are genuine.

One methodological point is noteworthy. The matching of IWS and DOT occupation codes was undertaken with the knowledge that the IWS occupations were both much more detailed and much more DOT-like in concept than, say, 3-digit Census occupations—and the hope that IWS-DOT matches would amount to more than previous attempts to match DOT and Census occupations (including my own work) had managed. That hope seems to have been confirmed. It is a pity there are not more worker-level variables on the IWS for the IWS-DOT matched job characteristics to explain!

REFERENCES

Aigner, Dennis, and Glen Cain. 1977. "Statistical Theories of Discrimination in Labor Markets." *Industrial and Labor Relations Review*, Vol. 30, No. 2 (January), pp. 175–87.

Anderson, Dave. " 'Super' Jets Question Today's Jets." *N.Y. Times*, Aug. 7, 1988.

Barron, John, and Mark Lowenstein. 1986. "On Imperfect Evaluation and Earnings Differentials." *Economic Inquiry*, Vol. 24, No. 4 (October), pp. 595–614.

Beach, Dale. 1975. *Personnel: The Management of People at Work*. 3d Edition. New York: MacMillan.

Bureau of National Affairs. 1981. "Wage and Salary Administration." Personnel Policies Forum No. 131.

Carlson, Norma. 1982. "Time Rates Tighten Their Grip on Manufacturing." *Monthly Labor Review*, Vol. 102, No. 5 (May), pp. 16–22.

Cleland, Sherill. 1955. *The Influence of Plant Size on Industrial Relations*. Princeton, N.J.: Industrial Relations Section, Princeton University.

Cornell, William. 1936. *Organization and Management in Industry and Business*. New York: Ronald Press.

Cox, John. 1971. "Time and Incentive Pay Practices in Urban Areas." *Monthly Labor Review*, Vol. 91, No. 12 (December), pp. 53–55.

Dickens, Williams, and Lawrence Katz. 1986. "Industrial and Occupational Wage Patterns and Theories of Wage Determination." NBER Working Paper 2014.

Freeman, Richard. 1982. "Union Wage Policies and Wage Dispersion Within Establishments." *Industrial and Labor Relations Review*, Vol. 36, No. 1 (October), pp. 3–21.

Garen, John. 1985. "Worker Heterogeneity, Job Screening, and Firm Size." *Journal of Political Economy*, Vol. 93, No. 4 (August), pp. 715–39.

Goldin, Claudia. 1986. "Monitoring Costs and Occupational Segregation by Sex." *Journal of Labor Economics*, Vol. 4, No. 1 (January), pp. 1–27.

Green, Jerry, and Nancy Stokey. 1983. "A Comparison of Tournaments and Contracts." *Journal of Political Economy*, Vol. 91, No. 3 (June), pp. 349–64.

Hamner, W. Clay. 1983. "How to Ruin Motivation with Pay." In Richard Steers and Lyman Porter, eds., *Motivation and Work Behavior*. 3d Edition. New York: McGraw-Hill, pp. 264–276.

Harris, Milton, and Arthur Raviv. 1979. "Optimal Incentive Contracts with Imperfect Information." *Journal of Economic Theory*, Vol. 20, No. 2 (April), pp. 231–59.

Holmstrom, Bengt. 1979. "Moral Hazard and Observability." *Bell Journal of Economics*, Vol. 10, No. 1 (Spring), pp. 74–91.

———. 1982. "Moral Hazard in Teams." *Bell Journal of Economics*, Vol. 13, No. 2 (Autumn), pp. 324–40.

International Labour Office. 1984. *Payment by Results*. Geneva: ILO.

Jacoby, Sanford. 1984. "The Development of Internal Labor Markets." In Paul Osterman, ed., *Internal Labor Markets*. Cambridge, Mass.: MIT Press.

King, Sandra. 1975. "Incentive Pay in Auto Repair Shops." *Monthly Labor Review*, Vol. 98, No. 9 (September), pp. 45–48.

Lansburgh, Richard, and William Spriegel. 1940. *Industrial Management*. 3d Edition. New York: John Wiley.

Lazear, Edward. 1986. "Salaries and Piece Rates." *Journal of Business*, Vol. 59, No. 3, pp. 405–31.

Lewis, L. Earl. 1960. "Extent of Incentive Pay in Manufacturing." *Monthly Labor Review*, Vol. 83, No. 5 (May), pp. 460–63.

Lundberg, Shelly, and Richard Startz. 1983. "Private Discrimination and Social Intervention in Competitive Labor Markets." *American Economic Review*, Vol. 73, No. 3 (June), pp. 340–47.

Maidment, Paul. 1987. "No Small Change: A Survey of Japan." *The Economist*, December 5, pp. S1–S34.

McKersie, Robert, Caroll Miller, and William Quarterman. 1964. "Some Indicators of Incentive Plan Prevalence." *Monthly Labor Review*, Vol. 84, No. 3 (May), pp. 271–76.

McLaughlin, David. 1986. "Pay for Performance: A Perspective." *Topics in Total Compensation*, Vol. 1, No. 1 (Fall), pp. 7–14.

Morse, Edward. 1986. "Productivity Rewards for Nonmanagement Employees." *Topics in Total Compensation*, Vol. 1, No. 1 (Fall), pp. 85–100.

Nalebuff, Barry, and Joseph Stiglitz. 1983. "Prizes and Incentives: Towards a General Theory of Compensation and Competition." *Bell Journal of Economics*, Vol. 14, No. 1 (Spring), pp. 21–43.

National Research Council, Panel on Technology and Women's Employment. 1986. *Computer Chips and Paper Clips*. Vol. 1. Washington, D.C.: National Academy Press.

Oi, Walter. 1983. "Heterogeneous Firms and the Organization of Production." *Economic Inquiry*, Vol. 21, No. 2 (April), pp. 147–71.

Pencavel, John. 1977. "Work Effort, On the Job Screening, and Alternative Methods of Remuneration." In Ronald Ehrenberg, ed., *Research in Labor Economics*, Vol. 1. Greenwich, Conn.: JAI Press, pp. 225–58.

Personick, Martin. 1987. "White-Collar Pay Determination Under Range-of-Rate Systems." *Monthly Labor Review*, Vol. 107, No. 12 (December), pp. 25–30.

Pryor, Frederic. 1984. "Incentives in Manufacturing: The Carrot and the Stick." *Monthly Labor Review*, Vol. 104, No. 7 (July), pp. 40–43.

Seiler, Eric. 1984. "Piece Rate vs. Time Rate: The Effect of Incentives on Earnings." *Review of Economics and Statistics*, Vol. 66, No. 3 (August), pp. 363–76.

Sekscenski, Edward. 1980. "Job Tenure Declines as Workforce Changes." BLS Special Labor Force Report 235.

Shaiken, Harley. 1987. "When the Computer Runs the Office." *New York Times*, March 22, sec. 3, p. 3.

Stigler, George, and Leonard Sayles. 1980. *Personnel:*

The Human Problems of Management. 3d Edition. Englewood Cliffs, N.J.: Prentice Hall.

U.S. Department of Commerce. 1979. *County Business Patterns 1977.* Washington, D.C.: GPO.

Weiss, Andrew. 1987. "Incentives and Worker Behavior: Some Evidence." In Haig Nalbantian, ed., *Incentives, Cooperation, and Risk Sharing.* Totowa, N.J.: Rowman & Littlefield, pp. 137–50.

PROFITABILITY AND COMPENSATION ADJUSTMENTS IN THE RETAIL FOOD INDUSTRY

CASEY ICHNIOWSKI and JOHN THOMAS DELANEY*

This paper uses longitudinal data provided by a large unionized grocery store chain to examine the relationship between profitability and compensation adjustments between 1976 and 1985. Consistent with the predictions of a Nash bargaining model, negotiated compensation adjustments were inversely related to the pre-negotiation operating income of the relevant stores. Concessionary compensation adjustments in response to relatively low levels of prior profitability occurred in the first year of contracts and subsequent compensation growth was unaffected by differences in prior profitability. Decreases in compensation rates led to significant improvements in subsequent economic performance. Estimates of this relationship, however, indicate that the impact of compensation adjustments on profitability changes was less than dollar-for-dollar.

COMPETITIVE pressures have increased dramatically in many industries in recent years. Although the sources of competition and firms' responses to competitive pressures vary across sectors of the economy, competition has led many unionized firms to seek concessions from their organized employees in the 1980s. For example, data compiled by the Bureau of National Affairs indicate that at least 500 concessionary agreements were negotiated in 1982 in industries including air transportation, manufacturing, and trucking (Cappelli 1985b; Cappelli and McKersie 1985). Concession agreements reduced wage rates and fringe benefits, and modified work rules that management deemed to be "restrictive."[1] Because concessions are intended to make firms more competitive, data on concession agreements provide an excellent opportunity to investigate the relationship between compensation adjustments and the economic performance of firms.

Data limitations have generally pre-

* Casey Ichniowski is Associate Professor of Business at Columbia University and John Delaney is Associate Professor of Business at the University of Iowa and at Columbia University. The authors are very grateful to the company that provided the data for permission to conduct this study, to Phyllis Dickhaus and Seung Lim for extensive help in constructing and analyzing the data set, and to John Abowd, Katharine Abraham, Peter Cappelli, Ron Ehrenberg, Anne Preston, and Susan Schwochau for helpful comments on an earlier draft.

Copies of the computer programs used to generate the results presented in this study are available from Casey Ichniowski at the Graduate School of Business, Columbia University, New York, NY 10027.

[1] Information on the incidence of concession bargaining is reported by Cappelli (1985b), Cappelli and McKersie (1985), and Becker (1988).

cluded tests of the relationship between measures of firm performance and changes in compensation and work rules in unionized operations.[2] Several studies have examined whether concessions have been sufficiently widespread to alter the differential between union and nonunion wages (see Freeman 1986). Other research has addressed whether concession bargaining is a new phenomenon (Cappelli 1983; Kassalow 1983), and whether there is a tradeoff between economic concessions and management's reserved rights (Becker 1988). At least two studies have considered the association between concessions and firm performance: Cappelli (1985b) investigated whether declining economic performance leads to concessionary behavior, and Becker (1987) examined the effects of concession agreements on shareholders' wealth.[3]

In this study, we examine the relationship between firm performance and compensation using unique, company-specific, longitudinal records on collective bargaining agreements and the financial performance of unionized stores in the retail food industry. This industry provides an especially appropriate sample for investigating the relationship between establishment-level performance and compensation decisions. Many retail food contracts are negotiated locally, and competitive pressures on retail food stores have varied over time and across regions of the country.

Competitive Pressures and Concession Bargaining in the Retail Food Industry

In the retail food industry, unionized firms and employees face several sources of increased competitive pressure. First, nonunion competition has increased substantially in many regions of the country in recent years. For example, between 1976 and 1981, the percentage of sales volume accounted for by nonunion food stores increased in 17 of 23 Standard Metropolitan Statistical Areas (SMSAs) included in one survey. In 1981, the average "nonunion concentration ratio" in these 17 SMSAs was 48.7%, an increase of 4.7 percentage points over the five-year period.[4]

Second, technological innovations have forced some unionized retail food companies to alter established work rules. Advances in boxing and prepacking in the meatpacking industry have made certain processing tasks less costly to perform at the packing site than at the retail store. Work restrictions and staffing requirements in the collective bargaining agreements of meatcutters in retail stores may impede the ability of unionized retail stores to take advantage of these cost savings. Third, regional demographic shifts can also affect the performance of retail food stores. For example, declining population in some regions of the country has reduced the demand for stores' products. Some combination of these changes precipitated a need for the negotiation of contractual adjustments in many retail food stores.

A Bargaining Model of Negotiated Wages and Profitability

The retail food industry has certain characteristics of a monopolistically com-

---

[2] In their review of the literature, Ehrenberg and Milkovich (1987) noted that empirical research generally has not addressed the fundamental relationship between the compensation policies that a firm pursues and its economic performance.

[3] In those studies data limitations precluded precise measurement of "concessionary behavior." Concession agreements are those for which parties reported that concessions were a topic of bargaining. It is not clear whether concessions were in fact negotiated, what the magnitude of concessions was, or whether some relatively insignificant concession was offset by large wage increases. Further, the measures of competitive pressure used by Cappelli are indirect, such as the difference between radial tire and bias tire plants in rubber worker contracts, or average plant wage levels in meatpacking negotiations. Similarly, Becker does not identify whether the concession agreement affects a large or small portion of the overall firm's business.

[4] These data are reported in annual volumes, *Market Scope,* published by the Progressive Grocer Company.

petitive market. Individual food stores face competition from other stores in the same area, but stores are differentiated by their geographical location. Within a geographical area a monopolistically competitive equilibrium will result in economic profits equal to zero. If there are economic rents associated with certain locations due to barriers to entry from zoning laws, space constraints, or other factors, however, some stores may earn monopoly profits in equilibrium.

The compensation of unionized retail food workers is based largely on negotiated wages.[5] Although models of profit-maximizing firms and competitive labor markets generally do not predict effects of firm profitability on wages,[6] standard bargaining models identify profitability as an important determinant of wages.

For example, the solution to the axiomatic Nash bargaining model, which coincides with predictions of other bargaining models, demonstrates the relationship between profits and collectively bargained wages. This standard bargaining model frames negotiation as a problem of maximizing the product of the union's utility and the firm's profits, each raised to a power measuring the relative bargaining power of the two parties:

$$(1) \quad \max [\pi - \pi_0]^\alpha [U(w,L) - U_0]^\beta$$

where $\pi = PQ - wL - rK$, and π_0 and U_0 equal firm profits and union utility, respectively, if the parties fail to reach agreement. For several general forms of the union's utility function in wages and employment,[7] this

maximization generates a first order condition of:

$$(2) \quad w_u = w_n + \tau(\pi/L)$$

which approximates to:

$$(3) \quad \ln w_u = \ln w_n + \tau(\pi/Lw_n)$$

where w_n is the wage associated with U_0, assumed equal to the alternative wage in nonunion employment. If Lw_n in equation (3) is relatively constant for the set of establishments and labor contracts in this study's narrowly defined industry sample, then profitability directly affects negotiated wages.

Although the specific interpretation of the parameter on the profitability term, τ, depends on the form of the union's utility function, τ is always positive. In general, negotiated wages increase as the union's relative bargaining power increases and as the importance of wages in the union's utility function increases.

In the framework of this simple bargaining model, increased competitive pressures in parts of the retail food industry should therefore affect negotiated wages. Exogenous shocks, such as increases in nonunion competition, cost-saving technologies adopted by competitors, or declining population, will shift the demand curve for an individual unionized store downward. If these shocks lead to a reduction in profits and if prior negotiated wages exceed w_n, negotiated wages in the next contract will fall relative to w_n.

If this demand shift results in negative profits, the reduction in wages may be crucial to the survival of the firm. When demand falls below average costs for all levels of output, the store has two options: it can negotiate a reduction in wages in the next contract sufficient to ensure positive profits, or it can close. Alternatively, if some portion of the new, lower demand curve is still above average costs of production, a reduction in output should still allow the firm to earn positive profits. In that event, the viability of the store is not so closely linked to wage concessions.

In this model, unions require information on establishment-level profits in order to benefit from store performance. This

---

[5] Output-based incentive pay does not exist in the 1975–85 sample that is analyzed below. This company, however, began to negotiate incentive plans in 1983. The total number of the company's contracts including incentive plans was one in 1983, eight in 1984, and 18 in 1985.

[6] Weiss (1966) showed that under the standard model of a profit-maximizing monopolist, the theoretical relationship between wages and profitability might be negative if high levels of profits in some firms are due to the firms' monopoly power.

[7] For example, Ben-Ner and Estrin (1989) and Simpson (1986) derived similar expressions for different assumed forms of the union's utility function.

information may not be available in practice. In particular, unless the firm consists of one establishment and is publicly owned, information on store performance is private. For theoretical, empirical, and institutional reasons, a firm is likely to share this private knowledge of the performance of its establishments only when profitability declines.

Theoretically, if there is asymmetric information on store profitability, the bargaining model implies that firms will have the strongest incentives to reveal information on establishment-level profitability when profits have declined.[8] This information should lead to lower negotiated wages. Empirically, Kleiner and Bouillon (1988) found that unionized firms that have more extensive information sharing programs pay higher wages without a significant increase in productivity. This relationship between information and higher wages may cause firms to conceal information on establishment performance. Moreover, labor law does not require profitable firms to reveal information on establishment-level performance during negotiations. Specifically, as long as the firm does not claim an inability to pay, it is not required to provide information demonstrating the honesty of its claim during negotiations (NLRB v. Truitt Manufacturing Co., 351 U.S. 149 (1956)).

If the firm acts on this incentive and does not provide profitability data when times are good, the union may suspect improvements in the financial condition of the establishments in which it operates. The union, however, must rely on publicly available signals, such as reported profitability for the entire firm, changes in competition from other firms, closings of the firm's own operations, or investment decisions by the firm in the specific establishments in which the union exists. If these signals are not perfect proxies for true profitability, which the firm is withholding, the relationship between profitability and wages should be less precise.

For example, if a firm withholds information on financial performance, it may use the threat of store closings in those regions where other stores have closed to negotiate lower wages when there is no real danger of closing (Cappelli 1985b: 101; Cappelli and McKersie 1985:232). Further, if the unionized firm has closed unprofitable stores in a region in response to nonunion entry, the demand facing each remaining store will be higher, as there will be fewer stores serving an unchanged market demand. Therefore, store closings may ensure that all remaining stores operate with positive profits.

In the absence of reliable information on profitability, union negotiators may find the threat of further store closings credible and agree to concessions even when they are not necessary. If employers use this strategy successfully, they may even go as far as closing a profitable store—as long as that closing leads to large enough concessions in remaining stores. These considerations derived from the simple bargaining model suggest several hypotheses to be tested. First, $\delta w_{u(t)}/\delta \pi_{t-1}$ should generally be positive. This relationship, however, should be especially precise and significant when $\pi_{t-1} < 0$.

Second, public signals that give the union a sign of establishments' true profitability, such as store closings in the region of the union contract, may affect negotiated wages. If the firm does provide profitability data when financial conditions are poor, and the data can be verified, then public information will provide no additional information beyond the actual profitability of the relevant stores. Any negative effects of regional store closings in models that control for actual store profitability, however, should be observed primarily in the sample of contracts covering profitable operations.

---

[8] Hollander and LaCroix (1986) developed this implication more formally to show how information sharing can lead to reduced firm wealth and a redistribution of firm income in favor of workers.

Data

A unionized company in the retail food industry provided us with detailed data files on its labor contracts and the performance of its stores. These data permit an analysis of the relationship between concession bargaining and store performance.

This company is a large well-known firm that operates across several states. In 1988, it had over 100,000 unionized employees. Unlike many American firms, this company is committed to operating its unionized establishments. For example, in order to achieve a cooperative relationship with its unions, an executive reported that the "riot act" had been read to store managers who were attempting to break their local unions. The company is also committed, however, to a strategy of "hard bargaining" to keep the labor costs of its unionized employees in line with the labor costs of its competitors. Its approach has been successful: it reduced its wage and fringe benefits costs each year over the period 1984–1988, but experienced only three strikes during that time.

Labor contract characteristics. The company has kept detailed records on all changes in labor contract provisions that affect the average straight time wage rate and the average rate of total compensation or base compensation rate (BCR) across all employees covered by each contract. Specifically, the BCR for a contract is the average total hourly compensation rate for that contract's employees. BCR includes all compensation except taxes and government-mandated insurance benefits.

For each newly negotiated clause across the entire set of contracts, the company provides a precise estimate of the contribution of that clause to the change in the BCR. These estimates are used to adjust the per-employee average BCR for the contract. At the end of the term of the contract, actual average BCR is compared to the estimates calculated from the clause-specific adjustments. Where the difference between the estimated BCR and the actual BCR is more than a few cents, the company has adjusted the clause-specific values that caused the discrepancy.[9] Below, we analyze a sample of

473 contract-years from 284 contracts covering the years 1976–1985 to identify the determinants of BCR changes, as well as the incidence and value of specific types of concessions.[10]

For each year of each contract, the company calculates the overall BCR and the contribution of each contract clause change to BCR. These detailed data permit an accurate, objective definition of "concessions." In contracts where overall BCR declines, there is an "overall concession" in absolute terms.[11] The data also allow the identification of specific "concession clauses" regardless of whether overall BCR increased or decreased. The contract data are matched to store performance and SMSA-specific measures.

Financial performance of stores. The company provided each store's annual operating income (before adjustments). Operating income does not correspond exactly to economic profits. It has not been possible to adjust these figures for those cost items that reduce operating profits in a given year but enhance expected future economic profitability.[12] Discrepancies be-

---

[9] Such adjustments are rare. Costing is achieved through a complex algorithm. According to this company's officials, the costing formula has been

extremely accurate—"to the penny" in one division of the firm for several years, and within a few cents per hour on average. The details of how clause-specific values are estimated are confidential. Discussions with the company's executives indicated that the formulas account for relevant distributions of employee characteristics (for example, seniority and wage grade) to calculate the actual value of a percentage change in wage rates, adjustments to wage progressions, adjustments to sick leave or vacation schedules, and other contract clauses. Predictions for certain clauses, such as multi-tier wage rates, the values of which are more difficult to estimate, are based on formulas for expected attrition by class of employee.

[10] The 284 contracts contain more than 473 contract-years. The usable number of contract-year observations is reduced, however, by missing data for some variables.

[11] Freeman (1986) discussed the importance of measuring concessions in relative terms (such as by comparing wage changes for comparable union and nonunion workers). Because our data are for the company's unionized employees, we measure concessions in absolute terms.

[12] This study does not investigate the effect of changes in union compensation on economic quasi-rents (see Abowd 1989). Among other differences, operating income is determined when labor is valued at negotiated compensation rates, whereas quasi-

tween operating profits and economic profits in this particular sample, however, will not be the result of differences in accounting practices or any other factor that varies only across industries or companies.

Because bargaining unit structures vary, contracts do not correspond directly to stores. All contracts in this sample cover only employees and stores of the company. The company did not negotiate any contracts jointly with other employers during this period. Contracts virtually always cover more than one store, and most contracts cover more than one store within the same local area. Most stores have two contracts—one for clerks and one for meatcutters. A nontrivial minority of stores have a third contract for employees in some specialty department of the store, such as bakery or liquor departments. Finally, a small number of stores have only one contract, usually because the store has no meatcutters contract.[13]

Discussions with company executives identified the exact stores covered by each contract. From this information, we constructed a bridge that specifies whether or not a store was covered by a contract, though not the extent of coverage in a particular store. Given this bridge between stores and contracts, the measure of performance calculated in the contract-based sample is the average profitability of the stores covered by a contract in each year. The measure of performance in the store-based sample is each store's operating income in each year.

Methods of Compensation Adjustment

Studies of concession bargaining docu-

ment that concessions may be negotiated for a wide variety of contractual provisions (Cappelli and McKersie 1985:232–33; Becker 1988:380). Because some cost is associated with virtually every contract provision, there is room for labor savings on almost every clause. Data limitations have prevented researchers from studying concessions on more than a handful of bargaining subjects, however, and measurement problems have precluded comparisons of the savings attributable to different concessionary clauses.

For example, Cappelli and McKersie's examination of 209 concession bargaining "incidents" divided concessions into three categories: work rule changes; wage/fringe freezes; and wage/fringe cuts. Becker's analysis of 70 concession incidents reported information on eight types of union concessions and nine types of union "gains" that were achieved in return for concessions. Neither these studies nor studies of concession bargaining generally have assessed the equivalence of various concessions and gains or determined the value of specific nonwage contract clause changes.

A clearer picture of the concession bargaining phenomenon requires a more comprehensive categorization and valuation of concessionary clauses. Identification of specific concessionary clauses ignores the importance and value of particular concessions. In addition, definitional problems arise in attempts to identify concessions (Freeman 1986; Becker 1988). Becker (1988) argued that unions are more likely to demand a *quid pro quo* or "gain" from employers in cases where concessions produce large savings. If management negotiates a wage increase in return for some work rule "concession," it is not obvious that negotiations are actually concessionary.

Concession bargaining is better measured by the sum of specific contractual concessions and gains. Because the company has reported the dollar-per-hour cost of its contract provisions, we are able to identify the extent to which concessions occur in specific clauses and across all contract provisions. We define a conces-

---

rents are calculated with labor valued at external wage rates.

[13] In our analysis, stores in a few regions that have a single joint "clerks and meatcutters" contract are treated as having two separate "contracts" because the company keeps BCR data for clerks and meatcutters separately in contracts covering both groups of employees. "One-contract stores" refers to those stores in which only one of the two employee groups—usually clerks—is employed.

sion as a reduction in the dollar-per-hour value of a specific contract provision from one contract to the next. Similarly, a concessionary contract occurs when the BCR declines from one contract to the subsequent contract. The company's data permit the most objective study of concession bargaining that has been possible to date.

Our investigation of the incidence and value of specific concessions is based on a sample of 284 contracts covering 473 contract-years. This sample is also used in the multivariate analyses reported below. The company's data identify the specific contract clause changes that occurred in the sample contracts. A coding scheme was developed that placed each change into one of 265 potential categories.[14] Figure 1 reports the incidence of concessions in 12 major categories (which are aggregates of the 265-category coding scheme) across the sample of contracts.

Contracts often contain more than one clause change in each of the 12 major categories because agreements run for more than one year, specific clause changes are phased in over time, and more specific subcategories of clauses have been aggregated into these twelve broad categories.[15] Unsurprisingly, the 284 contracts contained more clauses covering wages (about 4 per contract) than any other subject. In addition, 138 contracts contained multi-tier clauses. Of the 292 separate multi-tier clauses negotiated in these 138 contracts, 197 clauses instituted a lower tier for wage rates, and 95 instituted a lower tier for provisions other than wage rates.

The information on the dollar value of the clauses presented in Figure 1 suggests an important reason why concessions were distributed differently in different contracts. Each of the 12 categories contains a different potential for compensation increases and reductions. Where deep cuts

are necessary, they appear to come from reductions in wage rates and schedules, premium pay, time off, and staffing requirements. The adoption of multi-tier provisions covering wages also appears to offer substantial cost savings to the company. The possibility of large cost reductions is greater in these categories than others. Cost reductions, represented by negative values in Figure 1, however, were achieved in each of the 12 categories of clauses.

In the sample of 284 contracts, the mean clause value was negative in five of the major categories (premium pay rates, staffing provisions, two-tier wage clauses, other two-tier clauses, and other provisions). Two-tier provisions covering wages and other subjects, such as holiday pay and vacation eligibility, consistently provided cost reductions.[16] In certain circumstances, reductions in a contract's BCR achieved through a multi-tier provision can be considerable. Presumably, where the value of the savings associated with the multi-tier provision was particularly large, employee turnover was very high or the difference in the tiers was large. The latter case would imply that the pre-existing union wage scales were considerably higher than the wage necessary to attract new hires. Further, the figures on savings in BCR for the period of the given contract understate the savings associated with multi-tier benefits because savings from multi-tier clauses increase in future years and subsequent contracts as turnover continues.

Table 1 divides the data in Figure 1 into samples of concessionary and nonconcessionary contracts. Only clauses covering health and welfare provisions do not have a negative mean in the sample of concession contracts. Interestingly, however, there appears to be considerable variance in the value of specific contract clause changes in both samples. Dispersion among wage and health and welfare provisions is especially

---

[14] The categorization was guided by principles developed in labor contract scoring schemes devised in research on nonwage bargaining outcomes (see Kochan and Wheeler 1975; Kochan and Block 1977; Hendricks, Feuille, and Szerszen 1980).

[15] An appendix containing the categorization scheme is available from the authors.

[16] The few positive values associated with multi-tier clauses occurred in cases where a multi-tier provision was negotiated out of a contract, raising the pay of lower-tier workers, and in cases where lower-tier pay rates were increased.

Figure 1. The Value of the Company's Contract Clause Changes, by Major Category.

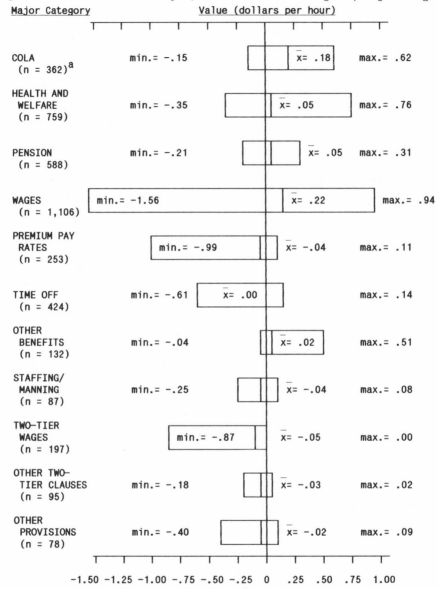

large in the sample of concessionary contracts. The data suggest that concessions in the contractual BCR may be less than concessions in specific contract items because of bargaining tradeoffs. This finding confirms that unions require some gains in return for give-backs (Becker 1988).

In both samples the minimum and maximum values of virtually every major category show that concessions and gains are not mutually exclusive within contracts. The large number of concessionary clauses in nonconcessionary contracts calls into question the use of concessions on specific clauses as a means of identifying

Table 1. The Value of the Company's Contract Clause Changes in Concession and Nonconcession Contracts.
(Dollars/Hour)

Contract Type and Major Category	No. of Clauses[a]	Mean	Standard Deviation	Minimum	Maximum
Concession Contracts					
COLA	12	−0.000	0.064	−0.1498	0.1497
HEALTH & WELFARE	89	0.035	0.110	−0.3468	0.5523
PENSION	31	−0.000	0.055	−0.2075	0.0779
WAGES	111	−0.123	0.423	−1.5609	0.9438
PREMIUM PAY RATES	43	−0.139	0.179	−0.7066	0.1031
TIME OFF	60	−0.070	0.074	−0.2266	0.0816
OTHER BENEFITS	9	−0.008	0.013	−0.0399	0
STAFFING/MANNING	22	−0.046	0.077	−0.2533	0
TWO-TIER WAGES	26	−0.092	0.174	−0.8683	0
OTHER TWO-TIER CLAUSES	47	−0.029	0.040	−0.1819	0.0200
OTHER PROVISIONS	19	−0.043	0.107	−0.4040	0.0002
Nonconcession Contracts					
COLA	350	0.185	0.113	−0.0724	0.6233
HEALTH & WELFARE	670	0.053	0.061	−0.1780	0.7587
PENSION	557	0.048	0.034	−0.0439	0.3073
WAGES	995	0.256	0.193	−0.2517	0.8529
PREMIUM PAY RATES	210	−0.025	0.104	−0.9880	0.1105
TIME OFF	364	0.012	0.043	−0.6147	0.1399
OTHER BENEFITS	123	0.022	0.057	−0.0075	0.5128
STAFFING/MANNING	65	−0.031	0.058	−0.2243	0.0772
TWO-TIER WAGES	171	−0.049	0.063	−0.4175	0
OTHER TWO-TIER CLAUSES	48	−0.032	0.033	−0.1229	0.0206
OTHER PROVISIONS	59	−0.010	0.050	−0.3172	0.0856

[a] Observations are the number of clauses in each subject area.

concession bargaining. The data for concessionary contracts also make it clear that very large decreases in BCR require wage concessions. In some circumstances, however, adjustments to premium pay rates or the adoption of a lower tier of wages can produce large savings in a contract's BCR. For example, a 1987 concessionary contract covering 5,198 clerks in 47 stores eliminated premium pay for working nights. This BCR reduction of 2.86 cents per hour, on average, was expected to generate labor cost savings of $575,000 ($12,234 per store) over the term of the contract.

Prior Economic Performance, Concessions, and Compensation Adjustments

In this section we estimate the effects of variables measuring economic pressure on annual changes in average hourly labor cost. The model is specified as:

$$(4) \quad \Delta \text{BCR}_t = \alpha + \beta 1(\text{PERF}_{pc} * \text{YEAR1}) + \beta 2(\text{PERF}_{pc} * \text{YEAR2}) + \beta 3(\text{PERF}_{pc} * \text{YEAR3}) + \beta 4(X)_t + \epsilon_t.$$

In equation (4), ΔBCR_t is a measure of the change in a contract's BCR in year t (either a continuous variable measuring the percentage change in BCR or a 0–1 variable indicating a reduction in BCR). PERF_{pc} represents measures of economic performance and competitive pressure for the stores covered by the contract during the final year of the previous contract. The two lagged measures of economic performance are the average profitability of all stores covered by the contract in the full calendar year before the negotiation of the contract and the percent of stores covered by a given contract that closed during the last calendar year before the negotiation of the contract. Finally, X_t represents a vector of other control variables.

The timing of the labor cost changes

and the indicators of economic pressure are measured carefully. Contracts in this sample are virtually all multi-year agreements. The average duration is 2.82 years and the vast majority of contracts have a duration of approximately three years. Measures of economic performance and competitive pressure in year t determine labor cost changes for the three years of a contract that begins in year t (that is, labor cost changes between t and $t+1$, between $t+1$ and $t+2$, and between $t+2$ and $t+3$). Profitability during the periods between $t+1$ and $t+3$ is in part determined by the labor cost adjustments that were negotiated in period t in response to estimates of profitability at that time.

The measures of prior economic performance will not necessarily have the same effect on negotiated changes in BCR across the different years of the contract. Therefore, in equation (4), the measures of prior economic performance are interacted with three dummy variables for the year of the contract (YEAR1, YEAR2, and YEAR3) to allow the lagged performance measures to have different effects on BCR changes in the different years of the labor contract. The dummy variables YEAR1 and YEAR2 are also included among the control variables in equation (4) with the YEAR3 dummy variable excluded as the reference category. These variables adjust for the fact that the lengths of the lags of the economic pressure indicators vary across observations. The YEAR variables will also capture differences in wage changes due to "front-loading" or "back-loading" of the collective bargaining agreements.

The vector of other control variables also includes eight dummy variables for the calendar year of the observation, the percent change in the manufacturing wage in the SMSA, the percent change in the SMSA's population, and the percent change in the SMSA's unemployment rate.[17]

Panel A of Table 2 presents estimates from three OLS models of the determinants of compensation changes. The dependent variable is $\ln(\text{BCR}_t/\text{BCR}_{t-1})$. When the three "lagged profitability $*$ contract year" interaction terms are entered (column 1), the coefficient on lagged profits for first-year BCR changes is positive and significant. The effects of lagged profits on BCR changes in the second and third contract years are insignificant.

When the three lagged store closing variables are entered (column 2), there is a positive effect of lagged store closings on first-year BCR changes. The effects of the lagged store closing variable on BCR changes in years two and three of the contracts are insignificant. The positive effect of the store closing variable on BCR changes in the first year of labor agreements may indicate that once the most unprofitable stores covered by a given contract have been closed in the year prior to negotiation, the union can seek larger wage increases because it no longer needs to be concerned about potential employment losses in the stores that were closed. In addition, it may anticipate increased demand for the remaining stores, and thus higher profits, after the store closings. In either case, the positive relationship between past store closings and first-year BCR changes does not support the hypothesis that past store closings are an implied threat of future store closings that tempers wage increases.

When both sets of interaction terms are entered together in the BCR change model (column 3), the results are similar to those in the column 1 and 2 models. Lagged profitability and lagged store closing variables have significant positive

---

[17] The average manufacturing wage in the state is used as the alternative wage measure in small SMSAs that are not continuously covered in the May volumes of *Employment and Earnings*. The unemployment rate variable is the annual percentage point change in the SMSA's unemployment rate, as reported in May volumes of *Employment and Earnings*. The population change variable is the percent change in SMSA population over a five-year period. The population data were reported in the *Statistical Abstract of the United States*. Observations occurring between 1975 and 1980 were assigned the percentage change in SMSA population for that five-year period. Observations occurring between 1980 and 1985 were assigned the percentage change in SMSA population for that five-year period.

Table 2. The Effects of Prior Profitability and Store Closings on Concessions in Overall Labor Costs.
(n = 473 Contract-Year Observations)

Panel A — Dependent Variable: ln(BCR$_t$/BCR$_{t-1}$)

OLS Estimates

Independent Variables	(1)	(2)	(3)
Lagged Average Store Profitability * YEAR1[a]	9.39E-8*** (3.37E-8)	—	11.17E-8*** (3.38E-8)
Lagged Average Store Profitability * YEAR2[a]	0.89E-8 (2.47E-8)	—	0.75E-8 (2.47E-8)
Lagged Average Store Profitability * YEAR3[a]	1.85E-8 (3.61E-8)	—	2.04E-8 (3.62E-8)
Lagged Percent of Stores Closed * YEAR1[a]	—	.120*** (.041)	.141*** (.041)
Lagged Percent of Stores Closed * YEAR2[a]	—	−.016 (.041)	−.015 (.041)
Lagged Percent of Stores Closed * YEAR3[a]	—	.003 (.043)	.004 (.043)
R^2	.230	.231	.250

Panel B — Dependent Variable: Pr(BCR$_t$ < BCR$_{t-1}$)

Probit Estimates

Independent Variables	(1)	(2)	(3)
Lagged Average Store Profitability * YEAR1[a]	− 1.33E-6† (0.86E-6)	—	− 1.35E-6† (0.87E-6)
Lagged Average Store Profitability * YEAR2[a]	− 0.84E-6 (1.02E-6)	—	− 0.50E-6 (1.14E-6)
Lagged Average Store Profitability * YEAR3[a]	0.45E-6 (1.67E-6)	—	0.40E-6 (1.69E-6)
Lagged Percent of Stores Closed * YEAR1[a]	—	.223 (1.169)	−.053 (1.221)
Lagged Percent of Stores Closed * YEAR2[a]	—	3.665** (1.865)	3.487* (1.893)
Lagged Percent of Stores Closed * YEAR3[a]	—	−.503 (3.068)	.396 (1.693)
− 2 * log-likelihood	106.42	106.92	109.62

Other controls for Table 1 models are eight dummy variables for calendar year of contract-year observation, two dummy variables measuring the first and middle contract-years of a contract, percent change in average hourly wage of manufacturing employees in the SMSA, percent change in SMSA unemployment rate, and percent change in SMSA population.

[a] Lag corresponds to the last full year prior to the start of the current labor contract.

* Significant at the .10 level; ** at the .05 level; *** at the .01 level (two-tailed tests).

† Significant at the .10 level in a one-tailed test.

effects on BCR changes during the first year of labor contracts.

Given the range of the lagged profits variable, the column 3 estimate of the effect of lagged profits on first-year BCR changes is considerable. For example, in the Table 1 sample, the average lagged profitability among contracts with positive lagged profits is $113,392, whereas the average lagged profitability among contracts with negative lagged profits is − $114,443. An increase in lagged profitability of $227,835 between these two

levels of profits would raise the BCR change variable by 2.5 percentage points, or 59% of the average BCR change in this sample. After the BCR adjustment in the first year of the contract, BCR changes in subsequent contract years are not significantly affected by differences in the levels of prior profitability.

The models in panel B of Table 2 respecify the dependent variable as Pr(BCR$_t$ < BCR$_{t-1}$). These models directly test whether measures of economic performance and competitive pressure affect the probability that there is an "overall concession" (an absolute reduction in BCR) from one year of the contract to the next. In the panel B models, the effects of lagged profits are concentrated in first years of contracts. The probability of a first-year BCR reduction declines as operating income increases in the covered stores. This negative effect of lagged profits on the probability of first-year BCR reductions is less significant than the effect of this variable in the panel A BCR change models. The coefficient on the "lagged profits * YEAR1" variable is significant at the .10 level in a one-tailed test in both the column 1 and column 3 models in panel B.[18]

The negative point estimate on the "lagged profits * YEAR1" variable in column 3 ($-1.353E$-6) also implies that differences in prior profitability in this sample can have considerable effects on the probability of a BCR concession. In this case, an increase of $227,835 in average lagged profits (the difference in mean profitability across the samples with positive and negative lagged profits) implies a 4.9 percentage point, or 42%, decrease in the probability of a concession when the profitability change is evaluated at the mean of the concession dependent variable in this sample ($\bar{x} = .116$).

The coefficients on the lagged store closing variables in the panel B concession probability models show a pattern different from that of the store closing coefficients in the panel A BCR change models. In the column 2 and 3 specifications in panel B, the lagged store closing variable is associated with higher probabilities of concessions during second contract years. When the dependent variable is specified

as the percent change in BCR (panel A), there is no significant difference in the observed year-two BCR changes for contracts experiencing different levels of store closings in the year prior to negotiations.

Although the estimated coefficients on the lagged store closing variables differ across models with different specifications for the dependent variable, the Table 1 estimates of the effect of lagged profitability generally present a consistent picture of how compensation adjusts to differences in economic performance. When profits are relatively low, compensation adjustments are relatively low and the likelihood of a concession is relatively high. The adjustments to low levels of profitability occur in the first year of the contract. After first-year compensation adjustments, compensation growth in other contract years is similar across contracts with different levels of prior profitability.

Thus, compensation established by contracts covering relatively unprofitable stores does not "catch up" to negotiated compensation in more profitable stores. BCR growth shifts to a lower path in the first year of the concessionary contract, and after this downward adjustment, the compensation growth profile in subsequent years is comparable to the profile for contracts covering more profitable operations.

Labor Cost Adjustments for Profitable and Unprofitable Operations

The finding that prior profitability is a significant determinant of concessions and changes in BCR is consistent with the economic propositions described above. Labor costs need to be adjusted where demand shocks lead to relatively low levels of profitability. Without concessions, the contracts associated with less profitable stores face more serious threats of store closings and job loss than the contracts associated with more profitable stores. More generally, the union's ability to negotiate wage increases is positively re-

---

[18] A one-tailed test is appropriate for coefficients on the lagged profits variables because the bargaining model predicts that profits should be positively related to compensation adjustments and negatively related to concession probabilities. Because lagged store closings would be negatively related to compensation changes if this variable signaled declining economic conditions in the region, but positively related to compensation changes if it signaled increased customer demand for the stores remaining open, a two-tailed test of significance is appropriate for the lagged store closing variable.

lated to profitability according to the bargaining model described earlier.

The bargaining model suggests that the effects of lagged profitability or store closings could be more pronounced on those contracts associated with unprofitable stores than on those associated with profitable stores. For example, if the company provides information on profitability only when profitability is declining, unions may rely on imperfect signals of profitability when profits are increasing. In models that control for profitability, store closings may add explanatory power to wage adjustment models only when profits are positive. If the company does provide profitability data when perfor-

mance is poor, the relationship between lagged profits and wage changes may be more precise for those contracts covering unprofitable operations than for those contracts covering profitable operations.

These possibilities are tested by estimating BCR change and concession probability models separately for the subsample of contract-years for which lagged profits are negative and the subsample for which lagged profits are positive. Table 3 presents estimates from models for these subsamples when $\ln(\text{BCR}_t/\text{BCR}_{t-1})$ is the dependent variable. Panel A presents estimates for the unprofitable sample, and panel B gives results for the profitable sample.

Table 3. The Effects of Prior Profitability and Store Closings on the Change in Overall Labor Costs.
(Dependent Variable: $\ln(\text{BCR}_t/\text{BCR}_{t-1})$; OLS Estimates)

Panel A — Sample with Negative Lagged Store Profitability			
(n = 195 Contract-Years)			
Independent Variables	**(1)**	**(2)**	**(3)**
Lagged Average Store Profitability * YEAR1[a]	20.50E-8*** (7.22E-8)	—	20.92E-8*** (7.19E-8)
Lagged Average Store Profitability * YEAR2[a]	0.37E-8 (4.50E-8)	—	0.58E-8 (4.48E-8)
Lagged Average Store Profitability * YEAR3[a]	2.39E-8 (7.75E-8)	—	2.34E-8 (7.72E-8)
Lagged Percent of Stores Closed * YEAR1[a]	—	.091** (.043)	.095** (.043)
Lagged Percent of Stores Closed * YEAR2[a]	—	−.014 (.046)	−.012 (.045)
Lagged Percent of Stores Closed * YEAR3[a]	—	.009 (.044)	.011 (.044)
R^2	.327	.314	.346
Panel B — Sample with Positive Lagged Store Profitability			
(n = 278 Contract-Years)			
Independent Variables	**(1)**	**(2)**	**(3)**
Lagged Average Store Profitability * YEAR1[a]	2.00E-8 (6.63E-8)	—	7.91E-8 (6.71E-8)
Lagged Average Store Profitability * YEAR2[a]	−0.84E-8 (5.58E-8)	—	−5.71E-8 (5.66E-8)
Lagged Average Store Profitability * YEAR3[a]	5.20E-8 (6.23E-8)	—	5.41E-8 (6.27E-8)
Lagged Percent of Stores Closed * YEAR1[a]	—	.424*** (.122)	.461*** (.126)
Lagged Percent of Stores Closed * YEAR2[a]	—	−.048 (.097)	−.047 (.101)
Lagged Percent of Stores Closed * YEAR3[a]	—	−.075 (.171)	−.045 (.176)
R^2	.192	.227	.233

[a] Information on control variables, lags, and significance levels is given in the notes to Table 2.

In the Table 3 models for the separate subsamples, lagged profitability has a significant positive effect on first-year BCR changes for the negative profit subsample (panel A, columns 1 and 3). In the positive profits subsample, the point estimate of the lagged profits effect on first-year BCR changes is also positive, but it is not significantly different from zero. Lagged profits has no significant effect on second- or third-year BCR changes in either the panel A or panel B subsample. The coefficients on the "lagged profits ∗ YEAR1" variable in panels A and B indicate a more precise effect of lagged profits on compensation adjustments when the prior profitability variable is negative—consistent with a hypothesis that union negotiators have access to more accurate estimates of financial performance when performance is relatively poor.[19]

Although the lagged profitability measure has a less precise effect on first-year BCR changes when lagged profitability is positive than when lagged profitability is negative, the results in panel B of Table 3 provide no support for the hypothesis that union negotiators respond to the publicly observable signal of store closings by accepting smaller BCR increases when lagged profits are positive. In particular, the lagged store closing variable has a significant positive effect on year-one BCR adjustments in the positive profits subsample (panel B, columns 2 and 3). The lagged store closing measure also has a positive effect on year-one BCR adjust-

ments in the negative profits subsample (panel A, columns 2 and 3). Management negotiators do not use past store closings as an implied threat of future job loss to moderate compensation adjustments in either the positive or negative profits subsample. To the contrary, the positive effects of the "lagged store closings ∗ YEAR1" interaction terms in both subsamples may indicate that once the most unprofitable stores covered by a given contract have been closed in the year prior to negotiation, the union can seek larger wage increases because it is no longer concerned about potential employment losses in the poor-performing stores that were closed.

When the dependent variable is respecified as the probability of a reduction in BCR in the Table 4 models, the pattern of results is very similar to the Table 3 results for the positive profits subsample (panel B). First-year concession probabilities are significantly lower when the lagged store closing variable is higher (panel B, columns 2 and 3). Although the point estimate of the effect of lagged profitability on first-year concession probabilities is negative, the effect is insignificant—consistent with the positive insignificant coefficient on the lagged profits variable on year-one BCR changes in Table 3, panel B. All other parameter estimates on the lagged profitability and store closing variables in Table 4, panel B are insignificant.

In panel A of Table 4, the respecification of the dependent variable as the probability of a BCR reduction leads to a pattern of results different from that observed in the Table 3, panel A change in BCR models. The effects of lagged profitability and lagged store closings on the probability of BCR concessions during year one of a contract are insignificantly different from zero in the Table 4, panel A models.

Overall, the results of BCR adjustment models for the full sample indicate that when the full range of the lagged operating income variable is considered, relatively low levels of prior period profitability lead to an initial downward adjustment of a contract's BCR growth profile in the

---

[19] Although the coefficients are consistent with the hypothesis that union negotiators have access to more accurate estimates of financial performance when performance is relatively poor, other interpretations should be acknowledged. For example, the operating income variable may be a less accurate indicator of true economic performance when operating income is positive, thereby producing a less precise estimate of the relationship between this proxy for economic profitability and compensation adjustments. Also, the estimates in panel A of Table 2 for the full sample imply that the average first-year BCR adjustment is higher when lagged operating income is positive than when lagged operating income is negative. Some signal of positive profitability may be responsible for higher BCR increases when lagged profits are positive than when lagged profits are negative.

Table 4. The Effects of Prior Profitability and Store Closings on the Probability
of an Overall Labor Cost Reduction.
(Dependent Variable: $\Pr(\text{BCR}_t < \text{BCR}_{t-1})$; Probit Estimates)

Panel A — Sample with Negative Lagged Store Profitability (n = 195 Contract-Years)			
Independent Variables	**(1)**	**(2)**	**(3)**
Lagged Average Store Profitability $*$ YEAR1[a]	−2.64E-6 (2.03E-6)	—	−2.55E-6 (2.01E-6)
Lagged Average Store Profitability $*$ YEAR2[a]	−0.43E-6 (1.95E-6)	—	0.45E-6 (2.10E-6)
Lagged Average Store Profitability $*$ YEAR3[a]	47.45E-6* (28.85E-6)	—	46.95E-6 (31.07E-6)
Lagged Percent of Stores Closed $*$ YEAR1[a]	—	1.148 (1.260)	1.076 (1.273)
Lagged Percent of Stores Closed $*$ YEAR2[a]	—	4.331 (2.741)	4.127 (2.712)
Lagged Percent of Stores Closed $*$ YEAR3[a]	—	−26.557 (56.002)	−4.066 (14.713)
−2 $*$ log-likelihood	65.27	64.75	68.28

Panel B — Sample with Positive Lagged Store Profitability (n = 278 Contract-Years)			
Independent Variables	**(1)**	**(2)**	**(3)**
Lagged Average Store Profitability $*$ YEAR1[a]	−0.56E-6 (1.89E-6)	—	−2.01E-6 (2.10E-6)
Lagged Average Store Profitability $*$ YEAR2[a]	−2.31E-6 (3.59E-6)	—	−1.17E-6 (3.84E-6)
Lagged Average Store Profitability $*$ YEAR3[a]	−8.80E-6 (8.74E-6)	—	−8.38E-6 (8.49E-6)
Lagged Percent of Stores Closed $*$ YEAR1[a]	—	−16.118** (6.613)	−17.355** (6.796)
Lagged Percent of Stores Closed $*$ YEAR2[a]	—	3.066 (2.885)	−2.677 (3.193)
Lagged Percent of Stores Closed $*$ YEAR3[a]	—	5.646 (6.371)	3.747 (6.856)
−2 $*$ log-likelihood	53.45	61.07	63.76

[a] Information on control variables, lags, and significance levels is given in the notes to Table 2.

first year of the labor contract. After this initial adjustment in year one, BCR growth profiles are similar across contracts covering stores with different levels of prior profitability. This particular pattern is again observed within the limited range of contracts covering stores that on average have negative operating incomes prior to negotiations. In contrast, within the positive range of the prior profitability measure, the effect of prior profitability on BCR adjustments is not significantly different from zero.

Do Compensation Adjustments Matter?

According to the results in Table 2,

negotiated changes in rates of compensation are positively related to prior financial performance and the probability of an overall concession is negatively related to prior financial performance. Concessionary adjustments should subsequently improve the economic performance of the covered stores. This section presents estimates of the response of profitability to prior compensation adjustments. Unlike the BCR-change analysis, in which BCR is determined in contracts, the relevant level of observation for an analysis of the effects of labor cost adjustments on subsequent profitability is the store. As in the analysis of the change in BCR, the relative timing of profitability changes and BCR adjustments is measured carefully. BCR_t has been measured as end-year BCR. We assume that BCR_t is the BCR that determines store profitability during year $t+1$ (π_{t+1}). As a result, in the models in this section, the change in profits ($\Delta\pi$) between t and $t+1$ is a function of the change in BCR (ΔBCR) between $t-1$ and t. As in the Table 2 models, store operating income is the measure of profitability.[20]

As noted above, each store may have up to three contracts. Therefore, the change in BCR from up to three different contracts—clerk, meatcutter, and other specialty department employee contracts—may affect a given store's profitability. The change in profitability models include three separate BCR change variables. The vector of control variables (X) in the change in profitability models includes two dummy variables for whether the store is a "one-contract" store or a "three-contract" store. The omitted category is the set of "two-contract" stores.

The vector of control variables also includes a set of year dummy variables; percent change in SMSA unemployment; percent change in SMSA population;[21] and a measure of the change in the company's local product market power. Progressive Grocer's *Market Scope* (1977, 1982, 1987) reports this company's sales and sales of all other retail food companies by SMSA for 1976, 1981, and 1986. The company's own concentration ratio is measured by the ratio of its own sales in an SMSA to total SMSA sales. The percentage change in this measure (ΔCONC) between 1976 and 1981 is applied to all observations in the given SMSA for the years 1976 through 1981. The percentage change in this measure between 1981 and 1986 is applied to all observations in the

given SMSA for the years 1982 through 1985. These company-specific sales measures are available for only 23 of the SMSAs in which the company operates. The analysis below is therefore restricted to store-years in these SMSAs.

The estimated profitability change model has the following form:

$$(5) \qquad \Delta\pi_{t,t+1} = \alpha + \beta 1(\Delta BCR_{t-1,t}) + \beta 2(X) + \epsilon$$

Because the change in profits between years t and $t+1$ and the change in BCR between $t-1$ and t can be negative, $\Delta\pi_{t,t+1}$ and $\Delta BCR_{t-1,t}$ are each specified as a simple arithmetic difference measured in dollars.

When the profit change equation is estimated, the results in column 1 of Table 5 are obtained. The coefficients on the three lagged change in BCR variables are all negative and significant for each of the three possible types of contracts. As expected, reductions in rates of compensation lead to a significant subsequent improvement in store operating income.

Although these effects are significant in the expected direction, the effects of changes in clerks' and meatcutters' BCR are perhaps smaller than expected. In particular, BCR changes are measured as changes in the dollar-per-hour BCR, and changes in stores' operating incomes are changes in annual profits. Assuming that scale effects are relatively unimportant, the coefficient on the change in BCR will be approximately equal in absolute value to the total number of annual hours for employees under a contract in the given store if a reduction in BCR increases subsequent profitability dollar-for-dollar.

Summary statistics from the company's reports for 1987 were used to estimate the average number of annual hours per store for typical clerk and meatcutter contracts. According to these reports, the company negotiated 60 contracts in 1987 covering 639 stores and involving approximately 1.56 million weekly hours (on average, 1,030,000 and 526,000 weekly hours were worked by clerks and meatcutters, respectively). Across these 639 stores, we estimated that clerks worked an average of

[20] As indicated in footnote 12, this analysis should be distinguished from an analysis of the effects of compensation changes on quasi-rent measures of performance. In particular, quasi-rents, unlike operating income, would be directly affected by changes in external market wage rates.

[21] The control variables measuring changes in SMSA population and unemployment rates are defined as they were for the Table 2 models. See footnote 17.

Table 5. The Effects of Labor Cost Adjustments on Subsequent Changes in Store Profitability.
(Dependent Variable: Store Profits$_{t+1}$ − Store Profits$_t$)
(n = 2,847 store-years)

Independent Variable	(1)	(2)
Dollar Change in Clerks' BCR[a]	−11,973*	−17,336***
	(6,263)	(6,743)
Dollar Change in Meatcutters' BCR[a]	−16,534***	−13,000**
	(4,967)	(5,573)
Dollar Change in Other BCR[a]	−84,129***	−56,710**
	(23,369)	(24,430)
SMSA Dummies	no	yes
R^2	.051	.068

[a] BCR changes are measured from the end of year $t-1$ to the end of year t in dollars.

Other control variables in the model are changes in the company's own SMSA-specific concentration ratio, a set of year dummies, percent change in SMSA population, percent change in SMSA unemployment rate, a dummy for whether a store is a one-contract store, and a dummy for whether a store is a three-contract store.

* Significant at the .10 level; ** at the .05 level; *** at the .01 level (two-tailed tests).

84,050 annual hours per store and meatcutters worked an average of 42,802 annual hours per store.[22]

According to the estimated coefficients in column 1 of Table 5, a one-dollar reduction in clerks' or meatcutters' BCR would not subsequently improve store performance by enough to indicate a dollar-for-dollar effect. For example, the column 1 coefficient on the meatcutters' BCR variable (−$16,534) corresponds to only 39% of the approximate number of meatcutters' hours per store calculated above.

There are at least three reasons for relatively small effects of changes in meatcutter and clerk BCRs. First, some of the difference may be attributable to efficiency wage explanations. As a store operates with reduced meatcutter or clerk compensation, it may incur costs in terms of turnover and recruitment, or in monitoring and disciplining a relatively lower-quality work force. Still, these costs would have to be quite large to account for the differences between the Table 5 BCR coefficients and a "dollar-for-dollar" effect.

Second, BCR changes are not measured

perfectly. Although BCR adjustments occur continuously throughout a contract, the ΔBCR variable measures changes from the end of year $t-1$ to the end of year t. The difference between the measure of ΔBCR and actual BCR changes may confound the estimate.

Finally, the model of changes in store profitability is probably incomplete. Cost items that affect operating income are not included in the model. In general, the model includes only limited determinants of the economic profitability of stores. If some omitted determinant of profitability is also correlated with BCR changes, then the coefficient on the BCR change variable will be biased. Further, it seems likely that the direction of this omitted variable bias on the BCR change variables would be positive. Factors that make certain regions or certain stores within regions relatively more profitable than others should be associated with relatively large increases in BCR.

The column 2 model attempts to address this possibility in a limited fashion through the inclusion of a set of SMSA dummy variables. If omitted determinants of profits are SMSA-specific and the true effects of BCR changes on subsequent changes in profitability are larger in absolute value than the column 1 estimates for meatcutters and clerks imply, then estimates in column 2 will be smaller—that

[22] The estimate is calculated by dividing the average weekly clerk and meatcutter contract hours by the number of stores covered by the contract and multiplying the result by 52. For example, annual meatcutter hours are calculated as [(525,974/639) * 52 = 42,802].

is, negative but larger in absolute value—than the estimates in column 1.

When the SMSA dummies are included in the store profitability model, the coefficient on the clerks' BCR change variable is reduced. The point estimate of this coefficient declines from −$11,973 in column 1 to −$17,336 in column 2. The point estimates of the coefficients on the meat-cutters' and other workers' BCR change variables, however, are greater in the column 2 model than in the column 1 model. Moreover, given the average annual hours calculations for a typical store and contract, the clerks' coefficient in column 2 is probably still too small to correspond to a dollar-for-dollar effect of BCR changes on profitability changes.

In short, estimated effects of BCR changes on subsequent profitability fall short of a "dollar-for-dollar" effect. Part of this estimated difference may be due to real losses in efficiency. Alternatively, part or all of the difference may be due to an incomplete specification of the profitability change model. Although the company's data do not permit us to sort out the relative importance of these two possibilities, the Table 5 models clearly indicate that changes in compensation affect future profits.

Conclusions

The analysis in this paper using one company's unique data sheds new light on the relationships among concession bargaining, firm profitability, and the closing of unionized operations. The data permit a more comprehensive examination than has previously been possible of the incidence and dollar-per-hour value of concessions in specific contract provisions. No previous study provides any estimate of the monetary value of changes in contract language.

Certain limitations apply to the extension of these results to other firms and other industries. First, this company is not the typical employer described in industrial relations texts today. It is, rather, committed to operating with unionized employees. Although this policy may be attributable to the high degree of unionization among the company's employees (see Kochan, Katz, and McKersie 1986), the firm is clearly trying to operate competitively with a unionized work force. The company's stance toward unions does not affect its valuation of contract clauses, however, and thus does not influence our analysis of the value of union concessions presented above.

Our results suggest that prior period profitability influences compensation rates negotiated in the current period. Compensation increases were smaller and concessions more likely where the prior profitability of the covered stores was lower. The company negotiated more moderate compensation increases and obtained concessions where such adjustments were more important to remain competitive. These compensation adjustments in response to differences in prior period profitability were negotiated only in the first years of contracts. After these first-year compensation adjustments, compensation growth in the second and third years of contracts was similar across contracts that were negotiated under different profitability conditions. Prior store closings, however, were not a threat to any contracts, profitable or unprofitable. In both the sample of contracts covering profitable stores and the sample of contracts covering unprofitable stores, prior period store closings had a *positive* effect on negotiated compensation adjustments.

Research on companies in other industries has reached somewhat different conclusions. Concessions are not always concentrated among firms and operations facing the strongest economic threats (see Cappelli 1985a). The results of our analysis, however, may be strongly influenced by the almost complete unionization of this company's employees and the company's evident determination to remain economically competitive using this unionized work force.

Other findings suggest some general observations about concession bargaining. First, concessions may be obtained on virtually any provision in a labor agreement. Some subjects, however, are more important sources of concessions because potential dollar cost reductions vary considerably across categories of contract clauses. Second, it appears that stores needing particularly drastic cost cuts to avoid closings probably have to reduce wages. Other contract clauses typically do not provide enough potential savings. Still, although most individual concessionary clauses produce small dollar-per-hour reductions in cost, those pennies add up. Consequently, it may be possible to design concession packages that achieve considerable savings without requiring workers to give up large hourly amounts.

Third, concerning multi-tier wage rates, which have received considerable attention in recent years, our results show that second and third tiers have been negotiated for many subjects of bargaining other than wages. The company's data show a wide variety of clauses that provide newly hired employees with less than is provided to other employees. For example, eligibility requirements for benefits have been changed, premium pay rates have been reduced, time off has been cut back, and benefits have been altered for new hires. Concession bargaining involves many more variations than have been commonly acknowledged.

Finally, changes in rates of compensation have the intended effect of improving the subsequent financial performance of establishments. Decreases in the rates of compensation in the contracts of all categories of employees investigated in this study have significant positive effects on subsequent economic performance. More convincing estimates of the magnitude of these effects, however, will require more detailed data.

REFERENCES

Abowd, John M. 1989. "The Effect of Wage Bargains on the Stock Market Value of the Firm." *American Economic Review,* Vol. 79, No. 4 (September), pp. 774–800.

Becker, Brian E. 1987. "Concession Bargaining: The Impact of Shareholders' Equity." *Industrial and Labor Relations Review,* Vol. 40, No. 2 (January), pp. 268–79.

———. 1988. "Concession Bargaining: The Meaning of Union Gains." *Academy of Management Journal,* Vol. 31, No. 2 (June), pp. 377–87.

Ben-Ner, Avner, and Saul Estrin. 1989. "Unions as Employee Representatives and as Employers: The Impact on Wages, Employment, and Productivity." Working paper, London School of Economics.

Cappelli, Peter. 1983. "Concession Bargaining and the National Economy." In Industrial Relations Research Association, *Proceedings of the Thirty-Fifth Annual Meeting.* Madison, Wis.: IRRA, pp. 362–71.

———. 1984. "Union Gains Under Concession Bargaining." In Industrial Relations Research Association, *Proceedings of the Thirty-Sixth Annual Meeting.* Madison, Wis.: IRRA, pp. 297–305.

———. 1985a. "Competitive Pressures and Labor Relations in the Airline Industry." *Industrial Relations,* Vol. 24, No. 3 (Fall), pp. 316–38.

———. 1985b. "Plant-Level Concession Bargaining." *Industrial and Labor Relations Review,* Vol. 39, No. 1 (October), pp. 90–104.

Cappelli, Peter, and Robert B. McKersie. 1985. "Labor and the Crisis in Collective Bargaining." In Thomas A. Kochan, ed., *Challenges and Choices Facing American Labor.* Cambridge, Mass.: MIT Press, pp. 227–45.

Ehrenberg, Ronald G., and George T. Milkovich. 1987. "Compensation and Firm Performance." In Morris M. Kleiner, Richard N. Block, Myron Roomkin, and Sidney W. Salsburg, eds., *Human Resources and the Performance of the Firm.* Madison, Wis.: Industrial Relations Research Association, pp. 87–122.

Freeman, Richard B. 1986. "In Search of Union Wage Concessions in Standard Data Sets." *Industrial Relations,* Vol. 25, No. 2 (Spring), pp. 131–45.

Hendricks, Wallace, Peter Feuille, and Carol Szerszen. 1980. "Regulation, Deregulation, and Collective Bargaining in Airlines." *Industrial and Labor Relations Review,* Vol. 34, No. 1 (October), pp. 67–81.

Hollander, Abraham, and Robert LaCroix. 1986. "Unionism, Information Disclosure and Profit-Sharing." *Southern Economic Journal,* Vol. 52, No. 3 (January), pp. 706–17.

Kassalow, Everett M. 1983. "Concession Bargaining—Something Old but Also Something New." In Industrial Relations Research Association, *Proceedings of the Thirty-Fifth Annual Meeting.* Madison, Wis.: IRRA, pp. 372–82.

Kleiner, Morris M., and Marvin L. Bouillon. 1988. "Providing Business Information to Production Workers: Correlates of Compensation and Profitability." *Industrial and Labor Relations Review,* Vol. 41, No. 4 (July), pp. 605–17.

Kochan, Thomas A., and Richard N. Block. 1977. "An Interindustry Analysis of Bargaining Outcomes: Preliminary Evidence from Two-Digit Industries." *Quarterly Journal of Economics,* Vol. 91, No. 3 (August), pp. 431–52.

Kochan, Thomas A., Harry C. Katz, and Robert B. McKersie. 1986. *The Transformation of American Industrial Relations.* New York: Basic Books.

Kochan, Thomas A., and Hoyt N. Wheeler. 1975. "Municipal Collective Bargaining: A Model and Analysis of Bargaining Outcomes." *Industrial and Labor Relations Review,* Vol. 29, No. 1 (October), pp. 46–66.

Progressive Grocer Company. 1987, 1982, 1977.

Market Scope. Stamford, Conn.: Progressive Grocer Company.

Simpson, Wayne. 1986. "Unions, Industrial Concentration, and Wages: A Re-examination." *Applied Economics,* Vol. 18, No. 3 (March), pp. 305–17.

U.S. Bureau of the Census. 1977–1987. *Statistical Abstract of the United States.* Washington, D.C.: GPO.

U.S. Department of Labor, Bureau of Labor Statistics. 1975–1985. *Employment and Earnings,* various May issues.

Weiss, Leonard. 1966. "Concentration and Labor Earnings." *American Economic Review,* Vol. 56, No. 1 (March), pp. 96–117.

THE EFFECTS OF HUMAN RESOURCE MANAGEMENT DECISIONS ON SHAREHOLDER VALUE

JOHN M. ABOWD, GEORGE T. MILKOVICH, and JOHN M. HANNON*

Using an event study methodology, the authors investigate whether human resource decisions of firms (such as decisions concerning compensation and benefits or staffing) announced in the *Wall Street Journal* in 1980 and 1987 discernibly affected either the level or variation of abnormal total shareholder return. They find no consistent pattern of increased or decreased valuation in response to any of five categories of HR announcements, even after controlling for the likely effect of such announcements on total compensation costs. On the other hand, announcements of permanent staff reductions and shutdowns or relocations were associated with significant increases in the variation of abnormal total shareholder return around the announcement date, which indicates that HR decisions in those two categories do affect shareholders' predictions of firms' performance.

THE relation between human resource decisions and organizational performance is a central issue in the study of managerial decision-making. Despite the considerable attention professionals and academics have given to the increased importance of effective human resource management, fewer researchers have focused on the effects of human resource management decisions on organization performance than on the determinants of the HR decisions themselves. (For a discussion of this point, see Dyer and Holder 1988; Schuler 1987; Kleiner et al. 1987; and Ulrich 1987.) One reason for the relative scarcity of this type of research may be the absence of well-developed theories, other than the price-theoretic models that emphasize the relation between unit compensation costs and employment, that relate strategic HR decisions to medium-term and long-term corporate outcomes. In addition, little effort has been made to create a taxonomy of the relevant HR strategies that might be used to measure the effects of alternative decisions on organizational performance.

The organizational performance outcomes most commonly considered are employee behaviors and attitudes. Studies of the effects of alternative gainsharing

* John Abowd is Professor of Labor Economics and Management, George Milkovich is Martin P. Catherwood Professor of Personnel and Human Resource Studies, and John Hannon is a Ph.D. candidate in Personnel and Human Resource Studies, all at Cornell University. John Abowd is also a Research Associate at the National Bureau of Economic Research. The financial support of the Alfred P. Sloan Foundation, The Center for Advanced Human Resource Studies, and the National Science Foundation (grant number SES-8813847 to Abowd) is gratefully acknowledged. The authors also thank Charles Brown, Barry Gerhart, and Kevin J. Murphy for comments on an earlier draft.

A data appendix lists all the citations from the *Wall Street Journal*. Security return data from the Center for Research in Security Prices must be licensed separately from the University of Chicago Graduate School of Business. Financial data from the COMPUSTAT system must be licensed separately from Standard and Poor's COMPUSTAT service.

plans on employee suggestions, performance, and satisfaction (Schuster 1983, 1984; Bullock and Lawler 1984), the effects of merit pay on performance and satisfaction (Pearce and Perry 1983; Heneman 1984), and the effects of flexible work schedules on attendance, absenteeism, and satisfaction (Gannon, Norland, and Robeson 1983) are all examples. Other research argues that the perceptions of organizational stakeholders (stockholders, employees, managers, and regulatory agencies) regarding the constituents of HR activities are the relevant outcomes (Tsui 1987). This type of analysis has been conducted using a variety of HR-related indexes as measures of performance (Fitzenz 1984), including productivity estimates (for example, the ratio of sales revenue to total employee salaries and the ratio of production volume to labor use) and staffing rates (for example, turnover rates, promotion rates, and offer/hire rates). A series of studies has applied cost-benefit analysis to some of these indexes (Boudreau, in press; Cascio 1987; Alexander and Barrick 1987).

Other authors have examined the relation of HR decisions to the economic performance of organizations. Economic performance has been defined using accounting measures (for example, net income, return on assets, and return on equity) and using financial market measures of shareholder wealth (holding period dividends plus capital gains). Research in this genre includes studies examining the effects of new collective bargaining agreements (Abowd 1989), concession bargaining (Becker 1987), strikes (Neumann 1980; Becker and Olson 1986; Tracy 1987, 1988), executive compensation (Baker, Jensen, and Murphy 1988; Brickley, Bhagat, and Lease 1985; Tehranian and Waegelein 1985; Gomez-Mejia, Tosi, and Hinkin 1987), and executive succession (Reinganum 1985; Etebari, Horrigan, and Landwehr 1987; Lubatkin, Chung, Rogers, and Owers 1989).

To summarize, research on the relation between human resource decisions and organizational performance appears to have focused most on immediate outcomes (behaviors and attitudes), less on intermediate outcomes (accounting measures, financial health, and economic outcomes), and hardly at all on ultimate outcomes like survival. (For a rare example of the third kind of investigation, see Thorndike 1949.) It may be, of course, that HR decisions operate directly on the immediate outcomes and only indirectly on the intermediate economic and ultimate survival outcomes.

In this study we attempt to analyze the effects of HR decisions on shareholder wealth. We do so recognizing that stock market measures of firm performance may have too much "noise" in many situations to permit detection of the direct effects of HR policies and practices. Recent evidence documenting the direct effects of labor relations events on the shareholder value of the firm suggests, however, that similar effects may be found for other HR decisions (Abowd 1989; Becker and Olson 1987; Ruback and Zimmerman 1984; Tracy 1988).

An important feature of these studies is their use of an economic model of the information content of the HR announcement. This model predicts which announcements should be associated with increased shareholder wealth (events associated with unexpected decreases in total compensation or increases in profitability) and which announcements should be associated with decreased shareholder wealth (events associated with unexpected increases in total compensation or decreases in profitability). These studies have focused on specific types of HR management events (primarily contract negotiations and strikes) and have used models appropriate for these events.

We have no general model that can classify HR events by their expected effects on shareholder wealth. Consequently, we use conventional event study methods in an effort to detect (1) any significant direct effects of HR announcements on shareholder wealth and (2) any evidence that market reactions of unpredictable direction occur.

Assessing HR Decision Effects Using the Event Study Methodology

We use the event study methodology

developed in accounting and finance (Ball and Brown 1968; Beaver 1968; Fama, Fisher, Jensen, and Roll 1969) and applied in the recent labor relations studies cited above. The basic premise of the event study is that capital markets react immediately to new information that materially affects the future profitability of the firm. An event is an announcement by the firm or an action in the marketplace that conveys incremental information to stock market participants allowing them to revise prior expectations regarding the prospects of a corporation or identifiable group of corporations (Patell 1976).

The efficient markets hypothesis implies that this new information will rapidly diffuse throughout the market, and some market participants will act on the information in a manner that changes the value of shareholders' wealth to reflect the consequences of the new information. A change in either the expected future cash flows or the riskiness of a firm's stock, which will affect the discount rate used to reduce case flows to present value, will result in a change in the price of the firm's common stock. If the change in expected cash flows or riskiness is expected to be advantageous, the price of the stock will rise. If the change in expected cash flows or riskiness is expected to be harmful, the price of the stock will decline.

Depending on the firm's capital structure, shareholder value may be equated with the total value of the firm or it may constitute some portion of total firm value. Regardless of the firm's capital structure, the event study methodology defines firm performance in terms of *changes* in shareholder value, which is generally called total shareholder return.

The Event Study Structure

Although event studies use many different techniques, they involve five general steps (see Bowman 1983; Brown and Warner 1980, 1985; and Schwert 1981). The steps are: (1) identify the events of interest; (2) model the normal (expected) total shareholder returns; (3) estimate the abnormal (unexpected) total shareholder returns; (4) organize and group the

abnormal returns according to event type; and (5) analyze summary measures for abnormal returns by event type.

The event of interest may be a single action affecting a group of firms simultaneously, such as a new regulatory agency announcement, or an action affecting different firms at various times, such as numerous firms making layoff announcements. The most critical component of the event measurement is the determination of the time when the public first learned that the event occurred (see Brown and Warner 1980, 1985). This date is called the event date.

The importance of correctly ascertaining the event date stems from a property of stock returns implied by the efficient markets hypothesis and empirically valid for total shareholder returns of firms with active capital markets—stock returns are neither serially correlated nor serially cross-correlated. Hence, on any given date a sample of abnormal returns has a zero mean. Further, a sample of cumulative abnormal returns (the sum of abnormal returns over a specified time interval) also has a zero mean. When abnormal returns and cumulative abnormal returns are computed for a group of firms that experienced a similar event, using the event date as the reference point, the average abnormal return for the group has a positive (negative) mean if the event is associated with the arrival of favorable (unfavorable) information on the market. Similar arguments hold for the cumulative abnormal return over a time interval that includes the event date. Other influences on total shareholder return are effectively controlled by the statistical properties cited above. When the direction of the effect cannot be predicted *ex ante*, the variance of abnormal returns and cumulative abnormal returns is greater on and around the event date than for a reference period before or after that date.

The estimation of the expected return is accomplished by statistical modeling of the relation between total shareholder return over a given holding period (typically one day or one month) with the total shareholder return for the same holding period arising from the capital market, a diversified portfolio of common stocks (typically a broad-based portfolio of common stocks traded on the New York Stock Exchange). The abnormal return is computed as the difference between the holding period total shareholder return and its estimated expected value, given the return on the market. The abnormal, or unexpected, return is computed for the reference period used to estimate the expected return model (typically 250 days for daily returns and 5 years for monthly returns) and an event period surrounding the event date (typically 21 days for daily returns and 7 months for monthly returns).

Formally, in our study the abnormal return was calculated using the following definitions (for daily return data):

$$(1) \quad R_{i,t} = (D_{i,t} + P_{i,t} - P_{i,t-1})/P_{i,t-1}$$

where $D_{i,t}$ = dividend per share over day t for security i and $P_{i,t}$ = price (ex dividend) of security i at the end of day $t;$ and

$$(2) \quad R_{i,t} = \alpha_i + \beta_i R_{m,t} + AR_{i,t}$$

where $R_{m,t}$ = return on the market portfolio for day $t;$ α_i and β_i = estimated intercept and slope for security $i;$ and $AR_{i,t}$ = abnormal return for security i on day t.

The price per share has been adjusted to reflect the effects of stock splits and stock dividends over the period $t-1$ to t. The return on the market portfolio is measured by the percentage change in the New York Stock Exchange value-weighted portfolio including dividends (Center for Research in Security Prices 1987). The estimated abnormal return (the residual from the estimated expected return model) was calculated as

$$(3) \quad AR_{i,t} = R_i - (\hat{\alpha}_i + \beta_i R_{m,t})$$

The intercept and slope of the expected return model were estimated over a 253-day period during the calendar year preceding the event date (called the estimation period). The same intercept and slope were used to calculate abnormal returns in the period surrounding the event date (called the event period). Abnormal returns have a zero mean over the estimation period because of the

properties of ordinary least squares, the technique used for estimation.

The abnormal returns were grouped according to a classification system developed for the HR events. Statistics, based on the abnormal returns, were computed for the event period, generally 5 days—2 days before the event, the event day itself, and 2 days after the event. Hence, when daily returns are used, $t = 0$ for the event day; the day before the announcement is $t = -1$; and the day after the announcement is $t = 1$. Abnormal returns were grouped by event type and day relative to the event day (t), and then averaged across firms. The average abnormal return for a day t is defined as:

$$(4) \quad AAR_t = \sum_{i=1}^{N} AR_{i,t}/N$$

where $AR_{i,t}$ = abnormal return for firm i on event day t and N = number of events in the group.

Average cumulative abnormal returns (average $CARs$) were also computed for the event period and an eight-day period preceding $t = -2$ (see Fama et al. 1969). The formula used was:

$$(5) \quad CAR_I = \sum_{t=t_1}^{t_2} AAR_t$$

where I is the relevant event group and t_1 and t_2 are the beginning day and ending day of the period.

To estimate changes in the variance of abnormal returns, we calculated variance ratio statistics based on the five-day event period and the 253-day estimation period. The statistic F_i was calculated according to the formula:

$$(6) \quad F_i = \frac{\sum_{t=-2}^{2} AR_{i,t}^2/5}{\sum_{t=t_1}^{t_2} AR_{i,t}^2/251}$$

where the period t_1 to t_2 delimits the estimation period. The numerator was divided by 5 (instead of 4) because the average abnormal return was not different from zero (and therefore was not estimated). The denominator is divided by 251 (or some number less than 251) to reflect the number of actual trading days used in the estimation of the expected return regression for company i (less two to account for the estimation of α and β).

Methodology for Evaluating HR Events

Definitions

Previous HR-based event studies have evaluated the effects of one specific type of event (for example, wage settlements or executive compensation plans) on shareholder value. In this study, we examine a broad range of human resource decisions for the years 1980 and 1987. The events were grouped into five major classes and nine distinct subcategories based on their likely effects on total compensation costs: (1) **general HR system changes**—no subcategories; (2) **compensation and benefits**—(a) increase, (b) decrease; (3) **staffing**—(a) permanent reduction, (b) temporary reduction, (c) recall or increase; (4) **relocation or shutdown**—(a) relocation, (b) shutdown; (5) **miscellaneous**—(a) health and safety; (b) all others (not estimated because of noncomparability across years).

Event Data: Source and Dating

The sample for this study includes all firms with traded securities on the New York Stock Exchange in 1980 or 1987. The source for events and the event dates is the *Wall Street Journal*. From our review of all 1980 and 1987 issues of the *WSJ*, we identified 452 events associated with 154 firms in 1980 and 195 events associated with 102 firms in 1987. The event date was taken as the date that the information was provided to the market via publication in the *WSJ*. (The Data Appendix lists all events for the calendar years 1980 and 1987 by event type and subcategory, including a synopsis of the *WSJ* articles.) Although deficiencies associated with the use of the *WSJ* and the *Wall Street Journal Index* have been noted (Thompson 1985;

Thompson, Olsen, and Dietrich 1987, 1988), the majority of event studies in accounting, finance, and labor relations have used one or both of these sources.

The total shareholder return and stock price information for those firms experiencing HR events was extracted from the Center for Research in Security Prices (CRSP) daily stock returns file (1987). In this study, the daily return, which reflects dividends paid plus the change in the price of the security for each trading day, was used. In order to account for the possibility that information was leaked to the market prior to the announcement of the event in the *Wall Street Journal,* an event window spanning two days before the event through two days after the event was evaluated. In order to allow for the possibility that the information slowly leaked into the market, an eight-day period beginning ten days before the event and ending three days before the event was also studied.

Expected Security Price Reactions

The announcement of a human resource decision has several potential effects. If an announced action is interpreted as an attempt to improve performance, it may be seen as beneficial. Alternatively, if it is perceived as an act of desperation, it may send a negative signal to the market and the firm's shareholders. Of course, shareholders and the market may be indifferent to the HR decisions described in the "events."

The major difficulty in categorizing the events is determining the element of new information or "surprise" in each announcement. Events that can be directly quantified (for example, earnings announcements or new collective bargains) are amenable to a statistical model separating the expected and unexpected components of the announcement. For the events we examine here, however, no direct model of the expected announcement is available. Instead, we categorize events by the direction of the effect on total compensation costs (when that effect can be determined); however, we must note that even when an event (such as a staffing increase or a compensation increase) is known to increase total compensation costs, the unexpected component of the increase is not necessarily positive.

We can speculate that certain information conveyed to the market through HR events would be unexpected. On the one hand, if the managers of the firm are always acting in the shareholders' best interest, the expected effect of any HR change is to increase the value of shareholders' wealth. This expected effect is capitalized into the security price gradually as the information about the general HR environment at the firm is revealed. The new information content—unexpected part—of every type of HR announcement, then, must be positive on average. On the other hand, the announcements also may contain some new information about the state of the product market (or other relevant economic factors). In these cases, the unexpected effects of the announcement will, on average, imply positive security price effects when the product market information is good and negative security price effects when the product market information is bad.

Consider the case of a permanent staffing reduction. The first-order effect of this change is to reduce total compensation costs and to reduce output (or at least productive capacity) within the organization. If the staffing reduction is in the shareholders' best interests, costs fall by more than the reduction in sales revenue, so that profits rise. On average, the unexpected component of the staffing change should have a positive effect on stock prices for this reason. If, however, the staffing reduction is greater than the market expectation based on economic conditions in the firm's industry, the unexpected component of the announcement also includes new information that the product market (or other economic conditions) are worse than expected. This part of the unexpected component of the staffing change will have a negative effect on stock prices. It is very difficult to model the net effect of such influences on stock prices without a comprehensive model for

decomposing the announcement into an expected component and unexpected components that reflect new information about HR policies and new information about the state of the product market.

Before considering the results of our event study, we report the results of a statistical analysis of the magnitude, variability, and sample size required for estimability of the average abnormal return caused by unexpected changes in sales, cost of goods sold, operating income, direct wage expense, and sales less direct wage expense. The experiment was conducted using 3,450 firms from Standard and Poor's COMPUSTAT annual financial data files. For each firm we calculated net sales, cost of goods sold, operating income, estimated direct wage expenses, and sales less direct wage expenses. We estimated the present value of the after-tax change in cash flow resulting from a one percent change in each of these quantities holding all other income statement items constant. The present value was calculated using horizons of one year, three years, and infinity. The abnormal return was estimated as the ratio of the present value of the change in cash flow divided by the December 1979 market value of the company's common stock.

This experiment, summarized in Table 1, reveals the difficulty of measuring the effect of HR events on stock prices when the effect on other economic factors can be perfectly controlled and when the effect on other factors cannot be controlled at all. The table shows the average abnormal return associated with the unexpected increase, the cross-sectional standard deviation of the average abnormal return, and an estimate of the number of events required to detect the abnormal return given the cross-sectional standard deviation and the average standard deviation of daily abnormal returns (.03; see Brown and Warner 1985).

An unexpected 1% increase in direct wage expenses that is expected to last only one year produces an average abnormal return of only $-.43\%$ and has enough variability to require 979 events for an

Table 1. Estimated Abnormal Returns from an Unexpected One Percent Increase in Sales, Costs, Operating Income, Direct Wages, and Sales Less Direct Wages for COMPUSTAT Companies in 1980.

Duration of Change	Sales	Costs	Operating Income	Direct Wages	Sales − Wages
1 year	2.18%	−1.75%	0.56%	−0.43%	1.78%
	(3.33)	(2.87)	(0.99)	(0.76)	(2.97)
	47	70	578	979	68
3 years	5.93%	−4.76%	1.53%	−1.17%	4.85%
	(9.06)	(7.79)	(2.69)	(2.07)	(8.08)
	14	19	89	143	19
Infinite	22.59%	−18.11%	5.84%	−4.47%	18.45%
	(34.48)	(29.68)	(10.24)	(7.89)	(30.75)
	10	11	18	22	12

Notes: The standard deviation of the abnormal return is in parentheses (stated as a percentage). The number in the third row of each panel is the estimated sample size required to detect the effect using a five-day window with daily abnormal returns with a standard deviation of .03 (Brown and Warner 1985).

Sources: Based on a sample of 3,450 COMPUSTAT firms (NYSE, AMEX, and OTC) using fiscal year 1979 data for Net Sales, Cost of Goods Sold, Operating Income, and Employees. Abnormal returns are stated as a percentage of the December 31, 1979 market value of all common stock outstanding.

Direct wage costs were estimated as $11,416 times employees. The annual earnings figure is the average annual earnings in private nonagricultural employment for 1979 derived from BLS data in CITIBASE.

Dollar values assume a 46% corporate income tax rate and are reduced to present value at 10.69%, which was the Moody's Baa rate in December 1979 (CITIBASE).

estimate that exceeds its standard error by two. If the HR event is of this order of magnitude and contains no information about the product market, it will be virtually impossible to detect the effect with stock price data. On the other hand, if the unexpected 1% increase in direct wage expenses is associated with a 1% increase in sales—that is, if the event signals an unexpected increase in profitable production—then only 68 events will be required to detect it even if the duration is only one year.

The signs of the abnormal returns in Table 1 can be reversed to discuss downturns. If a 1% decrease in direct wage costs (perhaps from an unexpected layoff of one percent of the work force) is expected to last three years, then the direct wage effect (+1.17%) may be detected with 143 events. If the HR event also signals a 1% downturn in sales, then the −4.85% effect is detectable with only 19 events.

The detectability of larger stock price changes arising from HR events involving larger unexpected changes in costs or direct wages can be estimated from the infinite horizon rows of Table 1. An unexpected change of 10% in direct wage costs that lasts only one year is essentially the same as a 1% change that lasts forever. It should therefore be detectable with 22 events, provided those events are not associated with the introduction of other information.

Finally, in order to provide some additional guidance regarding the magnitude of the estimated effects, we discuss the portfolio consequences of various abnormal returns. An average *CAR* of 1% means that a portfolio consisting of stocks about to experience the event will increase in value (on average) 1% between the close of business on day $t = -3$ and the close of business on day $t = 2$. If the event could be forecasted perfectly, then a 1% holding period return could be realized (gross of trading costs) by assembling such a portfolio on day $t = -3$ and liquidating the positions on day $t = 2$. Average *CAR*s of 1% for five-day event periods are economically significant, although not particularly large. For HR events, our estimated absolute *CAR*s ranged from .02% to 2.68%. For industrial relations events, absolute *CAR*s have been estimated in the 1.5% to 3% range. (See Ruback and Zimmerman 1984; Becker and Olson 1986; and Tracy 1988.)

Table 2. Mean Abnormal Returns for Human Resource Management Decisions, 1980: All Events.

Event Type	N	Day −2 Mean (S.Err.)	−1 Mean (S.Err.)	0 Mean (S.Err.)	1 Mean (S.Err.)	2 Mean (S.Err.)	Cumulative Abnormal Return −2 to +2	Cumulative Abnormal Return −10 to −3
Human Resource: General	29	.48% (.49%)	−.39% (.43%)	.39% (.65%)	−.65% (.42%)	−.51% (.43%)	−.67% (1.10%)	−1.10% (1.30%)
Compensation: Increase	29	−.69% (.39%)	−.35% (.73%)	.06% (.72%)	1.04%* (.41%)	−.26% (.37%)	−.20% (1.23%)	−.90% (1.45%)
Compensation: Decrease	28	.54% (.41%)	.52% (.49%)	.66% (.49%)	−.77% (.60%)	−.98% (.48%)	−.02% (1.11%)	−.15% (1.72%)
Staffing: Permanent Reduction	87	.33% (.26%)	.12% (.26%)	−.39%) (.26%)	−.28% (.23%)	−.19% (.22%)	−.42% (.55%)	−.74% (.67%)
Staffing: Temporary Reduction	157	−.28% (.19%)	−.36% (.20%)	−.17% (.23%)	−.19% (.17%)	−.20% (.22%)	−1.19%** (.45%)	.04% (.59%)
Staffing: Recall/Increase	24	.41% (.68%)	1.33% (1.03%)	−.28% (.39%)	−.09% (.33%)	−.41% (.32%)	.95% (1.37%)	−1.99% (1.06%)
Relocate	4	−1.86% (.76%)	−.61% (.65%)	1.39% (1.01%)	−.60% (.95%)	−1.00% (.41%)	−2.68% (1.75%)	−.36% (1.98%)
Shutdown	80	.39% (.35%)	−.20% (.27%)	.06% (.34%)	−.56%* (.25%)	.07% (.27%)	−.25% (.67%)	−.45% (.82%)
Health/Safety	14	.02% (.40%)	−1.07% (.50%)	−.62% (.40%)	.32% (.25%)	−.18% (.52%)	−1.52% (.95%)	.69% (1.26%)
Total	452	.06% (.12%)	−.12% (.13%)	−.08% (.13%)	−.24%* (.10%)	−.24%* (.11%)	−.62%* (.27%)	−.46% (.33%)

Notes: The abnormal returns were derived using an OLS market model regression equation.
* Significant at the .05 level; ** significant at the .01 level (two tails).
Sources: Event data were obtained by reading the *Wall Street Journal* for the year 1980. Stock price data were obtained from the Center for Research in Security Prices daily returns file.

Estimation Procedure

The usual procedure for calculating the expected total shareholder return from daily return data is to use an estimation period of about 250 days that ends about one month before the event period begins (see Brown and Warner 1985). We modified this procedure because of the relative frequency with which some HR events occur. Events such as permanent reduction announcements may, and did, occur once or more for a given firm in a particular year. For example, General Electric made five such work force reduction announcements in 1980. Furthermore, any number of combinations of event types may be experienced by firms in our study within a given period. For instance, in 1980, Firestone announced plans to shut down five plants (3/20/80)

and initiated permanent layoffs of white-collar workers (5/5/80).

To account for this potential multiplicity of HR events, which is attributable to the broad nature of the HR policies, we chose to modify the time frame for the market model estimation process. We have used returns for each firm from the preceding calendar year to generate our expected returns. This procedure reduces the potential for including confounding events in the estimation period. The abnormal return was then derived from the difference between the observed and the predicted returns. The abnormal return may be generated for any number of days before or after the event. We chose to analyze abnormal returns for days −2, −1, 0, 1, and 2. The cumulative abnormal return was computed for the 5-day period from day −2 through day +2. A second

Table 3. Mean Abnormal Returns for Human Resource Management Decisions, 1980: First Events.

Event Type	N	Day −2 Mean (S.Err.)	Day −1 Mean (S.Err.)	Day 0 Mean (S.Err.)	Day 1 Mean (S.Err.)	Day 2 Mean (S.Err.)	Cumulative Abnormal Return −2 to +2	Cumulative Abnormal Return −10 to −3
Human Resource: General	14	.84% (.90%)	−.16% (.75%)	.59% (1.10%)	−.70% (.59%)	−1.04% (.66%)	−.46% (1.84%)	−2.89% (2.04%)
Compensation: Increase	14	−.79% (.47%)	−.66% (1.14%)	1.74% (1.17%)	1.15%** (.36%)	−.26% (.49%)	1.18% (1.80%)	.07% (2.01%)
Compensation: Decrease	8	.62% (.93%)	−.32% (.74%)	−.86% (1.14%)	.06% (.79%)	.34% (.64%)	−.17% (1.94%)	−.39% (3.40%)
Staffing: Permanent Reduction	38	.19% (.39%)	.10% (.50%)	−.37%) (.50%)	−1.06%** (.37%)	.25% (.36%)	−.88% (.96%)	.42% (1.00%)
Staffing: Temporary Reduction	25	−.23% (.38%)	−1.05%* (.48%)	−.49% (.43%)	.14% (.30%)	−.49% (.67%)	−2.11%* (1.04%)	−1.34% (1.11%)
Staffing: Recall/Increase	3	1.38% (1.38%)	2.20% (5.25%)	.54% (.59%)	.76% (1.76%)	.95% (1.41%)	5.83% (5.90%)	−2.28% (2.84%)
Relocate	2	−2.32%* (.05%)	.18% (.73%)	2.98%* (.12%)	−1.61% (1.66%)	−1.32% (.36%)	−2.09% (1.85%)	.35% (3.73%)
Shutdown	43	.51% (.56%)	−.82%* (.39%)	.52% (.53%)	−.33% (.36%)	−.03% (.38%)	−.15% (1.01%)	−.65% (1.09%)
Health/Safety	7	.18% (.57%)	−.33% (.46%)	−1.00% (.61%)	−.15% (.30%)	−.20% (.75%)	−1.51% (1.25%)	−2.03% (1.61%)
Total	154	.19% (.22%)	−.44% (.24%)	.15% (.26%)	−.30% (.17%)	−.13% (.20%)	−.53% (.49%)	−.70% (.55%)

Notes and Sources: Same as for Table 2.

cumulative return spanning from day −10 through day −3 was also derived to examine the pre-event movement in the total shareholder return, if any.

Results

In this section we discuss the results for average cumulative abnormal returns and variance ratios for each of the analysis years. There is a separate discussion of the 1980 and 1987 studies. The *CAR* analyses were performed for all events and for the first event for each company. The variance ratio studies were performed using the first event for each company.

1980 Abnormal Returns

All events. In 1980 there were 452 HR events in 154 firms. Staffing–temporary reduction (157), staffing–permanent reduction (87), and shutdown (80) events occurred most frequently, as seen in Table 2.

In general, the results in this table

indicate that the stock market did not react predictably to most of the human resource interventions announced in 1980. Only the staffing–recall/increase subcategory had a relatively large positive average cumulative abnormal return (average *CAR*) for the 5-day period (+.95% ± 1.37%). The staffing–temporary reduction event had an average *CAR* of −1.19% ± .45%, which is the only statistically significant average *CAR* during the event period. The negative cumulative abnormal return for staffing–temporary reduction remains statistically significant when the data for all events in 1980 and 1987 are pooled (−1.11% ± .43%).

First events. In an attempt to isolate the effects of the human resource events under study, a second set of analyses was performed for the 1980 sample using only the first event for each firm. In 1980, there were 154 such events for 154 firms. When only the first event was considered, the shutdown (43), staffing–permanent

Table 4. Mean Abnormal Returns for Human Resource Management Decisions, 1987: All Events.

Event Type	N	Day −2 Mean (S.Err.)	−1 Mean (S.Err.)	0 Mean (S.Err.)	1 Mean (S.Err.)	2 Mean (S.Err.)	Cumulative Abnormal Return −2 to +2	Cumulative Abnormal Return −10 to −3
Human Resource: General	28	.08% (.29%)	.14% (.52%)	.22% (.31%)	.35% (.51%)	.32% (.40%)	1.10% (.93%)	−1.10% (.83%)
Compensation: Increase	10	.02% (.64%)	.53% (.74%)	.05% (.45%)	−.34% (.36%)	−1.11%** (.32%)	−.85% (1.19%)	−1.19% (1.92%)
Compensation: Decrease	18	−.09% (.48%)	−.46% (.50%)	−.09% (.48%)	.06% (.62%)	−.29% (.69%)	−.87% (1.25%)	−.25% (1.41%)
Staffing: Permanent Reduction	88	−.06% (.23%)	−.31% (.32%)	.13% (.27%)	.03% (.35%)	.56% (.35%)	.35% (.69%)	−.66% (.79%)
Staffing: Temporary Reduction	12	−.59% (.60%)	.49% (.65%)	−.24% (.23%)	−.18% (.49%)	.52% (.33%)	.00% (1.08%)	.96% (1.46%)
Staffing: Recall/Increase[a]	1							
Relocate	10	−.34% (.37%)	.10% (.35%)	−.20% (.37%)	.73% (.97%)	−.11% (.42%)	.18% (1.23%)	.33% (1.61%)
Shutdown	24	−.36% (.42%)	−.19% (.46%)	−.23% (.82%)	−.61% (.33%)	.40% (.40%)	−.98% (1.15%)	−1.04% (1.29%)
Health/Safety	4	−.39% (1.13%)	−1.00% (.98%)	−1.07% (1.30%)	.62% (.77%)	2.21% (1.48%)	2.51% (2.59%)	−2.85% (3.51%)
Total	195	−.14% (.14%)	−.15% (.19%)	.05% (.17%)	.02% (.20%)	.34% (.19%)	.12% (.40%)	−.65% (.46%)

[a] Insufficient sample size to perform significance tests for this category.

Other notes: Same as for Table 2.

Sources: Event data were obtained by reading the *Wall Street Journal* for the year 1987. Stock price data were obtained from the Center for Research in Security Prices daily returns file.

reduction (38), and staffing–temporary reduction (25) events were the most frequent, as shown in Table 3.

With the exception of the compensation–increase category, which was negative for the "all events" and positive for the "first events only," the associations observed for the overall sample have the same directions in the first event only sample. As in the all events sample, the first event only subset exhibits a large negative average *CAR* for the staffing–temporary reduction category. This negative average *CAR* is also significant for the pooled 1980 and 1987 first event analysis (−2.11% ± 1.00%).

1987 Abnormal Returns

All events. In 1987, there were a total of 195 events. Staffing–permanent reduction (88) was the predominant event type. General human resource (28) and shutdown (24) were the next most frequent event types, as can be seen in Table 4.

The 1987 results also show a general lack of predictability in the stock market reaction to the HR events. In three of the nine categories (compensation–increase, compensation–decrease, and shutdown) the direction of the relationship is the same as in 1980, although no average *CAR* is statistically significant at conventional levels.

First events. In 1987, there were 102 first events, as defined previously, for 102 firms. Considering only the first events, the staffing–permanent reduction (52)

Table 5. Mean Abnormal Returns for Human Resource Management Decisions, 1987: First Events.

Event Type	N	Day					Cumulative Abnormal Return	Cumulative Abnormal Return
		−2 Mean (S.Err.)	−1 Mean (S.Err.)	0 Mean (S.Err.)	1 Mean (S.Err.)	2 Mean (S.Err.)	−2 to +2	−10 to −3
Human Resource: General	12	.08% (.62%)	−.25% (.67%)	.31% (.58%)	.53% (.64%)	.44% (.68%)	1.11% (1.43%)	−1.41% (1.09%)
Compensation: Increase	5	.77% (.80%)	.13% (.75%)	.69% (.47%)	−.30% (.44%)	−.74% (.58%)	.54% (1.40%)	−1.80% (3.20%)
Compensation: Decrease	4	−.07% (1.82%)	.40% (.67%)	.54% (1.04%)	−.51% (1.62%)	−1.53% (1.65%)	−1.16% (3.19%)	−1.02% (3.88%)
Staffing: Permanent Reduction	52	−.19% (.34%)	−.86% (.45%)	.39%) (.39%)	−.12% (.53%)	.76% (.53%)	−.01% (1.01%)	−.94% (1.05%)
Staffing: Temporary Reduction[a]	1							
Staffing: Recall/Increase[a]	0							
Relocate	8	−.25% (.45%)	.46% (.27%)	−.26% (.45%)	.65% (1.22%)	.08% (.49%)	.67% (1.49%)	−.44% (1.92%)
Shutdown	18	−.77% (.46%)	−.44% (.55%)	−.45% (1.08%)	−.90%* (.36%)	.52% (.47%)	−2.04% (1.43%)	−1.57% (1.63%)
Health/Safety	2	−.18% (2.12%)	−1.55% (2.24%)	.26% (2.02%)	1.08% (.94%)	4.01% (2.56%)	3.62% (4.58%)	−5.28% (6.91%)
Total	102	−.21% (.22%)	−.52% (.27%)	.19% (.29%)	−.14% (.31%)	.53% (.31%)	−.15% (.63%)	−1.21% (.68%)

[a] Insufficient sample size to perform significance tests for this category.
Other notes: Same as for Table 2.
Sources: Same as for Table 4.

and shutdown (18) events occurred with the greatest frequency, as shown in Table 5.

Comparing the total 1987 sample with the first event only subset, we see that two important categories (compensation–increase and staffing–permanent reduction) have changes in average *CAR* signs. These changes are influential enough to result in different signs for the average *CAR* values for the all events sample (+.12%) and the first event only subset (−.15%). Again, no cumulative abnormal returns are statistically significant.

Variance Changes

In order to determine whether the variability of abnormal returns changes around the event date, we computed the ratio of abnormal return variances for the event period relative to the estimation period. Figure 1 displays a histogram of these variance ratios for the first event sample in 1980 compared to the theoretical F-distribution that would be obtained in the absence of variance shifts around the event. The many large values of the variance ratio that are apparent in the figure seem to rule out the hypothesis of no change in abnormal return variance. This impression is confirmed by the Kolmogorov D-statistic ($D = .111$, probability value $< .01$). The new information in the HR events is moving stock prices, but not in a predictable direction.

Figure 2 shows a similar histogram for the 1987 first event sample. Again, there are too many large variance ratios, compared to the theoretical F distribution, to accept the hypothesis of no variance change. The Kolmogorov D-statistic con-

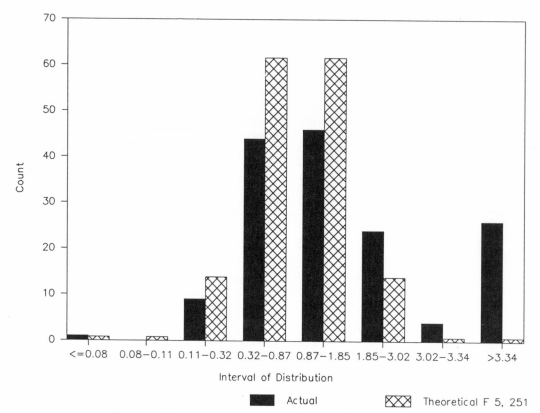

Figure 1. Distribution of Variance Ratios: 1980 First Events.

firms this conclusion (D = .147, probability value < .01).

Having concluded that there is evidence of a variance shift surrounding the event period in both 1980 and 1987, we examined lists of the events associated with the large variance shifts. For the year 1980 there were 26 events in the largest variance ratio category. Seven of these events were permanent staff reductions and nine were plant shutdowns. Although we were not able to predict the average effects of these events precisely, the variance ratios confirm that such events are associated with large swings in the stock price. Similarly, for 1987, there were 13 events in the largest variance ratio category. Nine were associated with permanent reductions in force, one was a shutdown, and one was a relocation. The results for 1987 are consistent with the 1980 variance results. Major reductions in staff or changes in plant location are associated with large abnormal returns of unpredictable direction. An analysis of the 1980 and 1987 variance ratios for all first events associated with permanent reductions of staff supports this conclusion (Shapiro-Wilk statistic = .869, probability value <.01 for 1980, and W = .150, probability value <.01 for 1987). Analysis of the 1980 and 1987 variance ratios for all first events associated with plant shutdowns was inconclusive.

A final issue that arises in connection with the finding that HR events increase the variance of abnormal returns around the announcement date is the possibility that HR decisions are selected for announcement in the *Wall Street Journal* precisely because of their likely impact on stock returns. We contacted the *WSJ* in an effort to determine the sources and coverage of HR news stories. The two primary sources are company press releases and reporters covering a geographic region or company. Most an-

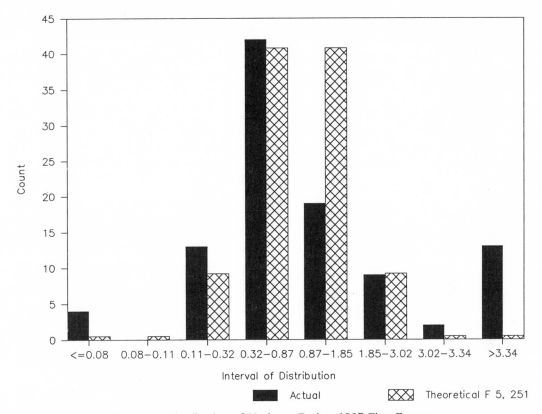

Figure 2. Distribution of Variance Ratios: 1987 First Events.

nouncements originate as press releases, and most descriptive stories originate from beat reporters; all stories are written by *WSJ* reporters. Press release information is investigated by the reporter and is not printed verbatim as distributed by the company. The *Journal*'s goal is to write a story on the same day the information is received, and almost all press releases about HR changes result in some news coverage. Some companies routinely disclose more information in the form of press releases and general interviews than other companies (private correspondence, 1989).

It seems likely that company policy regarding HR event press releases affects the probability of the event appearing in the *WSJ,* and hence that certain companies are more likely than others to appear in our analysis. It does not follow, however, that certain stories are more likely to appear for that company. The tests we performed for changing variances con-

trolled for the individual company's abnormal return variability; therefore, the possibility that high variance companies disclose more HR information would not bias our results.

Conclusion

In this study, we extended the use of the event study methodology to consider the effects of a variety of human resource decisions on shareholder return. Human resource announcements occur frequently, at least as compared to the accounting, control, and regulatory events that are often the focus of event studies. The magnitude and variability of the theoretical abnormal returns associated with unambiguous HR events—events that signal an unexpected increase or decrease in compensation costs holding other components of cash flow constant—are such that our task was a difficult one from the outset. Furthermore, most HR events apparently are not unambiguous new information. The temporary staff reduction event, which had a significant negative cumulative abnormal return, must contain some additional bad news about the product market, since by itself a staff reduction reduces compensation costs.

Like all other event studies, our conclusions rely on the assumptions that we have (1) properly identified and (2) adequately isolated true events. We believe, however, that human resource management announcements constitute valid events. Bowman (1983:561) has argued that "a very broad interpretation should be placed on what constitutes an event." Becker and Olson (1987) also suggest that capital market research supports the proposition that the market reacts to managerial decisions affecting cash flows and maximiz-

ing price per share. Certainly human resource management decisions meet these qualifications.

Our results indicate that the direction of the effect of HR management events is difficult to predict absent a more fully specified model for the unexpected change in total compensation expense and organizational efficiency associated with the announcement. Our finding of increased variance in abnormal shareholder return associated with HR announcements suggests, however, that these events do provide information that influences stock prices. In future research it might be useful to extend this concept to other HR intervention types, longer time periods, and broader samples than New York Stock Exchange firms, and to use models that explicitly consider the new information content of the announcements themselves.

Data Appendix

Table A1. Individual Events, 1980: Items from the *Wall Street Journal*.

OBS	COMPANY	EVENT DATE	EVENT DESCRIPTION
		PRIMARY CODE = HR	SECONDARY CODE = HR
1	AMERICAN ELECTRIC	80–08–15	WHAT DOES IT TAKE TO GET 900 WORKERS TO RELOCATE TO OHIO?
2	BANK AMERICA	80–09–24	IT PAYS TO STAY HEALTHY UNDER BANK'S PILOT PLAN
3	BETHLEHEM STEEL	80–07–29	GRADS TRAINED FOR FAST TRACK AT BETHLEHEM STEEL
4	CHRYSLER	80–06–30	CHRYSLER AND UNION SEEK TO DRIVE AWAY CURSE ON NEW AUTOS (Q CIRCLES)
5	CHRYSLER	80–07–16	CHRYSLER DIRECTORS FORCE GROUP TO EASE IMPACT OF CLOSINGS
6	CHRYSLER	80–10–07	CHRYSLER TELLS UAW IT IS TRYING TO SELL FOUR PARTS FACILITIES
7	COOPER JARRETT	80–08–01	COOPER JARRETT SEEKS MORE EMPLOYEE LOANS
8	DANA	80–06–24	DANA IS CITED FOR CONTEMPT IN CASE OVER UNION ELECTION
9	DELTA	80–07–07	FAMILY FEELING AT DELTA CREATES LOYAL WORKERS, ENMITY OF UNIONS
10	EASTERN AIR	80–09–03	EASTERN AIR GETS APPROVAL TO GROUND PREGNANT ATTENDANTS
11	FIRESTONE	80–03–19	FIRESTONE EMPLOYEES OFFERED $100 FOR BUYING U.S. CARS
12	FIRESTONE	80–08–13	LAID OFF FIRESTONE WORKERS FIND TALK, FRUSTRATION AND A FEW JOBS AT SEMINAR
13	FIRESTONE	80–11–19	FIRESTONE BECOMES STRONGER BY CUTTING CAPACITY, JOBS, PRODUCT LINES
14	FIRESTONE	80–11–28	CHALLENGE TO AFFIRMATIVE ACTION
15	FORD	80–06–16	CLOSING OF A FORD PLANT REFLECTS RISING WORRY OF CAR MAKERS: QUALITY
16	GEN. TIRE & RUBBER	80–06–04	FIRM WORKERS CAN GET $100 FOR BUYING U.S. CAR
17	GORMAN RUPP	80–02–07	BUY AMERICAN, RECEIVE A BONUS, EMPLOYEES TOLD

Table A1 (Continued)

OBS	COMPANY	EVENT DATE	EVENT DESCRIPTION
18	GRT ATL&PAC TEA CO	80–05–02	A&P'S NEW PRESIDENT ISN'T SIGNALLING ANY RE-TRENCHMENT WAVE DESPITE DEFICIT
19	GTE	80–03–07	GTE TRAINING CENTER (TO BE BUILT)
20	J.P. STEVENS	80–10–20	HOW THE TEXTILE UNION FINALLY WINS CONTRACTS AT J.P. STEVENS PLANTS
21	MANHATTAN INDUST	80–05–29	APPAREL MAKER SETS RESTRICTIONS TO HALT FRAUD BY EMPLOYEES
22	MOBIL	80–04–14	U.S. SUES MOBIL FOR EMPLOYEE TAX DATA SOUGHT IN IRS PROBE
23	PAINE WEBBER	80–01–31	PAINE WEBBER TRADING FOR OWN ACCOUNTS CUT SHARPLY TO EASE CLERICAL WORKLOAD
24	R.H. MACYS	80–10–10	MACY'S EXECUTIVE TRAINING SQUAD TEACHES FU-TURE RETAILERS
25	U.S. STEEL	80–09–16	U.S. STEEL SETS ACCORD ON HIRING OF WOMEN (25%)
26	U.S. STEEL	80–09–23	CLOSING OF A STEEL MILL HITS WORKERS IN U.S. WITH LITTLE WARNING (11/27/79)
27	VORNADO	80–04–09	VORNADO PLEADS "NO CONTEST" TO CHARGE OF ANTIUNION ACTION
28	WESTINGHOUSE	80–08–13	WESTINGHOUSE SETTLES MATERNITY LEAVE SUIT BY RESTORING SENIORITY
29	3M	80–07–07	3M USES PROMOTE-FROM-WITHIN POLICY TO BREED MANAGERS LIKE CHAIRMAN LEHR

PRIMARY CODE = COMP/BEN   SECONDARY CODE = INCREASE

OBS	COMPANY	EVENT DATE	EVENT DESCRIPTION
30	ALLIED CHEMICAL	80–01–18	ALLIED CHEMICAL CORP WORKERS ARE OFFERED HELP UNDER TRADE ACT
31	AMC	80–09–25	AMC WORKERS MAY GET AID
32	ATT	80–03–14	PHONE WORKERS UNION SAYS IT WILL SEEK WAGE BOOSTS OF BETWEEN 9.5 AND 18%
33	BRANIFF	80–11–26	BRANIFF PAY CUT PLAN IS REJECTED BY UNION; NECESSITY QUESTIONED
34	BRUNSWICK	80–10–24	ABOUT 5500 WORKERS MAY ASK U.S. FOR AID, LABOR AGENCY RULES
35	CHRYSLER	80–02–13	LABOR UNIT CLEARS 1800 AT CHRYSLER FOR U.S. ASSISTANCE
36	CITICORP	80–01–28	CITICORP PLANS TO BUY UP TO 2 MILLION SHARES FOR EMPLOYEES' PROGRAM
37	EASTERN AIR	80–01–04	EASTERN AIR WORKERS WILL RECEIVE STOCK, EASING LOSS OF CASH
38	EX-CELL-O	80–07–07	U.S. AID FOR WORKERS IDLED BY IMPORTS SET AT AUTO PARTS PLANT
39	FIRESTONE	80–08–01	SOME FORD, FIRESTONE, MATTEL WORKERS GET U.S. TRADE ACT AID
40	FORD	80–03–31	FORD EMPLOYEES AT 3 LOCATIONS RULED ELIGIBLE FOR U.S. AID (13,400)
41	FORD	80–04–21	U.S. TO AID 48,000 EMPLOYEES OF FORD; IMPORT RISE IS CITED
42	FORD	80–04–28	U.S. TO AID 131,000 FORD GM WORKERS HURT BY IMPORTS
43	FORD	80–06–10	U.S. LETS WORKERS AT FORD PLANT CLAIM AID DUE TO IMPORTS (4800)
44	FORD	80–08–01	SOME FORD, FIRESTONE, MATTEL WORKERS GET U.S. TRADE ACT AID
45	FORD	80–09–10	SOME FORD EMPLOYEES WILL GET FEDERAL AID AS A RESULT OF IMPORTS
46	FOREMOST-MCKESSON	80–03–11	FOREMOST-MCKESSON PENSIONS (ARE RAISED TO AC-COUNT FOR INFLATION 2500)
47	GM	80–05–06	U.S. TO COMPENSATE 900 GM WORKERS DUE TO IMPORT RISE
48	GM	80–10–24	ABOUT 5500 WORKERS MAY ASK U.S. FOR AID, LABOR AGENCY RULES
49	GM	80–10–29	LABOR AGENCY RULES 4810 GM EMPLOYEES QUALIFY FOR U.S. AID

Table A1 (Continued)

OBS	COMPANY	EVENT DATE	EVENT DESCRIPTION
50	GM	80–11–19	AGENCY RULES 5300 GM WORKERS MAY GET HELP DUE TO IMPORTS
51	GOODYEAR	80–04–25	GOODYEAR UNIT OFFERING BOUNTY FOR TECHNICIANS ($1000)
52	KAISER STEEL	80–09–18	USW LOCAL RETRACTS OFFER TO TAKE PAY CUTS TO AID KAISER STEEL
53	KODAK	80–05–30	KODAK GIVING EMPLOYEES 3% COST OF LIVING RAISES
54	LEAR-SIEGLER	80–10–24	ABOUT 5500 WORKERS MAY ASK U.S. FOR AID, LABOR AGENCY RULES
55	MATTEL	80–08–01	SOME FORD, FIRESTONE, MATTEL WORKERS GET U.S. TRADE ACT AID
56	RANCO	80–12–18	TRADE ADJUSTMENTS AID RULE AVAILABLE FOR 600 WORKING IN 2 INDUSTRIES
57	RIVERSIDE MFG	80–07–07	U.S. AID FOR WORKERS IDLED BY IMPORTS SET AT AUTO PARTS PLANT
58	TRW	80–05–12	WAGE-PRICE PROGRAM COSTS TRW $1M PLUS MANY HEADACHES

PRIMARY CODE = COMP/BEN   SECONDARY CODE = DECREASE

OBS	COMPANY	EVENT DATE	EVENT DESCRIPTION
59	BRANIFF	80–10–08	BRANIFF CHAIRMAN VOWS TO CUT HIS PAY 20% (10% FOR EMPLOYEES)
60	CHRYSLER	80–01–03	UAW WILL OFFER CONCESSIONS TO CHRYSLER TOMORROW, EXPECTS NEW ACCORD QUICKLY
61	CHRYSLER	80–01–07	CHRYSLER/UAW SET CONCESSION IN LABOR ACCORD
62	CHRYSLER	80–02–04	CHRYSLER/UAW LOCALS RATIFY REVISED PACT TO LOWER LABOR COSTS (111,000)
63	CHRYSLER	80–12–17	CHRYSLER ASKS UAW FOR A WAGE FREEZE TO HELP OBTAIN AID
64	CHRYSLER	80–12–23	UAW AGREES TO NEGOTIATE WITH CHRYSLER UP TO $600M IN WAGE CONCESSIONS
65	EASTERN AIR	80–12–04	EASTERN AIR EMPLOYEES MAY FIND CHRISTMAS TO BE A LITTLE BLEAKER
66	FIRESTONE	80–06–27	UNIROYAL & FIRESTONE BESET BY LOSSES, SLUMP IN TIRE SALES, ANNOUNCE PAY CUTS
67	FIRESTONE	80–10–02	FIRESTONE IS SEEKING A BUYER FOR 18 HOLES OF ITS GOLF COMPLEX (ELIMINATE PERK)
68	FIRESTONE	80–12–24	FIRESTONE EMPLOYEES IN MEMPHIS APPROVE PLANT'S SURVIVAL PLAN
69	FORD	80–03–10	FORD-UAW PACT FOUND TO VIOLATE WAGE GUIDELINES
70	FORD	80–04–17	FORD AGREES TO LIMIT SOME BOOSTS IN PAY TO MEET GUIDELINES
71	GEN. TIRE & RUBBER	80–11–05	AID REJECTED FOR 13,900 WHO CLAIM IMPORTS COST THEM THEIR JOB
72	GM	80–08–04	GM HALTS MERIT RAISES DUE TO 2ND QUARTER LOSS
73	GOODYEAR	80–11–05	AID REJECTED FOR 13,900 WHO CLAIM IMPORTS COST THEM THEIR JOB
74	INLAND STEEL	80–07–14	INLAND STEEL EMPLOYEES' WORK WEEK IS REDUCED (2300)
75	INTERLAKE	80–06–11	INTERLAKE SEEKS LID ON LABOR-COST BOOST IN STEEL UNION TALKS
76	J.C. PENNEY	80–04–08	J.C. PENNEY TO STOP ISSUING NEW COMMON FOR PROFIT SHARING PLAN
77	KAISER STEEL	80–08–22	UNION LOCAL TO ASK KAISER STEEL WORKERS TO ACCEPT WAGE CUT
78	KAISER STEEL	80–08–28	STEELWORKERS VOTE CUT IN SIZE OF PAY INCREASES AT KAISER STEEL MILL
79	TWA	80–01–01	TWA WILL SLASH SALARIES OF MANAGEMENT UP TO 25% OF AMOUNTS > $35,000 (800)
80	U.S. STEEL	80–05–20	MANAGEMENT REVOLT BEGINS AT U.S. STEEL OVER WAGE FREEZE
81	U.S. STEEL	80–11–05	AID REJECTED FOR 13,900 WHO CLAIM IMPORTS COST THEM THEIR JOB

Table A1 (Continued)

OBS	COMPANY	EVENT DATE	EVENT DESCRIPTION
82	UNION CARBIDE	80–11–05	AID REJECTED FOR 13,900 WHO CLAIM IMPORTS COST THEM THEIR JOB
83	UNIROYAL	80–06–27	UNIROYAL AND FIRESTONE BESET BY LOSSES, SLUMP IN TIRE SALES, ANNOUNCE PAY CUTS
84	UNIROYAL	80–07–24	URW APPROVES CUTS IN PAY AND BENEFITS TO AID UNIROYAL
85	WHEELING PITTSBURGH	80–02–15	WHEELING PITTSBURGH SAYS SOME WORKERS BACK PAY CUT (LOWER INCENTIVE PAY)
86	WHEELING PITTSBURGH	80–08–19	WHEELING PITTSBURGH WILL ASK 12,000 STEELWORKERS TO FORGO PAY BOOST

	PRIMARY CODE = STAFF		**SECONDARY CODE = PERM REDUCE**
87	AKZONA	80–07–21	AKZONA'S AMERICAN ENKA FURLOUGHS 180 EMPLOYEES
88	ALCOA	80–07–09	ALCOA IDLES INDEFINITELY UNITS IN TEXAS, INDIANA (130)
89	ALOCA	80–11–24	ALCOA TO CLOSE SECTIONS OF BRITISH ROLLING MILL; GM SLATES DISMISSALS
90	ALLIS CHALMERS	80–06–17	FIAT–ALLIS CHALMERS VENTURE SLASHES JOBS, PLANS SOME RELOCATION
91	AMERICAN CYNAMID	80–10–20	AMERICAN CYNAMID TO LAY OFF 200 DYE PLANT WORKERS
92	ARMCO	80–01–16	ARMCO TO LAY OFF MORE HOURLY EMPLOYEES (130)
93	ARMCO	80–05–29	ARMCO SLATES LAYOFF OF 190 MORE WORKERS AT MIDDLETOWN, OHIO
94	ARMSTRONG RUBBER	80–04–07	ARMSTRONG RUBBER SAYS IT WILL IDLE 10% OF EMPLOYEES IN 4 STATES (200)
95	ASARCO	80–06–26	ASARCO MINE IN ILLINOIS IS CLOSED, ABOUT 220 LAID OFF
96	ASARCO	80–07–24	ASARCO TO LAY OFF 116, CUT ZINC PLANT'S OUTPUT
97	B.F. GOODRICH	80–05–05	TIRE MAKERS TROUBLES START TO FORCE LAYOFFS IN WHITE COLLAR RANKS
98	B.F. GOODRICH	80–09–12	SOME GOODRICH EMPLOYEES TO PROFIT FROM QUITTING
99	BENDIX	80–06–24	BENDIX CORP REDUCES ITS MANAGEMENT STAFF (1600)
100	BETHLEHEM STEEL	80–05–05	BETHLEHEM STEEL AND JONES-LAUGHLIN CUT BACK OPERATIONS (1450)
101	BETHLEHEM STEEL	80–05–28	BETHLEHEM CLOSEDOWN OF BLAST FURNACE SET AT LACKAWANNA, NY (290)
102	BETHLEHEM STEEL	80–06–19	TWO STEELMAKERS ANNOUNCE FURTHER PRODUCTION CUTBACKS (700)
103	BORG WARNER	80–01–17	BORG WARNER UNIT IN BRITAIN TO DISMISS 600 WORKERS AT 2 PLANTS
104	CAMPBELL SOUP	80–04–11	CAMPBELL SOUP DIVISION PLANS LAYOFFS IN NEBRASKA (80)
105	CATERPILLAR	80–05–12	CATERPILLAR PLANS INDEFINITE LAYOFFS OF 3175 EMPLOYEES
106	CATERPILLAR	80–08–22	CATERPILLAR PLANS INDEFINITE LAYOFF OF 2,500 WORKERS
107	CESSNA	80–03–26	CESSNA TO LAY OFF 800 AT WALLACE DIV.
108	CHESSIE SYSTEM	80–05–21	CHESSIE SYSTEM SAYS IT WILL FURLOUGH 440 AT RACELAND, KY, UNIT
109	CHRYSLER	80–04–23	CHRYSLER TO LAY OFF 20% OF ITS SALARIED, OTHER STAFF TO SAVE $200M A YEAR
110	CHRYSLER	80–07–11	CHRYSLER WILL CLOSE SECOND WORK TURN AT ST. LOUIS FACILITY (2100) (U.S. AUTO)
111	CHRYSLER	80–07–21	CHRYSLER TO MAKE MORE REDUCTIONS IN ITS WORK FORCE (5400 WHITE COLLAR)
112	CHRYSLER	80–10–27	CHRYSLER CONSIDERING FURTHER CUTBACKS, IS USING A NEW STANDARD TO DECIDE
113	CHRYSLER	80–12–18	NEW CHRYSLER SURVIVAL PLAN WOULD STRIP $1 BILLION IN COSTS, MAY HARM FUTURE
114	COLONIAL PENN	80–01–18	COLONIAL PENN GROUP DROPS 300 EMPLOYEES IN COST CUT PROGRAM

Table A1 (Continued)

OBS	COMPANY	EVENT DATE	EVENT DESCRIPTION
115	CONTINENTAL AIR	80–06–17	CONTINENTAL AIR TO LAY OFF 1200 WORKERS AND REDUCE PASSENGER CAPACITY
116	CUMMINS ENGINE	80–01–09	CUMMINS ENGINE SETS LAYOFF OF ABOUT 1000
117	CUMMINS ENGINE	80–05–19	CUMMINS ENGINE SETS ADDED LAYOFF OF 1500
118	DANA	80–05–21	DANA UNIT TYRONE HYDRAULICS PLANS LAYOFF OF HALF ITS WORKERS (340)
119	DEERE & CO.	80–04–17	DEERE TO LAY OFF 390 WORKERS AT 3 UNITS DURING NEXT 30 DAYS
120	DEERE & CO.	80–05–16	DEERE WILL FURLOUGH ADDITIONAL 900 WORKERS
121	DEERE & CO.	80–05–29	DEERE PLANS TO LAY OFF 550 MORE AT IOWA PLANT WITHIN 3 MONTHS
122	DUPONT	80–05–13	DUPONT SLATES LAYOFF OF 400 AT FIBERS PLANT IN CHATTANOOGA, TENN.
123	EATON	80–06–05	EATON LAYS OFF 56 WORKERS INDEFINITELY
124	FIRESTONE	80–05–05	TIRE MAKERS TROUBLES START TO FORCE LAYOFFS IN WHITE COLLAR RANKS
125	FIRESTONE	80–05–27	FIRESTONE TO LAY OFF ADDITIONAL EMPLOYEES AT PLANTS SET TO CLOSE (1320)
126	GAF	80–05–29	GAF WILL SUSPEND AUTO PADDING OUTPUT AT A JOLIET, ILL., PLANT
127	GE	80–04–23	GE TO LAY OFF 250 FRIDAY
128	GE	80–05–13	GE TO LAY OFF 1200 MORE AT LOUISVILLE UNIT
129	GE	80–05–22	GE DELAYS TO MID JULY ITS LAYOFFS IN LOUISVILLE
130	GE	80–06–02	GE UNIT SLATES LAYOFFS (80)
131	GE	80–06–05	GE SLASHES ABOUT 400 SALARIED JOBS, OR 10%, AT LOUISVILLE FACILITY
132	GEN. TIRE & RUBBER	80–05–05	TIRE MAKERS TROUBLES START TO FORCE LAYOFFS IN WHITE COLLAR RANKS
133	GEORGIA PACIFIC	80–09–19	GEORGIA PACIFIC TO CLOSE BAG, SACK OPERATION AT PLANT IN ARKANSAS (75)
134	GM	80–03–28	GM ANNOUNCES ADDITIONAL CUTS IN ITS PRODUCTION (2100)
135	GM	80–04–25	GM MAY WIELD AX OVER ITS SALARIED STAFF FURTHER AS SALES SLIDE FORCES OUTPUT CUT
136	GM	80–04–28	GM'S 10% CUT OF SALARIED STAFF TO BRING INDUSTRY LAYOFFS CLOSE TO MID 70'S SLUMP (4,125)
137	GM	80–07–31	GM TO CUT WORK TURN AT PLANT IDLING 1,750
138	GM	80–11–24	TO CLOSE SECTIONS OF BRITISH ROLLING MILL; GM SLATES DISMISSALS
139	GOODYEAR	80–07–28	GOODYEAR UNIT TO CUT BIAS PLY TIRE OUTPUT AT FAYETTEVILLE, N.C.
140	GPU	80–09–15	GPU PLANS TO REDUCE ITS WORK FORCE BY 700
141	GULF & WESTERN	80–08–05	GULF & WESTERN TO CLOSE ONE SLAB ZINC LINE IDLING 690 EMPLOYEES
142	HERCULES	80–06–26	HERCULES DECIDES IT WON'T REBUILD UNIT AFTER FIRE, IDLING 700
143	INT'L. HARVESTER	80–04–24	INT'L. HARVESTER SAYS PAYLINE UNIT WILL LAY OFF 620, ADDED LAYOFFS POSSIBLE
144	INT'L. HARVESTER	80–05–19	INT'L. HARVESTER TO LAY OFF 285 AT LOUISVILLE PLANT
145	INT'L. HARVESTER	80–06–25	INT'L. HARVESTER TO LAY OFF 1200 OF ITS WORKERS AT PLANT IN INDIANA
146	INT'L. HARVESTER	80–11–18	INT'L. HARVESTER TO LAY OFF MORE AT CANADIAN UNIT
147	LTV	80–05–19	LTV LAYOFFS SLATED (350)
148	LTV	80–08–06	LTV UNIT TO SUSPEND PRODUCTION OF COAL AT MINE IDLING 390
149	MANAGEMENT ASSIST.	80–06–13	FIRM TO STOP MAKING WORK PROCESS LINE AS LOSSES CONTINUE (240)
150	MCDONNELL DOUGLAS	80–11–25	MCDONNELL DOUGLAS UNIT PLANS TO LAY OFF 800 WORKERS IN ONTARIO
151	MEMOREX	80–06–09	MEMOREX FIRES 220 OF ITS EMPLOYEES
152	MIRRO CORP.	80–05–16	MIRRO PLANS TO LAY OFF 200 WORKERS, EXPECTS DROP IN 2ND PERIOD NET

Table A1 (Continued)

OBS	COMPANY	EVENT DATE	EVENT DESCRIPTION
153	MONSANTO	80–03–20	MONSANTO UNIT TO TRIM NYLON FIBER PRODUCTION (SEVERAL HUNDRED)
154	PAN AM	80–08–22	PAN AM IS REDUCING PART OF ITS WORK FORCE (1,200)
155	PAN AM	80–09–02	PAN AM TO CUT 10% TO 14% OF SCHEDULE AND OVER 3,500 JOBS
156	RCA	80–12–18	NBC IS LIKELY TO LAY OFF MORE THAN 200, SLASH COSTS
157	REPUBLIC STEEL	80–06–19	TWO STEELMAKERS ANNOUNCE FURTHER PRODUCTION CUTBACKS (1000)
158	SCM	80–02–12	SCM PLANS TO LAY OFF EMPLOYEES IN SCOTLAND
159	SCM	80–07–03	SCM WILL LAY OFF 165 AT TYPEWRITER PLANT IN UPSTATE NY
160	SEARS	80–09–09	SEARS SETS EARLY RETIREMENT PLAN TO TARGET YOUTH INTO MERCHANDISING MANAGEMENT
161	SEARS	80–12–23	SEARS RAISES ESTIMATED EARLY RETIREMENT COST BY ABOUT $18M
162	SIGNAL CO.	80–05–16	SIGNAL'S MACK UNIT SAYS IT WILL LAY OFF 2863 OF ITS EMPLOYEES
163	TRANE CO.	80–12–10	TRANE SETS LAYOFFS OF SEVERAL HUNDRED
164	TWA	80–10–13	TWA MAKES CHANGES IN ORGANIZATIONAL PLAN, CUTTING 100 MANAGERS
165	U.S. STEEL	80–05–23	U.S. STEEL CONSIDERING MORE PRODUCTION CUTS IN THE PITTSBURGH AREA
166	U.S. STEEL	80–05–29	U.S. STEEL LAYOFFS WILL NEARLY CLOSE PLANT IN PITTSBURGH
167	U.S. STEEL	80–06–03	U.S. STEEL TO LAY OF 3000 MORE WORKERS AT ALABAMA PLANT
168	UNIROYAL	80–05–05	TIRE MAKERS TROUBLES START TO FORCE LAYOFFS IN WHITE COLLAR RANKS
169	UNITED AIR	80–06–16	UNITED AIRLINES LAYOFFS TO AFFECT 360 PILOTS AND 800 ATTENDANTS
170	VIRGINIA ELEC & POW	80–05–21	VIRGINIA ELEC. & POWER MOVES BACK POWER PLANT FINISH, WILL LAY OFF 2000
171	WHEELBRATOR-FRYE	80–11–10	WHEELBRATOR-FRYE ACTS QUICKLY TO CUT PULLMAN UNITS' STAFF
172	WHIRLPOOL	80–06–12	WHIRLPOOL TO LAY OFF 850 WORKERS AT PLANT
173	WHITE MOTORS	80–05–13	WHITE MOTORS SLATES RESTRUCTURING, LAYOFFS (350)

PRIMARY CODE = STAFF   SECONDARY CODE = TEMP REDUCE

OBS	COMPANY	EVENT DATE	EVENT DESCRIPTION
174	ALCOA	80–06–24	ALCOA CUTTING BACK ALUMINUM OUTPUT, SOFT DEMAND CITED
175	ALLIS CHALMERS	80–06–23	ALLIS CHALMERS PLANT IN MILWAUKEE SLATES 8-WEEK CLOSING (850)
176	AMC	80–02–22	FOUR AUTO ASSEMBLY PLANTS TO BE CLOSED TEMPORARILY
177	AMC	80–05–02	AUTO MAKERS CUT 2ND PERIOD PLANS FOR OUTPUT 10% (3,500)
178	AMC	80–05–09	AUTO MAKERS SET 8 MORE CLOSINGS FOR NEXT WEEK (8500)
179	AMC	80–05–23	ONLY AMC, FORD CLOSING PLANTS NEXT WEEK (7200)
180	AMC	80–06–06	AUTO MAKERS SET MORE CLOSEDOWNS FOR NEXT WEEK
181	AMC	80–06–20	U.S. CAR MAKERS SET MORE CLOSINGS FOR NEXT WEEK
182	AMC	80–06–27	AUTO FIRMS PLAN TO CUT OUTPUT 2.6% THIS WEEK
183	AMC	80–07–18	U.S. AUTO FIRMS TRIM OUTPUT 11% FROM WEEK AGO
184	AMC	80–08–08	LOWER AUTO OUTPUT THIS WEEK REFLECTS MANY PLANT CLOSINGS
185	AMC	80–08–29	GM PLANS TO LIFT OUTPUT OF CARS, TRUCKS AT 4 UNITS (AMC TO DECREASE)
186	AMC	80–10–24	FORD MOTOR TO CLOSE ITS PLANT IN SAN JOSE DURING NEXT WEEK (U.S. AUTO)
187	AMC	80–11–12	AMC WILL DROP WORK TURN, IDLING 2350 EMPLOYEES

Table A1 (Continued)

OBS	COMPANY	EVENT DATE	EVENT DESCRIPTION
188	AMC	80–12–19	CAR MAKERS PLAN MAJOR CLOSINGS IN EARLY JANUARY (U.S. AUTO)
189	AMC	80–12–26	CAR MAKERS IDLING 13 OF 40 FACILITIES FOR THE HOLIDAYS (U.S. AUTO)
190	ARMCO	80–06–18	ARMCO TO LAY OFF MORE WORKERS AT PLANT IN MIDDLETOWN, OHIO (142)
191	ARMCO	80–07–10	ARMCO ADDS TO LAYOFFS AT STEEL WORKS IN OHIO
192	BETHLEHEM STEEL	80–04–25	BETHLEHEM STEEL IS IDLING SEVERAL OF ITS MILLS AT SPARROWS POINT (1250)
193	BETHLEHEM STEEL	80–10–06	BETHLEHEM STEEL PUTS 500 ON WEEK'S LAYOFF
194	BLACK & DECKER	80–06–06	BLACK & DECKER PLANS TO LAY OFF ABOUT 2500
195	BURLINGTON NORTHERN	80–06–23	N&W, BURLINGTON TO IDLE 1764 CITING DROP IN SHIPMENTS
196	CATERPILLAR	80–11–20	CATERPILLAR LAYOFFS OF 3000 EMPLOYEES SCHEDULED FOR DEC. 1
197	CATERPILLAR	80–12–12	CATERPILLAR TRACTOR TO LAY OFF 9500 IN U.S. FOR A WEEK
198	CESSNA	80–06–20	CESSNA TO CLOSE PLANT IN KANSAS FOR AUGUST (2660)
199	CHAMPION SPARK PLUG	80–06–12	CHAMPION SPARK PLUG TO CLOSE PLANTS IDLING 3,800 FOR TWO WEEKS
200	CHARTER MEDIA	80–06–23	PHILADELPHIA BULLETIN PLANS LAYOFFS (150)
201	CHRYSLER	80–02–01	FURTHER AUTO CLOSINGS NEXT WEEK (U.S. AUTO)
202	CHRYSLER	80–02–06	CHRYSLER CANADA CLOSES PLANT
203	CHRYSLER	80–02–08	BIG 3 AUTOMAKERS SCHEDULE CLOSINGS AT PLANTS NEXT WEEK (U.S. AUTO)
204	CHRYSLER	80–02–15	CHRYSLER PLANS TO CLOSE CAR PLANT NEXT WEEK AND 2 TRUCK FACILITIES
205	CHRYSLER	80–04–11	U.S. CAR MAKERS SET CLOSING OF CUTBACKS AT 9 AUTO PLANTS (7,000)
206	CHRYSLER	80–05–16	CAR MAKERS ADD 11 PLANT CLOSINGS FOR NEXT WEEK (2300)
207	CHRYSLER	80–05–30	AUTO CONCERNS CUTS TO AFFECT 15 U.S. PLANTS (1600)
208	CHRYSLER	80–06–13	AUTO MAKERS CONTINUING BID TO CUT STOCKS, ARE IDLING 12 OPERATIONS NEXT WEEK
209	CHRYSLER	80–06–20	U.S. CAR MAKERS SET MORE CLOSINGS FOR NEXT WEEK
210	CHRYSLER	80–06–27	AUTO FIRMS PLAN TO CUT OUTPUT 2.6% THIS WEEK
211	CHRYSLER	80–07–03	FORD (CHRYSLER) WILL CLOSE EVERY U.S. PLANT BUT 1 NEXT WEEK (2000)
212	CHRYSLER	80–07–18	U.S. AUTO FIRMS TRIM OUTPUT 11% FROM WEEK AGO
213	CHRYSLER	80–07–25	FORD SETS CLOSINGS OF 6 PLANTS; 15600 WORKERS TO BE IDLED (U.S. AUTO)
214	CHRYSLER	80–08–08	LOWER AUTO OUTPUT THIS WEEK REFLECTS MANY PLANT CLOSINGS
215	CHRYSLER	80–08–15	FORD (CHRYSLER) WILL CLOSE TWO MORE PLANTS FOR ONE WEEK (U.S. AUTO)
216	CHRYSLER	80–08–29	GM PLANS TO LIFT OUTPUT OF CARS, TRUCKS AT 4 UNITS (CHRYSLER TO DECREASE)
217	CHRYSLER	80–09–12	FORD (CHRYSLER) ANNOUNCES 1-WEEK CLOSING OF 2 ASSEMBLY PLANTS (U.S. AUTO)
218	CHRYSLER	80–10–10	CHRYSLER WILL CLOSE TRUCK PLANT 1 WEEK TO TRIM INVENTORIES (U.S. AUTO)
219	CHRYSLER	80–10–17	FORD (CHRYSLER) ANNOUNCES 1-WEEK CLOSING OF 2 ASSEMBLY PLANTS (U.S. AUTO)
220	CHRYSLER	80–10–31	FORD & CHRYSLER PLAN SOME CLOSINGS TO TRIM INVENTORIES (U.S. AUTO)
221	CHRYSLER	80–11–07	CHRYSLER TO CLOSE TRUCK UNIT 1 WEEK, DROP A WORK TURN (1200)
222	CHRYSLER	80–11–14	FORD TO HALT OUTPUT AT TWO AUTO PLANTS TO CUT INVENTORIES (U.S. AUTO)
223	CHRYSLER	80–11–28	FORD, CHRYSLER PLAN TEMPORARY CLOSINGS AT CERTAIN FACILITIES (U.S. AUTO)

Table A1 (Continued)

OBS	COMPANY	EVENT DATE	EVENT DESCRIPTION
224	CHRYSLER	80–12–12	FORD IS SUSPENDING PRODUCTION 2 WEEKS AT PLANT IN SAN JOSE (U.S. AUTO)
225	CHRYSLER	80–12–19	CAR MAKERS PLAN MAJOR CLOSINGS IN EARLY JANUARY (U.S. AUTO)
226	CHRYSLER	80–12–24	CHRYSLER SETS EVEN DEEPER CUTS IN OUTPUT
227	CHRYSLER	80–12–26	CAR MAKERS IDLING 13 OF 40 FACILITIES FOR THE HOLIDAYS (U.S. AUTO)
228	CLEVELAND CLIFFS	80–06–16	CLEVELAND CLIFFS TO SUSPEND OPERATIONS AT 2 MINES IN MICHIGAN
229	COLT INDUSTRIES	80–09–03	COLT INDUSTRIES REPORTS LAYOFFS, EXPECTS DROP IN THIRD QUARTER PROFITS
230	CONSOL. FREIGHT	80–05–08	SOME PLANT CLOSINGS SET BY CONSOLIDATED FREIGHT UNIT (FREIGHTLINER) (2800)
231	CONSOL. FREIGHT	80–07–02	UNIT OF CONSOLIDATED FREIGHT TO REDUCE PRODUCTION OF TRUCKS
232	CONSOLIDATED FOODS	80–11–24	CONSOLIDATED FOODS SETS LAYOFFS OF 500 FOR WEEK
233	DEERE & CO.	80–05–02	DEERE PLANS TO LAY OFF 775 EMPLOYEES IN IOWA OVER NEXT 2 WEEKS
234	DEERE & CO.	80–06–02	DEERE WILL LAY OFF 1500 WORKERS IN IOWA
235	DEERE & CO.	80–06–18	DEERE TO CLOSE TWO IOWA FACTORIES FOR MOST OF OCTOBER (5800)
236	DEERE & CO.	80–07–03	DEERE TO STRETCH VACATION CLOSEDOWNS, PLANS MORE LAYOFFS
237	FORD	80–01–04	FORD WILL IDLE 34,000 WORKERS IN CLOSING 11 OF 13 AUTO PLANTS, 2 TRUCK OPERATIONS
238	FORD	80–01–18	GM & FORD TO CLOSE ADDITIONAL PLANTS NEXT WEEK TO REDUCE DEALER INVENTORIES
239	FORD	80–01–21	FORD MOTOR TO CLOSE 5 ASSEMBLY PLANTS AFFECTED BY STRIKE
240	FORD	80–01–25	FORD IS CLOSING TEMPORARILY 7 OF 13 AUTO PLANTS (15,600)
241	FORD	80–02–07	FORD UNIT IN FRANCE CUTS BACK PRODUCTION AT 2 PLANTS IN BORDEAUX
242	FORD	80–02–08	BIG 3 AUTOMAKERS SCHEDULE CLOSINGS AT PLANTS NEXT WEEK (U.S. AUTO)
243	FORD	80–02–22	FOUR AUTO ASSEMBLY PLANTS TO BE CLOSED TEMPORARILY (U.S. AUTO)
244	FORD	80–03–14	FORD TO CLOSE TEMPORARILY 3 CAR PLANTS NEXT WEEK, LAYOFF 10,800
245	FORD	80–03–14	FORD TO CLOSE TEMPORARILY 3 CAR PLANTS NEXT WEEK, LAYING OFF 10,800
246	FORD	80–04–11	U.S. CAR MAKERS SET CLOSING OR CUTBACKS AT 9 AUTO PLANTS (19,000)
247	FORD	80–04–18	CAR MAKERS PLAN 8 PLANT CLOSINGS FOR NEXT WEEK (10,800)
248	FORD	80–05–02	AUTO MAKERS CUT 2ND PERIOD PLANS FOR OUTPUT 10% (12,360)
249	FORD	80–05–05	FORD LIFTS PRICES (SOME ENGINE LINES IDLED) (2300)
250	FORD	80–05–09	AUTO MAKERS SET 8 MORE CLOSINGS FOR NEXT WEEK (6600)
251	FORD	80–05–16	CAR MAKERS ADD 11 PLANT CLOSINGS FOR NEXT WEEK
252	FORD	80–05–23	ONLY AMC, FORD CLOSING PLANTS NEXT WEEK (4570)
253	FORD	80–05–30	AUTO CONCERNS CUTS TO AFFECT 15 U.S. PLANTS (24,340)
254	FORD	80–06–06	AUTO MAKERS SET MORE CLOSEDOWNS FOR NEXT WEEK
255	FORD	80–06–13	AUTO MAKERS CONTINUING BID TO CUT STOCKS, ARE IDLING 12 OPERATIONS NEXT WEEK
256	FORD	80–06–20	U.S. CAR MAKERS SET MORE CLOSINGS FOR NEXT WEEK
257	FORD	80–06–27	AUTO FIRMS PLAN TO CUT OUTPUT 2.6% THIS WEEK
258	FORD	80–07–03	FORD WILL CLOSE EVERY U.S. PLANT BUT 1 NEXT WEEK
259	FORD	80–07–11	CHRYSLER (FORD) WILL CLOSE SECOND WORK TURN AT ST. LOUIS FACILITY (U.S. AUTO)

Table A1 (Continued)

OBS	COMPANY	EVENT DATE	EVENT DESCRIPTION
260	FORD	80–07–18	U.S. AUTO FIRMS TRIM OUTPUT 11% FROM WEEK AGO
261	FORD	80–07–25	FORD SETS CLOSINGS OF 6 PLANTS; 15600 WORKERS TO BE IDLED (U.S. AUTO)
262	FORD	80–08–08	LOWER AUTO OUTPUT THIS WEEK REFLECTS MANY PLANT CLOSINGS
263	FORD	80–08–15	FORD WILL CLOSE TWO MORE PLANTS FOR ONE WEEK (U.S. AUTO)
264	FORD	80–08–22	FORD TO IDLE 12,525 WORKERS AT SIX PLANTS (U.S. AUTO)
265	FORD	80–08–29	GM PLANS TO LIFT OUTPUT OF CARS, TRUCKS AT 4 UNITS (FORD TO DECREASE)
266	FORD	80–09–12	FORD WILL SUSPEND OUTPUT AT 2 PLANTS STARTING NEXT WEEK (U.S. AUTO)
267	FORD	80–09–26	FORD TO SUSPEND WORK AT 2 PLANTS DURING NEXT WEEK
268	FORD	80–10–03	FORD PLANS TO SHUT 2 AUTO PLANTS, IDLE 3000 WORKERS
269	FORD	80–10–17	FORD ANNOUNCES 1-WEEK CLOSING OF 2 ASSEMBLY PLANTS (U.S. AUTO)
270	FORD	80–10–24	FORD MOTOR TO CLOSE ITS PLANT IN SAN JOSE DURING NEXT WEEK (U.S. AUTO)
271	FORD	80–10–31	FORD & CHRYSLER PLAN SOME CLOSINGS TO TRIM INVENTORIES (U.S. AUTO)
272	FORD	80–11–06	BRITISH FORD THREATENS TO LAY OFF WORKERS INVOLVED IN WALKOUTS
273	FORD	80–11–14	FORD TO HALT OUTPUT AT TWO AUTO PLANTS TO CUT INVENTORIES (U.S. AUTO)
274	FORD	80–11–28	FORD, CHRYSLER PLAN TEMPORARY CLOSINGS AT CERTAIN FACILITIES (U.S. AUTO)
275	FORD	80–12–12	FORD IS SUSPENDING PRODUCTION 2 WEEKS AT PLANT IN SAN JOSE (U.S. AUTO)
276	FORD	80–12–19	CAR MAKERS PLAN MAJOR CLOSINGS IN EARLY JANUARY (U.S. AUTO)
277	FORD	80–12–26	CAR MAKERS IDLING 13 OF 40 FACILITIES FOR THE HOLIDAYS (U.S. AUTO)
278	GE	80–05–30	GE TO SUSPEND OUTPUT AT TRENTON, N.J., PLANT (350)
279	GM	80–01–18	GM & FORD TO CLOSE ADDITIONAL PLANTS NEXT WEEK TO REDUCE DEALER INVENTORIES
280	GM	80–02–01	FURTHER AUTO CLOSINGS NEXT WEEK (U.S. AUTO)
281	GM	80–02–08	BIG 3 AUTOMAKERS SCHEDULE CLOSINGS AT PLANTS NEXT WEEK (U.S. AUTO)
282	GM	80–02–22	FOUR AUTO ASSEMBLY PLANTS TO BE CLOSED TEMPORARILY (U.S. AUTO)
283	GM	80–03–04	GM PLANS TO LAY OFF 6500 OF ITS WORKERS, CLOSING 2 PLANTS (6 MONTHS)
284	GM	80–03–21	GM TO CLOSE 2 PLANTS FOR A WEEK, IDLING SOME 8400 WORKERS
285	GM	80–04–11	U.S. CAR MAKERS SET CLOSING OR CUTBACKS AT 9 AUTO PLANTS (17,000)
286	GM	80–04–17	GM PLANS TO CUT PRODUCTION AT 7 U.S. CAR AND TRUCK PLANTS, IDLING 12,000 WORKERS
287	GM	80–04–18	CAR MAKERS PLAN 8 PLANT CLOSINGS FOR NEXT WEEK (12,500)
288	GM	80–05–02	AUTO MAKERS SET 8 MORE CLOSINGS FOR NEXT WEEK (11,000)
289	GM	80–05–08	GM CANADA TO IDLE 10,400
290	GM	80–05–09	AUTO MAKERS SET 8 MORE CLOSINGS FOR NEXT WEEK (11,000)
291	GM	80–05–16	CAR MAKERS ADD 11 PLANT CLOSINGS FOR NEXT WEEK
292	GM	80–05–30	AUTO CONCERNS CUTS TO AFFECT 15 U.S. PLANTS (6,400)
293	GM	80–06–06	AUTO MAKERS SET MORE CLOSEDOWNS FOR NEXT WEEK

Table A1 (Continued)

OBS	COMPANY	EVENT DATE	EVENT DESCRIPTION
294	GM	80–06–13	AUTO MAKERS CONTINUING BID TO CUT STOCKS, ARE IDLING 12 OPERATIONS NEXT WEEK
295	GM	80–06–20	U.S. CAR MAKERS SET MORE CLOSINGS FOR NEXT WEEK
296	GM	80–06–27	AUTO FIRMS PLAN TO CUT OUTPUT 2.6% THIS WEEK
297	GM	80–07–03	FORD (GM) WILL CLOSE EVERY U.S. PLANT BUT 1 NEXT WEEK (1700)
298	GM	80–07–11	CHRYSLER (GM) WILL CLOSE SECOND WORK TURN AT ST. LOUIS FACILITY (U.S. AUTO)
299	GM	80–07–18	U.S. AUTO FIRMS TRIM OUTPUT 11% FROM WEEK AGO
300	GM	80–07–25	FORD SETS CLOSINGS OF 6 PLANTS; 15600 WORKERS TO BE IDLED (U.S. AUTO)
301	GM	80–08–01	CAR DEALERS TO CLEAR LOTS FOR 1981 MODELS
302	GM	80–08–08	LOWER AUTO OUTPUT THIS WEEK REFLECTS MANY PLANT CLOSINGS
303	GM	80–08–15	FORD (GM) WILL CLOSE TWO MORE PLANTS FOR ONE WEEK (U.S. AUTO)
304	GM	80–08–22	FORD (GM) TO IDLE 12,525 WORKERS AT SIX PLANTS (U.S. AUTO)
305	GM	80–12–19	CAR MAKERS PLAN MAJOR CLOSINGS IN EARLY JANUARY (U.S. AUTO)
306	GM	80–12–26	CAR MAKERS IDLING 12 OF 40 FACILITIES FOR THE HOLIDAYS (U.S. AUTO)
307	GOODYEAR	80–05–02	GOODYEAR UNIT TO CLOSE 4 PLANTS FOR 1 WEEK (6000)
308	GOODYEAR	80–06–10	GOODYEAR UNIT TO IDLE 5400 AND MOST OUTPUT FOR 3-WEEK PERIOD
309	HANNA MINING	80–06–03	HANNA MINING CLOSES PROJECT; 500 LAID OFF
310	HANNA MINING	80–09–03	NSP UNIT (HANNA MINING) TO SUSPEND OPERATIONS TO REDUCE INVENTORY
311	INT'L. HARVESTER	80–05–01	INT'L. HARVESTER OUTPUT SNAGGED AS WORKERS HONOR PICKET LINES
312	INT'L. HARVESTER	80–09–22	INT'L. HARVESTER WILL CLOSE 2 PLANTS TEMPORARILY (1700)
313	INT'L. PAPER	80–06–27	INT'L. PAPER SETS WEEK'S CLOSING OF PLANT
314	KEYSTONE CONSOLID.	80–06–04	KEYSTONE CONSOLIDATED TO IDLE WIRE OUTPUT AT FACILITY FOR ONE WEEK
315	LIBBY-OWENS	80–04–01	LIBBY-OWENS TO CLOSE 3 PLANTS (3400/WK)
316	LIBBY-OWENS	80–05–08	LIBBY-OWENS SLATES LAYOFF OF 900 MORE; CAR SALES SLUMP CITED
317	LTV	80–05–05	BETHLEHEM STEEL AND JONES-LAUGHLIN CUT BACK OPERATIONS (425)
318	LTV	80–05–30	LTV SUBSIDIARY PLANS CLOSINGS AND LAYOFFS AT OHIO, INDIANA UNITS
319	LTV	80–11–14	JONES & LAUGHLIN STEEL TO CLOSE PART OF PITTSBURGH WORKS (1000)
320	MCDONNELL DOUGLAS	80–09–05	MCDONNELL DOUGLAS SUBSIDIARY TO LAY OFF UP TO 200 IN TORONTO NEXT WEEK
321	NORFOLK & WESTERN	80–06–23	N&W, BURLINGTON TO IDLE 1764 CITING DROP IN SHIPMENTS
322	QUAKER OATS	80–10–23	QUAKER OATS TOY UNIT TO INCREASE LAYOFFS ON SLACKENED DEMAND
323	REPUBLIC STEEL	80–06–20	REPUBLIC STEEL TO CLOSE TEMPORARILY FURNACE IN CLEVELAND (250)
324	REYNOLDS METALS	80–07–07	REYNOLDS METALS TO IDLE FOUR ALUMINUM LINES (450)
325	SPRINGS MILLS INC.	80–05–23	SPRINGS MILLS LAYOFFS AT 6 FACILITIES (7000)
326	TEXAS INSTRUMENTS	80–12–03	MANY TEXAS INST. EMPLOYEES TO GET ORDERED VACATION DAYS AT END OF YEAR
327	TEXAS INSTRUMENTS	80–12–19	TEXAS INST. TO TRIM WORK WEEKS, CITES SOFT MARKET FOR COMPUTER PRODUCTS
328	U.S. STEEL	80–05–14	U.S. STEEL PLANS TO CLOSE 3 MORE BLAST FURNACES
329	UNITED TECHNOLOGIES	80–05–30	UNITED TECHNOLOGIES CARRIER UNIT TO LAY OFF 200 EMPLOYEES TODAY
330	WINNEBAGO	80–03–14	WINNEBAGO TO LAY OFF ABOUT 800 EMPLOYEES

Table A1 (Continued)

OBS	COMPANY	EVENT DATE	EVENT DESCRIPTION
	PRIMARY CODE = STAFF		**SECONDARY CODE = RECALL/INCREASE**
331	CHRYSLER	80–04–21	CHRYSLER CANCELS PLAN TO REDUCE PRODUCTION AT PLANT IN ST. LOUIS
332	CLEVELAND CLIFFS	80–11–18	CLEVELAND CLIFFS IRON IS PLANNING TO RESUME SOME OPERATIONS
333	COACHMAN IND.	80–09–15	COACHMAN INDUSTRIES RECALLS 200 WORKERS
334	CUMMINS ENGINE	80–03–10	CUMMINS ENGINE PLANS RECALL OF WORKERS (400)
335	CUMMINS ENGINE	80–10–27	CUMMINS ENGINE PLANS TO RECALL 375 WORKERS
336	CUMMINS ENGINE	80–11–26	CUMMINS ENGINE PLANS RECALL OF 420 WORKERS
337	DEERE & CO.	80–09–16	DEERE TO BOOST OUTPUT OF TRACTORS, RECALL 500 EMPLOYEES IN IOWA
338	ESMARK STAFF	80–11–21	ESMARK TO RE-OPEN A SWIFT BEEF FACILITY IN DES MOINES, IOWA (500)
339	FORD	80–11–07	CHRYSLER TO CLOSE TRUCK UNIT 1 WEEK, (FORD PLANS OT)
340	GM	80–02–19	GM PLANT WILL RECALL 1200 WORKERS
341	GM	80–02–25	GM TO CALL BACK SOME WORKERS, BOOST PRODUC-TION
342	GM	80–08–29	GM PLANS TO LIFT OUTPUT OF CARS, TRUCKS AT 4 UNITS (U.S. AUTO)
343	GM	80–09–11	GM WILL CALL BACK 1000 HOURLY EMPLOYEES FOR OLDSMOBILE PLANT
344	GM	80–10–03	FORD PLANS TO SHUT 2 AUTO PLANTS (GM PLANS EXTRA WORK TURNS)
345	GM	80–10–27	GM'S CADILLAC DIVISION WILL ADD WORK TURN, ENDING LAYOFF OF 3700
346	GM	80–11–06	GM INCREASES TRUCK PRODUCTION IN PONTIAC
347	GM	80–11–14	FORD TO HALT OUTPUT AT TWO AUTO PLANTS (U.S. AUTO) (GM TO UTILIZE OT)
348	GM	80–12–12	FORD IS SUSPENDING PRODUCTION 2 WEEKS AT PLANT (GM TO INCREASE)
349	HANNA MINING	80–10–10	HANNA MINING PLANS TO RE-OPEN PELLET LINE
350	INLAND STEEL	80–09–24	INLAND STEEL SAYS 1700 ARE TO RESUME 5-DAY WEEKS OCT. 6
351	INLAND STEEL	80–11–05	INLAND STEEL WILL RESUME ROLLING WORK AT A HOT STRIP MILL
352	TORO	80–10–02	TORO TO RECALL 675 OF 2000 LAID OFF
353	U.S. STEEL	80–08–21	U.S. STEEL PROPOSES TO RESTART FURNACES AT 3 SITES SOON
354	WINNEBAGO	80–04–30	WINNEBAGO TO RESUME MOTOR HOME OUTPUT
	PRIMARY CODE = SHUT/RELO		**SECONDARY CODE = RELOCATE**
355	AMERICAN EXPRESS	80–07–16	AMERICAN EXPRESS PLANS TO MOVE MOST OF DIVISION TO UTAH
356	CITICORP	80–03–13	SOUTH DAKOTA INVITES CITICORP TO MOVE ITS CREDIT CARD OPERATIONS (2900)
357	HERCULES	80–07–15	WILMINGTON WOOS HERCULES, CONVINCES FIRM NOT TO LEAVE (1200)
358	NCR	80–03–17	NCR TO BUILD FACILITY IN S.C., WILL CLOSE DELAWARE PLANT
	PRIMARY CODE = SHUT/RELO		**SECONDARY CODE = SHUTDOWN**
359	A.O. SMITH	80–08–01	A.O. SMITH IS CLOSING GRANITE CITY, ILL., PLANT
360	ALPHA PORTLAND	80–12–18	ALPHA PORTLAND CLOSES CEMENT MAKING PLANT
361	AMERICAN CYNAMID	80–08–06	AMERICAN CYNAMID IS PLANNING TO CLOSE OHIO TIRE YARN PLANT (350)
362	AMERICAN CYNAMID	80–10–21	AMERICAN CYNAMID TO CLOSE PLANT IN IOWA (120)
363	AMERICAN STANDARD	80–09–11	AMERICAN STANDARD UNIT TO CLOSE GEORGIA PLANT (250)
364	ARMSTRONG RUBBER	80–07–17	ARMSTRONG RUBBER WILL CLOSE FACTORY (600)
365	BAUSCH & LOMB	80–07–08	BAUSCH & LOMB TO END OPERATIONS AT 3 PLANTS
366	BETHLEHEM STEEL	80–09–04	BETHLEHEM STEEL PLANS CLOSING OF A SHIPYARD
367	BUNKER RAMO	80–08–25	BUNKER RAMO TO CLOSE TEXTILE PLANT, IDLE 75

Table A1 (Continued)

OBS	COMPANY	EVENT DATE	EVENT DESCRIPTION
368	CHAMPION HOME PROD	80–03–28	CHAMPION HOME PROD SAYS IT IS CLOSING 11 UNITS IN A MOVE TO CUT COSTS (450)
369	CHEVRON	80–02–20	CHEVRON CHEMICAL UNIT OF CA. WILL CLOSE (PUERTO RICO) FIBER PLANT
370	CHRYSLER	80–02–19	CHRYSLER PLANS TO CLOSE OHIO FOUNDRY IN APRIL (375)
371	CHRYSLER	80–05–13	CHRYSLER ANNOUNCES PERMANENT CLOSINGS FOR TRUCK FACILITY AND V8 ENGINE PLANT
372	CHRYSLER	80–05–19	CHRYSLER CLOSING IN JULY WILL SPELL END TO FIRM'S ROLE AS MAKER OF BIG CARS
373	CHRYSLER	80–07–22	CHRYSLER PLANS TO CLOSE SECOND PARTS FOUNDARY, IDLING ALMOST 1,300
374	COLLINS-AIKMAN	80–07–29	COLLINS-AIKMAN TO CLOSE PLANT IN COWPENS, S.C.
375	CROWN ZELLERBACH	80–07–11	CROWN ZELLERBACH TO CLOSE OREGON MILL
376	CROWN ZELLERBACH	80–07–31	CROWN ZELLERBACH PLANS TO CLOSE FACILITY (110)
377	CROWN ZELLERBACH	80–08–18	CROWN ZELLERBACH PLANS TO CLOSE PAPER TOWEL FACTORY, LAYING OFF 227
378	CYCLOPS	80–08–01	CYCLOPS MAY CLOSE FACTORY, WIPING OUT MOST OF 1979 EARNINGS (1,200)
379	CYCLOPS	80–02–22	CYCLOPS TO CLOSE PORTSMOUTH, OH. UNIT, SETS CHARGE ON PROFIT
380	DANA	80–05–14	DANA PLANNING TO CLOSE PERMANENTLY A TRUCK FRAME PLANT (875)
381	DANA	80–05–16	DANA TO CLOSE HARANA, ILL., FACILITY (200)
382	DANA	80–06–02	DANA WILL CLOSE TRUCK-AXLE FACILITY (1900)
383	DANA	80–06–03	DANA ANNOUNCES CLOSING OF HAVANA, ILL., TRUCK PARTS FACILITY
384	DENNY'S	80–08–06	DENNY'S PLANS TO CLOSE 150 DOUGHNUT STORES
385	DUPONT	80–02–12	DUPONT PLANS TO CLOSE PHILADELPHIA PAINT PLANT
386	FIRESTONE	80–03–20	FIRESTONE TO CLOSE 5 U.S. TIRE PLANTS TO CUT CAPACITY (7000)
387	FIRESTONE	80–03–31	FIRESTONE'S CANADA UNIT PLANS TO CLOSE A PLANT (650)
388	FIRESTONE	80–05–15	FIRESTONE TIRE PLANT IN BARBERTON, OHIO, TO BE CLOSED BY JULY 1 (300)
389	FIRESTONE	80–10–23	FIRESTONE WILL CLOSE ITS AKRON TRUCK TIRE PLANT IN 6 MONTHS
390	FIRESTONE	80–10–30	FIRESTONE DIVISION IS PLANNING TO CLOSE PLANT IN INDIANA (875)
391	FISHER FOODS	80–02–20	FISHER FOODS TO CLOSE LAST 5 STORES IN AREA OF YOUNGSTOWN, OHIO
392	FISHER FOODS	80–03–07	FISHER FOODS REPORTS LOSS AS PLAN TO CHARGE STORES PROVES COSTLY
393	FORD	80–01–11	FORD WILL CLOSE LA SITE LAYING OFF 1670
394	FORD	80–02–27	FORD PLANS TO CLOSE ENGINE-MAKING PLANT IDLING 1200 EMPLOYEES
395	FORD	80–04–08	FORD WEIGHS CLOSING PERMANENTLY SOME OF ITS PLANTS
396	FORD	80–04–16	FORD SET TO SLASH AUTO OPERATIONS IN N. AMERICA
397	FORD	80–05–12	FORD PLANS TO CLOSE 3 MORE PLANTS, CUT SOME BENEFITS (10350)
398	GEORGIA PACIFIC	80–04–22	GEORGIA PACIFIC CLOSES 4 PLANTS IN SOUTH, CUTS PRODUCTION AT ANOTHER (1000+)
399	GM	80–02–29	ST. LOUIS ENTREATS GM TO REBUILD PLANT RATHER THAN MOVE (5000)
400	GM	80–03–07	ST. LOUIS LEADERS LOSE PLEAS TO KEEP GM PLANT
401	GM	80–08–25	GM TO REDUCE TRUCK OUTPUT, CLOSE 1 PLANT (2000)
402	GREYHOUND	80–04–30	GREYHOUND TO CLOSE 3 OF 4 ARMOUR & CO BEEF SLAUGHTERING PLANTS (800)
403	GREYHOUND	80–09–10	GREYHOUND TO RETAIN 2 ARMOUR FACILITIES SLATED FOR CLOSING
404	INT'L. HARVESTER	80–10–09	INT'L. HARVESTER'S PLAN TO SELL UNIT FAILS; OUTPUT WILL STILL BE PHASED OUT

Table A1 (Continued)

OBS	COMPANY	EVENT DATE	EVENT DESCRIPTION
405	J.P. STEVENS	80–07–03	J.P. STEVENS TO CLOSE FABRIC PLANT IN CANADA (150)
406	JACK WINTER	80–08–29	JACK WINTER CLOSES ITS BLOUSE FACTORY
407	KERR-MCGEE	80–08–19	KERR-MCGEE CLOSES TWO URANIUM MINES (1450)
408	KIT MFG.	80–03–31	KIT MANUFACTURING CLOSES DOWN THREE MORE FACTORIES (150)
409	LIBBY-OWENS	80–03–25	LIBBY-OWENS SLATES OUTPUT CUT, CLOSING OF SHEET GLASS PLANT (350)
410	MILTON BRADLEY	80–11–24	MILTON BRADLEY SAYS IT WILL CLOSE PLANT ON CARIBBEAN ISLAND (200)
411	MOUNT VERNON MILLS	80–09–24	MOUNT VERNON MILLS TO CLOSE UNPROFITABLE PLANT IN COLUMBIA, S.C.
412	NATIONAL CAN	80–01–15	NATIONAL CAN TO CLOSE BALTIMORE PLANT FEB. 22 (120)
413	NATIONAL DISTILLERS	80–07–15	NATIONAL DISTILLERS BRIDGEPORT, CONN., MILL MAY BE CLOSED
414	PANTASOTE	80–06–13	PANTASOTE TO CLOSE OHIO PLANT NEXT MONTH (60)
415	PITNEY BOWES	80–07–08	PITNEY BOWES SAYS 2ND PERIOD NET IS CUT BY CLOSING OF ITS PLANT
416	POTLATCH	80–03–07	POTLATCH PLANS CLOSING OF A TISSUE PAPER MILL (94)
417	POTLATCH	80–03–28	POTLATCH WILL REDUCE PRODUCTION IN IDAHO (500)
418	QUESTOR	80–09–18	QUESTOR PLANS TO CLOSE 2 PLANTS, SEES LOSS FOR 1980 (300)
419	ROBERTSHAW	80–08–07	ROBERTSHAW WILL CLOSE 2 PLANTS, CONSOLIDATING BOTH INTO NEW DIVISION
420	SCOTT PAPER	80–06–19	SCOTT PAPER WILL CLOSE PLANT
421	SHAKLEE	80–05–19	SHAKLEE PLANS TO CLOSE 2 PLANTS AND PRUNE 2 PRODUCT LINES (300)
422	SIGNAL CO	80–11–30	SIGNAL'S MACK TRUCKS IS TO CLOSE ITS PLANT IN HAYWARD, CA. (700)
423	SINGER CO	80–10–07	SINGER WILL STOP CERTAIN PRODUCTION AT N.J. PLANT
424	ST. REGIS	80–01–04	ST. REGIS PAPER TO CLOSE YPSILANTI, MICH. PLANT (140)
425	ST. REGIS	80–04–21	ST. REGIS PAPER CURTAILS MORE OF ITS OPERATIONS
426	TEXFI INDUSTRIES	80–07–15	TEXFI PLANS TO CLOSE PLANT PRODUCING POLYESTER FIBER (440)
427	TODD SHIPYARDS	80–02–19	TODD SHIPYARDS PLANT WHERE RADIOACTIVITY LEAKED WILL BE CLOSED (50)
428	TRW	80–06–19	TRW CLOSING PLANT IN CHICAGO THIS FALL BUT LAYOFFS SET SOON
429	U.S. STEEL	80–02–29	U.S. STEEL IS BLOCKED FROM CLOSING DOWN YOUNGSTOWN MILLS (3500)
430	U.S. STEEL	80–03–24	U.S. STEEL MAY CLOSE YOUNGSTOWN WORKS, JUDGE DECIDES: ANTITRUST ISSUE REMAINS
431	U.S. STEEL	80–07–28	APPEALS COURT UPHOLDS RIGHT OF U.S. STEEL TO CLOSE 2 OHIO PLANTS
432	U.S. STEEL	80–10–30	U.S. STEEL IN REVERSAL TO KEEP OPEN PARTS OF PENN. PLANT
433	UNIROYAL	80–01–23	UNIROYAL PLANS TO CLOSE 2 PLANTS FOR TIRES IN U.S. (3,300)
434	VERMONT AMERICAN	80–08–08	VERMONT AMERICAN TO CLOSE VIRGINIA PLANT (75)
435	WARD FOODS	80–01–30	WARD FOODS CONSIDERS SHEDDING 3 BAKERIES
436	WESTINGHOUSE	80–07–28	WESTINGHOUSE TO CLOSE AIR CONDITIONING PLANT (480)
437	WESTINGHOUSE	80–09–30	WESTINGHOUSE PLANS TO CLOSE NUCLEAR PLANT PARTS FACILITY (1000)
438	WHITE MOTORS	80–01–29	WHITE MOTORS TO CLOSE EXTON, PA. FACILITY (625)

	PRIMARY CODE = MISC		**SECONDARY CODE = HEALTH/SAFE**
439	AMERICAN CYNAMID	80–09–09	MOST OSHA CITATIONS AGAINST AMERICAN CYNAMID DISMISSED BY OFFICIALS
440	CHRYSLER	80–11–10	CHRYSLER IS EXEMPTED BY OSHA FROM PART OF AIR SAFETY STANDARD

Table A1 (Continued)

OBS	COMPANY	EVENT DATE	EVENT DESCRIPTION
441	DOW CHEMICAL	80–07–25	HIGH INCIDENCE OF BRAIN TUMORS FOUND IN TEXAS PLANTS OF CARBIDE, DOW
442	GM	80–06–26	OSHA SEEKS TO PROSECUTE GM FOR WORKER'S DEATH
443	GOODYEAR	80–07–17	LOCAL CHARGES 70 DIED OF CANCERS CONTRACTED AT GOODYEAR PLANT
444	GOODYEAR	80–07–31	GOODYEAR TIRE IS SUED BY RUBBER WORKERS OVER CANCER, DEATHS
445	GOODYEAR	80–08–21	GOODYEAR SAYS STUDY REFUTES UNION CHARGES OVER CANCER INCIDENCES
446	PHILLIPS PETRO	80–07–22	GAS EXPLOSION INJURES 7 AT CHEMICAL FACILITY OF PHILLIPS PETRO
447	PHILLIPS PETRO	80–08–14	PHILLIPS PETRO FINE IN ACCIDENT SETTLEMENT IS REDUCED TO $3,600
448	PITTSTON CO.	80–07–09	PITTSTON UNIT WORKERS ARE INDICTED FOR FRAUD AND SAFETY VIOLATIONS
449	RESEARCH-COTTRELL	80–10–28	RESEARCH-COTTRELL TO PAY $85,000 FINE RELATED TO AN ACCIDENT
450	TENNECO	80–02–28	OSHA ACCUSES UNIT OF TENNECO OF 617 VIOLATIONS (NEWPORT NEWS SHIPPING)
451	UNION CARBIDE	80–07–25	HIGH INCIDENCE OF BRAIN TUMORS FOUND IN TEXAS PLANTS OF CARBIDE, DOW
452	WHIRLPOOL	80–02–27	JUSTICES UPHOLD LABOR AGENCY'S JOB-DANGER RULE

Table A2. Individual Events, 1987: Items from the *Wall Street Journal*.

OBS	COMPANY	EVENT DATE	EVENT DESCRIPTION
		PRIMARY CODE = HR	**SECONDARY CODE = HR**
1	ATT	87–01–04	ATT IS URGING TRANSFERS FOR SOME PREGNANT WOMEN
2	ATT	87–09–04	ATT STUDY SHOWS EARLY RETIREES SHARE A RANGE OF CHARACTER TRAITS
3	ATT	87–10–15	ATT MAY ASSIGN A SEPARATE STAFF TO SELL COMPUTERS
4	BARNETT BANK	87–04–03	STRATEGY, STRUCTURE, CULTURE (DESCRIPTIVE ARTICLE)
5	BOEING	87–10–22	BOEING MAY DELAY DEVELOPMENT OF ITS 7J7 JET, WORKERS TO BE REASSIGNED
6	CAP CITIES	87–07–10	CAP CITIES/ABC TO TEST JOB SEEKERS FOR DRUG USE
7	CHRYSLER	87–07–17	CHRYSLER CANADA UNIT ASKS UNION FOR FEWER JOB TITLES
8	DELTA	87–06–08	DELTA & WESTERN AIR PILOTS REACH ACCORD ON SENIORITY LIST
9	GE	87–05–12	GE WORKERS CLEAR CHANGES TO BOOST TV-PLANT OUTPUT
10	GE	87–08–10	CULTURE CLASS: GE'S MGMT. SCHOOL AIMS TO FOSTER UNIFIED CORP. GOALS
11	GM	87–04–07	ROY ROBERTS APPOINTED TO TOP PERSONNEL POST, GIVEN POWERFUL MESSAGE AND MISSION
12	GM	87–06–08	GM "TEAM CONCEPT" HITS ROUGH WATERS AT MODELE LOCATION
13	GM	87–06–19	GM CANADA WORKERS ACCEPT ACCORD, CLEAR WAY FOR PLANT'S SALE
14	GM	87–12–08	GM PLANT CLOSED DUE TO FIRST DAY OF HUNTING SEASON
15	GUILFORD IND	87–11–17	UNION WALKS OUT AGAINST GUILFORD OVER WORK RULES
16	IBM	87–01–13	IBM DISSIDENTS HOPE FOR INCREASED SUPPORT AS WORKFORCE IS CUT

Table A2 (Continued)

OBS	COMPANY	EVENT DATE	EVENT DESCRIPTION
17	IBM	87–04–27	SOME IBM WORKERS MAPPING STRATEGY TO PROMOTE UNIONS
18	IBM	87–09–18	IBM TO OFFER ITS EMPLOYEES REFERRALS ON EL-·DERLY CARE
19	INLAND STEEL	87–04–01	"LIFE OF A GRIEVER"—STEWARD SUMMARY
20	NW AIR	87–03–26	SOME NW AIR PILOTS THREATEN SLOWDOWN TO PROTEST PAY, SENIORITY GAPS
21	NW AIR	87–03–30	NW AIR TO DISCIPLINE PILOTS WHO STAGE PROTEST
22	OWENS CORNING	87–05–04	HOW A MANAGER MANAGES IN THE WAKE OF BIG STAFF CUTS
23	PHIL ELEC	87–04–01	PLANT CLOSED DUE TO OPERATORS SLEEPING ON THE JOB
24	SALOMON	87–08–20	SALOMON SECURITIES UNIT WON'T HIRE PENDING STUDY
25	TEXAS AIR	87–03–23	TEXAS AIR FACES EMPLOYEE RESISTANCE ON A GROWING NUMBER OF LABOR ISSUES
26	TEXAS AIR	87–05–15	TEXAS AIR ASKS ITS EMPLOYEES TO GO ON OFFENSIVE AGAINST CRITICS
27	UAL	87–04–07	UAL TO REVIEW PILOTS' UNION BID TO BUY UNITED AIRLINES
28	USG CORP	87–01–21	EMPLOYEES OF USG UNIT ARE TOLD TO STOP SMOKING

PRIMARY CODE = COMP/BEN   SECONDARY CODE = INCREASE

OBS	COMPANY	EVENT DATE	EVENT DESCRIPTION
29	AMER AIR	87–03–25	AMERICAN AIR ATTENDANTS WORK TO TOPPLE 2-TIER PAY
30	AMER AIR	87–12–24	AMER AIR FLIGHT ATTENDANT ACCORD WILL END 2-TIER WAGE
31	DRAVO	87–11–27	CONSTRUCTION FIRM TO END MOST TEMPORARY PAY CUTS (2,700)
32	FORD	87–02–19	FORD SCHEDULES PROFIT SHARING FOR 86', AVERAGE OVER $2100 A WORKER
33	HUDSON GENERAL	87–09–01	HUDSON OIL SETS ACCORD WITH U.S. OVER BACK WAGES
34	KODAK	87–03–16	KODAK SETS WAGE DIVIDEND
35	LTV	87–08–18	LTV IS ALLOWED TO PAY EARLY RETIREES SUPPLEMENT BENEFIT
36	NORFOLK-SOUTHERN	87–08–25	NORFOLK-SOUTHERN BETTERS SEVERANCE PLAN FOR TRAIN EMPLOYEES
37	NW AIR	87–11–18	NW AIR LIFTS SOME WORKERS' PAY TO EASE TENSIONS (2,900)
38	TIME	87–12–18	TIME INC. TO GIVE BONUSES OF $1,000 TO 2,200 WORKERS

PRIMARY CODE = COMP/BEN   SECONDARY CODE = DECREASE

OBS	COMPANY	EVENT DATE	EVENT DESCRIPTION
39	AMC	87–01–19	AMC IS SEEKING LABOR CONCESSIONS AT WISCONSIN PLANT
40	AMER AIR	87–03–16	AMERICAN AIR PAVES 2-TIER SCALE IN PACT WITH PILOTS
41	ASARCO	87–04–23	ASARCO ANNOUNCES RESTRUCTURING OF PENSION PLAN FOR SALARIED EMPLOYEES
42	CHRYSLER	87–04–27	CHRYSLER TRIMS BENEFIT FOR TOP AIDES, SLICES SOME OT PAY TO CUT COSTS
43	CHRYSLER	87–04–28	(PARAGRAPH RE:) COST CUTTING—LIMIT OT PAY AND MERIT PAY
44	FIRESTONE	87–03–10	FIRESTONE PLAN FOR PAY CUT CLEARED BY UNION WORKERS
45	FORD	87–08–28	FORD OFFERS UAW A CONTRACT PROPOSAL WITH EMPHASIS ON LUMP SUM PAYMENTS
46	GE	87–02–20	NBC TO SEEK CONCESSIONS FROM UNION
47	GM	87–03–03	GM CHANGES MERIT PAY FORMULA, CUTS PAY POOL
48	GM	87–05–26	GM NOW IS PLAGUED WITH DROP IN MORALE AS PAYROLLS ARE CUT

Table A2 (Continued)

OBS	COMPANY	EVENT DATE	EVENT DESCRIPTION
49	GM	87–08–13	GM PROPOSES A PACT BASED ON PERFORMANCE
50	GM	87–08–31	GM ASKS UAW FOR WIDE RANGE OF CONCESSIONS
51	GM	87–10–14	GM CHAIRMAN SMITH SAYS TENTATIVE PACT WILL HELP CUT COSTS
52	GM	87–12–18	GM PROFIT SHARING IS SEEN AS MAKING NO PAYMENT AGAIN
53	MELLON BANK	87–07–13	MELLON ORDERS FREEZE ON SALARIES AND HIRING
54	PAN AM	87–12–02	PAN AM PILOTS AGREE TO REDUCE WAGES FOR STOCK
55	TEXAS AIR	87–01–21	TEXAS AIR SEEKS BIG PAYCUTS AT ITS EASTERN UNIT
56	TEXAS AIR	87–10–06	TEXAS AIR CORP'S EASTERN UNIT SEEKS STEEP PAY CUTS FROM MACHINISTS' UNION
	PRIMARY CODE = STAFF		**SECONDARY CODE = PERM REDUCE**
57	ALLEGIS	87–07–07	ALLEGIS WILL CUT 250 UNITED JOBS IN REALIGNMENT
58	ATT	87–03–12	ATT TO ELIMINATE 600 ACCOUNTING, PAYROLL JOBS
59	ATT	87–04–16	(PARAGRAPH RE:) WORKFORCE REDUCTIONS Q1, 86', TO Q1, 87'
60	AUGAT	87–09–30	AUGAT PLANS TO CUT 130 JOBS
61	BANKAMERICA	87–02–02	BANKAMERICA PLANS FURTHER REDUCTIONS IN STAFF
62	BANKAMERICA	87–10–28	BANK COMPANY TRIMS 13% OF ITS MUNICIPAL BOND STAFF (50)
63	BELL ATLANTIC	87–09–21	BELL ATLANTIC OFFERS RETIREMENT INCENTIVES IN MOVE TO TRIM COSTS
64	BELL SOUTH	87–08–10	FIRM SETS 3RD PERIOD CHARGE FROM RETIREMENT PLAN COSTS (2400)
65	BORG WARNER	87–02–17	BORG WARNER TO REDUCE HEADQUARTERS STAFF 25% (88)
66	BURLINGTON IND	87–07–21	BURLINGTON REORGANIZATION TO ELIMINATE 525 STAFF AND RESEARCH JOBS
67	CANNON	87–01–07	CANNON GROUP CUTS FILM OUTPUT SCHEDULE, DISMISSES EMPLOYEES
68	CARPENTER TECH	87–03–04	CARPENTER TO REDUCE STAFF, IMPROVE PLANTS
69	CBS	87–03–09	CBS NEWS UNIT DISMISSES MORE THAN 200 EMPLOYEES
70	CHASE MAN	87–10–22	CHASE PLANS TO OFFER EARLY RETIREMENT TO 1000
71	CHRYSLER	87–10–28	CHRYSLER TO PARE 3,600 WORKERS, SOFT SALES CITED
72	CHRYSLER	87–11–11	CHRYSLER PLANS MORE LAYOFFS, UNION ASSERTS
73	CITICORP	87–11–18	CHRYSLER PLANS TO ELIMINATE 1,000 POSITIONS
74	CMS ENERGY	87–09–03	CMS ENERGY UNIT SAYS 551 WILL TAKE RETIREMENT OFFER
75	COCA COLA	87–12–10	COKE'S COLUMBIA UNIT TO DISMISS 500 IN PLAN TO SAVE $40M ANNUALLY
76	COMMODORE	87–04–27	COMMODORE LAYS OFF 50 OF 200 EMPLOYEES AT HEADQUARTERS
77	CONT ILL	87–11–10	BANKING FIRM TO TRIM EMPLOYMENT LEVELS BY 1,200
78	FIREMANS FUND	87–11–19	FIREMANS FUND UNIT TO DISMISS ALL 550 OF MASS. STAFF
79	FLOATING POINT	87–06–03	FLOATING POINT TO DISMISS 400, TAKE A CHARGE
80	GE	87–01–13	GE TO CUT 3400 JOBS AT ENGINE PLANTS, COMPETITION AND SLOWER DEMAND CITED
81	GE	87–01–14	GE PLANS TO IDLE 500 AT LOCOMOTIVE PLANT
82	GE	87–09–01	GE ENGINE DIVISION TO CUT 500 WHITE COLLAR WORKERS
83	GE	87–10–14	KIDDER PEABODY TRIMS MUNICIPAL STAFF BY 100
84	GE	87–10–15	NBC PLANS TO ELIMINATE 200 UNION MEMBERS' JOBS
85	GE	87–12–03	KIDDER PEABODY LAYOFFS BOLSTER THE VIEW MORE ARE LIKELY
86	GM	87–01–27	GM PLANS SHIFT IN PARTS MAKING TO OTHER FIRMS
87	GM	87–01–30	GM PUTS 3000 MORE WORKERS ON INDEFINITE LAYOFF
88	GM	87–02–02	GM WILL PHASE OUT DETROIT PARTS PLANT OF FISHER GUIDE UNIT
89	GM	87–02–12	GM CHAIRMAN SAYS COST CUTTING MOVES WILL SAVE NEARLY $3 BILLION IN 87'
90	GM	87–02–17	GM TO LAY OFF 70 MORE EMPLOYEES

Table A2 (Continued)

OBS	COMPANY	EVENT DATE	EVENT DESCRIPTION
91	GM	87–02–23	GM'S CANADIAN UNIT DISMISSES 99 WORKERS AT QUEBEC FACILITY
92	GM	87–04–24	GM PLANS PRODUCTION CUT AT PLANT SHARED WITH TOYOTA
93	GM	87–05–07	GM PLANS TO IDLE 6 FACILITIES AND LAY OFF 31,000 WORKERS
94	GM	87–05–15	GM AGAIN WILL IDLE PLANT TO CUT OUTPUT OF ITS PONTIAC FIERO
95	GM	87–07–01	GM TO LAY OFF 3,000 AS PART OF PHASE-OUT OF PRODUCTION PLANT
96	GM	87–08–21	GM TO SLASH OUTPUT 50% AT MISSOURI PLANT, IDLING 2,700 WORKERS
97	GM	87–11–04	GM IS AHEAD OF TIMETABLE FOR WHITE COLLAR LAYOFFS (32,800 TO DATE)
98	GREYHOUND	87–03–24	GREYHOUND BEGINS SHARP REDUCTION IN CORPO-RATE STAFF
99	GRUMMAN	87–01–19	GRUMMAN TO CUT TOTAL OF 1500 JOBS
100	HONEYWELL	87–11–13	HONEYWELL BULL TO CUT BY 10% U.S. JOB FORCE (1,300)
101	HP	87–10–09	HP COMPUTER, INSTRUMENT MAKER EXPECTS TO CUT WORK FORCE
102	IBM	87–01–20	IBM EXPECTS UP TO 1000 IN EUROPE TO RETIRE EARLY
103	IBM	87–04–08	CUTTING OUTPUT, IBM TELLS SOME WORKERS MOVE, RETIRE, OR QUIT
104	IBM	87–04–14	SUBTITLE: MORE REDUCTIONS-PROJECT 12,000 EARLY RETIRE UP FROM 10,000
105	KODAK	87–02–27	KODAK SETS LAYOFFS, TRANSFERS IN REVAMP OF ATEX, EIKONIX UNITS
106	LF ROTHSCHILD	87–12–08	LF ROTHSCHILD WILL DISMISS 700 EMPLOYEES
107	LOCKHEED	87–10–30	SOME LOCKHEED EMPLOYEES RUSH TO QUIT, AVERT IMPACT OF CRASH ON BENEFITS
108	LOMAS NETTLETON	87–08–11	LOMAS NETTLETON TO CUT STAFF BY 150 IN MORT-GAGE BANKING
109	MANF HAN	87–02–17	MANUFACTURERS HANOVER IS DISMISSING 150 MID-DLE MANAGERS TO REDUCE COSTS
110	MANF HAN	87–12–22	MANF HANOVER PLANS DEEP CUTBACKS (2,500)
111	MATTEL	87–06–04	MATTEL WILL TRIM 14% OF EMPLOYEES TO TRIM OVERHEAD
112	MCDONNELL DOUGLAS	87–10–13	INFORMATION SYSTEMS GROUP IN REVAMPING, LAYS OFF 300
113	MELLON BANK	87–05–08	MELLON IS OFFERING AN EARLY RETIREMENT TO 300 AT BANK UNIT
114	MELLON BANK	87–08–11	CHAIRMAN WILL CUT MELLON'S WORKFORCE BY 10%
115	MERRILL LYNCH	87–12–15	MERRILL LYNCH PLANS LAYOFFS TO SAVE UP TO $370 MILLION
116	N E UTILITIES	87–10–26	POWER FIRM'S CUTBACK PLAN WOULD ELIMINATE 600 JOBS
117	NEWELL	87–07–08	NEWELL CO., TO DISMISS 110 AT ANCHOR HOCKING CORP. (88)
118	NIAGARA MOHAWK	87–07–30	NIAGARA MOHAWK WILL CUT 389 JOBS IN EFFORT TO REDUCE COSTS
119	NORFOLK-SOUTHERN	87–03–04	NORFOLK-SOUTHERN PLANS TO CONSOLIDATE HEAD-QUARTERS STAFF
120	NORFOLK-SOUTHERN	87–12–17	RAIL WORKERS ARE OFFERED INCENTIVES TO LEAVE FIRM (1,200)
121	NORTON	87–01–15	NORTON TO REPORT $78.5 MILLION CHARGE, FIRE 300 EMPLOYEES
122	NTL SEMICONDUCT	87–10–29	NATIONAL SEMICONDUCTOR LAYS OFF 400 EMPLOY-EES
123	NTL SEMICONDUCT	87–11–17	DISMISSALS OF 500 ARE SET BY NATIONAL SEMICON-DUCTOR
124	OPPENHEIMER	87–10–19	OPPENHEIMER LAYS OFF 15 IN PUBLIC FINANCE DIVI-SION
125	OPPENHEIMER	87–11–05	OPPENHEIMER GROUP INC. LAYS OFF SOME EMPLOYEES

Table A2 (Continued)

OBS	COMPANY	EVENT DATE	EVENT DESCRIPTION
126	PACIFIC BELL	87-09-18	TWO PHONE CONCERNS OFFER MANAGERS PLANS FOR EARLY RETIREMENT
127	PAN AM	87-03-05	PAN AM SLASHES MANAGEMENT JOBS
128	PANHANDLE EASTERN	87-06-18	PANHANDLE EASTERN SETS OFFICE MOVE, CUT IN STAFF
129	PHILLIPS PETRO	87-12-17	PHILLIPS PLANS WORKER CUTS, CONSOLIDATION (2,250)
130	RAYTHEON	87-08-07	BEECH AIRCRAFT UNIT LAYS OFF 300 TO CUT COSTS
131	RJR	87-06-04	RJR UNIT, RJR REYNOLDS, PLANS INCENTIVE OFFER TO RETIRE EARLY
132	RJR	87-07-29	RJR NABISCO UNIT STAFF CUTS (EARLY RETIREMENT SUMMARY)
133	S NE TELEPHONE	87-09-18	TWO PHONE CONCERNS OFFER MANAGERS PLANS FOR EARLY RETIREMENT
134	SALOMON	87-09-22	SALOMON BROS SENIOR AIDES EXPECT LAYOFFS, RE-SHUFFLING OVER NEXT YEAR
135	SCOTT PAPER	87-12-03	COMPANY PLANNING LAYOFFS AT PHILADELPHIA LO-CATION
136	SOUTHERN N E	87-12-24	RETIREMENT PROGRAM CHOSEN BY 572, CHARGE IS SLATED
137	TEXAS AIR	87-04-20	TEXAS AIR TO LAY OFF 259 AT EASTERN, BUY 50% OF BAR HARBOR
138	UAL	87-02-02	UAL IS DISMISSING 1016 WORKERS
139	UNITED TECH	87-11-24	UNITED TECHNOLOGIES UNIT MULLS LAYOFFS AFTER UNION VOTE (2,000)
140	US WEST	87-01-19	US WEST INC. UNITS OFFER MANAGERS PLAN ON EARLY RETIREMENT
141	WENDY'S	87-05-21	WENDY'S INTERNATIONAL CUTS 20% OF ADMINISTRA-TIVE JOBS
142	XEROX	87-01-22	XEROX SAYS 1000 WORKERS CHOSE PLAN FOR EARLY RETIREMENT
143	ZENITH	87-09-22	EARLY RETIREMENT IS OFFERED AS MEASURE TO REDUCE COSTS
144	ZURIN	87-08-18	ZURIN MAKES CUTBACKS AT UNIT

	PRIMARY CODE = STAFF		**SECONDARY CODE = TEMP REDUCE**
145	CHRYSLER	87-10-30	CHRYSLER TO LAY OFF 400 HOURLY WORKERS AT WISCONSIN PLANT
146	FORD	87-06-12	FORD PLANT IN MICHIGAN TO CLOSE FOR 4 WEEKS, IDLING 900 EMPLOYEES
147	GM	87-01-13	GM TO HALVE OUTPUT AT PLANT IN LEEDS, MO.
148	GM	87-03-13	GM TO IDLE PLANT IN TEXAS, 2 WEEKS TO TRIM SUPPLY
149	GM	87-03-20	GM PLANS FURLOUGH OF 3,500 WORKERS TO TRIM INVENTORIES
150	GM	87-04-02	GM ANNOUNCES 1-WEEK SHUTDOWN OF 1/5 OF N.A. ASSEMBLY PLANTS
151	GM	87-04-03	GM PLANTS' FURLOUGHS GO FROM 6 TO 8
152	GM	87-05-22	GM IS CLOSING 3 PLANTS IN JUNE: STEP IDLES 13,600
153	GM	87-07-17	GM WILL CLOSE PLANT IN WILLOW RUN, MICH., FOR MODEL CHANGES
154	GM	87-07-24	GM TO CUT OUTPUT IN MOVES AFFECTING ABOUT 3,000 WORKERS
155	GM	87-11-05	GM WILL CUT MIDSIZED-CAR PRODUCTION, LAY OFF 6,400 WORKERS
156	GM	87-11-27	GM EXPANDS PERIOD OF PLANT SHUTDOWN SET FOR CHRISTMAS

	PRIMARY CODE = STAFF		**SECONDARY CODE = RECALL/INCREASE**
157	GM	87-02-27	GM WORKERS AT PLANT IN OHIO SET TO RETURN AFTER 1-WEEK LAYOFF

	PRIMARY CODE = SHUT/RELO		**SECONDARY CODE = RELOCATE**
158	AMER GENERAL	87-01-09	AMERICAN GENERAL PLANS MOVE

Table A2 (Continued)

OBS	COMPANY	EVENT DATE	EVENT DESCRIPTION
159	BEAR STEARNS	87–03–10	BEAR STEARNS PLANS TO MOVE HEADQUARTERS IN N.Y.
160	DONALDSON	87–07–09	DONALDSON TO MOVE 600 WORKERS IN N.J.
161	DREYFUS	87–09–30	DREYFUS MAY MOVE ALL OF ITS OPERATIONS OUTSIDE N.Y. TO CONSOLIDATE STAFF
162	DREYFUS	87–10–14	DREYFUS ALMOST SURE TO LEAVE MANHATTAN, DEVELOPER ASSERTS
163	J.C. PENNEY	87–04–29	PENNEYS WILL GO TO DALLAS, OFFICIALS IN N.Y. SAY
164	MOBIL	87–04–27	MOBIL PLANS TO FORSAKE N.Y.C. IN FAVOR OF VIRGINIA
165	MOBIL	87–06–23	MOBIL'S WARD WILL MOVE APPAREL BUYING DIVISION
166	RJR	87–01–12	RJR WANTS TO LEAVE WINSTON-SALEM, N.C., FOR ATLANTA
167	SINGER	87–08–20	THE MOVING VAN PULLS UP TO CURB UNWANTED TAKEOVER

PRIMARY CODE = SHUT/RELO   SECONDARY CODE = SHUTDOWN

OBS	COMPANY	EVENT DATE	EVENT DESCRIPTION
168	ALLEGHENY INTL	87–03–04	CLOSING OF 2 FACILITIES SLATED BY ALLEGHENY INC.
169	ARMSTRONG RUBBER	87–07–09	ARMTEK TO CLOSE TIRE PLANT AFTER DISPUTE WITH UNION
170	CARPENTER TECH	87–09–14	CARPENTER TO CLOSE PLANT
171	CHRYSLER	87–03–10	CHRYSLER SCHEDULES PRODUCTION PHASE OUT AT INDIANAPOLIS PLANT
172	DOMTAR	87–06–16	DOMTAR TO SELL OR CLOSE PAPER LINE AT U.S. SITE
173	FAIRCHILD	87–02–02	PLANT MAY BE SHUT BY FAIRCHILD
174	FIRESTONE	87–03–04	FIRESTONE TO CLOSE PLANTS IN ILLINOIS, OKLAHOMA, IOWA
175	FIRESTONE	87–07–16	TIRE MFG. TO END AT A FACILITY IN ONTARIO
176	FISHER FOODS	87–06–12	FISHER FOODS TO CLOSE AS MANY AS 19 STORES AND REPORT A CHARGE
177	FORD	87–03–11	FORD STEEL SUBSIDIARY TO CLOSE COKE OVENS AT DEARBORN, MICH.
178	GM	87–02–20	GM WILL IDLE PLANT IN OHIO (ALSO PHASE OUT 800 AT FLINT)
179	GM	87–03–06	GM PLANS CLOSINGS AT 3 PLANTS TO REDUCE ITS AUTO INVENTORIES
180	GM	87–08–05	GM TO CLOSE PARTS PLANT AS POTENTIAL SALE COLLAPSES
181	GTE	87–04–21	GTE CHIP PLANT IS TO BE CLOSED, PUT UP FOR SALE
182	HECKS	87–02–18	HECKS IN BID TO STOP LOSSES, WILL CLOSE 29 STORES
183	HORMEL	87–02–24	HORMEL INTENDS TO CLOSE PLANT IN OTTUMWA, IOWA
184	IBM	87–01–09	IBM CLOSES UNIT IN LATEST MOVE TO LOWER COSTS (REASSIGNED)
185	INT'L. CONTROLS	87–02–23	INT'L. CONTROLS CLOSES MOST OPERATIONS OF WESCAR FREIGHT UNIT
186	PROCTOR & GAMBLE	87–06–22	PROCTOR & GAMBLE SHUTS PLANT
187	SEARS	87–03–03	SEARS TO CLOSE 5 WAREHOUSES IN MOVE TO CUT COSTS
188	SQUARE D	87–12–15	SQUARE DUCT CLOSES TWO PLANTS
189	TODD SHIPYARDS	87–07–28	INSURANCE CANCELLATION LEADS FIRM TO WARN OF SHUTDOWN (WCI)
190	WESTINGHOUSE	87–02–02	WESTINGHOUSE TO CLOSE PLANT IN CONNECTICUT
191	WHEELING PITT	87–06–12	WHEELING PITT IS SET TO CLOSE SINTER PLANT

PRIMARY CODE = MISC   SECONDARY CODE = HEALTH/SAFE

OBS	COMPANY	EVENT DATE	EVENT DESCRIPTION
192	DUPONT	87–05–07	JURY FINDS DUPONT CONCEALED RECORDS ON WORKERS' HEALTH
193	FORD	87–11–10	FINES TOTALING $325K PAID FOR SAFETY RECORD VIOLATIONS
194	INTL PAPER	87–10–27	OSHA RECOMMENDS INTL PAPER BE FINED $242,000
195	SCOTT PAPER	87–12–07	SCOTT PAPER TO PAY $475K IN SETTLING CASE WITH OSHA

REFERENCES

Abowd, John M. 1989. "The Effects of Wage Bargains on the Stock Market Value of the Firm." *American Economic Review*, Vol. 79, No. 4 (September), pp. 774–800.

Alexander, Ralph A., and Murray R. Barrick. 1987. "Estimating the Standard Error of Projected Dollar Gains in Utility Analysis." *Journal of Applied Psychology*, Vol. 72, No. 3, pp. 475–79.

Baker, George P., Michael C. Jensen, and Kevin J. Murphy. 1988. "Compensation and Incentives: Practice vs. Theory." *Journal of Finance*, Vol. 43, No. 3, pp. 593–616.

Ball, R., P. Brown. 1968. "An Empirical Evaluation of Accounting Income Numbers." *Journal of Accounting Research*, Vol. 6, pp. 159–78.

Beaver, William H. 1968. "The Information Content of Annual Earnings Announcements." *Empirical Research in Accounting: Selected Studies* (supplement to the *Journal of Accounting Research*), Vol. 6 (supplement), pp. 67–92.

Becker, Brian E. 1987. "Concession Bargaining: The Impact of Shareholders' Equity." *Industrial and Labor Relations Review*, Vol. 40, No. 2, pp. 268–79.

Becker, Brian E., and Craig A. Olson. 1986. "The Impact of Strikes on Shareholder Equity." *Industrial and Labor Relations Review*, Vol. 39, No. 3, pp. 425–38.

———. 1987. "Labor Relations and Firm Performance." In Morris Kleiner et al., eds., *Human Resources and the Performance of the Firm*. Madison, Wis.: Industrial Relations Research Association, pp. 43–85.

Boudreau, John W. 1987. *Utility Analysis: A New Perspective on Human Resource Decision Making*. Unpublished paper No. 87–09, Center for Advanced Human Resource Studies, Ithaca, N.Y.

———. Forthcoming. "Utility Analysis in Human Resource Management Decisions." In M. D. Dunnette, ed., *Handbook of Industrial and Organizational Psychology*, 2nd edition. Palo Alto, Calif.: Consulting Psychologists Press.

Bowman, R. G. 1983. "Understanding and Conducting Event Studies." *Journal of Business Finance and Accounting*, Vol. 10, No. 4, pp. 561–84.

Brickley, James A., Sanjai Bhagat, and Ronald C. Lease. 1985. "The Impact of Long-Range Managerial Compensation Plans on Shareholder Wealth." *Journal of Accounting and Economics*, Vol. 7, pp. 115–29.

Brown, Stephen J., and Jerold B. Warner. 1980. "Measuring Security Price Performance." *Journal of Financial Economics*, Vol. 8, pp. 205–58.

———. 1985. "Using Daily Stock Returns: The Case of Event Studies." *Journal of Financial Economics*, Vol. 14, pp. 3–31.

Bullock, R. J., and Edward E. Lawler. 1984. "Gainsharing: A Few Questions and a Few Answers." *Human Resource Management*, Vol. 23, No. 1, pp. 23–40.

Cascio, W. F. 1987. *Costing Human Resources: The Financial Impact of Behavior in Organizations*. Boston: PWS-Kent.

Dyer, Lee, and Gerald W. Holder. 1988. "A Strategic Perspective of Human Resource Management." In Lee Dyer, ed., *Human Resource Management: Evolving Roles and Responsibilities*, ASPA/BNA Handbook of Human Resource management (Vol. 1). Washington, D.C.: Bureau of National Affairs, pp. 1–46.

Etebari, A., J. O. Horrigan, and J. L. Landwehr. 1987. "To Be or Not to Be—Reaction of Stock Returns to Sudden Deaths of Corporate Chief Executive Officers." *Journal of Business Finance and Accounting*, Vol. 14, No. 2, pp. 255–77.

Fama, Eugene F., Lawrence Fisher, Michael C. Jensen, and Richard Roll. 1969. "The Adjustment of Stock Prices to New Information." *International Economic Review*, Vol. 10, No. 1, pp. 1–21.

Fitz-enz, J. 1984. *How to Measure Human Resources Management*. New York: McGraw-Hill.

Gannon, M.J., D. L. Norland, and F. E. Robeson. 1983. "Shift Work Has Complex Effects on Lifestyles and Work Habits." *Personnel Administrator*, Vol. 25, pp. 93–97.

Gomez-Mejia, Luis R., Henry Tosi, and Timothy Hinkin. 1987. "Managerial Control, Performance, and Executive Compensation." *Academy of Management Journal*, Vol. 30, No. 1, pp. 51–70.

Heneman, R. L. 1984. *Pay and Performance: Exploring the Merit System*. New York: Pergamon.

Kleiner, Morris M., Richard N. Block, Myron Roomkin, and Sidney W. Salsburg, eds. 1987. *Human Resources and the Performance of the Firm*. Madison, Wis.: Industrial Relations Research Association.

Lubatkin, M. H., K. H. Chung, R. C. Rogers, and J. E. Owers. "Stockholder Reactions to CEO Changes in Large Corporations." *Academy of Management Journal*, Vol. 32, No. 1, pp. 47–68.

Patell, J. M. 1976. "Corporate Forecasts of Earnings per Share and Stock Price Behavior: Empirical Tests." *Journal of Accounting Research*, Vol. 14, pp. 246–76.

Pearce, Jane L., and James L. Perry. 1983. "Federal Merit Pay: A Longitudinal Analysis." *Public Administration Review*, Vol. 43, No. 4 (July–August), pp. 315–25.

Reinganum, Marc R. 1985. "The Effect of Executive Succession on Stockholder Wealth." *Administrative Science Quarterly*, Vol. 39, No. 1, pp. 46–60.

Ruback, Richard S., and Martin B. Zimmerman. 1984. "Unionization and Profitability: Evidence from the Capital Market." *Journal of Political Economy*, Vol. 92 (December), pp. 1134–57.

Schuler, Randall S. 1987. "Personnel and Human Resource Management Choices and Organizational Strategy." *Human Resource Planning*, Vol. 10, No. 1, pp. 1–17.

Schuster, Michael H. 1983. "Forty Years of Scanlon Plan Research: A Review of the Descriptive and Empirical Literature." In C. Crouch and F. Heller, eds., *International Yearbook of Organizational Democracy,* Vol. 1, pp. 53–71.

————. 1984. "The Scanlon Plan: A Longitudinal Analysis." *Journal of Applied Behavioral Science,* Vol. 20, No. 4, pp. 23–28.

Schwert, G. William. 1981. "Using Financial Data to Measure Effects of Regulation." *Journal of Law and Economics,* Vol. 24, pp. 121–58.

Tehranian, Hassan, and James F. Waegelein. 1985. "Market Reaction to Short-Term Executive Compensation Plan Adoption." *Journal of Accounting and Economics,* Vol. 7, pp. 131–44.

Thompson, R. 1985. "Conditioning the Return-Generating Process on Firm-Specific Events: A Discussion of Event Study Methods." *Journal of Financial and Quantitative Analysis,* Vol. 20, pp. 151–69.

Thompson, R. B., C. Olsen, and J. R. Dietrich. 1987. "Attributes of News About Firms: An Analysis of Firm-Specific News Reported in the *Wall Street Journal Index.*" *Journal of Accounting Research,* Vol. 25, No. 2, pp. 245–74.

————. 1988. "The Influence of Estimation Period News Events on Standardized Market Model Prediction Errors." *The Accounting Review,* Vol. 63, No. 3, pp. 448–71.

Thorndike, R. L. 1949. *Personnel Selection.* New York: John Wiley & Sons.

Tracy, Joseph S. 1987. "An Empirical Test of an Asymmetric Information Model of Strikes." *Journal of Labor Economics,* Vol. 5, pp. 149–73.

————. 1988. "Testing Strategic Bargaining Models Using Stock Market Data." Unpublished NBER Working Paper No. 2754 (October).

Tsui, Ann S. 1987. "Defining the Activities and Effectiveness of the Human Resource Department: A Multiple Constituency Approach." *Human Resource Management,* Vol. 26, No. 1, pp. 35–69.

Ulrich, David. 1987. "Organizational Capability as a Competitive Advantage: Human Resource Professionals as Strategic Partners." *Human Resource Planning,* Vol. 10, No. 4, pp. 169–84.

MERIT PAY PRACTICES: IMPLICATIONS FOR PAY-PERFORMANCE RELATIONSHIPS

DONALD P. SCHWAB and CRAIG A. OLSON*

This study uses a Monte Carlo simulation to examine how the relationship between pay and performance is affected by the pay system, measurement error in appraising performance, the consistency of true performance over time, and the rules governing promotion decisions. The authors find that conventional merit systems achieve a considerably better link between pay and performance than does a bonus system with periodic adjustments in base wages. A bonus system without periodic base wage adjustments also performs less well than conventional merit systems, because merit systems benefit from the consistency of true performance over time. One surprising finding is that even very substantial error in the measurement of performance has only a modest effect on the pay-performance correlation.

MUCH has been written recently about the promise of pay for performance systems as mechanisms to reduce fixed labor costs and to increase employee productivity (for example, Kanter 1987; O'Dell 1987). Gainsharing, profit sharing, top executive incentives, and merit pay all have received attention (see, for example, reviews by Ehrenberg and Milkovich 1987; Heneman, in press; Strauss 1986).

Of the systems that have attracted notice, merit pay is perhaps of particular interest. It is by far the most frequently employed method for linking pay to performance, especially among nonexempt employees. (Survey results of organizational practice are reported in, for example, Bureau of National Affairs 1981; Peck 1984). Further, there is substantial controversy about how effectively merit pay systems actually operate (see, for example, Heneman, in press). Studies of such systems in both private and public organizations provide disparate estimates of how closely they link employee performance and pay (Auster and Drazin 1987; Gerhart and Milkovich 1989; Heneman 1973; Johnson and Kasten 1983; Katz 1973; Kahn and Sherer 1988; Medoff and Abraham 1980, 1981; Schwab 1988). The

* Donald P. Schwab is Professor of Business and Craig Olson is Associate Professor of Business and Industrial Relations, both at the University of Wisconsin–Madison. The authors thank the Graduate School and the Vilas Foundation at the University of Wisconsin–Madison, and the National Bureau of Economic Research, for financial assistance. The simulation was constructed and run using hardware and software provided by a research contract between IBM Corporation and the Industrial Relations Research Institute. The authors also gratefully acknowledge critical comments on earlier drafts of this paper provided by Alison Barber, Charles Brown, W. Lee Hansen, Tom Mahoney, Anne Miner, and participants at a National Bureau of Economic Research Working Conference, Nov. 16–17, Cambridge, Mass.

An earlier version of this paper, reporting on an analysis of only two levels of merit policy and measurement error, was presented at the Academy of Management meetings, Anaheim, August 1988.

pay-performance relationship is critical because of its effect on organizational performance, on the rewards received by individuals, and on the efficient allocation of resources in the labor market.

The studies identified above are all case studies of single organizations. Thus, the disparate findings may result from at least three potential differences among the organizations studied. First, they may be partially due to differences in policies regarding the administration of the merit pay systems themselves. Second, they may be attributable to the quality of measures used to assess employee performance (measurement error). Finally, they may be due to other institutional features (such as promotion policies) that differ across organizations.

The major objective of the present study is to investigate how merit policies and other company attributes influence the relationship between employee performance and pay rewards. Findings from such an investigation should be of both scholarly interest and practical value. The study should be of interest to scholars concerned with wage determination, and it should also be of interest to human resource practitioners, since it may contribute to a better understanding of the operation of merit systems and suggest ways to make them more effective.

A Monte Carlo simulation was developed to accomplish the objective of the study. This methodology permits us to address three issues that most prior studies have been unable to examine. Most important, it permits us to manipulate merit policies and other institutional features of organizations that may influence the pay-performance relationship. Field surveys of single organizations are necessarily constrained to observing single values of institutional parameters. Thus, they cannot provide evidence of the effects these parameters may have on how effectively pay is linked to performance.

Second, the Monte Carlo simulation allows us to assess relationships longitudinally as well as cross-sectionally. Investigation of the former is particularly important because several features of merit

systems (developed below) have been hypothesized to attenuate pay-performance relationships over time.

Finally, the method permits us to observe the effects of measurement error on pay-performance outcomes directly. This is an especially attractive feature of simulations, because estimates derived from conventional survey methods (for example, estimates of interobserver or intertemporal unreliability) are crude at best.

Merit Pay Systems

Definition. Recent textbooks on compensation (for example, Hills 1987; Milkovich and Newman 1987; Wallace and Fay 1983) generally define merit pay systems as having four identifying characteristics:

1. Pay ranges are established for each job or group of similar jobs (the latter often established through job evaluation). These ranges, which have formal minimums and maximums, are typically standardized (in percentage terms) across jobs or job groups.

2. Individual progression within the pay range (usually at fixed intervals, such as once yearly) depends at least in part on observations of the employee's performance. Thus, merit pay systems differ from pay progression plans based solely on seniority, although seniority may be considered along with performance in merit systems. An employee's current location in the salary range may also be a part of the merit increase formula. Specifically, a given level of observed performance results in smaller pay increments as one moves higher in the pay range.

3. In textbook descriptions, performance is usually operationalized through performance appraisal systems whereby employee behavior is observed and then evaluated for its contribution to the organization. Typically, standards of success are not established *a priori*, a feature that differentiates merit systems from piece rate systems.

4. Finally, the pay increment obtained in any one time period is retained over time by building it into the employee's base

salary. The latter characteristic differentiates merit systems from both bonus and individual or group incentive systems in which the pay increment is an inducement that does not increase base pay.

Merit policy variations. Surveys provide evidence that organizational practice is more heterogeneous than the above characterization suggests, and that what goes under the heading of merit systems varies rather widely (see, for example, Bureau of National Affairs 1981; Peck 1984). For example, a substantial number of private sector firms purportedly using merit systems do not use performance appraisals to measure performance (Evans 1970), and merit systems in universities may not have formal range minimums or maximums (Schwab 1988). Further, Hansen (1988) summarized 50 American Association of University Professors (AAUP) contracts with universities and found that one-shot bonus systems (in which the increment is not built into base pay) outnumbered conventional merit systems by a ratio of 3 to 1. These one-shot bonus systems appear to be increasingly used in the private sector as well (Bureau of National Affairs 1984; O'Dell 1987).

In the present study, rules governing salary increments were varied along several dimensions. Of particular interest was a contrast between one-shot bonus systems and more conventional merit systems. Increased use of one-time bonuses is probably attributable to the belief that they more closely link pay to performance. For example, Lawler (1971, 1981) has argued that conventional merit systems attenuate the relationship between current period performance and pay increases by building pay increments into base pay.

Yet another consideration suggesting that merit systems may erode the connection between performance and pay is that many merit pay policies link the magnitude of the pay increment not only to performance but to location in the salary range. Holding performance constant, such policies reduce the magnitude of the pay increment as one approaches the pay range ceiling. If the prescriptive literature

is any guide, this is common practice in merit pay plans (see, for example, Basnight 1980; Doyel and Johnson 1985; Stokes 1981).

Of course, different policies linking pay to performance also have different implications for total wage bills, especially over time. In the absence of base pay adjustments, for example, one-shot bonus systems would necessarily generate a lower total wage bill because bonus payments are not built into base pay. Policies making pay increments a partial function of location in the salary range are specifically designed to control wage costs (see, for example, Hills 1987:344–45; Milkovich and Newman 1987:354–55).

The present study thus varies merit policies along three dimensions. First, we vary whether pay increments are built into base pay; second, we vary whether pay increments are a function of location in the salary range; and finally, we vary the rules for raising average pay levels in order to investigate the effects of such rules on total wage cost.

Measurement Error

There is widespread skepticism about the ability of organizations to accurately (validly) observe employees' "true" performance, especially with the performance appraisal procedures typically employed (for reviews, see Ilgen and Feldman 1983; Landy and Farr 1980). Both academics and practitioners generally view the difficulty of reliably measuring employee performance as a substantial obstacle to implementing effective merit systems. Representative of scholars who have addressed the subject, Hills, Madigan, Scott, and Markham (1987) stated that "the measure of . . . performance is *the* critical component of any merit system," and concluded that such measures frequently fail because they "reveal evidence of errors or other deficiencies" (p. 55). Illustrative of practitioners' concerns is Winstanley's (1978:49) observation, "One of the reasons we old-timers are very pessimistic about management's ability to relate pay to performance is based on the fact of industrial life; the validity [accuracy] of performance appraisals is very low."

It is well known that measurement error in performance evaluation will attenuate the relationship between pay and true performance. Indeed, recognizing this, current compensation textbook discussions of merit systems focus almost exclusively on the quality of alternative procedures for appraising performance (see, for example, Hills 1987:327–43; Milkovich and Newman 1987:332–51). Little is known, however, about the magnitude of attenuation of the pay-performance relationship that is actually produced by measurement error. Particularly little is known about this effect across time and in combination with other institutional differences in the merit systems.

As previously noted, the methodology used in the present study is especially useful for investigating the implications of measurement error in merit pay systems. The simulation manipulates the relationship between performance as observed through performance appraisals and true performance scores. The effects of alternative models on relationships between performance and pay are then observed.

Institutional Context

Since this study is intended to simulate what might be expected in a real internal labor market, the parameters and characteristics of its labor force are important design elements. For several reasons, we chose to study job hierarchies representing entry level through middle managers and professional/technical employees.[1] The Bureau of National Affairs (1981) survey

found that nearly 90% of responding firms used some form of merit system among these groups (the highest level of use among all occupational groups). Further, empirical studies of the relationship between merit pay and performance in noneducational organizations have frequently focused on these types of employees (for example, Auster and Drazin 1987; Gerhart and Milkovich 1989; Medoff and Abraham 1980, 1981; Kahn and Sherer 1988). These studies were of substantial help in developing the parameters and estimates of the error terms in the research reported here.

The employment consequences and structural characteristics of such hierarchies have been of considerable interest to researchers. Private sector firms and some government bureaucracies are typically organized in hierarchies characterized by Althauser and Kalleberg (1981) as firm internal labor markets (FILMs). In such markets, access to a hierarchy occurs largely at the bottom; higher-level job opportunities tend to be filled internally through promotion from lower-level jobs.

FILMs with these general characteristics have been observed in several investigations of managerial and professional hierarchies (for example, Foulkes 1980:143; Osterman 1984). Over time, a labor force in such a FILM would be characterized by turnover throughout the hierarchy. External replacements,[2] if necessary, would be hired primarily into the entry level of the hierarchy, and replacements for vacancies above entry level would be obtained from incumbents at lower levels in the hierarchy, when possible.

Promotion rules. Pay increments are typically provided when employees are promoted in FILMs of the sort described. This institutional practice will influence relationships observed between pay and performance along with merit pay policies. The effect of promotion policies on pay-performance relationships, in turn,

---

[1] Top managers are excluded because the human resource policies applicable to their positions are likely to differ substantially from the policies applicable among bottom- to middle-level managers and professionals. Reward practices, in particular, differ between top management and others; the former typically have a variety of contingent payment schemes not available to middle- and lower-level managers and professionals. Top managers are also frequently exempted from the performance appraisal-based merit systems of the group studied here (Bureau of National Affairs 1983).

---

[2] Entrants from another FILM in the same organization (for example, clerical jobs) would also be considered external in this context.

will depend partially on the role of employee performance in promotion decisions. Since the importance of performance versus other criteria, such as seniority, is disputed empirically (compare Abraham and Medoff 1985 and Mills 1985), in this study we vary the relationships between performance and promotions.

Performance over time. The nature of the institutional work environment, along with employee characteristics, likely influences the constancy of employee performance over time. For example, changes in supervision, co-workers, and technology may all affect employee performance from one period to the next. This effect, in turn, will influence pay-performance relationships, especially longitudinal relationships. Because we were unable to obtain empirical estimates of how employee performance varies over time, we varied it as a part of the methodology.

Summary

The major objective of the present study is to investigate how merit policies, along with several other institutional rules and characteristics, influence the relationship between employee performance and pay. More specifically, the study was designed to examine the effects on the pay-performance relationship of (1) different merit and bonus pay systems, (2) the amount of error present in the measures of employee performance, (3) promotion practices, and (4) the consistency of employee performance across time.

Method

Overview

The methodology used in this study can be thought of in experimental terms. A set of 640 managerial/professional firm internal labor market (FILM) labor forces (n = 100), all identical (subject to several uncorrelated error terms), was created by Monte Carlo simulation (see below). Each labor force was then assigned to one combination of (1) pay system, (2) measurement error, (3) promotion system, and (4) correlation of performance with performance over time. The labor forces created were assigned to these combinations in a design that was crossed (each level of one independent variable occurred with each level of every other independent variable) and balanced (an equal number of labor forces [K = 20] were assigned to each combination of independent variables). Relationships between pay and performance produced by these combinations of conditions were observed in the cross-section and over time. The variance in the relationships was studied as a function of each of the four factors we manipulated and as a function of the interactions between those factors.

We began the simulation by specifying a labor force for each FILM. Members of the labor force were assigned pay levels, observed and true performance, and organizational characteristics such as tenure and job level. Each FILM was then followed over the ten time periods. In addition to the imposition of the experimental manipulations, each FILM experienced turnover to, and hiring from, the external labor market. Analysis was performed on two samples consisting of (1) all employees in a FILM in any given time period and (2) all who remained with their FILMs for the full ten periods. The general method is described below and a detailed description of the method is contained in the Appendix.

Manipulations

Pay systems. Four systems were designed to address the pay issues identified above. To help isolate the potential effects of merit increases that are built into base pay and merit increases that are made a partial function of location in the salary range, we constructed two merit systems to contrast with one-shot bonuses. In one, hereafter called conventional, (a) the merit increment was built into base pay and (b) range minimums and maximums were enforced (pay increments were adjusted up or down to keep pay within the salary range of the job level). In the other, hereafter called uncapped, merit was built into base pay, but no range minimums or maximums were enforced for merit increments (although they were specified to make external hiring decisions comparable—see below). Range minimums only (with the same values as those for the merit systems) were specified for the one-shot bonus system, where periodic salary increments were not built into subsequent base pay.

Effects on wage costs were investigated through several steps. Without adjustments in the rate ranges, employees would eventually, albeit at different rates of progress from individual to individual, approach the salary maximum and be unable to obtain further increases in the conventional merit system. Absent unlimited promotion opportunities, a weakening of the relationship between performance and pay is inevitable in such a system. Further, a consequence of this pattern for our simulation would be substantial variance between the conventional and uncapped merit systems in the total wage bill after the completion of a number of periods, a difference we wished to avoid.

In practice, the problem of "salary ceilings" is typically addressed by periodic increases in nominal salary ranges. We adopted this practice in the present study. In each time period, pay range minimums and maximums were increased by the average used to transform performance into merit or bonus payments. This step permitted pay growth opportunity for high performers and was designed to keep total wage costs between the two merit systems roughly comparable over time.

An analogous total wage bill comparability problem occurred for the one-shot bonus system. In the absence of some sort of upward adjustment in pay, total pay costs for the bonus system would in time be less than pay costs for the two merit systems. Although we were unable to find empirical literature describing outcomes from bonus systems over time, it seems reasonable to suppose that some upward adjustment in nominal pay levels would ordinarily be necessary to retain, and

certainly to attract, a labor force. As a consequence of these factors, we developed a second one-shot bonus system (hereafter called the across-the-board bonus system). In this case, pay increments were not built into base pay, but in each time period base pay for each employee was increased by an average comparable to the increase in pay minimums and maximums in the conventional merit system.

Measurement error. The amount of error present in the performance measures of all four pay systems was manipulated. We could not, of course, estimate the amount of measurement error present in the performance appraisals of field studies. Borman's (1978) research suggests, however, that a correlation of .60 between observed and true performance may push the upper limits of validity. This value was chosen to represent low measurement error. A value of .30 was chosen, arbitrarily, to represent high measurement error.

Promotion rules. In a recent review of the promotion literature, Markham, Harlan, and Hackett (1987) noted that little is known about how organizations select candidates for promotion. Further, as noted earlier, there is controversy regarding the importance of performance versus other criteria for promotion. Since this study is concerned primarily with merit pay systems, we investigate only two promotion practices. These two practices were chosen to represent opposite extremes in terms of the expected relationship between promotions and performance. In one, promotion is perfectly related to observed performance, and in the other, employees are chosen for promotion randomly.

Performance over time. As in the case of measurement error, we had little empirical evidence for specifying the amount, or even the functional form, of the relationship to be expected between employee performance over time. It seemed plausible, however, to suppose that each employee has some characteristic level of performance different from that of other employees (as suggested by the performance heterogeneity found in wage studies using panel data), but that each employee's performance is also subject to some random period-to-period variation. Consequently, we specified a true performance model that was equal to a constant value plus a random component. The variance of the random component was set so that the correlation between true performance levels over time was the same between any two time periods and equal to either .8 or .5. In addition to the random component, true performance was adjusted upward by .1 of a standard deviation. The latter increase in performance over time is consistent with increasing performance due to growth in human capital.

Initial Specification of the Labor Force

The relationship observed between performance and pay over time obviously depends in part on the strength of the initial relationship between those variables and others. Thus, specification of initial relationships among employee variables was important, and one of the more difficult tasks we confronted in the construction of the simulation. We chose to begin by making relationships among several dimensions conform to our best estimate of what is observed among FILMs of the sort simulated. To that end, we studied cross-sectional data found in the field research of Auster and Drazin (1987), Gerhart and Milkovich (1989), and Kahn and Sherer (1988).

Six characteristics of the employees in the FILM were initially defined: (1) firm tenure, (2) job tenure, (3) job level, (4) observed performance, (5) true performance, and (6) annual salary. The initial specification involved the first four variables. The correlation matrix for these variables is shown in the Appendix and the values chosen are comparable to the correlations found in the studies identified above. These vectors were then transformed and rescaled to conform to plausible distributions of values observed in the field data.[3] For example, the hierarchical structure of the FILM was created by placing employees in one of seven job levels. The proportion of employees in each job level (from lowest to highest) was .30, .30, .15, .09, .09, .04, and .03.[4] (Again, for a description of all the distributions, see the Appendix.)

Initial pay levels were made a linear function of observed performance, firm tenure, job tenure, job level, and squared terms for the tenure variables. With an error term introduced, the R^2 of the equation was set approximately equal to .50. Next, a pay range of 50%, typical for these kinds of jobs (Personick 1984), was set for each job level, with approximately 90% overlap between job levels. A small number of employees had to have their job levels or pay adjusted to bring job level and pay range in line (see the Appendix for the exact pay ranges and for details on the adjustment procedure).

Finally, a measure of true performance was created that is correlated with observed performance consistent with the two manipulated levels of measurement error.

Procedure Across Time

At the beginning of each period, true performance was defined as a function of a constant value and a random component. Observed performance for the period was then set to be a function of true performance for the period.

Turnover occurred at the beginning of each period. The turnover rate was set at approximately 10%, a value suggested by Price's (1977) review. The probability of turnover for an employee was made a negative function of firm tenure, consistent with wide observation (for example, Cotten and Tuttle 1986; Price 1977), and

---

[3] These authors provided data beyond what was summarized in their papers. We gratefully acknowledge their assistance.

[4] These proportions are roughly comparable to those obtained in studies of managerial hierarchies by Gerhart and Milkovich (1989), Rosenbaum (1979), and Stewman and Konda (1983).

the hazard function was defined by a Weibull distribution.

Vacancies created by turnover were then filled by promoting current eligible employees (those with at least one period of experience in their current job level) from the level immediately below using one of the two promotion policies. Promoted employees were given a 15% pay increment subject to the constraints of the pay system (see the Appendix for details). If there were more opportunities than eligible internal candidates, vacancies were filled with candidates hired from the external labor market.

Pay increases were granted to employees not promoted based on one of the four pay system treatments. (1) In the conventional merit system, pay range minimums and maximums were adjusted upward each period before merit increases were provided. The pay increase was made a function of observed performance subject to the constraint that the new salary level had to fall within the new job level salary range. (2) The uncapped merit treatment was identical to the conventional merit system except that increases were not constrained by salary grade minimums and maximums. (3) In the across-the-board bonus system, base pay was adjusted up each period before the bonus was determined. The base pay adjustment each period was sized to keep the total wage bill of the system comparable to that of the merit systems. The bonus payment was a function of observed performance. (4) In the straight bonus system, increments were determined by observed performance unconstrained by the minimums and maximums of the salary grades.

Vacancies in the lowest level created either by turnover or promotion were filled at the end of the period from the external market, as were vacancies at higher levels if the number of internal eligible employees was insufficient.

Dependent Variables

Two dependent variables were generated because of our interest in longitudinal as well as cross-sectional pay-performance relationships. Both are represented by correlations across employees in each FILM. Also, both include measures of true performance rather than observed performance, since one objective of the study was to investigate effects of measurement error on pay returns to performance.

The first variable, called cross-sectional, is the correlation of performance in a period with the pay increase associated with that performance. C (for performance) and A (for pay), in Figure 1, represent the values that would serve as inputs for this correlation in the fifth time period. The cross-sectional correlation thus indicates how well the FILM relates periodic pay increments to period performance. It is analogous to a correlation typically reported in field studies of pay-performance relationships except for the fact that we used true rather than observed performance.

The second variable, called longitudinal, is the correlation of accumulated pay increase and accumulated true performance in any time period. The shaded area under the pay and performance curves in Figure 1 shows the values that would serve as one employee's inputs to this correlation in the fifth time period. The cumulative nature of both components of the variable provides information about how closely the FILM has linked pay increments to performance over time.[5] Given the numerous sources of error that can creep into pay systems over time, we expected that the cross-sectional correlations would exceed the longitudinal correlations.

---

[5] Another possible method for assessing the longitudinal relationship was to correlate accumulated performance and accumulated total pay (including starting pay level). This correlation would generally be lower than the longitudinal correlation, because starting salary was imperfectly correlated with initial productivity. This alternative method for assessing the longitudinal relationship was also calculated. As expected, it resulted in pay-performance correlations lower than those obtained longitudinally but with otherwise analogous "behavior."

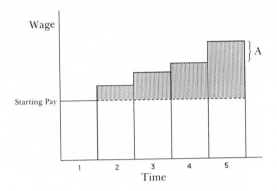

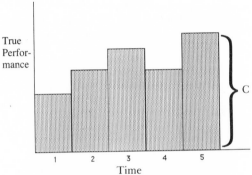

Figure 1. Description of the Dependent Variables.

Samples

Two samples were used in the analysis reported below. One consists of those employees who were in a FILM and remained with it for the full ten periods. Hereafter called stayers, it is analogous to samples reported in most field research. The average size of this sample was 66.4.

The second sample consists of all employees present in a FILM in any time period. Thus, in addition to the stayers in a period, it includes employees who might leave before the tenth period or who were hired after the first period. Hereafter called total, it would likely be the sample an organization would use for internal evaluation. The average size of this sample was 90.8.

Results

Total wage bill. As noted, we sought to make the total costs of three of the four pay systems roughly comparable by manip-

ulating the way dollars were allocated to pay increments (merit or bonus) and periodic increases in rate range minimums and maximums. Table 1 shows that this effort was successful. Each of the four systems had an average wage bill of just over $2.4 million in the first time period. By the tenth time period, conventional merit, uncapped merit, and across-the-board bonus had an average wage bill of just over $2.9 million. The cost of the straight bonus system declined to an average of $2.15 million because all new hires were brought in at the range minimum for their job level.

Pay system outcomes. The two methods for assessing relationships between employee pay and performance produced different correlations, and in the direction expected. In the total sample, the highest relationship (grand mean = .387) was obtained between cross-sectional true performance and pay increase. The average correlation for longitudinal pay and per-

Table 1. Mean Wage Bill (in units of $10,000) by Time Period and Pay System for 640 Managerial/Professional Firm Internal Labor Markets:A Simulation. (Standard Deviations in Parentheses)

Period	Capped Merit	Uncapped Merit	Across-the-Board Bonus	Straight Bonus
1	242 (2.57)	241 (.52)	243 (2.30)	243 (1.29)
2	245 (2.20)	244 (1.92)	245 (2.33)	238 (1.18)
3	249 (2.36)	248 (1.67)	250 (1.59)	233 (1.03)
4	253 (2.77)	252 (1.67)	253 (2.86)	230 (1.32)
5	258 (3.64)	257 (2.02)	258 (3.03)	227 (1.56)
6	264 (1.53)	262 (1.49)	265 (2.26)	223 (2.34)
7	270 (3.14)	270 (1.36)	270 (2.54)	221 (1.41)
8	278 (2.22)	276 (2.30)	277 (2.49)	219 (2.80)
9	285 (3.35)	284 (2.17)	284 (1.96)	215 (1.79)
10	292 (2.86)	291 (2.36)	291 (3.39)	215 (1.43)

Table 2. Summary of Analysis of Variance.

		F-Values			
		Total Sample		Stayer Sample	
Variable	DF	Longitudinal Pay-Performance	Cross-Sectional Pay-Performance	Longitudinal Pay-Performance	Cross-Sectional Pay-Performance
A. Time	9	1047.16**	23.73**	23.70**	3.77**
B. Pay System	3	113.53**	90.29**	833.58**	33.20**
C. Promotion	1	1143.26**	2364.80**	3110.89**	1452.98**
D. r(True/Obs. Perf.)	1	125.48**	458.34**	434.71**	479.30**
E. r(True/True Perf.)	1	17.45**	3.59	1138.59**	10.86**
A by B	27	2.50**	2.00*	15.78**	.86
A by C	9	29.26**	1.77	2.10	1.65
A by D	9	8.54**	1.24	.54	1.47
A by E	9	27.21**	.73	14.62**	1.50
B by C	3	21.66**	2.70	44.79**	2.70
B by D	3	1.32	.38	7.93**	.46
B by E	3	6.59**	3.26*	10.73**	2.51
C by D	1	1.26	12.18**	.49	10.30**
C by E	1	.002	.68	2.07	2.11
D by E	1	6.86**	.16	.37	.77
Explained	1	145.69**	42.36**	100.87**	26.79**
Residual Sum of Square		346,285	473,788	640,874	671,559
Total Sum of Square		993,072	731,063	1,472,812	903,087

* Significant at the .01 level; ** at the .001 level.

formance was .244. In the stayer sample the longitudinal and cross-sectional correlations were higher than in the total sample and almost identical (.447 for the longitudinal correlation and .422 for the cross-sectional correlation).

Analysis of variance was used to assess the effects of the treatments on the dependent variables. Each dependent variable was analyzed as a function of treatment main effects and interactions. Given the number of treatments, up to five-way interactions were permissible. For the analysis reported here, three-way and higher order interactions were pooled into the error sum of squares.

Table 2 shows a summary of the treatment main effects and two-way interactions for the two dependent variables and the two samples. Since the major focus of the study is the consequences of alternative reward systems through time, other treatments are discussed primarily only as they interact with variations in pay systems.[6]

Table 2 shows that there were statistically significant differences among the four pay systems in the correlation between true performance and pay, both in the cross-section and longitudinally. The mean correlations are shown in Table 3. In the cross-section for the total sample, the mean correlations for the conventional merit system and the across-the-board bonus are almost identical, as are the correlations for the uncapped merit and straight bonus. Among the stayers, the results are very similar for three of the four pay systems in the cross-section. Both merit systems outperformed both bonus systems longitudinally.

Table 2 also shows that there were statistically significant (p < .001) main time effects in the two samples for both measures of the relationship between pay and performance. Results for the first,

---

[6] Main effects for the other manipulated variables were completely as expected. The promotion rule ranking eligible employees from highest to lowest

performers produced higher pay-performance correlations than the rule choosing employees randomly. Similarly, higher pay-performance correlations were obtained when the measurement of performance contained less error and when true performance correlated more highly with true performance over time. All main effects for both dependent variables are statistically significant (p < .001).

Table 3. Average Pay-Performance Correlations Across Pay System, by Dependent Variable and Selected Times.

Dependent Variable	Merit		Bonus	
	Con-ventional	Un-capped	Across-the-Board	Straight
Total Sample				
longitudinal	.254	.262	.217	.245
cross-section	.373	.404	.367	.406
Stayers				
longitudinal	.504	.508	.357	.417
cross-section	.420	.434	.402	.432

sixth, and tenth time periods are shown in Table 4. In the total sample the average longitudinal correlation changed in a nonlinear fashion from .426 to .174 to .269. As the stayer data suggest, however, this change is due to the correlations for the new hires; among the stayers there is a modest linear increase in the longitudinal correlations over the ten periods. In the cross-section there is a modest decline over time for the total sample (.426 to .382 to .371) and a very modest U-shaped relationship among the stayers.

Of particular interest, given the purposes of this study, are pay system–time interactions. Table 2 shows that these interactions were significant in both samples for the longitudinal correlation and in the total sample for the cross-sectional correlation. Table 5 summarizes these results. It shows the average correlations by pay system for the first period (when the two correlations are the same), the sixth period, and the tenth period.

For the total sample the patterns over time across all four pay systems are

Table 4. Average Pay-Performance Correlations Across Time, by Dependent Variable.

Dependent Variable	Time Period		
	1	6	10
Total Sample			
longitudinal	.426	.174	.269
cross-section	.426	.382	.371
Stayers			
longitudinal	.428	.450	.476
cross-section	.428	.419	.434

similar, as the statistically significant but relatively small F-values suggest. Each system shows a nonlinear decline in the longitudinal correlation between pay and performance and a modest linear decline for the cross-sectional correlation. After the first period, the pay-performance correlation for the across-the-board bonus system is generally lower than that for the other three pay systems. Among only the stayers, the differences between the pay systems are more striking for the longitudinal correlation. The pay-performance correlation increases in all the pay systems except the across-the-board bonus, and the increases are much greater for the merit systems than for the straight bonus. By the tenth period, the longitudinal pay-performance correlation is .558 for the merit systems and .449 for the straight bonus.

The most noteworthy pattern over time in the longitudinal correlation is the difference between the bonus and merit systems. In later time periods the longitudinal pay-performance correlation is higher in the two merit systems than in the straight bonus system because, on average, high (low) performers obtain larger (smaller) prior pay increments and hence greater (lesser) subsequent pay increases in the merit systems. The declining correlations in the across-the-board bonus system are due to the pay adjustment that, over time, increasingly attenuates the longitudinal pay-performance relationship.

Measurement error. Given the gap between the two error specifications in this study (.3 and .6), one might anticipate a substantial resulting difference in the cross-section correlation between pay increase and performance, at least in the first period. Table 6 shows, on the contrary, that in both samples superior performance measurement results in only a .05 correlation point advantage over inferior measurement in the first time period. The small size of this difference is probably largely due to differences in starting salary level, holding performance level constant.

The modest difference associated with measurement error remains to period ten

Table 5. Average Pay-Performance Correlations Across Pay System, by Selected Dependent Variable and Time.

Time Period	Dependent Variable	Merit		Bonus	
		Conventional	Uncapped	Across-the-Board	Straight
Total Sample					
1st	Both	.420	.433	.424	.428
6th	Cross-section	.362	.408	.359	.399
	Longitudinal	.181	.191	.145	.178
10th	Cross-section	.350	.389	.345	.400
	Longitudinal	.277	.282	.238	.278
Stayers					
1st	Both	.421	.435	.425	.430
6th	Cross-section	.418	.438	.397	.422
	Longitudinal	.515	.522	.349	.414
10th	Cross-section	.435	.437	.409	.454
	Longitudinal	.557	.559	.340	.449

among stayers. In the total sample, however, it disappears because the effect of measurement error is overwhelmed by the modest relationship between pay and performance for new hires from the external labor market.

Discussion

Our major objective has been to investigate the effects of variations in merit pay systems and other firm internal labor market (FILM) characteristics on the relationship between employees' pay and their productivity, both in the cross-section and across time. To do so, we simulated a large number of managerial/professional labor forces using Monte Carlo techniques, experimentally manipulated certain pay system and other FILM characteristics, and, finally, observed the resulting relationships between pay and performance.

Table 6. Average Pay-Performance Correlations Across Measurement Error in the First and Tenth Periods.

Time Period	Measurement Error	
	.3	.6
Total Sample		
First	.401	.451
Tenth	.268	.270
Stayers		
First	.403	.454
Tenth	.443	.509

Several observations about the methodology are appropriate before discussing the results and major implications. As noted above, the use of a simulation allows us to assess the effects of variation in merit and other institutional practices and to study the effects of measurement error on the pay-performance relationship. Neither of these subjects could be effectively examined in case studies of the sort previously reported.

The use of a simulation methodology also carries disadvantages, of course. Most important, results from simulations will misrepresent what one could expect from field research unless the specification of the model mirrors institutional "reality" in important respects. To specify a realistic model, we obtained probable cross-sectional relationships between employee variables from prior field research. The similarity across these studies in relationships among important variables (for example, the relationship between observed performance and pay) provides some confidence in the generalizability of the relationships obtained here. Moreover, we sought to specify dynamic relationships (both the rates and functional form of turnover, for example) consistent with results from field studies.

There are, nevertheless, limits to the probable external validity of the findings. Although we varied several FILM characteristics other than merit rules, some of the variables that we held constant unquestionably influence pay-performance relationships in organizations. For example, variation in promotion opportunities, the size of promotion pay increments, and the relationship between promotion and performance would all combine to influence the strength of the relationship between pay and performance. These, in turn, are functions of still other variables, such as turnover rates and changes in organizations' size and shape through time (see, for example, Stewman and Konda 1983).

It is particularly important to note that our results were obtained in a stable labor force environment. Labor force growth or decline would tend to strengthen or weaken the pay-performance relationship because, on average, promotion is positively correlated with performance. Further, the salary maximum cap on the conventional merit system would be relatively less (more) influential if the labor force were increasing (decreasing).

It is also important to note that we made employee performance growth a function of experience, but not of the monetary rewards received. The results may, thus, over- or under-estimate actual relationships if performance is endogenous to reward system rules. We believe that our method is an appropriate first step because of ambiguity about how pay may influence performance (compare Adams 1964 with Vroom 1964) and because of the modest relationships observed between pay and performance in field studies (for example, Schwab, Olian-Gotlieb, and Heneman 1979).

Subject to the potential constraints identified, a number of interesting results were obtained from this exercise. The modest size of the pay-performance relationships we observed is an important result both theoretically and practically. Performance variation never accounted for much more than 25% of the variance in pay increments in any pay system, even in the cross-section. Although these results are not particularly surprising in light of the results of prior field research and nonempirical speculation, they serve as a reminder that policies designed to link individual pay to productivity confront formidable obstacles.

At the same time, not too much should be made of the absolute magnitudes of the pay-performance relationship obtained here. Our sample of field studies that served as major inputs to parameter specification was small. Further, the correlations produced between starting pay and initial performance in our simulation were somewhat lower than the cross-sectional results reported in these field studies. These relationships have a direct effect on both the longitudinal and cross-sectional pay-performance correlations reported here.

Greater confidence can be placed in the *relative* effects we found for different pay practices and the other FILM characteristics that we manipulated. The magnitude of the pay-performance relationship at the beginning of the simulation was similar across pay systems and the other manipulated parameters, and other FILM characteristics that influenced the pay-performance relationship (such as turnover rates) were held constant across treatment conditions. Thus, the statistically significant differences between pay systems observed here can be safely attributed to differences built into our simulation.

Two results of this exercise are unexpected. The first unexpected outcome concerns the contrast between merit and one-shot bonus systems. Two arguments have been offered to suggest that bonus systems should outperform merit systems in relating pay to performance. First, attenuation of the pay-performance relationship in merit systems is expected because pay increments are built into subsequent base pay. This feature of merit pay, it has been reasoned, should at least attenuate the relationship between recent pay increments and performance (see, for example, Lawler 1981). Second, merit systems may constrain pay increases within salary ranges, again weakening the relationship between pay and performance.

This study provides no support for the first expectation. In the total sample the uncapped merit system linked current pay increments to current performance about as well as the straight bonus systems (and better than the across-the-board bonus system) in all time periods. The conventional merit system also performed as well as the straight bonus system longitudinally. In the sample of employees who remained in a FILM for the full ten periods (the "stayers"), both merit systems outperformed even the straight bonus longitudinally. As noted, we believe this result is due to the fact that true performance is fairly consistent over time and that the merit system, but not the bonus system, benefits from this consistency.

Very little support was found for the second explanation. Constraining merit pay increments to maintain the integrity of job level salary ranges did generally attenuate the pay-performance relationship in the cross-section relative to that in the uncapped system, but the differences between the two merit systems amounted to less than .01 in the longitudinal relationship between pay and performance. It should be noted, however, that the difference between the capped and uncapped merit systems is a function of the frequency and magnitude of the salary range adjustments in the capped merit system. In the present study, ranges were adjusted each period by the average value of the merit wage increase matrix. Reducing the size of the adjustment or adjusting the ranges less frequently would be expected to produce more dramatic differences between the capped and uncapped merit pay systems.

The second major unexpected result of this study has to do with the relative effects of measurement error. As noted earlier, both the practitioner literature and the academic human resource literature suggest that error in the measurement of performance is a major, if not the most serious, difficulty in maintaining a viable merit system. Measurement error obviously attenuates the relationship between true performance and pay; but we have found that effect to be relatively small.

We compared results when the correlation between true and observed performance was .6 (representing "accurate" measurement) and when it was .3 (representing "inaccurate" measurement). The resulting variation in the pay-performance relationship, however assessed, was substantially smaller than the difference between these two levels of measurement error when the other variables manipulated and left free to vary were included in the simulation. Indeed, in the total sample the pay-performance correlations produced in the presence of the two levels of measurement merged over time.[7] In the stayer sample, the effect of measurement error persisted over time, but was never large.

This study also brings some evidence to bear on the relative costs of the alternative pay systems. One rationale for range constraints on pay increases is to control total labor costs (see, for example, Milkovich and Newman 1987:395). Our results show that conventional merit systems are not necessarily less costly than systems that do not constrain pay increments. An uncapped merit system can result in costs comparable to those of conventional merit systems in an environment where periodic range increases are implemented in response to pressure on range ceilings or the cost of living if the organization is willing to increase variance below the mean wage as well as above it.[8] Further, where nominal wage increases are necessary to attract or retain a labor force, our results indicate that a bonus system may be no less costly than an uncapped merit system.

One other matter that deserves attention is the high sensitivity of the results to

---

[7] There are, of course, other reasons to be concerned about error in the performance measures used in individual pay systems. Employee perceptions of procedural justice may be as important as distributive justice in terms of their affective responses to pay systems (Folger and Greenberg 1985). The research here obviously addresses only issues associated with distributive justice.

[8] There may, however, be psychological costs to the uncapped systems, since there is evidence suggesting that both pay administrators and employees feel it is equitable for those earning more, performance constant, to receive smaller increments (see, for example, Birnbaum 1983).

the sample studied. Large differences in the pay-performance relationship as a function of pay system were observed only among stayers, and only in the longitudinal analysis. In the total sample, effect sizes were relatively modest, even though highly significant in a statistical sense. These differences by sample, in turn, suggest that the rules for paying new entrants and the quality of entrants can have a substantial impact on the apparent effectiveness of pay systems designed to differentially reward employees once they are in the organization.

This study has allowed us to address a number of issues about the effects of pay systems on the pay-performance relationship that are very difficult to approach in field research. It may have been supposed that since we determined the relationships between the different variables when building the simulation, the results from the simulation were easy to predict and could not have contributed substantially to the understanding of pay systems. On the contrary, however, this study has provided some evidence at variance with assumptions commonly expressed in the academic literature and by many practitioners. First, we find that merit systems perform very well when compared to bonus systems when individual performance is assumed to be fairly consistent over time. Second, we find that measurement error in evaluations of employees' performance has only a modest effect on the pay-performance relationship in the context of the institutional pay-setting process. Although the magnitude of these effects is undoubtedly sensitive to the construction of the simulation, these results have important implications for organizational practice and future research on pay systems.

Appendix

Description of the Simulation

Each of the 32 cells in the 4×2^3 design included 20 firms with 100-employee labor forces in the managerial/professional internal labor market that were followed for ten time periods. This appendix describes how these labor forces were established at the beginning of the simulation and the construction of the ten-period simulation.

Initial Conditions of the Organizations

The initial characteristics of the 100 employees in each firm were defined along six dimensions: (1) firm tenure, (2) job tenure, (3) true performance, (4) observed performance, (5) annual salary, and (6) job level within the organization. Several steps were followed to create these data. First, a 100×4 matrix of standard, normally distributed variables was created in which the four columns correspond to the data that were subsequently transformed into observed performance, firm tenure, job tenure, and job level. (See Figure A1.)

Transformations. Resulting standard, normally distributed values were transformed in several steps. First, employees were assigned to one of the seven job levels based on the value of the normally distributed vector corresponding to job level. The breakpoints used to create the organizational structure were $-.524$, $.253$, $.6745$, 1.00, 1.476, and 2.05. This process created a hierarchical job structure. The initial salary grades for the seven levels were as shown in Figure A2.

Second, firm tenure was created by dividing the employees into intervals with the distributions shown in Figure A3. The tenure classification was based on the value of the normal vector corresponding to firm tenure. Individuals were then uniformly distributed within their assigned interval. Third, job tenure was constructed using the same process as that used to create firm tenure (see Figure A4). Finally, job tenure was set equal to organizational tenure where the preceding steps produced a value for job tenure that was greater than that for firm tenure.

Initial pay. A two-step process was used to construct pay for each employee at t_0. First, an initial value was constructed as a linear function of observed performance, firm tenure, firm tenure squared, job tenure, and job level. Second, a normally distributed random error term was then added to this linear function to produce an R^2 of approximately .5 when pay was regressed on the tenure, performance, and job level variables. The R^2 from this process was only approximately .5 and the regression weights from an OLS wage estimate are only roughly comparable to the linear weights shown above because the regression weights depend on the correlations between the independent variables.

Pay constructed in the preceding steps created a few values that fell outside the salary ranges for the individual's job level. In these cases the individuals were moved to the nearest job level with a salary grade that included their pay. For the very small number of individuals with pay either above the salary maximum for grade seven or below the

Observed Performance	1.0	.04	.00	.12
Firm Tenure		1.0	.60	.35
Job Tenure			1.0	.15
Job Level				1.0

Figure A1. The Correlation Matrix.

Level 1	Min.	Max.	% of Work Force
Level 1	15,000	25,000	30
Level 2	16,875	28,125	30
Level 3	18,984	31,641	15
Level 4	21,357	35,596	9
Level 5	24,027	40,045	9
Level 6	27,030	45,051	5
Level 7	30,409	50,682	2

Figure A2. Initial Salary Grades for the Seven Job Levels.

minimum for grade one, pay was adjusted to equal the maximum (minimum) for grade seven (one).

Performance. Observed performance was equal to the random normal vector created in the first step of the simulation. True performance was created such that the correlation between true and observed performance was equal to one of the two treatment values (see below). Like observed performance, true performance was normally distributed.

The Simulation Process

The following sequence of events occurred in each time period for each organization in each of the cells: (1) true and observed performance for the period were determined; (2) turnover in the organization occurred; (3) promotion decisions were made to fill the vacancies created by turnover in job levels 2 through 7; (4) wage or bonus decisions (or both) were made; (5) vacancies not filled in levels 2 through 7 by promotion were filled with external labor market hires; and (6) vacancies in level 1 created by either turnover or promotion were filled from the external labor market. The organization then began the next time period and the preceding six steps were repeated for a total of ten periods. The remainder of this appendix describes these six steps in greater detail.

True and observed performance. True performance in period t for an individual was equal to:

$$TP_t = (t-1)(.1) + ITP + (1-rho^2)^{1/2} * v_t,$$

where ITP is underlying true performance for the employee, rho equals the correlation of true performance between periods (.8 or .5), and v is a random variable drawn from the standard, normal distribu-

Firm Tenure	Cumulative Percentage of Sample
<=2.5	9
<=7.5	30
<=12.5	51
<=17.5	70
<=22.5	82
<=27.5	90
<=32.5	96
<=37.5	98

Figure A3. Distribution of Employees by Firm Tenure.

Job Tenure	Cumulative Percentage of Sample
<=1.5	22
<=3.0	42
<=4.5	60
<=6.0	82
<=7.5	90
<=9.0	98

Figure A4. Distribution of Employees by Job Tenure.

tion. This formula ensures that the variance in true performance is constant from one period to the next. The intercept of .1 shifts the true performance of the employee upward by .1 of a standard deviation. This shift moves an employee who is at the mean to the 54th percentile of the performance distribution from the preceding period.

Observed performance was created from TP and the variance of observed performance was also held constant. The correlation between true and observed performance in any period was set equal to .34 or .67. When true or observed performance was then transformed into Performance Appraisal Scores (see below), the correlation between true and observed Performance Appraisal Scores was equal to one of the two manipulation levels, .3 or .6.

Turnover. The probability of turnover for each employee was a decreasing function of firm tenure and was equal to the following Weibull function:

$$Pr(turnover) = (.25)(.7)(Firm\ tenure)^{(.7-1)}$$

The turnover probability for each individual was compared with a random draw from a [0,1] uniform distribution. The individual left the organization if this random number was less than or equal to his or her turnover probability.

Promotions. Two promotion policies were followed. Under each policy the pool of eligible applicants for promotion to a higher level were those one level lower with at least one period of job tenure. Under the first policy, openings were filled in each level by promoting those with the highest observed level of performance. Under the second policy, those promoted were randomly selected from the eligible pool. If there was an insufficient number of eligible individuals to fill openings created by turnover, the remaining openings were filled from the external labor market using the method described below.

Wage decisions. In all four pay policy cells, individuals who were promoted moved up one salary grade and received a 15% wage increase, subject to constraints (salary grade minimums and maximums) of the pay system. The pay increase for those not promoted depended on the salary system treatment.

In the conventional merit treatment, salary minimums and maximums for each of the seven salary grades were increased by 3.5% each year. The salary increase for an individual who was not promoted was based on a merit pay system subject to the new minimum and maximum of the individual's salary grade. A forced, five-point performance appraisal score was created based on observed performance.

The distribution across the five performance ranges and the merit increases for each range were as shown in Figure A5. When these merit increases moved employees out of their salary range, their salary was adjusted upward (downward) to the salary range minimum (maximum).

The uncapped merit treatment was identical to the capped merit system except that merit and promotion wage increases were not constrained by the salary grade minimums and maximums.

In the across-the-board bonus system, a 3.5% increase was given in periods 2 through 10 for those not promoted. These increases were not constrained by the minimum and maximum salary grades. In addition, in periods 1 through 10 bonus payments were given based on the performance appraisal results. The across-the-board increase in periods 2 through 10 ensures that the total wage bill in this bonus system is comparable to the wage bill in the merit systems.

In the straight bonus system there was no adjustment in base pay except through the promotion process. Bonus payments were based on the

performance appraisal results. For employees who were promoted, the bonus was based on the new base salary. Bonuses were unconstrained by the minimums and maximums of the salary grades.

External hires. Vacancies in level one (the lowest level) created by either turnover or promotion were filled from the external labor market. In addition, if the number of eligible incumbents in a level was not sufficient to fill vacancies in the next highest level, the unfilled vacancies were also filled from the external labor market. The mean and standard deviations of observed performance of those hired from the external labor market were equal to the mean and standard deviations of incumbents in the grade at the start of the period (before turnover occurs). Thus, hires from the external labor market had only a minimal impact on the average quality of the work force. New hires were paid the salary grade minimum.

Descriptive Statistics

Tables A1 and A2 provide descriptive statistics across the 32 cells for each time period for a sample run of the simulation program. Table 1 reports data on firm size following turnover, the number of employees who turned over, the number promoted, mean observed and true performance, and mean cumulative true and observed performance. Table 2 reports the mean number of employees at each job level for each of the ten periods. In both of these tables the standard deviation reported is for the 32 cell means and not the standard deviation across all of the firms in a cell (32 treatment cells × 20 firms).

	Performance Appraisal Score			
	1–2	2–3	3–4	4–5
Percent of Work Force	20	25	35	20
Merit Increase (%)	2	3	4	5

Figure A5. Percent of Work Force and Merit Increase by Performance Appraisal Scores.

Table A1. Mean Values Across All 32 Cells by Time Period.
(Standard Deviations in Parentheses)

Period	Firm Size	No. T/O	No. Promoted	Observed Perf.	True Perf.	Cum. TP	Cum OP
1	91.84	8.16	5.66	−.01	.001	.001	−.010
	(0.56)	(0.56)	(0.47)	(.027)	(.022)	(.022)	(.027)
2	91.41	8.59	5.78	.098	.100	.103	.091
	(.66)	(.66)	(.54)	(.030)	(.025)	(.039)	(.043)
3	91.09	8.91	5.96	.186	.192	.289	.272
	(.54)	(.54)	(.38)	(.038)	(.025)	(.055)	(.069)
4	90.74	9.26	6.08	.229	.301	.568	.551
	(.53)	(.53)	(.55)	(.028)	(.019)	(.061)	(.081)
5	90.61	9.39	6.05	.401	.403	.931	.915
	(.85)	(.85)	(.71)	(.031)	(.020)	(.073)	(.090)
6	90.54	9.46	6.08	.514	.511	1.366	1.355
	(.71)	(.71)	(.50)	(.029)	(.027)	(.089)	(.099)
7	90.58	9.42	5.99	.609	.610	1.871	1.859
	(.67)	(.67)	(.48)	(.024)	(.023)	(.104)	(.112)
8	90.52	9.48	6.01	.720	.727	2.450	2.433
	(.72)	(.72)	(.61)	(.032)	(.022)	(.119)	(.129)
9	90.44	9.56	6.05	.828	.837	3.089	3.063
	(.79)	(.79)	(.64)	(.028)	(.025)	(.134)	(.140)
10	90.51	9.49	6.02	.955	.955	3.797	3.777
	(.79)	(.79)	(.59)	(.037)	(.026)	(.146)	(.155)

Table A2. Mean Number of Workers Across the 32 Cells by Job Level and Time Period.
(Standard Deviations in Parentheses)

Period	1	2	3	4	5	6	7
1	24.20	24.51	16.10	10.41	9.14	5.21	2.28
	(0.88)	(1.09)	(0.90)	(0.68)	(0.61)	(0.53)	(0.27)
2	23.97	24.44	16.04	10.36	9.12	5.20	2.28
	(0.88)	(0.92)	(0.91)	(0.69)	(0.65)	(0.53)	(0.27)
3	23.69	24.41	16.03	10.35	9.13	5.21	2.28
	(0.80)	(0.97)	(0.91)	(0.68)	(0.62)	(0.54)	(0.27)
4	23.44	24.41	16.02	10.29	9.08	5.22	2.28
	(0.81)	(0.90)	(0.86)	(0.68)	(0.57)	(0.55)	(0.27)
5	23.24	24.50	16.02	10.30	9.12	5.16	2.28
	(1.03)	(0.96)	(0.84)	(0.64)	(0.64)	(0.54)	(0.27)
6	23.17	24.45	16.00	10.32	9.11	5.21	2.27
	(0.81)	(0.98)	(0.89)	(0.68)	(0.64)	(0.55)	(0.27)
7	23.17	24.43	16.00	10.38	9.12	5.21	2.28
	(0.90)	(0.91)	(0.89)	(0.67)	(0.62)	(0.54)	(0.27)
8	23.09	24.48	16.02	10.31	9.11	5.23	2.28
	(0.90)	(0.89)	(0.82)	(0.72)	(0.61)	(0.53)	(0.27)
9	23.06	24.49	16.01	10.33	9.07	5.22	2.27
	(0.98)	(1.03)	(0.81)	(0.72)	(0.60)	(0.53)	(0.26)
10	23.08	24.42	16.06	10.37	9.09	5.21	2.28
	(0.84)	(1.04)	(0.81)	(0.67)	(0.65)	(0.54)	(0.27)

REFERENCES

Abraham, K. G., and J. L. Medoff. 1985. "Length of Service and Promotions in Union and Nonunion Work Groups." *Industrial and Labor Relations Review,* Vol. 38, No. 3, pp. 408–20.

Adams, J. S. 1963. "Toward an Understanding of Inequity." *Journal of Abnormal and Social Psychology,* Vol. 67, No. 5, pp. 422–36.

Althauser, R. P., and A. L. Kalleberg. 1981. "Firms, Occupations and the Structure of Labor Markets." In I. Berg, ed., *Sociological Perspectives on Labor Markets.* New York: Academic Press, pp. 119–49.

Auster, E. R., and R. Drazin. 1987. *The Persistence of Sex Inequality at Higher Levels in the Hierarchy: An Intraorganizational Perspective.* Unpublished paper, Columbia University.

Basnight, T. A. 1980. "Designing Master, or 'Ideal', Pay-Performance Matrices." *Compensation Review,* Vol. 12, No. 4, pp. 44–50.

Birnbaum, M. H. 1983. "Perceived Equity of Salary Policies." *Journal of Applied Psychology,* Vol. 68, No. 1, pp. 49–59.

Borman, W. C. 1978. "Exploring Upper Limits of Reliability and Validity in Job Performance Ratings." *Journal of Applied Psychology,* Vol. 63, No. 2, pp. 135–44.

Bureau of National Affairs. 1984. *Productivity Improvement Programs.* Personnel Policies Forum. Washington, D.C.: BNA.

Bureau of National Affairs. 1981. *Wage and Salary Administration.* Personnel Policies Forum. Washington, D.C.: BNA.

Cotton, J. L., and J. M. Tuttle. 1986. "Employee Turnover: A Meta-Analysis and Review with Implications for Research." *Academy of Management Review,* Vol. 11, No. 1, pp. 55–70.

Doyel, H. W., and J. L. Johnson. 1985. "Pay Increase Guidelines with Merit." *Personnel Journal,* Vol. 64, No. 6, pp. 46–49.

Ehrenberg, R. G., and G. T. Milkovich. 1987. "Compensation and Firm Performance." In M. Kleiner et al., eds., *Human Resources and the Performance of the Firm.* Madison, Wis.: IRRA, pp. 87–122.

Evans, W. A. 1970. "Pay for Performance: Fact or Fable." *Personnel Journal,* Vol. 49, No. 9, pp. 726–31.

Folger, R., and J. Greenberg. 1985. "Procedural Justice: An Interpretive Analysis of Personnel Systems." In K. Rowland and G. Ferris, eds., *Research in Personnel and Human Resources Management,* Vol. 3. Greenwich, Conn.: JAI Press, pp. 141–83.

Foulkes, F. K. 1980. *Personnel Policies in Large Nonunion Companies.* Englewood Cliffs, N.J.: Prentice-Hall.

Gerhart, B. A., and G. T. Milkovich. 1989. "Salaries, Salary Growth, and Promotions of Men and Women in a Large Private Firm." In R. T. Michael and H. I. Hartmann, eds., *Pay Equity: Empirical Inquiries.* Washington, D.C.: National Academy Press, pp. 23–43.

Hansen, W. L. 1988. "Merit Pay in Structured and Unstructured Salary Systems." *Academe,* Vol. 74, No. 6, pp. 10–13.

Heneman, R. L. In press. "Merit Pay Research." In K. M. Rowland and G. R. Ferris, eds., *Research in Personnel and Human Resource Management,* Vol. 8. Greenwich, Conn.: JAI Press.

Heneman, H. G., III. 1973. "Impact of Performance on Managerial Pay Levels and Pay Changes."

Journal of Applied Psychology, Vol. 58, No. 1, pp. 128–30.

Hills, F. S. 1987. *Compensation Decision Making.* Chicago: Dryden.

Hills, F. S., R. M. Madigan, K. D. Scott, and S. E. Markham. 1987. "Tracking the Merit of Merit Pay." *Personnel Administrator,* Vol. 32. No. 3, pp. 50–57.

Hills, F. S., D. K. Scott, S. E. Markham, and M. J. Vest. 1987. "Merit Pay: Just or Unjust Desserts." *Personnel Administrator,* Vol. 32, No. 1, pp. 53–59.

Ilgen, D. R., and J. M. Feldman. 1983. "Performance Appraisal: A Process Focus." In B. Staw and L. L. Cummings, eds., *Research in Organizational Behavior,* Vol. 5, pp. 141–97.

Johnson, M., and K. Kasten. 1983. "Meritorious Work and Faculty Rewards: An Empirical Test of the Relationship." *Research in Higher Education,* Vol. 19, No. 1, pp. 49–71.

Kahn, L., and P. Sherer. 1988. "How Does Merit Pay Induce Higher Performance? A Test of Expectancy and Efficiency Wage Theories." Paper delivered at the National Academy Meetings, Anaheim, Calif.

Kanter, R. M. 1987. "From Status to Contribution: Some Organizational Implications of the Changing Basis of Pay." *Personnel,* Vol. 82, No. 1, pp. 12–37.

Katz, D. A. 1973. "Faculty Salaries, Promotions, and Productivity at a Large University." *American Economic Review,* Vol. 63, No. 3, pp. 469–77.

Landy, F. J., and J. L. Farr. 1980. "Performance Rating." *Psychological Bulletin,* Vol. 87, No. 1, pp. 72–107.

Lawler, E. E. 1981. "Merit Pay: Fact or Fiction?" *Pay and Organization Development.* Reading, Mass.: Addison-Wesley.

Lawler, E. E. 1971. *Pay and Organizational Effectiveness.* New York: McGraw-Hill.

Markham, W. T., S. L. Harlan, and E. J. Hackett. 1987. "Promotion Opportunity in Organizations: Causes and Consequences." In K. M. Rowland and G. R. Ferris, *Research in Personnel and Human Resource Management,* Vol. 5. Greenwich, Conn.: JAI Press.

Medoff, J. L., and K. G. Abraham. 1981. "Are Those Paid More Really More Productive? The Case of Experience." *Journal of Human Resources,* Vol. 16, No. 2, pp. 186–216.

Medoff, J. L., and K. G. Abraham. 1980. "Experi-

ence, Performance, and Earnings." *The Quarterly Journal of Economics,* Vol. 95, No. 4, pp. 703–36.

Milkovich, G. T., and J. M. Newman. 1987. *Compensation.* Plano, Tex.: Business Publications.

Mills, D. Q. 1985. "Seniority Versus Ability in Promotion Decisions." *Industrial and Labor Relations Review,* Vol. 38, No. 3, pp. 421–425.

O'Dell, C. 1987. *People, Performance and Pay.* Houston, Tex.: American Productivity Center.

Osterman, P. 1984. "White-collar Internal Labor Markets." In P. Osterman, ed., *Internal Labor Markets.* Cambridge, Mass.: MIT Press, pp. 163–89.

Peck, C. 1984. *Pay and Performance.* New York: The Conference Board, Research Bulletin No. 155.

Personick, M. E. 1984. "White-Collar Pay Determination Under Range-of-Rate Systems." *Monthly Labor Review,* Vol. 107, No. 12, pp. 25–30.

Price, J. L. 1977. *The Study of Turnover.* Ames, Iowa: Iowa State University Press.

Rosenbaum, J. E. 1979. "Organizational Career Mobility: Promotion Chances in a Corporation During Periods of Growth and Contraction." *American Journal of Sociology,* Vol. 85, No. 1, pp. 21–48.

Schwab, D. P. 1988. "Predicting Salary Levels and Salary Increments: An Examination of Merit System Equities." Paper delivered at the National Academy Meetings, Anaheim, Calif.

Schwab, Donald P., Judy D. Olian-Gottlieb, and Herbert G. Heneman III. 1979. "Between-Subjects Expectancy Theory Research: A Statistical Review of Studies Predicting Effort and Performance." *Psychological Bulletin,* Vol. 86, No. 1, p. 139–47.

Stewman, S., and S. L. Konda. 1983. "Careers and Organizational Labor Markets: Demographic Models of Organizational Behavior." *American Journal of Sociology,* Vol. 88, No. 4, pp. 637–85.

Stokes, D. M. 1981. "A New Mathematical Approach to Merit-Based Compensation Systems." *Compensation Review,* Vol. 13, No. 4, pp. 43–55.

Strauss, G. 1986. *Participatory and Gainsharing Systems: History and Hope.* Paper presented at the Johnson Foundation Wingspread Conference, Racine, Wis.

Vroom, V. H. 1964. *Work and Motivation.* New York: Wiley.

Wallace, M. J., Jr., and C. H. Fay. 1983. *Compensation Theory and Practice.* Boston: Kent.

Winstanley, N. B. 1972. Comment on Pattern's "Pay for Performance or Placation." *Personnel Administrator,* Vol. 23, No. 5, pp. 49–52.

PROFIT SHARING AND EMPLOYMENT STABILITY

JAMES CHELIUS and ROBERT S. SMITH*

This paper tests the hypothesis that workers whose compensation packages contain a profit-sharing component are less susceptible to layoff in the face of negative shocks to product demand than are workers paid a fixed, time-based wage. The theory is tested on two data sets, one a household survey and the other a survey of small businesses conducted by the authors. The characteristics of profit sharing among small businesses by and large meet the theoretical requirements for stabilizing employment, and the authors do find evidence in both samples to support the hypothesis; the evidence, however, is of borderline statistical significance and is therefore more suggestive than definitive.

A N intriguing policy prescription gener-ated from economic theory recently is the advocacy of profit sharing as a means to combat unemployment. The idea that extensive use of profit sharing in compensating workers could reduce unemployment publicly surfaced with the publication, in 1984, of Martin Weitzman's *The*

Share Economy (Weitzman 1984). Since then, a lively debate has developed in Great Britain, where the government has implemented a policy to stimulate the use of profit sharing for purposes of combating unemployment.[1] In the United States, this policy prescription has been debated (Mitchell 1987; Nuti 1987) but not yet widely researched. Some Democratic politicians began to raise the policy issue in at least a tentative way, however, during the 1988 Presidential campaign (Murray 1987).

The major purpose of this paper is to empirically investigate the effects of profit sharing on the employment of nonsupervisory workers in firms facing reduced demand. After considering whether the characteristics of profit-sharing plans in the United States typically meet the requisite conditions for employment stabilization, we present tests of the theory on two quite different sets of data. First, the effects of profit sharing on employment stability in the face of negative demand

* James Chelius is Professor of Industrial Relations, Institute of Management and Labor Relations, Rutgers University, and Robert S. Smith is Professor of Industrial and Labor Relations, New York State School of Industrial and Labor Relations, Cornell University.

The authors thank Denny Dennis of the NFIB Foundation and David Wray and John Bell of the Profit Sharing Research Foundation for providing access to their memberships for purposes of the survey. John Matzner, Research Director of the National Foundation for Unemployment Compensation and Workers' Compensation, provided invaluable services as a coordinator among all parties involved in the survey, including the U.S. Small Business Administration, which granted funds in support of this project. The authors also thank Phil Ulan for research assistance and Professors Ronald Ehrenberg, Daniel Hamermesh, Douglas Kruse, and Martin Weitzman for helpful comments.

Readers interested in obtaining the data used in this study should contact Robert Smith, School of Industrial and Labor Relations, Cornell University, Ithaca, NY 14853.

[1] See Parliament of the United Kingdom (1986); Blanchflower and Oswald (1987a); Estrin, Grout, and Wadhwani (1987); Jackman (1987); Standing (1988); and Estrin and Wilson (1989).

shocks are directly estimated with data from a special survey of approximately 4,000 small businesses in the United States. Second, the effects of profit sharing on the probability of being laid off are investigated using a household data set.

Profit Sharing and the Demand for Labor

Profit Sharing with a Wage Guarantee: the Long Run

Judging from the predominance of their use in the United States, it would seem that time-based nominal wages that are generally downward-inflexible are preferred by firms and workers. It can be argued, however, that such wage guarantees come at a high social cost: persistent unemployment caused by the adjustment (in the short run, at least) of employment levels, rather than wages, to negative demand shocks. Would a system that combined a fixed wage guarantee with a profit-sharing component yield more employment stability?

In answering this question theoretically, we must first remember that no matter what "mix" of guaranteed and share wages a firm offers its workers, workers' expected total compensation with an employer must be enough to attract (and keep) them away from alternative places of employment. It is true that if employees prefer wage stability, which entails the risk of employment variability over a business cycle, to a system that yields variable earnings (and perhaps greater stability of employment), then the latter system would have to be accompanied by a compensating wage differential to offset its perceived disadvantages to workers. The central point, however, is that the total compensation a share firm must pay its workers is ultimately market-determined.[2] In what

follows, this market-clearing level of compensation will be denoted by W^*.

If a profit-sharing firm wants to offer W_g as a guaranteed time-based wage, it must select its profit-sharing parameter (s", say) so that when the share component is added to W_g the sum brings workers' expected pay up to W^*. In the simple case in which the profit-sharing pool is split equally among workers, the total payments to each worker must satisfy the following condition:

$$(1) \quad W_g + \frac{s"(PQ^* - W_g L^* - CK^*)}{L^*} = W^*$$

where P is the price at which output can be sold and Q^*, L^*, and K^* are, respectively, the profit-maximizing levels of output, labor, and capital. The expression in parentheses in equation (1), of course, is expected profits as calculated before share payments are made to workers; multiplying it by s" and dividing it by L^* yields the per-worker bonus.

Thus, in deciding its optimum scale of output and optimum levels and mix of capital and labor, a firm paying its workers under a hybrid profit-sharing system will regard the market wage rate (W^*) as its long-run cost of obtaining labor. Once its optimum output and levels of inputs are determined, it can set its guaranteed wage and profit-sharing parameter passively— solving equation (1) to ensure that its workers' earnings are equivalent to this market-determined wage.

It is important to understand that, at the firm's profit-maximizing level of employment, the marginal revenue product of labor (product price, P, times labor's marginal physical product, MP_L)[3] must equal the market wage. If the marginal

---

[2] Firms might choose to offer profit sharing and pay a compensating differential if they believe that such a pay system will enhance worker productivity or reduce turnover costs by raising worker loyalty to the firm. Our survey, as well as one by Mitchell and Broderick (1988), suggests that increased productivity and employee loyalty are commonly, but by no means universally, thought to accompany profit

sharing. A comprehensive review of empirical findings regarding profit sharing's effects on employee productivity is presented by Weitzman and Kruse (1989), who find a positive association between profit sharing and productivity; they believe, however, that the results of the various studies are more suggestive than definitive.

[3] For expositional convenience, the profit-maximizing conditions are discussed in the context of a competitive firm.

revenue product of labor exceeds the market wage for labor (W^*) the firm will want to expand its operations, hire more labor, and produce more output in the long run. Similarly, if the firm's marginal revenue product of labor is less than the going wage, it could improve its long-run profits by planning to reduce employment and its scale of output.[4] Thus, the only time the firm is satisfied with its long-run levels of output and employment is when the marginal revenue product of labor is equal to the market wage:

$$(2) \qquad P\ MP_L = W^*$$

Profit-Sharing with a Wage Guarantee: The Short Run

In the short run (when K^*, W_g, and s" are all fixed), a firm with a hybrid profit-sharing system will find that, abstracting from hiring costs, if it adds an extra worker to its work force it bears the cost of the guaranteed wage, W_g, plus a fraction (s") of the resulting addition to profit. Thus, its marginal cost of labor (MC_L) is as follows:

$$(3) \quad MC_L = W_g + s"\ (P\ MP_L - W_g)$$

In equation (3), the expression $P\ MP_L - W_g$ represents the *addition* to the firm's profits (before sharing) caused by hiring one more worker. Because the marginal revenue product of labor is equal to the market wage for a profit-maximizing firm, and because the guaranteed wage must lie below the market wage, the term $P\ MP_L - W_g$ must clearly be greater than zero when the firm is producing its long-run, profit-maximizing level of output.

The firm will want to hire an additional worker in the short run if the marginal revenue product of labor exceeds the marginal cost. That is, the firm will want to continue hiring as long as the following condition is met:

$$(4) \quad P\ MP_L > W_g + s"(P\ MP_L - W_g)$$

Rearranging expression (4), it can be shown that the firm paying on a profit-sharing basis will find it can enhance profits by hiring an additional worker as long as labor's marginal revenue product exceeds the guaranteed wage:

$$(5) \qquad P\ MP_L(1-s") > W_g(1-s"),$$
$$\text{or } P\ MP_L > W_g$$

Intuitively, as long as $P\ MP_L > W_g$, the firm is able to keep a fraction $(1-s")$ of any additional net revenues generated by a new employee.

Implications for Employment

At first blush, it is tempting to conclude that a profit-sharing firm will be "labor-hungry" and always on the lookout for workers to add to its payrolls. A powerful incentive to hire more labor would appear to exist, even at the optimum. Indeed, the notion that profit-sharing firms will always be labor-hungry and will therefore exhibit greater employment growth is very explicit in Weitzman (1984).

Theory, however, does not support the implication that profit-sharing firms will behave differently from those paying time-based wages in the long run. Both types of firms must have roughly equal compensation levels in the long run,[5] and facing the same long-run prices for capital and labor will cause them to choose the same K^* and L^*. In the short run, a profit-sharing firm in a market with full employment faces two problems in expanding beyond L^*: attracting new workers and keeping the ones it has. Both problems are created by the fact that, with MP_L falling and s" fixed, hiring beyond L^* reduces total compensation per worker *below* W^*.[6]

---

[4] If the firm finds it is not maximizing profits, it will recalculate its optimum output and employment levels and reset its share parameter to yield—at these new levels—a level of compensation its employees could obtain elsewhere.

[5] If profit-sharing firms must pay a compensating wage differential, then total compensation in profit-sharing firms must be higher. The main point, however, is that long-run compensation levels are market-determined.

[6] Because MP_L falls as more workers are hired, additions to the pool of profits set aside for profit sharing are smaller than the average bonus paid

The really important implication to come out of our analysis of the profit-sharing firm concerns how it will behave in a business downturn. Suppose we assume that a firm operating at its long-run profit-maximizing scale of output is faced with a decline in product demand. If it pays its workers entirely with guaranteed (fixed) wages equal to the market wage (W^*), its original marginal revenue product of labor will equal W^*; thus, when the fall in product-market demand reduces labor's marginal revenue product, the latter will fall below W^* and the firm will lay off workers.

The firm paying under a profit-sharing system will not be as quick to reduce employment. If the profit-sharing firm starts from a position in which labor's marginal revenue product equals W^*, its guaranteed wage will lie below the original marginal revenue product of labor:

(6) $P\, MP_L > W_g$

The business downturn facing the firm will cause a fall in labor's marginal revenue product (the left-hand side of expression 6), but the firm will not have incentives to reduce its employment level unless the *new* marginal revenue product falls below W_g. Layoffs do not automatically result from a fall in product demand, therefore, and theory thus predicts that workers in some profit-sharing firms—those in which marginal revenue productivity does not fall below W_g—are "cushioned" against being let go when the firm faces adversity.

Share workers' earnings, of course, are depressed by the fall in total revenues and the absence of layoffs (a smaller pool is shared by the same number of employees). Workers in the firm may want to leave when their earnings are cut, but if the recessionary fall in product demand that created this situation is economy-wide, there may be few job offers elsewhere; thus, moving to a new job may be difficult. Under a profit-sharing system, then, workers have a good measure of

employment stability over a business cycle, but the earnings of those who remain employed are likely to be more variable than they would be under the more conventional wage system.[7]

It is important to note that to have a measurable effect on employment in sectors facing reduced demand, profit-sharing payments must be both cyclically variable and substantial in size. The larger the bonuses paid by a firm operating at its optimum level in the long run, the greater is the "gap" between labor's marginal revenue product and W_g, and the greater the employment security that is afforded employees.

Employment security, however, is also the result of a compensation package with a *variable* component in it. Although a profit-sharing scheme with a fixed share parameter (s" above) guarantees procyclically variable bonuses, it will be seen below that most U.S. firms with profit sharing do not calculate share payments using a fixed parameter. To the extent that share distributions are purely *ad hoc* (as opposed to being calculated according to a predetermined formula), and the firm decides to keep per-worker distributions constant over a business cycle, profit sharing loses its employment stabilizing effects. A fixed per-worker share payment will have the same effects on employment as a fixed wage.

Empirical Studies of Profit Sharing and Labor Demand

Perhaps the most obvious country in which to study the employment effects of profit sharing is Japan. Large firms in Japan pay their "regular" employees (who constitute half to three-quarters of their workers) a guaranteed salary plus a semi-annual bonus that typically amounts to

---

out—which serves to decrease the amounts paid per worker.

[7] Weitzman advocates the use of tax incentives to induce *widespread* adoption of "share" wage systems. If a substantial number of employees were paid share wages, he argues, the economy as a whole would be more recession-proof because employment would be more stable. Hence, actual wage reduction might be fairly rare. Cooper (1988) analyzes the normative aspects of widespread profit sharing.

about 25 percent of yearly pay. These bonuses, although large, are not completely tied to profits. In fact, two estimates of the elasticity of bonuses with respect to profits (Freeman and Weitzman 1987; Wadhwani 1985) suggest that these elasticities are only in the range of 0.10 to 0.15. Thus, if profits were to fall to zero from their normal levels, and if bonuses are normally 25 percent of pay, a mere 2 to 4 percent reduction in employee compensation would ensue. Although this reduction may be enough to generate some employment stability, it is not clear how much of an effect can be reasonably anticipated.

Freeman and Weitzman (1987) used aggregate, time series data to analyze employment effects in Japan, and they found that employment responded positively to the size of per-worker bonuses and negatively to the level of wages, holding aggregate employer revenues and previous employment levels constant. One interpretation of this finding is that employment grew when profit sharing was used more extensively. Because Freeman and Weitzman measured actual bonuses rather than the share parameter (s" in equation 1 above), however, it could be argued that bonuses acted as a more precise control for yearly business conditions than revenues alone. If so, it might be the case that the level of bonuses and the level of employment were both responding to a common causal variable.

Wadhwani (1985) tested the proposition that greater flexibility in Japanese compensation helps to stabilize prices and output in addition to employment. He presented evidence that neither the rate of price inflation nor the deviation of actual from potential output is lower in Japan than elsewhere. The underutilization of labor in Japan does seem to be smaller than in other countries, but Wadhwani noted that this could be due to a host of other factors.

Both papers using Japanese data employed highly aggregated, time series data. Empirical tests using firm-level, cross-sectional data have been conducted by British economists. Eastrin and Wilson (1986) and Bradley and Estrin (1987)

found higher employment *levels*, other things equal, in profit-sharing firms, but they are inclined to attribute most of this phenomenon to increased worker productivity. Jones and Pliskin (1989) found much more modest effects. Blanchflower and Oswald (1987b) investigated the more central question of whether employment *changes* in firms with decreasing demand were affected by profit sharing, and they found no such effects. Estrin and Wilson (1989) found no direct effect of profit sharing on employment changes, but did find that profit-sharing firms had more flexible pay. None of these findings, however, may be especially relevant to the American experience, because the typical bonus in British profit sharing firms is comparatively small (just 3 percent of pay, as compared to about 7 percent in the United States), and temporary layoffs are in any case not a common characteristic of the British economy.

Kruse (1987) analyzed the yearly employment changes of 849 U.S. manufacturing firms and 533 nonmanufacturing firms in the context of both increases and decreases in the overall unemployment rate. He found that employment in firms with profit-sharing plans[8] responded similarly to employment elsewhere when nationwide unemployment fell; however, when unemployment rose, employment in profit-sharing firms fell less than in other firms (but significantly so only in manufacturing). Although the findings with respect to unemployment increases can be viewed as reasonably supportive of the theory, the findings for periods of falling unemployment are anomalous (although not inconsistent with the results we report below). If layoffs are significantly lower in profit-sharing firms than in other firms during downturns, recalls (and hence employment increases) should be significantly lower during recoveries.

---

[8] His data only permitted an identification of tax-qualified (deferred) profit-sharing plans, but these form the vast majority of plans in the United States.

Characteristics of Profit-Sharing Plans in the Small Business Sector

Except for data on its members published by the Profit Sharing Council of America (PSCA), regularly available data on profit sharing are virtually nonexistent. The PSCA data are informative for some purposes, but they cannot yield estimates of the fraction of firms that have adopted profit sharing. Also, because PSCA members are self-selected, it cannot be assumed that the characteristics of their plans are typical.

A special survey was conducted for the current study. The respondents were among the members of two organizations: the National Federation of Independent Businesses (NFIB) and the PSCA. The NFIB is an association of small businesses, and it regularly conducts monthly and quarterly surveys of its members. Questionnaires were sent to roughly 7,000 of the 13,000 NFIB members responding to one of its monthly or quarterly surveys in 1987; these 7,000 employers represented those reporting over 5 employees. The response rate to our mailed questionnaire was roughly 53% (3,702 responses), as compared to the typical monthly/quarterly survey response rate of 33%.

To enrich the profit-sharing component of the sample, some 450 PSCA members—the membership believed to have 100 or fewer employees—were surveyed. The response rate among the PSCA members was roughly 61%, with 286 responding.

Focusing on nonsupervisory workers, the questionnaire we mailed asked for information on changes in employment, wages, product prices, and sales volume in 1987; it also inquired about relative and absolute wage levels. For employers with profit-sharing plans, questions were asked about the type of plan, the relative size of normal distributions, and the extent to which the per-worker distributions varied with profits. Some attitudinal questions on profit sharing were also asked. (Copies of the questionnaire will be supplied by the authors upon request.) Questionnaires were mailed in June 1988, and a follow-up mailing to nonrespondents was conducted in July.

Descriptive data on important characteristics of profit-sharing plans in our sample are displayed in Table 1. Among the 3,702 NFIB respondents, 28% (1,041 employers) reported that they had a profit-sharing plan. This percentage is very close

Table 1. Profit-Sharing Characteristics of Some Members of the National Federation of Independent Businesses (NFIB) and the Profit Sharing Council of America (PSCA).

Characteristic	NFIB Sample (n = 3,702)	PSCA Sample (n = 286)	Full Sample (n = 3,988)
Employers with Profit Sharing	28%	93%	33%
Of the Employers with Profit Sharing:			
Employers with deferred plans	69%	85%	73%
Employers with cash plans	18	4	15
Combination of deferred and cash distributions	13	11	12
Employers with no pension separate from profit sharing	80%	77%	79%
Profit sharing as a percentage of payroll (median firm)	7%	8.5%	7.6%
Distribution completely discretionary	73%	78%	74%
Distribution by formula	20	11	18
Formula plus discretionary	7	10	8
Median decrease in per-worker distributions when profits fall by 50%	−48%	−42%	−47%

to the 25% of *employees* in small firms who reported, in the Quality of Employment Survey (to be discussed later), having a profit-sharing plan in 1977.[9]

Most profit-sharing plans are "deferred" plans, under which share distributions are paid into an account to which the employee has only limited access until separation or retirement.[10] Some 69% of the NFIB profit-sharing firms and 85% of PSCA members have deferred plans. Only 4% of PSCA members have cash plans, under which distributions are paid to employees entirely in cash; the comparable figure for NFIB profit sharers is 18%. The remaining profit sharers in each organization have hybrid systems, under which both cash and deferred account distributions are made.

A deferred account profit-sharing plan serves essentially as a defined contribution pension, under which employer contributions are made on a contingency basis. Roughly 83% of all profit-sharing employers in our sample said they "agree" or "strongly agree" with the statement, "Our profit sharing plan was set up primarily as a way to fund employee pensions without locking our firm into fixed yearly contributions." Slightly over 79% of profit sharers in our sample do not have a pension plan for nonsupervisory employees that is distinct from their profit-sharing plan.

The implications of profit sharing for employment stability depend, of course, on how *employers'* marginal labor costs are affected, especially in business downturns. In turn, the behavior of marginal labor costs is affected by the proportion of compensation coming from profit-sharing distributions and the downward flexibility of these distributions when profits fall.

---

[9] Of those workers in the 1977 Quality of Employment Survey who worked in firms of under 100 employees, 25% listed profit sharing among the elements of their compensation package. This is the same percentage reported by all workers, regardless of firm size.

[10] Under the Tax Reform Act of 1986, employees can withdraw funds from their accounts, but they must pay a 10% penalty plus personal income tax on amounts withdrawn before separation or retirement.

For the median NFIB firm with profit sharing, share distributions are reported as typically comprising a bit over 7% of payroll costs. For the median PSCA firm, the reported percentage is about 8.5%. The latter figure is comparable to data published for the PSCA's *entire* membership (Hewitt Associates 1987), whereas the former is larger than the 5% reported by the Chamber of Commerce from its surveys of firms with over 100 employees (U.S. Chamber of Commerce 1982–84).

How downwardly flexible are share distributions? Roughly three-quarters of profit-sharing employers make completely discretionary distributions each year, whereas only 18% rely entirely on a predetermined percentage of profits (the remainder employ a mixture of the two methods). Although only the formula method guarantees the downward flexibility in per-worker distributions needed for employment stability, 63% of discretionary sharers indicated that "payments per employee rise when profits rise and fall when profits fall." Another 30% of employers with discretionary payments indicated that they try to keep per-employee distributions constant, but will declare distributions that are less if profits are unusually low. For *all* profit sharers, only 7% stated that distributions per employee were invariant to increases or decreases in profits.

Despite the well-known pitfalls of hypothetical questions, we asked profit-sharing employers by how much their distributions per nonsupervisory worker would fall (from average levels) if profits fell 50% below average. In response, 12% of NFIB shares and 18% of PSCA sharers said there would be no change in per-worker distributions; the remainder indicated profit-sharing payments would be reduced. The median NFIB employer reported that a reduction of 48% would take place, and in the PSCA sample the median reduction reported was 42%.

The results of our survey convey the strong general impression that profit sharing, although mostly discretionary, is conducted in such a way that per-employee distributions do fluctuate with profit levels. The downward flexibility this fluctuation implies suggests that, in most cases, profit-sharing plans should serve to stabilize employment in the face of negative demand shocks. Despite this apparent flexibility, however, a large minority (42%) of profit sharers agreed that "in practice it is difficult to reduce profit-sharing contributions in bad years because of employee morale." Further, there was a curious failure by many employers to perceive that reductions in per-worker profit-sharing distributions represent a reduction in labor costs; only half of profit sharers agreed that "profit sharing is a vehicle for generating some flexibility in labor costs per nonsupervisory worker."[11]

Empirical Analyses

Perhaps the two most striking facts to emerge from our data sets are that profit-sharing firms facing declining sales reduced employment less than did firms without profit sharing, and workers with profit sharing were less likely to have experienced layoff. In our survey of firms, we were able to identify those that had experienced sales declines in 1987; profit-sharing firms in this group reduced nonsupervisory employment by 8%, whereas non-sharers reduced employment by 10%. In our sample of nonsupervisory workers (from the 1977 Quality of Employment Survey) we found that only 4% of those with profit sharing had been laid off during the previous 12 months, as compared to 7% of workers without profit sharing.

These simple differences are provocative, but they are surely not an adequate test of our central hypothesis that, other things equal, a profit-sharing firm is less likely than a non-profit-sharing firm to lay off workers in the face of declining demand. The simple differences take no

account of the magnitudes of negative demand shocks, nor do they control for correlates of profit sharing that might be affecting these differences. In short, the simple differences do not provide adequate assurance that we have held "other things equal." The tests described below are attempts to determine whether the simple results above survive once we have controlled for these other factors as best we can.

Basic Analyses: Employer Data

We wish to test the hypothesis that for a given negative shock to product demand, profit-sharing firms will exhibit smaller reductions in employment than will firms without profit sharing. In testing this hypothesis, it is important to be able to distinguish the incentives for employment stability *inherent* in profit sharing from firms' employment policies that might otherwise *cause* them to adopt profit sharing. For example, if firms wanting to foster stronger worker-firm attachments tend to be the ones that adopt profit sharing, and if for the same reasons they also pursue "no-layoff" policies, there is a risk that the researcher will confound the causes and effects of profit sharing in testing the hypothesis.

Table 2 displays, for NFIB members, some data on the differences between profit-sharing firms and other firms.[12] Perhaps the most striking difference is that profit sharers have more employees than firms without profit sharing.[13] There are also tendencies for profit-sharing firms to have higher-wage workers and lower quit rates. Further, the guaranteed wage for profit sharers seems to be set at the market level, so workers in profit-

---

[11] It is interesting that one large corporation not in our sample, Union Carbide (Chemicals and Plastics Group), in outlining the benefits of its new profit-sharing plan to employees, argues that profit sharing "provides greater job security and opportunity by reducing compensation costs during a business downturn" (Union Carbide Corporation 1989).

[12] Because PSCA firms are self-selected members of a profit-sharing organization, they may be unrepresentative of the universe of profit sharers, especially among the small business sector. Therefore, Table 2 focuses on NFIB members.

[13] It is possible that one motivation for small firms to adopt profit sharing is to reduce income disparities between the owner and workers, who often work side-by-side. This rationale is clearly most compelling for the most successful small firms, which tend also to be larger.

Table 2. Comparison of Profit-Sharing and
Other Firms, NFIB Sample.

Characteristic	Profit Sharing (n = 928)	No Profit Sharing (n = 2069)
Number of Full-Time Nonsupervisory Employees, Beginning of 1987 (mean)	19.3	12.1
Number of Part-Time Employees, Beginning of 1987 (mean)	3.2	2.9
Quit Rate (mean)	.13	.18
Percentage of Employment in:		
Construction	13	15
Manufacturing	27	18
Transportation, travel, communication	4	4
Wholesale trade	17	10
Retail trade	18	29
Agriculture, landscaping, veterinarian	2	3
Finance, insurance, real estate	8	6
Personal and business services	5	9
Professional services	7	6
Median Nonsupervisory Wage Rate	$8.63	$7.55
Median Wage Relative to Market	1.0	1.0

sharing firms would appear to earn more,
on average, than comparable workers in
other firms. There are also differences in
the incidence of profit sharing across
one-digit industries, with the incidence of
profit sharing relatively high in manufacturing and wholesale trade, and relatively
low in retail trade.

Unfortunately, there are no theoretically or empirically satisfying models of
profit-sharing adoption.[14] Some 59% of

---

[14] In an attempt to find out why firms did *not* use
profit sharing, several questions about nonuse were
asked. More than one reason could be given by each
firm, so the percentages obtained are not additive.
Nevertheless, 33% of non-adopters believed it would
raise unit costs of output, 22% cited lack of
knowledge about profit sharing, 20% said it would be
"too much trouble," and 19% feared opening the
books to employee scrutiny.

NFIB profit sharers believed, however,
that sharing increases employee loyalty,
and 70% of PSCA members thought so;
thus, it is plausible that firms wanting
strong employee-employer attachments
would adopt profit sharing. Further, if
there are other, unobserved causes underlying the adoption of profit sharing, it is
not unreasonable to think that such causes
might be common to industries or firm
size groups. Hence, data on quit rates,
firm size, and industry must clearly be
included in any serious test of the above
hypothesis.

In testing the hypothesis above, we
assumed that the change in employment
(ΔE) accompanying a given change in sales
volume (ΔV) was affected by the presence
or absence of profit sharing as well as by
other factors influencing the adjustment
of a firm's work force:

$$(7) \qquad \Delta E = f(\Delta V, PS, Q, X, \Delta W).$$

In equation (7), *PS* is a dichotomous
variable indicating the presence ($PS = 1$) or
absence ($PS = 0$) of profit sharing. The
remaining variables in equation (7) are
discussed below.

The variable Q represents the firm's
quit rate, and it is expected that Q
negatively influences ΔE for two reasons.
First, if quits are either welcomed (as in a
business slump) or unexpected, they tend
to reduce the work force without the need
for layoffs or firings. Second, firms that
undertake policies designed to increase
worker-firm attachment—perhaps because of firm-specific human capital investments—may be loath to make quick
adjustments in their work force levels in
the face of either increases or decreases in
sales. To separate the direct economic
incentives of profit sharing from the
effects on employment adjustments that
would be caused anyway by a firm's
"attachment" policy, some proxy for the
latter policy is necessary; in our empirical
estimates, each firm's quit rate (Q) in 1987
serves this purpose.

Vector X in equation (7) contains industry and size indicators, which could be
correlated with employment adjustments;
for reasons suggested in Table 2 and

discussed above, these factors must be taken account of in isolating the incentive effects of profit sharing. The variable ΔW in equation (7) stands for the percentage-point change in the firm's (guaranteed) wage rate for nonsupervisory workers over the year.

The basic functional form chosen for use in empirically estimating equation (7) was the simplest possible:

$$(8) \quad \ln(E_t) = \beta_0 + \beta_1 \ln(E_{t-1})$$
$$+ \beta_2(\Delta V) + \beta_3(\Delta V')$$
$$+ \beta_4(PS) + \beta_5 Q$$
$$+ \beta_6(\Delta W) + \delta X + e$$

The variables E_t and E_{t-1} are, respectively, the number of full-time nonsupervisory employees with the firm at the end and beginning of 1987. Percentage-point declines in sales volume within the range of zero to 50 percent are given by ΔV, and $\Delta V'$ is a dichotomous variable indicating sales volume declines in excess of 50%. The quit rate, Q, is the number of nonsupervisory employees who quit during 1987 divided by the total number of full- and part-time workers at the beginning of the year. The vector X contains two dichotomous size variables; X_1 takes the value of unity if $E_{t-1} > 20$, and X_2 takes the value of unity if $E_{t-1} > 50$. It also contains dichotomous variables representing industry (see Table 2 for the industries included in the list).

Among the 3,702 firms in our NFIB sample, 490 (13.2%) reported a decline in dollar sales volume in 1987. With a median decline in sales of 12.2 percent, firms reduced employment by 9.6 percent. However, the results of estimating equation (8), which are presented in Table 3, suggest that declines in employment among profit-sharing firms averaged some 4 percentage points below declines elsewhere once other factors were controlled for.[15] This differ-

Table 3. Estimates of Equation (8) on NFIB Firms with Sales Declines. (Dependent Variable: $\ln E_t$) (Mean of $E_t = 12.91$)

Independent Variable	Mean Value	Estimated Coefficients (Standard Errors)
$\ln E_{t-1}$	$E_{t-1} = 14.28$	.975 (.021)
ΔV	-12.35	.005** (.001)
$\Delta V'$	.02	$-.276$** (.092)
PS	.29	.042* (.029)
Q	.14	$-.106$** (.061)
ΔW	2.20	.014 (.004)
N_1 (>20 Employees)	.21	.031 (.044)
N_2 (>50 Employees)	.04	$-.132$* (.070)
One-Digit Industry Controls		Yes
R^2		.93
Observations		433

* Significantly different from zero at the .10 level, with a one-tail test on the coefficient of PS and a two-tail test on the coefficient of N_2.
** Significantly different from zero at the .05 level (one-tail test).

ence is statistically significant, but only at the .10 level.

How credible are these estimates? For the most part, the estimated coefficients on other variables in equation (8) are sensible. The coefficient on $\ln E_{t-1}$ is very close to unity (insignificantly different from 1 at the .05 level) as one would expect.[16] The coefficients on ΔV and $\delta V'$

---

[15] Regressions on subsamples that included PSCA members yielded results that were similar in magnitude and significance to the ones obtained from the NFIB-only data set. Despite the similarity of results, we believed it was of paramount importance that our test be as free as possible from unobserved factors that might be simultaneously correlated with the adoption of profit sharing and a "no layoff" policy.

NFIB profit sharers are probably a more representative group than PSCA members of profit-sharing firms generally; therefore, we believed that there was a lower probability of confounding the incentive with the "attachment policy" effects of profit sharing. Because preliminary analyses indicated that PSCA members had smaller employment declines than NFIB members with profit sharing, we believed that prudence dictated tests that excluded PSCA members.

[16] This result suggests that the dependent variable

are consistent in implying that, for every percentage-point drop in sales, employment falls by roughly 0.5 percentage points.[17] Moreover, quits (Q) have their expected negative effect on ending employment.

The most troubling result in Table 3 is the positive coefficient on ΔW, which is surely the result of ΔW's endogeneity with employment changes. Our estimate of equation (8) implicitly assumed that ΔW was exogenous to the firm, but it is entirely possible that in the presence of information lags, implicit contracts, or other sources of labor market rigidities, even small firms can deviate from market wage changes in the short run (delaying, for example, wage changes if product demand is slack).

In sum, the estimate of equation (8) yields strong evidence that employment changes are determined largely by changes in business volume. As predicted by theory, however, profit-sharing firms appear to reduce employment less than other firms during business downturns. This estimated difference is only weakly significant in a statistical sense, but it does corroborate the simple difference noted at the beginning of this section.

Tests That More Finely Characterize Profit Sharing

The test above utilized a simple dichotomous measure of profit sharing. Our survey, however, asked questions designed to obtain information on the two charac-teristics of profit sharing that are most closely linked in theory to employment stability: the size and variability of distributions per employee. Profit-sharing measures that incorporate these characteristics are useful in testing our hypothesis, because there are *a priori* reasons to expect some profit-sharing plans (those with large and variable distributions) to work better than others at stabilizing employment.

To obtain some idea of the size of profit-sharing distributions, we asked employers to indicate (for nonsupervisory workers) the ratio of profit sharing to payroll in typical years. Assigning the value of zero to non-sharers, this ratio was inserted in place of the PS variable in estimates of equation (8) to test whether firms in which profit sharing is larger exhibit more employment stability in the face of negative demand shocks. The results offered no statistically significant evidence that the *size* of distributions affected employment stability in the face of reduced product demand.

In attempting to assess the *variability* of profit-sharing distributions, we asked employers to indicate whether they (a) varied per-worker distributions with profits, (b) kept per-worker distributions constant, or (c) kept distributions constant unless business was unusually bad. Firms with more variable distributions should have more stable employment in downswings, but regressions using the above trichotomous classification of sharers found estimates of all three coefficients to be similar.[18]

One question asked profit-sharing employers how they believed sharing affected their labor costs. Those who agreed that sharing makes labor costs more variable were put into one group and those who disagreed or were uncertain were put into a second. Dichotomous variables indicating both groups replaced the PS variable

---

could have been the *change* in employment and that perhaps some sort of weighted least squares analysis could have been employed. It was not clear, however, whether larger or smaller firms had greater errors in reported employment changes. Normally, one places greater weight on employment changes in larger firms (due to the law of large numbers), but in this case we noted a definite tendency of larger firms in the sample to round off reported employment to the nearest five. We therefore adhered to our original approach, which we believed to be both less restrictive and less likely to introduce additional error into the estimation procedure.

[17] The implication holds for the coefficient of $\Delta V'$ if the volume declines in firms with $\Delta V' = 1$ are close to 50%.

[18] The only category with a coefficient achieving statistical significance, though, was the one in which distributions were variable. Since 61% of profit sharers were in this category, however, the higher significance levels were probably the result of larger sample size.

in estimates of (8). In this test we found that, contrary to expectations, those who perceived that sharing increases labor cost flexibility exhibited *less* employment stability in the face of business slumps.

The general support for our hypothesis in the tests using a simple dichotomous measure of profit sharing, coupled with the general failure of the tests using more detailed characteristics of profit-sharing plans, leaves us with two related questions. Is the greater employment stability exhibited by profit-sharing firms during business slumps due to some characteristics of profit-sharing adopters that we were unable to capture? Or, is the failure of the more detailed profit-sharing measures to support the major hypothesis attributable to data problems?

In addressing the first question, it must be remembered that we used data on the quit rate, industry, and firm size in the estimating equations. We also employed data on wage (skill) levels, relative wages, overtime, and the length of time it takes for workers to become fully productive (all of which are proxies for specific human capital investments) in regressions not reported in the paper. These latter variables always exhibited insignificant effects on employment changes, and their inclusion did not alter the estimated effects of profit sharing. It is difficult to explain why firms with "no layoff" policies would be especially inclined to adopt profit sharing unless they do so because they realize sharing will reduce the costs of this policy. Additionally, if "good" employers have both profit sharing *and* "no layoff" policies, would not the separate results of these latter policies be captured by the quit rate?

There are, however, some strong indications that profit sharers had difficulty consistently characterizing their plans. Of those who answered that they held per-worker distributions constant "no matter whether profits rise or fall," 33% indicated on another question that they would cut distributions in the face of a 50% fall in profits; moreover, 70% indicated agreement with the statement that profit sharing was a way of funding employee pensions "without locking the firm into fixed yearly contributions." Of those firms indicating that per-worker distributions vary with profits, only 54% indicated agreement with the statement that "profit sharing provides some flexibility in labor costs" (ironically, 45% of those characterizing their distributions as "fixed" agreed). Among those who stated they calculated distributions as a "specific percentage of profits" (a sufficient condition for distributional flexibility), only 69% indicated on another question that "payments per employee rise when profits rise and they fall when profits fall."

Thus, it is plausible to argue that the generally weak results associated with the more detailed characteristics of profit-sharing plans were caused by errors-in-variables problems that tended to bias the relevant coefficients toward zero. The simplest and most objective characteristic of profit sharing is its presence or absence, and it is in the analysis using this basic distinction that the strongest evidence for the hypothesis tested here was obtained.

Further Tests Using Employer Data

The tests discussed above employed a very simple methodology and functional form. They also ignored some subsidiary hypotheses that can be easily derived from the theory. This section briefly describes some further tests and describes their results.

First, as noted above, there is clear evidence of simultaneity between employment and wage changes. To explicitly allow for the endogeneity of ΔW, we employed a two-stage least squares procedure, in which ΔW was instrumented by the other exogenous variables in equation (8) plus measures of the wage rate, wages relative to the market, and a union variable. The estimated coefficient on ΔW did turn negative, but it was insignificant; more important, the estimated coefficient of profit sharing was unaffected in size, sign, and significance.

Second, equation (8) merely estimates an *average* effect of profit sharing on employment changes, given the decline in sales volume. Although the assumption that employment changes vary by some constant may be practical in giving us one easily interpretable estimate of profit sharing's effects, it is surely not rigorously defensible. Referring back to equation (6), a profit-sharing firm will not lay off workers as long as its marginal revenue product of labor is above the guaranteed wage; once the marginal revenue product falls below the guaranteed wage, however, sharers—like non-sharers—also engage in layoffs. Thus, for "small" changes in product demand, we should observe that the effects of profit sharing on employment grow with declines in sales (that is, up to some point, larger negative demand shocks lead to a larger difference in layoffs between a sharer and a non-sharer). When the demand shock is large enough to close (or make negative) the share firm's original gap between marginal revenue product and the guaranteed wage, however, there will be a constant difference between the employment reductions of a sharer and a non-sharer.

To properly test the theoretical implication that profit-sharing effects on employment changes are proportional to "small" negative demand shocks, but are constant for larger ones, requires methods that can identify the boundary line between "large" and "small" shocks. Because this boundary line is surely firm-specific and highly dependent on both the size and variability of profit-sharing distributions, and because of the evidence we found that employers in our sample have difficulty consistently characterizing their profit-sharing plans, we regard the identification of the boundary line as outside the scope of our capabilities. We did perform a preliminary test using the median sales volume decrease as the boundary line, and the results were inconclusive. That is, the "constant" effect (for large sales declines) was about the same as in Table 3 but not statistically significant, and the proportional effect for small changes was both insignificant and of the wrong sign.

Finally, two subsidiary hypotheses were tested. One was that, because layoffs are smaller for profit sharers than for other

firms when product demand falls, their additions to employment should be significantly smaller when demand recovers. Recalling our theoretical conclusions about the long run, the other hypothesis was that in the face of long-run growth in demand, sharers and non-sharers would have similar employment increases. Testing these hypotheses requires that we have access to measures of both *changes* in sales volume and the principal *reason* for these changes.

In the survey, we were able to determine the direction and magnitude of a firm's sales volume over the year. Further, if positive growth had occurred over the year, we asked respondents to indicate whether that growth (a) largely represented recovery from a prior slump, (b) was mainly due to price increases, or (c) reflected new growth in the real volume of goods or services. Those with sales increases due mainly to recovery formed "Subsample R," and firms experiencing growth in their real sales volume were placed in "Subsample G."

The two subsidiary hypotheses concerning firms experiencing sales growth were tested using a variant of equation (8) in which the sales volume decrease variables were replaced by exactly analogous increase variables. The results for both samples are displayed in Table 4. The estimated coefficient on the profit-sharing variable in the long-run growth sample ("G") is positive but about half the size of the estimated coefficient in Table 3; further, consistent with the theory, it is insignificantly different from zero. Contrary to expectations, however, the coefficient on *PS* in sample "R" is positive and also insignificant. Because of its small size, and because respondents may have had difficulties distinguishing "recovery growth" from other sources of growth, we are not persuaded that much stock can be placed in sample "R's" results; it is worth noting, however, that our results for demand downswings and upswings are broadly consistent with those of Kruse (1987).

Tests Using Household Data

Given the lack of decisive evidence from

Table 4. Estimates of Equation (8) on NFIB Firms with Increasing Sales. (Dependent Variable: $\ln E_t$)

Independent Variable	Estimated Coefficients (Standard Errors)	
	Sample "R"	Sample "G"
$\ln E_{t-1}$	.958 (.025)	.989 (.013)
ΔV	.006** (.002)	.004** (.001)
$\Delta V'$	−.023 (.092)	.216** (.048)
PS	.016 (.034)	.023 (.018)
Q	.038 (.055)	.027 (.024)
ΔW	.005 (.006)	.002 (.003)
N_1	.033 (.059)	−.011 (.029)
N_2	.068 (.087)	−.105** (.043)
One-Digit Industry Controls	Yes	Yes
R^2	.96	.93
Observations	199	1,060

** Significantly different from zero at the .05 level (one-tail test).

our employer survey, prudence suggests that the theoretical implications be tested on completely different data if possible. One data set permitting such tests is the Quality of Employment Survey (QES) of 1977—a household survey that included data on a variety of elements in respondents' compensation packages, including the existence of profit sharing.[19]

Testing for the effects of profit sharing

[19] Those interviewed for the QES in 1977 were placed in one of two partially overlapping samples: the 1977 cross-section and the 1973–77 panel. Of the 1,514 respondents in the 1977 cross-section, 435 were in the panel. Besides these latter 435, there were an additional 457 respondents in the 1973–77 panel, and these 457 were added to the cross-sectional sample. The other fringe benefits upon which data were collected included paid vacations, medical insurance and other health benefits, life insurance, retirement programs, sick leave, training/education programs, thrift plans, free or discounted merchandise, stock options, clothing allowances, legal aid, and day care.

on employment stability among individuals necessarily involves analyzing the probability of being laid off if one's employer experiences a negative demand shock. The 1977 QES asked each respondent, "Were you laid off from your present employer during the previous twelve months?" Because of the way this question was framed, the analyses described below had to exclude workers with less than one year's experience with their current employer. The data are for full-time, private sector, nonconstruction, nonsupervisory employees.

It can be seen from the first row of Table 5, which offers some descriptive summaries of the data, that one-quarter of the sample's nonsupervisory workers participated in a profit-sharing plan—a fraction reassuringly close to the coverage found in our employer-based sample. Most interesting, however, are the data in row two of Table 5 and noted at the

Table 5. Comparison of Nonsupervisory, Nonconstruction Workers with and without Profit Sharing (Excluding Workers with Less Than 1 Year's Tenure with Current Employer).

Characteristic	With Profit-Sharing	Without Profit-Sharing
Number (percent)	102 (25%)	302 (75%)
Percent Laid Off	4%	7%
Percent with Pensions	82%	74%
Annualized Hourly/ Weekly/Monthly Pay	$11,828	$11,683
Percent with over 5 Years of Tenure with Current Employer	48%	60%
Average Total Labor Market Experience	18 years	20 years
Percent Male	64%	63%
Percent Minority	11%	16%
Percent Unionized	23%	49%
Percent in Establishments with over 500 Employees	34%	36%
Percent Skilled or Technical	29%	26%
Percent Clerical	39%	20%

Source: 1977 Quality of Employment Survey (computations by authors).

beginning of section 3: *nonsupervisory workers with profit sharing were about half as likely as those without profit sharing to have been laid off during the previous year.*

By itself, of course, the above finding is not evidence that profit sharing stabilizes employment, because other factors affecting layoffs could be correlated with the presence of profit sharing. A proper test of the hypothesis that, *ceteris paribus*, profit sharing reduces layoff probabilities must take account of (a) product demand conditions facing firms, (b) policies or incentives of firms regarding employment adjustments to given demand shocks, and (c) personal characteristics affecting layoffs in firms deciding to use that adjustment mechanism.

Product demand changes. Because layoffs within a year can be affected by monthly changes in product demand, an indicator of these monthly changes is required. Data on production, shipments, and sales are available monthly for only a few industries, so the best available measure of monthly changes in production volume at the detailed industry level is employment.[20] In this test, product market conditions affecting layoffs were measured by the largest ratio of each industry's employment "high" to its *subsequent* "low" during the year prior to interview.[21]

Firm-level incentives concerning layoffs. Controls for firm-level incentives to lay off

workers, given external demand conditions, should clearly include the profit-sharing variable. It should also include indices of firm-specific human capital investments.

Because firms that have large investments in their workers will tend to work them overtime, one could argue that "overtime hours usually worked" is a good index for specific human capital. Data on usual overtime hours were collected on the 1977 QES, but it is not clear what employees had in mind when they answered. If they responded by indicating only their *recent* overtime hours, instead of some long-run average, then "cyclical" and "specific human capital" effects may be confounded. This possible conflation poses no particular problems for our analysis, in which the focus is on the effects of profit sharing, but it does suggest that there is an ambiguous sign expectation on the coefficient of "overtime."

Firms that have relatively large investments in their workers, and those that have relatively high costs of monitoring the effort of their workers, are thought to adopt policies that induce long-term worker-firm attachments. In these firms, which usually have internal labor markets, layoffs risk severing (and shortening) these attachments; therefore, layoffs in these firms may be avoided. Such firms are typically large and offer pensions as a "reward" for long-term attachment. They also often extend generous fringe benefits, such as sick pay, to their workers. Thus, controls for firm size and for the presence of pensions and sick pay were utilized in the estimating equation. It is expected that, other things equal, layoffs will be lower in large firms and in ones that offer pensions and sick pay.

To control for the effects of unionization on layoffs, a dichotomous variable indicating union coverage was included in the estimating equation. One-digit occupational dummy variables were also included in the estimating equation to capture the effects of both general shifts in demand and occupational differences in firm-specific training investments. Finally, another way to control for the effects of

---

[20] Unfortunately, the effects of this variable will overlap the effects of those in other categories—including profit sharing—if firms in the same industry tend to follow similar hiring, training, and compensation practices. This overlap will make it more difficult to estimate the layoff effects of profit sharing if the incidence of share firms clusters so much by industry that industry-wide employment is affected. Unfortunately, there were too few QES respondents in most Census-coded industries to draw reliable inferences about the clustering of profit sharing.

[21] Since QES respondents were interviewed in October to December 1977, the "prior year" was defined as October 1976 to September 1977. If monthly employment levels in the industry had more than one peak, the largest peak-to-trough measure was used. Industry employment data at the three- and four-digit level were taken from U.S. Bureau of Labor Statistics (1983) and converted to Census industry codes for merging with the QES data.

specific training is to estimate the difference between one's current and one's "market" wage—a difference that is thought to grow with the extent of firm-specific human capital. This factor can be incorporated by including each respondent's earnings *and* the market determinants of earnings (experience, education, and other demographic variables) in the estimating equation.

Personal characteristics affecting layoffs. Given the widespread practice of laying off workers in inverse order of their seniority within the firm, the most obvious personal characteristic of relevance to whom is laid off is job tenure. Two job tenure categories were defined in the sample:[22] 1–5 years, and over 5 years. Gender and race dummies were also included to capture any effects of these characteristics on layoffs.

Discussion of the results. Two specifications of a "layoff" equation were estimated using a probit technique, and the results are shown in Table 6. In both models we find, as we did with our employer-based data, that employment adjustments are largely driven by business volume changes (see the coefficient on the "high-to-low employment change" variable). Other factors having effects on layoff probabilities are firm size, worker tenure, and union status.[23]

For our purposes, the notable results in Table 6 are the negative coefficients on the profit-sharing variables. These negative coefficients, both of which are larger than their standard errors, imply that—other things equal—profit sharing does tend to reduce the probability of layoff. Further, the estimated magnitude of the decline in layoff probability is large: the probit coefficients imply a 3 percentage-point reduction in layoff probability (from a sample mean value for non-sharing firms of 7%). In other words, the point estimates from our probit analyses imply

the same differences observed in the raw data in Table 5.

As with our employer-based tests, however, the evidence corroborating economic theory is not conclusive. One estimated coefficient of the profit-sharing variable is barely significant at the .10 level, and the other fails to achieve significance at that level. As before, then, the point estimates are consistent with theory, but they only hover around significance at the .10 level.

Summary and Conclusions

Tests of the hypothesis that workers whose pay is partially in the form of profit sharing have greater job security in the face of business downturns were performed on two completely different data sets separated in time by a decade. Although in both cases the level of statistical significance can be characterized as marginal (.10 level with one-tail tests), the fact that there was support for the theory in both bodies of data is clearly worth stressing.

It is fair to say that we found no strong indications from our employer-based data that the characteristics of profit-sharing plans exert much of an effect on job security. Most plans, at least among small businesses, appear to have distributions that vary with profits even though explicit formulas are not widely used. Moreover, it would appear that most employers implicitly promise distributions in "normal" periods that are large enough to offer some increased job security.[24] Thus, the measure of profit sharing offering most support for the theory was the simple measure of its presence or absence.

Finally, we tested two subsidiary hypotheses on our employer data. In the face of long-run growth, share and non-share firms made similar additions to employ-

---

[22] As explained earlier, all workers in the subsample analyzed had worked with their current employers for at least a year.

[23] The "union" result is consistent with the prevailing view that wages are more rigid in the union sector and that therefore *quantity* adjustments in labor utilization are more necessary.

[24] Union Carbide's profit-sharing plan referred to in footnote 11 holds "guaranteed" pay to 95% of what employees would normally receive. The corporation, which believes that profit sharing will improve employment stability, apparently believes that a 5% reduction in compensation is sufficient to avoid layoffs in most situations. (See Union Carbide Corporation 1989.)

Table 6. Probit Estimates of the Effects of Profit Sharing on Layoffs.
(Dependent Variable: Laid Off Last Year (= 1), Not Laid Off (= 0))

Independent Variable	Model I: 423 Observations			Model II: 404 Observations		
	Coef-ficient	(Standard Error)	t-Value	Coef-ficient	(Standard Error)	t-Value
Intercept	−6.531	(2.001)	−3.26	−6.714	(2.155)	−3.12
High to Low Employment Change	4.419	(1.869)	2.36	4.234	(1.950)	2.17
Tenure Less Than 6 Years	0.366	(0.225)	1.63	0.353	(0.264)	1.34
Union Coverage	0.596	(0.275)	2.17	0.624	().297)	2.10
Male	0.383	(0.279)	1.37	0.481	(0.305)	1.58
Nonwhite	−0.860	(0.476)	−1.81	−0.872	(0.501)	−1.74
Usual Overtime Hours	−0.002	(0.017)	0.10	−0.001	(0.018)	0.06
Large Firm (> 500 Employees)	−0.423	(0.257)	−1.65	−0.547	(0.277)	−1.98
Skilled or Technical Worker	−0.311	(0.269)	−1.16	−0.366	(0.282)	−1.30
Clerical Worker	0.020	(0.338)	−0.06	0.081	(0.362)	0.22
Unskilled or Service Worker	−0.292	(0.358)	−0.82	−0.303	(0.380)	−0.80
Receives Sick Pay	−0.239	(0.225)	−1.06	−0.204	(0.236)	−0.87
Has Pension	0.186	(0.302)	0.62	0.114	(0.318)	0.36
Has Profit Sharing	−0.369	(0.305)	−1.21	−0.411	(0.312)	−1.32
Experience				0.053	(0.041)	1.29
Experience Squared ($\times 10^{-2}$)				−0.135	(0.087)	−1.55
High School Education				0.069	(0.272)	0.25
Some College				−0.402	(0.384)	−1.05
Wage/Salary Annualized (in Thousands)				0.007	(0.014)	0.51

ment (as expected from theory). Our data yielded no evidence, however, that profit-sharing firms recovering from a prior slump in sales added fewer workers, as would be expected if they had laid off fewer during the slump.

What, then, can be made of these results? First, if there are any effects of profit sharing on employment, they are observed primarily in periods of business downturns. Second, evidence of increased job security during downswings, however borderline in terms of conventional levels of statistical significance, cannot be dismissed; evidence of that association was found in two different data sets (in both gross measures and multivariate analyses) and was, moreover, consistent with evidence from the only other U.S. study on this topic (Kruse 1987).

Third, it seems likely that although there are tendencies for profit sharing to stabilize employment in downswings, the tendencies are not uniformly present across employers—driving up the standard errors of estimated effects. As we indicated, small employers had difficulty characterizing their profit-sharing plans in a consistent way, and about half of small business owners with profit sharing did not perceive that flexibility in labor costs is implied by distributions that are tied to profits. Thus, on the one hand, the inconsistency of the effects found on employment may be related to employers' inconsistent (incomplete?) perceptions of profit sharing itself. On the other hand, it must be remembered that adjustments firms make to reduced demand are neither always smooth (whole plants or sections of plants may be closed) nor limited to employment changes. Our lack of data on how hours per worker changed, and our inability to identify which firms were likely to make discontinuous changes in employment, both suggest that results of marginal significance were perhaps the best one could expect.

REFERENCES

Blanchflower, David, and Andrew Oswald. 1987a. "Profit Sharing—Can It Work?" *Oxford Economic Papers,* Vol. 39, pp. 1–19.
———. 1987b. "Shares for Employees: A Test of Their Effects." Discussion paper no. 273, Centre for Labour Economics, London School of Economics, February.
Bradley, Keith, and Saul Estrin. 1987. "Profit Sharing in the Retail Trade Sector: The Relative Performance of the John Lewis Partnership." Discussion paper no. 279, Centre for Labour Economics, London School of Economics, May.
Cooper, Russell. 1988. "Will Share Contracts Increase Economic Welfare?" *American Economic Review,* Vol. 78, No. 1 (March), pp. 138–54.
Estrin, Saul, Paul Grout, and Sushil Wadhwani. 1987. "Profit Sharing and Employee Share Ownership." *Economic Policy,* Vol. 4 (April), pp. 14–62.
Estrin, Saul, and Nick Wilson. 1986. "The Micro-Economic Effects of Profit Sharing: The British Experience." Discussion paper no. 247, Centre for Labour Economics, London School of Economics, July.
———. 1989. "Profit Sharing, the Marginal Cost of Labour and Employment Variability." Unpublished paper, Department of Economics, London School of Economics.
Freeman, Richard, and Martin Weitzman. 1987. "Bonuses and Employment in Japan." *Journal of the Japanese and International Economies,* Vol. 1, pp. 168–94.
Hewitt Associates. 1987. *1987 Profit Sharing Survey.* Chicago: Profit Sharing Council of America.
———. 1977. *1977 Profit Sharing Survey.* Chicago: Profit Sharing Council of America.
Jackman, Richard. 1987. "Profit-Sharing in a Unionised Economy with Imperfect Competition." Discussion Paper No. 290, Centre for Labour Economics, London School of Economics, August.
Jones, Derek C., and Jeffrey Pliskin. 1989. "British Evidence on the Employment Effects of Profit Sharing." *Industrial Relations,* Vol. 28, No. 2 (Spring), pp. 276–98.
Kruse, Douglas. 1987. "Profit-Sharing and Economic Variability: Microeconomic Evidence." Mimeo,

Department of Economics, Harvard University, November.
Mitchell, Daniel J. B. 1987. "The Share Economy and Industrial Relations." *Industrial Relations,* Vol. 26, No. 1 (Winter), pp. 1–17.
Mitchell, Daniel, and Renae Broderick. 1988. "Flexible Pay Systems in the American Context: History, Policy, Research, and Implications." Mimeo, Institute of Industrial Relations, University of California–Los Angeles, April.
Murray, Alan. 1987. "Sharing the Wealth: Democrats Latch on to Bonus Pay System in Search for New Ideas." *Wall Street Journal,* April 24, pp. 1, 27.
Nuti, Domenico Mario. 1987. "Profit-Sharing and Employment: Claims and Overclaims." *Industrial Relations,* Vol. 26, No. 1 (Winter), pp. 18–29.
Parliament of the United Kingdom. 1986. "Profit Related Pay." A consultative document presented by the Chancellor of the Exchequer, July.
Quinn, Robert P., and Graham L. Staines. 1979. *The 1977 Quality of Employment Survey.* Ann Arbor: Institute for Social Research, University of Michigan.
Standing, Guy. 1988. "Would Revenue-Sharing Pay Cure Unemployment?" *International Labour Review,* Vol. 127, No. 1, pp. 1–18.
Union Carbide Corporation. 1989. "Chemicals and Plastics Profit Sharing Plan." Danbury, Conn.: Union Carbide Corporation.
U.S. Bureau of Labor Statistics. 1983. *Supplement to Employment and Earnings.* Washington, D.C.: U.S. Department of Labor, Bureau of Labor Statistics, July.
U.S. Chamber of Commerce. 1973–84. *Employee Benefits.* Washington, D.C.: Economic Policy Division, U.S. Chamber of Commerce.
Wadhwani, S. 1985. "The Macroeconomic Implications of Profit Sharing: Some Empirical Evidence." Discussion paper no. 220, Centre for Labour Economics, London School of Economics, June.
Weitzman, Martin L. 1984. *The Share Economy.* Cambridge Mass.: Harvard University Press.
Weitzman, Martin, and Douglas Kruse, 1989. "Profit Sharing and Productivity." Unpublished paper, Department of Economics, Harvard University.

COMPENSATION POLICY AND FIRM PERFORMANCE: AN ANNOTATED BIBLIOGRAPHY OF MACHINE-READABLE DATA FILES

JULIE L. HOTCHKISS*

This paper presents detailed descriptions of 24 machine-readable data files that could be used in empirical studies of the relationship between compensation policy and firm performance. Also included are the addresses of the organizations (mostly government agencies) that create and distribute the files and, in most cases, of specific persons to contact in order to obtain the data. The author also provides information on data available from six private consulting firms.

MOST compensation policy studies have focused on the direct effect different policies have on *employee* performance, and have thus been concerned directly or indirectly with the principal-agent problem. As a direct consequence of its effect on employee performance, however, compensation policy must also have an influence on the performance of the *firm*. Specifically, a trade-off between monitoring costs and reduced shirking is inherent in any compensation policy, and this trade-off plays an important role in determining the final revenue or profit enjoyed by the firm.

Fewer studies have addressed the secondary effect of compensation policy on firm performance than have addressed the primary effect on employee performance. Undoubtedly, analysts have been discouraged from examining the effect of com-

pensation policy on firm performance by the apparent lack of suitable data. The purpose of this paper is to present information about machine-readable data sets that could be used for a wide range of research on the effect of compensation policy on firm performance.

This paper does not, of course, contain information on every data set ever used in studies of compensation policy. Instead, I attempt to present information on *current* data files that are *publicly* available in *machine-readable* form. In addition, some data sets not available in machine-readable form are included mainly because of their novelty. I omit information on the physical characteristics of each file (whether it is on tape or diskette, the number of tapes, how the information is blocked, whether it is in ASCII format, and so on). This information is easily obtained from the contacts listed.

One can imagine what the ideal data set for the analysis of the effect of compensation policy on firm performance would contain. First, it would have information on both the individual worker and the establishment (the employer). The individual information would consist of the usual

* Julie Hotchkiss is Senior Associate and Assistant Professor of Economics with the Policy Research Program in the College of Business Administration at Georgia State University. The author thanks Ronald Ehrenberg, Daniel Hamermesh, participants in the Cornell conference "Do Compensation Policies Matter?" and all of the contacts listed in the paper for their comments and corrections.

demographic variables;[1] the occupation or duties of the workers; the number of hours of work; the worker's wages and fringe benefits; and information on any other forms of compensation, such as profit sharing, pensions, and cost-of-living adjustments. This information would cover a number of periods for the same individuals, enabling researchers to examine, for example, how often people change employers and how that behavior might be related to types of compensation.

Ideal information pertaining to the employer would allow one to examine the compensation *structure* of the firm. For example, one would want to know how the compensation rates are distributed among the employees, and what form internal pay hierarchies take. Another dimension of interest is the *level* of compensation, and how employee compensation figures in the firm's cost structure. A third dimension of interest is the different ways in which various forms of compensation are brought together to make up the total compensation package. The policies that dictate compensation increases within a firm, or occupational group, would also be of interest. Finally, one might be interested in the administration of compensation, two important aspects of which are the amount of information made available to employees and the degree to which employees participate in the determination of compensation.[2]

Of course, an important piece of information would be the identity of the firm. Once the firm's identity is known, it is possible to merge in objective performance measurements, such as stock market returns, which are easily comparable across firms. In addition, it would be desirable to have all of the above information for the same firms over several periods of time, in order to examine the effect of changes in compensation policy.

There are different levels at which one might desire to undertake an analysis of compensation policy. The data sets below were included because each one meets one or more of the above criteria. Some data sets are more "ideal" than others, and some are clearly useful only when merged with other data sets. Most easily available employer data sets contain information at the industry level rather than the firm level, clearly making them less than ideal, but nonetheless useful for some purposes. Each data set was conceived by its originators for a specific purpose, and therefore has particular strengths. The points of strength of each data set may not be apparent in what follows because the discussion will focus on the particular usefulness of the data set for analysis of compensation policy issues.

Detailed information on each data set follows. For quick reference, Table 1 summarizes the characteristics of each data set.

Area Wage Surveys (AWS). Conducted by the Bureau of Labor Statistics. Washington, D.C.: The Bureau [producer and distributor].

Universe. The universe consists of manufacturing; transportation and utilities; wholesale and retail trade; finance, insurance, and real estate; and selected service industries. The minimum employment size cut-off varies by industry from 50 to 100.

Geographic coverage. Local, regional, and national data are obtained from 90 metropolitan areas. Alaska and Hawaii are excluded.

Time period. Data are collected annually for some areas and biennially for others. The program has been running since the 1950s, but data availability and compatibility across years are not certain.

File size. There are 11,300 establishments in a sample representing all Primary Metropolitan Statistical Areas and Metropolitan Statistical Areas in the United States.

Contact. Ken Hoffman, project manager for the Area Wage Survey, Office of Compensation and Working Conditions, Bureau of Labor Statistics, 441 G Street, NW, Washington, D.C., 20212 (202/523-1536).

Discussion. The AWS consists of a number of surveys, each covering a different area. The data are produced in printed form and

---

[1] "Usual demographic variables" include gender, race, age, level of education, geographic location, marital status, and number of children present.

[2] For a more detailed discussion of the different dimensions of employee compensation, see Ronald G. Ehrenberg and George T. Milkovich, "Compensation and Firm Performance," in Morris M. Kleiner et al., eds., *Human Resources and Performance of the Firm* (Madison, Wis.: Industrial Relations Research Association, 1987), pp. 87–122.

Table 1. Summary of Attributes of Data Sets Covering Compensation Policy and Firm Performance.

Data Set Name	Longitud.[a]	Rep. Level[b]	Employer Comp. Struct.	Employer Wages/Salary	Employer Other Comp.[c]	Employer Perform. Measure[d]	Employee Demo. Variables	Employee Occup./Duties	Employee Wages/Salary	Employee Hrs./Sched.	Employee Other Comp.[c]
Area Wage Surveys	no	area	no	yes	1, 2, 5, 9	no	—	broad	—	yes	—
Census of Manufacturers	yes	indus.	no	yes	no	3, 6	—	—	—	—	—
Collective Bargaining Agreements	yes	indus.	—	—	—	—	—	—	gains	—	—
COMPUSTAT	yes	firm	no	no	no	4, 6, 8, 9	—	—	—	—	—
CRSP Stock Files	yes	firm	no	no	no	4	—	—	—	—	—
Current Population Survey, May	no	indus.	no	—	—	—	yes	yes	yes	yes	no
Dictionary of Occupational Titles	—	occup.	—	—	—	—	—	yes	—	—	—
Employee Benefits in Gov't	no	sector	no	yes	1, 2, 4, 5, 7, 10, 11	no	—	broad	—	no	—
Employee Benefits in the Private Sector	no	sector	no	yes	1, 2, 5, 10, 11	no	—	broad	—	no	—
Employer Expenditures for Employee Comp.	yes	firm	no	yes	1, 2, 5, 7, 9, 10, 16, 17, 18	no	—	2 types	—	yes	—
Employment Opportunity Pilot Project	no	firm	yes	yes	no	1, 7	few	yes	yes	yes	—
Form 5500	yes	firm	no	no	1, 2, 7, 9, 12, 18	no	—	—	—	—	—
Industry Wage Surveys	no	indus.	yes	yes	1, 2, 5, 9	no	—	broad	—	yes	—
Labour Statistics	yes	country	no	yes	no	no	—	—	—	—	—
Longitudinal Research Database	yes	firm	no	yes	no	2, 3, 5, 6, 9	—	—	—	—	—
Manufacturers' Shipments, Inventories, and Orders	yes	indus.	no	—	—	5	—	—	—	—	—
National Longitudinal Survey	yes	indus.	no	—	—	—	yes	yes	yes	yes	no
National Medical Care Expenditure Survey	no	indus.	no	—	—	—	yes	yes	yes	yes	1, 6, 7
NSPATC	yes	occup.	no	yes	no	—	—	—	—	some	—

(continued)

Table 1. (Continued)

| | Data Set Attributes | | | | | | | | | | |
| | Employer | | | | | | Employee | | | | |
Data Set Name	Longitud.[a]	Rep. Level[b]	Comp. Struct.	Wages/ Salary	Other Comp.[c]	Perform. Measure[d]	Demo. Variables	Occup./ Duties	Wages/ Salary	Hrs./ Sched.	Other Comp.[c]
Panel Study of Income Dynamics	yes	indus.	no	—	—	—	yes	yes	yes	yes	1, 2, 3, 4, 5
Quality of Employment	yes	occup.	—	—	—	—	yes	yes	yes	yes	1, 3, 9, 10, 12, 13, 14, 15
Survey of Income and Program Participation	yes	indus.	no	—	—	—	yes	yes	yes	yes	1
The Public School Survey	no	school	simple	—	7, 19	student perform.	few	yes	yes	yes	—
Time Use Longitudinal Panel Study	yes	indus.	no	—	—	—	yes	yes	yes	yes	6, 8

[a] A data set is considered longitudinal if matching across at least two time periods can be accomplished.

[b] The representation level under "Employee" is always the individual.

[c] Codes: (1) pension plan; (2) life insurance; (3) maternity leave; (4) job security; (5) paid vacation; (6) commissions; (7) bonuses; (8) piece-rate payment; (9) health insurance; (10) various types of personal leave; (11) flexible benefits; (12) profit sharing/stock options; (13) dental benefits; (14) eye care benefits; (15) legal aid services; (16) severance pay; (17) welfare funds; (18) supplementary unemployment; (19) release time.

[d] Codes: (1) revenue; (2) output; (3) value added; (4) stock prices or dividends paid; (5) value of shipments; (6) assets; (7) projections of growth; (8) liabilities; (9) sales.

requests for machine-readable data files are reviewed and processed individually. Straight-time earnings data for all establishments are reported for selected occupational categories. Indexes of earnings and percent increases are reported for selected occupational groups. The following is an example of the kinds of information that may be included under the "establishment practices and employee benefits" category (these are likely to vary across surveys): minimum entrance salaries; late-shift pay provisions for full-time (FT) manufacturing, production, and related workers; scheduled weekly hours and days; annual paid vacations for FT workers; insurance, health, and retirement plans offered to FT workers; health plan participation by FT workers; and other benefits offered to FT workers. Beginning in 1988, these data are updated every three to four years only.

Data on scheduled workweeks, shift differentials, and supplementary benefits are obtained only once every three years. The focus of employee health and welfare benefits is on incidence rather than costs or detailed plan provisions.

This data set does not contain employee information, establishment (or area) performance measures, or any identification of establishments.

Collective Bargaining Agreements, 1985–87.
Conducted by the Bureau of Labor Statistics. Washington, D.C.: The Bureau [producer and distributor], 1988.

Universe. The universe consists of collective bargaining units of at least 1,000 workers.

Geographic coverage. Collective bargaining units from across the United States are included. There are no breaks or classifications in the data on a geographic basis.

Time period. Data are collected annually.

File size. The data are available for all 2-digit industries.

Contact. Harriette Weinstein, Project Director, Collective Bargaining Statistics, The Bureau of Labor Statistics, Department of Labor, 441 G Street, NW, Washington, D.C. 20212 (202/523-1308).

Discussion. The published data contain information on the average percent adjustment in the wage rate negotiated by the bargaining units for each year of the contract, plus the annual average over the life of the contract. Individual settlement data are collected and maintained. The information is confidential, and requests for its use are evaluated individually. The data are produced in printed form, but individually tailored machine-readable data sets can be arranged.

Census of Manufacturers (COM): Geographic Area and Industry File, 1982 [machine-readable data file]. Conducted by the Bureau of the Census. Washington: The Bureau [producer and distributor], 1985.

Universe. The universe is all operating establishments (approximately 345,000) employing one person or more primarily engaged in manufacturing and 10,000 auxiliaries of manufacturers. Data are provided on a summary basis for the United States as a whole, each state, the District of Columbia, Standard Metropolitan Statistical Areas, counties, and selected places with 450 manufacturing employees or more.

Geographic coverage. Coverage includes all states in the United States and the District of Columbia.

Time period. The COM is conducted every five years and each census contains information pertaining to a one-year time period. The most recent survey was conducted in 1987, but is not yet available to the public.

File size. Data are provided on approximately 450 manufacturing industries.

Contact. Data file information: Data User Services Division, Customer Services (Tapes), Bureau of the Census, Washington, D.C., 20233 (301/763-4100). Technical documentation: Data User Services Division, Data Access and Use Staff, Bureau of the Census, same address (301/763-2074). Subject matter: Industry Division, Bureau of the Census, same address (301/763-1503).

Discussion. Censuses of manufacturers for the United States were conducted every ten years from 1810 to 1900. Annual information has been made available every five years since 1905. (From 1919 to 1939 the census was taken every two years.) The following variables are included in the COM: employment and payroll, shipments, cost of materials, value added, inventories, expenditures, assets, rents, depreciations, and purchased services. This data set is presented in successive cross-sections (every five years). It contains no employee information and no information on compensation forms other than total payroll. This data set is probably most useful for combining industry-level variables with other data sets. Similar information has been collected by the Bureau for the Retail Trade, Wholesale Trade, Services, Minerals, and Construction Sectors.

COMPUSTAT II [machine-readable data file]. New York: Standard & Poor's Compustat Services, Inc. [producer and distributor], 1988.

Universe. The universe consists of companies with stocks that are traded on the New York, American, and Regional Stock Exchange in the

United States, as well as firms trading over-the-counter or solely in Canada.

Geographic coverage. The United States and Canada.

Time period. For most companies, 20 years of annual data and 40 quarters (10 years) of quarterly data are available.

File size. Depending on the data file, the number of companies within a file ranges from 150 to 6,250. The annual files include 175 data items, and the quarterly files include 100 data items.

Contact. Standard & Poor's Compustat Services, Inc., 1221 Avenue of the Americas, New York, NY 10020 (212/512-4900). *Corporate office:* 7400 South Alton Court, Englewood, CO 80112 (303/771-6510).

Discussion. The COMPUSTAT data file has no employee information beyond total expenditures on employees, and is most useful for information pertaining to firm performance. The tax-payer identification number is reported, so these data can be combined with other files reporting this number.

The following files are available from COMPUSTAT: *Primary industrial:* 800 companies of greatest investor interest (traded on the NYSE). Annually and quarterly. *Supplementary industrial:* 800 companies of less investor interest. Annually and quarterly. *Tertiary:* 800 companies not included in the first two files; some non-industrial. Annually and quarterly. *Full-coverage:* 4,000 companies filing 10-K's with the Securities and Exchange Commission. Annually and quarterly. *Over-the-counter:* 800 companies with stock that is traded over-the-counter. Annually only. *Canadian file:* 225 major Canadian companies. Annually only. *Bank file:* 150 bank holding companies. Annually and quarterly.

The following broad categories of information are available, each broken down in varying degrees depending on the data file: Income Statement (sales and income), Earnings Per Share Information, Balance Sheet (assets, liabilities and net worth, stockholders' equity), Statement of Changes in Financial Position (sources and uses of funds), and Market Information.

Current Population Survey (CPS), May Supplement, 1969–

[machine-readable data file]. Conducted by the Bureau of the Census for the Bureau of Labor Statistics. Washington, D.C.: Census Bureau [producer and distributor], 1969–.

Universe. The universe consists of all persons in the civilian, noninstitutional population of the United States living in households.

Geographic coverage. The sample covers all states and the District of Columbia and is designed to be nationally representative.

Time period. Information in the data set pertains to the week preceding the interview. Interviews are conducted annually.

File size. Data are arranged in a rectangular format by individual. There are 165,498 records.

Contact. General information: Demographic Surveys Division, Current Population Surveys Branch, Bureau of the Census, Washington, D.C., 20233 (301/763-2773). Data purchase: Data User Services Division, Customer Services (Tapes), same address (301/763–4100).

Discussion. The Census Bureau conducts monthly surveys focusing on different issues. The largest sample of the United States population is found in the March supplement; it is the strongest supplement in the variety of demographic variables and sheer size, and the only supplement that includes income information. The May supplement might be more useful for compensation analysis, because in addition to the usual demographic variables, it contains information on the individual's work schedule and information on dual jobs when they are relevant. Other variables of interest in the May and March supplements are detailed categorization of the individual's occupation and industry of employment, and union coverage and membership. The CPS is most often used for cross-sectional analysis, although individuals may be matched for four-month periods separated by eight months of no interviews. The Census Bureau does make available some already-matched data files. The CPS contains no employer identification or performance measure.

The CPS may also be obtained through the Bureau of Labor Statistics at a somewhat lower cost.

Center for Research in Security Prices (CRSP) Stock Files, 1925–

[machine-readable data file]. Conducted by the Center for Research in Security Prices. University of Chicago, Graduate School of Business: Center for Research in Security Prices [producer and distributor], 1925–.

Universe. Depending on the file of interest, the universe consists of all companies with stock that is traded on the New York Stock Exchange or the American Exchange (or both) or over-the-counter.

Geographic coverage. Only companies located in areas subject to U.S. Security Exchange Commission (SEC) regulation are included.

Time period. The data are presented on a daily basis since July 1962 and on a monthly basis since December 1925.

File size. Data are presented for every

company ever traded on the NYSE. Firms may have multiple securities representing equity claims. The information is accompanied by identifying SIC code.

Contact. Center for Research in Security Prices, Graduate School of Business, University of Chicago, 1101 East 58th Street, Chicago, Illinois, 60637 (312/702-7275).

Discussion. Five kinds of data are presented for each company: (1) identifying information (for example, name, CUSIP number, and SIC code), (2) distribution information (for example, cash dividends and stock dividends), (3) history of the number of shares outstanding, (4) price history and industry history, and (5) name history.

This data set is purely performance-measure oriented. There is no information on employees or compensation policy.

Dictionary of Occupational Titles (DOT), 4th edition, 1977 [machine-readable file]. National Academy of Science, Committee on Occupational Classification and Analysis [principal investigator]; U.S. Department of Labor, Washington, D.C. [producer]; Inter-University Consortium for Political and Social Research, Ann Arbor, Michigan [distributor]. 1981.

Universe. The universe is occupational categories.

Geographic coverage. NA.

Time period. NA.

File size. The file includes 574 occupational categories and 145 descriptive variables for each.

Contact. Obtaining file: Inter-University Consortium for Political and Social Research, P.O. Box 1248, Ann Arbor, Michigan, 48106 (member services: 313/763-5010).

Discussion. This information is clearly most useful for supplementing other data sets. It contains no firm-specific information, but is dedicated solely to the presentation of consistent descriptive characterizations of 574 occupational categories. The DOT occupational codes can be linked to the characteristics of the individuals in those occupations gathered from the census of 1970.

Employee Benefits in Medium and Large Firms, 1986 [machine-readable data file]. Conducted by the Bureau of Labor Statistics. Washington, D.C.: The Bureau [producer and distributor], 1987.

Universe. The universe is private sector establishments employing at least 50, 100, or 250 workers depending on the industry. Industrial coverage includes mining; construction; manufacturing; transportation, communications, electric, gas and sanitary services;

wholesale trade; retail trade; finance, insurance, and real estate; and selected services.

Geographic coverage. The coverage is nationwide, excluding Hawaii and Alaska.

Time period. Data were collected from January to June (inclusive), reflecting a one-time average reference period of April 1986. Other surveys available on magnetic tape were performed annually from 1981 to 1985. A 1988 survey was available as of 1989.

File size. The survey includes about 1,503 establishments.

Contact. Office of Compensation and Working Conditions, Bureau of Labor Statistics, 441 G Street, NW, Washington, D.C., 20212 (202/523-9241).

Discussion. Data were collected for the following three broad occupational groups: professional-administrative, technical-clerical, and production. Excluded from the survey are executive employees; part-time, temporary, and seasonal employees; and employees in constant travel status. Information is included on the provision and incidence of the following benefits: paid lunch periods, rest periods, holidays, vacations, personal leave, funeral leave, military leave, jury-duty leave, and sick leave; sickness and accident, long-term disability, health, and life insurance; retirement and capital accumulation plans; flexible benefits; and reimbursement accounts. The survey includes no employee information, establishment performance measures, or identification of establishments.

Employee Benefits in State and Local Governments, 1987 [machine-readable data file]. Conducted by the Bureau of Labor Statistics. Washington, D.C.: The Bureau [producer and distributor], 1988.

Universe. The universe is state and local government establishments employing at least 50 workers.

Geographic coverage. The coverage is nationwide, excluding Hawaii and Alaska.

Time period. Data were collected from January to June (inclusive), reflecting an average reference period of April 1987.

File size. The survey includes 869 government units: 24 states and 845 local government establishments.

Contact. Office of Compensation and Working Conditions, Bureau of Labor Statistics, 441 G Street, NW, Washington, D.C., 20212 (202/523-9241).

Discussion. Data were collected for the following three broad occupational groups: regular employees, teachers, and police and firefighters. Excluded from the survey are executive employees; part-time, temporary, and seasonal employees; employees in constant travel status;

elected officials, legislators, and judges; and volunteers. Information is included on the provision and incidence of the following benefits: paid lunch periods, rest periods, holidays, vacations, personal leave, funeral leave, military leave, jury-duty leave, and sick leave; sickness and accident, long-term disability, health, and life insurance; retirement and capital accumulation plans; flexible benefits; and reimbursement accounts. Information on benefits in an additional category, including severance pay, child care, supplemental unemployment insurance, and nonproduction bonuses, is also included. Not included are employee information, establishment performance measures, or identification of establishments.

Employer Expenditures for Employee Compensation (EEEC), 1977 [machine-readable data file]. Conducted by the Bureau of the Census. Washington: The Bureau [producer and distributor], 1978.

Universe: The universe consists of private non-farm firms of all sizes. Each firm has associated with it a four-digit SIC code. The 1976 data set was the only one with a universe restricted by size of the firm—only firms with 20 or more employees were eligible to be included in that sample.

Geographic coverage. The Bureau sampled the entire United States.

Time period. Data are provided in annual summary form. There were seven surveys of the same type conducted in 1966, 1968, 1970, 1972, 1974, 1976, and 1977.

File size. 3,320 firms are included in the 1977 survey.

Contact. Paul Scheible, Bureau of Labor Statistics, 441 G Street, Washington, D.C. 20212 (202/523-1165).

Discussion. For each firm, all expenditure information is provided for two groups of workers: office and non-office. Each firm is identified only by its four-digit standard industry code (SIC). To preserve the confidentiality of each large firm, which may be identified by its SIC, employment, and state codes, the data are split into two reports. No performance measures are included in the data set.

For each firm and each worker category the following information is provided: *Expenditures:* total payroll as well as expenditures on benefits (paid vacation, holiday, sick leave, and personal time; bonuses; severance pay; life, accident, and health insurance; retirement plans; supplementary unemployment benefits; welfare funds; and all legally required insurance payments). *Hours:* total man-hours; hours spent away from work for sick leave, vacation,

holidays, and other causes. Also included is information on whether employees contribute to the various benefits covered in the data set and whether employee groups are covered by a union agreement. A state location code is also included for each firm.

Employment Opportunity Pilot Project (EOPP) Employers' Survey, 1981 [machine-readable data file]. Conducted by the Gallup Social Science Research Group under contract to the National Center for Research in Vocational Education. Ohio: The National Center [producer and distributor], 1987.

Universe: The universe consists of firms with ten or more employees in selected geographic areas.

Geographic coverage. Employers were surveyed by telephone in 30 sites or communities. The states represented in the survey are Ohio, Texas, Louisiana, Alabama, Kentucky, Colorado, Wisconsin, Washington, Missouri, Virginia, and Florida.

Time period. The data set contains information on each establishment pertaining to the fourth quarter of 1981.

File size. The data set contains information on 3,482 firms. A supplementary data set is available that is employee-based and contains data on about 5,400 employees.

Contact. Kevin Hollenbeck, The National Center for Research and Vocational Education, 1960 Kenny Rd., Columbus, Ohio, 43210 (800/848-4815 or 614/486-3655, ext. 355).

Discussion. This survey is the second of two waves of employer surveys. The first survey was conducted by Westat, Inc. under contract to SRI and the University of Wisconsin. Data from that wave are also available, but the second wave of data is supported by the National Center.

This data set contains three categories of information. The first concerns information on the firm itself. For both full-time and part-time employees as groups, the following information is supplied (for both groups): the number of employees, hours of work, percentage covered by a collective bargaining agreement, and average hourly wage (not including benefits). The reporting of gross sales or receipts and the firm's projections of growth might be used as performance measures.

The second category of information concerns the structure of compensation within the firm. The following structural information is supplied for the job that was last filled by the firm: starting wage, current wage (of person who filled the job), top wage (for this type of job), and how long it takes someone to reach the top of the wage scale for this job.

The third category of information includes some demographic and productivity variables for the individual who was last hired by the firm: gender, age, schooling, cost of training, job title, tenure with the firm, estimated relative productivity, and how long it took to fill this person's position. Other information includes the number of hires, rehires, vacancies, and separations for both temporary and permanent employees.

Form 5500 Annual Return/Reports, 1984–1986 [machine-readable data file]. Washington, D.C.: U.S. Department of Labor [producer and distributor], 1988.

Universe. The universe is all establishments providing any one or more of the benefit plans listed in the "Discussion" (below).

Geographic coverage. Establishments filing Form 5500 are located throughout the United States.

Time period. The reports are in annual summary form.

File size. The data set contains information on all firms that are required by the Internal Revenue Service to file a form in the Annual Return/Report Form 5500 series (5500, 5500C, and 5500R) pursuant to the Employee Retirement Income Security Act of 1974.

Contact. Edward L. Toles, U.S. Department of Labor, 200 Constitution Ave. NW, Room N-5510, Washington, D.C., 20210 (202/523-8769).

Discussion. These data are most useful for matching with the COMPUSTAT data set, which contains financial information for all firms that issue publicly traded stock. Issuing publicly traded stock is not, however, a necessary attribute of firms included in the 5500 data set. The employer identification number (EIN) is included in both of the mentioned data sets, allowing one to match the information.

In addition to the EIN, the name and address of the firm are included. The benefit plans asked about on the form are supplemental unemployment, health insurance, life insurance, defined pension benefit plans, defined contribution plans (profit-sharing, stock bonus, target benefit, other money purchase), and other pension plans.

The following information is included for each plan the firm offers: type of plan (for example, collectively bargained, single-employer); number of participants (active and separated); changes in plan; termination of plan; type of funding arrangement; all plan assets and liabilities; all plan income and expenses; number of employees—total number excluded from plan, number eligible, number participating; and integration of plan with

Social Security and Railroad Retirement. Actuarial information is also supplied as reported on Schedule B of the 5500 form.

Industry Wage Surveys (IWS). Conducted by the Bureau of Labor Statistics. Washington, D.C.: The Bureau [producer and distributor].

Universe. The universe includes manufacturing and some nonmanufacturing industries. Minimum employment in establishments covered varies by industry from 5 to 250 employees.

Geographic coverage. Nationwide coverage of approximately 30 selected industries; studies of an additional 10 industries are limited to selected metropolitan areas.

Time period. Data are collected during selected months on a 2- to 6-year cycle.

File size. The sample comprises about 12,000 establishments representing 40 industries.

Contact. Phil Doyle, project manager of the Industry Wage Surveys, Office of Wages and Industrial Relations, Bureau of Labor Statistics, 441 G Street, NW, Washington, D.C., 20212 (202/523-1309).

Discussion. The data are available in published form and may be requested for a specific industry; the IWS is *not* a comprehensive data set containing information on a number of different industries at one time. Machine-readable data are not readily available; requests are reviewed and processed on an individual basis. Within the industry surveyed, hourly earnings and structure of pay (time-based versus incentive pay) are reported by occupation category. Weekly earnings are presented for some white-collar industries (for example, banks and data processing). Data on the method of wage payment are not presented for these industries.

The data provide information on the percentage of workers covered by varying levels of the following benefit categories: paid holidays, paid vacations, health, insurance, and retirement plans, and other selected benefits that may be specific to the industry. Depending on the survey, some regional occupational earnings distributions are reported. Information is also included on the method of wage payment and on scheduled weekly hours for the entire industry across regions. Employee information pertains to production workers in manufacturing industries and office or service workers in nonmanufacturing industries. Not included are employee information, establishment performance measures, or identification of establishments.

Labour Statistics (LABORSTA) [machine-readable data file]. Conducted by the International Labour Office. Geneva, Switzerland: the ILO [producer and distributor].

Universe. The universe is the country.

Geographic coverage. The coverage is international—countries from all over the world are represented.

Time period. Data are collected annually. Data for all included countries go back to at least 1969; some data are available starting with 1945, and some data are reported quarterly since 1976.

File size. The survey includes about 188 countries.

Contact. Patrick Cornu, Bureau of Statistics, International Labour Office; 4, route des Morillons, CH-1211 Geneve 22, Switzerland (41-22-799-6554).

Discussion. The data reported in this file, the same as those found in the ILO's *Yearbook of Labour Statistics,* include: total population, employment, unemployment, hours of work, wages, labor cost, consumer prices, occupational injuries, and industrial disputes. Complete documentation and all of the data are most easily provided by the ILO in SAS format, created on an IBM370 machine. These data are currently provided free of charge by the ILO upon request. This data set contains no individual-level data. The variables hours, wages, and prices are available by industry and occupation in a different data set called OCTINQ (October Inquiry); these data are reported on an annual basis since 1983 (hours and wages) and 1985 (prices).

Longitudinal Research Database (LRD) [machine-readable data file]. Washington, D.C.: Center for Economic Studies, Bureau of the Census [producer and distributor].

Universe. The universe consists of all establishments in the manufacturing industry.

Geographic coverage. Establishments from all over the United States are included.

Time period. Data are reported on an annual basis from 1972 to 1986, and are updated annually.

File size. The annual survey data cover over 6,000 multi-unit firms.

Contact. For information about the series: Robert H. McGuckin, Chief, Center of Economic Studies, Room 3442, FOB 3, U.S. Bureau of the Census, Washington, D.C. 20233 (301/763–2337).

Discussion. This data file contains linked data from 5 different censuses and 11 different annual surveys, constructed by pooling information from the Census of Manufacturers (COM) and the Annual Survey of Manufacturers (ASM). Due to confidentiality requirements, research requests are processed by the Center's staff, unless special arrangements are

made. The advantage of this data file over the COM is the level of disaggregation—data are maintained at the establishment level.

Some of the input variables included for all establishments are total employment; number of production workers; production worker hours; total salaries and wages; production worker wages; other employee wages; total supplemental labor costs; costs of materials; costs of contract work; cost of purchased services; building and machinery repairs; cost of purchased communications services; inventory stocks at the beginning and end of the year for finished products; work-in-progress and materials; capital expenditures for building and equipment; rental payments; and building and machinery depreciation, retirements, rents, and repairs. The output data include value of shipments reported for each 7-digit product in COM years and for each 5-digit product class in the ASM years, value added, miscellaneous receipts, and value of resales and receipts for contract work.

The LRD contains no employee-characteristics information, although some research at the Center has used Current Population Survey information in conjunction with LRD-based information.

Manufacturers' Shipments, Inventories, and Orders M3-1 (88) Published and Unpublished Data (MSIO), 1958–1988 [machine-readable data file]. Conducted by the Bureau of the Census. Washington: The Bureau [producer and distributor].

Universe. The universe consists of all manufacturing companies. The sample consists of most manufacturing companies with 1,000 or more employees, and some smaller companies.

Geographic coverage. Companies from all over the United States were used.

Time period. The data are presented on a monthly, quarterly, and annual basis.

File size. The data set contains information for most 2-digit standard industry code (SIC) manufacturing industries.

Contact. Data file information: Data User Services Division, Customer Services (Tapes), Bureau of the Census, Washington, D.C., 20233 (301/763-4100). Technical documentation: Data User Services Division, Data Access and Use Staff, Bureau of the Census, same address (301/763-2074). Subject matter: Industry Division, Bureau of the Census, same address (301/763-2502).

Discussion. This data set contains the following variables for most 2-digit SIC manufacturing industries: value of shipments, new orders, unfilled orders, total inventories, materials and supplies inventories, work-in-process inventories, and finished goods inventories. The

MSIO contains data in successive cross-sections, contains no employee or cost information, and therefore is probably most useful as a supplement to other data sets.

National Longitudinal Survey of Labor Market Experience (NLS), 1966– [machine-readable data files and CD-ROMs]. Conducted by the National Opinion Research Center and the U.S. Bureau of the Census; principal investigator, Randall J. Olsen. The Ohio State University: Center for Human Resources Research [producer]; Inter-University Consortium for Political and Social Research, Ann Arbor, Michigan [distributor], 1966–.

Universe: The data are arranged by individuals and consist of five cohorts: older men (ages 45–59), interviewed 1966–83; young men (ages 14–24), interviewed 1966–81; mature women (ages 30–44), interviewed 1967–present; young women (ages 14–24), interviewed 1968–present; and youth of both sexes, interviewed 1979–present.

Geographic coverage. Each cohort is designed to be a nationally representative sample of the United States population (within the relevant age group).

Time period. Cohorts were originally interviewed on an annual basis. Beginning in 1970, the older men were interviewed biennially; biennial interviews for young men began in 1972; biennial interviews for mature women began in 1970; biennial interviews for young women began in 1974. The youth cohort (NLSY) has been interviewed annually since 1979.

File size. Data for each of the first four cohorts include about 5,000 individuals, and the NLSY contains information on over 12,000 individuals.

Contact. National Longitudinal Survey Users' Office, Center for Human Resource Research, 921 Chatham Lane, Suite 200, Columbus, Ohio, 43221-2418 (614/263-1682-7309). Bitnet Address: USERSVC@OHSTHR. Also available at no charge are copies of the *NLS Handbook* and the *NLS Bibliography*.

Discussion. The NLS contains the usual demographic variables for each individual, with the exception that geographic location codes are available *under restricted use* for the youth cohort only. The individual's occupation, industry, wage or salary, union status, and hours of employment are included, but establishment-level identification and firm performance measures are not included. Information is also available on intrafirm, interfirm, and geographic mobility. The longitudinal nature of the NLS allows one to follow this information over several years. Individuals are not asked about forms of compensation other than wages and salary.

Two data files containing information on the children of the youth sample are also available, as well as a week-by-week Workhistory Tape for the 1979 youth cohort.

National Medical Care Expenditure Survey, 1977 [machine-readable data file]. Conducted by the National Opinion Research Center of the University of Chicago and Abt Associates, Inc. of Cambridge, Massachusetts. North Carolina: Research Triangle Institute [contracting agency]; Washington, D.C.: National Center for Heath Services Research [producer]; Springfield, Virginia: National Technical Information Service [distributor], 1977.

Universe. The universe is the civilian, noninstitutionalized population of the fifty states and the District of Columbia.

Geographic coverage. The sample is designed to be nationally representative of the United States population.

Time period. The survey questions pertain to the year 1977.

File size. The sample consists of approximately 14,000 households containing a total of 40,320 persons.

Contact. National Technical Information Service, U.S. Department of Commerce, Springfield, Virginia, 22161 (703/487-4660). Also, Inter-University Consortium for Political and Social Research, P.O. Box 1248, Ann Arbor, Michigan, 48106 (313/763-5010).

Discussion. This data set contains the usual demographic variables for each individual. Compensation information includes wages or salary; pension plan coverage; commissions; bonuses; overtime; health insurance premiums; and the source and amount of premium payments and benefits covered. The data set is purely cross-sectional in nature and contains only establishment-level information on firm size and industry. This survey is accompanied by a firm survey that is used simply to verify information supplied by respondents. Similar surveys were performed in 1980 and 1987.

National Survey of Professional, Administrative, Technical and Clerical Pay (PATC), 1960–. Conducted by the Bureau of Labor Statistics. Washington, D.C: The Bureau.

Universe. Data are collected at the establishment level and reported by levels of selected occupations. Minimum employment in establishments varies by industry from 50 to 250.

Geographic coverage. The survey is designed to be nationally representative of the United States, except Alaska and Hawaii.

Time period. Interviews are conducted annually, in March.

File size. The sample comprises about 3,500 establishments. Twenty-five to 30 occupations are covered. The number of work levels for occupations ranges from 1 to 8, and as a result, information is reported for about 125 occupational work levels.

Contact. General information: Office of Compensation and Working Conditions, Bureau of Labor Statistics, Department of Labor, 441 G. Street, NW, Washington, D.C., 20212 (202/523-1570). Obtaining data: Bureau of Labor Statistics, 230 S. Dearborn St., Chicago, Illinois, 60604 (312/353-1443).

Discussion. For each level of occupation, information is presented almost exclusively on wages. There is some limited information on hours of work and salary distributions. The PATC survey will be called the "White-Collar Pay Survey" in the future.

Panel Study of Income Dynamics (PSID), 1968– [machine-readable data file]. Conducted by Survey Research Center under contract to the Office of Economic Opportunity. Ann Arbor, Michigan: Survey Research Center, Ann Arbor, Michigan [producer]; Inter-University Consortium for Political and Social Research, Ann Arbor [distributor], 1968–.

Universe. The data set is arranged in a relational format containing information pertaining to the family and the individual.

Geographic coverage. The study originally included families from 40 states and currently covers all 50 states and some areas outside the continental United States.

Time period. Interviews are conducted annually. Information pertains to annual summaries of family and individual activity.

File size. Originally, 4,702 families were interviewed; currently, about 7,200 families are interviewed.

Contact. Data management and analysis: Institute for Social Research, The University of Michigan, P.O. Box 1248, Ann Arbor, Michigan, 48106-1248 (313/763-5169). Order information: Sales Fulfillment Section, same address (313/763-5166).

Discussion. The PSID is of longitudinal nature. It contains the usual demographic variables, as well as variables on labor force participation and detailed family income measures. Starting in 1984, information regarding monthly dating of labor force events has been included, with detailed information on employer and position changes, as well as information on the receipt of life insurance, maternity leave, and job security from employer(s). Information on retirement plans includes the following: pension plan coverage, pension eligibility formula, determination of benefits, and availability of and contributions made to a company retirement plan. Availability of paid vacation is also included. This information is not updated annually. The individual's occupation, industry, wage or salary, union status, and hours of employment are included (and updated annually), but no establishment-level identification or firm performance measure is included. Recent topics included in the data are family assets (1984, 1989), kinship and help networks (1988), and health (1986)

The National Science Foundation currently provides most of the funding for the data collection.

Quality of Employment Surveys, 1977 [machine-readable data file]. Conducted by the Survey Research Center under contract with the Office of the Assistant Secretary for Policy Evaluation and Research of the U.S. Department of Labor; principal investigators, Robert P. Guinn and Graham Staines. Ann Arbor: Survey Research Center, Institute for Social Research [producer and distributor], 1978.

Universe. The sample is designed to represent all employed adults.

Geographic coverage. The survey covers all 48 contiguous states in the United States.

Time period. The reference year is 1976. Two previous surveys were conducted by the Center: one in 1969 and another in 1973.

File size. The 1977 sample contains information on 1,515 respondents.

Contact. Inter-University Consortium for Political and Social Research, P.O. Box 1248, Ann Arbor, Michigan, 48106 (member services: 313/763-5010).

Discussion. The survey contains a set of "core" questions that can be traced across all three surveys, but each successive survey was expanded and changed to include new variables in addition to the core. The 1977 survey provides cross-sectional information for 1977, but also has a panel structure in that some of the 1973 participants were re-surveyed in 1977. The data set contains the usual demographic variables, as well as the weight and height of participants. Other variables of interest are information on stability of job, interfirm mobility, flexibility of schedule, hours worked per week, work schedule, other use of time on the job besides working, union membership, total family income, basis of pay (hourly, salary, commission, out-of-profits, by job, piece rate, and other), and earnings. The worker is also asked to indicate by which fringe benefits he or she is covered. The range of benefits covered by the survey is extensive. There are also many attitudinal and subjective evaluation questions. The only information given about the employer is the approximate size of the firms the individual works in (in addition to the industry); there is no firm performance measure or firm identification.

Survey of Income and Program Participation (SIPP), June 1983–July 1986 [machine-readable data file]. Prepared by the Bureau of the Census. Washington, D.C.: The Bureau [producer and distributor], 1983–86.

Universe. The data are arranged in either relational or rectangular format and contain information on the individual, the family, and the household.

Geographic coverage. The sample is designed to be nationally representative of the noninstitutional civilian population of the United States. Hawaii and Alaska are not included, and not every state is identifiable.

Time period. Interviews were conducted for everyone on a rotating basis three times a year. Questions pertain to the four months preceding the interview. Answers reflect monthly behavior, weekly behavior, or both.

File size. The original sample contained 21,000 households. Slightly fewer than 21,000 households were added in February 1985 and again in January 1986, so that the sample in 1986 exceeded 60,000 households.

Contact. General information: Daniel Kasprzyk (301/763-5784) or David McMillen (301/763-5592) in the Population Division, Bureau of the Census, Washington, D.C., 20233. Questionnaire content: Jack McNeil (301/763-7946) or John Coder (301/763-5060) in the Population Division. Technical documentation: Data User Services Division, Data Access and Use Staff (301/763-2074). Data File: Data User Services Division, Customer Services (Tapes) (301/763-4100).

Discussion. The SIPP data set is very strong in demographic and income source information. In common with all household surveys, however, it contains virtually no employer information. The individual is asked for an estimate of the size of the firm in numbers of employees. This question is asked in the Wave IV topical module questionnaire only. The only information on compensation forms other than wage and salary is also obtained in the Wave IV topical module; the individual is asked whether he or she is part of a pension plan, what determines the level of retirement benefits, how much the individual contributes to the plan, whether the plan is a profit sharing plan, and how the individual would receive benefits (for example, in a lump sum payment). The individual's occupation, industry, wage or salary, and hours of employment are included, but no establishment-level identification or firm performance measures are included. Except for information obtained in topical

modules, the SIPP data set is longitudinal in nature.

The 1985 Public School Survey, 1984 [machine-readable data file]. Conducted by Research Triangle Institute. Washington, D.C.: U.S. Department of Education, Office of Educational Research and Improvement [producer and distributor], 1985.

Universe. The data file has two parts representing the universes of public schools and of public school teachers.

Geographic coverage. The sample is designed to be nationally representative.

Time period. Questions are asked pertaining to the fall of 1984.

File size. The sample consists of 2,801 schools and 10,650 teachers.

Contact. Charles Hammer, U.S. Department of Education, Office of Educational Research and Improvement Information Systems and Media Services, 555 New Jersey Ave., NW, Washington D.C., 20208-1327 (202/357-6330 or 800/424-1616).

Discussion. There are two parts to the data file: the school data and the teacher data. The data tape permits linkage between teachers and the schools in which they teach.

The school data contain information on the following: enrollment, minority enrollment, staffing, provision of and enrollment in advanced placement programs, graduates applying to college, student performance on the Scholastic Aptitude Test (SAT) and American College Test (ACT), use of aides and volunteers, use of computers, and incentive programs for teachers.

The teacher data contain information on the following: training, experience, subjects being taught, incentives, certification and endorsement, assistance of aides and volunteers, salaries, working hours, additional employment, age, gender and racial-ethnic background.

This data file would be of particular interest to those interested in teacher compensation (participation in different types of incentive programs) and the "productivity" of public schools, which might be measured by SAT and ACT scores as well as participation in advance-placement courses

Time Use Longitudinal Panel Study (TULPS), 1975–1981 [machine-readable data file]. Principal investigators, F. Thomas Juster, Martha S. Hill, Frank P. Stafford, and Jacquelynne Eccles. Survey Research Center, Institute for Social Research, Ann Arbor, Michigan [producer]; Inter-University Consortium for Political and Social Research, Ann Arbor [distributor], 1983.

Universe. The universe consists of individuals who were 18 years of age or older in 1975 and the spouses of those who are married.

Geographic coverage. The data set is designed to be nationally representative of the population 18 years and older of the United States. The sample excludes Hawaii and Alaska.

Time period. The survey was designed as two sets of interviews. The first set comprised four interviews from October 1975 to September 1976. The second set consisted of four interviews from February 1981 to December 1981. The responses are presented as summaries of time use during the 24 hours preceding the interview. The data sets are based on time diaries kept by the participants.

File size. The panel consists of 620 respondents and roughly 400 spouses (a subset of the original sample of the 1,519 respondents and 900 spouses who started the four 1975–76 waves).

Contact. Inter-University Consortium for Political and Social Research, P.O. Box 1248, Ann Arbor, Michigan, 48106 (member services: 313/763-5010).

Discussion. This data file contains useful information pertaining to time spent at various activities on the job (such as coffee breaks and lunch), as well as information about training on-the-job. The usual demographic variables are included for each individual. Other variables of interest include union membership, income sources, wages, earnings satisfaction, attendance, work history, occupation, industry, job characteristics, and work schedule. There is no information on the firm itself (that is, no firm performance measures or firm identification). Information on the type of compensation (for example, commission or piece-rate) received by the individual is supplied.

Private Consulting Firms Conducting National Surveys

A number of private consulting firms conduct surveys regarding payment levels and payment schemes for different categories of employees. The primary consumers of these surveys are the firms participating in the surveys and others who are interested in establishing pay schemes within their organizations that are competitive with those of other firms. For example, suppose a firm is creating a new position that will require certain skills and will entail certain responsibilities. The firm can use the surveys to determine what employees with similar skills and job duties are being paid at other establishments, and structure the pay of the new position accordingly.

Some consulting firms make the results of their surveys available only to the survey participants, and all charge a substantial fee for the information they provide. The companies listed below make at least some information available to nonparticipants. Most information is reported in some summary form (for example, means or medians, in tables or charts). Since the firms surveyed are not identified and since the information is not presented on an individual level, these surveys are probably most useful in conjunction with other data sets that may need to be supplemented with an estimate of the compensation for various occupations in different industries or by geographic region.

Abbot, Langer and Associates, 548 First Street, Crete, Ill. 60417 (312/672-4200).

1. Compensation of legal and related jobs (non-law firms). Information on current salaries and total compensation of attorneys, legal administrators, para-legal assistants, and legal secretaries in business, industry, and not-for-profit organizations, reported by position held, type of employer, size of employer, supervisory responsibility, length of experience, age and year of degree, field of specialization, number of attorneys in firm, and geographic area.

2. Salaries and bonuses in the service department— 1988. Data on starting, maximum, and actual salaries; bonuses; and profit-sharing from 200 companies covering about 11,000 employees in 40 jobs in the service field. These data are presented by type of employer and size of employer. A supplement entitled "Fringe Benefits, Working Conditions, and Billing Practices in the Service Department—1988" provides supplementary information in the named areas.

3. Compensation in nonprofit organizations. Analysis of salaries, salary ranges, and total compensation in the nonprofit sector. Employee compensation is analyzed by length of experience, level of education, level of supervisory responsibility, and type of nonprofit organization.

4. Compensation and benefits in research and development. Means, medians, first and third quartiles, and first and ninth deciles of salary ranges, current salaries, and total income (salary plus cash bonuses) for over 5,200 R&D

employees, ranging from entry-level Technician to R & D Director. These data are reported by type of employer, size of employer, supervisory responsibility, discipline, level of education, experience, education versus experience, functions, and location. An additional section reports on normal workweek and overtime, holiday, vacation, insurance, sick leave, and pension practices.

5. *Compensation in manufacturing; compensation in the security/loss prevention field; compensation of professional engineers—1988.* These three separate reports contain the following information for their respective groups: salaries, salary ranges, and total cash compensation of management, engineering, and technical personnel by type of employer, size of employer, professional level, supervisory responsibility, length of experience, level of education, type of training, region, city, and state.

Mercer-Meidinger-Hansen, Inc., 1417 Lake Cook Rd., Deerfield, Ill. 60015 (312/948-8104).

This company conducts national surveys in the following human resources job categories: data processing; environmental and hazardous waste; finance, accounting, and legal; hospital management; human resource management; investment management; life insurance officer; materials and logistics management; micro/mini-computer; multisystems management; oil and gas industry; telecommunications industry; and telecommunications department. Most of the compensation information for each of these groups is reported by geographic location and industry, and it sometimes includes the relationship of compensation to gross sales, assets, premiums, the budget, and employment. In addition, this company provides reports on geographic salary differentials and salary planning and incentives. The survey participants are listed for each survey.

Hewitt Associates, 100 Half Day Rd., Lincolnshire, Ill. 60015-9971 (312/295-5000).

1. *Flexible compensation programs and practices (1987).* Data on the flexible compensation programs of more than 200 employers nationwide. Examines practices in plan design, program requirements, administration, and communication for choice-making programs and spending accounts.

2. *Summary of ERISA reporting requirements (1987).* Detailed explanation of employee benefit plan reporting requirements under ERISA. Sample reporting forms are included.

3. *Survey of short- and long-term management incentive plans (1988).* Details on the prevalence and design of incentive arrangements for top management of more than 150 companies with annual sales of $50 to $500 million.

4. *The 10-100 survey (1987).* Data on base salary and bonus amounts for top management of manufacturing organizations with annual revenues between $10 and $100 million. Covers 27 positions at the corporate level, 22 at the subsidiary/division level, and 13 at the plant level.

Administrative Management Society, 4622 Street Rd., Trevose, Penn. 19047 (215/953-1040).

There are three reports produced by this company that each present average salary rates, starting salaries, and salary rates by company size, region, industry, and city. The information has been gathered from over 2,500 North American companies representing 250,000 employees. Each report covers a group of occupations: the Office Salaries Report covers 20 clerical, secretarial, and administrative positions; the Data Processing Report covers 20 key exempt and nonexempt data processing positions; and the Management Salaries Report covers 16 middle-level management positions and four supervisory positions.

The three surveys on which the reports are based have been conducted annually for several years. Each report also includes a summary of each position description, salary budget increases for the current year, and projections of salary budget increases for the following year.

Executive Compensation Service, Two Executive Dr., Fort Lee, N.J. 07024 (201/585-9808).

The ECS annually presents 22 domestic reports and 21 reports covering European practices. The domestic reports offer salary, salary range, and bonus information for the following categories: top management, middle management, supervisory management (by region and by industry), professional and scientific personnel (by region and by industry), sales and marketing personnel, technician and skilled trades personnel, office personnel, and hospital and health care personnel. Supplemental reports are offered that provide information on the highest paid 33% of each position in the top management data base and also in the middle management data base. Reports are also available that provide results of regression analyses relating salary and total compensation to size indicators relevant to each middle-management position (total company sales, total assets, and so on); regression results relating top management compensation to company size are also available.

The European reports provide salary and bonus data for 9 top management titles, 21 middle management titles, and 24 employee level titles; these data are presented separately for each of the 17 countries included.

All data are reported via statistical tables, charts, and graphs.

The Hay Group, Compensation Information Center, Philadelphia, Penn. 19103 (215/875-2660).

The Hay Group conducts more than 50 major surveys annually, but only the Compensation Survey Reports described below are available to nonparticipants. Compensation Survey Reports are provided for the following occupations *within the manufacturing sector*: accounting and finance, human resources, engineering, legal, sales, and data processing/information services. Each report contains job tables for each position (summarizing salary range midpoint, base salary, and total compensation); job analyses derived according to both region and industry; contingent compensation analyses that examine the forms of at-risk compensation used by each respondent; staffing and budget ratios; salary administration data; and relationships of functional pay to the all-jobs marketplace.